Leith's
COOKERY SCHOOL

Leith's

COOKERY SCHOOL

Prue Leith and Caroline Waldegrave

Macdonald Illustrated

For W.A.W. and C.R.K.

The authors wish to thank the cooks, chefs, writers and friends who have been, albeit unknowingly, contributors to this book. We have not, of course, plagiarized anyone's recipes, but it is hard not to think 'Troisgros brothers' when one eats a plate of exquisitely arranged sorbets, or 'Michel Guérard' when cooking chicken in vinegar, or 'Anne Willan' when seeing our picture of the classic Tarte Normande. All cooks are influenced, inspired and taught by other cooks, and we are no exception, except perhaps in admitting it!

In addition to cookery-writers, we would particularly like to thank Scott Ewing for help on the technical chapters; Richard Harvey, Master of Wine, wine merchant and lecturer at Leith's School of Food and Wine, for his expert eye on the Wine chapter; the publishers Fontana for permission to reprint tried-and-true basic recipes, such as Mayonnaise and Apple Sauce, from *Leith's Cookbook*; the cookery teachers (particularly Sally Procter, co-principal) of Leith's School for patient testing of recipes; Jane Harrington for cooking the dishes for the photographs; and Marie Lathia for battling with the word-processor.

A Macdonald Illustrated Book

First published in Great Britain in hard back, in 1985 by Macdonald & Co (Publishers) Ltd, London & Sydney
First published in paper back in 1990 by Macdonald & Co (Publishers) Ltd
A member of Maxwell Macmillan Pergamon Publishing Corporation

British Library Cataloguing in Publication Data
Leith, Prudence
Leith's cookery school.
1. Cookery
I. Title
II. Waldegrave, Caroline
641.5 TX717

ISBN 0-356-19583-X

This book was designed and produced by
Quarto Publishing Ltd
The Old Brewery, 6 Blundell Street
London N7 9BH

Senior Editor Tessa Rose
Editor Linda Sonntag

Art Editor Marnie Searchwell
Designers Michelle Stamp
Sue Pressley
Alun Jones

Photography John Heseltine
Illustrations Ann Savage

Art Director Alastair Campbell
Editorial Director Jim Miles

Typeset by Fleetfoto Typesetting Ltd, London
Colour origination by Universal Colour Scanning Ltd, Hong Kong
Printed by LeeFung Asco Printers Ltd, Hong Kong

Macdonald & Co (Publishers) Ltd
Orbit House
1 New Fetter Lane
London EC4A 1AR.

The publishers wish to acknowledge the help of Berry Bros & Rudd Ltd, Collier Campbell and Christian Fischbacher (London) Ltd, David Mellor and Magimix for the loan of glassware, fabrics and kitchen equipment, with very special thanks to Reject China Shops.

CONTENTS

METHODS AND TECHNIQUES

INTRODUCTION

This book sets out to do what sounds like the impossible — to teach cooking as it is taught in a first class chef's college or cookery school, but without a teacher at the learner's elbow to guide their every step. Instead there is — this book.

Caroline Waldegrave, my co-author, and I both know it can be done. We see perhaps 100 cookery students each year pass through practical courses at Leith's School of Food and Wine, and there is no doubt that what sorts the good cooks from the hopeless ones is not manual dexterity, intellectual prowess, the money to buy the best ingredients or even a creative imagination. It is the will to learn, the desire to do things well rather than just passably, and the enthusiasm of the good food lover that makes the difference.

Many of our best cooks have been what are so unencouragingly called 'mature students' — women, and occasionally men, who have decided midway through a career that they made a dreadful mistake at 18, and have now given up job, income and often a life of considerable ease to slave, literally, over a hot kitchen stove.

So, let us assume that you, dear reader, genuinely want to learn to cook, but do not have the time, money or maybe inclination, to attend a practical cookery school. Why shouldn't you just pick up any cookbook and start cooking? After all, this will teach you more than reading any amount of essays on the subject, and the more you cook the better you will get at cooking.

But this book attempts to give you what Leith's School of Food and Wine gives its students — which is quite simply the confidence of the professional. If you learn how to hold you knife to chop the herbs, how to fillet a flat fish, how to bone a chicken, *why* the hollandaise curdled, cooking will provide you with increasing enjoyment and diminishing irritation.

For anyone with imagination, cooking can be the most absorbing and satisfying of pleasures. Of course cooking is not all high-flown inspiration and creation. Some of it, like family supper night after night, can be deadly boring. But even here, the properly trained cook is at an advantage. The competent operator will turn out scrambled eggs for supper with maximum efficiency and minimum mess, and manage it all within the television commercial break. If it is to be burgers *again*, the good cook might wring some pleasure out of the chore by making them from fresh ingredients and serving them with homemade relishes or tomato ketchup.

So this book then, is for *potentially* good cooks. To get the most out of the course you need an interest in food, the desire to master the art, and a degree of discipline. The course is designed, as all our school courses are, round menus. You learn by cooking a meal, rather as you learn French in a 'language lab' by the 'total absorption', or in-at-the-deep-end method.

The Menu Lessons do not progress by easy stages from very simple to elaborately sophisticated, because the reader-cook is unlikely to want to live on salads and grills for the first months and end up cooking elaborate and fancy meals night after night at the end of the course. But the book is logically planned and it is wise to start on Menu Lesson 1 and move onwards and upwards, gaining skills and mastering techniques as you go. All new methods are thoroughly explained as the reader-cook meets them for the first time, and the Introduction and the second half of the book consolidate the lessons with more detailed information on broader subjects — reading a recipe, menu planning, serving style, cooking methods, stocks and sauces, baking with yeast, the culinary properties of the egg, etc. These chapters should be read by the cook when they are referred to in the Menu Lessons.

The Menu Lessons correspond to the lectures and demonstrations attended by cookery school students — they make doing the actual cooking easier, because they explain the whys and wherefores. It is much easier to get things right if you have a clear idea of what you are trying to achieve at the outset.

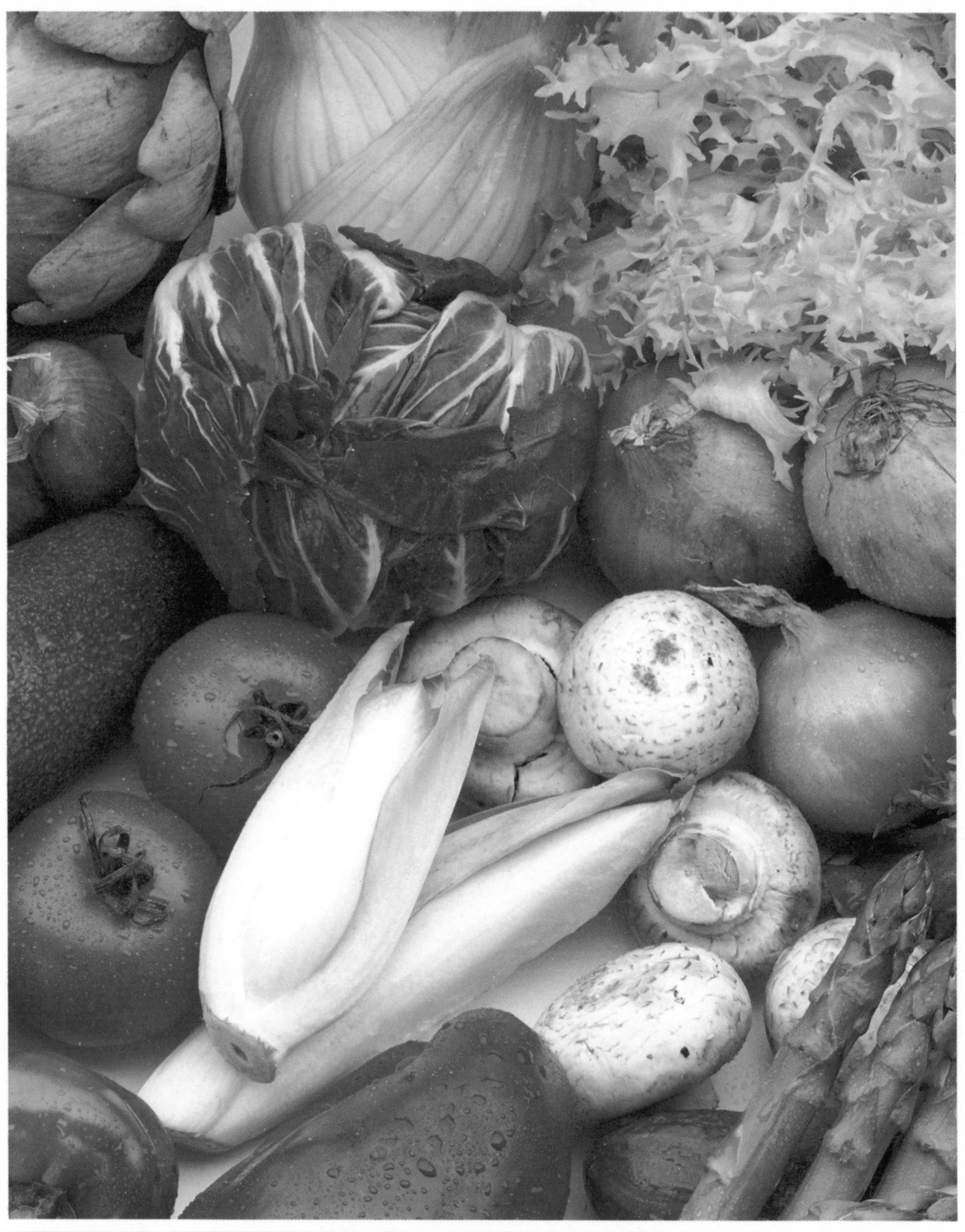

Fresh, high-quality ingredients are the basis of all good cooking — remember that vegetables in the supermarket may have been picked months before.

SHOPPING AND STORING

Today's cook must inevitably make some compromises and sacrifices when shopping. It is not always possible to hunt down the very best unsalted butter, the most perfect curly endive or the fattest Greek olives in the time available. And besides, no cook has an unlimited budget. But real care and fastidiousness in choosing food does pay. The frustration of unpacking bruised tomatoes is compounded by the knowledge that it is one's own carelessness (in failing to pick good fruit or in allowing the check-out assistant to bruise it, for example) that has caused the waste — of food, of money, and perhaps of time if more must now be bought.

At the risk of sounding obvious, or even pedantic, here are a few points to bear in mind:

BUYING FOOD

There are several points to remember when shopping for food:

1 Make a list before setting out and stick to it. Impulse buying can be wasteful if a bargain food such as fresh fruit or meat cannot be used promptly. Of course, substitution for the listed items can be made but it is not wise to buy ill-considered extras.

2 Try not to shop for food on an empty stomach — hunger leads to overbuying. The best time to shop is immediately after breakfast. There is then the added advantage of the likely availability of the broadest range of the freshest produce.

3 Take a pocket calculator to help compare prices of similar items of different size and quantity when buying expensive items and shopping around for the best food prices.

4 Keep a notepad on the kitchen wall and write down things that are running low before they run out, thus avoiding shopping for basics at convenience stores which charge more for them. Be sure to check the list before setting out.

5 Put all purchases away as soon as possible, especially fresh and frozen foods which deteriorate rapidly. Before filling the refrigerator, check what is left in it and move less fresh food to the front or, if necessary, throw it away.

Good food and fine cooking are based on freshness. To make sure that food is fresh, there are a few things to remember for successful shopping:

1 A shop with a large turnover is likely to have fresher food than one which tries to stock everything for a few customers. If buying unusual ingredients, buy them from shops in which they are not regarded as strange and where, therefore, large quantities of them are sold — for example buy fresh curry spices from an Indian delicatessen, phyllo pastry or vine leaves from a Greek one.

2 Try to buy from a store whose management is reliable and helpful and whose products taste good and weigh what the ticket says they should weigh. For instance, someone who sells poor quality cuts of lamb is unlikely to sell good quality mince or poultry. The general look of the shop, its cleanliness and that of the staff as well as their attitude tells something about the management's standards and the food they sell.

3 Complain firmly but politely if things are not right, and return food if it is below standard. A conscientious store manager will do his best to satisfy his customers. But he cannot put something right if no one tells him about it. If the butcher or an assistant mistakenly sells pigs liver as more expensive calves liver and the cook only notices at home when it is too late for an exchange, he or she should nonetheless tell the butcher as soon as possible. He has no reason not to believe his customer and every reason to ensure that it does not happen again.

4 If things are perfect, say so. Shopkeepers naturally tend to favour friendly customers who compliment the wares on which they build their livelihood and reputation, who respect their premises and who pay promptly. They may help you with advice on which cuts of meat are best and how much to buy for a recipe, what special items may be in the cold room and perhaps even by grinding your kitchen knives.

5 Bulk buying can mean price saving and less shopping, but it has a less positive side. For instance, the 'bargain' is often not a bargain at all. 'Giant size' packs may not always mean that the food in them is cheaper, measure for measure, than in smaller packages. Buying a quarter or half of a lamb for the freezer would be inappropriate for people who only eat roasts and steaks. The less prime cuts could stay in the freezer for months, even years, after the grilling meat has been eaten.

Bulk buying can even make the cook's job harder as variety is important to the appetite. This compounds the difficulty of getting through large quantities of the same food while it is at its best. For example, supplies of flour and cereals can go stale if kept for months; dried fruit and pulses get tougher or run the risk of mildew and even cans of food can become rusty, leaky and 'blown'. Be warned, too, that some 'bargain offer' bulk purchases are from little known brand names that are often of inferior quality. In such cases, it is wise to buy a single pack to try it out before buying more.

STORING FOOD

VEGETABLES that appear in the supermarket as if they has just been picked that morning are often the result of a commercial illusion created by packing and refrigeration technology. Some of the vegetables, especially imported ones, may be weeks or months old. At home, spoilage will be rapid unless some of the professionals' techniques are employed.

In the refrigerator almost all vegetables store well in polythene bags or plastic boxes. The low temperatures prevent spoilage and the polythene bags prevent dehydration. The air in a refrigerator is surprisingly dry and quickly causes limpness. This is especially true for root vegetables such as carrots, and for leafy ones such as lettuce.

If refrigerator space cannot be found for all the vegetables, use a cool, dark place for the rest as heat and light will hasten their spoilage. To protect freshness, wrap the vegetables in newspaper or brown paper or put them in a cardboard box with a lid. Do not use airtight containers such as polythene bags or plastic boxes as the warmer temperatures will cause the vegetables to sweat and then rot. Be sure to prevent tomatoes and other fruit from touching each other if they are to be stored for more than a day or two. The points of contact will go bad first.

Tender lettuces, leafy herbs and watercress will go limp if they cannot retain or replace water. Almost any green vegetables will wilt in a day if stored in a rack in the kitchen of a centrally heated house. Store them, if possible, in polythene bags in the warmest part of the refrigerator, usually the plastic drawer or compartments. Herbs can be kept like flowers in a jug of water as can celery stalks. Watercress should be totally submerged in water or put to stand in a jug of water, stalks up and leaves down. Keep everything as cool as possible even if it cannot be refrigerated.

DRIED PULSES such as black-eyed peas, lentils, lima beans and red kidney beans should be bought from a shop with a sufficiently rapid turnover to ensure fresh stocks. There is a great difference between beans dried last season and those dried two or three years ago. As a rule, the smaller the bean the better, because they are less inclined to break up on cooking and have a sweeter taste and a less floury texture than larger beans. Store dried beans and peas in airtight containers; they go stale in the open. Don't buy more than two months' worth at once.

FRUIT such as berries cannot be stored satisfactorily for more than one or two days even in the refrigerator. If they cannot be used in time, freeze and use them for ice creams, purées and pies. Citrus and hard fruits can be stored, like vegetables, either in polythene bags in the refrigerator or outside the refrigerator in paper bags or a cardboard box in a cool place. Never use polythene bags in warm temperatures. They would cause the fruit to rot more rapidly.

To store citrus or hard fruit for more than a week, wrap each piece separately in newspaper before putting them in a plastic bag in the refrigerator or in a box in a cool place. If under-ripe, some varieties of apples, quinces and pears will keep like this for months. Oranges will keep for about three weeks, tangerines and limes for about two weeks, lemons and grapefruit for about a month. Bitter (Seville) oranges may not keep more than a week, but they can be frozen as their spoilt texture will not harm the marmalade or jam for which they are intended.

Bananas should not be wrapped or refrigerated but hung in a cool place. Avocado pears should not be chilled either. Both develop black skins if refrigerated and their ability to ripen is impaired.

Bunches of grapes and stone fruit can be stored wrapped or open in the refrigerator, or wrapped separately in newspaper and kept in the dark in a cool place.

Be sure to store strong-smelling fruit such as cut pineapple or melon well wrapped in the refrigerator. Their fragrance will affect the flavour and smell of cheese, butter and milk.

CHEESE should be chosen by its texture and smell; there should be no sign of sweating on the surface and the smell, even if strong, should never be rancid or yeasty. Sample the cheese in the shop if possible. Once home, cheese should be kept covered in foil which, unlike plastic wrap, does not cause it to sweat. Plastic wrap will do no harm while the cheese is refrigerated but it will sweat unpleasantly if at all warm. In the refrigerator on the warmest shelf, soft cheese can be stored for up5 days and hard cheese up to two. After refrigeration, unwrap the cheese and let it warm up and 'breathe' for about an hour to bring out its fragrance and flavour before eating it.

Outside the refrigerator, store soft cheese in a cool place (below 10°C/50°F) for a day or two, and hard cheese up to 5 days. The cut surface of a large cheese can be protected by a sheet of plastic wrap, but do not cover the whole cheese.

OTHER DAIRY PRODUCTS such as milk, cream and butter should be kept in a cool place and preferably in the refrigerator. All of them should be stored well covered with plastic wrap or with lids in place to protect them from the flavour and fragrance of other foods.

EGGS can be stored for a few weeks at room temperature but will keep very much longer when refrigerated. Remember to remove refrigerated eggs an hour or so before using them for cake making and whisking — room temperature eggs whisk to a greater volume than cold ones. Cracked eggs and separated eggs should be stored in the refrigerator covered with plastic to prevent drying out. Egg yolks can also be covered with a thin layer of water or milk to seal them off from the air if they are destined for scrambled eggs or omelettes.

MEAT AND POULTRY If stored at higher than 16°C/60°F, meat should be eaten in 24 hours. If kept at 10°C/50°F in, say, an unrefrigerated larder, meat will keep satisfactorily for 48 hours and domesticated poultry for 24 hours. If meat is refrigerated at 2°C/35°F, it will keep for up to a week, but it will dry out. Poultry, even if refrigerated, should not be kept more than four days. Liver and other offal and sliced or minced meat should be eaten as fresh as possible, preferably on the day of purchase.

If meat and poultry cannot be eaten within these limits, they should be frozen or salted. If they have to be stored, immediately remove them from any plastic covering as this will cause them to sweat, become slimy and decompose due to bacterial growth.

To counteract the hardening and drying out of meat and poultry, spread a thin layer of butter or margarine over the surface of the flesh to form a seal or cover it loosely with foil.

FISH does not improve on storage. If it is to be kept longer than 12 hours, it should be frozen. If necessary it can be kept, at most, one to two days in the coldest part of the refrigerator. Scatter cubed or cracked ice over it, replacing the ice as necessary, and cover the container to prevent the smell of fish tainting other food in the refrigerator. If this method of storage is not possible, wrap the fish in a cold wet cloth and keep it as cool as possible.

SMOKED FISH AND SMOKED ROE can be stored in a covered container in the refrigerator for a few days or hung in a cool dry place. Freeze if they need to be stored for longer. This will slightly impair the texture, but will not affect flavour if eaten within one month.

CAVIAR AND OTHER LIGHTLY SALTED FISH ROES should be eaten within a week of opening. If more heavily salted, roes will keep refrigerated for longer but are better the sooner they are eaten.

FRESH HARD FISH ROES (EGGS) OR SOFT ROES (SPERM) should be eaten as fresh as possible or be frozen and then defrosted just before they are needed.

SEAFOOD, which includes crustaceans such as lobster and crabs, and molluscs, such as oysters and mussels, perishes quickly. For this reason, seafood is generally sold alive, frozen or already cooked. Cook freshly killed or thawed shellfish immediately. After cooking, seafood can be stored refrigerated for up to four days but the quality of the taste deteriorates significantly after a day or so.

To store live shellfish, put oysters (curved side down to prevent them losing their juices), mussels, lobsters or crabs in an open basket, box or bucket and cover them with a damp cloth. Keep them in the bottom of the refrigerator at about 5°C/41°F. Eat as soon as possible as they lose weight and condition after a few days.

READING A RECIPE

Almost the most difficult aspect of cooking for many cooks is knowing how much salt to put into anything. 'A pinch' says the recipe, or 'season to taste', which can be daunting if not downright unhelpful. Unfortunately, there are two answers: the nutritionist's advice would be 'add as little as you can get away with', whereas the gastronome's or classic cook's might be: 'as much as you can get away with' — or the maximum amount of salt that the dish will bear without the diner being able to taste it. Food salted by the cook should never taste salty, or 'of salt'. But it will not taste of much at all if there is no salt in it. Salt, from a cook's point of view, is there to bring out the flavour of the food. A vegetable soup, however well made with the best ingredients, will be 'tasteless' without salt. It is surprising how much salt it will need before it tastes full-bodied.

But what do recipes mean by 'a pinch'? They mean all the salt you can pick up by digging three fingers deep into the salt pot — about half a teaspoon in fact. 'A teaspoon' of anything means a level 5ml teaspoon (that is a largish old-fashioned medicine spoon or teaspoon, not a modern shallow slimline one). All spoon measurements in recipes are level ones.

And how much does 'chopped parsley' or 'tarragon sprigs' or 'icing sugar for decoration' imply? Generally, if the quantity is not specified, the ingredient is not there primarily for the flavour, but for the look of the dish, and the cook can judge by reading the recipe. 'Chopped parsley' on the top should, in our opinion, be just enough to give the dish a fresh and cared-for look, not so much as to hide the ingredients underneath from view. The 'dust with icing sugar' instruction can be obeyed according to the likes of the cook. Some things, like plain un-chocolated profiteroles, look best heavily dredged with an even layer of icing sugar. Others, like complicated chocolate cakes or apple crumbles with uneven crusty tops, look best lightly powdered. Perhaps the best advice is to do it lightly, take a look, and add some more if you think it needs it.

And what does 'preheat the oven' mean? It means get it to the required heat before putting the food in it.

What does 'separate the eggs' mean? Not, as one student at Leith's quite reasonably assumed, putting the brown eggs on one side of the table and the white ones on the other. (For how to separate eggs, see page 280).

And what about 'baste' and 'sweat', 'sauté' and 'dégorge'? Reading a recipe, for a novice as yet uninitiated into the secret language of the cult, can be very frustrating. 'Why can't they write English?' must be the constant cry of the learner-cook. But the fact is that shortcut terms are essential to cooking as any jargon is to its trade. Once mastered, the words are a help — instead of having to plough through a long paragraph instructing: 'heat the butter until melted but not foaming, add the chopped onions, cover them closely to prevent the escape of steam, and cook over gentle heat until they are soft, cooked and transparent, but on no account browned or crisply fried,' the cook need only read 'sweat the onions,' which makes for more cooking and less reading time.

A glossary of the most common and useful cooking terms is on p.344. The keen cook should learn them by heart. The understanding of them will make such classics as Escoffier's *Le Guide Culinaire*, the *Larousse Gastronomique*, Herring's *Dictionary of Gastronomy* and *Le Répertoire de la Cuisine* books of pleasure and information, rather than incomprehensible tomes.

SWEATING ONIONS
Cook chopped onions very slowly in melted butter. Cover with a piece of greaseproof paper to create a steamy atmosphere. The onions should be soft, cooked and transparent, but not brown.

TRADITIONAL DISHES

Inexperienced cooks are often nervous of getting the serving of such special-event food as caviar and smoked salmon wrong in some small detail. Of course it should not matter, but if the cook knows what is supposed to be done, then he or she can decide whether to break the rules or not.

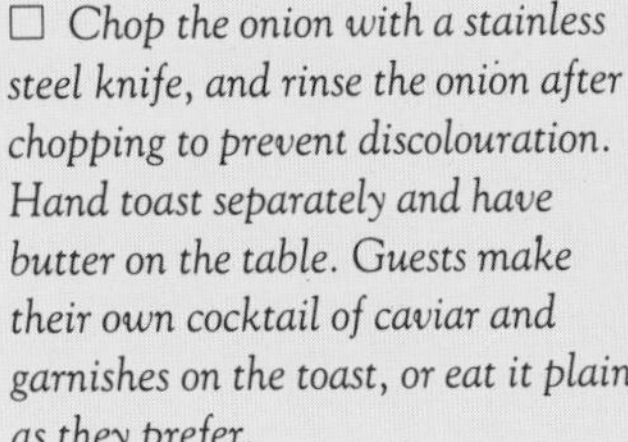

☐ *Chop the onion with a stainless steel knife, and rinse the onion after chopping to prevent discolouration. Hand toast separately and have butter on the table. Guests make their own cocktail of caviar and garnishes on the toast, or eat it plain as they prefer.*

CAVIAR *25g/1oz per person*

Leave the caviar in its original pot. Chill it, and stand on a napkin. Serve a teaspoon onto each guest's plate, and offer, from another platter, wedges of lemon, chopped hard-boiled egg white and sieved yolk (in separate piles) chopped parsley and chopped raw onion.

BROWN SHRIMPS *150ml/¼pt per person*

Serve the shrimps in piles, unshelled, on individual plates with hot bread, good butter, lemon wedges and salt and black pepper. The guests shell their own shrimps. Provide finger bowls.

POTTED SHRIMPS *One small pot per person*

Warm the pots gently in the oven, and when the butter is just melted, or at least soft, turn out onto individual plates. Offer toast (no butter) and lemon wedges separately, and a knife and fork to eat them with. This is the traditional way of serving shrimps, but today they are sometimes turned out cold and eaten, like pâté, *on* rather than with the toast. They are better just warm however. Do not re-chill them once melted.

GULLS EGGS *2 per person*

Hardboil the eggs by boiling them for 8 minutes. *PLOVERS EGGS (4 per person)* boil for 6 minutes. *QUAILS EGGS (6 per person)* boil for 4 minutes. Serve in a basket lined with lettuce leaves or a napkin, and offer sea or rock salt, celery salt or oriental salt, black pepper and cayenne pepper separately. Serve brown bread and butter. The guests peel the eggs and eat them in their fingers.

OYSTERS *Nine or 12 per person*

Serve 6 each if there is a big meal to come, but oyster lovers like a lot! Order the oysters and ask for them to be opened only when you are there to collect them, or as late as possible. Keep refrigerated until serving. If the fishmonger has not loosened the oysters from the bottom shell do so with a sharp knife. Check that there no bits of shell or grit on the saucer-shaped bottom shells on which they lie but leave any seawater or juices with them. Discard the top shells. Put the oysters onto oyster plates, or failing them, onto dinner plates covered by a napkin to keep them from tipping or rolling. Hand Tabasco sauce, or chilli pepper, black pepper, white pepper, wedges of lemon and vinegar separately and serve with brown bread and butter. The diner eats the oysters with a fork, and drinks the juice from the shell as from a cup.

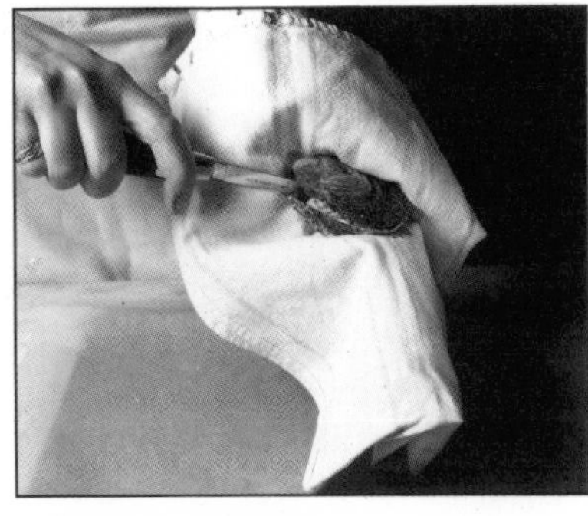

OPENING OYSTERS
Protect your hand with a cloth. Lay the oyster rounded side down in it to catch the juices. Insert an oyster knife between the shells near the hinge, and lever them apart.

OURSINS *(Sea urchins) 3 per person*

Serve exactly as oysters, with the same accompaniments, but with a teaspoon for the guest to extract the flesh. The fishmonger cuts off the top of the shell, like the top of a boiled egg.

SMOKED SALMON *75g/3oz per person*

Arrange slices in a single layer on dinner plates. Hand lemon wedges or halves and brown bread and butter separately. To slice smoked salmon: use a salmon or ham knife. Put the fish skin-side down on the board. Slice the top thin layer of smoked skin-like flesh off, then feel for the row of lateral bones whose tips will be sticking like pins straight up in a row between the two fillets of flesh, in a line running the length of the fish. Pull them out, one by one, with tweezers or pliers. Then slice the flesh horizontally in paper thin pieces. Keep covered or painted with salad oil.

SMOKED TROUT *1 per person*

Use scissors to cut the smoked skin carefully round the neck and tail before loosening it with the fingers and peeling it off, leaving head and tail intact. Serve on individual plates with lemon wedges, handing brown bread and butter and horseradish sauce (p.231) separately.

SMOKED MACKEREL *Half a fish per person*

Peel the fish and carefully lift the fillets off the backbone. There will be four of them. Arrange two per person on plates with lemon wedges and hand mustard, mayonnaise (p.61) or horseradish sauce separately.

ASPARAGUS *Allow 6 fat or 12 thin spears per person*

Cut off the woody ends. Peel the fibrous stalks. Wash well. Tie in bundles. Boil in an asparagus cooker (the stalks stand in the water, the tips cook in the steam) or simmer lying down in salted water in a frying pan, until the stalk is tender halfway down. Drain well. Serve from a platter lined with a napkin to absorb the moisture. Hand melted clarified butter, hollandaise or beurre blanc separately if hot; vinaigrette if cold.

ARTICHOKES *1 per person*

Twist and pull the stalk off the artichoke very close to the base so that it will stand without rolling. See illustrations. Trim off straight the tips of the bottom few rows of leaves if they are hard or cracked and anyway if the tip spines are prickly. Leave the smaller higher leaves. Boil for 45 minutes in salted water with a cut-up lemon and 1tbsp oil in it. When a leaf (not an outside one) will pull out easily, drain the artichokes upside down. When cool enough to handle, prise open the middle leaves and lift out the central cluster of tiny leaves. Using a teaspoon scrape out the fibrous ‘choke’ and discard it. Serve the artichokes on individual plates on a folded napkin. Give each guest a small pot of clarified melted butter if the artichokes are hot, or vinaigrette dressing if cold. The guest pulls the leaves off the flowerhead, dips the flesh end into the butter or sauce eats the softer part with his fingers and discards the leaves.

SMOKED SALMON

1 Cut a thin layer, lifting the side bones away from the smoked salmon side.

2 Trim off the fatty edge.

3 Feel along the flesh with fingertips to locate the remaining row of small lateral bones, and extract them with tweezers or hook them out with a potato peeler.

PREPARING AN ARTICHOKE

1 Cut off the tips of the artichoke's leaves with a kitchen knife. Use scissors to trim the lower leaves.

2 Make a shallow cut around the stalk about 2cm/1 inch from the head. The idea is to just score the stalk, not to sever it.

1

2

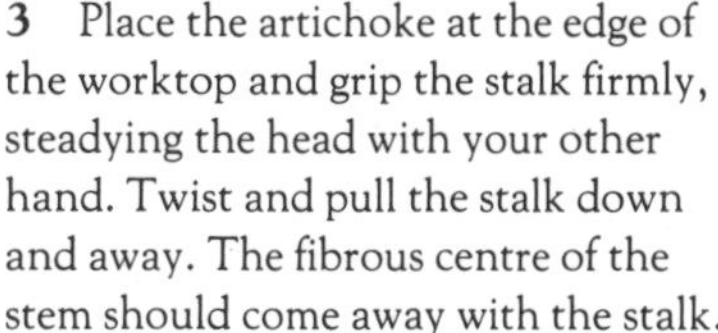

3 Place the artichoke at the edge of the worktop and grip the stalk firmly, steadying the head with your other hand. Twist and pull the stalk down and away. The fibrous centre of the stem should come away with the stalk.

4 Trim off the rest of the stalk with a kitchen knife.

3

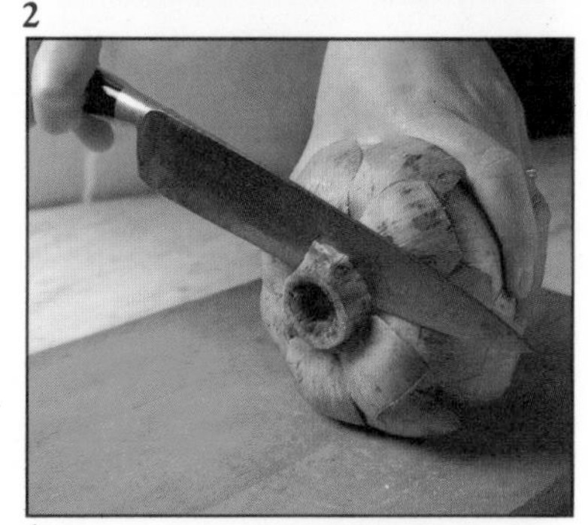

4

5 When cooked, gently separate the tops of the outer leaves and pull out the central bud of small leaves.

6 Use a teaspoon to scrape out the fibrous 'choke' from the heart.

5

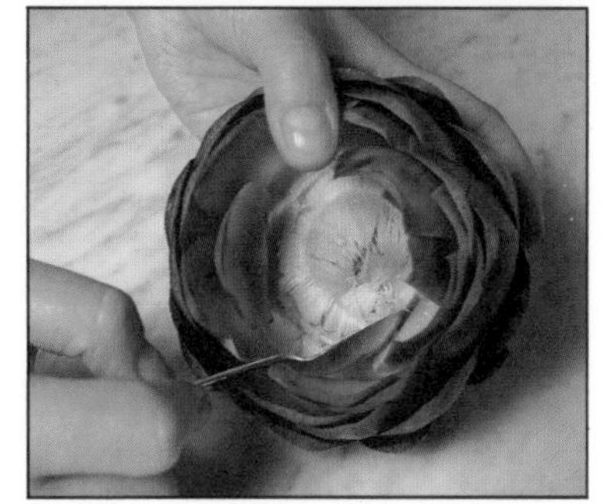

6

MENU PLANNING

The menu lessons in this book are all carefully planned, but it may be useful to include a few guidelines here for menu planning if the cook is to make the decisions. In any event, outside factors such as the availability or cost of ingredients, the time allotted for preparation, or the likes and dislikes of family and friends are bound to force some changes.

The most obvious rule, but the most important, must be to KEEP IT SIMPLE. There is no point in attempting so much that the quality of execution is threatened. Not many cooks can produce half a dozen things sublimely well all at once. So plan things so that at least two-thirds of the preparation and cooking can be done in advance, so that the meal is feasible — no good planning two hot baked courses both requiring warmed dinner plates if there is only one oven, or ending up trying to stir-fry the last-minute vegetables at the same time as assembling a complicated main course. Make a plan of action, right down to: 7.55 — dish the potatoes, add the mint. 8.00 — take the wine from the fridge etc.

Don't be too proud to stick the plan of action on the wall and follow it, slave-like. Professional cooks do it all the time and it saves their sanity. It also saves a lot of time.

BALANCE IS ALL It is possible to have a seven course meal of such exquisite balance that the guests go home at midnight feeling fit for a day's work, and equally to produce two courses so out of kilter as to make everyone feel bloated and ill, and fit for nothing.

The commonest problem is simply too much rich food. The French, great cooks and great gastronomes that they are, are heavily to blame. Even the famous Nouvelle Cuisine is butter-laden and cream-laden, scarce in vegetables and high in protein. The secret is not to abandon creamy or buttery dishes, but to limit their size and number.

If the first and second courses of a dinner party have contained little fat, and have been on the small side, then an exquisite coffee cream pudding or a wickedly fattening meringue will be greeted with real pleasure, instead of weary groans and sighs, and will be eaten with appreciation, not guilt. A little is genuinely better than a lot, and hosts need never feel they must provide second helpings of everything. Very often guests are relieved to be given modest amounts to eat. Most of us eat more than is healthy, and it is nice to be let off the ritual of refusing second helpings and feeling churlish and rude, or accepting them and feeling guilty and gross.

The best way to check for nutritional balance is to run through the proposed courses to see that cream, fat, or large amounts of butter do not appear in more than one of them, and that the animal protein content is nicely balanced with vegetables or fruit to provide fibre and vitamins. At a hotel banquet, I once had a meal that, though it looked innocent enough, was so high in fat and animal protein, it should have been labelled 'Dangerous to health'. It was a pork and liver terrine served with toast and butter, a roast shoulder of lamb, roast potatoes, spring vegetables, crème caramel and, finally, Angels on horseback.

Chatting merrily we ate everything, without noticing that the cholesterol count was inordinately high. It was only when feeling much the worse for wear the next day that I thought to properly consider the balance of that meal: the terrine, garnished as it was with watercress, looked innocent enough, even healthy. But it was made with fatty pork, and served with plenty of butter on the toast. Plain, slightly pink and perfectly cooked lamb, especially served with plenty of vegetables seemed positively virtuous, but lamb shoulder is wonderfully flavoursome and moist precisely *because* it is very fatty, and the brilliant vegetables had got their sheen from a liberal dousing in butter. Only the roast potatoes openly showed their colours — everyone knows roast potatoes are fatty and fattening — but then, they are impossible to resist. Crème caramel, that innocent looking nursery pudding, is made of eggs, cream, milk and sugar. Oysters and bacon, the main ingredients of the 'angels', are both high in cholesterol and they sat on delicious little fried bread croûtes, probably fried in beef dripping.

The main things to aim for are plenty of fresh vegetables and fruit, some starch, and not too many fatty foods or meaty ones.

MENU CONTENT There are also a few mental checks that you should run through when planning a menu, as much for the gastronomic pleasure and interest of the diner as for healthy eating:

1 Avoid too many eggs in the meal. It is easy to forget that custards, cakes, and many pastries contain eggs, and if the first course is, say, an egg mousse or a quiche it would be wiser to have a fruit dessert.

2 Check that the vegetables are sufficiently interesting. Avoid having two members of the brassicca family (like cauliflower and sprouts).

3 Check that the first course and the dessert are not both predominantly fruit (such as melon to start and fruit salad to finish).

4 Check that fish does not appear twice, such as a seafood salad followed by a baked seabass.

5 Check that no two courses contain similar poultry or meat, such as chicken liver pâté followed by Coq au vin.

6 Check that the meal contains good colour, texture and taste contrast.

7 Check that the wines, if served, are in the right order and are suitable to accompany the food. In brief: red should follow white; older wines should follow younger ones; strong big wines should follow delicate light ones; white wines go with fish, white meat and delicate poultry; red wines go with red meat, poultry, game and cheese. (For wine see p.25.)

COLOUR Unless you are deliberately designing a dish or a menu to suit a colour theme such as a red fruit salad of red cherries, strawberries, raspberries, redcurrants, water melon, red plums etc., then the best rule is contrast without garishness. The commonest problem is too white a meal — pale soup, chicken, cauliflower, rice, meringues and cream. But never include brightly coloured food just for the colour alone. Those awful wet tomatoes one gets in steakhouses to cheer up a brown steak with brown chips, are just such an example. I agree the steak could do with the colour, but I would rather see a sprig of edible watercress, or a well-grilled tomato half, than the meaningless tasteless whole tomato.

TEXTURE Again, contrast is the thing. If the casserole is soft, and it is to be served with mashed potatoes to mop up the gravy, then provide something crunchy to go with it — not too-cooked carrots for example, or crisp French beans. Beware of the 'all baby-food' meal, too. Some cooks have found their electric food processors, which chop, purée and grind so magically, too seductive to resist and the result can be a smooth pâté, followed by lasagne, followed by Floating islands — so that one longs for something to get one's teeth into, literally.

The use of unusual oils and vinegars can often subtly enhance the flavour of a dish. Raspberry vinegar *(top left)* adds light fresh flavour to dressings. Tarragon vinegar *(top right)* is good with white meat salads. Walnut oil *(above left)* is expensive and aromatic, while hazelnut oil *(above right)* is more delicately flavoured.

TASTE Beware of over-complication. If carrots taste delicious flavoured with ginger, and cabbage is good with caraway, and beetroot is helped by a pinch of cumin, it does not follow that all those vegetables, so treated, will be good together. Too many distinct tastes numb the palate leading to an overall confusion rather like mixing together every colour in the paint box. As a general rule, the aim of British and French cooks has been to let the intrinsic taste of the main ingredient dominate, with a minimum of masking or flavour-changing. The aim is quite different to, say, that of Indian cooking where the subtle, complicated and careful mixing of spices is designed to alter, sometimes unrecognizably, the original ingredients.

There are exceptions in British cooking, where strong tastes are added, usually as an optional accompaniment, to contrast and complement food, such as the serving of chutney with cold meats, mustard with roasts etc. But, generally, seasonings are added to enhance and emphasize the true taste of the main ingredient. Fernand Point, great chef and father of the 20th-century gastronomic revival, said: 'I believe above all else that a chicken should taste of chicken, the very best, most perfect chicken, the most carefully bred, the healthiest chicken in its prime, prepared with infinite care and cooked in such a way that nothing of its essence be lost.'

Which brings me to the whole problem of taste. What tastes *right?* How does one know if it tastes right? I think that, for the beginner cook who lacks confidence in his or her judgement, the only way to learn to taste — and cooks learn to taste food just as wine-tasters learn to taste wine — is to consciously think about the food while tasting it. It is very easy to swallow a mouthful without noticing anything about it — whether it was too salty, too weak, too strong, too sweet, or even what it tasted of.

While cooking the Menu Lessons in this book, taste everything at every stage, and try to distinguish the flavours in your mouth. We have often noticed at Leith's school that students are shy to say what they detect in tasting a dish and yet, when pressed to take a guess, they will guess right. Students of wine have the same problem — they are perhaps so overawed by the image of the erudite wine taster that they forget he is using the same equipment as the rest of us — taste buds and nose.

A simple way to gain confidence in your ability to taste is to conduct this experiment: make a jug of simple lemonade by mixing 300ml/½pt water with 1½ tbsp sugar dissolved in a cup of hot water, and the juice of 2 small lemons. Now pour two glasses. Chill one and leave the other at room temperature. The warmer one will taste both sweeter, when it first touches the tongue, and more acid and generally stronger than the iced one after swallowing. This is because cold impairs the action of the taste buds — which is why ice cream mixtures are always over-sweetened and over-flavoured. Next, with the drinks at the same temperature, add a teaspoon of sherry to one glass and a drop of peppermint essence to the other. See if you can detect the difference. Then add a shake of cinnamon to the sherry-flavoured drink and a grating of nutmeg to the other. Keep your eyes shut, muddle them up and see if you can still detect the various flavours. Continue to complicate the tastes until you are thoroughly muddled. You will be astonished at how acute your sense of taste is.

The thing to remember is that most foods have more than one taste. Braised red cabbage for example, will be sweet (from the apples and sugar) and at the same time sour (from the apples and vinegar), and this is quite apart from the taste of cabbage, garlic and anything else in the pot.

The use of herbs offers endless horizons of culinary pleasure. *From top to bottom:* Coriander adds an exotic flavour to salads. Mint gives a unique, refreshing taste to vegetables. Rosemary should be used sparingly, but its clean woody taste is ideal for poultry and meat. And basil's pungent flavour enhances vegetable salads.

Another, perhaps obvious thing to remember is that taste is one of life's great pleasures, and for the cook to neglect its possibilities is senseless. Many wonderful flavours can be enjoyed without any effort on the part of the cook. It does seem sad that, for example, when so many different flavours of salad oil, different types of vinegar and different varieties of mustards or herbs are available, that most of us still make all our vinaigrette dressings with the same oil, the same vinegar, the same flavourings, and still use parsley to excess and other herbs hardly at all.

Even salts are interesting. Try tasting, side by side, unadulterated cooking salt (rock salt or sea salt) and so-called 'table salt' containing magnesium sulphate (which is what makes it free-flowing) or iodised salt. The difference may not be apparent in strong-flavoured dishes, but a stick of celery dipped into salt, a potato crisp sprinkled with it or a salad made with nothing but olive oil and salt will taste much better if pure salt is used. Unusual oils (hazelnut, walnut, sesame, virgin olive) are more expensive than the tasteless salad oils such as corn oil, rape seed oil and arachide (groundnut or peanut) and one would not want to use them as frequently and as lavishly as one does the cheaper oils, but for an instantly new and different taste, a tablespoon of hazelnut oil in the salad or a sprinkling of sesame oil on stir-fried vegetables will work wonders. Or try frying in olive oil — the taste is evocatively Mediterranean.

Try different mustards or vinegars for sauces and dressings. Mustards come in many guises, and though it is obviously not feasible to have too many pots on the go at once, it is unadventurous, to say the least, to keep buying the same brands year after year. A good compromise would be to have English mustard in dry form (it keeps almost indefinitely and produces fresher stronger mustard than the ready-made variety) and to experiment with more exotic mustards, one at a time, bought in jars. Nouvelle cuisine chefs have fallen so in love with raspberry vinegar (see p. 274) that there has been a sort of culinary backlash with fashionable chefs now despising it (as they despise the kiwi fruit because of its popularity a few years ago) but gastronomy should not be a slave to fashion. If it tasted wonderful two years ago, it still will today. And both raspberry vinegar and kiwi fruit (and its fashionable successors the mangosteen, rambutan, mango, passionfruit and lychee) should have an occasional place in our kitchens if our pockets can stand the strain.

A walk round a good food store or delicatessen can be an eye-opener. It is worthwhile trying, for example, honeys made from specified flowers or different parts of the country. They vary astonishingly. Look for the Bee-keepers' Association symbol on the label. There is a lot of illegally labelled blended honey available which, though perfectly good, does not have the delicacy of a single-flower or single-hive honey.

Yoghurt, too, can be a surprise. Supermarkets are now selling many varieties of yoghurt, including the wonderfully flavoured Greek variety. This, with a spoon of good runny honey on top, and perhaps a few unshelled sweet Jordan almonds, must be one of the easiest and most delicious puddings.

Salad herbs and edible flowers are a marvellous pleasure ground for the cook. In the Paris markets you can buy electric-orange coloured nasturtium flowers, as well as pumpkin flowers and courgette flowers. The former go in salads, and the last two are stuffed and steamed. It is worth buying a book on edible leaves and flowers, both wild and cultivated. They afford endless possibilities for experiment.

Even without access to Paris markets, gardens and hedgerows, the cook's lot, at least in the bigger towns, is improving. Supermarkets now carry all sorts of fresh pasta — and it is worth buying them one by one and trying them — dozens of varieties of good cheeses, including many new English and traditional French goats' cheeses, and a few strange new salad vegetables which provide inspiration for the creative cook. Try a slice of goats' cheese, grilled briefly to brown the top and to warm it through, served on a bed of unusual saladini, or small leaves, such as mâche (lamb's lettuce or corn salad), radicchio (the red lettuce), chicory and endive, dressed only with a little walnut oil and sprinkled with sea salt. Nothing could be more delicious, prettier or easier to achieve.

PRESENTATION

The way we present food, or dish it up, influences the diner's attitude to it enormously. However delicious a bought wrapped sandwich is, and however wholesome a bottle of fresh milk, neither looks too good plonked on a table just like that. The same milk in a glass jug, the same sandwich cut into quarters and put on a plate, crusts down and filling up, will immediately look more appealing.

The same principle applies to all food. There are attractive ways and unattractive ways of presentation, and it is surprisingly easy to get it right. Many a good cook does not have the reputation he or she deserves, simply because the food *looks* unappetizing. Sadly, the reverse is true also, especially in restaurants and hotels. Wonderfully presented food may cry out to be eaten, only to prove disappointingly bland or stale.

So presentation, decoration or what professionals rather unattractively call 'garnishing' won't do as a substitute for good cooking, but if the cook has got the taste right, it does seem a pity to stop there. Why not get the look right too?

Chefs have a saying: 'the customer buys with his eyes'. So does any diner. Perhaps not with money, but his first impression is the one he will probably stay with. If the dish looks good, he will be predisposed to find it tasting good. If it looks dull or unattractive, it will need to be sublimely good to get him to change his mind.

So what constitutes good dishing up? There are, as in most matters of design and style, some golden rules:

KEEP IT SIMPLE Over-garnished and elaborately decorated food rarely looks right. Even grand and complicated buffet pieces, like whole salmon in aspic or glazed boars' heads, are more effective if the design is basically restrained and ordered. The simply dressed salmon on p.59 looks more edible, less artificial and less 'messed about' than it would if covered with a deep layer of aspic, rosettes of mayonnaise, tomatoes cut into waterlilies, radish roses, cucumber curls, lemon wedges and everything else the cook can lay hands on.

KEEP IT FRESH Nothing looks more off-putting than tired food. If salad wilts when dressed in advance, if sauté potatoes become dull and dry when kept warm for hours, and whipped cream goes buttery in a warm room, don't risk it. The slight trouble — if the cook is organized — of last-minute salad-tossing or dishing up is a price worth paying.

KEEP IT RELEVANT A sprig of fresh watercress complements lamb cutlets nicely. The texture, taste and colour all do something for the lamb. But scratchy sprigs of parsley, though they might provide the colour, are unpleasant to eat. Gherkins cut into fans do nothing for salads, tomato slices do not improve the look of a platter of sandwiches — they rather serve to confuse and distract the eye. It is better by far to dish up a plate of chicken mayonnaise with a couple of suitable salads (rice salad and tomato salad, for example) to provide the colour and contrast needed, than to adorn it with undressed tomato waterlilies or inedible baskets fashioned out of lemon skins and filled with frozen sweetcorn.

There are, happily, some simple tricks to good presentation. Of course they are not hard and fast rules, but they allow the cook to confidently and speedily dish up food, almost without thinking, knowing that it will look appetizing. Almost all of them apply whether the food is homely and comforting, and best served in earthenware or wooden bowls, or sophisticated and elegant, gracing the best bone china.

CENTRE HEIGHT Dishes served on platters, such as chicken sauté, meringues, profiteroles or even a bean salad, are best given 'centre height' — arranged so the mound of food is higher in the middle with sides sloping down. Coat carefully and evenly with the sauce, if any. Do not overload with food, which makes dishing up difficult. Once breached, an over-large pile of food looks unattractive.

CONTRASTING ROWS Biscuits, petits fours, little cakes, cocktail canapés all look good if arranged in rows (each row consisting of one variety) rather than dotted about. Pay attention to contrasting colour, taking care, say, not to put two rows of chocolate biscuits side by side, or two rows of white sandwiches.

DIAGONAL LINES Diamond shapes and diagonal lines are easier to achieve than straight ones. Somehow the eye is more conscious of unevenness in verticals, horizontals and rectangles.

NOT TOO MANY COLOURS As with any design, it is easier to get a pleasing effect if the colours are controlled — say, just green and white, or just pink and green, or chocolate and coffee colours or even two shades of one colour. Coffee icing and hazel nuts give a cake an elegant restrained look. Adding multi-coloured icings to a cake, or every available garnish on a salad tends to look garish. There are exceptions of course: a colourful salad Niçoise can be as pleasing to the eye as a dish of candy-coated chocolate drops.

CONTRASTING THE SIMPLE AND THE ELABORATE If the dish or bowl is elaborately decorated, contrastingly simple food tends to show it off better. A Victorian fruit epergne with ornate stem and silver carving will look stunning filled with fresh strawberries. Conversely, a plain white plate sets off pretty food design to perfection. The modern nouvelle cuisine presentation of food, individually plated for each person in a careful pattern, works better on a plain plate.

UNEVEN NUMBERS As a rule uneven numbers of, say, rosettes of cream on a cake, baked apples in a long dish, or portions of meat on a platter look better than even numbers. This is especially true of small numbers. Five and three invariably look better than four, but there is little difference in effect between 11 and 12.

A GENEROUS LOOK Tiny piped cream stars, or sparsely dotted nuts, or mean-looking chocolate curls (or caraque) on a cake look amateurish and rather stingy.

AVOID CLUMSINESS On the other hand, the temptation to cram the last spoon of rice into the bowl, or squeeze the last slice of pâté onto the dish leads to a clumsy look, and is rather daunting to the diner.

THE GOLDEN RULES

KEEP IT SIMPLE

KEEP IT FRESH

KEEP IT RELEVANT

PRESENTATION TRICKS

CENTRE HEIGHT

CONTRASTING ROWS

NOT TOO MANY COLOURS

SIMPLE WITH ELABORATE

UNEVEN NUMBERS

GENEROUS LOOK

AVOID CLUMSINESS

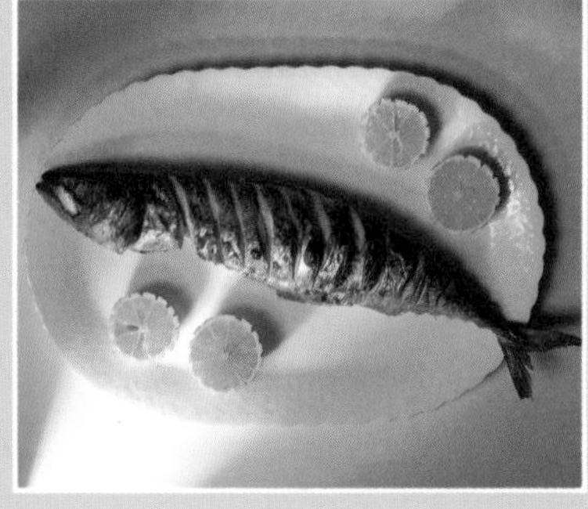

BEST SIDE UPPERMOST

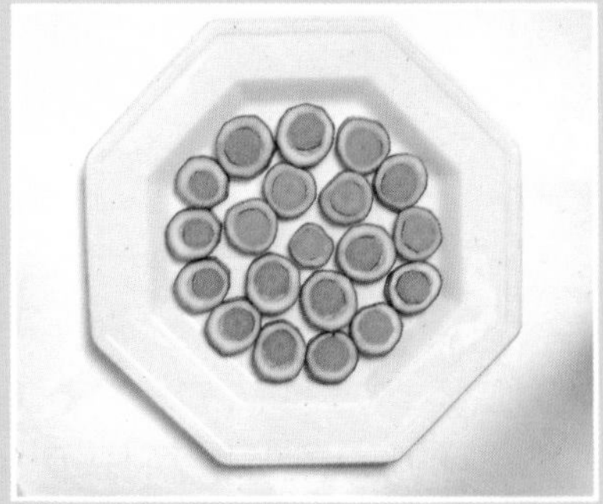

WITTY FOOD

OVERLAPPING Chops, steaks, sliced meats, even rashers of bacon look best evenly overlapping. This way, more of them can be fitted comfortably on the serving dish than if placed side by side.

BEST SIDE UPPERMOST Usually the side of a steak or a cutlet that is grilled or fried first looks the best, and should be placed uppermost. Bones are generally unsightly and, if they cannot be clipped off or removed, should be tucked out of the way.

WITTY FOOD It is sometimes amusing, and attractive, to produce food which raises a smile or intrigues the diner. The courgettes stuffed with carrots in our picture are a good example, as are bowls of cold soup with names written on them — a neat way of combining first course and place name.

WINE

Wine, of course, is not obligatory at a meal. Strong tasting curries, for example, are often better served with dry cider or beer.

But wine matters as much as food in many meals — especially formal ones — and the cook, who is likely also to be the wine buyer, should know a little about it. It is a fascinating subject, well worth the daunting plunge of first buying a book on wine and settling down to study it. As this is essentially a cook book there is space only for the barest introduction to the subject.

The taste of wine is, crudely put, either sour or sweet, or a combination of the two. On top of that, the wine may be heavy or light, young or well aged, or be described by reference to anything that the taste of the wine brings to mind — flowery, stony, fruity, woody, etc. Wines from certain regions have recognizable characteristics given them by the grape variety grown, the soil it is grown in, the weather, the method of fermentation and so on. These distinctions are becoming more confused as countries, especially those with a new wine industry, grow each others' grape varieties and adopt each others' methods of vinification. But broadly, it goes something like this:

WHITE WINES

GERMANY AND ALSACE grow wonderful, white, fruity, flowery, straw coloured wines such as the Sylvanas, the Riesling of the Moselle or Rhine (Hock) or the Gewürztraminers of Alsace. If they are young and labelled light, dry or Spätlese or 'table wine' they will still be sweeter than the dry table whites of the rest of France, but perfectly dry enough, and most suitable, for serving with shellfish, cold smoked meats, fish and salads.

Germany's greatest and most expensive wines are made from the same grapes but picked so late they are ripe to the point of rottenness, producing dark gold, very sweet and wonderfully flavoured dessert wines, to be drunk with pudding, or better still after it, when nothing can interfere with the incomparable taste that lingers in the mouth, ending as you swallow it, with a little kick of acidity that prevents the sweetness from cloying. These wines are labelled 'Auslese', 'Beerenauslese' (which is even sweeter) and Trockenbeerenauslese (the sweetest of all).

FRANCE mainly grows drier, less fruity wines. The Muscadets and Sancerres of the Loire are usually drunk very young, and they are light, refreshing and tart. Their high acidity makes them particularly suitable for drinking with oily salads or fried fish.

The white wines of Chablis and Burgundy are more expensive, with more 'class' or 'nobility' — by which wine tasters mean more subtle, complicated and interesting tastes. Chablis is classically served with shellfish, and white Burgundy with all white meats, fish and poultry.

Great white Burgundies, with some age and from a fine vineyard such as the famous Montrachet, are powerful enough to drink with stronger tasting foods such as goose or roast pork and onion sauce. The white wines of the Macon (such as the famous Pouilly Fuissé) are worth a try — fresh, grapey and tart, and good with most first courses. There are some excellent, big and powerful white Rhônes like Hermitage Blanc. The dry white wines of Bordeaux are generally less interesting than those of Burgundy, though pleasant and smooth to drink. The great white wines of Bordeaux are the dessert wines of Sauternes and Barsac, made like the German Auslese, with late-picked overripe grapes. They are famous the world over, and a sip of well chilled Château d'Yquem after dinner or with the strawberries is one of the great gastronomic experiences.

France's most famous, and generally most expensive, white wine is champagne. It is given a second fermentation in the bottle to produce the characteristic sparkle. Surprisingly, it is made from predominantly black grapes, but with the skins (which produce the colour in red wine) removed before fermentation. Champagne is most frequently drunk as an aperitif, occasionally through the meal (a good vintage champagne has enough body and character to hold its own with almost any food) and sometimes with the dessert or pudding. Pink champagne is slightly heavier, and generally served as an aperitif. Almost all the wine-growing countries make sparkling wines, but none compare with good champagne.

SPAIN produces increasingly good reliable white wines, but they tend to be uninteresting.

ITALY, on the other hand, produces many popular and diverse wines. Soave or Frascati must be true beginners' wine — fresh, good flavour and easy to drink.

PORTUGAL's most famous white wine export is the well publicized Vinho Verde, which indeed has a faintly green colour. It is light, refreshing and rather acid — good with oily first courses.

YUGOSLAVIA AND SOUTH AFRICA both produce German-style wines, the Yugoslavs exporting Riesling (though from a different grape to the German one), and the South Africans producing a good reliable uniform Steen.

ENGLISH wines are German-style too, some excellent, some appalling.

SOUTH AMERICAN white wines tend to be flat and not very good value.

NORTH AMERICAN white wines from California, if they are good, tend to be expensive in Europe. They follow the dry style of France.

RED WINES

FRANCE produces, without question, the world's greatest red wines, and the only argument is whether Bordeaux or Burgundy carries off the honours. The top growths in both areas fetch astronomical prices and are truly amazing wines — subtle, full, memorable.

Burgundy, being a smaller area, produces less wine than Bordeaux and by and large fetches higher prices. On the other hand, the common run of Burgundies are easier to drink — less hard, less full of acid and tannin, than the cheaper clarets.

Most Rhône red wines are still very good value, pleasant and soft, and ready to drink while yet young. The great Rhônes, such as Côte Rôtie and Hermitage are expensive, incredibly deep flavoured and delicious and need, like all top red wines, long ageing in the bottle.

Beaujolais, apart from the famous 'nouveau' which is, at least in our opinion, a bad and expensive buy, is a wonderfully light, fruity red wine, surprisingly good when served young and chilled at an outdoor lunch. Well-aged Beaujolais from a top individual village, such as Moulin-à-Vent, will rival good Burgundy — Beaujolais is not all light and frivolous.

ITALY produces the famous Chianti, and many great red wines. But the Italian penchant for very sunny, rather 'cooked' red wines often means that, to English tastes, cheaper Italian wines are unpleasantly oxidized — brownish in colour and acrid tasting. Buy young wines from a supermarket with a good turnover.

SPAIN has greatly improved its vinification methods, and their reds are reliably sound, fruity and sunny, big, pleasant and fairly alcoholic. Excellent with unsophisticated country stews and casseroles.

AUSTRALIA, SOUTH AFRICA, CALIFORNIA AND SOUTH AMERICA export some excellent red wines, modelled on the European Clarets, Burgundies and Rhônes, but often with a sunnier, fruitier, fuller flavour. The experts would say they lack complexity, but most are good satisfying wines. Very good buys can be had if older vintages are bought. Most 'new country' reds are drunk young, when they would benefit from some mellowing in the bottle.

ROSE WINES

Mateus Rosé from Portugal is the most widely distributed rosé, but the best dry rosés come from France, notably from Anjou, the Rhône and Provence. But all countries that make red wine, make rosé, and the style tends to follow their red wine style, only lighter, and generally sold young. Serve chilled with first courses, lunchtime main courses (especially if salad-y and light) or with hot fish dishes.

A good set of wine glasses should contain *(from left to right)*: the champagne flute ; the all-purpose Paris goblet—available in 3½oz (liqueur), 5oz (sherry), 8oz (white wine) and 12oz (red wine) sizes. The last three tulip-shaped glasses are best for wine — the 6oz for dessert wine or sherry, the 12oz for red wine and the 8oz for white wine.

CHOOSING, STORING AND SERVING

WHICH VINTAGE? Most of us drink blended non-vintage 'everyday' wines except on special occasions, but when buying more expensive wines, no knowledge at all can be a dangerous thing. In Europe, where the weather can play havoc with any wine-grower's ambitions, it is worth referring to a chart to show what year was good for which region. But in the Southern hemisphere, and in California, the weather is reliably sunny and modern methods mean uniform wines. So the date on the bottle is more an indication of age, and therefore maturity, than of quality.

STORING Most wine today is bought young and drunk almost at once. But if it is to be stored, especially if it is to be laid down to gain some maturity — which would nearly always apply to good quality reds (not whites) — it should be put somewhere cool and dark. (Heat can spoil the flavour, light spoils the colour.) Dampness doesn't matter — if anything it is good for the wine — but take care not to store wine in a damp cellar in its cardboard box, which will rot, and make sure the labels are not against a damp floor or they will become illegible.

Lie all wine bottles on their sides, stacked in rows one on top of the other, head-to-tail, to keep them steady, or put them in wine bins or, if they are in wooden crates, leave them unpacked but with the crate positioned so the bottles are lying, not standing. The reason for this is so that the wine stays in contact with the cork and prevents it drying out, shrinking, and allowing the entrance of air, which will oxidize the wine.

SERVING TEMPERATURE Most red wines are served at 'room temperature', but that need not be as hot as the most modern central heating. The word 'chambré' (brought to room temperature) does not mean, as many wine waiters seem to think it does, heated over the boiler or in a bath of hot water like a baby's bottle. It is better to have the wine on the cool side than positively warm — it will lose its chill very quickly in the glass anyway. If it has been in a cold cellar, stand it in the dining room for an hour or two before dinner. A few red wines (young Beaujolais for example) are occasionally served chilled on hot summer days, and rosé and white wines are always chilled. But do not near-freeze them. The cold inhibits the performance of the tastebuds, and really icy wine has little taste. One or two hours in a domestic refrigerator, half-an-hour in a good cold one set just above freezing (or even 15 minutes in the freezer as long as someone remembers to take it out before the cork blows) will do. Do not leave white wines for weeks in the refrigerator — they might precipitate crystals, which, though harmless, are a nuisance and look unattractive.

Champagnes and sparkling wines are usually served colder than other whites. They are certainly less explosive to open if they are well chilled.

DECANTING Decanting (pouring the wine from the bottle into a carafe or decanter, or another bottle) is done primarily to eliminate sediment and is only necessary with some well-aged red wines. White and rosé wines are not decanted. Some experts believe that young wines benefit from decanting because the aeration they receive provides an instant ageing action, making the wine mellower and softer. Opinions differ, but as the taste of both young and old wines can change dramatically in the glass, and some, regardless of maturity, seem to be perfect on pulling the cork, the easiest rule might be to decant wines with sediment and not to bother with the others. Professionals decant wine with the aid of a candle lit behind the pouring wine so that they can see, as they slowly pour it, when they are down to the sediment. But if the pourer takes care to keep the wine as still and horizontal as possible without spilling it when pulling the cork, and to pour with care, the candle is not really necessary. Just watch very carefully when getting towards the end of the bottle, and stop at first speck of sediment. If sediment does get shaken pour the wine through a filter paper.

OPENING WINE The first requisite is a good corkscrew. The next is to centre it well, and not to turn so much that the screw goes right through the cork and sprinkles cork bits into the wine. If opening well-aged red wine, decant it as described. Otherwise, just open the bottle, wipe the neck to remove any sticky bits and pour the wine. For convenience corks may be pulled in advance and put back in the bottle neck, but this should not be done more than three hours before dinner. A very few wines, such as the strong Italian Barolos, do benefit from being kept open at room temperature for up to six hours — their flavour seems to soften and grow.

All wines risk deterioration if left exposed to air for long. Open white wines, if kept refrigerated, keep longer than reds — if the bottles are full and re-corked they may be perfectly good three days later. Reds are unlikely to keep (even re-corked and refrigerated) more than 24 hours.

Leftover wine should be used quickly either for drinking or cooking. If it must be kept at all pour it into small screw-topped bottles so that as much air as possible is eliminated.

SHERRY AND PORT Medium or dry sherry is sometimes served with clear soup, and port is often served with cheese, especially Stilton. However, the practice of pouring the port into a scooped-out Stilton is horrific — it makes the cheese look disgusting, curdled and purple, and anyone then wanting it as the Stilton makers intended is thwarted.

There is a popular pleasant white or pale pink wine from the Rhône, Muscat de Beaumes de Venise, which is a dessert wine for drinking with pudding or fruit. It is high in alcohol having been fortified with brandy.

TO OPEN CHAMPAGNE

1 Chill it really well. Press on the cork with your thumb while peeling off foil and loosening wires. This will prevent the cork blowing out if the champagne is a little lively.

2 Hold the bottle at an angle, grip the cork firmly in one hand,twist the bottle — not the cork — with the other, and ease the cork out.

3 If the champagne bubbles up when the cork comes out, briefly dip a finger into the top of the bottle. The bubbles will subside.

4 If the bottle is opened at an angle, the champagne will not fizz over as easily as it would if the bottle was held upright.

1

2

3

4

CHOOSING WINE

Wine 'rules' are broken all the time by experienced wine drinkers, but it takes confidence. We would suggest at least for the beginner, an almost slavish devotion to the serving guidelines set out here.

HORS D'OEUVRES, SOUPS AND SALADS

HORS D'OEUVRES, COLD MEATS OR SALADS	Tart and spicy whites, eg Gewürztraminer (Alsace), Muscadet or Sancerre (Loire)	CLEAR SOUPS	Dry sherry or white Burgundy
		CREAMY SOUPS	Any dry white

SHELLFISH

PLAIN	Dry, light whites, eg Chablis (good with oysters), light white Burgundy, Riesling (including Moselle)	IN RICH SAUCES	'Big' dry whites, eg dry white Bordeaux, powerful white Burgundy, eg Meursault or Montagny, white Rhône, eg Hermitage Blanc

FISH

PLAIN	Light, dry whites with some acidity, eg Loire	SMOKED, GRILLED OR FRIED	Dry light whites, eg white Burgundy, white Bordeaux, Vinho Verde (Portugal), Muscadet or Sancerre (Loire)
IN RICH SAUCES	As shellfish in rich sauces		

POULTRY

PLAIN OR DELICATE	Good, heavy whites, eg white Burgundy, white Rhône	WITH RICH SAUCES OR STUFFING	As plain poultry; or reds, eg Beaujolais, Rhône or Claret

WHITE MEAT

PORK AND VEAL	Full-bodied white, eg Spanish Rioja, Rhône, Italian whites; or light reds, eg young Rhône, Beaujolais	PORK AND HAM	Powerful white Burgundy or Rosé, eg Tavel, Côtes de Provence

RED MEAT AND GAME

GRILLED AND ROAST MEATS	Good, smooth red wines, eg Beaujolais, Burgundy, Claret, Southern hemisphere, California	MEAT CASSEROLES AND STEWS	As grilled and roast meats; but rougher, cheaper white can be very pleasant. Or dark, powerful wines from Roussillon or Cahors
GAME	Mature, full-bodied reds, eg good Claret, Burgundy, Rhône		

CHEESE, PUDINGS AND FRUIT

CHEESE	Any red	PUDDINGS AND FRUIT	Sauternes, Barsac, German dessert wines, Muscat de Beaumes de Venise, not-too-dry champagne

SERVING STYLE

How much formal convention is followed at an informal family table or at a simple supper with friends, depends of course on the character and personal style of the host or hosts. But it is useful to know how things ought to be done, so that, at an elegant dinner party or if cooking for someone else, the cook at least won't make any blunders.

LAYING THE TABLE As a rule, cutlery is laid so that the diner works from the outside in — his first course knife will be furthest from his plate, and on the right, because he is to pick it up with his right hand. His first course fork will be on his left, and furthest from his plate. Similarly, if the first course is soup, the soup spoon will be on the right (because he will use his right hand), at the extreme outside of his cutlery collection.

If a knife-and-fork first course is followed by soup, the soup spoon will be in second place, and so on, working inwards to dessert spoon and fork, or cheese knife. Dessert or pudding cutlery is sometimes (in homes, though seldom in restaurants) put across the top of the diner's place, the spoon above or beyond the fork and the handles pointing toward the hand that will pick them up — ie spoon handle towards right hand, fork handle towards left hand.

Logic prevails in the same way with glasses, which are set out just beyond the knife tip, in a diagonal row, first one (say for a white wine to go with the first course) nearest, next wine glass (say for the red to go with the main course) a little further away, and the dessert wine glass at the end of the row. The bread plate is placed on the diner's left, to the left of the cutlery. Napkins either go on this plate, or in the middle of the diner's place if the first course is not yet on the table. Individual ashtrays, fingerbowls, salt cellars are placed within comfortable reach.

The commonest mistakes students make in laying tables are to fail to

When laying the table, cutlery should be arranged with the implements to be used first on the outside. Make sure that you line up the bases of all the pieces, and that there is enough room for the dinner plate. Here, from right to left are a soup spoon, bread knife, dinner knife, dessert spoon, dessert fork and dinner fork. Glasses, on the other hand, are arranged so that the first to be used is closest to the diner. Here the innermost glass is for sherry, the next for red wine, and the outermost for port. Other arrangements are dictated by the menu.

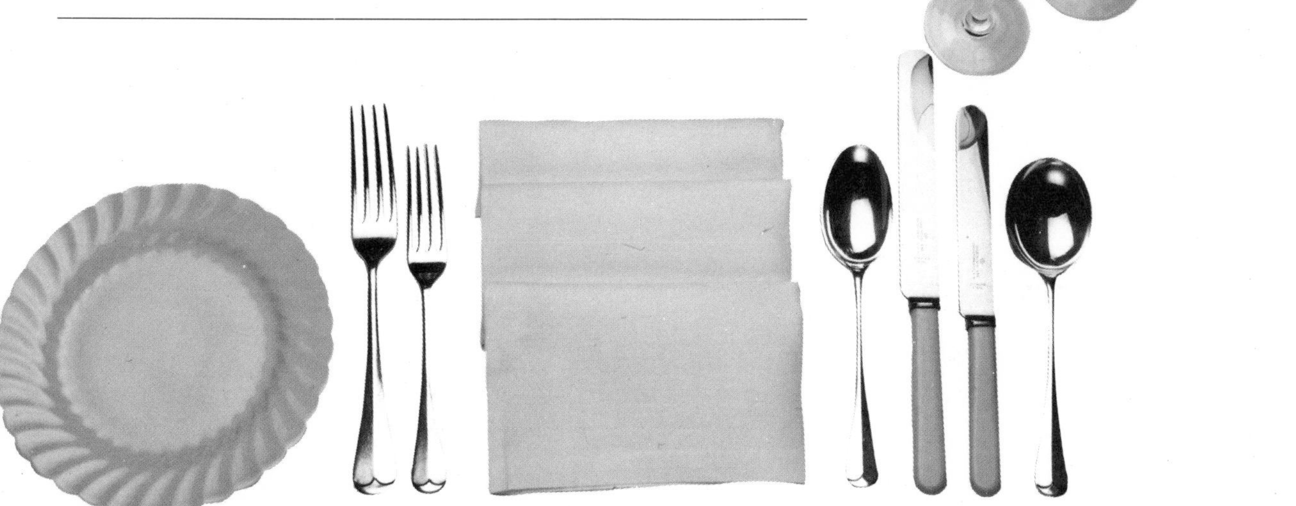

leave enough space between the banks of cutlery for the dinner plate to fit comfortably (leaving the guest scrambing under his plate for a knife or fork), to line up the tips of the cutlery instead of the bases, which gives an untidy unprofessional look, and to arrange flowers or candles in such a way that diners cannot see each other across the table. Low flowers are best, and candles should be checked to make sure they do not confuse sight lines. Nothing is so irritating as having to peer round an obstruction to carry on a conversation.

THE ETIQUETTE OF SERVING At a family supper, everyone may help himself, pass along the loaded plates, pass up the dirties, and stack for the washer-up. But, at a formal dinner, what is meant to happen is this: women are served before men, starting with the most important female guest end ending with the hostess. Usually the top female guest will be seated on the right of the host. The men are then served, the most important male guest (who will be seated at the right of the hostess) being served first, then the others and, lastly, the host. Once everyone is served the hostess (or host in the absence of one) starts to eat which is a signal for everyone else to tuck in.

HOW MUCH TO GIVE? A daunting plateful tends to take away the appetite, so do not over-help guests to food. Take trouble to arrange things neatly and attractively on the plate. Place the first spoonful (say the meat) to one side, not in the middle, then work round with vegetables and garnishes, keeping the piles separate. Slops and drips look bad, so take time when spooning a sauce to let any excess run off the spoon before moving away from the main dish and make sure the serving dish and diner's plate are as close together as possible.

If waiting formally, by the diner's side, hold the platter with one hand almost over his plate and use a spoon and fork in the other hand to serve him. This is called 'banquet service'. If the diner is helping himself, hold the platter *very low* close to the table and close to his plate, to the side of it, so he can manage the awkward business of turning and wielding spoon and fork. This is called 'silver service'. If waiting formally, the server always serves food, or offers it, from the diner's left and clears dirty plates from his right. But in awkward or crowded corners it is better to forget convention and do whatever is least likely to disturb conversation.

SERVING WINE The wine should be served at the same time as the food, or even before, but not too long afterwards — the waiting is a strain for the guests dying for a drink, and drinking is permitted straight away even if eating is not. The host tastes it — if he has not already done so — then everyone is served, ladies then men.

Good waiters, or hosts, do not constantly top up glasses, but do so positively when they are down to about a third. Glasses should not be filled more than two thirds full — the idea is to leave room for the drinker to be able to get his nose into the glass to smell it without getting the tip wet! It also means he can swill the wine about, which encourages the release of its bouquet.

CLEARING THE TABLE This should happen as unobtrusively as possible. Nothing should be touched until everyone has finished his food and indicated the fact by putting knife and fork firmly together. Then the plates are removed, but not stacked one on top of t'other or scraped within sight of the diners. Such unattractive operations should be performed out of sight. When the plates are cleared, everything connected with the just-removed course is cleared too — salt and pepper, mustard, sauces, salad dishes and, if the savoury courses are now over, bread plates and bread and butter. Nothing connected with the pudding should go on the table before everything pertaining to the previous course is off it. The same goes for coffee — it should not appear, nor should the bitter mints or petits fours, until the pudding has vanished, with its sauce jugs, cream etc.

CREATIVITY AND IMAGINATION

There are few everyday outlets for creativity like cooking. Cooks, whether professional or dometic, have at least one, sometimes two, chances a day to do something satisfyingly creative, to put their personal stamp on a production, however modest, and to give great pleasure to other people. As the cook becomes more experienced, and clings less tenaciously to this, or to other cookbooks, the opportunities for original and imaginative cooking will broaden. As the cook learns what flavours work with what, what combinations are pleasing and satisfying, failures will be fewer and triumphs greater. But a word of warning: no one becomes a good cook by trying to 'be creative' from the kick-off. My heart sinks like a stone when some amateur tells me: 'Oh, I never use cookbooks. I like to create. I just fling in a bit of this and a bit of that, and I use my imagination. Cookbooks are for pedants.' One knows at once what that cook's food tastes like — the product of heavy libations of wine from one hand and indiscriminate doses of herbs from the other. Good, even great, cooks have devoted their lives to putting on paper the products of their own and their colleagues' experience. They have not been too proud to weigh and measure, to correct and adjust recipes, to make dishes again and again, just so that less experienced cooks can, with their aid, turn out delicious food. It does not make sense to run before you can walk. So stick like a limpet to the recipes or Menu Lessons. Do your best to do as you are told and when, flushed with success, you are tempted to 'create', why not cook another menu from the book, get another triumph under your belt, then another and another. 'Creating', until you know what you are doing, and even sometimes then, can be a heartbreaking business. Disappointing food is the surest way to dampen a cook's enthusiasm, so why risk it?

In our opinion, the best way for cooks to start experimenting is with leftovers — at least they had their moment of glory, and may have a second coming. If they don't, and end up in the bin, well, at least it is not as ruinous as experimenting with the best that money can buy.

This is not to say, of course, that you must always slavishly follow a recipe. If you cannot get blackcurrants, redcurrants will probably do. If you like a recipe for chicken the chances are that it will work for guineafowl. We are pleading for the attitude of a dedicated and serious student, not that of a slave, like the lady who told me that she had followed my recipe for lemon meringue pie three times, then said: 'It is still too lemony.' When I suggested she might have cut the lemon juice down a bit after the first time she said: 'Oh no, I'm sure the recipe is right. It must be me. I always get things wrong.' No, dear lady, you just lacked the confidence to trust your own judgement. Confidence is what you need, and confidence, surprisingly, is quite easy to get. It comes with success, and success comes with cooking. So stop reading, and start cooking, and have a good time while you are at it.

THE MENU LESSONS

PHOTOGRAPH ON P.50

MENU LESSON 1

Soupe de poissons

Lamb kebabs with yoghurt and mint dressing

Saffron rice

Orange and watercress salad

Almost crème brûlée

A fish soup is a lesson in imagination. Go to the market or fish stall, survey the fish on the slab and buy a selection to suit pocket and mood. Or make the fish soup as directed, and experiment next time. Plenty of garlic, both in the soup and the rouille with which the soup is enriched, gives an authentic South of France flavour, but less can be used.

The lamb kebabs are truly simple, demonstrating the advantage of a good marinade.

The Crème brûlée is always delicious — with that much cream, eggs and sugar it cannot but be. But the skill of perfect timing to get a good skin on the custard, and careful even grilling of the brûlée top, are not always easily mastered. So take time, and follow the instructions pedantically.

WORK PLAN

- The Crème brûlée custard can be made the day before, and the sugar top should be grilled about 2 hours before dinner. This gives the top time to set to crackly caramel, but not to melt again stickily.
- The soup should be made on the day of eating, but it can be allowed to cool for later reheating — take care not to boil it, though, or the fish will disintegrate and overcook.
- The rouille keeps well overnight, covered in polythene wrap.
- The marinading of the kebabs can be done well in advance, but last-minute grilling is essential for pink and tender lamb.
- The yoghurt dressing can be made in advance, as can the saffron rice.
- Prepare the salad on the day of serving, but dress it not more than 30 minutes ahead of time.

SOUPE DE POISSONS

INGREDIENTS *(Serves 8)*

Fish trimmings (head, skin, bones)
1.5kg/3lb mixed white fish, filleted (grey mullet, monkfish, John Dory, conger eel, haddock, cod, plaice, sole etc.)
1 onion, chopped
2 carrots, chopped
1 stick celery, chopped
2 litres/3½ pt water
10-12 live mussels
3tbsp virgin olive oil
2 large mild onions, sliced
2 cloves garlic, crushed
White of 2 leeks, sliced
1 × 5cm/2 inch strip orange peel
2 sprigs of fennel
3 Provençale tomatoes, peeled and quartered
Generous pinch of saffron filaments
Salt and cayenne pepper

1 FIRST PREPARE A GOOD FISH STOCK Put the fish trimmings into a large saucepan with the chopped onion, carrot and celery. Cover with the water. Bring to the boil and simmer slowly for 30 minutes. Skim as necessary. Strain into a clean saucepan. Reduce, by boiling rapidly, to 1.7litres/3pt.

2 While the stock simmers, PREPARE THE ROUILLE Simmer the pepper and chilli in the water for 10 minutes. Drain and dry well. Grind the pepper, garlic, pimento and chilli in a pestle and mortar to a smooth paste or blend finely in a coffee grinder or liquidizer. Beat in the olive oil drop by drop so that it is incorporated smoothly without separating. Add enough breadcrumbs to make the sauce hold its shape, and add the Tabasco if the chilli was omitted. Taste and season with salt if necessary. Set aside.

3 CLEAN THE MUSSELS Scrub them well, removing their 'beards' and discarding any that do not shut when tapped on the sink edge.

FOR THE ROUILLE
1 green pepper, destalked and de-seeded
1 dry chilli, or a few drops of Tabasco
150ml/¼pt water
2 garlic cloves, crushed
1 canned pimento cap
3tbsp virgin olive oil
1tbsp dry white breadcrumbs

TO SERVE
8 small slices of French bread, dried in the oven
Coarsely grated Gruyère cheese

☐ *Mediterranean fish soups are made with any and all the fish available in the seafront markets. Rough bouillabaisse will contain tiny bony fish too small for filleting, large chunks of bigger fish, prawns, squid — whatever is available. Classic recipes tend to demand gurnard, galinette, weaver, brill, rascasse, spiny lobster, red mullet and John Dory. The flavour of the soup will of course vary with its fish, but any combination will be good. If good red sweet tomatoes from a sunny climate are not available, add a little sugar and 1tsp tomato purée to the soup, or use canned Italian tomatoes.*

4 Heat the olive oil in a large saucepan. Add the onion, garlic, leeks, orange peel and fennel. Cook until the vegetables are soft.

5 Add the fish stock, tomatoes and saffron. Bring to the boil.

6 Cut the fish fillets into bite-sized pieces.

7 Simmer the soup, add the fish and mussels. Poach for 4 minutes or until all the mussel shells have opened. Discard any that do not open. Taste and season. (It may need a little Tabasco or cayenne pepper.)

8 Spread the rouille onto the crusts of bread. Place in the bottom of a warm soup tureen. Pour over the soup and hand the grated Gruyère cheese and any extra rouille separately.

CLEANING MUSSELS
1 Clean the shells thoroughly by scrubbing with a stiff brush. Discard any that do not close when tapped on sink edge or table top.

2 Scrape and pull away their seaweed-like 'beards'. Rinse in a bowl of clean water.

LAMB KEBABS WITH YOGHURT AND MINT DRESSING

INGREDIENTS (Serves 4)
900g/2lb boned leg of lamb
2 red peppers

FOR THE MARINADE
150ml/¼pt red wine
1tbsp lemon juice
1tbsp oil
8 whole allspice
1 heaped tsp cumin
1 sprig of fresh thyme
½ onion, sliced
6 black peppercorns

FOR THE YOGHURT AND MINT DRESSING
150ml/¼pt low fat plain yoghurt
½ clove crushed garlic
2tbsp chopped fresh mint
Salt and freshly ground black pepper

1 Cut the meat into 5cm/2 inch lean cubes. Marinade, preferably overnight, in the marinade ingredients, well mixed. Keep refrigerated and turn occasionally.

2 MAKE THE DRESSING by simply mixing the ingredients together. Season to taste. Turn into a ramekin or serving bowl.

3 Heat the grill.

4 Cut the red peppers into large pieces and skewer on long skewers alternately with the pieces of lamb.

5 Grill for 6 minutes. Do not worry if the edges of the peppers char. They taste very good that way. Serve on a bed of saffron rice.

NOTE Rosemary twigs make excellent skewers for lamb kebabs. Remove the leaves from the part of the stem that will be driven through the meat but retain a head of leaves at the top of the stem. This will give the meat a wonderful flavour during cooking.

SAFFRON RICE

INGREDIENTS (Serves 4)
225g/8oz long grain rice
425ml/¾pt water, boiling
Large pinch of saffron powder
Salt

1 Rinse the rice, drain it and put into a heavy bottomed pan with the water, saffron and salt.

2 Cover and simmer slowly without removing the lid for 25 minutes, by which time the liquid should be completely absorbed and the rice cooked.

ORANGE AND WATERCRESS SALAD

INGREDIENTS (Serves 4)
6 oranges
Large bunch of watercress
French dressing (optional), see p.139.

1 Peel the oranges with a knife as you would an apple, making sure that all the pith is removed.

2 Cut across (not parallel to the segments) into thin slices or cut into segments. Reserve the juice.

3 Wash and drain the watercress. Remove the tough stalks and discard them.

4 Lay the slices of orange in a glass or bowl.

5 Arrange the watercress on top of the oranges and sprinkle evenly with dressing or orange juice or both.

PREPARING ORANGES
1 With a sharp knife cut off both ends of the orange to expose the flesh.

2 Peel the orange as you would an apple, removing rind and pith in one operation. Do not leave any traces of pith on the flesh.

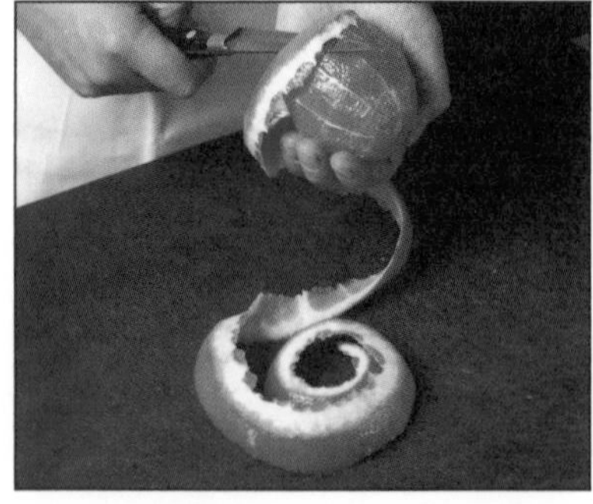

3 Do not squeeze the orange, which should lie in the cupped hand. Use plenty of backwards and forwards sawing action but the minimum of pressure.

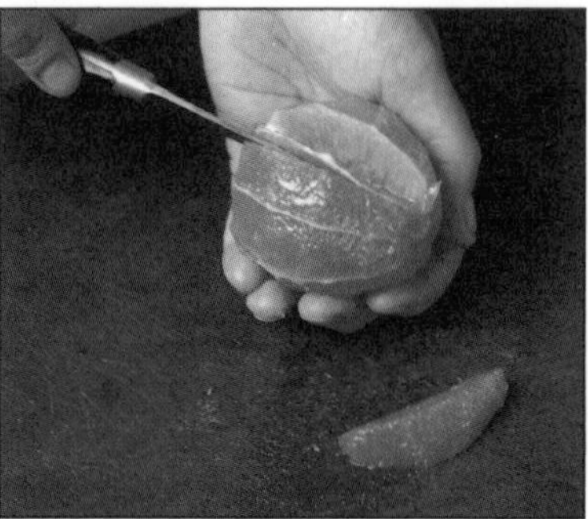

4 Cut along each side of the longitudinal membranes to release pith-free segments.

5 Alternatively, cut in fine slices across the core of the whole orange.

ALMOST CREME BRULEE

INGREDIENTS (Serves 4)
290ml/½pt double cream
1 vanilla pod OR 1tsp vanilla flavouring
1 egg plus 3 egg yolks
1tbsp caster sugar

FOR THE TOPPING
Caster sugar

☐ *Crème brûlée is also good made in individual ramekin dishes, rather than one large dish. Brown sugar can be used for the caramel top, and is easier to get looking good, but it gives a different flavour and is not considered correct by classic cooks.*

(Crème brûlée is best started a day in advance)

1 Put the cream with the vanilla pod into a pan and heat up to scalding point, making sure it does not boil. Remove the vanilla pod.

2 Set the oven to 170°C/325°F/Gas 3.

3 Beat the egg and egg yolks with the caster sugar and stir in the hot cream. Place the mixture in the top of a double saucepan, or in a bowl over a pan of simmering water, on a gentle heat. Stir all the time until the custard is thick enough to coat the back of the spoon. If using vanilla flavouring add it now.

4 Pour the custard into an ovenproof serving dish and bake for 8 minutes to create a good skin on top. Refrigerate overnight. On no account break the top skin.

5 Next day heat the grill.

6 Sprinkle the top of the custard with an even 5mm/¼ inch layer of caster sugar: to do this stand the dish on a tray or large sheet of greaseproof paper and sift the sugar over the dish and tray or paper. This way you will get an even layer. Collect the sugar falling wide for re-use.

7 When the grill is blazing hot put the custard under it, as close as possible to the heat. The sugar will melt and caramelize before the custard underneath it boils. Watch carefully, turning the custard if the sugar is browning unevenly.

8 Allow to cool completely before serving. The top should be hard and crackly. To serve, crack the top with the serving spoon and give each diner some custard (which should be creamy and barely set) and a piece of caramel.

NOTE True Crème brûlée is made with yolks only and gives a rich, not quite set, custard. It is beloved of many people but others find it too sickly. The texture of the custard should be that of clotted cream. Recipe on p.281; see also Cheat's crème brûlée on the same page.

PHOTOGRAPH ON P.51

MENU LESSON 2

Spinach roulade with smoked salmon

Chicken breasts with leek and watercress sauce

Pasta (see p.124)

Turned carrots

Fresh pineapple and kirsch

Both first and second courses of this most delicious and elegant meal contain cream, so resist the temptation to offer any more with the pineapple. The roulade may be dished up à la nouvelle cuisine in slices on separate plates if preferred but as this treatment is especially pretty and attractive for the chicken breasts, it may be more convenient to cut and serve the roulade in the dining room. Serve smallish slices — it is important that the guests leave room for the chicken.

The skills taught in this Menu Lesson are the careful timing and trimming of the roulade — it looks professional, neat and attractive if cut and rolled with care. Timing is important with the chicken breasts too. If they are just firm to the touch, palest pink without a hint of mauve when cut, then the cook has got it right. Do not be tempted to make the dish in advance. Last-minute poaching makes the difference between a perfect and a pedestrian result. Also, do not be tempted to use a processor for the sauce. It needs a liquidizer or old-fashioned pushing through a sieve for a velvety smooth texture.

Cutting the pineapple is trickier than it looks, and is seldom perfectly done at the first attempt. The tricks are first to cut the top and bottom off thickly so that the fruit left is cylindrical rather than barrel-shaped, and secondly to keep the knife tip as close to the skin as you dare when cutting between flesh and skin. The fear of breaking the skin usually makes the beginner cut too deeply into the fruit. Do not worry about piercing the skin and cutting your palm — it won't happen (see illustrations on p.42).

WORK PLAN

- The roulade reheats successfully in oven or microwave, but the chicken is best made at the last minute.
- The pineapple will benefit from steeping in Kirsch and sugar.

SPINACH ROULADE WITH SMOKED SALMON

INGREDIENTS (Serves 4)
450g/1lb fresh spinach (or 170g/6oz frozen spinach)
15g/½oz butter
Salt and freshly ground black pepper
4 eggs, separated
Pinch of nutmeg

FOR THE FILLING
2 cartons soured cream
110g/4oz smoked salmon, chopped
2tsp fresh chopped dill

1 TO PREPARE THE SPINACH, remove the stalks and wash thoroughly. Bring a pan of water to the boil with a pinch of salt. Add the spinach and boil rapidly for 2-3 minutes until the leaves are limp, bright green and just cooked. Drain thoroughly by squeezing between two plates. Chop finely and push through a sieve (or purée in a processor or liquidizer if available). Beat in the butter.

2 Set the oven to 190°C/375°F/Gas 5. Take a large roasting tin and cut a double layer of greaseproof paper slightly larger than the tin. Lay this in the tin. Do not worry if the ends stick up untidily around the sides. Brush lightly with oil or melted butter.

3 TO MAKE THE ROULADE Gradually beat the egg yolks into the spinach and season well with salt, pepper and nutmeg.

4 Whisk the egg whites until stiff but not dry and fold them into the spinach. Pour this mixture into the prepared roasting tin. Spread it flat.

5 Bake for 10-12 minutes or until the top feels dry and springy to the touch.

PREPARING SPINACH

1 To remove the tough stalks from spinach, fold leaves in half.

2 Grip the leaf close to the stalk and tear away the stalk briskly and firmly.

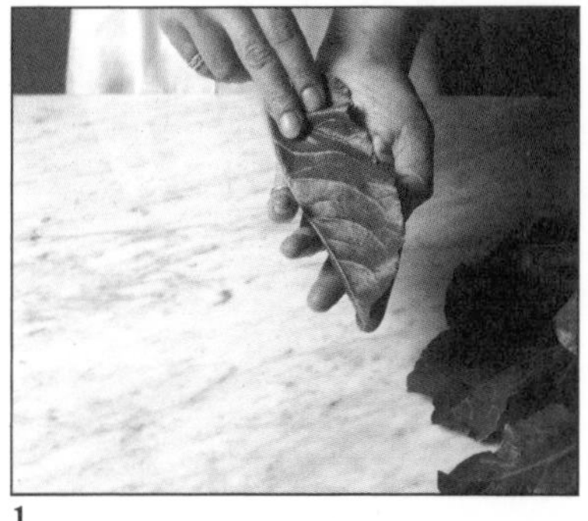
1

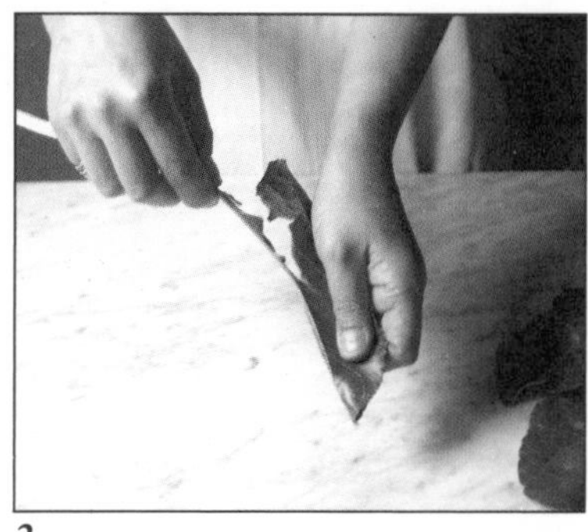
2

6 Mix the filling ingredients together.

7 Turn the roulade out onto a piece of greaseproof paper. Remove the backing of paper and trim roulade, as shown.

8 Spread the filling onto the roulade and roll it up.

9 Wet the paper, wrap the roulade up in it and return to the oven for 5 minutes to reheat. Serve on a warm, flat dish or wooden board.

SPINACH ROULADE

1 Lay a double layer of greaseproof paper in the tin. Brush with oil or melted butter. Pour in the mixture and spread flat. Bake for 10 minutes.

2 Place a piece of greaseproof paper on a tea towel. Sprinkle with grated Parmesan cheese. Turn the roulade out onto it. Remove the original backing paper. Trim the edges.

3 Spread the filling onto the roulade and roll up as you would a Swiss roll, removing the paper as you go.

CHICKEN BREASTS WITH LEEK AND WATERCRESS SAUCE

INGREDIENTS (Serves 4)
4 chicken breasts, boned and skinned
30g/1oz truffle (optional), finely sliced
15g/½oz butter
85g/3oz white of leeks, finely chopped
1 small shallot, finely chopped
½ bunch of watercress, carefully picked over
2tbsp port
290ml/½pt white stock (see p.268)
75ml/2½fl oz double cream
2 egg yolks
3tbsp water

1 With a sharp knife, make a horizontal incision in the thickest part of each chicken breast and insert slices of truffle.

2 Melt the butter, add the leeks and shallot and cook slowly until soft but not brown. Add all but two sprigs of the watercress, the port, stock and cream and simmer for 10 minutes.

3 Add the chicken breasts and poach, covered, for 12 minutes. Turn the chicken over half way through cooking. Remove from the pan, returning any watercress or leeks stuck to the breasts to the saucepan. Keep warm while you make the sauce.

4 Chop the remaining watercress very finely.

5 Liquidize the poaching liquid and vegetables until very smooth. Pour into a clean saucepan. Bring to just below boiling point.

6 Mix the egg yolks with the water, add a little of the hot sauce to the yolks and return the lot to the saucepan. Stir over a moderate heat until thickened. It is essential that the sauce does not get near boiling point — it would curdle. Stir in the remaining chopped watercress to improve the colour.

7 Arrange the chicken breasts, split in two if liked, on individual warmed plates. Spoon over the sauce.

TURNED CARROTS

INGREDIENTS (Serves 4)
900g/2lb carrots
Salt and freshly ground black pepper
Knob of butter

1 Peel and turn the carrots (see p.150).

2 Steam over a pan of boiling water until tender.

3 Serve with salt, pepper and a little melted butter.

NOTE The turned carrots can be served on the same plate as the chicken breasts or separately, as preferred.

FRESH PINEAPPLE AND KIRSCH

INGREDIENTS (Serves 4)
1 large pineapple
Kirsch
Caster sugar

☐ *The best pineapples available in Europe or North America are not picked until ripe, when they are flown to their destination. They have the central cone of leaves intact. Pineapples that ripen on a long sea voyage have their central leaves removed to prevent sprouting during storage.*

1 Cut the top and bottom off the pineapple so that you are left with a cylinder of fruit. Do not throw away the leafy top.

2 With a sharp knife cut round inside the skin, working first from one end and then from the other, so that you can push the fruit out in one piece. Try not to pierce or tear the skin.

3 Slice the pineapple. Remove the core, if woody, from each slice with an apple corer.

4 Stand the cylindrical pineapple skin in a shallow bowl. Put the fruit back in, sprinkling with Kirsch and caster sugar as you go. Replace the top.

PREPARING A PINEAPPLE
1 Cut off the top and bottom with a sharp knife. Cut these end slices thickly so what is left is not barrel-shaped but cylindrical.

2 Cut round inside the skin, working first from one end, then the other, until you can push the fruit out in one piece. Try to cut as close to the skin as possible.

3 Slice the fruit and remove the central core with an apple corer if at all woody.

PHOTOGRAPH ON P.54

The principal pitfalls for the cook in this menu are under-seasoning the fish terrine, which will then be bland and dull, overcooking the lamb, which needs to be evenly pink inside, and allowing the potatoes to stick and break up in the pan. The latter can only be avoided by using the right pan—a good oldfashioned heavy one or a modern non-stick one.

Cutting vegetables into even matchsticks takes care, practice, and more than anything, patience. But a perfect julienne looks very professional.

MENU LESSON 3

Fish terrine with chive dressing

Collops of lamb with onion and mint purée

Julienne of vegetables

Pommes à la Parisienne

Arranged fruit salad with mango sauce

WORK PLAN

- The terrine and sauce are best made between 8 and 24 hours in advance
- The lamb must be cooked at the last minute but can be prepared, the purée made etc. well in advance.
- All vegetables are better prepared and cooked as late as possible. If cutting them into julienne more than an hour or so ahead, keep them covered in clingfilm, not soaking in water which can, if prolonged, make them lose flavour. (See note after the 'Julienne' recipe.)
- Pommes à la Parisienne easily develop a 'reheated' taste if re-fried but will keep warm for half an hour or so without coming to harm.
- Because none of the fruit will discolour, it can be prepared, and the sauce made, a few hours in advance. But do not over-chill. Fruit loses flavour if too cold.

FISH TERRINE WITH CHIVE DRESSING

INGREDIENTS (Serves 4)
675g/1½lb filleted sole, skinned (see p.116)
2tsp green peppercorns
1 large carrot
45g/1½oz French beans, topped and tailed
3 egg whites
290ml/½pt double cream
Salt and ground white pepper
Continued overleaf

1 Put the raw sole fillets into a food processor and pound well or chop finely and push through a sieve. (Quite a task!)

2 Rinse the green peppercorns under running cold water for one minute. Drain well. Peel the carrot and cut into sticks about the size of the beans. Steam the carrots and beans over boiling water (or boil in salted water) until *very* tender. Rinse under cold water and drain on absorbent paper.

3 Set the oven to 175°C/350°F/Gas 4.

4 Put the pounded, or sieved, fish into a bowl. Season with salt and set in a roasting tin of ice to keep the mixture chilled. Beat well and gradually add first the egg whites and then the cream, making sure that the mixture does not become too runny. It should hold its shape. The egg whites and cream can be added in the processor but they must be very cold and not over-beaten. If too warm the mixture will split (curdle) and there is no way to rescue it. The described method is foolproof and guarantees a good-textured terrine. Taste, and season accordingly. If unable to taste

FOR THE DRESSING
2 egg yolks
Salt and freshly ground black pepper
1 large bunch chives, chopped
290ml/½pt oil
Juice of ½ lemon
1 carton soured cream

TO GARNISH
4 small sprigs watercress

raw fish — (actually it tastes delicious — think of Japanese Sashimi) cook a teaspoon in a non-stick pan and taste.

5 Lightly oil a loaf tin or terrine and spoon in a quarter of the fish mixture. Spread it flat with a spatula. Arrange 4 parallel lines of green beans down the length of the tin. Cover with a second quarter of the fish mixture. Spread flat. Arrange 4 lines of carrot sticks immediately above the beans. Cover with a third quarter of the fish mixture. Spread flat. Arrange 4 parallel lines of green peppercorns immediately above the carrots. Cover with the remaining fish mixture. Spread flat. Cover with a piece of damp greaseproof paper.

6 Stand the terrine in a roasting tin half filled with nearly boiling water and bake for 35 minutes. Leave to cool.

7 MAKING THE DRESSING Put the egg yolks into a liquidizer, add salt and pepper and whizz for 1 minute. Add the chives (which must be very dry) and gradually add the oil. The sauce should become fairly thick. (If it begins to curdle do not worry — the soured cream will act as a stabilizer.) Add the lemon juice and then the remaining oil. Add the soured cream and whizz briefly. Taste and adjust seasoning.

8 TO SERVE Invert a plate or wooden board over the terrine and turn the whole thing over. Give a gentle shake and remove the tin. Cut into even slices. Pour enough of the chive dressing to just cover the base of 4 medium-sized plates. Cover with one or two slices of fish terrine and garnish with a small sprig of watercress.

COLLOPS OF LAMB WITH ONION AND MINT PUREE

INGREDIENTS (Serves 4)
Two 7-bone best ends of lamb, chined
A few sprigs fresh mint
30g/1oz unsalted butter

FOR THE PUREE
1 large mild onion
55g/2oz butter
2tbsp chopped fresh mint
Salt and freshly ground black pepper

FOR THE GRAVY
2 sticks celery
2 sprigs fresh thyme
½ onion
2tsp redcurrant jelly
1tbsp port
1tbsp orange juice
1tbsp arrowroot

1 Set the oven to 200°C/400°F/Gas 6.

2 With a small knife remove the 'eye' of the best-ends in one piece. Trim away any fat. Slice into 12 collops (small slices). Place in a bowl with plenty of roughly chopped mint, cover and refrigerate for at least a few hours, preferably overnight.

3 Put the bones into a roasting pan and bake in the hot oven for 45 minutes or until well browned.

4 Meanwhile, prepare the onion and mint purée: chop the onion very finely. Cook slowly in the butter until soft but not coloured; may take up to 40 minutes. Push through a sieve. Add the mint and season to taste.

5 When the lamb bones are browned remove them, with as little fat as possible, into a large saucepan. Cover with 1.1 litre/2pt water. Add the celery, thyme and onion. Bring slowly up to the boil, skimming off the scum. Simmer for 1½ hours — skimming every so often. Strain into a clean pan. It should measure about 425ml/¾pt. If it is more reduce by boiling rapidly.

6 Add the jelly, port and orange juice. Boil rapidly for 3 minutes.

7 Slake (ie mix) the arrowroot with a little cold water, add some of the hot stock and return the mixture to the saucepan. Bring to the boil, stirring continuously. Boil for no more than 1½ minutes. Taste and season with salt and pepper. Keep warm.

8 Reheat the onion and mint purée.

9 Fry the collops, fairly slowly, in the unsalted butter for 2 minutes a side.

10 Spoon enough gravy to flood the base of each diner's plate. Arrange 3 collops on the gravy and place a spoonful of the purée on top of each.

NOTE If serving the complete menu, the vegetables can also be served on the individual plates, or arranged on the same large serving plate as the meat.

COLLOPS OF LAMB

1 Lay the rack skin-side down and, with fingers and knife, remove the line of gristle to be found under the meat at the thick end.

2 Separate the chine-bone (split back-bone) from the ribs along the line where the butcher has sawn through the rib-bones.

3 Starting at the layer end of the rack, remove the half-moon shaped piece of cartilage from between the layers of flesh and fat — it is the edge of the shoulder blade.

4 With a sharp knife (and making small cuts close to the rib-bones) ease the bones, in one piece, away from the meat.

5 Gradually separate the whole 'eye' of the meat (the fat-free cylinder) from the bones.

6 Using a sharp flexible knife remove all fat and membrane from the meat.

7 Finally, slice into neat rounds or 'collops'.

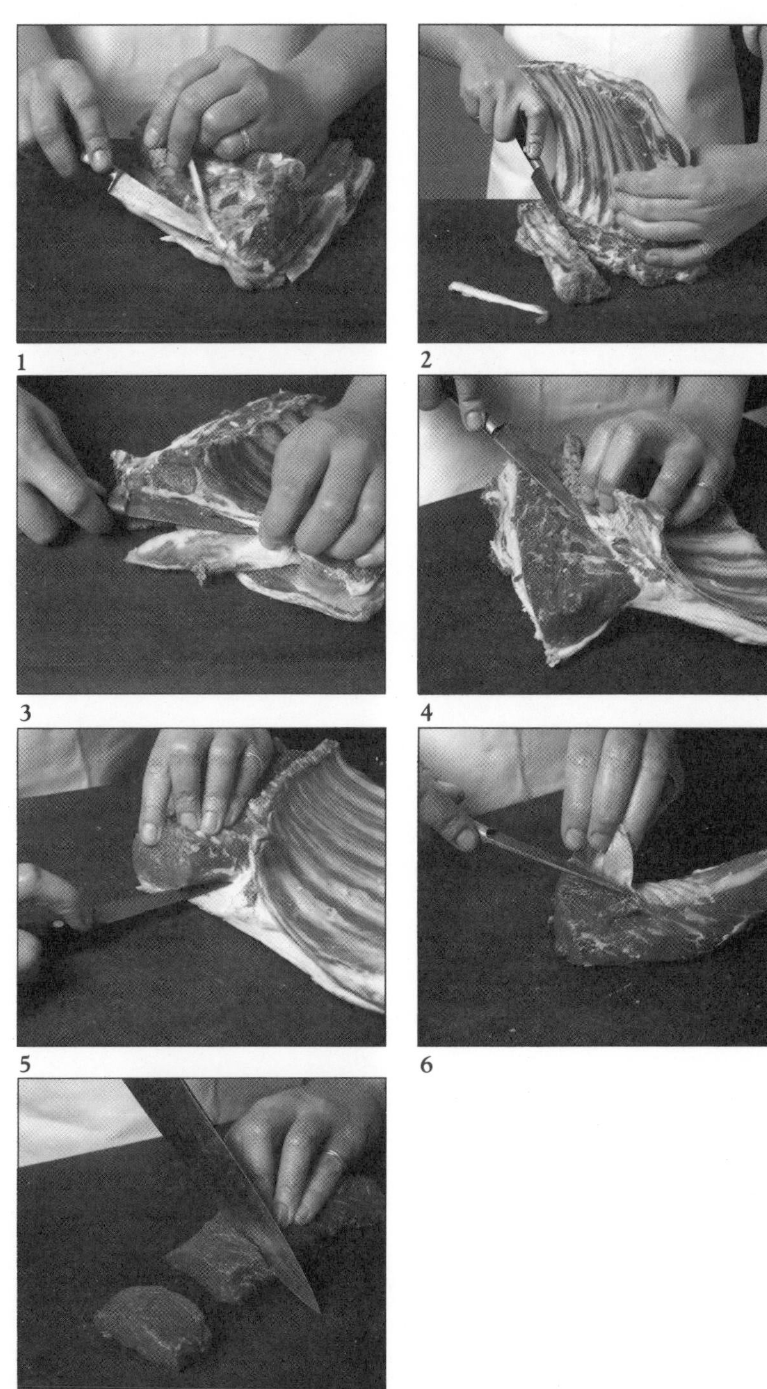

1 2 3 4 5 6 7

JULIENNE OF VEGETABLES

INGREDIENTS (Serves 4)
340g/12oz carrots
340g/12oz courgettes
340g/12oz leeks
Ground ginger
Fresh thyme
Salt and pepper
Melted butter

☐ *An oldfashioned steamer with compartmental vegetable baskets is perfect for the vegetable julienne. Failing that, use foil to make loose parcels and place in the top half of the steamer.*

1 Peel the carrots and cut the ends off the courgettes. Using the white part only of the leeks, cut all the vegetables into 'julienne' strips the size of a matchstick. Keep the vegetables separate.

2 Wash the vegetables well and steam them, separately, over boiling water until tender but not over-soft. Season the carrots with salt, pepper and ground ginger; the courgettes with salt, pepper and thyme and the leeks with salt and pepper.

3 Arrange the vegetables in 3 neat rows on a large dish. Brush with melted butter and serve immediately.

NOTE If necessary the vegetables can be prepared and even cooked a few hours before the dinner. Having steamed them refresh them under running cold water until completely cold. Drain well on absorbent paper. Arrange them on the dish, dot with butter and cover with clingwrap. Reheat in a microwave oven until the clingwrap puffs up and feels hot to the touch. If you have only a conventional oven, cover with tin foil instead of plastic and reheat at 200°C/400°F/Gas 6 for 20 minutes.

JULIENNE VEGETABLES
1 Square off the sides of root vegetables so that they are block-shaped.

2 Slice finely, using a good, sharp knife.

3 Stack the slices and slice again into 'matchsticks'. Split washed leeks, cut into 5cm/2 inch lengths, and slice lengthwise. Soaking Julienne vegetables in iced water makes them curly.

POMMES A LA PARISIENNE

INGREDIENTS (Serves 4)
4 large potatoes
2tbsp oil
Knob of butter
Salt

1 Peel the potatoes and scoop into small balls with a melon baller as shown. As you prepare the balls drop them into a bowl of cold water (this prevents discolouring). Float a plate on top to keep them submerged.

2 Heat the oil in a sauté pan and add the butter. Dry the potato balls well and toss them in the pan until completely coated with fat. Fry very slowly until they are browned and tender, shaking the pan frequently to prevent them sticking.

3 Drain well, sprinkle with salt and serve immediately.

NOTE Allow 15 Parisienne potatoes per head. The larger the potatoes, the easier it is to scoop them into balls without too much waste.

POMMES A LA PARISIENNE
1 Push the melon baller deep into the flesh of the peeled potato.

2 Work it in as deep as possible before twisting the wrist to extract perfectly round balls.

ARRANGED FRUIT SALAD WITH MANGO SAUCE

INGREDIENTS (Serves 4)
2 kiwi fruit
1 punnet strawberries or raspberries
110g/4oz seedless green grapes
A few sprigs of mint

FOR THE SAUCE
1 ripe mango
2 passionfruit
2tbsp water

☐ *Any fruit which will not go brown in the air can be used for the Arranged fruit salad. An alternative sauce would be the Coulis rouge on p.130.*

1 Peel and slice the kiwi fruit. Hull the strawberries or leave the raspberries whole. Take the grapes off the stalks.

2 Skin the mango and remove the flesh from the stone. Blend the flesh with the passionfruit pulp and water in a food processor or liquidizer. Pour (strain if the sauce is fibrous) onto the base of 4 dessert plates. If using a liquidizer, strain out the passionfruit seeds,which otherwise will get crushed. (A processor leaves them whole, which many people find attractive, but crushed seeds look like pepper or dust.)

3 Arrange the fruit attractively on each plate. Garnish with a little sprig of mint (optional) and cover lightly with clingwrap until ready to serve.

PHOTOGRAPH ON P.55

This is a highly sophisticated cook's dinner requiring time, dedication and, regrettably, money. The skills learnt are fairly advanced — a velvety mousseline, careful preparation of sweetbreads, a delicate purée. But the results are well worth the effort.

MENU LESSON 4

Scallop mousse with crayfish sauce

Sweetbreads with spinach and pear purée

Noodles

Broccoli (see p.56)

Yoghurt, honey and dates

or

Muscovado cream

WORK PLAN

Although the mousse and the sweetbreads *can* be kept warm, there is no doubt that last-minute cooking means perfection. It is a menu for the organized gourmet. However, a food processor makes short work of the mousse and the purée, and the pudding is simplicity itself. So, well in advance:

- Make the sauce but do not add the crayfish.
- Prepare but do not cook the scallop mousse.
- Soak, blanch and egg-and-crumb the sweetbreads.
- Make the spinach and pear purée.
- Prepare the yoghurt, honey and dates.

This will leave perhaps 30 minutes of last-minute work (cooking the mousse, frying the sweetbreads, heating the purée and boiling noodles and broccoli).

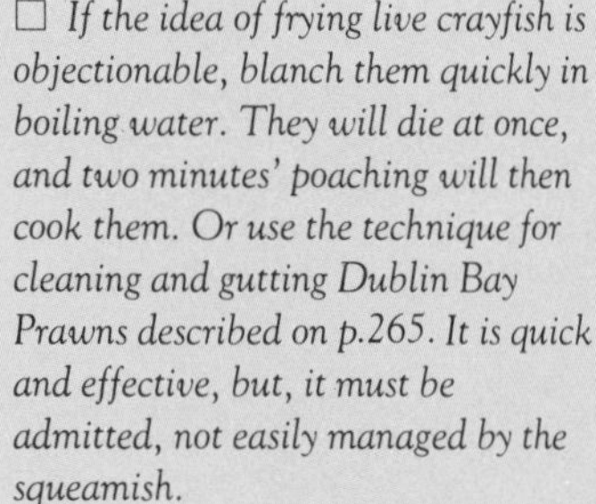

☐ *If the idea of frying live crayfish is objectionable, blanch them quickly in boiling water. They will die at once, and two minutes' poaching will then cook them. Or use the technique for cleaning and gutting Dublin Bay Prawns described on p.265. It is quick and effective, but, it must be admitted, not easily managed by the squeamish.*

SCALLOP MOUSSE WITH CRAYFISH SAUCE

This recipe and the following one have been adapted from Michel Guérard's *Cuisine Gourmande* (Macmillan 1977).

INGREDIENTS (Serves 4)
225g/8oz scallops, chilled
Salt and white pepper
1 egg, chilled
350ml/12fl oz double cream, chilled
30g/1oz butter, melted
290ml/½pt crayfish sauce

1 Remove the tough muscle (found opposite the roe) from the scallops. Process the scallops briefly with salt and pepper. When smooth add the egg and process for 1 minute. Refrigerate until fairly firm, about 30 minutes.

2 Now process in the cream. The mousse should be fairly thick. Do not overheat or allow the mixture to warm up — it would separate. Check the seasoning.

3 Set the oven to 220°C/425°F/Gas 7. Brush 4 ramekins with melted butter and fill with the scallop mousse. Place in a roasting tin half filled with hot water and bake for 30 minutes. Once cooked, keep warm in the bain marie, out of the oven.

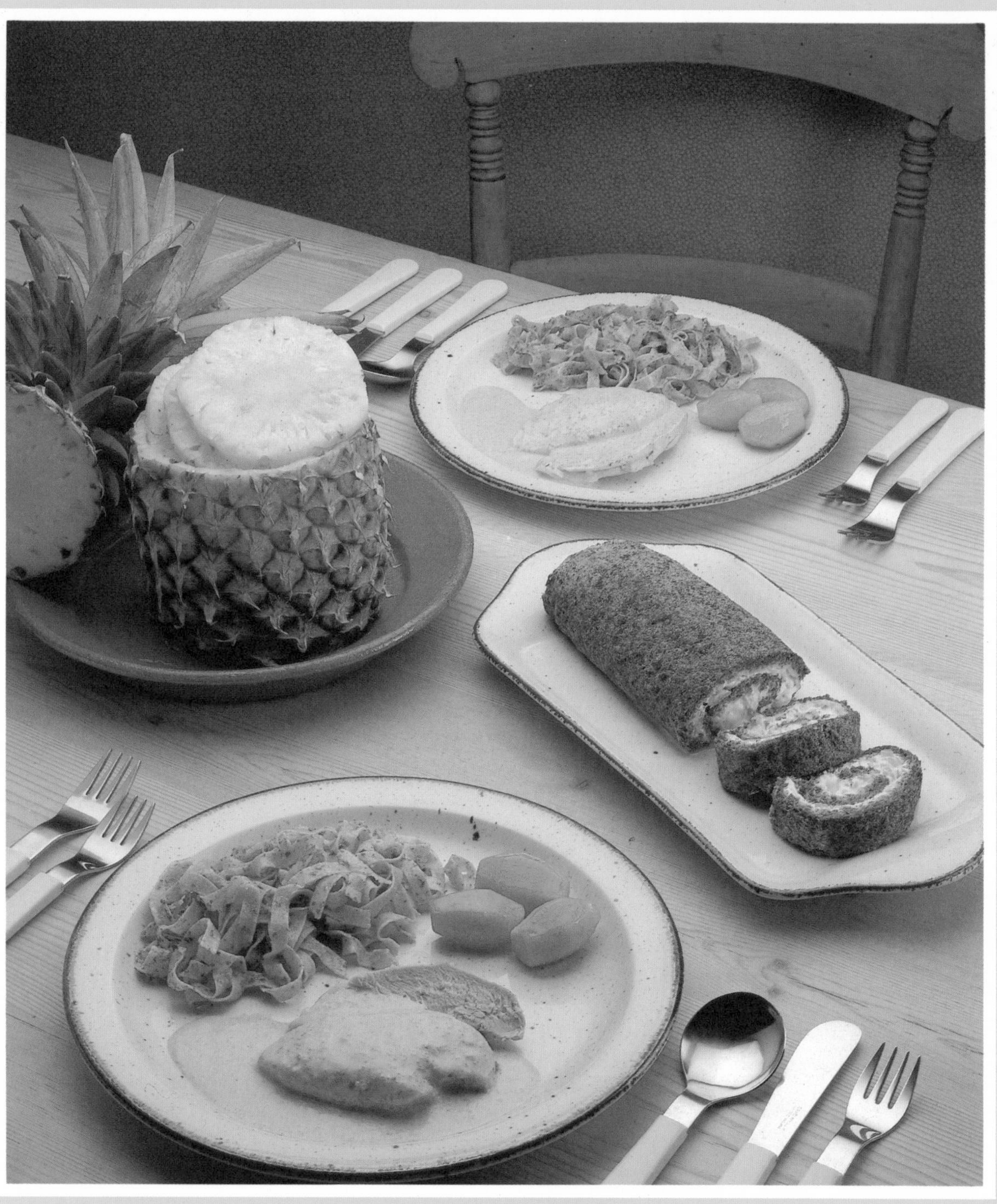

MENU LESSON 2 *(see p.40)*
The richness of some ingredients contrasts with the plainness of others. *Clockwise from top left:* Pineapple and kirsch, chicken breasts in leek and watercress sauce with pasta and carrots, spinach roulade.

PREPARING SWEETBREADS
1 Soak sweetbreads in several changes of fresh cold water until the water no longer turns pink. Then blanch them in near-boiling water for 5 minutes.

2 Pick over the sweetbreads, removing larger pieces of skin and membrane.

3 Squeeze the sweetbreads or put them between sheets of cloth or paper, weighted down to press out liquid. Leave weighted for 20 minutes.

NOODLES

INGREDIENTS (Serves 4)
225g/8oz egg noodles
2tbsp olive oil
Salt and freshly ground black pepper

1 Boil the pasta in plenty of rapidly boiling salted water, with 1tbsp oil, until tender but not soft. Drain well and rinse with boiling water to prevent the pasta sticking together.

2 Serve turned in the second tablespoon of oil and seasoned with plenty of freshly ground black pepper.

NOTE Fresh noodles (pasta) will cook, depending on size, in anything from 1 to 5 minutes. Dried pasta will take from 10 to 20 minutes.

YOGHURT, HONEY AND DATES

INGREDIENTS (Serves 4)
570ml/1pt Greek yoghurt
110g/ 4oz Fresh dates
4tbsp Thick cream
4tbsp Good quality runny honey
55g/2oz Jordan almonds, unblanched

1 For each person put 2 heaped tbsp of Greek yoghurt in a pudding bowl.

2 Stone the dates, skin and chop roughly. Put a few on the top of each helping of yoghurt.

3 Spoon a good dollop of thick cream over the top and then trickle over a little runny honey.

4 Scatter a few almonds on top, and serve at once.

NOTE The dessert can be acceptable or astonishingly good depending on the quality of the ingredients. Ordinary yoghurt, honey, dates, cream and almonds will give a perfectly good result. But the best Greek yoghurt, a single-flower honey, fresh dates, Jersey or Guernsey cream, and new season's Jordan almonds turn a nursery pudding into Ambrosia.

MUSCOVADO CREAM

INGREDIENTS (Serves 4)
290ml/½pt Greek yoghurt
290ml/½pt Double cream
2tbsp Muscovado or molasses sugar

1 Mix whipped double cream half and half with good Greek yoghurt.

2 Pour into a glass bowl or individual glasses.

3 Sprinkle the top heavily with a good raw brown sugar such as Muscovado or molasses sugar.

4 Leave overnight in the refrigerator for the sugar to melt before serving.

PHOTOGRAPH ON P.58

Apart from the pretty and colourful omelette, this menu is good old fashioned home cooking, teaching the techniques of casseroling, of suet crust pastry and of English steamed puddings. Do not serve potatoes or rice with the casserole if you can help it — the suet crust will provide the necessary gravy-mopping-up starch. Remember the pudding is a proper steamed sponge and, though light, is high in calories, especially if served, as it should be, with cream or custard. Serve small portions.

MENU LESSON 5

Three-flavour omelette

Beef casserole with suet crust

Broccoli

Green salad (see p.139)

Steamed lemon pudding

WORK PLAN

- The omelette should be made an hour or so in advance to give it time to cool to lukewarm, but resist the temptation to make it too much ahead of time as it is best not refrigerated.
- The casserole can be cooked well ahead, and the suet crust added when reheating.
- Broccoli, like all green vegetables, can be cooked, refreshed, cooked and reheated in a microwave (covered with cling film) at the last minute. But it should not be cooked more than a few hours ahead, both cooking and cooling should be swift, and reheating should be last-minute.
- Steamed puddings reheat very well, especially in a steamer or microwave oven.

THREE-FLAVOUR OMELETTE

INGREDIENTS (Serves 4)
9 eggs
Olive oil
450g/1lb ripe tomatoes, peeled, seeded and chopped
Fresh thyme
Salt and pepper
450g/1lb spinach, well washed
2 cloves garlic, peeled
Nutmeg
75g/2½oz grated Gruyère cheese
9tbsp cream

TO SERVE
Virgin green olive oil and black olives

1 Preheat the oven to 180°C/350°F/Gas 4.

2 Get out 3 bowls and break 3 eggs into each bowl.

3 Heat a little oil in a frying pan, add the tomatoes, thyme, salt and pepper and cook fairly briskly to a dryish purée. Stir frequently to prevent it sticking or burning. Allow to cool.

4 Wash and remove the stalks from the spinach. Cook in oil with the peeled but whole cloves of garlic, salt, pepper and nutmeg. Stir with a wooden spoon and cook until all the moisture has evaporated. Remove the garlic. Set aside to cool. Chop well.

5 Add the cheese to one bowl of eggs, the tomato purée to the second bowl and the finely chopped spinach to the third bowl. Add 3tbsp cream to each mixture and whisk them well. Taste and season as required.

6 Oil the inside of a terrine or loaf tin and pour in the tomato mixture. Place the dish in a bain-marie half filled with very hot water and bake until the tomato mixture is just set. This can take up to 45 minutes.

7 Gently pour in the cheese mixture. Bake for 10-15 minutes until set.

Continued on p.56

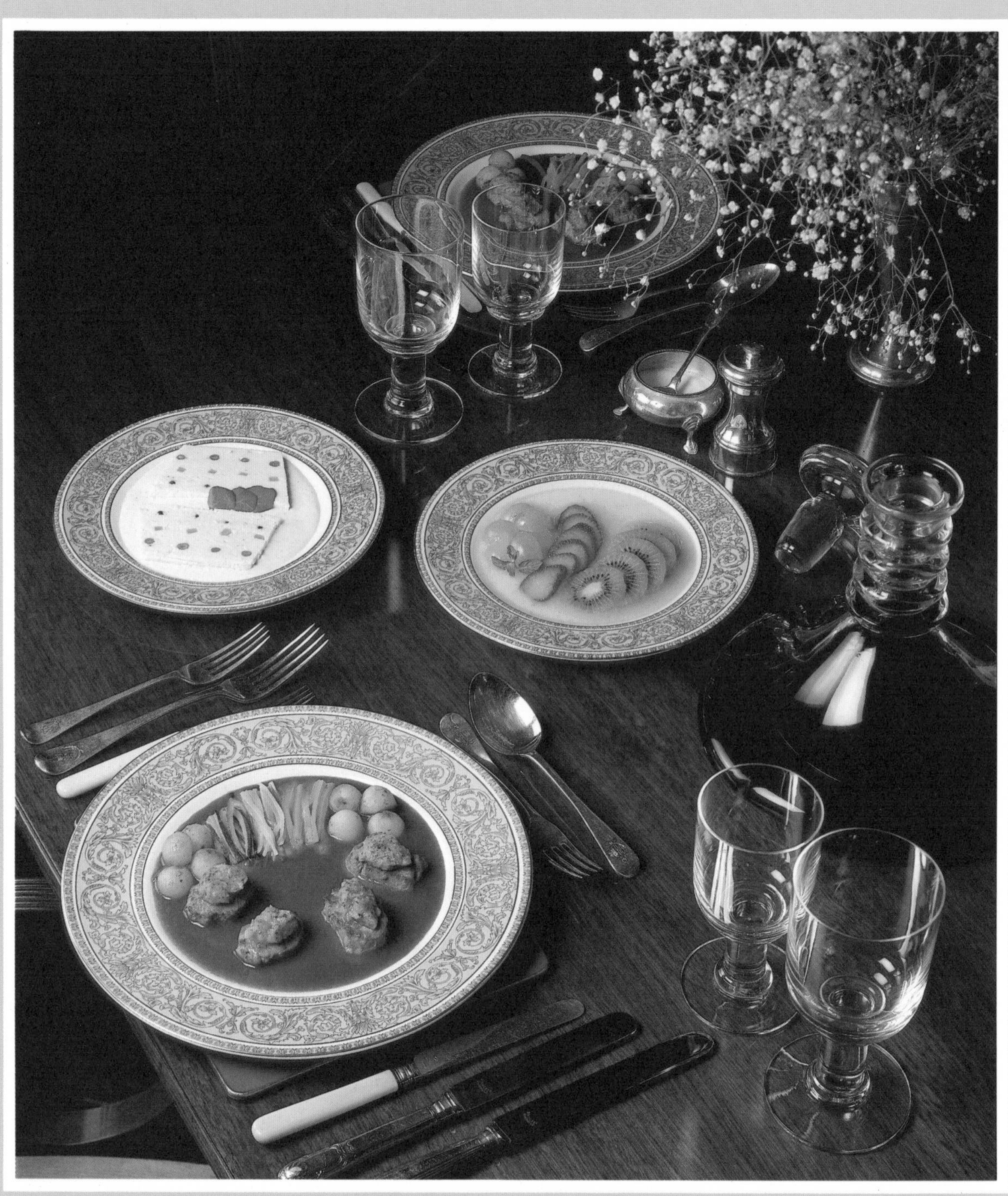

MENU LESSON 3 *(see p.43)*
This owes its inspiration to France. *Clockwise from top left:* Slices of fish terrine on chive dressing, fruit salad with mango sauce, collops of lamb with onion and mint purée together with julienne of vegetables and pommes à la Parisienne.

MENU LESSON 4 *(see p.48)*
You'll need all your skills for this. It requires time and dedication. *Clockwise from top left:* Yoghurt, honey and dates, noodles, broccoli, scallop mousse with crayfish sauce and sweetbreads with spinach and pear purée. *Inset:* Muscovado cream.

8 Add the spinach mixture and return to the oven for 20-25 minutes. The whole baking process can take up to 1½ hours.

9 Leave to cool for 30 minutes. Turn out onto a wooden board and slice. Serve on individual plates sprinkled with olive oil and garnished with the black olives.

BEEF CASSEROLE WITH SUET CRUST

INGREDIENTS (Serves 4)
675g/1½lb chuck steak
1tbsp beef dripping
12 small button onions or shallots
30g/1oz butter
1 clove garlic
2tsp flour
290ml/½pt red wine
290ml/½pt brown stock (see p.268)
Bouquet garni (bay leaf, sprig of thyme, parsley stalk and a stick of celery tied up with string)
Salt and freshly ground black pepper
45g/1½oz rindless fatty bacon
110g/4oz button mushrooms

FOR THE TOP
340g/12oz flour quality suet pastry (see p.79)

1 Set the oven to 150°C/300°F/Gas 2.

2 Cut the beef into 3cm/1½ inch cubes, discarding any fat.

3 Melt the dripping in a thick bottomed casserole pan and brown the beef pieces very well a few at a time. They must be really dark brown on all sides. Put them into a bowl as they are done. If the bottom of the pan becomes very dark or too dry, deglaze it: pour in a little of the wine, swish it about, scraping off the sediment stuck to the bottom, and pour over the meat. Heat up a little more fat and continue to brown the meat. When it is all brown repeat the déglacage (adding the wine and scraping the pan).

4 Peel the shallots by dunking them in boiling water for 6 seconds and then removing the skins. Dry them and fry in half the butter until well browned.

5 Add the garlic and stir in the flour. Cook, stirring, for 1 minute.

6 Add the wine and stock. Stir until boiling, again scraping the bottom of the pan.

7 Put the meat and sauce together in a casserole and add the bouquet garni. Season. Cover and put in the oven for 2 hours.

8 Meanwhile prepare the bacon and mushrooms: dice the bacon and wipe the mushrooms but do not peel or remove the stalks. Cut into quarters if large. Melt the remaining butter in a frying pan and when foaming add the bacon and mushrooms and cook fairly fast until delicately browned. Lift them out and add to the stew when it has been in the oven for 2 hours.

9 Increase the oven temperature to 200°C/400°F/Gas 6.

10 On a floured surface, roll the suet pastry to a shape that neatly fits the casserole dish, but does not cover the dish rim.

11 Drop the pastry on top of the stew and continue to bake, uncovered, for a further 30 minutes.

BROCCOLI

INGREDIENTS (Serves 4-6)
675g/1½lb broccoli (about 110g/4oz per person if serving as a second vegetable)
Butter
Salt and pepper

1 Wash the broccoli. Remove any tough leaves and split the stalks if very thick.

2 Place upright (so that the very tips are steamed rather than boiled) in a narrow tall pan of rapidly boiling salted water. Cook, uncovered, until tender. The timing naturally depends on the size of the broccoli, but on average it takes somewhere between 6 and 10 minutes to cook.

3 Serve with a little melted butter and black pepper.

PREPARING BROCCOLI

1 Cut off very tough stalk-ends. Split the stalks if very thick.

2 Use a potato peeler to peel stalk ends. This allows the stalk to cook as quickly as the flower if a narrow pan or asparagus steamer is not available. Or, the heads can be cut from the stalks and the stalks sliced finely into rings, which will cook in about 4 minutes in rapidly boiling water.

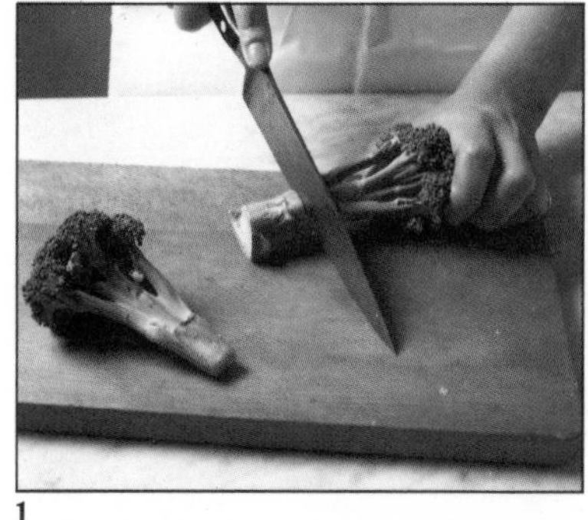
1

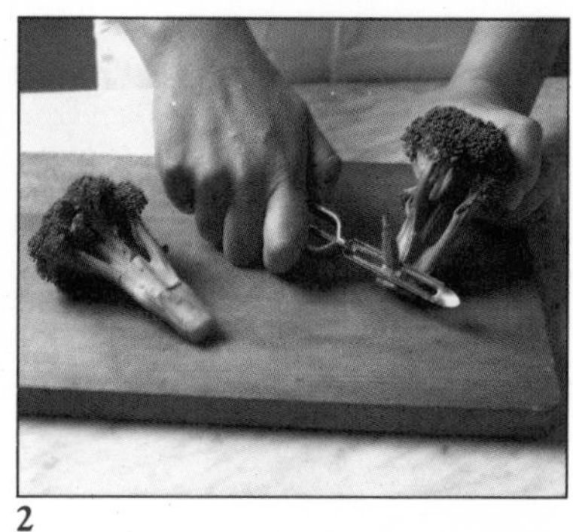
2

STEAMED LEMON PUDDING

INGREDIENTS (Serves 4)
110g/4oz butter
110g/4oz caster sugar
Grated rind and juice of 1 lemon
2 eggs, beaten
110g/4oz self-raising flour
milk

□ *When buying lemons (or other citrus fruit) choose thin-skinned ones that are heavy for their size. They contain more juice than thick-skinned types. To extract maximum juice, warm them briefly in oven or microwave (a few seconds only if using the latter) before squeezing.*

1 Grease a pudding basin with a knob of butter.

2 Cream the butter, and when very soft add the sugar and grated lemon rind. Beat until light and fluffy.

3 Gradually add the eggs, beating well between each addition. Beat in the lemon juice, adding a little flour if it looks as though it may curdle.

4 Sift and fold in the flour. Add enough milk to give a dropping consistency.

5 Turn into the pudding basin. Cover with greased greaseproof paper with a pleat (for expansion when the pudding rises) and tie down.

6 Steam gently in a double saucepan, with the water below boiling, for 2½ hours. Make sure the water does not boil dry.

7 Turn out and serve with custard or cream.

COVERING STEAMED PUDDING

1 Make a large pleat in a doubled piece of greaseproof paper.

2 Cover the bowl with the pleat running across the top. The pleat allows the pudding to expand during cooking.

1

2

3 Cut a long piece of string, wet it and fold it in half. Run this around the rim of the bowl, pulling the cut ends through the loop. Pull tight.

4 Make a knot on the opposite side of the bowl, leaving enough string free to act as a handle. Cut off excess paper, leaving a frill about 2.5cm/1 inch wide.

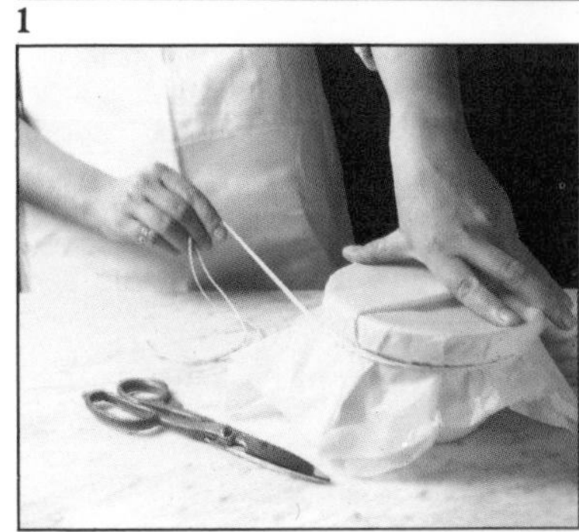
3

4

MENU LESSON 5 *(see p.53)*
Here at last is plain old fashioned cooking — omelette, casserole, vegetables, salad and steamed pudding. *Clockwise from top left:* Custard, beef casserole with suet crust, steamed lemon pudding, green salad, three-flavour omelette and broccoli.

MENU LESSON 6 *(see p.60)*
The perfect meal for a summer buffet — cold soup and a large whole fish. *Clockwise from top left:* Custard, cucumber and dill salad, boned whole salmon mayonnaise, avocado soup, summer pudding and *(centre)* potato and chive salad.

PHOTOGRAPH ON P.59

This Menu Lesson teaches the cook the simple technique of an uncooked blender soup. The soup is a perfect buffet party one, easy to do, pretty and popular and thick enough not to slop easily.

Whole fish, perfectly cooked, are a buffet classic. Our Menu Lesson assumes a whole salmon, but the technique is good for any whole round fish. The joy is that, whatever the fish size, the method of cooking in the cooling court-bouillon will work because: the larger the fish, the bigger the fish kettle; the greater the quantity of liquid, the longer heating up will take. So a bigger fish will get a proportionately longer cooking time.

The salads are easy to achieve but require carefully balanced seasoning.

Summer pudding is a classic of English home cooking. A good one is rare, but not hard to achieve if the instructions are meticulously followed.

MENU LESSON 6

Avocado pear soup

Boned whole salmon mayonnaise

New potato and chive salad

Cucumber and dill salad

Summer pudding

WORK PLAN

• Making the soup takes a matter of minutes. It will keep its fresh colour for an hour or two if refrigerated, but for no longer.

• The salmon can be cooked the day before eating and left in its court-bouillon overnight. Decorate it on the day of serving.

• The salads can be prepared several hours ahead but should not be dressed until an hour or so before time.

• Summer pudding *should* be made the day before, and turned out on the day.

AVOCADO PEAR SOUP

INGREDIENTS (Serves 4)
4 avocado pears
1 small onion
Salt and freshly ground black pepper
720ml/1 ¼pt cold white stock (see p 268)
Juice of 1 lemon

TO GARNISH
2tbsp soured cream
1tbsp chopped chives

1 Skin and stone the avocado pears. Mash to a purée in a bowl with a fork, or chop roughly on a board.

2 Chop the onion.

3 Liquidize together the avocado pears, onion, salt, pepper, stock and lemon juice. Chill.

4 Serve in individual bowls with a spoonful of soured cream and a sprinkle of chopped chives.

BONED WHOLE SALMON MAYONNAISE

INGREDIENTS (Serves 6)
1.8kg/4lb salmon, cleaned (see p.264)

FOR THE COURT-BOUILLON
1 onion, sliced
1 bay leaf
1 parsley stalk, bruised
6 peppercorns

1 Put all the court-bouillon ingredients into a large fish kettle and add enough water to come 7½cm/3 inches up the sides.

2 Add the salmon. Bring slowly to the boil. Reduce the heat and poach for 1 minute. Leave the salmon to cool in the court-bouillon without a lid. The salmon will cook in the cooling court-bouillon. Check it every 20 minutes or so to make sure that it is not overcooking. A fish like this is cooked when the dorsal fin (the large one in the centre of the back) pulls out easily and when it will skin readily. Allow it to get completely cold. If it is cooked before the liquid is cold, stand the whole kettle in cold water to hurry up the cooling process. The fish is much more moist if it is not lifted out of the liquid until cold.

FOR THE FILLING AND DECORATION
150ml/ ¼pt mayonnaise
1 large cucumber
2 lemons
Bunch of watercress
Fish aspic (see p.64)

3 Skin the fish, leaving the head and tail intact. Carefully remove the two top fillets and remove the backbone. Sandwich them back in place with mayonnaise.

4 Skin the cucumber and cut it into very fine strips. Blanch in boiling water for 1 minute and refresh under running cold water. Drain well.

5 Decorate the salmon with a lattice of cucumber skin: if you are using the aspic, dip the cucumber in a little of it before arranging on the fish. This helps stick the strips in place. Leave to set. Using a large basting spoon held near the bowl and not at the handle end, coat the fish with just-liquid but nearly set aspic. Getting the aspic at the point of setting, but not yet solid, is tricky. Have ready a bowl of warm water and a bowl of iced water with a few cubes of ice floating in it. Put the aspic into a metal jug and stand it in one or other bowl according to whether it needs melting over gentle heat, or thickening by cooling. Stir gently to assist even warming or cooling, but do not whisk or stir vigorously or the aspic will trap bubbles. Do not be tempted to use the aspic until the texture is perfect — too thin and it will simply run off the food. Too cool and it will be uneven, lumpy and too thick. Patience is all. Leave to set.

6 Coat again if necessary to achieve a thin but even shine — not a thick coat.

7 Add lemon wedges to the dish and perhaps a collar of watercress to cover the join between head and body.

NOTE 1 If a large fish is cooked before the court-bouillon is cold, and the kettle is too large to stand in a sink to cool rapidly, lift out the fish, and immediately drop a piece of plastic wrap over it, lightly but closely (with no air pockets). This will allow the fish to cool without becoming dry. A polythene covering that traps warm air between fish and plastic can lead to food poisoning. See p.331.

NOTE 2 The serving plate can be flooded with a shallow layer of aspic and allowed to set. The salmon is then served on a sea of aspic. Any left-over aspic can be finely chopped (on damp greaseproof paper) with a wet knife, or set on a shallow tray and cut into neat dice with a knife. But if the aspic is not crystal clear it is not wise to do this — chopping emphasizes its murkiness.

MAYONNAISE

INGREDIENTS
2 egg yolks
1tsp pale (preferably Dijon) mustard
290ml/ ½pt olive oil OR 150ml/ ¼pt each olive and salad oil
Squeeze of lemon juice
1tbsp wine vinegar
Salt and pepper

1 Put the yolks into a bowl with the mustard and beat well with a wooden spoon.

2 Add the oil, literally drop by drop, beating all the time. The mixture should be very thick by the time half the oil is added.

3 Beat in the lemon juice.

4 Resume pouring in the oil, going rather more confidently now, but alternating the dribbles of oil with small quantities of vinegar.

5 Add salt and pepper to taste.

NOTE If the mixture curdles, another egg yolk should be beaten in a separate bowl, and the curdled mixture beaten drop by drop into it.

MENU LESSON 7 *(see p.66)*
An unusual and delicious lunch or the perfect late-night supper — and an object lesson in bread and pastry making. *Clockwise from top left:* Shortbread, green fruit salad, smoked chicken pizza made with mozzarella and one with fromage blanc.

MENU LESSON 8 *(see p.69)*
A taxing meal for the cook — if it is to be prepared to perfection. *Clockwise from top left:* Strawberry meringue basket, grilled pepper salad, veal kidney and wild mushroom feuilletées with carrot and cardamom purée, and green salad.

FISH ASPIC

INGREDIENTS (Serves 4)
1 onion
1 carrot
1 stick celery
Bones, head and skin of 2 medium-sized white fish
110g/4oz minced lean shin of beef
1 bay leaf
6 black peppercorns
1 glass white wine
55g/2oz gelatine
2 egg whites and 2 egg shells, crushed

1 Cut the onion, carrot and celery into small chunks. Put into a saucepan with the fish heads, bones and skin. Add the mince, bay leaf, peppercorns and wine. Pour over 850ml/1½pt cold water. Bring to the boil, skim, and simmer *very* slowly for 30 minutes. Strain and leave to get cold.

2 Put the stock into a large very clean saucepan, sprinkle over the gelatine and put the saucepan over a gentle heat.

3 Place the crushed shells in a bowl, add the egg white and whisk until frothy. Pour into the warming stock and keep whisking steadily with a balloon whisk until the mixture boils and rises. The longer this takes the clearer the aspic will be. Stop whisking immediately and draw the pan off the heat. Allow the mixture to subside. Take care not to break the crust formed by the egg white.

4 Bring the aspic to the boil again (without whisking). Allow to subside. Repeat once more (the egg white will trap the sediment in the stock and clear the aspic). Allow to cool for 5 minutes.

5 Fix a double layer of *white* kitchen paper or fine muslin in a sieve over a very clean basin and carefully strain the aspic through it. Do not worry if, or when, the egg white crust slips into the sieve. If the aspic is not absolutely clear it can be strained once more. Do not hurry the process — stirring and swirling produces murky aspic. Taste and season if necessary, using ground white pepper, salt and possibly a drop of sherry. Leave to chill and set.

NOTE Do not leave the warm aspic to cool for too long before straining lest it set in the paper or sieve, clogging the filter.

☐ *Granulated commercial aspic can be used if you do not wish to make your own fish aspic.*

NEW POTATO AND CHIVE SALAD

INGREDIENTS (Serves 4)
675g/1½lb new potatoes
Sprig of mint
4tbsp French dressing (see p.139)
3tbsp soured cream
1tbsp mayonnaise
2tbsp fresh chopped chives

1 Boil the potatoes with the mint in a pan of boiling salted water until just tender. (If using very small new potatoes they are good left unpeeled. If they are large they should be peeled *after* boiling.) Drain well. Cut up if large.

2 Toss in the French dressing while still hot. Leave to cool.

3 Mix the soured cream and the mayonnaise together. Add half the chives.

4 Turn the potatoes in this creamy dressing and tip into a salad bowl.

5 Sprinkle liberally with the rest of the chopped chives.

CUCUMBER AND DILL SALAD

INGREDIENTS (Serves 4)
1 cucumber
Salt and freshly ground black pepper
1tbsp chopped fresh dill
2tbsp white wine vinegar
½tsp salt

1 Peel and slice the cucumber. Sprinkle the slices with salt and leave, in a colander, for 20 minutes.

2 Rinse well, drain and dry the cucumber thoroughly. Arrange in overlapping slices in a circular dish.

3 Sprinkle with the dill and vinegar. Season with freshly ground black pepper. Leave for at least 30 minutes before serving.

DE-SEEDING CUCUMBER
For greater elegance, remove the cucumber seeds. To do this, split the cucumber lengthwise. Use a melon-baller or teaspoon to remove the seeds in one steady movement. Then follow the recipe, but do not attempt to arrange the slices in rows — it would take all day.

SUMMER PUDDING

INGREDIENTS
900g /2lb mixture of raspberries, strawberries, cherries (stoned), redcurrants, blackcurrants and blackberries
150ml/¼pt water
225g/8oz sugar
285g/10oz dessert apples, peeled and sliced
6-8 slices stale white bread, with crusts removed

TO SERVE
Cream or custard (p.280)

1 Put the apples into a large saucepan. Add the water and heat until just simmering. Cook slowly, covered, until the apple slices look glassy and are limp.

2 Add the rest of the fruit and threequarters of the sugar, stir gently, and again bring the pan slowly to boiling point, when the red fruit will be barely cooked, and plenty of juice will have run from it. Taste and add the rest of the sugar if necessary.

3 Dip pieces of crustless stale bread in the juice and use them to line a pudding basin. See illustration.

4 Fill up with the drained but still juicy fruit, and weigh down with a saucer and a weight (perhaps a can of fruit) to press out any excess juice. Stand the basin in a bowl to catch any drips.

5 Chill until firm (overnight is best). Turn out, and use the collected juice as a last-minute sauce to give the pudding a shine.

6 Serve with plenty of cream or custard.

SUMMER PUDDING

1 Dip pieces of stale white bread, from which the crusts have been removed, into the juices that have run from the cooked soft fruit.

2 Use a square piece of dipped bread to line the bottom of a pudding basin, then use triangles or fingers of dipped bread for the sides, overlapping the pieces slightly.

3 Use a perforated spoon to fill the basin with the fruit so as to avoid filling it with too much liquid.

4 Cover with more soaked bread, and weight the pudding using a saucer and a heavy weight to press out excess juice.

1

2

3

4

PHOTOGRAPH ON P.62

The simple techniques of breadmaking (for the pizza), getting a perfect fruit salad syrup and baking a high-butter pastry, are covered in this Menu Lesson. The menu would make an unusual and delicious lunch, or perhaps a late night supper for theatre-goers.

MENU LESSON 7

Smoked chicken pizza

Green fruit salad

Shortbread

WORK PLAN

• The pizzas can be prepared well in advance up to and including step 6. They can then be put into a very cold refrigerator to inhibit further working of the yeast and baked later, 20 minutes or so before serving.

• The syrup for the fruit salad, and most of the fruit can be prepared ahead — even the apples can be added two or three hours before serving if the dish is kept chilled.

• The shortbread can be made days in advance. But even if starting from scratch the whole meal, including the shopping, would not take more than half a morning to produce.

SMOKED CHICKEN PIZZA

INGREDIENTS (Serves 4)

FOR THE DOUGH
1tsp fresh yeast
175ml/6fl oz lukewarm water
450g/1lb plain flour
½tsp salt
2tbsp olive oil

FOR THE FILLINGS
4tbsp tomato purée
1tbsp fresh basil
85g/3oz smoked chicken breast, sliced
1kg/2lb tin Italian tomatoes
4tbsp fromage blanc, labne or 1 small mozzarella
Salt and freshly ground black pepper
Chopped oregano or marjoram

1 MAKE THE DOUGH Dissolve the yeast in warm water. Sift the flour and the salt together and mix to a soft dough with the yeasty water. Mix in the olive oil with a knife and then knead for 10 minutes until smooth and elastic.

2 Grease 2 deep sandwich (or moule-à-manquer) tins with a little more oil and divide the dough between the tins. Put in a warm place to rise (say, for about an hour over the boiler). Push the dough flat on the bottom of the tins and press to come up the sides. Put the tins back in the warm place for about half an hour to rise again until puffy.

3 Set the oven to 250°C/500°F/Gas 9.

4 Push down the dough again with the back of a large spoon or with your knuckles and once again press the edges up the sides of the tin.

5 FOR THE FILLINGS Mix the tomato purée and basil together and spread this all over the bottom of the dough. Arrange the smoked chicken breast over the tomato purée.

6 Drain the tomatoes. Cut them in half and drain well on absorbent paper or by leaving in a sieve for 15 minutes. Put them into the pizzas with the labne or mozzarella if using them. Sprinkle with the oregano or marjoram and season.

7 Bake for 15 minutes. Spoon over the fromage blanc if using that and bake again until browned, about 5 more minutes.

☐ *Mozzarella is the usual cheese for pizza but the Lebanese labne or the French fromage blanc are excellent too. Because fromage blanc browns rapidly, it is added towards the end of the cooking time, rather than with the other topping ingredients.*

☐ *The rather sophisticated topping of this pizza can of course be substituted with any, or all, of the traditional ingredients — thinly spread tomato purée, sliced tomatoes, mozzarella cheese, anchovies, spicy sausage, black olives, mushrooms, etc. Dust a little marjoram or oregano on top and add a sprinkling of olive oil before baking. Larger flat pizzas can be baked using baking sheets instead of cake tins.*

KNEADING DOUGH
1 Stretch and pull the dough, using the heel of your hand to pull.

2 Then fold it over and push together. Repeat the stretching, pulling, and pushing with the knuckles until the dough is smooth and elastic. This should take about 10 minutes.

3 Test that the dough is ready by pressing it with your finger.

4 It should spring back to its previous stage while you watch. If the indentation remains the dough is not yet elastic enough and needs more kneading.

GREEN FRUIT SALAD

INGREDIENTS (Serves 4)
2 green apples
1 small ripe green melon
110g/4oz seedless white grapes
2 kiwi fruit

FOR THE SUGAR SYRUP
150ml/¼pt water
55g/2oz granulated sugar
Squeeze lemon juice
2tbsp kirsch (optional)

1 MAKE THE SUGAR SYRUP Bring the ingredients slowly to the boil. The water should not boil before the sugar has dissolved or it may crystallize into lumps that will not dissolve.

2 Boil hard for a minute or two to get a perfectly clear syrup.

3 Leave to cool.

4 PREPARE THE FRUIT Do not peel the apple, but core it and cut into thin slices. Put immediately into the syrup.

5 Using a melon baller, scoop the melon flesh into balls, or simply cut into even sized cubes.

6 Wash and de-seed the grapes as shown overleaf.

7 Peel and slice the kiwi fruit.

8 Put all the prepared fruit into the syrup with the kirsch, if used. Chill well.

NOTE 1 Green fruit salad looks very pretty if served in the scooped out melon, or in a clear glass bowl.

NOTE 2 The syrup used here is a standard syrup suitable for poaching fruit, adding to fruit salad and for when 'sugar syrup' is called for in a recipe. Sweeter syrups are sometimes needed (for candying fruit for example) with up to 450g/1lb sugar to every 570ml/1pt water. Equally, a thin sugar syrup (perhaps for fresh fruit that is low in acidity) might have only 110g/4oz sugar to the pint.

NOTE 3 Syrups may be flavoured by the addition of fresh mint leaves, bay leaves, crushed cardamom pods, cinnamon sticks, lemon or orange peel etc. Just include the flavouring when making the syrup. Allow to cool, then strain.

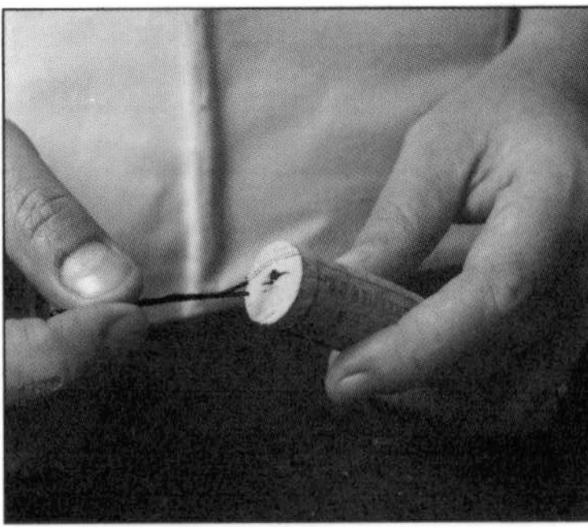

DE-SEEDING GRAPES
1 Make a hole in the end of a wine cork and insert the ends of a clean hair grip firmly into it.

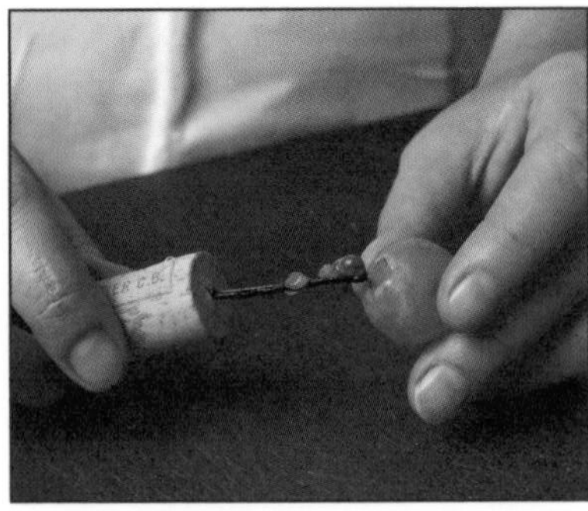

2 Use the rounded end of the hair grip to hook out the grape seeds. (The cork, though not essential, makes using the hair grip easier and ensures finding it again.)

SHORTBREAD

INGREDIENTS (Serves 4)
110g/4oz unsalted butter
55g/2oz caster sugar
170g/6oz plain flour
30g/1oz split almonds

1 Set the oven to 190°C/375°F/Gas 5.

2 Beat the butter and sugar together until soft and creamy.

3 Work in the flour by degrees, with a minimum of beating.

4 Pat the paste into a smooth ball, then into a square about 1cm/½ inch thick.

5 Slip a floured baking sheet under the paste.

6 Prick with a fork and cut into fingers. Sprinkle with caster sugar. Decorate with split almonds, pressing them in gently.

7 Bake to a pale biscuit colour (about 20 minutes). Leave 2 minutes then lift onto a cooling rack to crisp up and cool.

8 Store in an airtight container only when stone-cold.

PHOTOGRAPH ON P.63

The pepper salad of this menu is simplicity itself but depends on some dedication on the part of the cook if it is to be perfect. First, it is far more interesting and flavoursome if the peppers are red (ripe and sweet), yellow (the blandest of the peppers) and green (the least ripe and most astringent), rather than all one colour. Next, though the grilling of the peppers and the removal of the outer membrane is not strictly necessary, the dish is the better for it.

The secret of good kidneys is not to overcook them. They become tough and strong flavoured if cooked beyond pinkness.

Read the chapter on meringues on p.286 if attempting the meringue cake for the first time.

MENU LESSON 8

Grilled pepper salad

Veal kidney and wild mushroom feuilletées

Green salad (see p.139)

Carrot and cardamom purée

Strawberry meringue basket

WORK PLAN

- The pepper salad may be made several hours in advance and will benefit from an hour or two in the oil.
- The pastry can be made in advance and baked an hour or two before eating but the kidneys must be a last-minute matter.
- The purée reheats well and the meringue can be made (but not filled) the day before serving.

GRILLED PEPPER SALAD

INGREDIENTS (Serves 4)
6 large peppers (red, yellow and green)
3 eggs
6 anchovy fillets
2tbsp olive oil
Freshly ground black pepper

1 Cut the peppers in quarters, deseed and skin them: place them under a very hot grill until the skin has blistered and blackened evenly all over. Then, scrape the skin off the peppers. Cut away the stalks and membranes.

2 Hard boil the eggs. With a needle or egg prick, prick a hole in the rounded end of the egg. This allows the release of trapped air which would otherwise expand, bursting the shell. Put into a saucepan of boiling, salted water and simmer for 10 to 12 minutes depending on the size of the eggs. Drain and leave under running cold water for 2 minutes. This prevents the egg overcooking and an unattractive greeny-black ring forming around the yolk. The less vigorous the bubbles when boiling the egg the tenderer the whites will be. Boiling produces rubber-like egg white.

3 Remove the shells and cut the eggs into quarters lengthwise, using a stainless steel knife (a carbon steel knife will discolour the white, leaving grey streaks and patches).

4 Cut the flesh into shapes like petals, and arrange them like a flower on a flat round dish, garnishing with the hard boiled eggs and anchovy fillets. Pour over the olive oil and sprinkle with a little black pepper.

VEAL KIDNEY AND WILD MUSHROOM FEUILLETEES

INGREDIENTS (Serves 4)
340g/12oz flour-quantity puff pastry (see p.85)
1 beaten egg

FOR THE FILLING
290ml/½pt white wine
340g/12oz veal kidneys
55g/2oz ceps, sliced
55g/2oz small chanterelles
55g/2oz small morels
70g/2½oz unsalted butter
2tsp Dijon mustard
1tbsp chopped fresh parsley
Squeeze of lemon juice
Salt and freshly ground black pepper
6tbsp double cream

☐ *These feuilletées are wonderful if the pastry is homemade, light and buttery. But frozen puff pastry is a good product and need not be scorned by the busy cook.*

1 Set the oven to 220°C/425°F/Gas 7.

2 TO MAKE THE PASTRY CASES Roll the pastry into a large rectangle. Cut into four 10cm/4 inch diamond shapes (ie each side should measure 10cm/4 inches). With a knife cut a line about 1.25cm/½ inch from the edge of each diamond, without cutting all the way through the pastry. This inner diamond will become the lid of the feuilletées. Make a design in this diamond with the knife. 'Knock up' the sides of the feuilletées (see illustration). Place them on a damp baking tray and brush with egg. Chill for 15 minutes.

3 Bake in a preheated oven for 20 minutes or until the pastry is puffed up and brown. With a sharp knife remove the 'lids' and scoop out any uncooked pastry. Transfer the cases and lids to a wire rack to cool.

4 Reduce the oven to 180°C/350°F/Gas 4.

5 Meanwhile, PREPARE THE FILLING Put the wine into a saucepan and reduce, by boiling rapidly, to half its original quantity.

6 Remove the membranes and cores from the kidneys and slice them fairly finely, as shown.

7 Fry all the mushrooms slowly in a little of the butter for about 4 minutes. Set aside.

8 Slowly fry the kidneys, a handful at a time, in the remaining butter.

MAKING FEUILLETEES

1 Cut a margin 1.25cm/½ inch from the edge of each diamond, cutting into but not through the paste. Pattern the border, indenting the paste. Decorate the inner diamond in the same way.

2 Use the floured blade of the knife to tap or 'knock up' the edges — slightly separating the many layers of paste to encourage them to rise in the oven.

3 Place on a damp baking sheet and brush with egg, taking care not to wet the edges, as this will prevent the pastry from rising and separating into its many 'leaves'.

4 When baked and still hot, use a sharp knife to cut round and lift the 'lids'.

5 Pull out any uncooked pastry from inside the feuilletées. Return to the oven to dry out further if necessary. Cool on a wire rack.

☐ Wild mushrooms are not easy to obtain. Fortunately cultivated ones are excellent, especially the flat dark type.

9 Return the mushrooms to the frying pan with the barely cooked kidneys. Add the wine, mustard, parsley, lemon juice, salt and pepper, and cream. Bring to the boil and boil for 1 minute.

10 Return the pastry cases to the oven to reheat.

11 Divide the filling between the 4 pastry cases. Put on the lids and serve immediately.

PREPARING VEAL OR OX KIDNEY

1 Remove as much of the white 'core' as possible with scissors.

2 Slice the kidney thinly. Veal kidney (which is smaller and paler) is usually cooked at this stage. Ox kidney is chopped smaller for mixing with other meats.

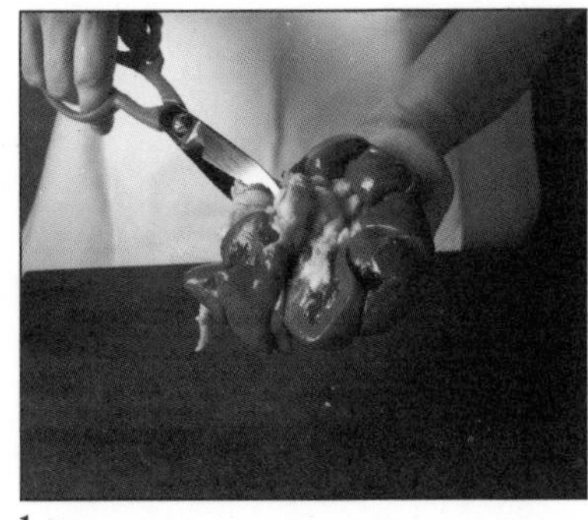

1

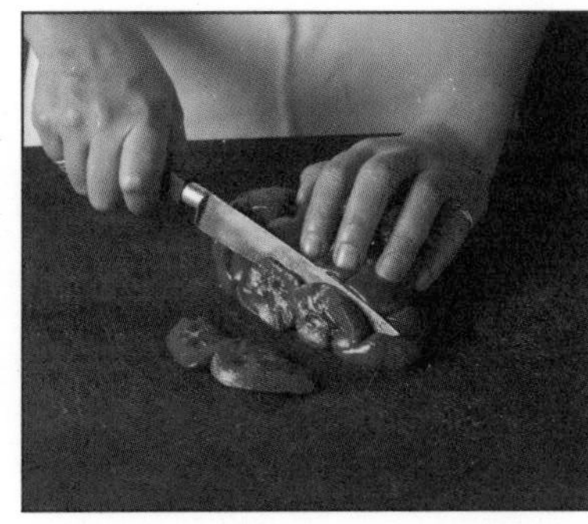

2

CARROT AND CARDAMOM PUREE

INGREDIENTS (Serves 4)
450g/1lb carrots
570ml/1pt water
2 cardamom pods, cracked
1 bay leaf
2tbsp Greek yoghurt
1tbsp chopped fresh chervil
Salt and freshly ground black pepper

1 Peel and slice the carrots. Cook in the water, with the cardamom pods and bay leaf, until very tender (about 12 minutes).

2 Remove the cardamoms and bay leaf. Allow the carrots to cool slightly. Liquidize with the Greek yoghurt.

3 Add the chervil and season to taste.

NOTE For a variation in the carrot purée try flavouring it, instead of with cardamom, with finely grated orange rind, with chopped mint, or with ground cumin.

STRAWBERRY MERINGUE BASKET

INGREDIENTS (Serves 4)

FOR THE MERINGUE CUITE
8 egg whites
450g/1lb icing sugar
6 drops vanilla flavouring

FOR THE FILLING
450g/1lb fresh strawberries, hulled
425ml/¾pt double cream, whipped

This is a classic meringue cuite recipe. For further details see p.288.

In order to make this 18cm/7 inch diameter basket, you will need to make the meringue in two batches — it is too great a quantity to be managed at once.

1 Set the oven to 130°C/275°F/Gas 1. Line 2 large baking sheets, with silicone 'bakewell' paper. Draw two 18cm/7 inch diameter circles on each piece of paper and turn over.

2 Make up the first batch of meringue cuite. Put half the egg whites with half the sifted sugar into a mixing bowl and set over, not in, a pan of simmering water. Whisk, with a large hand balloon whisk or electric hand whisk, until the meringue is thick and will hold its shape. This may well take up to 10 minutes of vigorous beating. (A very good imitation meringue cuite can be made by whisking the egg whites and sugar together in a powerful mixer without bothering with heating the meringue. But hand whisks tend to overheat in the time it takes to achieve the correct solidity of meringue if not beaten over heat.)

☐ As an alternative to double cream for the meringue, the cook might make crème fraîche (see p.125). It has to be made a day in advance, but its slightly acid taste goes well with the very sweet meringue.

3 Add half the vanilla flavouring. Remove the bowl and whisk for a further 2 minutes.

4 Remove the meringue from the heat and put into a forcing bag fitted with a 0.75cm/½ inch plain nozzle. Squeeze gently to get rid of any pockets of air. Hold the bag, upright, in your right hand, and using your left hand to guide the nozzle, pipe a circular base on the first baking sheet, using one of your pencilled circles as a guide (see illustrations overleaf). Pipe 3 18cm/7 inch empty rings on the 3 remaining pencilled circles.

5 Bake for 45 to 60 minutes until dry and crisp. Cool on a wire rack.

6 Make up the second batch of meringue cuite using the remaining ingredients. Return the round of cooked meringue to the baking sheet. Use a little uncooked mixture to fix the hoops on the round, one of top of the other.

7 Put the remaining mixture into a forcing bag fitted with a rose nozzle. Cover the hoops with the meringue.

8 Bake at the same temperature for 45-50 minutes until set and crisp. Cool.

9 Fill with the lightly whipped cream and strawberries just before serving.

MERINGUE BASKET
1 Pencil 4 18cm/7 inch circles on silicone 'bakewell' paper and oil the paper. Using the pencil lines as the outer limit, pipe empty rings and one circular disc, starting at the middle. Bake until dry and crisp.

2 Using uncooked meringue as glue, stack the empty rings on the base. Pipe more meringue up the sides of the basket, working in straight lines from bottom to top.

3 Use any extra meringue to pipe scrolls or shells or rosettes along the top edge. Bake again for about 45 minutes until crisp. (See feature on piping, pp.300-301.)

PHOTOGRAPH ON P.82

MENU LESSON 9

Scallop and mangetout salad

Pork fillets with red and green peppers

Pommes Anna

Fresh peas

Apple strudel

This menu may sound like an odd combination of ideas in that the first course is a sophisticated 'salade tiède', the main course is a peasant curry (served without the traditional accompaniments) and the pudding is a hearty Austrian pie. But being brave about combinations is no bad thing. It is true that frequently stepping out of style is a mistake — the leap from garlicky Provençale ratatouille to nursery bread-and-butter pudding could dismay the discerning palate. However, the combinations in the following recipes — seafood followed by pork, pork followed by apple pie — are in fact tried and traditional ones.

The techniques emphasized are those of careful timing in the cooking of easily spoilt ingredients (scallops and mangetouts), the tricky art of a perfect Pommes Anna, neither anaemic nor over-brown, and the exciting and satisfying business of strudel pastry.

WORK PLAN

- The mangetouts can be cooked, the french dressing made, the scallops cleaned and sliced and the lamb's lettuce washed and dried, but the salad cannot be put together until the last minute.
- The pork dish could be completely precooked and then reheated when required. Alternatively it could be kept warm for half an hour or so.
- The pommes Anna can sit for half an hour.
- The peas must be cooked at precisely the right time.
- The strudel can be made on the morning of a dinner party but tends to stodginess if made the day before.

SCALLOP AND MANGETOUT SALAD

INGREDIENTS (Serves 4)
12 fresh scallops
225g/8oz mangetouts, topped and tailed
Handful of lamb's lettuce
1tbsp fresh chopped mint
French dressing (see p.139)
1tbsp lemon juice
2tbsp very small fried croutons

1 Clean the scallops, saving any juices and removing the muscular white frill found opposite the orange roe. Rinse off any black matter. Separate the roes from the body. Slice the white part of the scallops into 2 or 3 horizontally, but leave the roes whole.

2 Blanch (put into a saucepan of boiling salted water) the mangetouts for 3-4 minutes. Refresh (run under cold water until cold. This will prevent further cooking and set the colour). Drain well.

3 Wash and drain the lamb's lettuce.

4 Add the mint to the French dressing, and in it toss together the mangetouts and lamb's lettuce and place on 4 side plates.

5 Put the scallops into a pan with the lemon juice and their own juices. Put on a well fitting lid and gently shake and toss them over a moderate heat for 30 seconds, or until they have lost their glassiness, and become very slightly firmer to the touch.

6 Tip the warm scallops, with the juices, over the mangetouts, scatter on the croûtons and serve immediately.

☐ *Frozen scallops can be used if fresh ones cannot be had. Try to get them frozen with the coral — it is frequently absent from frozen packs.*

PORK FILLETS WITH RED AND GREEN PEPPERS

INGREDIENTS (Serves 4)
675g/1½lb pork fillet
1 clove garlic
1 large onion
1 red pepper
1 green pepper
2tbsp sunflower oil
1tsp ground cumin
1tsp ground coriander
1tsp ground cinnamon
1tsp ground turmeric
½tsp ground mild chilli powder
Water
110g/4oz ricotta or curd cheese
1tbsp roughly chopped fresh mint

1 Trim off any fat and membrane from the pork fillet with a sharp, flexible knife. Cut the meat into 0.5cm/¼ inch slices.

2 Peel and crush the garlic. Put the peeled clove on a piece of greaseproof paper and place a small pile of salt beside it. Using an ordinary cutlery knife, squash the garlic using a little of the salt to encourage the flow of juice and to obtain a creamy consistency.

3 Slice the onion, as shown.

4 Discard the stalks and seeds of the peppers and slice the flesh.

5 Heat the oil in a large sauté pan and in it brown the meat, a few pieces at a time, until evenly coloured all over. Remove the meat to a plate.

6 Add the garlic, onions and peppers to the pan and allow to soften without browning for 2-3 minutes. Add the dry spices and cook for a further 2 minutes. Stir regularly and add a little extra oil if they are in danger of getting too dry or burnt.

7 Take the pan off the heat. Return the pork and add enough water to just cover the meat and vegetables. Return to the heat and bring gradually up to the boil, stirring continually.

8 Add the cheese and stir until melted. (If using ricotta cheese beat it with a little cold water, add some of the hot juices from the pan, mix well and return to the pan. This inhibits the tendency to lump.)

9 Simmer for about 10 minutes or until the meat is tender. Add the mint and serve immediately.

SLICING ONIONS
1 Split the unskinned onion in half through the top and tail.

2 Pull away the onion skin from the pointed top, leaving the root end intact. This will prevent the 'leaves' of onion slipping while being sliced. Repeat with the second half-onion.

3 Put each onion-half, cut-side down, on the board and slice widthways, from tip to root. Use the knuckles as a guide, moving them back a little after each cut. Use a downwards and forwards cutting action, keeping the knife-tip touching the board.

POMMES ANNA

INGREDIENTS (Serves 4)
675g/1½lb potatoes
55g/2oz butter, clarified (see next recipe)
Salt and pepper
Grated nutmeg

1 Clarify the butter, as shown.

2 Heat the oven to 190°C/375°F/Gas 5. Brush a small heavy frying pan with the butter.

3 Wash, peel and slice the potatoes very finely.

4 Arrange a neat layer of overlapping slices on the bottom of the frying pan, starting in the middle. Brush the potatoes with the melted butter and season well with salt, pepper and nutmeg.

5 Continue to layer the potatoes, butter and seasoning until all the potatoes have been used. Finish with butter and seasoning.

6 Hold the pan over direct medium heat for 2 minutes to brown the bottom layer of potatoes.

7 Take off and cover with greaseproof paper and a lid (or foil). Bake in the oven for about 45 minutes.

8 When the potatoes are tender, slide a flexible palette knife under the potatoes to loosen them, invert a serving plate over the pan and turn the potatoes out so that the neat first layer is now on top.

NOTE Clarified butter is used here because the recipe calls for high heat which would burn the milk solids and impurities in unclarified butter. It is also used where a clean good looking butter is needed (such as melted butter for serving with asparagus, or to seal the top of a pâté).

CLARIFIED BUTTER

There are many complicated recipes for clarifying butter, but the method shown here is simple and completely foolproof. The object is to get rid of salts and milk solids in the butter so that it will be crystal clear and can be brought to high temperatures without burning.

TO CLARIFY BUTTER
1 Melt the butter in a heavy saucepan and allow it to foam for a minute or so, but not to burn. When the foaming begins to die down, remove from the heat and leave to settle for 20 seconds.

2 Pour through a strainer lined with fine muslin cloth or a pressed paper kitchen cloth. The butter will emerge clear.

FRESH PEAS

INGREDIENTS (Serves 4)
900g/2lb fresh peas
Pinch of salt
Pinch of sugar
Sprig of fresh mint
Knob of butter
Freshly ground black pepper

1 Hull the peas and boil in a pan of salted water to which a pinch of sugar and a sprig of mint has been added. They will take about 3 minutes to cook.

2 Drain in a colander and serve with melted butter and freshly ground black pepper.

NOTE Young peas from the garden are best served this way. Older, sturdier peas are better puréed. Frozen peas are a better buy than most fresh peas from the shop.

APPLE STRUDEL

INGREDIENTS (Serves 4)
285g/10oz flour-quantity strudel pastry (see next recipe)

FOR THE FILLING
675g/1½lb cooking apples
Handful of currants, sultanas and raisins
30g/1oz brown sugar
½tsp cinnamon
½tsp ground cloves
2tbsp browned crumbs
Grated rind 1 lemon
55g/2oz melted butter
Icing sugar

1 First, make the pastry, and keep it well wrapped in cling-film.

2 PREPARE THE FILLING Peel, score and slice the apples very finely (if they are too thick they will pierce the pastry and fail to cook properly) and mix together with the dried fruit, sugar, spices, crumbs and lemon rind.

3 Now roll and pull the pastry, as shown. This stage is satisfyingly dramatic, but needs plenty of space — like the dining room table. Put a tablecloth over a large table and dredge it lightly with flour. Put the strudel pastry on top and roll out.

4 Trim off the thick edges and brush immediately with melted butter.

5 Sprinkle the filling evenly over the pastry and roll up.

6 Tip the strudel onto the baking sheet. Brush with the remaining butter.

7 Bake in the oven until golden brown (about 40 minutes). Dust with icing sugar while still hot.

NOTE If the strudel has been made in advance it can be reheated for 5 minutes in the oven to warm through.

STRUDEL PASTRY

INGREDIENTS (Serves 4)
285g/10oz plain flour
Pinch of salt
1 egg
150ml/¼pt water
1tsp oil

1 Sift the flour and salt into a bowl.

2 Beat the egg and add the water and oil. First with a knife and then with one hand mix the water and egg into the flour, adding more water if necessary to make a soft dough.

3 Beat the paste until smooth and elastic, as shown. Put it into a clean floured bowl. Cover and leave in a warm place for 15 minutes.

4 The pastry is now ready for rolling and pulling, as described.

☐ *Bought filo (or phylo) pastry is obtainable from some supermarkets and from Greek speciality food shops. It comes ready rolled and in convenient leaves. It can be frozen.*

BEATING STRUDEL PASTE
1 Lift the dough up in one hand and with a flick of the wrist throw it onto a lightly floured marble slab or board without letting go of it.

2 Gather it up again and repeat the flinging down. Keep doing this for a few minutes. The paste will gradually become more elastic and less sticky.

3 Keep folding and flicking until the paste is smooth, shiny and elastic. Cover and leave in a warm place for 15 minutes.

MAKING APPLE STRUDEL
1 On a table covered by a large floured cloth, roll the paste out as thinly as possible.

2 Now put your hands, lightly floured, under the paste and gently pull and stretch it keeping your hands fairly flat. Carefully work all round the table, gently pulling the paste until it is evenly paper-thin.

3 Trim off the thick edges. Do not worry about the odd tear hole.

4 Brush immediately with butter to prevent the paste drying out — it becomes brittle alarmingly quickly.

5 Sprinkle the filling on the paste, leaving a clear margin. Use the cloth to help roll it up like a Swiss roll, trying to maintain a fairly tight, even roll.

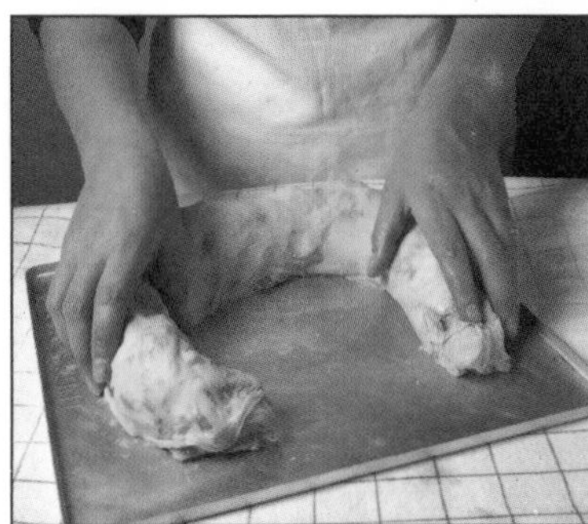

6 Tip the strudel onto a greased baking sheet and curve it gently into a horse-shoe shape. Brush with butter and bake.

PHOTOGRAPH ON P.83

This is a classic English steak pudding, followed by a super-rich ice cream. So serve fairly small portions, and perhaps offer a salad or second green vegetable. See p.323 for detailed information on ice cream making. The main lessons covered are the making of suet crust (read also the note on p.305 in Pastries), the principles of steaming and the technique of parfait or mousse-based ice cream.

MENU LESSON 10

Steak and kidney pudding with smoked oysters

Brussels sprouts (see p.106)

Ginger ice cream

WORK PLAN

• The steak pudding can be made in advance and reheated (for 40 minutes) in a steamer, but the pastry is at its best when freshly made. So, if possible, prepare the filling as much as a day in advance, but arrange matters so that the suet pastry is made just before steaming, and the pudding is eaten within an hour or so of being ready.

• Brussels sprouts smell appalling if washed and prepared (but kept raw) in advance. So, if they cannot be prepared and cooked at the last minute, prepare and boil them in advance. Cool under running cold water. Drain very well and reheat briefly in the microwave, covered in cling film. Do not keep sprouts warm — they discolour and become bitter.

• All ice creams are best a few hours after freezing but this one will still be excellent after a few days, or even weeks of freezer storage. If it becomes too hard and icy, chop it into pieces and re-whisk it in a processor, while still frozen.

STEAK AND KIDNEY PUDDING WITH SMOKED OYSTERS

INGREDIENTS (Serves 4)
675g/1½lb chuck steak
225g/8oz lambs' kidney
Flour
Salt and pepper
340g/12oz flour-quantity suet pastry (see next recipe)
1 small can smoked oysters, drained
2tsp chopped onions
2tsp chopped fresh parsley

1 Cut the steak into cubes about 1.5cm/¾ inch square.

2 Chop the kidneys, discarding any sinew. (See illustration.)

3 Place both steak and kidney in a large sieve. Pour over flour and shake until the meat is lightly coated.

4 Line the pudding basin with the prepared suet pastry.

5 Fill the lined basin with the meat and add the smoked oysters. Sprinkle plenty of seasoning, chopped onion and parsley in between the layers.

6 Add water to come three quarters of the way up the filling.

7 Roll the remaining third of suet pastry 0.5cm/¼ inch thick and cover the pudding filling.

8 Cover the pudding with a piece of greaseproof paper, pleated down the centre (this is to allow room for the pastry to expand), and a similarly pleated piece of foil. Tie down with string.

☐ *The smoked oysters (and indeed the kidney) can be left out of the pie. Mushrooms could be substituted for oysters in the Steak pudding.*

9 Place in a saucepan of boiling water with a tightly closed lid, or in a steamer, for 5 hours, taking care to top up with boiling water occasionally. (If using the saucepan method, the water should come two thirds up the side of the pudding basin. If too full the water bubbles over the top. If too empty it risks boiling dry.)

10 Remove the paper and tin foil and serve the pudding from the bowl.

NOTE 1 Traditionally, steak and kidney puddings served from the bowl are presented wrapped in a white linen napkin. Alternatively, they can be unmoulded onto a large deeply-lipped dish and cut like a cake.

NOTE 2 As the filling of the pudding may, with long cooking, dry out somewhat, it is worth having a gravy boat of hot beef stock handy to moisten the meat when serving.

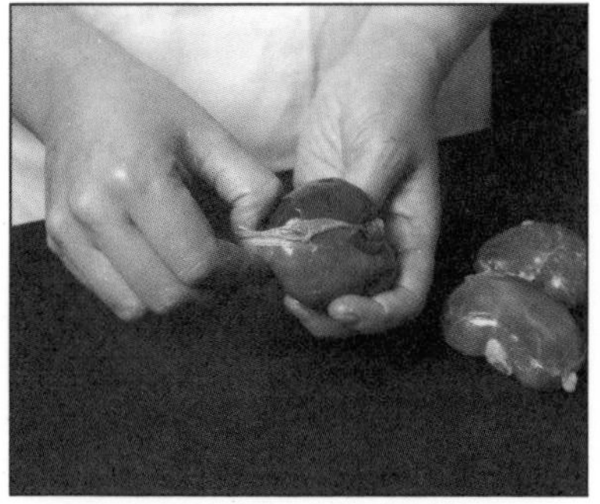

PREPARING LAMBS' KIDNEYS
1 Nick the membrane with a knife and pull it off.

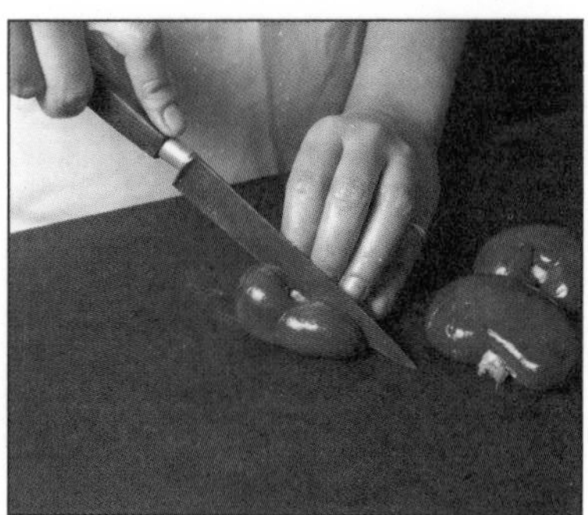

2 Cut the kidneys lengthways through the core to give even halves.

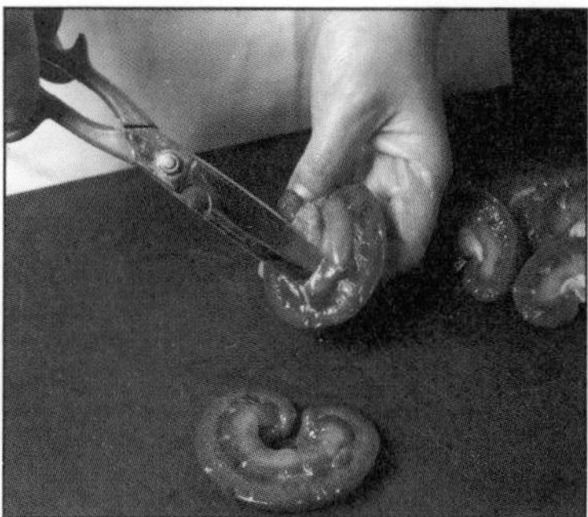

3 Use scissors to remove all the white gristle and fat from the centre (the 'core'). Tuck the scissor points right in to snip out as much of the core as possible.

SUET PASTRY

INGREDIENTS
Butter for greasing
340g/12oz self-raising flour
Salt
170g/6oz shredded beef suet
Water to mix

1 Grease a pudding basin.

2 Sift the flour with a good pinch of salt into a bowl. Rub in the shredded suet and add enough water to mix, first with a knife, and then with one hand, to a soft dough.

3 Roll out the pastry and line the pudding basin as shown.

4 Fill the pastry bag with the desired mixture.

LINING A PUDDING BASIN
1 Cut a third from the prepared suet paste and reserve it.

2 Roll the rest out on a lightly floured board to a round about 1cm/½ inch thick.

3 Flour the round well on top then fold it lightly in half, bringing the far edge towards you when you fold.

4 Gently roll it to a round again, pushing the flat folded edge into a curved shape.

5 Use floured hands to separate the two layers of pastry to give a bag-shape.

6 Carefully lift the 'bag' and ease gently into the greased pudding basin.

7 Trim off the excess paste leaving 2cm/1 inch above the edge. Fill.

8 Roll out the remaining third of the paste to make a round lid. Put in place, wet the edges and press them together securely.

GINGER ICE CREAM

INGREDIENTS (Serves 4)
45g/1½oz granulated sugar
75ml/2½fl oz water
2 egg yolks
1tsp ground ginger
2 pieces stem ginger, cut into fine strips
290ml/½pt double cream, lightly whipped

1 Dissolve the sugar in the water over a gentle heat. When completely clear, boil rapidly for 3 minutes. Cool for 1 minute.

2 Put the egg yolks into a large bowl with the ground ginger. Whisk with an electric hand whisk or balloon whisk and pour on the hot sugar syrup while whisking. (Do not allow the syrup to touch the whisk — it cools on contact and sets solid.) Keep whisking until thick and stone cold.

3 Fold in the strips of ginger and the whipped cream. Turn into a soufflé dish and freeze.

4 Remove from the freezer 20 minutes before it is to be eaten and scoop into a glass bowl.

NOTE This is a good example of a parfait or frozen mousse that needs no re-beating once frozen. If however the mixture was not sufficiently thick and mousse-like when freezing, it might freeze unevenly, too hard or with icy shreds in it. If this happens chop it into pieces and beat until smooth in the processor. Then refreeze.

MENU LESSON 11

Artichoke and pâté de foie gras salad

Braised saddle of venison

Amandine potatoes

Carrot and celeriac purée

Strawberry mille feuilles

PHOTOGRAPH ON P.83

This Menu Lesson teaches the technique of braising game — a skill requiring care and judgement. It also attempts the perfect vegetable purée and the French pastry that should be the lightest and most delicious of confections, Mille feuilles (literally 'a thousand leaves').

WORK PLAN

- Most braised foods reheat perfectly and venison is no exception. It can be cooked the day before eating if convenient.
- The salad is best done as late as possible, though the artichokes could certainly be cooked a few hours in advance.
- Amandine potatoes are perfectly horrid reheated so, though they can be prepared in advance, they must be fried at the last minute.
- The vegetable purées are best freshly made but they do heat up and keep warm very well.
- Bake the pastry for the Mille feuilles on the day of serving, but assemble it as late as possible.

ARTICHOKE AND PATE DE FOIE GRAS SALAD

INGREDIENTS (Serves 4)
2 handfuls slightly bitter salad leaves such as radicchio, young spinach, lamb's lettuce or chicory
French dressing (see p.139)
4 artichoke bottoms, still warm from boiling, or reheated in warm stock (see Note)
55g/2oz pâté de foie gras

1 Wash, pick over and pull the salad leaves to smallish pieces. Dry well. Toss in a little of the French dressing and arrange on 4 side plates.

2 Slice the still warm artichoke bottoms and toss in the remaining dressing. Pile on top of the salad leaves.

3 Slice the foie gras into 4 and arrange a slice on top of each salad. Serve immediately.

NOTE Many cooks say that the leaves and chokes of the artichokes should be removed and the bottoms then cooked in acidulated, salted water for 25 minutes or until tender. It seems rather a waste of the delicious leaves which one might as well cook at the same time and reserve for later eating or for soup. Whole artichokes should be cooked in acidulated, salted water for about 45 minutes or until the outside leaves will pull out easily. The essential thing for this salad is that the bottoms are tender. For further details on cooking artichokes see p.16.

☐ *Foie gras pâté is very expensive, and any smooth rich pâté that will slice neatly may be used instead, though it will not of course have the flavour of the real thing.*

MENU LESSON 9 *(see p.73)*
The leap from a peasant curry to hearty Austrian pudding may dismay the purist, but the structure of this meal (*below*) is a tried and tested one. *Clockwise from top left:* Fresh peas, scallop and mangetout salad, apple strudel, Pommes Anna and pork fillets with peppers.

MENU LESSON 11 *(see p.81)*
Braising game requires care — this is your chance to practise it (*right*). *Clockwise from top left:* Strawberry mille feuilles, carrot and celeriac purée, artichoke and pâté de foie gras salad, braised saddle of venison and amandine potatoes.

MENU LESSON 10 *(see p.78)*
This is a classic British meal (*left*) with Brussels sprouts, steak and kidney pudding and ice cream. *Clockwise from top left:* Ginger ice cream, Brussels sprouts and steak and kidney pudding with smoked oysters.

BRAISED SADDLE OF VENISON

INGREDIENTS (Serves 8)
2kg/4lb piece of venison loin or half a very small saddle
Oil
30g/1oz butter
2 onions, sliced
110g/4oz carrots, peeled and sliced
4 sticks celery, cut into chunks
Salt and freshly ground black pepper
1 bay leaf
Fresh thyme
290ml/½pt red wine
290ml/½pt brown stock (see p.268)
15g/½oz butter
15g/½oz flour
1tbsp cranberry jelly

1 Heat the oven to 150°C/300°F/Gas 2.

2 Prepare the venison by trimming away all the membrane, skin and sinew. This will take some time but is well worth the effort.

3 Heat a little oil in a very large ovenproof casserole. When hot, add the butter and brown the venison well on all sides. Remove from the casserole.

4 Add the onions, carrots and celery and cook slowly until lightly browned.

5 Season with salt and pepper, add the bay leaf and sprig of thyme. Lay the venison on top of the vegetables. Add the wine and stock.

6 Bring slowly to simmering point, cover tightly and put in the oven for 2 hours or until the meat is tender.

7 When cooked, lift out the meat and keep warm while making the sauce: strain the liquid from the vegetables into a saucepan. Reduce, by boiling rapidly, to about 290ml/½pt.

8 TO MAKE A BEURRE MANIE Soften the butter with a knife and whisk in the flour. Whisk this into the liquid bit by bit, stirring, and bring to the boil. The idea is that the flour is evenly distributed throughout the sauce as the butter melts. Boil for 1 minute.

9 Add the cranberry jelly to the sauce and adjust the seasoning.

10 Lift the venison off the bone and carve into neat collops. Arrange in overlapping slices and spoon over the hot sauce.

AMANDINE POTATOES

INGREDIENTS (Serves 4)
450g/1lb potatoes
Salt and white pepper
3tbsp milk
15g/½oz butter
Beaten egg
Chopped or flaked almonds
Oil for deep frying

1 Peel the potatoes and cut into even sized, fairly large chunks.

2 Cook in boiling salted water until soft. Drain well. Return to the saucepan and place over a moderate heat for a few minutes to dry.

3 Push the potatoes through a stout sieve or through a fine mincer. Push the mound of potatoes to one side of the saucepan and pour the milk into the exposed side of the pan. Put this side over a direct heat and add a lump of butter. When the milk is boiling, beat it into the potato. You want a fairly firm purée. Allow to cool.

4 Roll the potatoes into balls about the size of a walnut. Roll first in the beaten egg and then in the almonds.

5 Heat the oil until a scrap of bread will frizzle and brown in 30 seconds (185°C/360°F).

6 Place the potato balls (do not allow them to touch each other) in the chip basket.

7 Fry until golden brown. Drain well on absorbent paper and serve immediately.

NOTE If they have to be kept warm do not cover them or pile them on top of each other as they will become soggy.

☐ *Do not attempt this menu for more than four people on the first occasion.*

CARROT AND CELERIAC PUREE

INGREDIENTS (Serves 4)
450g/1lb carrots
225g/8oz celeriac
Milk
Butter
Salt and freshly ground black pepper

1 Peel and slice the carrots and cook in boiling salted water until very tender (about 12 minutes). Drain and push through a sieve.

2 Peel and cut up the celeriac into even sized chunks. Simmer in just enough milk to cover. When tender (after about 15 minutes) drain and push through a sieve. Reserve the milk.

3 Mix together the carrot and celeriac purée. Add enough milk and butter to make a soft but firm purée. Season to taste with salt and pepper.

NOTE Both these purées, unlike potato purée (which rapidly becomes gluey) can be beaten in a food processor.

STRAWBERRY MILLE FEUILLES

INGREDIENTS (Serves 4)
225g/8oz flour-quantity puff pastry (see next recipe)
About 340g/12oz good strawberry jam
290ml/½pt double cream, stiffly whipped
225g/8oz strawberries

1 Set the oven to 220°C/425°F/Gas 7.

2 On a floured board roll the pastry into 3 rectangles about 10×20cm 4×8 inches, and about the thickness of a large coin. Place on a wet baking sheet. Prick, very lightly, with a fork — this will help it rise evenly.

3 Leave to relax, covered, for 20 minutes. Bake for about 15 minutes or until brown and puffy.

4 Carefully split each piece of pastry in 2 horizontally and return to the oven, cut side up, to dry out for 3 minutes. Leave to cool on a wire rack.

5 Neaten the pastry edges with a sharp knife. Choose the piece of pastry with the smoothest base, and reserve. Spread a thin layer of jam on the 5 remaining strips and cover thinly with cream. Place them on top of each other and cover with the 6th, reserved, piece of pastry, smooth side uppermost. Press down gently but firmly.

6 Melt the rest of the jam but do not allow it to boil. Brush the top layer of pastry with warm jam. Arrange the strawberries, sliced if necessary, on top of the jam and then brush or spoon on enough of the still warm jam glaze to make the strawberries glisten.

☐ *Frozen puff pastry may be substituted for homemade pastry by the cook in a hurry. The trick is to roll it very thinly and make sure it is baked right through or it will be soggy.*

PUFF PASTRY

INGREDIENTS (Serves 4)
225g/8oz plain flour
Pinch of salt
30g/1oz lard
425ml/¾pt icy water
140-200g/5-7oz butter

1 If you have never made puff pastry before, use the smaller amount of butter: this will give a normal pastry. If you have some experience, more butter will produce a lighter, very rich pastry.

2 Sift the flour with a pinch of salt. Rub in the lard. Add the icy water and mix with a knife to a doughy consistency. Turn on to the table and knead quickly until smooth. Wrap in polythene or a cloth and leave in the refrigerator for 30 minutes to relax.

3 Lightly flour the table top or board and roll the dough into a rectangle about 13×25cm/5×10 inches. See the illustrations on p.88 for the rest of the process.

MENU LESSON 12 *(see p.89)*
It's time for slimmers. Here is a nouvelle cuisine menu for weight-watchers who like to eat — and cook — well. *Clockwise from top left:* Cassis cream pie, fennel and walnut salad, pine nuts and duck breast salad, red butter sauce and grilled lobster.

MAKING PUFF PASTRY

1 Roll the puff-paste to a rectangle 13×25cm/5×10 inches and then roll the middle third out a little wider than the rest to create side flaps as shown.

2 Tap the butter lightly with a floured rolling pin to get it into a flattened block about 10×8cm/ 4×3 inches. Put this 'block' on the centre of the pastry and fold the side flaps over to enclose it.

3 Fold both top and bottom over to tightly enclose the butter. Press the sides together with the length of the rolling pin to prevent the butter escaping.

4 Give the parcel a half-turn (90°) so that once more the long sides are on left and right and the short sides nearest and farthest from you.

5 Tap the parcel with the rolling pin to flatten the butter a little, then roll out quickly and lightly until the paste is three times as long as it is wide.

6 Fold it very evenly in three again, first folding the third closest to you, then folding the far third towards you. Seal the edges again by pressing firmly with the length of the rolling pin.

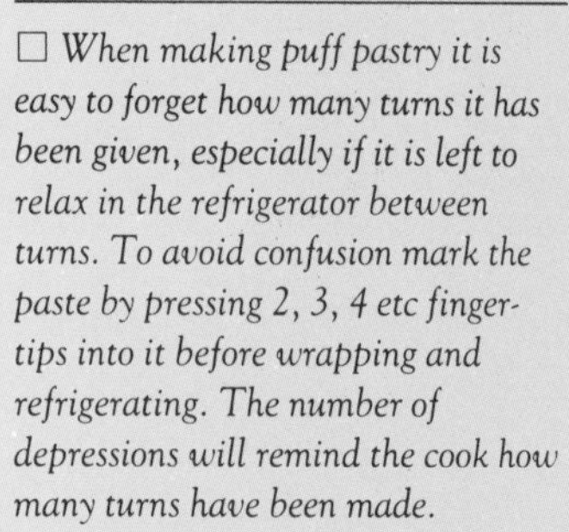

☐ *When making puff pastry it is easy to forget how many turns it has been given, especially if it is left to relax in the refrigerator between turns. To avoid confusion mark the paste by pressing 2, 3, 4 etc finger-tips into it before wrapping and refrigerating. The number of depressions will remind the cook how many turns have been made.*

7 Again give it a half turn (90°) so that the short sides are at top and bottom and the long sides are to the left and right. Wrap the paste and let it rest in a cool place for 30 minutes or so.

8 Again roll out. Repeat the whole process of rolling and folding until the paste has had 6 rolls and folds in all. Allow it to rest, well-wrapped, if the butter shows signs of melting or squeezing out.

PHOTOGRAPH ON P.87

MENU LESSON 12

Pine nuts and duck breast salad

Grilled lobster with red butter sauce

Fennel and walnut salad

Cassis cream pie

This is a very elegant nouvelle cuisine menu and none the worse for that. The lesson teaches careful presentation of a salade tiède (a salad served with warm ingredients added at the last minute), the making of a butter-mounted sauce, the daunting sounding but surprisingly easy business of killing a live lobster, and finally that most sophisticated of mousses, the Cassis cream pie. The latter involves two almost identical mousses beaten over heat and the production of a mirror-like glaze.

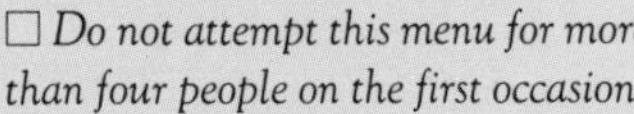

☐ *Do not attempt this menu for more than four people on the first occasion.*

WORK PLAN

- Start with the dessert. It can be made in the morning for an evening dinner, or the cake and cream base may be frozen and thawed and glazed on the day of baking.
- Prepare both dressings and salads but do not put them together. (The pine nuts and duck breast must be fried just before serving.)
- Step 1 of the sauce for the lobster can be done in advance but the cooking of the lobster must be a last-minute business.

PINE NUTS AND DUCK BREAST SALAD

INGREDIENTS (Serves 4)

2 handfuls bitter salad leaves (eg mâche, watercress, chicory, radicchio)
2 tbsp French dressing, made with walnut oil (see p.139)
1tbsp unsalted butter
1 raw duck breast, skinned and split horizontally into 2
55g/2oz pine nuts

1 Wash, pick over and pull into smallish pieces the bitter salad leaves. Dry well. Toss in the dressing and arrange on 4 side plates.

2 Heat the butter in a frying pan until it has ceased to foam. Add the duck breast pieces and fry fairly fast to brown on both sides — about 3 minutes in all. They are done when they feel firm when pressed and are pink, not blue, when cut. Lift out onto a board.

3 Put the pine nuts into the frying pan and shake over the heat until pale brown and crisp.

4 Slice the duck diagonally into thin slices. Return them, and any juices, to the pan, toss briefly and scatter over the salads. Serve at once.

CLEANING LOBSTER

1 To kill lobster for grilling, locate the well-defined cross on the back of the head.

2 Pierce firmly with a sharp, heavy knife. The lobster will die instantly, although it might still move alarmingly.

3 Continue the cut down the back to split the lobster in half lengthways.

4 Turn it around and split the head.

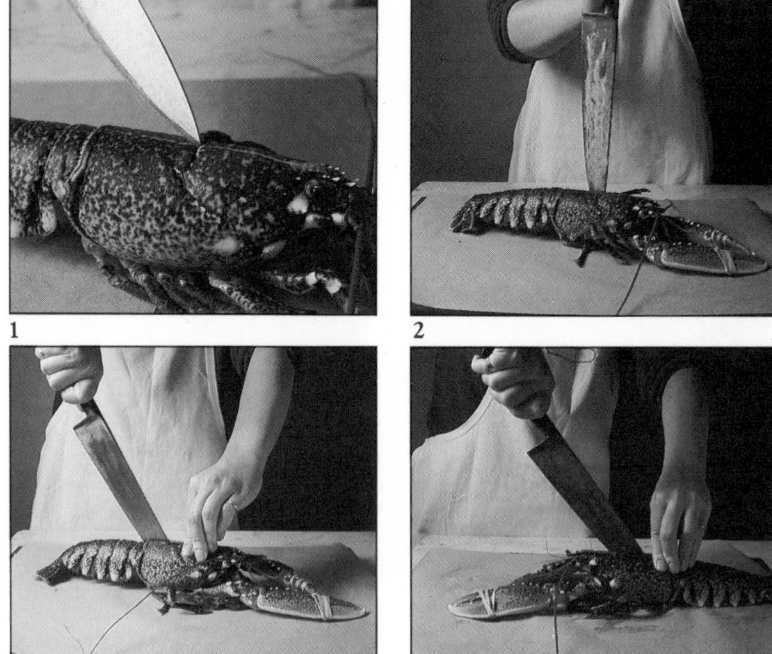

1 2 3 4

GRILLED LOBSTER WITH RED BUTTER SAUCE

INGREDIENTS (Serves 4)
4 small live lobsters
Cayenne pepper
Unsalted butter, melted

FOR THE SAUCE
1 shallot, finely chopped
425ml/¾pt dry white wine
1tsp fish glaze (see p.270)
110g/4oz unsalted butter, chilled and cut into small lumps
The coral from the lobster, if available
3tbsp double cream
1tsp tomato purée

TO GARNISH
Watercress

☐ *If killing a live lobster as described is too daunting, get the fishmonger to do it for you, and to remove the stomach sac and intestine, but do this on the day of cooking. Freshness is all.*

1 PREPARE THE BUTTER SAUCE Put the shallot into a small saucepan with the white wine. Cook slowly until the liquid is reduced by half. Strain into a clean pan. Add the fish glaze and set aside.

2 Next kill the lobsters (see above).

3 Lay the lobsters out flat and split in half lengthwise. Remove the stomach sac from near the head and the threadlike intestine.

4 Heat up the grill.

5 Brush the lobster with butter and season with cayenne pepper. Place under the grill, cut side uppermost first, for about 5 to 10 minutes a side (depending on size) or until the lobster is a good bright red.

6 While the lobster is cooking, continue with the butter sauce. Mix 1 tsp butter with the coral. Set aside.

7 When the lobsters are cooked, crack the claws (without removing from the body) in a claw-cracker or by covering with a cloth and hitting with a rolling pin. Keep the lobsters warm while finishing the sauce.

8 Warm up the reduced wine and fish glaze. Using a wire whisk and plenty of vigorous continuous whisking, add the butter bit by bit. The process should take about 1½ to 2 minutes and the sauce should thicken considerably. Do not allow it to get too hot.

9 Whisk in the coral butter and cream, and any pan juices from the grill. Add a little tomato purée to colour. Season as required.

10 Arrange the lobsters on a large oval dish. Garnish with watercress and hand the sauce separately.

5 Extract the cartilaginous stomach sac from near the head. It will probably have been split by the knife so look for the other half in the second half-shell.

6 Pull it away and discard it.

7 Pull away and discard the thin thread-like intestine (possibly in pieces) that runs from head to tail.

8 Scoop out the soft greeny-grey or creamy tomalley or liver if it is to be used in a sauce. Or leave it in place for grilling. Do not discard — it is delicious. Remove the greeny-black roe, if any, to the sauce. Or leave in place if preferred. It turns bright red when cooked, and tastes excellent.

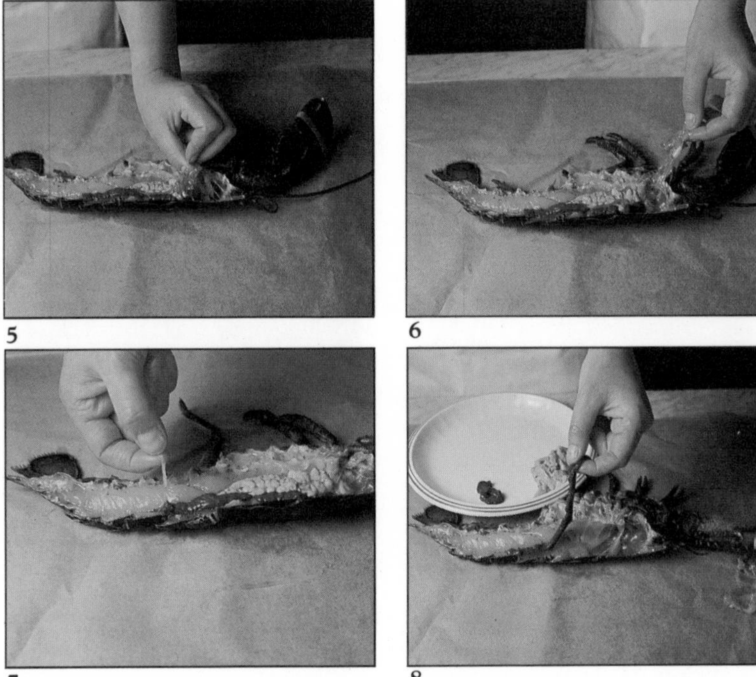

5 6 7 8

FENNEL AND WALNUT SALAD

INGREDIENTS (Serves 4)
2 large or 3 small bulbs of fennel
110g/4oz fresh shelled walnuts
1tbsp chopped marjoram
French dressing made with hazelnut oil (see p.139)

1 Remove the feathery green tops of the fennel and put aside. Wash, then finely slice the fennel heads, discarding any tough outer leaves or discoloured bits.

2 Blanch the fennel in boiling water for 3 to 4 minutes to soften slightly. Refresh by running under cold water until cool. Drain well on absorbent paper, or dry in a tea towel.

3 Chop the nuts coarsely.

4 Mix together the fennel, nuts and marjoram and moisten with a little French dressing. Pile into a salad bowl.

5 Chop the green leaves of the fennel and scatter them over the salad.

CASSIS CREAM PIE

INGREDIENTS (Serves 4)

FOR THE BASE
2 eggs, separated
55g/2oz caster sugar
30g/1oz plain flour, sifted
1tbsp blackcurrant jelly or sieved jam

Continued overleaf

1 Set the oven to 220°C/425°F/Gas 7.

2 Grease and flour a 20cm/8 inch diameter loose-bottomed cake tin.

3 MAKE THE BASE Set a bowl over a pan of simmering water and put into it the yolks and half the caster sugar. Keeping the water simmering under the bowl but not touching the bottom of it, whisk the mixture with an electric or balloon whisk until it is pale, mousse-like and very thick. Remove from the heat.

4 Whisk the egg whites until stiff and fold in the rest of the sugar.

5 Fold the yolk and white mixtures together, then fold in the flour.

6 Turn into the cake tin and bake for 15 minutes until evenly brown and slightly shrunk from the tin sides.

CASSIS CREAM PIE

FOR THE MOUSSE AND GLAZE
340g/12oz blackcurrants
5tbsp crème de cassis liqueur
3 eggs, separated
110g/4oz caster sugar
15g/½oz gelatine
150ml/¼pt double cream
2tbsp blackcurrant jelly or sieved jam

7 Remove the cake from the tin and cool, upside down, on a wire rack.

8 When cold, spread evenly with the blackcurrant jelly or jam.

9 Wash the cake tin and oil its sides. The mousse will set in this.

10 MAKE THE BLACKCURRANT PUREE by simmering the fruit with 2tbsp of water. Keep stirring and boiling as much as possible until the juice has evaporated without the fruit catching and burning the bottom of the pan.

11 Push the fruit through a sieve to extract the seeds, scraping the paste-like purée from the back of the sieve with a clean (not covered in blackcurrant seeds) spoon. Take one third of the purée and reserve it for the top. Mix the rest with 2tbsp cassis.

12 MAKE THE MOUSSE Once again set a bowl over simmering water and whisk the yolks, 2tbsp cassis and two thirds of the sugar. It will be more liquid than the first mixture and will take longer — it should thicken sufficiently to leave a ribbon-like trail when the whisk is lifted. Remove from the heat and whisk occasionally as it cools.

13 Put 3tbsp water into a small saucepan and sprinkle over the gelatine. Leave to soak for 10 minutes.

14 Stir the blackcurrant purée into the egg yolk mixture.

15 Put the gelatine over very gentle heat to dissolve it. When runny and clear, stir into the blackcurrant mixture.

16 Whip the cream until it will just hold its shape and fold into the mousse.

17 Whisk the egg whites until stiff and fold in the remaining sugar.

18 Fold the blackcurrant mousse and the meringue mixtures together lightly and without overmixing — a few airpockets is preferable to a mixture with all the air stirred out of it.

19 Fit the cooled and jam-spread cake back into the cake tin, and pour the mousse into it. Level the top and freeze until very solid.

20 To remove the mousse from the tin loosen the sides by wrapping the cake tin in a cloth dipped in very hot water. Push the nearly or completely frozen mousse out of the tin on the loose bottom. With a fish slice ease the pie onto a serving plate. Allow to thaw in the refrigerator. (The only reason the pie is frozen is to make getting it out of the tin easier. But if a deep flan ring on a baking sheet is used instead of the tin, or a spring-form cake pan — one that has sides that unclip — then freezing is not necessary.)

21 TO MAKE THE GLAZED TOP Gently heat together the reserved blackcurrant purée and the sieved jam or jelly. Stir until melted then boil hard for a few seconds to get a shiny clear syrup.

22 Cool the glaze until just liquid, then pour over the now set mousse, and ease carefully to the edges with a palette knife. Prick any air bubbles with the tip of a knife.

☐ *The cream pie seems immensely complicated, but if followed step by step it is surprisingly easy.*

PHOTOGRAPH ON P.94

Papayas are traditionally served for breakfast in hot countries and they make an excellent first course. The chicken is a spicy, curry flavoured dish, good with the nutty flavoured Basmati rice. Bread-and-butter pudding gives an otherwise Indian-influenced menu a more colonial flavour. The techniques learnt in this menu include the tricky one of cooking separate grain Basmati rice, the grinding and frying of spices and the mastery of perfect smooth-as-silk and crusty topped bread-and-butter pudding.

MENU LESSON 13

Fresh papaya and lime

Chicken with whole spices

Basmati rice

Broccoli (see p.56)

Apricot bread-and-butter pudding

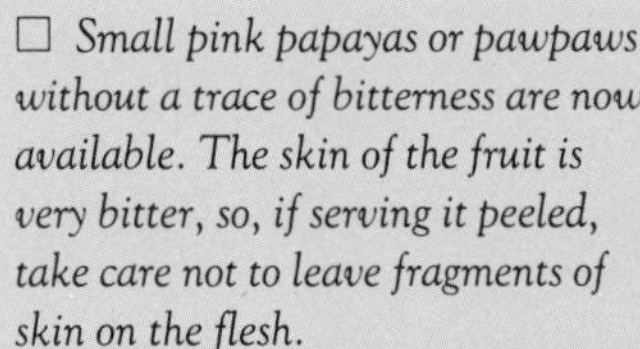

☐ *Small pink papayas or pawpaws without a trace of bitterness are now available. The skin of the fruit is very bitter, so, if serving it peeled, take care not to leave fragments of skin on the flesh.*

WORK PLAN

- The papaya can be cut in advance and chilled under clingfilm. But try to arrange matters so that the chicken is freshly cooked with freshly ground spices, the rice is just ready when you are and the pudding is baking as the main course is eaten. It can be reheated, but it never quite regains the perfect puffed-up crusty top.
- See also the note on Broccoli on p.53.

FRESH PAPAYA AND LIME

INGREDIENTS (Serves 4)
2 fresh papayas
2 limes

1 Simply cut 2 ripe papayas in half, lengthways, remove the pips and serve each half with 2 lime wedges. If the papaya is not perfectly sweet offer granulated sugar — the gritty texture is good with the creamy flesh.

NOTE A slice or two of Parma or Bayonne ham would go well with the fruit too, if preferred.

CHICKEN WITH WHOLE SPICES

INGREDIENTS (Serves 4-6)
One 1.8kg/4lb chicken
70g/2½oz unsalted butter
½tsp ground ginger
2tsp turmeric
5 onions, sliced
4 crushed cardamoms
0.75cm/½-inch splintered cinnamon
3 cloves
Good pinch of ground mace
Good pinch of cayenne pepper
¾tsp black pepper
1 bay leaf
1tsp mustard seed
2 cloves garlic

1 Joint the chicken into 8 pieces as illustrated on p.96.

2 Remove the skin from all the chicken joints. Melt half the butter in a large sauté pan and when the bubbles have disappeared, fry the chicken pieces with the ginger and turmeric. Take care not to go too fast (the butter will burn) and not too slowly (the juices will escape from the chicken). Remove the joints to a plate.

3 Melt another tablespoon of butter in the pan and slowly cook the onions until soft but not browned. Remove them to the chicken plate.

4 Meanwhile crush the cardamoms, cinnamon, cloves, mace, cayenne, pepper, bay leaf and mustard seeds together in a pestle and mortar, or coffee grinder, taking care to get them to coarse, not fine, grains.

5 CRUSH THE GARLIC Peel the cloves of garlic and place on a piece of greaseproof paper (to stop the smell permeating the chopping board). Pile a little salt beside the garlic. Using an ordinary cutlery knife mash the garlic, with a little salt, to a smooth purée.

Continued on p.96

MENU LESSON 13 *(see p.93)*
A tropical meal with some homely touches. *Clockwise from top left:* Broccoli, apricot bread-and-butter pudding, chicken with whole spices on a bed of Basmati rice, and papaya and lime.

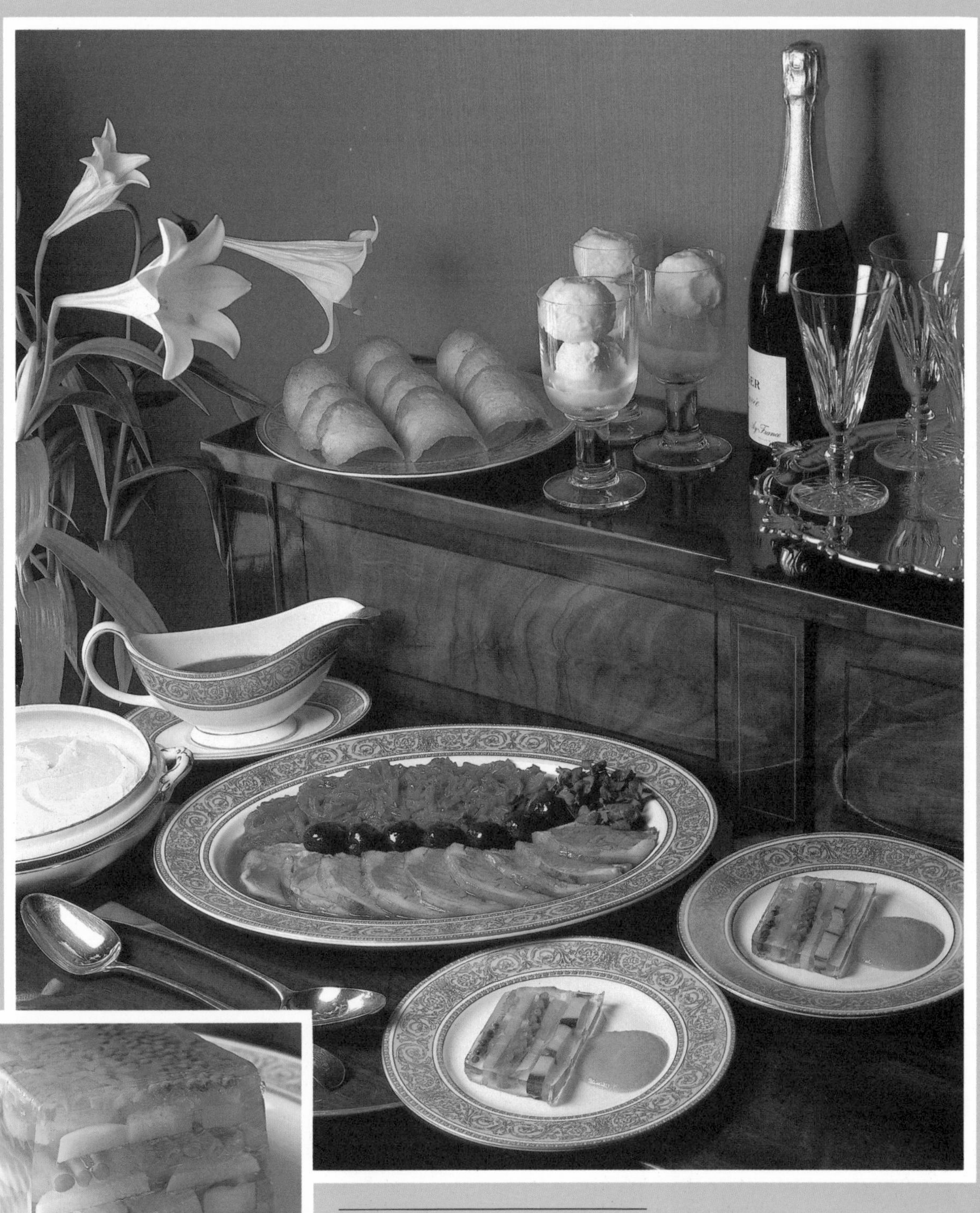

MENU LESSON 14 *(see p.98)*
This contrasts *nouvelle* presentation with *ancienne cuisine*. *Clockwise from top left:* Tuiles aux amandes, Champagne sorbet, vegetables in aspic, pork with prunes and braised red cabbage, mashed potatoes and gravy.

☐ *Smaller chickens can be jointed into four with the wings, thighs and drumsticks left intact.*

6 Add the garlic, crushed spices, and any remaining butter to the sauté pan. Shake and jerk the pan back and forth over fierce heat to keep the spices moving. When sizzling vigorously, immediately reduce the temperature to low. Return the chicken and onions to the pan and cook, covered, for 45 minutes or until the chicken is very tender.

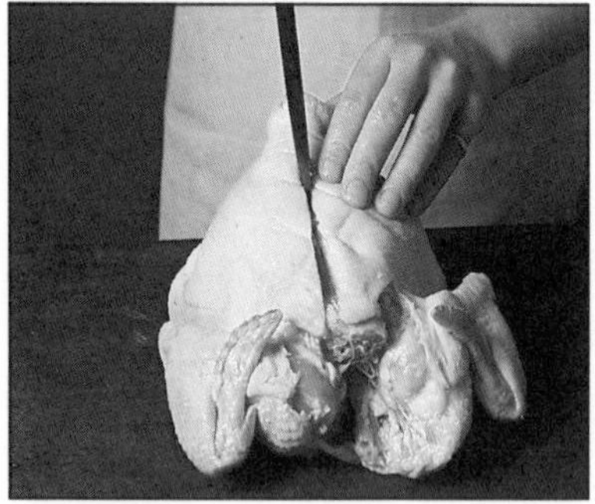

JOINTING A CHICKEN

1 Turn the chicken over so the backbone is uppermost. Cut through to the bone along the line of the spine.

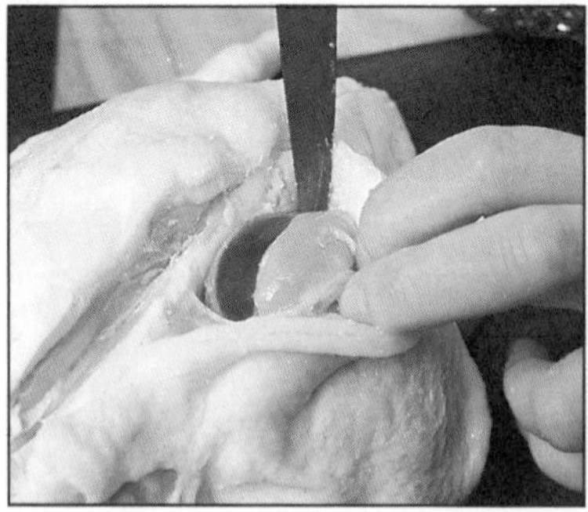

2 Where the thigh joins the backbone there is a fleshy 'oyster' on each side. Cut round them to loosen them from the carcass so that they come away when the legs are severed.

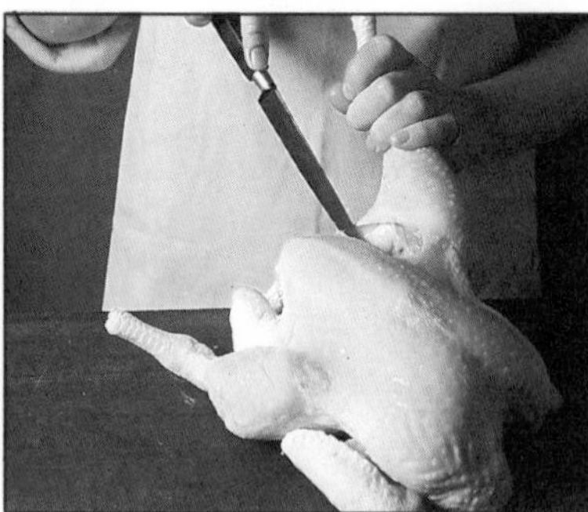

3 Turn the bird over and pull a leg away from the body. Cut through the skin only, as far round the leg as possible, close to the body.

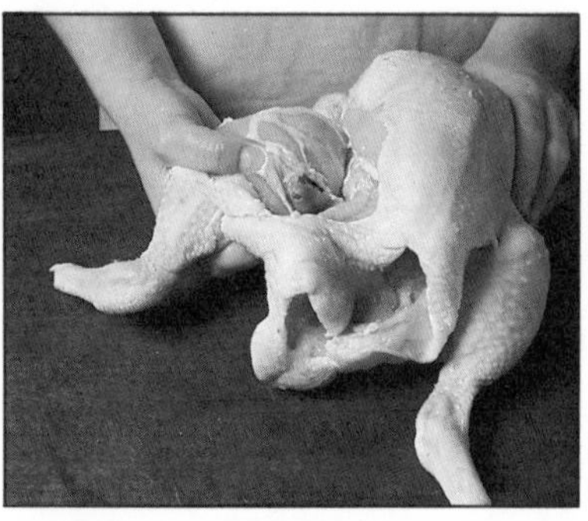

4 Pull the leg away from the body and twist it down so that the thigh bone pops out of its socket on the carcass and is exposed.

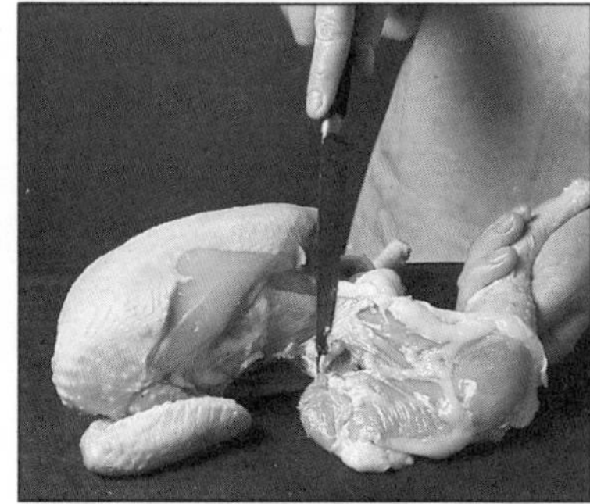

5 Cut the leg off, taking care to go between thigh, bone and carcass and to bring the 'oyster' away with the leg. (Turn over briefly to check.) Repeat the process for the other leg.

6 Now for the breast. Carefully cut down each side of the breast bone to free the breast flesh a little.

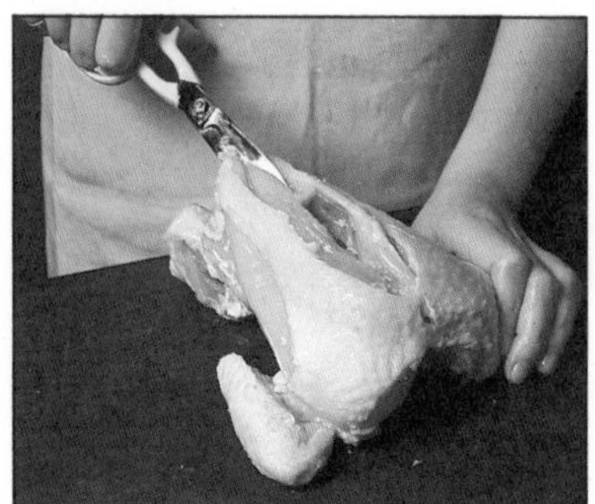

7 Use scissors to cut through the small bones close to the breast. Cut away the breast bone.

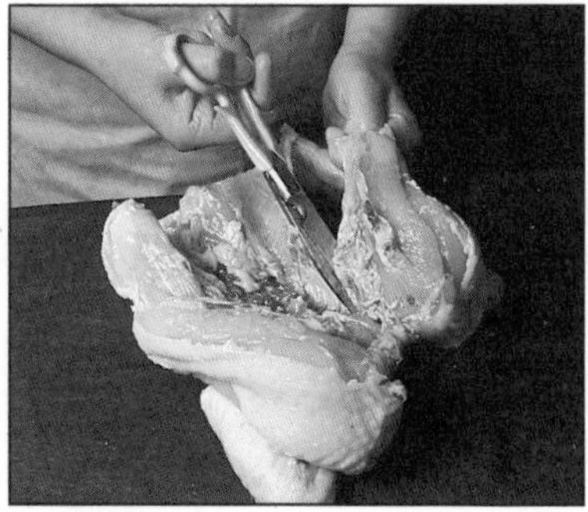

8 Open up the bird. Cut each wing and breast off the carcass with scissors, starting at the tail end and cutting up to and through the wing bone near the neck.

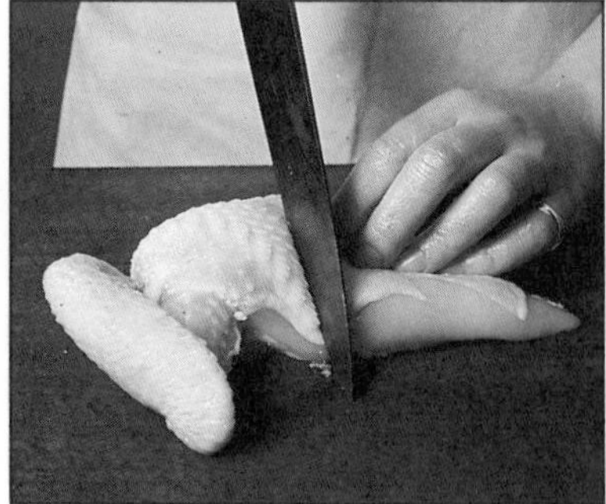

9 Cut the wing joint in two, leaving abut one third of the breast attached to the wing.

10 Cut off the almost meatless pinions (which can go in the stock-pot with the carcass) from each wing.

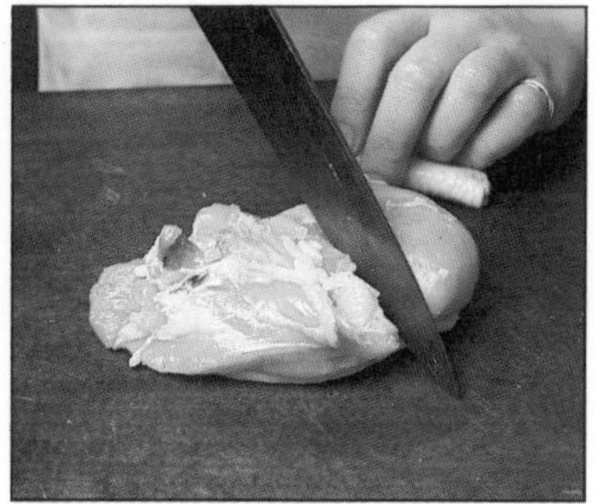

11 Lay the legs skin-side down on the board and cut through where the thigh and lower leg bones meet.

12 With the heel end of a heavy knife (or a cleaver) chop the feet bones off the drumsticks.

BASMATI RICE

INGREDIENTS (Serves 4)
225g/8oz Basmati rice
1 stick cinnamon
4 cardamom pods, crushed
1tsp mustard seeds
Salt and freshly ground black pepper

☐ *Basmati rice is considered the best flavoured long grain rice, but it comes unpolished and raw which calls for some care and effort on the part of the cook. Commercially available 'polished' or 'parboiled' or 'easy-cook' rice has been treated so that it seldom sticks or becomes gluey.*

1 Wash the rice under cold water and then leave to soak in more cold water for 30 minutes.

2 Drain and wash thoroughly. Place in a saucepan, just cover with water (so that the top grains are wet), add the cinnamon, cardamom and mustard seeds. Season with plenty of salt and pepper.

3 Bring to the boil, cover and cook slowly until the rice is tender. It will take between 7 and 10 minutes to cook. Drain, if necessary, and serve fairly quickly.

NOTE Many recipes call for a cooking time of 25 minutes for rice cooked by this method but that assumes that the rice has not been given the preliminary soaking, and rather more water is used to cover it. Place the unsoaked (dry or just rinsed) rice in a pan. Push your finger into the rice to touch the bottom of the pan and note the level it comes to on your finger. Use your thumb to mark the place. Now lightly touch the *surface* of the rice with your fingertip and add enough water to reach the original point on your finger marked by your thumb.

APRICOT BREAD-AND-BUTTER PUDDING

INGREDIENTS (Serves 4)
3 large slices plain bread
45g/1½oz butter
3tbsp chopped dried apricots
2 eggs
1 yolk
1tbsp sugar
290ml/½pt creamy milk
½tsp vanilla flavouring
Ground cinnamon

☐ *A more traditional bread-and-butter pudding is made with dried currants and raisins rather than chopped apricots.*

1 Cut the crust off the bread and spread with butter. Cut into fingers. Layer in a shallow ovenproof dish, butter side up, and sprinkle with the apricots as you proceed.

2 MAKE THE CUSTARD Mix the eggs and yolk with the sugar and stir in the milk and vanilla flavouring.

3 Pour the custard carefully over the bread and leave to soak for 30 minutes. Sprinkle with ground cinnamon.

4 Heat the oven to 180°C/350°F/Gas 4.

5 Place the pudding in a roasting tin of hot water and cook in the middle of the oven for about 45 minutes or until the custard is set and the top brown and crusty.

NOTE The pudding may be baked without the bain marie (hot water bath) quite successfully, but if used it will ensure a smooth, not bubbly custard.

PHOTOGRAPH ON P.95

The first course of this Menu Lesson concentrates on exquisite nouvelle cuisine presentation, and carefully balanced delicate flavours. The loin of pork and red cabbage are contrastingly ancienne cuisine and robust. Mashing potatoes is an under-learnt art and this lesson takes the cook step by step through the process. Champagne sorbet is tricky but sublime. Read the chapter on sorbets (p.323) before embarking on this recipe.

The baking and shaping of the tuiles needs precision and precise timing. So get everything ready in advance, shut the kitchen door and take the telephone off the hook.

MENU LESSON 14

Vegetables in aspic with red pepper sauce

Loin of pork braised with port and prunes

Mashed potatoes

Braised red cabbage

Champagne sorbet

Tuiles aux amandes

WORK PLAN

- The vegetable terrine and sauce should, ideally, be made four or five hours before serving. But these jellied terrines are frequently made the day before serving and it would take an exceptionally discerning palate to detect the difference. But longer storage than 24 hours means the terrine begins to lose its fresh taste.
- The loin of pork reheats well, and will keep warm quite happily for an hour or two.
- Braised red cabbage positively improves with keeping.
- Mashed potatoes are at their best within hours of making, though they can and do reheat successfully.
- Champagne sorbet is best within three days of making but because of the high proportion of alcohol in the mixture it never freezes rock hard, and keeps its soft texture better than most sorbets.
- Make the Tuiles aux amandes not more than three days ahead, and keep in an airtight tin. They are irresistible straight from the oven.

VEGETABLES IN ASPIC WITH RED PEPPER SAUCE

INGREDIENTS (Serves 8)

FOR THE SAUCE
1 large sweet red pepper
1 onion, sliced
2tbsp olive oil
2 tomatoes, peeled, quartered and deseeded
1 clove garlic
1 bouquet garni
Salt and pepper

1 PREPARE THE PEPPER SAUCE Cut the pepper in quarters and singe the pieces all over by holding over a direct flame or under a hot grill until very black. Peel off the outer membrane.

2 Cook the onion in the oil until just beginning to brown and soften. Add the tomatoes, pepper, garlic and bouquet garni. Add 3tbsp water. Bring to the boil. Cover and simmer for 20 minutes.

3 Remove the bouquet garni. Liquidize or push through a sieve. Season with salt and pepper. Leave to cool.

VEGETABLES IN ASPIC

FOR THE TERRINE (Serves 4)
2 small artichokes, washed and with the stems removed
1 slice lemon
1 tsp oil
110g/4oz carrots, peeled and sliced
Pinch of sugar
110g/4oz courgettes, half-peeled to give a striped effect, and sliced
Sprig of thyme
110g/4oz white turnips, peeled and sliced
55g/2oz French beans, topped and tailed
110g/4oz asparagus
590ml/1pt beef aspic (see next recipe)
½ pimento finely diced
2tsp green peppercorns, well rinsed
4 sprigs of basil
Salt

☐ *Vegetables for the jellied terrine need to be very well cooked so that they cut easily, but must remain bright in colour. To achieve this cook them separately in plenty of very fast-boiling well salted water and drain, rinse and refresh under cold water quickly.*

4 COOK ALL THE VEGETABLES
ARTICHOKES Place in a pan of boiling salted water with a slice of lemon and 1tsp oil. Cook uncovered for 45 minutes or until large leaf will pull out easily. Cool. Remove all leaves and the 'choke' and slice the hearts.
CARROTS Cook in boiling salted, lightly sugared water until tender. Refresh under running cold water. Drain very well.
COURGETTES Cook in boiling salted water, with a sprig of thyme, until tender. Refresh under running cold water. Drain very well.
TURNIPS Cook in a small quantity of lightly salted boiling water until tender.
FRENCH BEANS Cook in boiling salted water until tender. Refresh under running cold water. Drain very well.
ASPARAGUS Peel the tough ends of the asparagus stalks with a potato peeler or scrape them with a knife. Tie in a bundle. Cook in boiling salted water until tender. Refresh under running cold water and drain very well.

5 Melt the aspic very slowly and ladle enough of it into a well chilled small loaf tin or 1 litre (2pt) terrine to just cover the base. Any bubbles can be burst with the point of a knife. Leave to set in the refrigerator.

6 In separate bowls, mix the pimento and green peppercorns with a little aspic and arrange two neat alternate parallel lines of each down the length of the terrine. Leave to set.

7 Pour in a thin layer of aspic. Leave to set.

8 Mix the carrots with a little aspic and arrange them on top of the set jelly. Leave to set.

9 Continue to layer up the vegetables and aspic finishing with a layer of basil sprigs. Allow to cool, then refrigerate until required.

10 TO SERVE Remove the terrine from the refrigerator about half an hour before serving time so that it does not have a rubbery texture. Dip the bottom of the mould briefly in hot water. Place a plate over the mould and turn plate and mould over together. Remove the mould. Hand the sweet pepper sauce separately.

TO 'STRIPE' COURGETTES
1 Peel the skin off courgettes, leaving alternate strips unpeeled for a pretty effect. Cook small courgettes whole like this and slice larger ones thickly.

PEELING ASPARAGUS
1 Use a knife or a potato peeler to peel the tough skin from the bottom few inches of asparagus stalks. This will enable the whole stalk to cook quickly to edible tenderness.

2 If using a potato peeler, make sure that you peel away from you.

CLEARING ASPIC
1 Whisk the crushed egg shells and whites until frothy, and whisk into the slowly warming stock.

2 Whisk steadily until mixture boils and rises. Stop whisking and allow mixture to subside taking care not to break the crust of the egg whites. Bring to boil again without whisking and allow to subside. Repeat.

3 Fix a double layer of white kitchen paper or fine muslin in a sieve over a clean basin. Carefully strain the aspic without 'hurrying' it. Do not worry if the egg white slips into the sieve.

BEEF ASPIC

INGREDIENTS
570ml/1pt well flavoured brown stock, chilled (see p.268) (For white aspic use chicken instead of beef stock)
2 egg shells
2 egg whites
15g/½oz gelatine

1 Lift or skim any fat from the stock. Taste and add salt and pepper as required.

2 Put the stock into a large saucepan and sprinkle on the gelatine if you need it (use the full quantity if the cold stock is liquid, half if it is hardly set, none if firmly set). Put the pan over gentle heat.

3 Clear the aspic, as shown above. Leave mixture to cool for 5 minutes before straining. Repeat the straining if the aspic is not crystal clear.

4 This should make about 1 pint of aspic. Leave to chill and set.

NOTE Do not leave the warm aspic to cool for too long before straining it as it will set in the sieve, if cool.

☐ *The longer it takes to whisk the egg shells and whites into the warming stock the better, for the clearer the aspic will be.*

TO MAKE ASPIC DICE
1 Fill a flat-bottomed container with a shallow layer of liquid aspic. Place it very level in the refrigerator to set. Then cut into neat dice.

2 Use a fish slice, reversed so that it can act more as a 'plough' than a lifter, to remove the dice.

LOIN OF PORK BRAISED WITH PORT AND PRUNES

INGREDIENTS (Serves 8)
One 1.8kg/4lb boned and rolled loin of pork
Oil for frying
15g/½oz butter
1 onion, finely chopped
110g/4oz prunes, soaked overnight in black tea
570ml/1pt brown stock *(see p.268)*
150ml/¼pt port
1 bay leaf
2 sprigs fresh thyme
1tbsp redcurrant jelly
Salt and freshly ground black pepper
5tbsp double cream
1 small bunch watercress

1 Set the oven to 150°C/300°F/Gas 2.

2 Heat the oil in a flameproof casserole dish. Add the butter and, when foaming, the pork. Fry until lightly browned all over. Add the onion and fry until golden.

3 Add the prunes, stock, port, bay leaf, thyme and redcurrant jelly. Season with salt and pepper. Bring to the boil, cover, and place in the oven. Bake for 2 hours.

4 Remove the pork from the casserole and keep warm. Strain the cooking liquid. Skim off any fat and boil rapidly until reduced to about 290ml/½pt. It should be syrupy. Add the cream. Keep warm.

5 Stone the prunes. Slice the pork and arrange in overlapping slices on a warm plate. Spoon over some of the sauce. Garnish with the prunes and watercress and hand the remaining sauce separately.

MASHED POTATOES

INGREDIENTS (Serves 4)
675g/1½lb potatoes
Butter
Milk or single cream
Salt and ground white pepper
Grated nutmeg

The consistency of mashed potatoes can vary from the firm texture referred to as pommes purée to the creamy, buttery soft mixture called pommes mousseline.

1 Peel the potatoes and cut into even sized, fairly large chunks. If they are too small they absorb too much water, and lose flavour in boiling.

2 Cook in boiling salted water until soft. Do not undercook — they will not mash. Do not overcook — the potatoes will be too watery. Drain well, return to the saucepan and stir over a moderate heat for a few minutes to dry.

3 Push the potatoes through a sieve (or mince through a fine mincer plate), which guarantees a lump-free result.

4 Push the mound of potato to one side of the saucepan and pour a little milk into the exposed side of the pan. Put this side over a direct heat and get the milk boiling. Add a good lump of butter. Beat the milk and butter into the potato.

5 Continue with more milk, cream or butter until the required consistency is reached. Add salt, pepper and nutmeg to taste.

☐ *Never use a processor to mash potatoes. They become gluey. Heating the milk before beating it in also helps to prevent a gluey consistency.*

BRAISED RED CABBAGE

INGREDIENTS (Serves 4)
1 small red cabbage
1 onion, sliced
30g/1oz butter
1 cooking apple, peeled and sliced
1 dessert apple, peeled and sliced
2tsp brown sugar
2tsp vinegar
Pinch of ground cloves
Salt and freshly ground black pepper

1 Shred the cabbage and discard the hard stalks. Rinse well.

2 In a large pan, fry the onion in the butter until it begins to soften.

3 Add the drained but still wet cabbage, apples, sugar, vinegar and cloves, and season with salt and pepper.

4 Cover tightly and cook very slowly, mixing well and stirring every 15 minutes or so. Cook for 2 hours, or until the whole mass is shiny, dark, soft and greatly reduced in bulk. (During the cooking it may be necessary to add a little water.)

5 Taste and add more salt, pepper or sugar if necessary.

CHAMPAGNE SORBET

INGREDIENTS (Serves 4)
425ml/¾pt water
340g/12oz granulated sugar
425ml/¾pt champagne
Juice of 1 lemon and 1 small orange

1 Turn the freezer to coldest.

2 Put the water and sugar in a heavy pan and dissolve slowly on a gentle heat.

3 When the sugar has completely dissolved, boil rapidly until the syrup is tacky and a short thread can be formed if the syrup is pulled between finger and thumb.

4 Add the champagne and fruit juice and allow to cool.

5 Freeze overnight or until icy, then whisk until smooth. Return to the freezer. The sorbet will not freeze solidly due to the high alcohol content, and should not be removed from the freezer until it is to be served. For this reason, serve in well chilled goblets.

NOTE An electric ice cream machine makes short work of this sometimes tricky sorbet. To ensure freezing without the benefit of a machine, the wine can be brought to the boil and cooled before being added to the syrup. This eliminates the alcohol, which is one of the factors preventing solid freezing. But traditionally the champagne is not boiled precisely because it is meant to be soft and alcoholic, and is much nicer so. The boiled version however, provided champagne is used to start with, does taste very good despite the loss of alcohol.

☐ *As this sorbet does not set rock hard (the high proportion of sugar and alcohol prevent solid freezing), make sure the the glasses or serving bowls are well chilled. Should the sorbet become crystalline or grainy, rewhisk it (preferably in a chilled processor bowl) while frozen.*

TUILES AUX AMANDES

INGREDIENTS (Serves 4)
30g/1oz blanched almonds
2 egg whites
110g/4oz caster sugar
55g/2oz plain flour
½tsp vanilla flavouring
55g/2oz melted butter

1 Set the oven to 180°C/350°F/Gas 4. Lightly grease at least three baking sheets and a rolling pin.

2 Cut the almonds into fine slivers or shreds.

3 Place the egg whites in a bowl. Beat in the sugar with a fork. The egg white should be frothy but by no means snowy. Sift in the flour and add the vanilla and almonds. Mix with the fork.

4 Cool the butter (it should be melted but not hot) and add it to the mixture. Stir well.

5 Place the mixture in teaspoonfuls at least 13cm/5 inches apart on the baking sheets and flatten well.

6 Bake in the oven until a good brown at the edges and pale biscuit coloured in the middle (about 6 minutes). Remove from the oven and cool for a few seconds.

7 Lift the biscuits off carefully with a palette knife. Lay them, while still warm and pliable, over the rolling pin to form them into a slightly curved shape. As soon as they are stone cold put them into an airtight tin or plastic bag to keep them crisp.

☐ *The use of silicone-coated paper to line the baking trays makes removing and shaping the tuiles very easy.*

PHOTOGRAPH ON P.115

Grouse is the most delicious of game birds if cooked to perfection and served with the traditional trimmings of crisp game chips, creamy bread sauce, buttery crumbs and redcurrant jelly. But it takes concentration and effort to get all to the table at the right moment, so it is sensible to have a reheatable soup to start, and an easy refreshing dessert. The usual pitfalls of this menu are overcooked grouse (it takes courage not to put the birds in to roast until 30 minutes before serving), overcooked Brussels sprouts, and soggy breadcrumbs.

MENU LESSON 15

Prawn bisque

Roast grouse, croûtes and gravy

Game chips

Bread sauce

Fried crumbs

Brussels sprouts

Tangerines in caramel

Brandy snaps

WORK PLAN

Make the soup, game chips, bread sauce , crumbs, tangerines and brandy snaps (which will keep, unfilled, in a tin) in advance, leaving only the grouse and sprouts for last minute cooking.

PRAWN BISQUE

INGREDIENTS (Serves 4)
900g/2lb unshelled raw prawns
2tbsp oil
110g/4oz butter
2 shallots, chopped
Juice of ½ lemon
3tbsp brandy
1 bay leaf
1 parsley stalk
Blade of mace
1.1 litres/2pt well flavoured fish stock
30g/1oz flour
Salt and pepper
Tabasco sauce
3tbsp cream

☐ *If there is no roe to be found, 1tbsp tomato purée whisked into the bisque will give a better colour.*

1 Wash the prawns, reserving any roe.

2 In a large heavy pan heat the oil, add 30g/1oz of the butter and fry the prawns and roe for 2 minutes or until they begin to change colour. Add the shallots, lemon juice and brandy and continue to cook for a further 2 minutes or until the prawns are a bright pink. Allow to cool until the prawns can be handled.

3 Shell the prawns, keeping the shells. Reserve the pan with its juices, and any roe from the prawns.

4 Simmer the prawn shells, bay leaf, parsley stalk and blade of mace in the stock for 30 minutes (this will help to give the bisque flavour and colour).

5 Meanwhile blend or pound together nearly all the prawns with about 45g/1½oz butter and any reserved roe. Keep the remaining prawns for garnish.

6 Melt the remaining butter (about 45g/1½oz). Add the flour and cook for 30 seconds. Strain in the stock and bring slowly to the boil, stirring constantly. Simmer for 2 minutes, strain in the pan juices, and whisk in the prawn butter.

7 Season with salt, pepper and Tabasco. Add the cream and finally the reserved prawns.

ROAST GROUSE

INGREDIENTS (Serves 4)
4 grouse, drawn (do not discard the liver)
4 rashers rindless streaky bacon
30g/1oz butter
Salt and freshly ground black pepper
1tsp flour
290ml/½pt game stock or, if unavailable, white stock (p.268)
4 croutes (see below)
Cress to garnish

Allow 1 young grouse per head. Grouse are often served very rare like steak but this recipe is for pink (medium) grouse.

1 Heat the oven to 190°C/375°F/Gas 5.

2 Clean the livers and place inside each grouse. Place in a roasting pan.

3 Cut the rashers of bacon in half and lay two pieces over the breast of each grouse. Dot with a little butter and season with salt and pepper.

4 Roast for 25 minutes. Remove the bacon after about 15 minutes to allow the breasts to brown thoroughly. Turn off the oven.

5 Remove the grouse to a plate and keep warm in the cooling oven while you make the gravy.

6 Tip off all but 1 scant tbsp of the fat from the roasting pan. Try not to lose any of the meat juices.

7 Add the flour and cook for 1 minute until a russet brown.

8 Cool for a minute, then add the stock and bring to the boil, stirring continuously with a spoon, scraping the bottom of the pan to loosen the sediment as it comes to the boil. Boil thoroughly until syrupy in consistency. Add any meat juices that have run from the grouse. Taste and season and strain into a warmed gravy boat.

9 Scrape the liver from the grouse and spread it onto the uncooked side of the croûtes.

10 Arrange the grouse on a serving plate and garnish with the croûtes and cress.

CROUTES FOR ROAST GAME BIRDS

When roasting small game birds such as pigeon or woodcock, the 'trails' (entrails) are left inside and only the gizzard removed. After roasting, the liver, juices, etc. are spread on the uncooked side of a slice of bread which has been fried or toasted on one side only. The roasted bird is served on this croûte.
Larger birds like pheasant and grouse are drawn before roasting, but the liver may be returned to the body cavity to cook with the bird. This, plus any other scrapings from the inside of the bird, is spread on the uncooked side of the croûte, which is then cut diagonally in half and served as a garnish to the whole roast bird.

GAME CHIPS

INGREDIENTS (Serves 4)
450g/1lb large potatoes
Oil for deep frying
Salt

1 Wash and peel the potatoes. If you want even sized chips trim each potato into a cylinder shape.

2 Slice them very finely, preferably on a mandoline. Soak in cold water to remove the excess starch (this will prevent them from discolouring or sticking together).

☐ *Wear a scarf or chef's hat when deep frying — it keeps the smell of fat out of your hair.*

3 Heat the oil in a deep fryer until a crumb will sizzle vigorously in it.

4 Dry the chips very thoroughly on a tea towel.

5 Lower a basket of chips into the hot fat. They are cooked when they rise to the surface and are golden brown.

6 Drain on absorbent paper, sprinkle with salt and serve.

GAME CHIPS
1 Take care when using a mandoline to keep fingers out of the way of the blade. Strong plastic mandolines are faster and more durable than wooden ones.

2 Game chips that look less like bought potato chips can be made by shaving the peeled potato with a swivel peeler.

BREAD SAUCE

INGREDIENTS (Serves 4)
1 large peeled onion
6 cloves
290ml/½pt milk
1 bay leaf
A pinch of white pepper
Pinch of nutmeg
Salt
55g/2oz fresh white breadcrumbs
55g/2oz butter
2tbsp cream (optional)

1 Cut the onion in half. Stick the cloves into the onion pieces and put with the milk and bay leaf in a saucepan.

2 Add the pepper, a pinch of nutmeg, and a good pinch of salt. Leave to stand for 30 minutes or more if you can. If not, bring very slowly to the boil, and then simmer for 10 minutes. If you have had time to let the milk infuse (stand with its flavourings) you will not need to simmer it. But bring it to the boil very slowly just the same.

3 Lift out the studded onion halves and add the breadcrumbs. Add the butter and cream.

4 Reheat the sauce carefully, without boiling.

5 If it has become too thick by the time it is needed, beat in more hot milk. It should be creamy. If it is too thin, boil, stirring continually, until the correct consistency has been achieved.

FRIED CRUMBS

INGREDIENTS
55g/2oz butter
4tbsp dry white breadcrumbs

☐ *The secret of good breadcrumbs is very slow frying and patient stirring and turning in the butter.*

Melt the butter and very slowly fry the crumbs in it stirring frequently until they have absorbed most of the butter, and are golden in colour and crisp. Serve in a warm bowl, handed to the diners with the sauce or sauces.

NOTE Fresh white crumbs can be used, but rather more butter will be needed as they are very absorbent, and great care should be taken to fry slowly, so that the crumbs become crisp before they turn brown.

BRUSSELS SPROUTS

INGREDIENTS *(Serves 4)*
675g/1½lb very small Brussels sprouts
Butter
Salt and freshly ground black pepper

☐ *The secret of sprouts is fast-boiling water before the sprouts go in, and tiny sprouts the size of small marbles.*

1 Wash and trim the sprouts, paring the stalk and removing the outside leaves if necessary.

2 Tip into a large pan of boiling salted water and cook, uncovered, until just tender but not soggy: the flavour changes disastrously if boiled too long. The timing naturally depends on the size of the sprouts but they will take somewhere between 6 and 9 minutes.

3 Drain thoroughly and serve immediately with a little melted butter and a couple of grinds of black pepper.

NOTE Do not be tempted to cut a cross into the stem of the sprouts. This was a recommended procedure when sprouts were cooked to a grey sogginess. If the sprouts are very small and young, and rapidly boiled in an open pan, splitting the stalks is not necessary.

TANGERINES IN CARAMEL

INGREDIENTS *(Serves 4)*
8 small seedless tangerines
170g/6oz granulated sugar
425ml/¾pt water

TO SERVE
Caramel shards (optional, see illustrations below)

☐ *Take care when buying the tangerines — eat one in the shop to ensure it is not full of seeds.*

1 Wash and dry 2 tangerines. Pare the rind with a potato peeler, making sure that there is no pith on the back of the strips. Cut into fine needle shreds.

2 Put the sugar and half the water into a heavy saucepan. Warm gently to dissolve the sugar. Increase the temperature and boil rapidly until beginning to brown. Add the needle shreds.

3 When thoroughly caramelized, stand back and pour in the remaining water. Take care — it will fizz most alarmingly.

4 Bring back to the boil, stir well to dissolve any lumps of caramel and simmer until thick and syrupy. Leave to cool.

5 Peel the tangerines and remove as much of the pith as possible. Leave them whole.

6 Place the tangerines in a glass bowl. Pour over the cold caramel sauce and needle shreds. Chill well.

TO MAKE CARAMEL SHARDS
1 To avoid crystallization when syrups are boiling, add a little lemon juice or cream of tartar. Alternatively, substitute pure glucose for 20 per cent or more of the sugar. Or constantly brush the sides of the pan with clean water to wash down any sugar crystals.

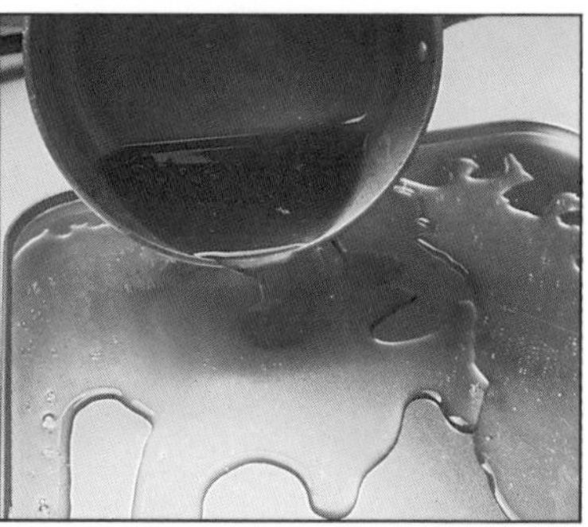

2 Boil sugar syrup to a caramel — either a pale one as on the right of the baking tray above, or darker. Pour quickly onto an oiled tray. Once brown, caramel burns easily.

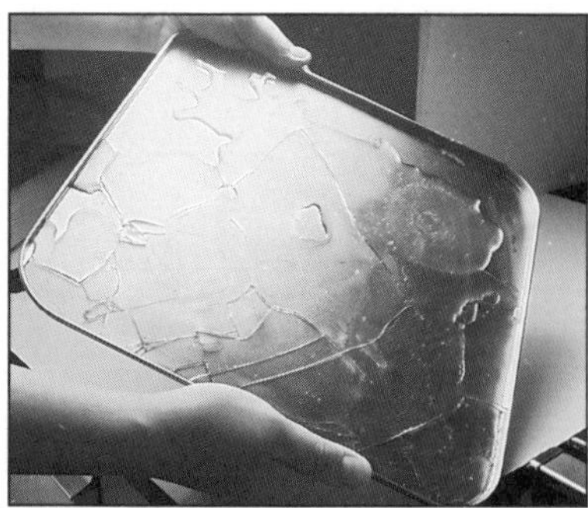

3 When cold bend the tray slightly to crack the caramel. If the tray is too rigid, break the caramel into shards with a heavy object, such as the end of a rolling pin. Once cold, sprinkle on caramel tangerines if you wish, or store in an airtight jar.

BRANDY SNAPS

INGREDIENTS (Serves 4)
110g/4oz sugar
110g/4oz butter
110g/4oz or 4tbsp golden syrup
Juice of ½ lemon
110g/4oz flour
Large pinch of ground ginger

TO SERVE
Whipped cream or ice cream

1 Set the oven to 190°C/375°F/Gas 5. Grease a baking sheet, palette knife and the handle of a thick wooden spoon.

2 Melt the sugar, butter and syrup together. Remove from the heat.

3 Sift in the flour, stirring well. Add the lemon juice and ginger.

4 Put the mixture on the baking sheet in small teaspoonfuls about 15cm/6 inches apart. Bake for 5-7 minutes. They should go golden brown but still be soft. Watch carefully — they burn easily.

5 Remove from the oven, shape and fill, as shown.

NOTE 1 Brandy snaps should not be filled with wettish mixtures like whipped cream or ice cream until shortly before serving, or the biscuit will quickly lose its crispness. Similarly, if brandy snap cups are not to be served immediately they must, once cool, be put into an airtight container for storage. They become soggy if left out.

NOTE 2 Do not bake too many snaps at a time as once they are cold they will be too brittle to shape — though they can be made pliable again if briefly returned to the oven.

BRANDY SNAP CUPS
The mixture for these is exactly the same as for brandy snaps but the biscuits are shaped round one end of a wide rolling pin or a narrow jam jar or bottle. They are also filled with whipped cream.

MINIATURE BRANDY SNAPS (served as petits fours after dinner) are shaped over a skewer. These are not generally filled.

SHAPING BRANDY SNAPS

1 When cooked brandy snaps are cool enough to handle, but still hot and pliable, ease them off the baking sheet with a palette knife.

2 Fold them around the greased handle of a wooden spoon. Hold one edge against the handle with a finger and gently curl each snap around the handle using a cupped hand.

3 Once set they can be gently slid off the handle. If they cool too quickly and cannot be moulded, return them briefly to the oven to soften. Cool on a wire rack.

4 Use a piping bag fitted with a medium-sized fluted nozzle to fill both ends of the brandy snaps. For brandy snap cups, shape the snaps over the greased end of a jam jar or rolling pin.

1

2

3

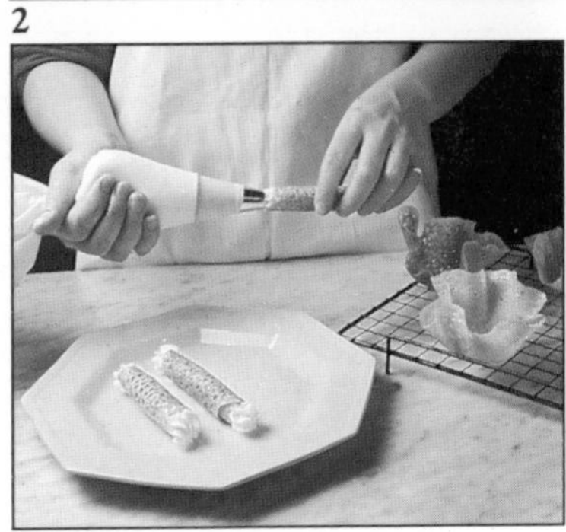

4

PHOTOGRAPH ON P.114

MENU LESSON 16

Pot au feu

Mashed potatoes (p.101)

Green salad (p.139)

Chocolate profiteroles

This menu is a lesson in classic stewing or poaching. Pot au feu, like Bollito in Italy, Boiled beef and carrots in England, and Boiled New England dinner in the US, can be a glorious thing, or a disaster. The trick is in the slow, slow, slow cooking and the religious skimming off of fat and scum. Pot au feu cooked in the bottom oven of an Aga cooks so slowly that the scum and fat come to the surface without bubbling at all, and so cannot affect the clarity of the broth below. They can be skimmed off at the end of the cooking time, which would probably be all night. But most cooks cannot afford the fuel for such long slow cooking, and anyway do not have ovens as gentle as that. With greater heat the liquid will bubble, and fat and scum will be constantly bubbled through the stock, giving it a murky look and a fatty taste. To avoid this there is nothing for it but constant skimming, and as gentle a simmer as the cook can contrive. The gentle cooking also produces succulent, tender and non-stringy meat.

To go with such homely fare, what better than perfect mashed potatoes, creamy and smooth to mop up the broth?

The second part of the Menu Lesson is classic too, and the cook should read the notes on choux pastry on p.306 before embarking on the paste. It is in fact one of the easiest of French pastries, rising as if by magic, and beloved by everyone for its buttery crispness. The pitfalls are allowing the butter/water mixture to boil too long (so altering the proportions), not being quick and vigorous enough with tipping in and beating the flour (which leads to lumps), and adding too much egg to the mixture, which gives an unmanageable dough and rather flat hard choux buns. But obedience to the recipe instructions will ensure crisp, risen, brown and delicious profiteroles.

WORK PLAN

- If making the profiteroles more than 8 hours in advance, freeze them (empty and un-iced) as they quickly become stale. They can be crisped up in the oven, filled and iced 2 or 3 hours before serving.
- Pot au feu reheats excellently. But take care when cooling and heating large pots of meat and liquid that they do not go bad. See the note on food poisoning on p.331, and follow the cooling instructions.
- Mashed potatoes reheat well, especially in a microwave oven, and green salad may be prepared a few hours ahead of time, but should not be dressed more than half an hour before serving.

POT AU FEU

INGREDIENTS (Serves 4)
1kg/2¼lb silverside or topside of beef, tied into a compact shape
1kg/2¼lb beef bones in 5-8cm/2-3 inch pieces
2.25litres/4pt water
2tsp salt
6 peppercorns
3 cloves
3 onions, peeled
225g/8oz carrots, peeled and cut into short lengths
Continued on next page

1 Put the bones into the bottom of a large pot. Place the meat on top. Add the water, salt, and peppercorns. Place on a gentle heat and very gradually bring to simmering point. This should take 30 minutes. Skim constantly.

2 Once the stock is simmering, dépouille: add 150ml/¼pt very cold water to the boiling stock. This will help to bring scum and fat to the surface. Skim quickly and thoroughly. Continue to simmer and dépouille until the stock is very clear.

3 Stick the 3 cloves into one of the onions, like nails. Add the vegetables, skim off any further scum. With a clean damp cloth clean the edges of the saucepan of any scum.

110g/4oz turnips, peeled and quartered
225g/8oz small leeks, cleaned
1 very small parsnip, peeled and chopped
2 sticks celery, trimmed and chopped

TO SERVE
Chopped parsley

4 Cook, very slowly, half covered with a lid for about 3 hours. The pot must barely simmer.

5 TO SERVE, remove the cloves from the onion. Lift out the beef, slice it thickly (or leave whole to carve at table) and place in a serving dish with the vegetables. Cover and keep warm.

6 Skim any fat from the broth (or lay a sheet or two of absorbent paper on the surface to lift off any grease spots). Strain most of the broth into a tureen and serve as soup. Ladle the rest, with the peppercorns, over the meat and vegetables to moisten them and dust the top with chopped parsley.

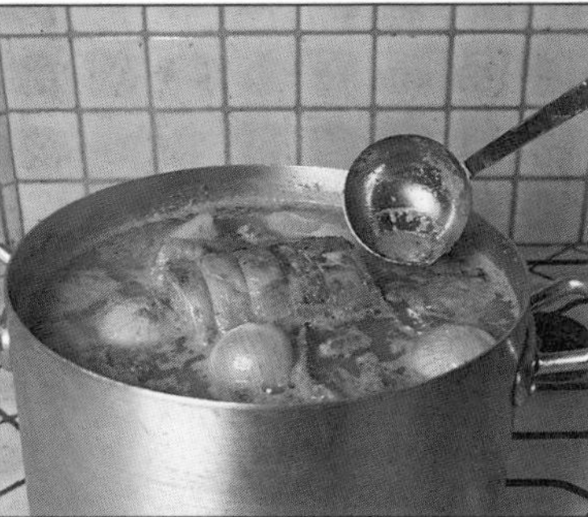

TO DEPOUILLE LIQUIDS
Add a splash of very cold water to the simmering liquid. This will bring fat and scum to the surface. Skim off quickly. Repeat every 15 minutes or as more scum and surface fat forms.

CHOCOLATE PROFITEROLES

INGREDIENTS (Serves 4)
3 egg-quantity choux paste (see next recipe)
570ml/1pt double cream
170g/6oz chocolate
4tbsp water
15g/½oz butter
1tbsp icing sugar

1 Set the oven to 200°C/400°F/Gas 6.

2 Pipe or spoon the choux mixture on to a wet baking sheet.

3 Bake for 20-30 minutes.

4 Remove from the oven and make a small hole in the side of each profiterole. Return to the oven for 5 minutes.

TO MAKE PROFITEROLES
1 Spoon or pipe the mixture onto a wet baking sheet, making small mounds, well apart to allow for swelling in the oven.

2 When they are baked to a good brown colour (if too pale they will become soggy when cool) remove from the oven and make a hole the size of a pea in the side of each profiterole. Return to the oven, hole side uppermost, to allow the insides to dry out as the steam escapes through the hole.

3 Cool on a wire rack. Quickly freeze them (once cold) if they are not to be served the same day.

☐ *If no piping bag is available for filling the profiteroles, they can be split, allowed to dry out and cool, and filled with cream. The icing is then spooned over the top. However, they are then difficult to eat in the fingers, but for a sit-down meal this would not matter.*

5 Whip the cream stiffly and mix in about 1tbsp sifted icing sugar. When the profiteroles are cold, fill with the cream, using a forcing bag fitted with a small plain nozzle inserted into the holes in their sides.

6 Melt the chocolate with the water and butter. Stir, without boiling, until smooth and shiny.

7 Dip the tops of the profiteroles deeply in the chocolate and allow to cool and harden.

NOTE The chocolate mixture could be served separately as a hot sauce, with the cream-filled profiteroles lightly dusted with icing sugar.

CHOUX PASTRY

INGREDIENTS
85g/3oz butter
220ml/7½fl oz water
105g/3¾oz plain flour, well sifted
Pinch of salt
3 eggs, lightly beaten

1 Put the butter and water together in a heavy saucepan and bring to a vigorous boil.

2 Draw off the heat and immediately tip in the flour and beat the mixture hard until smooth.

3 Add the salt, then stand the bottom of the saucepan in a basin or sink of cold water to speed up cooling. Cool for a few minutes.

4 Beat in enough egg to produce a mixture of dropping consistency.

TO MAKE CHOUX PASTE
1 Put the water and the butter, cut into 3-4 pieces, into a heavy saucepan and place over a gentle heat.

2 Bring to the boil slowly so that by the time the liquid boils all the butter has melted.

3 As soon as the liquid is boiling fast, tip in all the flour and remove the pan from the heat.

4 Beat vigorously until a smooth paste is formed. The trick is to beat out the lumps before they are cooked solid by the heat. Once the paste curls away from the sides of the pan, stop.

5 Allow the paste to cool slightly then beat in the liquid egg, a little at a time. It may not be necessary to add all the egg.

6 Continue adding egg until you have a soft dropping consistency. The mixture will be shiny and smooth and will fall reluctantly from a spoon if it is given a sharp jerk.

PHOTOGRAPH ON P.118

This is a light and pretty looking menu, either for the professional cook or for the home cook who can leave the table to fry the duck breasts — they cannot be done in advance. The techniques covered in the Menu Lesson are the careful balancing of tastes (too much strawberry makes the dressing taste like dessert, too little and the fruitiness is not there), the last-minute well judged sautéing of the duck breasts, and the making of a whisked sabayon — the whisking of eggs over heat to produce a stable frothy emulsion.

MENU LESSON 17

Avocado pear with strawberry vinaigrette

Duck breasts with green peppercorn sauce

Mâche and endive salad

Poached pears with sabayon and sorbet

WORK PLAN

• The vinaigrette can be made several hours ahead of time but loses its pink colour if made the day before.
• The avocado will discolour if cut more than half an hour in advance.
• The duck breasts are a last-minute affair, but the sauce can be made in advance and reheated.
• The sorbet can be made 24 hours ahead of time and the sabayon will stand without separating for 2 hours, but such an elegant dessert needs to be dished up at the last minute.

AVOCADO PEAR WITH STRAWBERRY VINAIGRETTE

INGREDIENTS (Serves 4)
2 avocado pears
6tbsp oil
1tsp lemon juice
55g/2oz ripe strawberries
Salt and pepper
Pinch of sugar

1 MAKE THE DRESSING Liquidize almost all the oil, lemon juice, strawberries, salt, pepper and sugar together. Taste and add more sugar, lemon juice, strawberries, salt or pepper as needed.

2 Cut the avocado pears in half lengthways (or widthways, see p.112) and remove the stones and skin. Lay, rounded side up, on a board, slice and fan out. Brush them with the remaining oil.

TO STONE AND PEEL
1 Split the avocado and carefully twist to separate the two halves. Pierce the avocado stone with a sharp knife and twist to extract it.

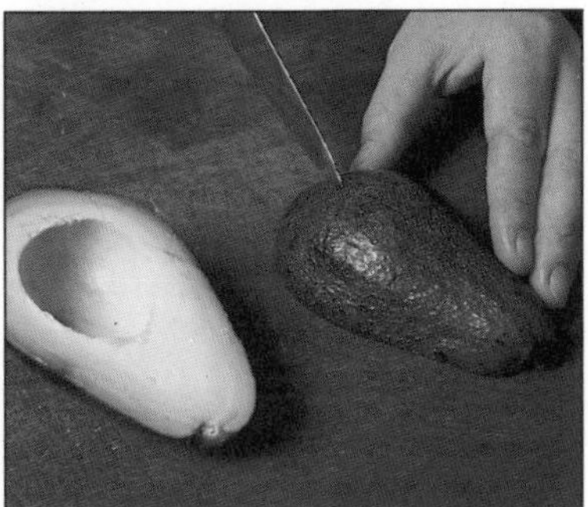

2 Turn each half of the avocado face down and cut just through the skin from top to tail.

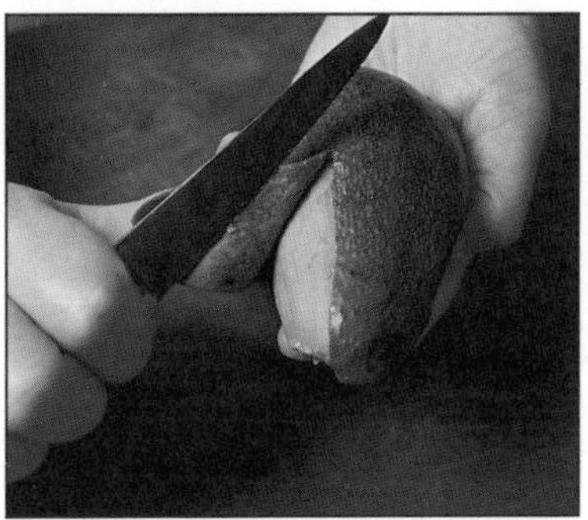

3 Carefully peel back the skin using the knife blade. Gripped firmly with the thumb, the skin should come away without tearing.

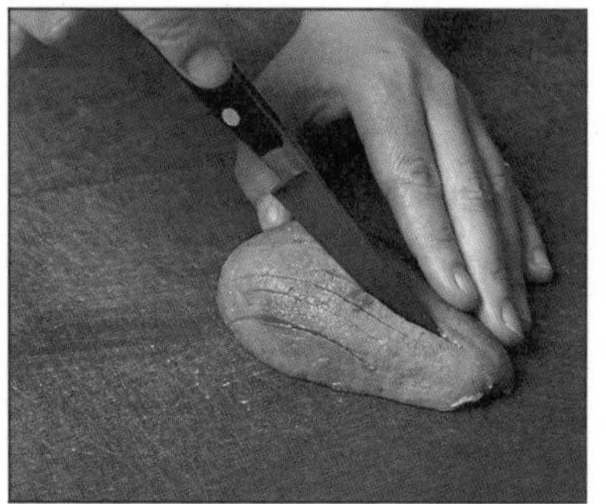

TO MAKE 'FANS'
1 For a fan-shape, cut through the flesh lengthwise in parallel slices without cutting through the pointed end.

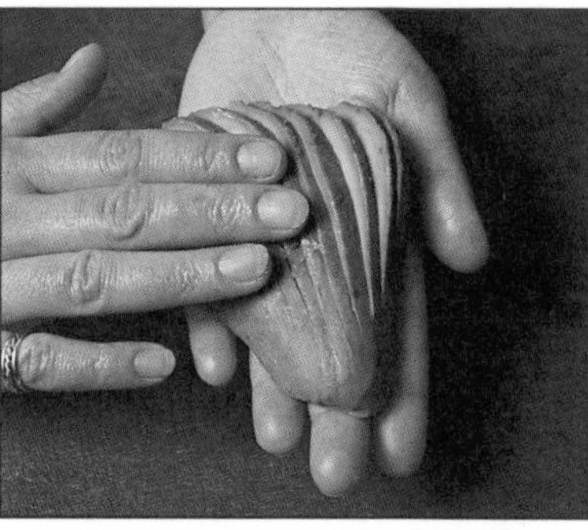

2 Place the sliced half pear on your palm and gently press down and away with the flat of your hand to fan out the slices.

3 Lay the fanned out pear on the plate, being careful not to damage the velvety outer surface with your finger-tips.

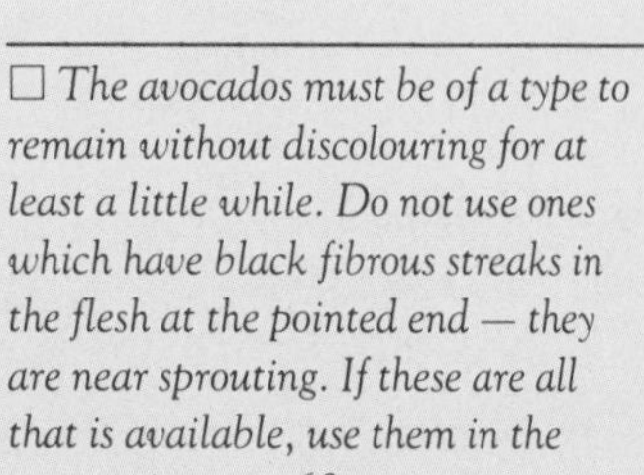

☐ *The avocados must be of a type to remain without discolouring for at least a little while. Do not use ones which have black fibrous streaks in the flesh at the pointed end — they are near sprouting. If these are all that is available, use them in the soup recipe on p.60.*

SLICING WIDTHWAYS
1 For neat separate slices, lay the avocado half on a palette knife and cut widthways into slices about 3mm/⅛ inch thick.

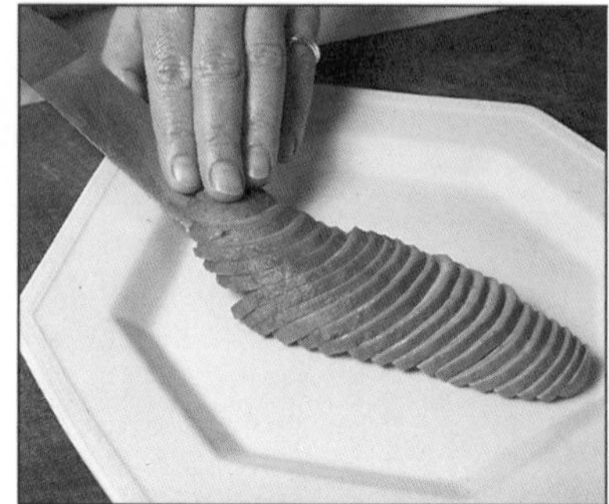

2 Then use the knife to lift them into place. Slide the sliced pear on to the plate, gently pressing down to achieve the ranked effect.

3 Pour the dressing on to 4 side plates making sure that the base of each plate is completely covered. Arrange the sliced avocado pears on top of the strawberry dressing.

DUCK BREASTS WITH GREEN PEPPERCORN SAUCE

INGREDIENTS (Serves 4)
4 large duck breasts, skinned
45g/1½oz unsalted butter

FOR THE SAUCE
150ml/¼pt dry white wine
3tbsp brandy
8tbsp white stock (p.268)
290ml/½pt double cream
2tbsp wine vinegar
1tsp sugar
1tbsp port
20g/¾oz green peppercorns, well rinsed
20g/¾oz tinned red pimento cut into dice
Salt and pepper

As this is a complicated recipe we have (as suggested in the work plan) given first the method for the sauce and then instructions for cooking the duck breasts and garnish. This assumes the sauce will be reheated at the last minute.

1 TO MAKE THE SAUCE Put the wine and brandy in a heavy pan and boil gently for about 5 minutes or until reduced to a third of the original volume.

2 Add the stock and boil for 5 minutes. Add the cream and boil for about 15 minutes (stirring occasionally so that it does not catch on the bottom) or until the sauce has reduced by about a third and is of pouring consistency (ie about as thick as single cream).

FOR THE GARNISH
2 firm dessert apples, peeled and cut into 8
30g/1oz unsalted butter

☐ *The duck breasts, if large and thick, could be split horizontally for quicker frying.*

3 Put the vinegar and sugar into a small saucepan. Boil for 30 seconds or until it smells caramelized and is reduced to about 1tbsp. Cool for 1 minute and pour in the cream sauce. Stir well. It may be necessary to put it back over the heat to re-melt the caramel. Add the port, peppercorns and pimento. Season. Set aside until ready for use.

TO COOK THE DUCK BREASTS AND THE APPLE GARNISH
These must be cooked while the first course is eaten.

1 Melt the 45g/1½oz unsalted butter in a large heavy frying pan. When it stops foaming add the duck breasts and fry fairly fast on both sides. Reduce the heat and fry slowly for 8 to 10 minutes.

2 Melt the butter for the garnish in a second frying pan and fry the apples very slowly until golden brown.

3 TO SERVE Reheat the sauce in a double saucepan.

4 Slice the duck breasts, lengthwise, into fairly thin slices. They should be rose pink.

5 Flood the base of 4 large plates with the sauce. Arrange a fan of sliced duck breast on each plate and garnish with 3 or 4 pieces of apple.

MACHE AND ENDIVE SALAD

INGREDIENTS (Serves 4)
225g/8oz mâche (lamb's lettuce or corn salad)
1 small curly endive
French dressing made from walnut oil (see p.139)
1 bunch chives, finely chopped

1 Wash and spin dry the leaves.

2 Just before serving toss in the French dressing with the chives.

POACHED PEARS WITH SABAYON AND SORBET

INGREDIENTS (Serves 4)
4 Conference pears
570ml/1pt sugar syrup (see p.67)
4 egg yolks
3tbsp caster sugar
55ml/2fl oz eau de vie Poire William (pear brandy)
150ml/¼pt double cream, lightly whipped
Pear sorbet (see p.131)
A few sprigs of mint to garnish

☐ *If the combination of pears, pear sorbet and sabayon sauce is too complicated, the sorbet can be omitted — but the three together are very good indeed.*

1 Peel the pears very neatly without removing the stalks. Remove the core with a teaspoon. Choose a tall narrow pan. Place the pears, stalks upwards, in the pan. Add the sugar syrup and cover with a lid. The pears should be completely covered by the sugar syrup. If this is not possible, wet the pears in the syrup thoroughly and boil the syrup fast for a few minutes so that it bubbles over their entire surface. Turn the pears during cooking with wooden (rather than metal) spoons to prevent damage.

2 Simmer slowly until very tender and glassy. The longer and slower the pears are cooked the better. Remove from the syrup, allow to cool and then refrigerate until cold.

3 PREPARE THE SABAYON SAUCE while the pears are poaching. Put the egg yolks and sugar into a bowl. Set over a saucepan of simmering water. Do not let the base of the bowl touch the water. Whisk, for at least 10 minutes, until thick and creamy. Remove from the heat and whisk repeatedly until cool. Add the Poire William and cream. Chill.

4 TO SERVE, flood the base of 4 pudding plates with the sabayon sauce. Slice the pears in such a way that they can be re-arranged as a whole, but slightly flattened, pear. Garnish each plate with a large scoop of pear sorbet and a sprig of mint.

MENU LESSON 15 *(see p.103)*
The traditional game bird deserves all the traditional dressings (*right*). *Clockwise from top left:* Tangerines in caramel, roast grouse with game chips and croûtes, Brussels sprouts, gravy, prawn bisque, bread sauce, brandy snaps and fried crumbs.

MENU LESSON 16 *(see p.108)*
Classic stewing is the lesson from this menu (*above*), showing the French, Italian, British and American approach to the same technique. *Clockwise from top left:* Green salad, pot-au-feu, chocolate profiteroles, pot au feu broth and mashed potatoes.

PHOTOGRAPH ON P.119

MENU LESSON 18

Fried fillets of sole with cucumber

Pommes allumettes

Chicory and radicchio salad

Lemon meringue pie

This is a good lunchtime menu of two courses only, but the cook concentrates on two methods of frying — the classic 'meunière' (or Miller's wife method — when food is lightly floured before frying in butter) and deep frying for this rather elegant version of potato chips.

Lemon meringue pie is not the easiest of baked pies, so take time to work carefully and thoughtfully, clearing up (there is a great deal of washing up!) as you go.

WORK PLAN

• The lemon meringue pie can be prepared and cooked in advance, but most of this menu requires some last-minute work. The fish and cucumber require last-minute frying, though the cucumber can be blanched first. The potatoes can be cut in advance and kept under water but must be dried and fried just before serving.

• The salad can be washed and spun-dry in advance but should not be dressed more than half an hour in advance.

FRIED FILLETS OF SOLE WITH CUCUMBER

INGREDIENTS (serves 4, giving each diner 3 fillets)
3 large lemon soles
1 large cucumber
Seasoned flour
85-110g/3-4oz butter
Salt and pepper
2tsp lemon juice
2tsp chopped parsley

☐ *If filleting Dover sole, see the illustrations on p.264. For lemon sole, follow the instructions here.*

1 Skin and fillet the soles into 12 neat fillets.

2 Peel the cucumber and, using a melon-baller, scoop the flesh into balls (see illustrations on p.47). Place these in a pan of boiling salted water for 2–3 minutes. Drain and dry well.

3 Dip the fillets in seasoned flour. Lay them on a plate but do not allow them to touch each other — they will become soggy and will not fry well.

4 Heat 1 good tbsp butter in a frying pan. When foaming, put in the fillets — not too many at a time. Turn them over when a golden brown; allow about 1½ minutes on each side. Dish onto a shallow platter and keep warm. (Halfway through the cooking, if the butter over-browns, it will be necessary to wipe the pan out and reheat with fresh butter.)

5 Melt more butter in the pan. Add the cucumber balls and fry quite briskly until a delicate brown. Allow the pan to cool for a minute. Add salt, pepper, parsley and lemon juice. Boil up and tip over the fish. Serve.

FILLETING RAW LEMON SOLE

1 Trim off the fins with scissors.

2 Lay the fish dark side up on a paper-covered board. Using a sharp filleting knife, cut behind the gills and down to the backbone along the length of the fish.

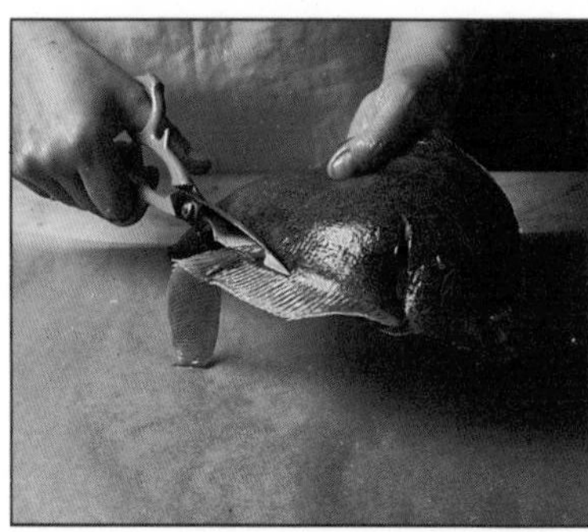

1

2

3 Holding the knife almost flat against the bones, stroke the flesh away from the bones, easing it away gently with one hand. Repeat the process for the other side of the fish.

4 Lay the fillets skin-side down on the board. Grip the tail with one hand and 'push' the flesh away from the skin with a knife held in the other. Use salt to stop your fingers slipping.

3

4

POMMES ALLUMETTES

INGREDIENTS (Serves 4)
450g/1lb potatoes
Oil for deep frying
Salt

1 Wash and peel the potatoes. Cut them into tiny even matchsticks and soak in cold water for 15 minutes. This is to remove the excess starch and will prevent the potatoes from sticking together. Dry them thoroughly with a tea towel.

2 Heat the oil until a crumb dropped in the fat sizzles vigorously. Fry the chips until golden brown and crisp (2 - 3 minutes). Drain on absorbent paper. Sprinkle with salt and serve at once.

POMMES ALLUMETTES
1 Cut the potatoes into rectangular, or near-rectangular, blocks.

2 Slice thinly and evenly.

3 Stack the slices (but not too high as the slices will tend to slip and topple over) and slice across into sticks.

☐ *The most important factor in deep frying is hot clean fat. See p.252 for more detailed instructions on deep frying. Wear a hat or scarf to protect your hair from the smell of deep frying. Put the cut potatoes into cold water to prevent discolouring and to remove excess starch. However, if they are left exposed to the air and do discolour, just rinse them well and proceed — the colour will vanish on cooking.*

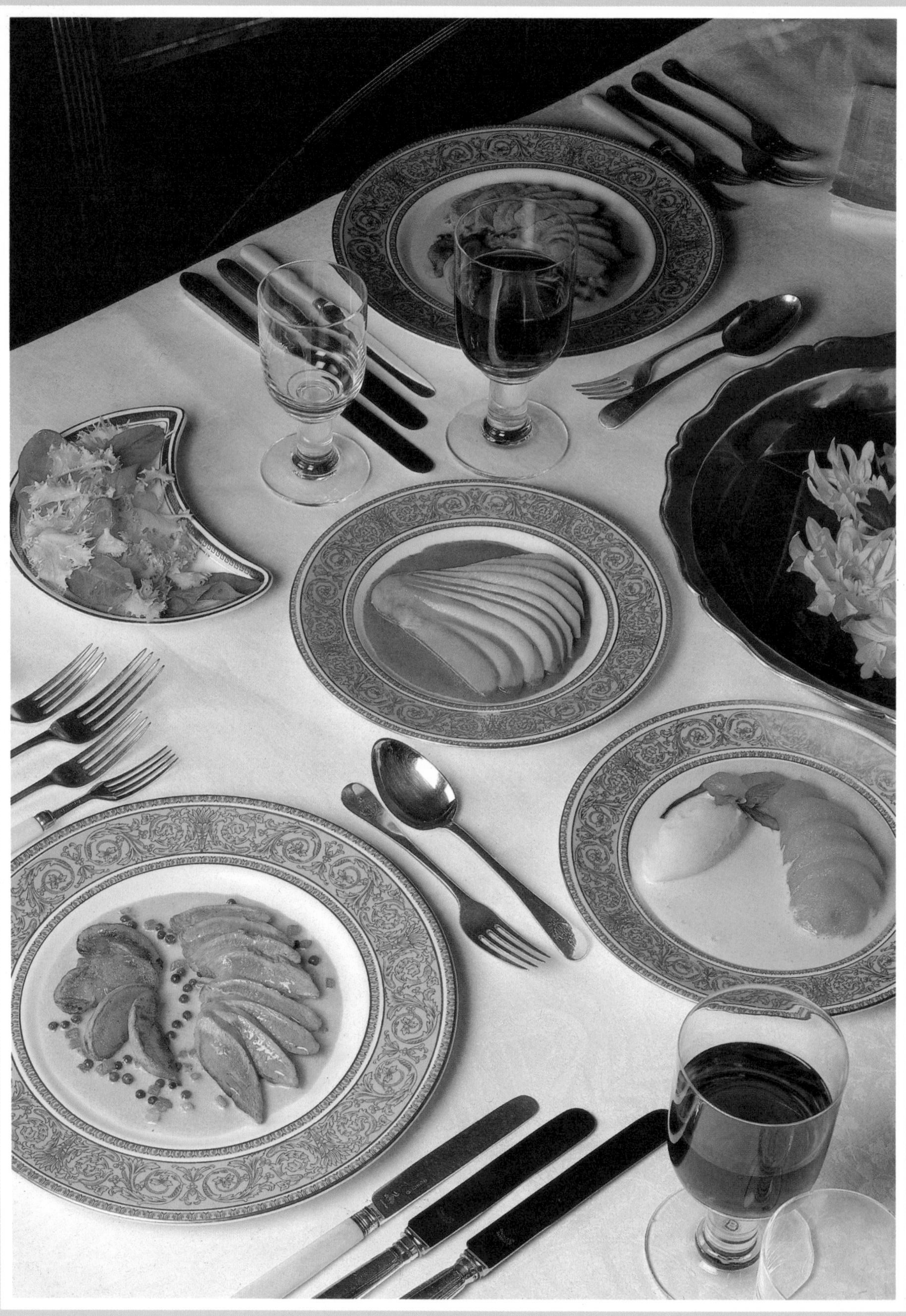

MENU LESSON 17 *(see p.111)*
A light and pretty menu (*left*), but you'll have to leave the table to cook the duck breasts. They can't be done in advance. *Clockwise from top left:* Mâche and endive salad, avocado pear with strawberry vinaigrette, poached pear with sabayon and sorbet, and duck breasts with peppercorn sauce.

MENU LESSON 18 *(see p.116)*
A good lunchtime menu (*above*), but the cook has to master two methods of frying — meunière and deep frying. *Clockwise from top left:* Lemon meringue pie, chicory and radicchio salad, fried fillets of sole with cucumber and pommes allumettes.

CHICORY AND RADICCHIO SALAD

INGREDIENTS (Serves 4)
2 heads chicory
3 radicchio lettuces
French dressing (see p.139)

☐ *The central core of many chicories is very bitter. Taste and remove if necessary.*

1 Wash the chicory and split the heads down the middle. Remove the small cone-shaped bud from the centre of the base of the chicory — it can be bitter (see p.125). Slice the leaves fairly finely.

2 Wash and spin-dry the radicchio.

3 Arrange the lettuce around the edge of a large dish with the chicory in the centre. Spoon over the French dressing.

LEMON MERINGUE PIE

INGREDIENTS (Serves 4)
110g/4oz flour quantity shortcrust pastry (see p.168)

FOR THE FILLING
30g/1oz cornflour
290ml/½pt milk
30g/1oz caster sugar
2 egg yolks
Grated rind and juice of 1 lemon

FOR THE MERINGUE
2 egg whites
110g/4oz caster sugar
A little extra caster sugar

1 Roll out the pastry and use it to line a 15cm/6 inch flan ring (see p.190). Leave to relax in the refrigerator for about 30 minutes.

2 Heat the oven to 190°C/375°F/Gas 5.

3 Bake the pastry case blind (see p.191).

4 Meanwhile, MAKE THE FILLING Slake, that is, mix, the cornflour with 1tbsp milk.

5 Heat the remaining milk. Pour this onto the cornflour paste. Stir well and return the mixture to the pan. Boil for 3 – 4 minutes, stirring continuously. Add the sugar.

6 Allow to cool slightly, then beat in the egg yolks, lemon rind and juice.

7 Pour immediately into the pastry case. If it is left in the saucepan it will go lumpy as it cools. Return to the oven for 2 minutes to set.

8 Reduce the oven to 170°C/325°F/Gas 3.

9 FOR THE MERINGUE Put the egg whites into a clean dry bowl and, with a large dry balloon whisk or electric hand whisk, whisk until stiff but not dry (see p.283). Whisk slowly to begin with and gradually build up speed. Do not stop whisking or leave the whites standing.

10 Add 2tsp sugar (that is, 1tsp per egg white) and whisk again until very shiny.

11 Fold in the remaining sugar, or whisk in briefly. Pile the meringue onto the pie. It is essential to cover the filling completely as the pie will weep. Dust with a little extra caster sugar.

12 Place in the oven for 10 minutes or until the meringue is a pale biscuit colour.

NOTE 1 Lemon curd (see p.282) makes a good alternative to the lemon custard filling but should not be too thick a layer — it is very strong flavoured.

NOTE 2 When making meringue with an electric machine, half the sugar can be added at the first stage and the rest folded in just before baking.

☐ *The trick for a perfect lemon meringue pie is to make sure the meringue thickly covers the whole surface of the lemon — otherwise it looks unattractively wet.*

PHOTOGRAPH ON P.122

Perfect scambled eggs are more difficult to achieve than many cooks realize. Here the cook learns the correct method for creamy smooth eggs. The pigeon balls (which are stuffed with butter) are simply made, but perfect evenly shaped balls take time and care to produce. The cook learns the technique of wrapping a farce round chilled butter and of steaming to preserve the bright colour of the mint. Producing a faultless Tarte Tatin is a triumph well worth the trouble this upside-down pie involves. Altogether a tricky menu for the more confident cook.

MENU LESSON 19

Scrambled eggs with smoked salmon

Minted pigeon balls

Fresh tomato sauce (see p.212)

Pasta

Bitter salad

Tarte des demoiselles Tatin with crème fraîche

WORK PLAN

- The tarte is at its best lukewarm so make it an hour or so ahead of time.
- Prepare the crème fraîche the day before, or buy it on the day.
- The tomato sauce and salad (not dressed) keep well once prepared.
- Pasta, cooked and buttered or oiled, will stay warm for half an hour without coming to grief.
- The pigeon balls can be prepared several hours in advance and kept refrigerated. But it is important to steam them (and to scramble the eggs, of course) at the last minute.

SCRAMBLED EGGS WITH SMOKED SALMON

INGREDIENTS (Serves 4 as a first course, 2 as a main course snack)
4 eggs
A little butter
Salt and freshly ground black pepper
55g/2oz chopped smoked salmon

1 Beat the eggs and strain to remove the threads.

2 Melt the butter in a saucepan. Tip in the eggs, season with a little salt and pepper. Stir until just beginning to thicken. Add the smoked salmon and serve before it has time to overcook and become grainy and watery.

NOTE This is delicious served with strips of hot pitta bread for a first course or on wholemeal toast as a snack.

SCRAMBLED EGGS

1 For 'wet' scrambled eggs proceed slowly and stop stirring just before the eggs set. They continue to cook while being served.

2 For 'dry' scrambled eggs continue a few seconds more and stop when still moist but no longer runny.

1

2

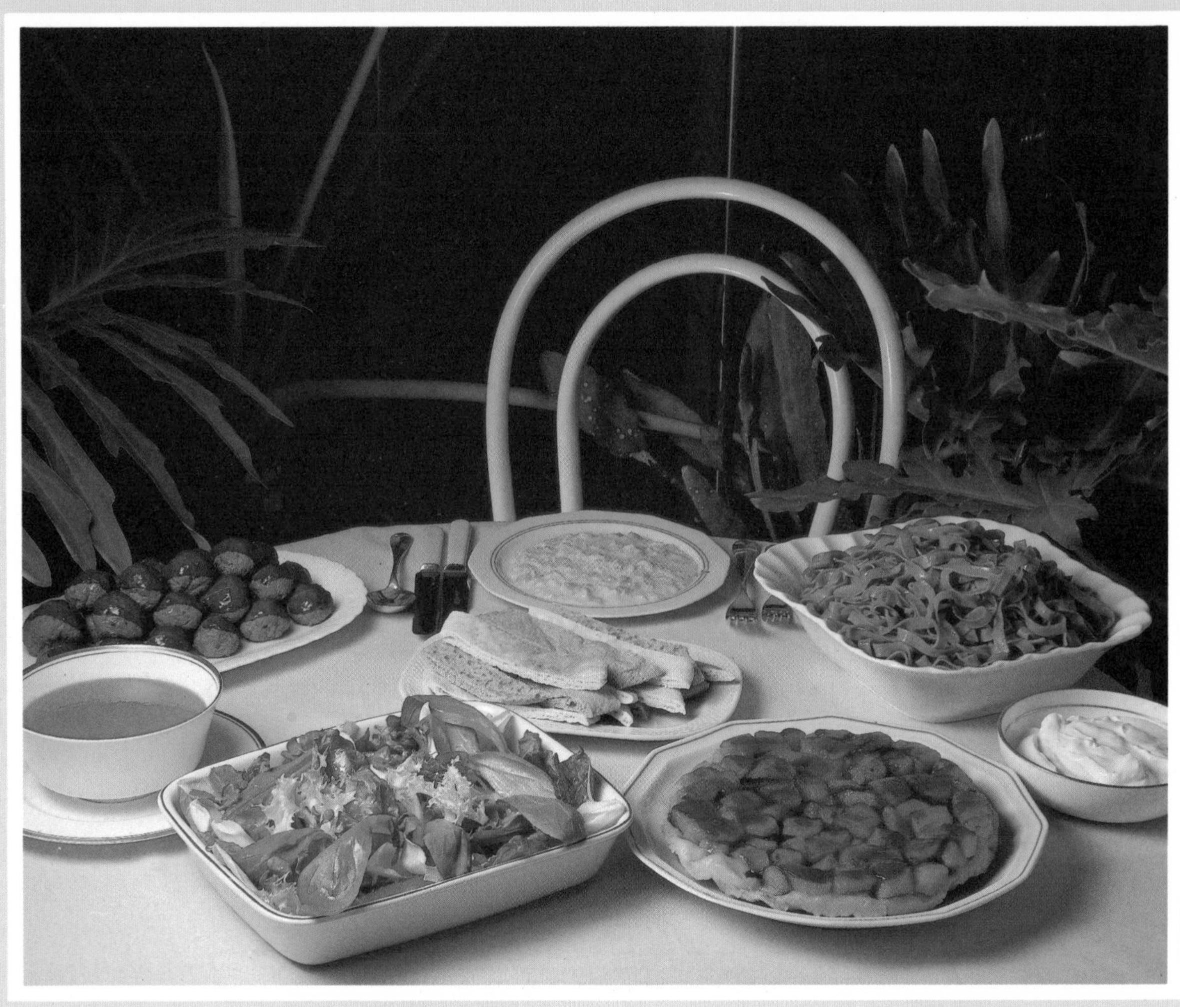

MENU LESSON 19 *(see p.121)*
Anyone can make scrambled eggs — but can they? They are more difficult to perfect than many cooks realize. *Clockwise from top left:* Minted pigeon balls, scrambled eggs with smoked salmon, pasta, crème fraîche, tarte des demoiselles Tatin, bitter salad, fresh tomato sauce and (*centre*) pitta bread.

MENU LESSON 20 *(see p.128)*
This is an inexpensive menu, but it teaches several lessons — careful tasting, judicious seasoning and neat presentation. *Clockwise from top left:* Spinach timbale with tomato and thyme dressing, trois sorbets, baked gnocchi, collops of pork with prunes, carrots and turnips, and green salad.

MINTED PIGEON BALLS

INGREDIENTS (Serves 4)
3 pigeons
85g/3oz unsalted butter, well chilled
2 small shallots
170g/6oz piece streaky bacon
Fresh thyme and a few leaves of rosemary
A little brandy
Fresh mint leaves
Salt and freshly ground black pepper

☐ *The pigeon balls, made rather smaller than here, can also be served as a first course or as hot cocktail party snacks.*

1 Skin the pigeons and take the flesh off the bones. Keep the carcases for stock or soup for another dish.

2 Cut 75g/2½oz of the butter first into cubes, then roll into 30 little balls the size of a hazelnut (or use a small melon-baller to scoop out the balls) and put them in the freezer.

3 Chop the shallot finely and cook in the remaining butter until soft.

4 Put the pigeon flesh, bacon, shallot, thyme and rosemary together in the food processor and work until smooth (or mince finely).

5 Moisten your fingers with brandy and shape the farce (pigeon mixture) around the butter balls. Place a mint leaf firmly on each ball.

6 Put the balls on a steamer rack over boiling water and steam, covered, for 8 minutes. Serve immediately.

PASTA

INGREDIENTS (Serves 4)
450g/1lb strong flour
Pinch of salt
5 eggs
1tbsp oil

1 Sift the flour and salt on to a wooden board. Make a well in the centre and drop in the eggs and oil.

2 Using the fingers of one hand mix together the eggs and oil, and gradually draw in the flour. The mixture should be a very stiff dough.

3 Knead until smooth and elastic (about 15 minutes). Wrap in polythene and leave to relax in a cool place for 1 hour.

4 Roll one small piece of dough out at a time until paper thin. Cut into the required sized noodles.

5 To dry, hang over a chair back if long noodles, or on a wire rack or dry tea-towel if small ones, for at least 30 minutes before boiling.

NOTE To flavour pasta simply add any of the following flavourings with the eggs:
TOMATO PASTA Add approximately 2 tsp tomato purée.
HERB PASTA Add plenty of chopped very fresh herbs to taste. For example: parsley, thyme and tarragon.
BEETROOT PASTA Add 1 small, cooked, puréed beetroot.
CHOCOLATE PASTA Add 55g/2oz melted, cooked chocolate. This is delicious served as a hot pudding with cream.

BITTER SALAD

INGREDIENTS (Serves 4)
Any or all of the slightly bitter leaves: watercress, radicchio, young kale, curly endive, young spinach, chicory, lamb's lettuce.

FOR THE DRESSING
3tbsp salad oil
1tbsp olive oil
1tbsp red wine vinegar
1tsp French mustard
Salt and pepper

1 Put the dressing ingredients into a screw topped jar and shake well.

2 Wash and dry the salad leaves, discarding any tough stalks.

3 Toss the salad in the dressing and tip into a clean bowl.

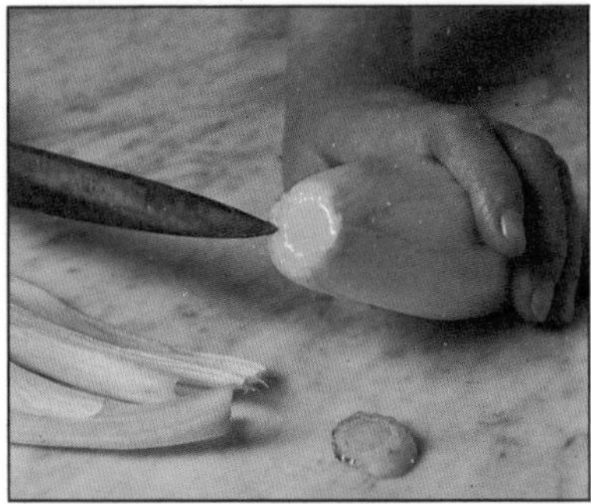

CORING CHICORY
1 Slice off the root. (The milky ring marks the edge of the core.)

2 Remove any tough outer leaves. Then, insert the knife and cut carefully around the core.

3 Ease out the cone-shaped core.

TARTE DES DEMOISELLES TATIN

INGREDIENTS (Serves 4)
900g/2lb dessert apples (preferably Russets)
55g/2oz butter
55g/2oz soft dark brown sugar
Grated rind of 1 lemon
170g/6oz rich shortcrust pastry (see p.192)
85g/3oz granulated sugar

TO SERVE
Crème fraîche or whipped cream

□ *If the tarte, on turning out, does not have quite the glazed brown top it should, melt a little sugar, boil it to a caramel (see p.106) and pour over.*

1 Set the oven to 200°C/400°F/Gas 6.

2 Peel, core and cut the apples into chunks. Melt the butter in the bottom of a cake tin,preferably a moule à manquér, add the sugar and hold over direct heat to caramelize slightly. Add the apples and lemon rind and turn in the butter and sugar until well coloured. Do not worry if there are a few sugar lumps — they will dissolve in the oven. Press the apples down firmly. The tin should be absolutely full.

3 Roll out the pastry and cover the cake tin with it.

4 Bake for 30 minutes, or until the pastry is golden brown.

5 Loosen the pastry and carefully tip any excess juice into a saucepan.

6 Turn the pie upside down onto a plate. Cool to lukewarm.

7 Not more than an hour before serving, add the granulated sugar to the juices in the pan and put over gentle heat to dissolve. Once clear, boil rapidly to a clear toffee and immediately pour evenly over the apples (take great care when boiling sugar — it is dangerously hot). Leave to set to a cracknel as it cools.

8 Once the top is hard serve as soon as possible (the toffee will dissolve after an hour or so, and run out of the tart). Hand the whipped cream or crème fraîche separately.

CREME FRAICHE

INGREDIENTS
570ml/1pt whipping cream
1½tbsp buttermilk

1 Put the cream and buttermilk into a large saucepan. Put over a gentle heat and bring it up to 24° -29°C (75° -85°F), but no hotter or it will not work. At this point it will feel just warm.

2 Remove from the heat, cover and leave in a warm place (such as an airing cupboard) overnight.

NOTE 1 To whip crème fraîche put it in the refrigerator, and put a bowl and a whisk into the freezer for half an hour before use. It will not whip very stiffly.

NOTE 2 Crème fraîche does have a slightly sour or tart flavour. Many people like it sweetened with a little sifted icing sugar.

MENU LESSON 21 *(see p.133)*
Reversing the usual pattern this menu follows a hot starter with a cold main course. *Clockwise from top left:* New potato salad with sour cream, carrot and Gruyère timbales with tomato sauce, ceviche, fennel and red pepper salad and red and blackcurrant flan.

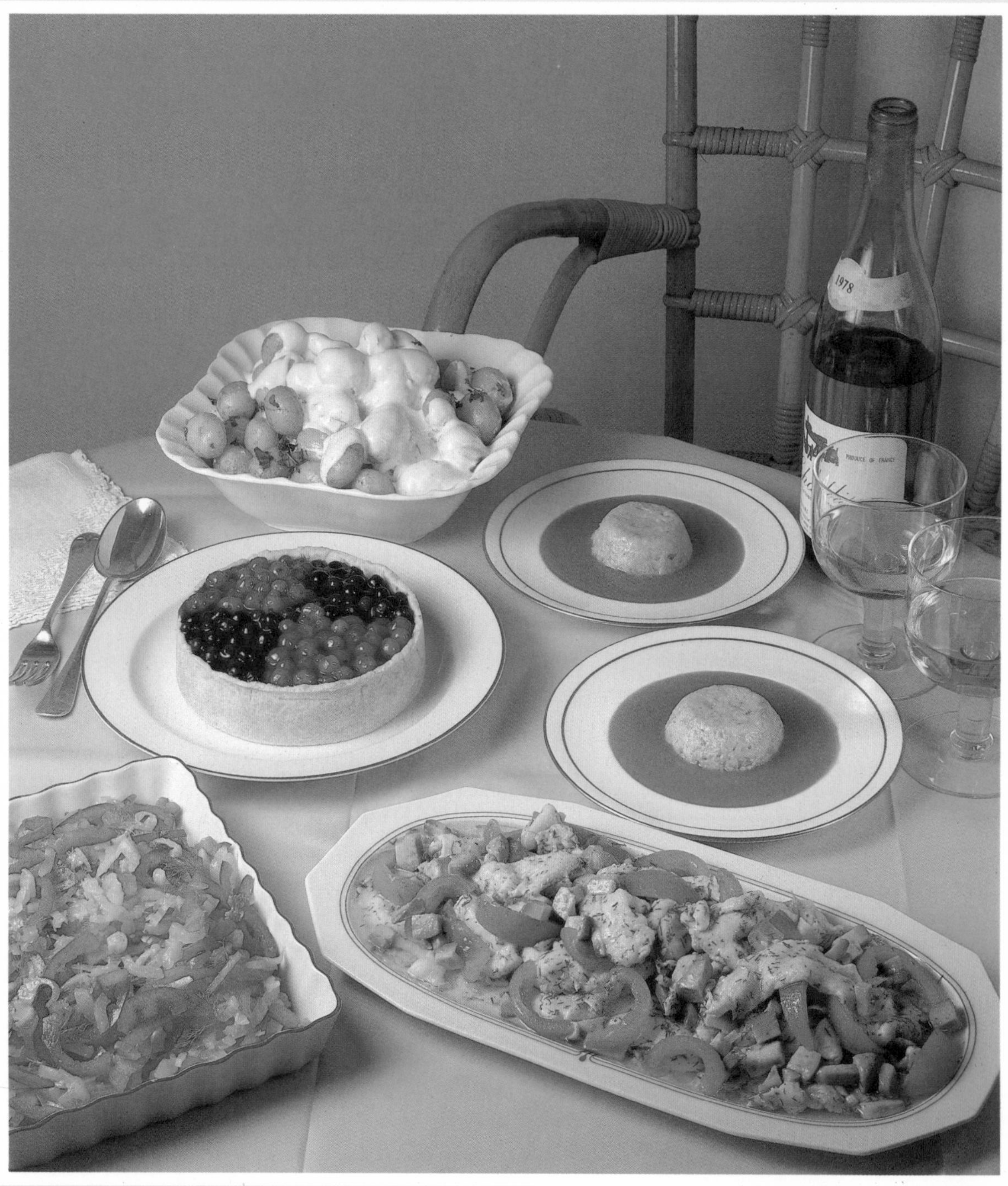

MENU LESSON 22 *(see p.136)*
This sophisticated, good-looking, light summer meal is easy to prepare. *Clockwise from top left:* Pinwheel cookies, green salad, sauté potatoes, tomato, mozzarella and avocado pear salad, blackcurrant fool and (*centre*) rack of lamb with herbs.

PHOTOGRAPH ON P.123

This menu is simple, elegant and not too expensive. The spinach purée must be well and carefully seasoned if it is not to be overpowered by the piquant dressing. The pork and sorbet recipes emphasize the same lessons — careful tasting, judicious seasoning and neat precise presentation. The technique that the cook will find the hardest is that of 'turning' vegetables — a skill that is rarely mastered at the first attempt. But persistence will be rewarded with the satisfaction of professional looking, neat and uniform vegetables.

MENU LESSON 20

Spinach timbales with tomato and thyme dressing

Collops of pork studded with prunes

Baked gnocchi

Green salad (see p.139)

Trois sorbets

WORK PLAN

- The spinach timbales and their dressing can be made in advance — they are best eaten cooled to lukewarm. If allowed to become stone cold, reheat them gently by standing in a dish or roasting pan of hot water.
- The preparation, but not the cooking of the pork and gnocchi, can be done ahead of time.
- The sorbets are best made between 6 and 24 hours ahead of time.

SPINACH TIMBALES WITH TOMATO AND THYME DRESSING

INGREDIENTS (Serves 4)
675g/1½lb fresh spinach
30g/1oz butter
85g/3oz fresh white breadcrumbs
2 eggs, beaten
1 egg yolk
Pinch of ground nutmeg
Salt and freshly ground black pepper
345ml/12fl oz milk

FOR THE TOMATO AND THYME DRESSING
12 fresh tomatoes
1tsp sunflower oil
Chopped fresh thyme
2tbsp plain yoghurt
1tsp lemon juice

1 PREPARE THE DRESSING Prick the tomatoes with a sharp knife to puncture the skin then dip them into boiling water for 10 seconds. Peel. Cut into quarters and remove the seeds. Chop finely.

2 Heat the oil in a frying pan, add the tomatoes and cook rapidly until almost all the liquid has evaporated, taking care not to allow the mixture to 'catch'.

3 Add the very finely chopped thyme. Allow to cool and mix with the yoghurt and lemon juice. Set aside.

4 MAKE THE TIMBALES Wash the spinach well and remove the tough stalks. Put, still wet, into a saucepan with a lid and, holding the pan in one hand and the lid on with the other, shake and toss the spinach over a gentle heat until it is soft and reduced in quantity.

5 Drain well and remove about 15 of the best and biggest leaves carefully. Drain these on absorbent paper.

6 Squeeze all the water from the remaining spinach, pressing it between two plates. Tip on to a board and chop very finely. Butter 4 ramekin or small soufflé dishes and line with the whole spinach leaves.

7 In a saucepan melt the butter, add the spinach and stir until fairly dry looking. Take off the heat and add the breadcrumbs, eggs, egg yolk, nutmeg and seasoning.

8 Heat the milk and stir it into the mixture.

9 Spoon the spinach mixture into the moulds and cover with buttered foil or greaseproof paper.

10 Heat the oven to 180°C/350°F/Gas 4. Stand the ramekins in a roasting pan full of boiling water. Transfer both roasting tin and spinach mould to the oven and bake for 25 minutes or until the mixture is firm.

11 Turn out onto a serving dish or onto individual plates. Spoon a little of the tomato dressing onto each plate and serve the timbales whilst still warm.

COLLOPS OF PORK STUDDED WITH PRUNES

INGREDIENTS (Serves 4)
8 thick pork medallions cut from the fillet, each weighing about 70g/2½oz
8 prunes
Salt and freshly ground black pepper
Flour
Oil
Butter
150ml/¼pt white wine
150ml/¼pt brown stock (see p.268)
30g/1oz unsalted butter, cut into 4 and chilled

TO GARNISH
8 prunes
8 turned carrots
8 turned turnips
Butter
Parsley

1 PREPARE THE PRUNES Put all 16 into a saucepan of cold water. Bring up to the boil. Tip half the water into a bowl and add 8 of the prunes. Leave them to soak for 30 minutes. Meanwhile cook the remaining 8 prunes (for the garnish) until tender — about 20 minutes if they were very hard. Drain, cut in half and reserve.

2 With a sharp knife pierce the medallions in two places and push half a prune (from the uncooked lot) into each hole. Season the medallions with salt and pepper and dust lightly with flour. Put them on a plate without allowing them to touch (the flour coating will be spoiled by moisture if they do).

3 TURN THE CARROTS AND TURNIPS Cut them into 5cm/2 inch long pieces. Square off the sides so you have a rectangular block. With a short, firm, sharp knife shave (or 'turn') the side edges of the block so that you get a multi-sided barrel shape, slightly fatter in the middle than towards the ends. This is difficult to do at first so do not despair if they are not a great success to begin with (see p.150 for illustration). Cook until tender and drain well.

4 Heat a little oil in a very large heavy frying pan. When hot add the butter. Add the medallions and cook quickly to lightly brown them on both sides. Reduce the temperature and sauté slowly, constantly basting them with the fat in the pan. Stop when they feel just firm (neither squashy nor unyieldingly hard) to the touch — about 10 minutes.

5 Remove the medallions and keep warm while you prepare the sauce in the frying pan and reheat the garnish: tip off *all* the fat from the frying pan, add the wine and reduce, by boiling rapidly, by about half. Add the stock and boil hard for 2 minutes. Strain through a sieve into a small saucepan and place over a moderate heat.

6 'MOUNT' THE SAUCE with the butter. Whisk in the pieces of butter one by one. Keep the sauce as hot as possible without boiling. The butter should be whisked to a smooth emulsion. Adding too much butter at once will lead to the sauce separating. It should thicken a little and have a shiny appearance.

7 Flood the base of 4 warmed meat plates with the sauce. Arrange the pork medallions, turned vegetables and prunes on top of the sauce and sprinkle with the chopped parsley.

☐ *If 'turning' vegetables does not come easily, try the technique whenever you can: if preparing potatoes for puréeing, or courgettes or carrots for soup or stock, turn them first, just for the practice.*

BAKED GNOCCHI

INGREDIENTS (Serves 4)
290ml/½pt milk
55g/2oz semolina
Salt and pepper
Pinch of grated nutmeg
55g/2oz freshly grated Parmesan cheese
1 beaten egg
Oil and butter for greasing baking tray and dish

1 Bring the milk to the boil in a heavy based saucepan. Sprinkle in the semolina and stir while it thickens to a heavy paste. Cook gently, stirring occasionally, for 10 minutes. Take care — it can bubble and splash.

2 Remove from the heat, beat in the salt, pepper, nutmeg and all but 1tbsp of the cheese. Grease a small baking sheet and spread the gnocchi dough onto it using first the back of a spoon then, as it cools, pat it flat with your hand. Allow to cool.

3 Stamp out rounds with a cookie cutter, or cut into diamond shapes.

4 Butter an ovenproof dish, put in the gnocchi, brush the tops with beaten egg and scatter over the remaining cheese.

5 Heat the oven to 200°C/400°F/Gas 6. Bake for 15 minutes or until brown on top.

NOTE Single cream poured all over the gnocchi before baking (it will take about 290ml/½pt) gives a softer more luxurious dish that can be served for a first course. But the more usual gnocchi, as here, are served dry as an accompaniment to meat dishes.

TROIS SORBETS

INGREDIENTS (Serves 4)
Pear sorbet (see next recipe)
Passionfruit sorbet (see p.132)
Redcurrant sorbet (see p.132)

FOR THE COULIS ROUGE
225g/8oz raspberries
1tbsp water
1tbsp caster sugar

FOR THE DECORATION (optional)
1 small punnet fresh raspberries
1 small punnet fresh strawberries
1 large seedless orange OR 2tbsp half-whipped double cream

1 PREPARE THE COULIS ROUGE Put all the ingredients into a thick bottomed saucepan. Bring slowly to the boil to allow the sugar to dissolve. Then boil hard for one minute to make the sauce clear and shiny. Leave to cool, then refrigerate.

2 If using the fruit for decoration, hull the strawberries and slice them if large. Peel the orange and cut it into segments as illustrated on p.38. Put all the fruit in the refrigerator, keeping the varieties separate.

3 Chill 4 dessert plates in the refrigerator. Put a baking sheet into the freezer.

4 MOULD THE SORBETS, as illustrated, with 2 dessert spoons. Put the egg shaped sorbets onto the frozen baking tray and return to the freezer until ready to dish up.

SHAPING SORBETS
1 Use two matching dessert spoons (or teaspoons for smaller egg shapes). Fill one spoon with sorbet mixture.

2 Use the other, reversed so the back of the spoon is uppermost, to pat down and smooth the top.

3 Then press down gently while pushing the top spoon down and away from you, thus scraping off the excess on the far side.

4 Scoop up the sorbet in the top spoon (the one in your right hand).

5 And place it back in the left-hand spoon, scraping off the excess down and towards you with the right-hand spoon as you do so.

6 Repeat until you have a smooth, even egg-shape. Lay the sorbets carefully on a well chilled plate to serve.

5 Pour the sauce onto the plates first, then arrange the sorbet as shown and either feather the sauce with the half-whipped double cream (see p.325 for instructions), or, if using the fruits for decoration, put a neat pile of each fruit on each plate between the sorbets. Serve at once.

NOTE Other fresh fruits and sorbets may be combined, with or without a fruit sauce. For example, sorbets of Kiwi fruits, mango and strawberries could be accompanied by matching fruits, or champagne and China tea sorbets could be accompanied by black and white halved and seeded grapes and a few fresh mint leaves.

PEAR SORBET

INGREDIENTS (Serves 4)
4 William pears
155g/5½oz icing sugar
Juice of 2 lemons
1 egg white

1 Peel, core and quarter the pears.

2 Put the pears into a saucepan with the sugar and enough water to just cover. Poach gently for 10–15 minutes.

3 Remove the pears and reduce the cooking liquor by rapid boiling until thick and syrupy. (It should feel tacky and silky when tested between finger and thumb). Purée the pears, sugar, syrup and lemon juice in a liquidizer or food processor.

4 Allow to cool and then freeze.

5 When nearly frozen return the sorbet to the chilled bowl of a food processor and process briefly. Whisk the egg white until stiff but not dry and add it, by degrees, while the processor is on. The sorbet should double in bulk. In the absence of a food processor fold the lightly whisked egg white into the nearly frozen pear purée.

6 Freeze until firm.

NOTE This is an excellent method of sorbet making using a processor. But these ices can also be made by any of the methods described on p.326.

POURING FROM PROCESSORS
Keep the processor-blade from falling out of the up-turned bowl by holding it in place with a finger in the spindle hole under the bowl.

PASSIONFRUIT SORBET

INGREDIENTS (Serves 4)
170g/6oz granulated sugar
425ml/¾pt water
Pared rind and juice of 1 lemon
450g/1lb passionfruit pulp — 25-30 passionfruit
½ egg white

1 Dissolve the sugar in the water over gentle heat. Add the lemon rind. Boil rapidly for 8–10 minutes or until the syrup feels very tacky and a short thread will form between finger and thumb.

2 Strain the sugar syrup into the passionfruit and add the lemon juice. Cool and freeze.

3 When nearly frozen, process the sorbet briefly in a chilled food processor bowl. Whisk the egg white until stiff but not dry and add it, by degrees, to the mixture while the processor is on. In the absence of a processor, whisk the egg white by hand and fold it into the half-frozen mixture. (Do not use a liquidizer as this breaks up the black seeds.)

4 Freeze again until firm. Whisk briefly with a fork every hour or so as the mixture freezes, to ensure a smooth texture.

NOTE Passionfruit pulp can be strained to remove the seeds, but though they are tasteless, they lend a pleasant crunchiness to the texture.

REDCURRANT SORBET

INGREDIENTS (Serves 4)
225g/8oz granulated sugar
290ml/½pt water
450g/1lb redcurrants
7g/¼oz gelatine
Juice of ½ orange

1 Dissolve the sugar in the water over a low heat. When completely dissolved boil until the syrup feels very tacky when tested between finger and thumb. This will take between 8 and 10 minutes.

2 Using a fork, strip the redcurrants from the stalks. Liquidize, then push through a sieve. You should get about 570ml/1pt of redcurrant juice.

3 Put 2tbsp juice into a small saucepan and sprinkle over the gelatine. Leave to 'sponge' for 3 minutes.

4 Add the orange juice to the redcurrant purée. Mix with the sugar syrup.

5 Dissolve the gelatine, without boiling, over a gentle heat and add it to the redcurrant mixture.

6 Cool and freeze until almost frozen.

7 Re-whisk in a chilled bowl until smooth, then refreeze until solid. Or freeze until solid then cut into blocks and whisk in a processor until creamy and smooth. Refreeze.

PHOTOGRAPH ON P.126

This menu reverses the usual pattern, with the first (hot) course followed by a cold main course. It would be particularly suitable for a late summer lunch when black and redcurrants are in season. The techniques used include the gentle poaching au bain marie of the timbales and the marinading of the raw fish for the ceviche.

The flan is an interesting recipe. The pastry shell is protected from the juices of the fruits by a thin layer of sponge cake and the fruits are softened by maceration rather than by cooking.

Getting a good, deep jam glaze on the flan is a skill worth learning — the amateur cook instinctively goes easy on the jam fearing that a lot of it will make the flan sickly. But in fact the sugar in the glaze is almost the only sweetening that the very tart fruit will get, and it needs it. Also, a good clear smooth shine on a fruit flan is one of the joys of the French pâtissier's window.

MENU LESSON 21

Carrot and Gruyère timbales with fresh tomato sauce

Ceviche

Fennel and red pepper salad

New potato salad with sour cream

Redcurrant and blackcurrant flan

WORK PLAN

- The Ceviche must be prepared in advance and the flan keeps well for up to 8 hours. It could easily be made several hours in advance.
- Neither salad will come to any harm if dressed a few hours in advance.
- The tomato sauce can be made, if necessary, several days before.
- This leaves only the timbales for last-minute cooking, and even they can be put together, if not cooked, ahead of time.

CARROT AND GRUYERE TIMBALES

INGREDIENTS (Serves 4)
170g/6oz grated carrot
85g/3oz grated Gruyère cheese
1 egg
Salt and freshly ground black pepper
¼tsp dry English mustard
2tbsp double cream
Butter

TO SERVE
Fresh tomato sauce (see p.212)

1 Set the oven to 190°C/375°F/Gas 5.

2 Blanch the carrot in boiling salted water for 30 seconds. Refresh under running cold water and drain very well. Mix together the carrot, cheese, egg, salt, pepper, mustard and cream. Beat well.

3 Butter 4 deep moulds or small tea cups and pour in the carrot and cheese mixture. Cover with greaseproof paper and put the moulds into a roasting tin half filled with very hot water.

4 Bake for 20 minutes.

5 Reheat the tomato sauce if it is cold.

6 Carefully turn each mould out onto a warm serving dish and hand the sauce separately.

CEVICHE

INGREDIENTS (Serves 4)
340g/12oz fillet of monkfish, halibut or sole
1 onion, sliced
Juice of 2 lemons or 4 limes
Large bunch of fresh dill, chopped

1 Trim the monkfish and cut into the thinnest possible slices. If using halibut or sole cut it into fine strips.

2 Put the fish, onion, lime juice and dill together and leave in a cool place for 6 hours, giving an occasional stir. (If the fish is really finely sliced, as little as 30 minutes will do; it is ready as soon as it looks 'cooked' — opaque white rather than glassy.)

☐ *Use only the freshest fish for ceviche. It is eaten raw and any pronounced 'fishy' smell will ruin it.*

3 Remove the onion and season with salt and pepper.

NOTE Extra ingredients can be added, just before serving, such as slices of avocado pear; fresh, seeded and chopped red and and green chillies; peeled, seeded tomatoes or sliced red or green peppers.

PREPARING TOMATOES

1 Make a small cross in the skin of each tomato where the stalk was attached to the fruit.

2 Dunk in boiling water for 10 seconds (more if under-ripe, less if very soft) and immediately transfer to cold water to stop further cooking. Peel off the skins, starting at the 'nicked' point near the stalk. They should come away easily.

3 Cut the tomatoes from top to bottom in quarters and push out the seeds and fleshy core with your thumb.

4 Cut each quarter into even halves or into finer 'julienne' slices if preferred.

1

2

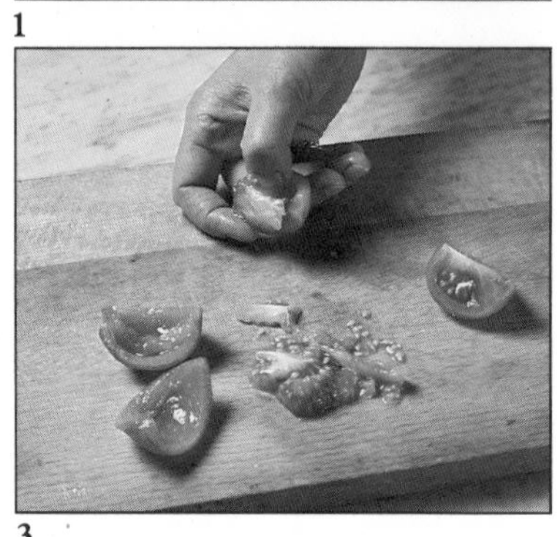

3

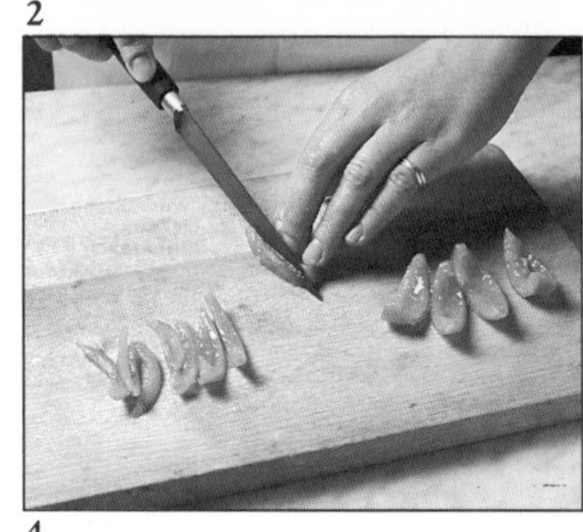

4

FENNEL AND RED PEPPER SALAD

INGREDIENTS (Serves 4)
2 small heads fennel
1 red pepper
French dressing (see p.139)

1 Remove the feathery green tops of the fennel and put aside. Finely slice the fennel heads.

2 Blanch in boiling salted water for 2 minutes. Rinse, until cold, under running cold water. Drain well.

3 Remove and discard the seeds and inner pith from the pepper. Cut the flesh into thin strips.

4 Toss the fennel and pepper together in the French dressing. Tip into a clean salad bowl. Chop the fennel leaves and scatter over the salad.

PREPARING FENNEL

1 Remove discoloured or leathery outer leaves. Split the head in half lengthwise.

2 Remove inner thick core. It may be sliced thinly if liked, or discarded.

1

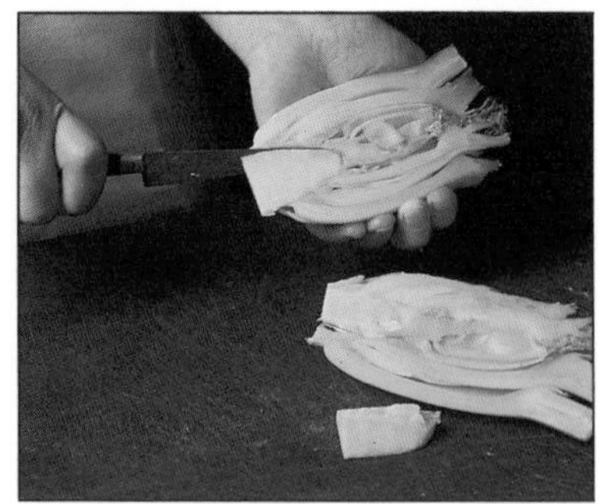

2

NEW POTATO SALAD WITH SOURED CREAM

INGREDIENTS (Serves 4)
450g/1lb new potatoes, scrubbed
A few sprigs of mint
140g/5oz soured cream
1 clove garlic, crushed
1tbsp salad oil
Salt and freshly ground black pepper

1 Boil the potatoes in salted water until tender. Drain. When cold tip into a serving dish.

2 Roughly chop the mint and scatter over the potatoes.

3 Mix all the remaining ingredients together and season with salt and pepper. Pour over the potatoes.

REDCURRANT AND BLACKCURRANT FLAN

INGREDIENTS (Serves 4)
170g/6oz flour-quantity sweet pastry (see next recipe)

FOR THE SPONGE LINING
1 egg
55g/1oz caster sugar
55g/1oz flour, sifted

FOR THE FILLING
170g/6oz redcurrants, fresh or frozen
170g/6oz blackcurrants, fresh or frozen
85g/3oz caster sugar

FOR THE GLAZE
3tbsp redcurrant jelly

TO SERVE
Whipped cream

☐ *Frozen black and redcurrants can be used instead of fresh ones in the flan, as can drained tinned ones.*

1 Strip the redcurrants and blackcurrants off the stalks by holding each sprig of berries by the stalk in one hand and using a fork in the other to dislodge the berries. (If they are frozen, thaw and drain them.)

2 Put the black and redcurrants in separate bowls and add half the sugar to each bowl, shaking to distribute the sugar without crushing the fruit. Leave for 4 hours. (Alternatively, simmer the fruits very gently with the sugar and a few spoons of water for 3 or 4 minutes to soften and cook them.

3 Make up the pastry and use it to line a deep 18cm/7 inch diameter flan ring (see p.190). Refrigerate for 20 minutes.

4 Set the oven to 200°C/400°F/Gas 6.

5 Bake the flan case blind (see p.191) for 15 minutes.

6 MAKE THE SPONGE LINING while the flan case is in the oven. Put the egg and sugar into a bowl and set it over (not in) a pan of simmering water. Whisk steadily until the mixture is thick and mousse-like and the whisk will leave a ribbon-like trail when lifted. Remove from the heat and fold in the sifted flour. Remove the 'blind beans' from the half-cooked flan case. Pour the mixture in and return to the oven.

7 Bake for a further 10 minutes, then remove the flan ring and reduce the oven to 190°C/375°F/Gas 5 and continue cooking until the pastry case is crisp and pale biscuit-coloured, then remove and allow to cool.

8 Strain the fruit well (tipping both juices into a small saucepan) and arrange the black and redcurrants in alternate quarters of the flan.

9 Add the redcurrant jelly to the juice and boil rapidly until syrupy and smooth. Cool until near setting, then spoon over the tart to give it a good clear glaze.

10 Serve with whipped cream, handed separately.

SWEET PASTRY

INGREDIENTS
170g/6oz plain flour
Large pinch of salt
½tsp baking powder
100g/3½oz unsalted butter
55g/2oz caster sugar
1 egg yolk
55ml/2fl oz double cream

1 Sift the flour, salt and baking powder into a large bowl.

2 Rub in the butter until the mixture looks like coarse breadcrumbs. Stir in the sugar.

3 Mix the egg yolk with the cream and add to the mixture.

4 Mix to a firm dough — first with a knife and finally with one hand. Chill, wrapped, for 30 minutes before using (or allow to relax after rolling out but before baking).

PHOTOGRAPH ON P.127

The techniques involved in this light summer menu (making a vinaigrette, roasting lamb, sautéing potatoes to perfection, cooking a simple custard) are not difficult; the time plan is straightforward and the result is a sophisticated good looking and delicious meal.

MENU LESSON 22

Tomato, mozzarella and avocado pear salad

Rack of lamb with herbs

Sauté potatoes

Green salad

Blackcurrant fool

Pinwheel cookies

WORK PLAN

The fool and cookies can be made well in advance; the tomatoes and cheese can be sliced several hours ahead of time but the rest of the meal should be cooked as near to the last minute as possible. Avocado pears go brown if left to stand too long, meat overcooks and loses flavour, potatoes become leathery and salads soggy.

TOMATO, MOZZARELLA AND AVOCADO PEAR SALAD

INGREDIENTS
3 sweet flavoured tomatoes
225g/8oz mozzarella cheese
1 ripe avocado pear

FOR THE DRESSING
4tbsp very fresh walnut oil
2tsp wine vinegar
A few sprigs of fresh basil
Salt and freshly ground black pepper

☐ *Keep mozzarella cheese in a bowl of chilled water until ready for use.*

1 Peel the tomatoes as shown on p.134, and slice.

2 Slice the mozzarella cheese into similar sized pieces.

3 Cut the avocado pear in half. To remove the stone, pierce it with a sharp, firm knife, turn the knife and twist out the stone. Skin the avocado pear and slice.

4 Arrange overlapping slices of tomato, mozzarella and avocado pear on a large flat plate.

5 Mix together the walnut oil and wine vinegar. Season with salt and pepper. Pour it over the salad and add the basil leaves. Cover closely with cling wrap to exclude the air (this will help prevent the avocado pear from going brown) and refrigerate until ready to serve.

RACK OF LAMB WITH HERBS

INGREDIENTS (Serves 4)
Two 7-bone best ends of lamb
55g/2oz butter
2tbsp mixed chopped thyme, mint and rosemary
2tsp Dijon mustard
Freshly ground black pepper
1 glass red wine

TO GARNISH
Bunch of watercress

1 Prepare the racks of lamb, or ask the butcher to do so. The racks must be chined (see p.45). The bones must be shortened, and most of the fat should be removed. For a fancier roast you could make the racks into a 'guard of honour' (see illustrations).

2 Set the oven to 220°C/425°F/Gas 7.

3 Mix the butter with the herbs and mustard. Spread it over the rounded fat side of the lamb. Season with plenty of pepper.

4 Place the racks, curved side up, in a roasting pan and roast for 30 minutes.

5 Halfway through the cooking, pour the wine into the pan next to the meat and add 150ml/¼pt water.

6 When the meat is cooked, remove it to a warmed serving dish and return it to the turned-off oven while preparing the gravy.

7 With a large basting spoon carefully skim off all the fat from the roasting pan without losing any of the meat juices. To lift the last vestige of fat: lay a sheet of absorbent paper on the surface of the liquid and lift off. Boil rapidly until a little less than 290ml/½pt of gravy is left.

8 Place the two racks on a warmed serving dish. Garnish with the watercress. Add any meat juices that have run from the meat to the gravy and pour into a warmed sauceboat.

NOTE This is an unthickened gravy. For one made with flour see p.229.

☐ *Do not season meat for roasting with salt as this tends to draw out the juices.*

RACK OF LAMB

1 Remove the gristle, chine- and blade-bones from the rack as shown on p.45. Turn the rack skin-side up and cut through to the bones about 4cm/1½ inch from the bone-ends.

2 Remove the end piece of skin, fat and meat by lifting and scraping with a knife.

3 Stand the rack on its end and cut the flesh and fat in neat blocks from between the bone-tips.

4 Lay the rack down on the board and scrape the bone ends clean. Try to remove all traces of meat and membrane.

1

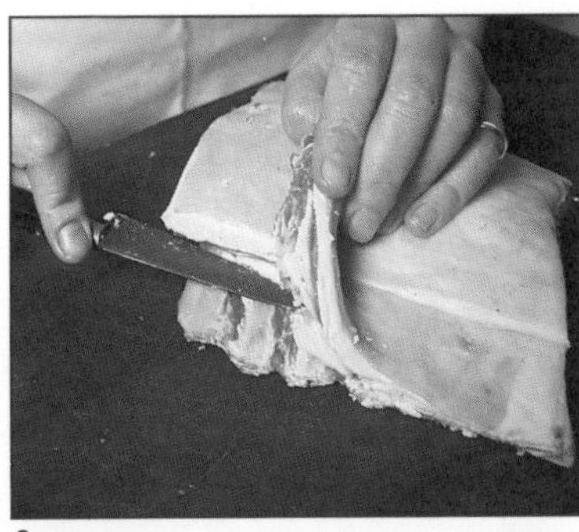

2

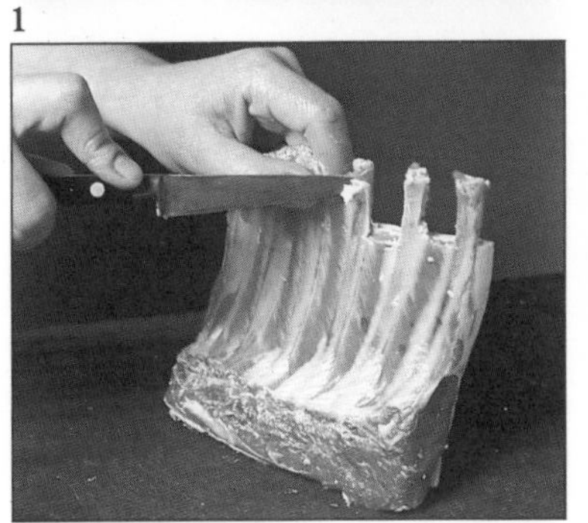

3

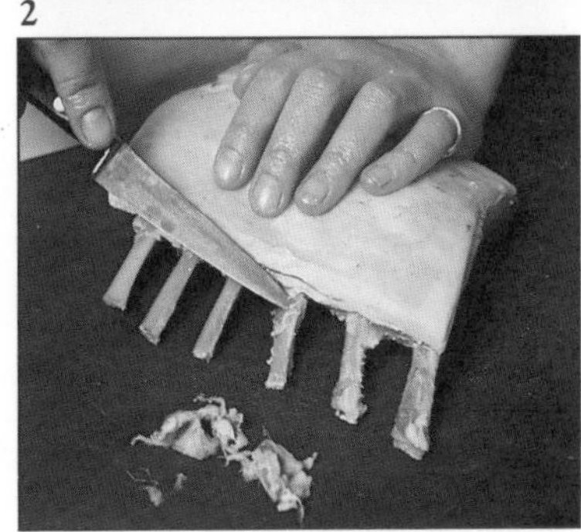

4

5 With the rack skin-side up, ease up a corner of the skin. Pull it away, using the knife to help the process.

6 Trim off any excess fat to leave only a thin covering. The rack can now be covered with mustard, as in our recipe, or criss-crossed as below and roasted plain.

5

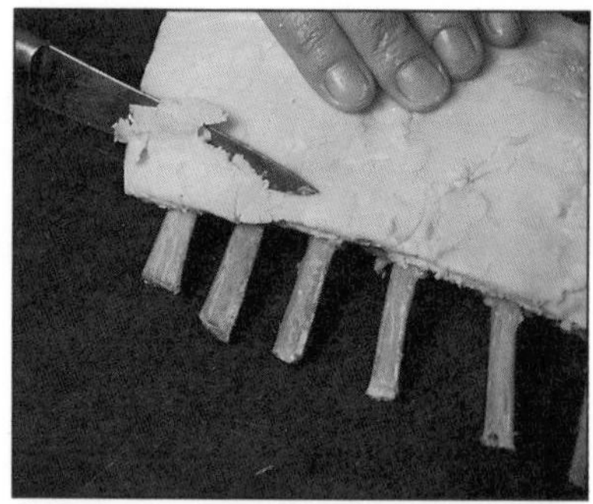

6

GUARD OF HONOUR
1 If you want a more impressive presentation, mark two matching racks (from the same animal if possible) with a criss-cross pattern cut into the fat.

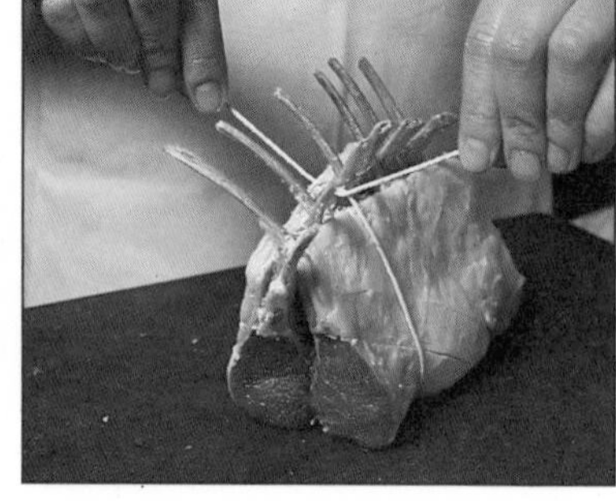

2 Interlock the two racks and tie at intervals with string.

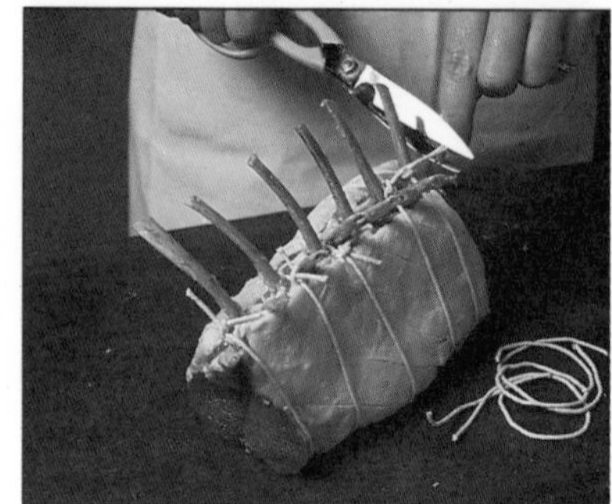

3 Trim off ends of string and roast standing, bones upward. You can prevent the rib-ends from burning by wrapping each one in foil.

SAUTE POTATOES

INGREDIENTS (Serves 4)
675g/1½lb potatoes
2tbsp oil
45g/1½oz butter
Salt and freshly ground black pepper
1tbsp chopped fresh rosemary (optional but good)

☐ *The secret of perfect sauté potatoes is very slow frying. Fast frying gives leathery, instead of crumbly, potatoes.*

1 Wash and peel the potatoes, put into cold salted water, bring to the boil and cook, covered, until just tender. Drain. Cut the potatoes into 2cm/1 inch irregular chunks.

2 Heat the oil and butter gently together in a large sauté pan. When the bubbles have disappeared and the foaming has stopped add all the potatoes at once. (The oil is used for its economy and to provide crispness. The butter is used to give colour and flavour to the potatoes.) Do not allow the pan to get too hot or the butter will burn.

3 Add the salt and pepper. Gently shake the potatoes occasionally to prevent them sticking while they slowly fry to a golden brown. Turn them every so often to ensure an even colour. They will break up a little — they should be fairly dry and crumbly. Do not use more fat than in the recipe and do not fry them too fast — in either case they will become leathery. Good sauté potatoes can take 30 minutes of slow careful frying.

4 When golden and evenly brown add the rosemary, cook for half a minute more and tip into a warmed serving dish.

GREEN SALAD

INGREDIENTS (Serves 4)
1 lettuce (any kind)
French dressing (see below)
Choice of the following:
green pepper, cucumber, fennel, celery, chicory, spring onions, watercress, green beans, peas
1tsp each chopped fresh mint and chives

1 PREPARE THE SALAD INGREDIENTS, which could include
LETTUCE Do not twist or wring the leaves together, which bruises them, but break each lettuce leaf into small pieces individually. Wash, drain and shake or spin dry. (A salad spin-dryer is a useful gadget.)
GREEN PEPPER Wash, cut off the top and remove the seeds (they are very hot). Slice finely.
CUCUMBER Wash. Peel or not, as desired. Slice finely.
FENNEL Wash, cut into quarters. Remove the thick stalk. Slice finely. Reserve the feathery green tops.
CELERY Wash and chop together with a few young leaves.
CHICORY Wipe clean. Remove the tough core with a sharp knife (see illustration p.125). Cut each head at an angle into 3 or 4 pieces, then separate the leaves.
SPRING ONIONS Wash and peel. Chop half the green stalks finely. Keep the white part with the rest of the salad.
WATERCRESS Wash and pick over, discarding the thick stalks and any yellow leaves.
BEANS AND PEAS Cook in boiling salted water until just tender and cool under running cold water. Drain well and pat dry.

2 Add the chopped herbs and the chopped spring onion tops (if used) to the dressing.

3 Mix the salad ingredients together and just before serving toss them in enough French dressing to lightly coat (and therefore flavour) the salad but not so much as to swamp it. Lift into a clean salad bowl. Sprinkle with the feathery tops of the fennel (if used).

BASIC FRENCH DRESSING

INGREDIENTS
3 parts oil
1 part wine vinegar
Salt and pepper

☐ *Basic French dressing can be made and refrigerated. Small quantities can then be flavoured as required.*

Put all the ingredients together in a screw topped jar. Before using shake until well emulsified.

NOTE 1 This dressing can be flavoured with crushed garlic, mustard, sugar, chopped fresh herbs, etc. as desired.

NOTE 2 If kept refrigerated the dressing will more easily form an emulsion when whisked or shaken, and has a slightly thicker consistency. If over-chilled, however, the oil will have an unpleasantly stringy texture and will need gentle warming in the jar under a hot tap.

FRENCH DRESSING

Our recipe is for a basic French dressing but each time a dressing is made the following factors should be considered.

TYPE OF OIL (see p.21). With walnut or hazelnut oil use 5 parts oil to 1 part vinegar; with olive oil (only use virgin oil) use 4 parts oil to 1 part vinegar or lemon juice; with other salad oils use proportions as in the recipe. Do not use any strong flavoured oil (eg sesame, coconut) except in small quantities.

TYPE OF VINEGAR
Always use a good quality wine vinegar. There are many varieties of flavoured vinegars readily available and they should be used in slightly smaller proportions than in the recipe.

WINE SERVED WITH THE SALAD
If good wine is to be served at the same time as the salad keep the acidity of the dressing down to a minimum. Too acid a dressing interferes with the taste of the wine.

BLACKCURRANT FOOL

INGREDIENTS (Serves 4)
225g/8oz blackcurrants
1tbsp water
55g/2oz caster sugar to taste
290ml/½pt egg custard (see next recipe)
150ml/¼pt double cream, lightly whipped

1 Wash the blackcurrants if dusty, and remove stalks but do not 'top and tail'.

2 Add the water and sugar. Stew gently for about 4 to 5 minutes until soft. Liquidize and push through a sieve. Allow to cool.

3 Stir in the custard and half the cream. Turn into a glass bowl and 'marble' or swirl in the remaining cream.

EGG CUSTARD

INGREDIENTS
290ml/½pt milk
20g/¾oz cornflour
2 egg yolks
45g/1½oz caster sugar
3 drops vanilla flavouring
3tbsp cream

This is a thickened custard for use with fools, trifles etc. A more sophisticated, flourless, version is on p.232 and a thicker one for filling profiteroles and éclairs etc. is on p.281. Notes on thickening liquids are on p.279.

1 Mix 1tbsp of the milk with the cornflour and egg yolks. Put the rest into a thick pan to heat. When boiling add the hot milk to the cornflour mixture and then pour this mixture back into the pan.

2 Stir continuously over the heat until the sauce thickens. Boil, stirring, for 30 seconds. Remove from the heat, add the sugar and mix. Allow to cool for 2 minutes and add the vanilla flavouring and cream.

PINWHEEL COOKIES

INGREDIENTS (Serves 4)
100g/3½oz butter
110g/4oz caster sugar
1 egg, lightly beaten
170g/6oz self-raising flour
30g/1oz dark sweetened chocolate

☐ The pinwheel cookes are speedily made in a food processor. Just beat the dough ingredients together, remove half the mixture and add the melted chocolate (or cocoa powder) to the other half and mix.

1 Beat the butter and sugar together until pale and fluffy. Gradually beat in the egg.

2 Work in the flour and divide the mixture in half.

3 Melt the chocolate over a pan of simmering water and work into it one half of the mixture.

4 Spoon the two mixtures onto sheets of clingwrap, wrap up and chill for 30 minutes.

5 Set the oven to 180°C/350°F/Gas 4.

6 Roll out the two doughs to two rectangles about 20×5cm/8×2 inches. To do this without the paste sticking or breaking (it is very rich in fat and therefore liable to do so) follow the instructions with the illustrations opposite.

7 Lay the chocolate dough over the plain biscuit dough, as shown, and roll up.

8 Freeze for one hour to harden.

9 When firm, slice the roll into thin biscuits and bake for 10 to 12 minutes or until evenly pale brown.

PINWHEEL COOKIES

1 Put the chocolate-flavoured dough between two sheets of polythene and gently roll out thinly, through the plastic.

2 Cut off uneven edges and fill any gaps to make an even rectangle. Repeat the process with the plain biscuit-dough.

3 Remove the top sheet of plastic from the rolled-out pastes.

4 Lift the chocolate paste and lay it, bare-side down, on top of the plain paste.

5 Carefully peel off the backing plastic (now on top) from the chocolate dough.

6 Using the remaining under-sheet of plastic to help, roll the dough up together into a tight roll. Keep the plastic parallel to the chocolate dough while you pull it away from you.

7 Cut off the end of the roll and slice the dough into even rounds. Place well apart on greased baking sheets. Bake for 10-12 minutes until a pale, even brown.

8 Leave to cool 2 minutes then lift onto wire rack to cool and become crisp. When completely cold, store in an airtight container.

PHOTOGRAPH ON P.146

This menu emphasizes the importance of attractive presentation, and the first course is arranged on individual plates. But of course one big serving platter could be used instead. Calves liver is simple to cook but it takes practice and some skill to get it right. If the pan is too hot, the liver tends to brown unevenly. If it is too cool the blood leaks from the liver leaving it dry and unattractive. Test for 'doneness' by feeling with a finger (see steaks p.249). The liver should retain some tenderness. If it feels rigidly firm it will be grey and overcooked. Calves liver should have at least a vestige of pink juices inside.

Orange tuiles require concentration and timing. They must be removed at the moment when they are just brown, and shaped at exactly the right temperature — when they are still pliable but not too hot to handle. But their look, and taste, justifies the care they demand.

The ice cream recipe is easily made with an electric hand whisk but small quantities (as here) can be tackled by hand. The sugar syrup must be watched carefully — a minute too long at the boil and it will be caramel.

MENU LESSON 23

Prawn salad

Calves liver with mint and ginger

Boulangère potatoes

Hot raw beetroot

Rich vanilla ice cream

Orange tuiles

WORK PLAN

• The salad can be made a few hours in advance, but should not be over-refrigerated. The tastes are delicate and easily lost by too much chilling.
• The potatoes can be made in advance and kept warm for an hour or so. The beetroot keeps warm well but as it only requires a minute or two's heating anyway, it could be prepared in advance and cooked at the last minute.
• The ice cream may of course be made in advance and is so rich that the texture does not deteriorate in the freezer even if kept for several weeks. The tuiles are wonderful freshly made but are still good if kept in an airtight tin after making.
• The liver is definitely a last-minute affair — liver spoils fast if kept warm and is ruined by reheating.

PRAWN SALAD

INGREDIENTS (Serves 4)
110g/4oz Mediterranean prawns
1 avocado pear
2 oranges
110g/4oz cooked mangetouts
110g/4oz cooked cauliflower florets
Chopped chives
Chopped parsley
French dressing (see p.139)
Salt and freshly ground black pepper

1 Pick over and shell the prawns. Remove the black vein, using a small sharp knife (see p.193).

2 Peel, stone and slice the avocado pear.

3 Peel the oranges, as you would an apple, leaving no pith on the flesh, and cut into segments (see p.38).

4 Toss all the ingredients together in the French dressing. Season well.

5 Serve on individual plates and hand brown bread and butter separately.

PREPARING COOKED PRAWNS
1 Remove the tail by pinching it firmly and pulling it. The tail may be left on if preferred.

2 Carefully peel off the shell and legs and pull away the intestinal thread that runs down the back.

3 The head can be left intact, or it can be gently pulled off the body.

CALVES LIVER WITH MINT AND GINGER

INGREDIENTS (Serves 4)
450g/1lb calves liver
55g/2oz unsalted butter for frying
Salt and freshly ground black pepper

FOR THE SAUCE
150ml/¼pt white veal stock (see p.268)
1 glass red wine
2.5cm/1 inch piece of root ginger, peeled and chopped
1 small onion or shallot, chopped
1tbsp chopped fresh mint
30g/1oz button mushrooms, chopped
2tbsp soured cream

TO GARNISH
Bunch of watercress

1 Prepare the liver and cut into fine slices. Set aside.

2 PREPARE THE SAUCE Put the stock, wine, ginger and shallot together in a small saucepan. Increase the temperature and boil rapidly until reduced to just under half. Strain into a clean saucepan. Add the mint and mushrooms and simmer slowly for 5 minutes.

3 Heat the butter in a frying pan until it stops foaming. Season the liver with salt and pepper and fry quickly in the hot butter until just firm to the touch, but by no means hard. Arrange on a warm serving dish.

4 Pour the sauce into the liver pan and reheat, stirring. Remove from the heat, whisk in the soured cream and pour over the liver. Garnish with a small bunch of watercress and serve immediately.

□ *If the butcher is slicing the liver for you, make sure he does it evenly and thinly. If you cannot trust him, buy a corner piece and do it yourself.*

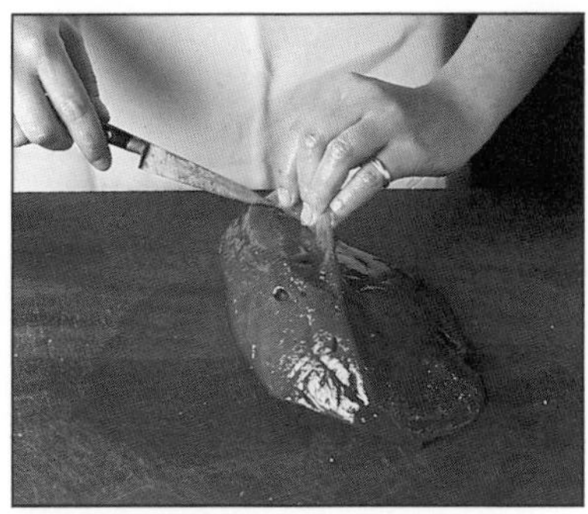

PREPARING CALVES LIVER
1 With a small sharp knife remove the fine membrane that covers the liver. Hold the knife against the liver and gently pull away the skin.

2 Cut into very fine slices with a long, thin knife. Remove any 'tubes' carefully — they are unpleasantly tough when cooked.

BOULANGERE POTATOES

INGREDIENTS (Serves 4)
675g/1½lb potatoes, thinly sliced
55g/2oz butter
1 onion, thinly sliced
Continued on p.144

1 Heat the oven to 190°C/375°F/Gas 5.

2 Butter a pie dish and arrange the potatoes in layers with the onion, adding a little salt and pepper as you go.

Salt and freshly ground black pepper
290ml/½pt chicken stock

☐ *Don't worry if the Boulangère potatoes discolour as you slice them. Just rinse them well. The colour will disappear on cooking.*

3 Arrange the top layer of potatoes in overlapping slices.

4 Dot with the rest of the butter and pour in the stock.

5 Bake in the oven for about 1-1½ hours or until the potatoes are tender and the top browned.

HOT RAW BEETROOT

INGREDIENTS (Serves 4)
450g/1lb raw beetroot
55g/2oz butter
Salt and coarsely ground black pepper
Squeeze of lemon

☐ *Wear rubber gloves to prevent the beetroot staining hands and nails — beetroot juice is almost indelible.*

1 Peel the beetroot and put it through the julienne blade of a processor or grate it on a coarse cheese grater or mandoline.

2 Melt the butter. Toss the beetroot in it for 2 minutes until hot, but by no means cooked.

3 Season with salt, pepper and a sprinkle of lemon juice.

NOTE Raw beetroot in a mustardy vinaigrette is very good too.

RICH VANILLA ICE CREAM

INGREDIENTS (Serves 4)
80g/3oz sugar
3tbsp water
1 vanilla pod or 1tsp vanilla flavouring
425ml/¾pt double or single cream
3 egg yolks (see p.280 for separating eggs)

1 Put the sugar and water into a saucepan and dissolve over a gentle heat.

2 Put the vanilla pod and cream in another saucepan and infuse over gentle heat for 2-3 minutes. Strain and cool. (If using vanilla flavouring do not heat the cream but simply add the vanilla.)

3 When the sugar has dissolved, bring the syrup to boiling point and boil for 2 – 3 minutes 'to the thread'. Allow to cool for 1 minute.

BOILING SUGAR 'TO THREAD'

1 To test density of sugar syrup dip your fingers into cold water and take a pinch of boiling syrup from a spoon. At 103°C/217°F a 'short thread' (1cm/½ inch) should form when fingers and thumb are drawn apart.

2 When the thread does not break until it is 2½-5cm/1-2 inches long it is at 'long thread' and the sugar syrup will be at 110°C/230°F.

1

2

4 Pour the sugar syrup on to the egg yolks (taking care not to hit the wires of the whisk where it would cool and set stickily) and whisk until the mixture is thick and mousse-like, and will leave a ribbon trail when the whisk is lifted.

5 Cool, whisking occasionally. Fold in the cream and freeze.

6 When the ice cream is half-frozen whisk again and return to the freezer.

ORANGE TUILES

INGREDIENTS (Serves 4)
2 egg whites
110g/4oz caster sugar
55g/2oz butter
55g/2oz plain flour
Grated rind of 1 orange

1 Set the oven to 190°C/375°F/Gas 5. Grease a baking sheet.

2 Whisk the egg whites until stiff. Add the sugar and beat until smooth.

3 Melt the butter. Add it to the egg white mixture by degrees with the sifted flour. Fold in the orange rind.

4 Spread out teaspoonfuls, well apart, on the prepared baking sheet and bake until pale brown (5-6 minutes).

5 Shape the tuiles on an oiled rolling pin or the handle of a large wooden spoon.

6 When cold, store in an airtight container.

SHAPING TUILES
1 Thinly spread teaspoons of mixture (well apart) on a greased baking sheet. Bake 5-6 minutes.

2 When brown, loosen the tuiles from the sheet while still hot and pliable. Shape them round an oiled rolling pin, using a cupped hand to press them on to it.

3 As they cool they harden and become crisp. Slide them off the pin and cool on a wire rack.

☐ *Silicone-coated paper used to line the baking trays makes lifting the tuiles very easy.*

MENU LESSON 23 *(see p.142)*
The importance of attractive presentation is emphasized in this menu. *Clockwise from top left:* Hot raw beetroot, boulangère potatoes, rich vanilla ice cream, orange tuiles, prawn salad, calves liver with mint and ginger and buttered brown bread.

MENU LESSON 24 *(see p.148)*
One of the most sophisticated menus in the book, but the result is simple, pretty and delicious. *Clockwise from top left:* Iced borscht with cumin, China tea sorbet in filigree baskets, and seafood feuilletées with steamed turned carrots and potatoes.

PHOTOGRAPH ON P.147

MENU LESSON 24

Iced borscht with cumin

Seafood feuilletées with spinach

Steamed turned carrots and potatoes

China tea sorbet in filigree baskets

This Menu Lesson is one of the most sophisticated in the book, requiring some care on the part of the cook, but the result is simple, light, pretty and delicious. It is important to make neat, evenly sized feuilletées, so take trouble over marking them with a knife blade, to glaze them carefully so they look wonderfully professional, and (most importantly) not to overcook the fish for the filling.

Turning carrots is a chef's trick that is surprisingly difficult to master. If time is short, neat bâtons (rectangular stumpy sticks) or even blocks will do, or the carrots can be peeled and grooved along their length with a canelle knife so that the slices have a pretty decorative border.

The tea sorbet is unusual and intriguing, and very refreshing. An electric sorbetière gives a creamy consistency; making it by the freeze-and-beat method sometimes produces a more grainy granita-like texture, which is pleasant too. Serve in chilled glasses if not making the filigree baskets.

WORK PLAN

- Get the sorbet and soup made well in advance, and turn the vegetables in peace so that there is time to get them right. Keep them under water until it is time to cook them.
- Make the feuilletées on the morning of the dinner or, if that is not possible, not more than a day before. (Keep them in an airtight box overnight.)
- The spinach can be cooked an hour or two in advance.
- This means that just before dinner the cook must simultaneously steam the vegetables, poach the fish and make the sauce, then quickly reheat the spinach and put the feuilletées together. But it sounds more complicated than it is, and can be managed without panic if everything else — table, warm plates, drinks, flowers etc. are already taken care of.

ICED BORSCHT WITH CUMIN

INGREDIENTS (Serves 4)
450g/1lb raw beetroot
570ml/1pt water
Salt and freshly ground black pepper
30g/1oz butter
1 large onion, sliced
225g/8oz raw potatoes, peeled and sliced
425ml/¾pt milk
1tsp cumin seeds OR ½tsp ground cumin
1 chicken stock cube
Juice of ½ lemon
190ml/⅓pt cream
290ml/½pt soured cream
1tbsp chopped fresh chives

1 Wash the beetroot but do not peel them. Boil them in the water with a good pinch of salt for 3 hours or until very tender. Do not throw away the water, but peel the beets, discarding the skins.

2 Melt the butter in a heavy saucepan and in it slowly fry the onion until just turning colour. Add the sliced potatoes and cook over gentle heat for a further 5 minutes.

3 Add the milk, cumin and chicken stock cube. Simmer slowly until the potato is cooked.

4 Put the beetroot and cooking liquid through a liquidizer, vegetable mill or sieve. Then liquidize or sieve the contents of the saucepan. Mix with the beetroot.

5 Add the lemon juice and plenty of pepper. Taste for seasoning, adding salt if needed. Stir in the cream.

6 Chill well. Serve the soup in individual soup plates or cups, with a good dollop of soured cream in each serving, and the top sprinkled with the chives.

☐ *The borscht is good with fresh thyme instead of the cumin, and is delicious hot or cold.*

SEAFOOD FEUILLETEES WITH SPINACH

INGREDIENTS (Serves 4)
340g/12oz flour-quantity puff pastry (see p.85)
1 beaten egg

FOR THE FILLING
900g/2lb fresh spinach
570ml/1pt fish stock (see p.269)
Salt and pepper
110g/4oz cooked prawns
225g/8oz plaice fillets, skinned
110g/4oz scallops
85g/3oz raw scampi
15g/½oz butter
Nutmeg

FOR THE WHITE WINE SAUCE
2 shallots, finely chopped
225g/8oz unsalted butter
100ml/3½fl oz white wine
1tbsp double cream
Juice of ¼ lemon
Salt and ground white pepper

1 Set the oven to 220°C/425°F/Gas 7.

2 MAKE THE FEUILLETEES Roll the pastry into a large rectangle and cut it into 10cm/4 inch diamonds (ie each side should measure 10cm/4 inches). Place them on a dampened baking sheet. Brush with beaten egg. With a sharp knife trace a line about 1.25cm/½ inch from the edge of each diamond, without cutting all the way through the pastry. The central diamonds will form the 'hats' on the pastry cases. Make a design inside this diamond with the knife. Flour the blade of a knife and use this to 'knock up' the sides of the pastry (see illustration on p.70). Chill for 15 minutes.

3 Bake in the heated oven for 20 minutes, or until puffed up and brown. With a knife, outline and remove the 'hats' and scoop out any uncooked dough inside. Transfer the cases and hats to a rack to cool. Reduce the oven to 130°C/275°F/Gas 1.

4 PREPARE THE FILLING Wash the spinach very well and remove the stalks. Put into a pan, with salt, cover and cook gently, shaking the pan occasionally for 5 to 7 minutes. The spinach will reduce in quantity by about two thirds. Refresh under running cold water and drain thoroughly by squeezing between two plates.

5 Put the fish stock into a large shallow pan. Bring up to scalding point and add the fish fillets, poach for 2 minutes, then add the scallops and scampi and poach for a further 2 minutes. Remove from the pan with a slotted spoon. Strain the stock and reduce by rapid boiling to a syrupy 'fish glaze'.

6 MAKE THE WHITE WINE SAUCE Sweat the shallots very slowly in 15g/½oz butter. Add the wine and 1tsp fish glaze. Reduce to half quantity by boiling. Cut the remaining butter into small pieces and gradually whisk it in over a low heat. Sometimes take the pan off the heat — the sauce is inclined to separate if overheated. Work fairly quickly however, as otherwise the sauce will be only just warm and reheating it risks curdling it. Try to keep it just below boiling point. Add the lemon juice and double cream. Taste and add extra fish glaze, and salt and pepper if necessary. Stand the finished sauce in a pan of hot water.

☐ *Frozen puff pastry can be used for the feuilletées. It does not have the rich butteriness of perfect homemade pastry but it is a good product nonetheless.*

7 Reheat the spinach in the butter and season with salt, pepper and nutmeg. Spread some inside each pastry case. Cut the plaice fillets into 3 or 4 diagonal pieces. Arrange with the other seafood on the spinach. Warm in the oven for about 10 minutes.

8 Just before serving, spoon a generous tablespoon of sauce over each feuilletée. Set a hat on top. Hand the rest of the sauce separately in a warmed sauce boat.

STEAMED TURNED CARROTS AND POTATOES

INGREDIENTS (Serves 4)
450g/1lb carrots
450g/1lb potatoes
Salt and freshly ground black pepper
Knob of butter

1 Peel and turn the carrots and potatoes as illustrated overleaf.

2 Steam over a pan of boiling water until tender — about 15 to 20 minutes if they are acorn-sized.

3 Serve with salt, pepper and a very little melted butter.

☐ *If 'turning' vegetables does not come easily, try the technique whenever you can: if preparing potatoes for puréeing, or courgettes or carrots for soup or stock, turn them first, just for the practice.*

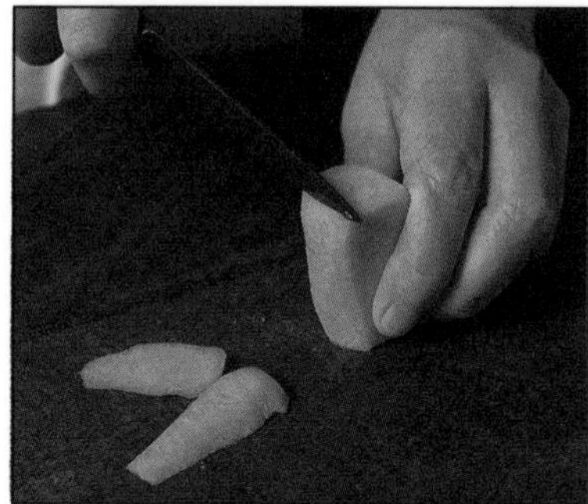

TURNING VEGETABLES
1 Cut into 5cm/2 inch long pieces. Square off the sides to give a rectangular block.

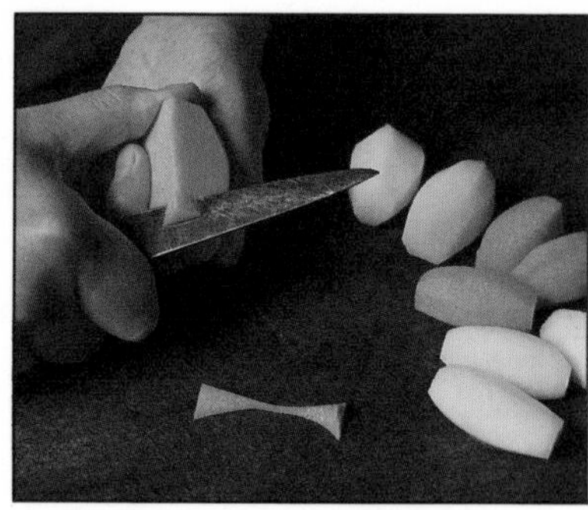

2 Shave off the edges lengthwise, rounding the cuts slightly to give barrel-shapes. Other vegetables, like turnips, can also be prepared in this way.

CHINA TEA SORBET IN FILIGREE BASKETS

INGREDIENTS (Serves 4)
570ml/1pt water
170g/6oz granulated sugar
Thinly pared rind of 2 large lemons (no pith)
Juice of 2 lemons
2tbsp black China tea leaves (eg Lapsang Souchong)

FOR THE FILIGREE BASKETS (optional)
2 egg whites
110g/4oz caster sugar
125g/4½oz plain flour
½tsp vanilla flavouring

1 Put the water, sugar, rind and lemon juice into a saucepan. Boil for 5 minutes.

2 Add the tea. Allow to cool, then strain.

3 Freeze. Whisk frequently during the freezing process to ensure an even consistency, or freeze in an electric sorbetière, or churn (see p.323).

4 TO MAKE THE FILIGREE BASKETS Cut a template out of cardboard to match the shape illustrated. For a basket big enough to hold a ball of sorbet the stencil should be about 5cm/2 inches deep and about 20cm/8 inches long at its widest.

5 Grease and flour a greaseproof paper-lined baking sheet and mark the shape of the template in the flour coating.

6 Set the oven to 200°C/400°F/Gas 6.

7 Whisk the egg whites and sugar together until the whisk will leave a ribbon-like trail when lifted.

8 Sift in the flour, add the vanilla and beat until smooth.

9 Put the mixture into a piping bag fitted with a nozzle with a 'mouth' about 2mm/ $\frac{1}{10}$ inch across, or into a paper piping bag made as illustrated on p.324.

10 Pipe the shapes onto the floured paper.

FILIGREE BASKETS
1 First make the template. Draw a curved line on cardboard round one side of an upturned plate.

2 Draw round a smaller plate or saucer to give two parallel curved lines. Square off the ends and cut out the template to give the shape shown in the next picture.

1

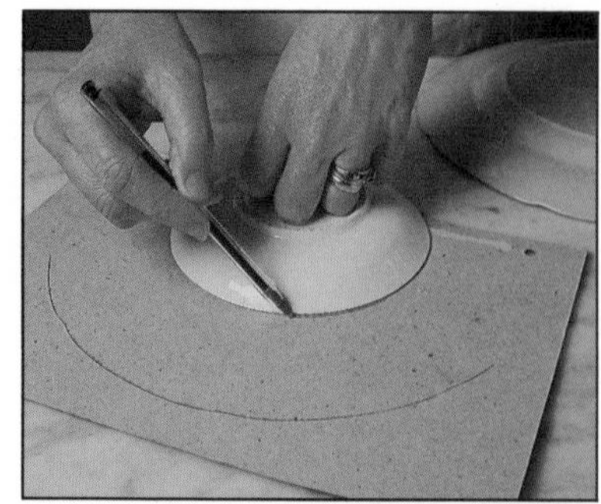

2

3 Lay the template on greased and floured greaseproof paper on a baking sheet and mark the shape with a hard object.

4 Make the biscuit mixture and fill a paper piping bag with it. (For instructions on how to make the bag, see p.324.)

5 Do not overfill the bag. Fold down well to prevent mixture squeezing out of the top.

6 For the first design, pipe around the outline of the marked shape, then fill in the middle with a lattice design. For a basket with a scalloped top, pipe overlapping circles in one continuous movement.

7 Pipe a zig-zag between parallel lines at the narrow edge.

8 Bake only until very pale brown, then ease carefully off the paper with a palette knife.

9 While still hot and pliable, bend to a basket shape and drop into a cup to hold in shape while cooling.

10 Once cold the biscuit will be crisp and rigid and can be extracted. If the shapes cool too fast and become too hard to bend, return them briefly to the oven to soften again.

3 4 5 6 7 8 9 10

11 Bake for 4 to 6 minutes or until just pale brown.

12 Remove from the oven and ease the biscuits off the tray. Have ready 6 smallish conical shaped teacups.

13 Return the biscuits to the hot oven for 30 seconds or just long enough for them to become very pliable again. While hot, curl them round and drop them into the teacups. Allow to cool.

14 Once cold, store in an airtight container until needed.

MENU LESSON 25

Paper-thin raw beef with mustard and horseradish sauce

Vinegar chicken

Pommes Anna (see p.74)

Broad beans

Candied lemon tart

PHOTOGRAPH ON P.155

This menu contains three recipes very dear to the hearts of today's fashionable top-flight French chefs. All require time and a degree of dedication. (The broad beans for example are not only shelled to remove the pod but re-shelled to remove the purplish skins, leaving only the brilliant green inner beans.) But the recipes are very rewarding. The skills learnt are fairly sophisticated. To cut the beef perfectly and painstakingly and to remove every thread of sinew and membrane, takes the beginner more time than the experienced chef, but it is a long process for anyone.

The vinegar chicken is our adaptation of a Michel Guérard recipe to which we have added reduced cream, giving it a milder, richer flavour. The cook learns, perhaps with surprise, that you can boil cream and add vinegar to it without curdling, that half a dozen garlic cloves is not too much for a single chicken, and that with care a perfect buttery mound of over-lapping potatoes can be assembled.

The candied lemon tart is the prince of French fruit flans — freshly made lemon filling in a rich sweet shortcrust.

☐ *If following this menu exactly, go easy on the portions, it is fiendishly rich in animal fats and protein. Except for a very special occasion it might be wise to replace the beef with a simple salad starter (perhaps a julienne of carrot, leek and white mushrooms in a lemony vinaigrette, or a tomato and basil salad), or to omit a first course altogether.*

WORK PLAN

- The steak can be cut, flattened and de-sinewed a few hours in advance, but the slices should not be left one on top of the other — they will discolour. Also, they will need dishing onto clean plates if any blood has leaked from them.
- The dressing can be prepared a few hours in advance.
- The chicken keeps warm for an hour or so satisfactorily but is not good reheated.
- The broad beans can be blanched and skinned a few hours in advance, to be reheated at the last minute in butter in a pan.
- Pommes Anna need to be timed to avoid reheating, although the dish keeps warm well for an hour or so.
- The tart can be made two days before serving. However, it should be decorated at the last minute.

PAPER-THIN RAW BEEF WITH MUSTARD AND HORSERADISH SAUCE

INGREDIENTS (Serves 4)
675g/1½lb fillet steak

This recipe allows 170g/6oz beef per head, which would be adequate for a main course. Halve the recipe quantities for a first course.

1 Cut the fillet steak, across the grain, into very fine slices. Flatten the slices between two pieces of clingfilm using a mallet or rolling pin. Carefully remove all sinews with tweezers or small sharp knife.

FOR THE SAUCE
3tbsp plain yoghurt
3tbsp double cream
3tbsp mayonnaise (see p.61)
1tbsp Dijon mustard
1 level tsp creamed horseradish (see p.231)
Lemon juice

☐ *Chill the beef until almost, but not quite, frozen — it will be easier to slice finely if firm rather than lax and wobbly.*

2 Spread the slices, without overlapping, on large dinner plates.

3 Mix together the first four sauce ingredients.

4 Flavour to taste with the horseradish and lemon juice. Hand the sauce separately.

NOTE Our recipe specifies fillet steak, but any lean tender beef will do. Fillet ends, which are cheaper than steaks, are excellent.

VINEGAR CHICKEN

INGREDIENTS (Serves 4)
One 1.8kg/4lb chicken, jointed into 8 pieces (see p.96)
30g/1oz butter
5 large garlic cloves, unpeeled
5tbsp wine vinegar
290ml/½pt dry white wine
2tbsp brandy
2tsp pale French mustard
1 heaped tsp tomato purée
290ml/½pt very fresh double cream
2 tomatoes, peeled and seeded
Chervil leaves

☐ *Make sure the cream for the chicken dish is very fresh. Less than fresh cream is inclined to curdle in the sauce.*

1 Heat the butter and brown the chicken pieces in it, skin side first. Add the unpeeled garlic and cover the pan. Cook gently for 20 minutes or until the chicken is tender. Pour off all but 1tbsp fat.

2 Add the vinegar to the pan, stirring well and scraping any sediment from the bottom. Boil rapidly until the liquid is reduced to about 2tbsp. Lift out the chicken and keep warm.

3 Add the wine, brandy, mustard and tomato purée to the remaining vinegar in the pan, mix well and boil to a thick sauce (about 5 minutes at a fast boil).

4 In a small heavy bottomed saucepan boil the cream until reduced by half, stirring frequently to prevent burning. Take off the heat and fit a small wire sieve over the saucepan. Push the vinegar sauce through this, pressing the garlic cloves well to extract their pulp.

5 Mix the sauce and add salt and pepper as necessary. Cut the tomato into thin strips and stir into the sauce with the chervil. Arrange the chicken on a hot serving dish, and spoon over the sauce.

NOTE The deliciousness of this dish — and it *is* delicious — depends on the vigorous reduction of the vinegar and wine. If the acids are not properly boiled down the sauce is too sharp.

BROAD BEANS

INGREDIENTS (Serves 4)
450g/1lb shelled broad beans (about 2kg/4lb unpodded weight)
Salt and freshly ground black pepper
Melted butter
1tsp chopped fresh savory

1 Boil the beans in salted water for 4 — 8 minutes or until tender.

2 Run under cold water until cold enough to handle. Slip off the pale purplish green skins and discard.

3 Reheat the beans in a frying pan with the salt, pepper, savory and butter. Toss very carefully as they are inclined to break up.

NOTE Frozen broad beans are perhaps better for this dish, unless truly fresh ones can be had from the garden.

MENU LESSON 25 *(see p.152)*
This menu (*below right*) contains three recipes that are fashionable with today's top-flight chefs. *Clockwise from top left:* Paper-thin raw beef with mustard and horseradish sauce, vinegar chicken, broad beans, candied lemon tart and pommes Anna.

MENU LESSON 26 *(see p.157)*
Here is an unusual combination of the simple and the sophisticated (*right*). *Clockwise from top left:* Apple sauce, boudin noir with hot potato and bacon salad, anchovy butter, spinach soufflé, poached apricots with kernels and (*centre*) macaroons.

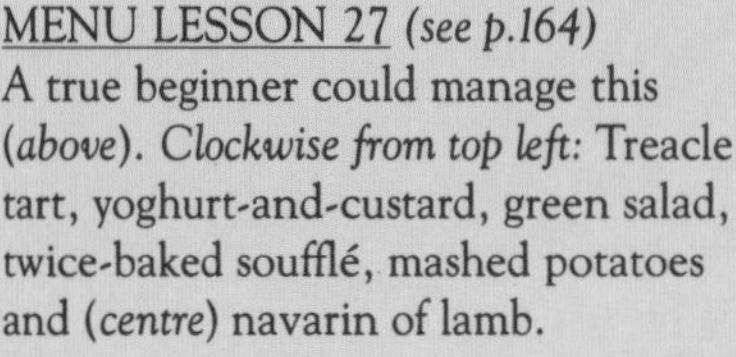

MENU LESSON 27 *(see p.164)*
A true beginner could manage this (*above*). *Clockwise from top left:* Treacle tart, yoghurt-and-custard, green salad, twice-baked soufflé, mashed potatoes and (*centre*) navarin of lamb.

CANDIED LEMON TART

INGREDIENTS (Serves 4)
170g/6oz flour-quantity pâte sucrée (see next recipe)
4 eggs
1 egg yolk
200g/7oz caster sugar
150ml/ ¼pt double cream
Juice and rind of 2 lemons
Icing sugar

TO GLAZE
1 lemon
150ml/ ¼pt sugar syrup (see p.67)

1 Set the oven to 170°C/325°F/Gas 3.

2 Line a 18cm/7 inch flan ring with pâte sucrée. Relax for 30 minutes and then bake blind (see p.191) for 15 minutes. Leave to cool on a wire rack. Reduce the oven to 150°C/300°F/Gas 2.

3 FOR THE FILLING Mix the eggs and extra yolk with the sugar and beat lightly with a whisk until smooth. Add the cream and whisk again. Add the lemon juice and rind. It will thicken alarmingly but do not worry.

4 Put the pastry case back onto a baking sheet and spoon in the lemon filling. Bake for 50 minutes — if it becomes too brown cover the top with a piece of tin foil.

5 While the pie is cooking, prepare the glazed lemon rind. With a potato peeler, pare the rind from the lemon very finely, making sure that there is no pith on the back of the strips. Cut into very fine shreds.

6 Simmer these shreds in the sugar syrup until tender, glassy and candied. Leave to cool on greaseproof paper.

7 When the tart is cooked remove the flan ring and leave to cool.

8 When cool, dust thickly and evenly with sifted icing sugar and arrange the candied shreds on top.

PATE SUCREE

INGREDIENTS
170g/6oz plain flour
A pinch of salt
85g/3oz butter, softened
3 egg yolks
85g/3oz caster sugar
2 drops vanilla flavouring

1 Sift the flour onto a board with the salt. Make a large well in the centre and put the butter in it. Place the egg yolks and sugar on the butter with the vanilla flavouring.

2 'Peck' the butter, yolks and sugar together, as shown. Gradually draw in the flour and knead lightly.

3 If the pastry is very soft, chill before rolling or pressing out to the required shape.

NOTE 1 Pâte sucrée must be allowed to relax for 30 minutes before baking, either before or after rolling out.

NOTE 2 The pastry can be made in a food processor by simply processing all the ingredients together until the paste forms a ball. Do not overwork or the warmth of friction will melt the butter. Chill before rolling or pressing out.

PATE SUCREE
1 Make a ring of sifted flour on the work surface, and put the softened butter in the centre. Make a shallow 'well' in the butter with your fingertips and put the yolks, sugar and vanilla flavouring into it.

2 With the fingertips of one hand, 'peck' the butter mixture until combined and smooth, then gradually draw in the surrounding flour and knead lightly to a smooth ball.

1

2

PHOTOGRAPH ON P.155

This menu is an unusual combination of the sophisticated and the simple. The surprisingly easy lessons of the soufflé are learned. The soufflé is served with anchovy butter, which melts on contact, giving the soufflé richness and an interesting, unusual flavour.

MENU LESSON 26

Spinach soufflé with anchovy butter

Boudin noir

Hot potato and bacon salad

Apple sauce

Poached apricots with kernels

Macaroons

WORK PLAN

- The first things to prepare are the anchovy butter and the apple sauce (which can be refrigerated or frozen), the poached apricots, which will keep refrigerated for 3 or 4 days, and the macaroons, which keep well in a biscuit tin.
- The spinach soufflé base can be made several hours in advance but should (if it has been refrigerated) be rewarmed carefully to soften the mixture before folding in the egg whites. The soufflé, of course, must be timed to emerge from the oven as the guests sit down. (It is better to get them seated with a glass of wine and let them wait a few minutes for the soufflé — they will not notice — than to have the soufflé wait on them and become overcooked in the oven or sunken out of it.)
- Poach the boudin noir and dress the hot potatoes while the soufflé is cooking.

SPINACH SOUFFLE WITH ANCHOVY BUTTER

INGREDIENTS (Serves 4)
110g/4oz sorrel
340g/12oz spinach
Salt and pepper
55g/2oz butter
Dried white breadcrumbs
55g/2oz flour
290ml/½pt milk
Pinch of cayenne
½tsp mustard
55g/2oz strong Cheddar or Gruyère cheese
4 eggs
1tbsp Parmesan cheese

TO SERVE
Anchovy butter (see next recipe)

1 To prepare the sorrel and spinach, remove the stalks and wash the leaves very carefully. Place in a pan of boiling salted water for 2 minutes. Drain very well, squeezing water out through a colander or sieve or between two plates. Chop finely.

2 Set the oven to 200°C/400°F/Gas 6. Lightly butter a 15cm/6 inch soufflé dish or 4 large ramekins. Coat the sides lightly with breadcrumbs.

3 Melt the butter in a saucepan and stir in the flour. Add the milk and bring to the boil, stirring continuously. Boil for one minute.

4 Take the sauce off the heat, stir in the salt and pepper, cayenne, mustard, cheese, spinach and sorrel. Cool slightly.

5 Separate the eggs, adding the yolks to the spinach mixture. Whisk the egg whites until stiff but not dry, and mix a spoonful thoroughly into the spinach mixture. Then gently fold in the rest.

Continued on p.160

MENU LESSON 28 *(see p.169)*
Again, this menu teaches the importance of good presentation. *Clockwise from top left:* Mangetout peas, salmon in pastry, noix au café, tarragon sauce, smoked chicken salad, and cucumber and dill salad.

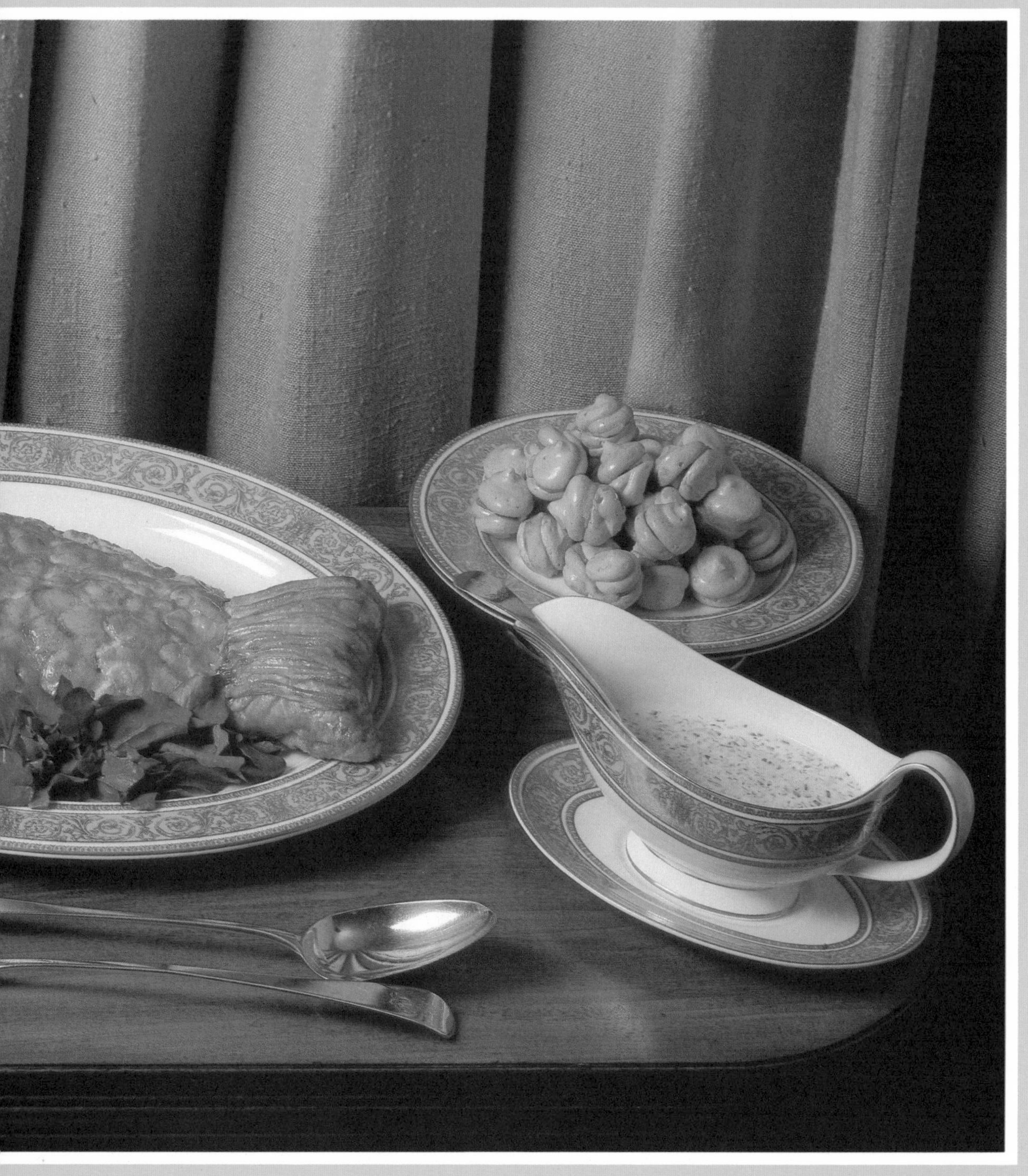

□ See p.41 for the efficient de-stalking of spinach.

6 Pour into the soufflé dish or ramekins, which should not be quite full. With a knife cut through the mixture several times to ensure that there are no large pockets of air. Sprinkle the top with Parmesan cheese.

7 Bake for 20 to 25 minutes or until the soufflé is still moist in the middle but crisp around the edges. (It should not wobble alarmingly when given a slight shove, nor be absolutely rigid.)

8 Hand the anchovy butter separately.

ANCHOVY BUTTER

INGREDIENTS
1 clove garlic
4 anchovy fillets
110g/4oz butter
Freshly ground black pepper
2tsp anchovy essence

1 Crush the garlic. Add the anchovy fillets and pound to a paste. Beat in the butter and season with the pepper and anchovy essence.

2 Spoon the mixture onto a small piece of foil or greaseproof paper. Roll up into a cylinder shape. Chill until hard. To serve, unwrap and cut into slices.

BOUDIN NOIR

INGREDIENTS (Serves 4)
About 675g/1½lb small boudin noir (black pudding or blood sausage)
Hot potato and bacon salad (see next recipe)
Chopped parsley

1 Poach the whole boudin noir, without pricking them, in barely simmering water until warm all the way through. They will probably take 10 minutes.

2 Lift them from the water, and carefully skin them. Slice diagonally in thick slices and arrange the slices, overlapping, down one side of the serving dish, with the hot potato and bacon salad down the other. To slice a curved object, like this sausage, evenly, see slicing a banana on p.207. Sprinkle with parsley and serve at once.

□ Raw beetroot cut or grated into fine julienne strips and tossed in oil until just hot (1-2 minutes) and served with a sprinkling of caraway seeds makes another good accompaniment to the boudin noir. If served with the sausage on a black or purple plate the effect is spectacular.

CHOPPING PARSLEY
1 Hold the tip of a large, heavy knife down with one hand and firmly move the handle up and down with the other, using a sharp cutting action.

2 Use the blade to scrape the parsley into a pile every now and then so that each chop cuts the maximum amount of parsley. Continue until the leaves are finely and evenly chopped.

HOT POTATO AND BACON SALAD

INGREDIENTS (Serves 4)
675g/1½lb potatoes
Sprig of mint
110g/4oz back bacon rashers
French dressing (see p.139)
2tbsp chopped chives
Salt and freshly ground black pepper

1 Peel the potatoes, cut in half and cook in a saucepan of salted water with the mint.

2 While the potatoes cook, remove the rind from the bacon and grill the rashers until crisp but not brittle. Keep warm.

3 Drain the potatoes. Cut into cubes and toss in the French dressing.

4 Cut the bacon into strips and add to the potatoes. Toss in half the chives. Season with salt and pepper. Transfer to a clean dish and sprinkle with the remaining chives, or arrange on a dish beside the boudin noir.

APPLE SAUCE

INGREDIENTS (Serves 4)
450g/1lb cooking apples
Finely grated rind of ¼ lemon
3tbsp water
1tsp sugar
15g/½oz butter

1 Peel, quarter, core and slice the apples.

2 Place in a heavy saucepan with the lemon rind, water and sugar. Cover with a lid and cook very slowly until the apples are soft, shaking the pan frequently to prevent sticking and catching.

3 Beat in the butter. Serve hot or cold.

POACHED APRICOTS WITH KERNELS

INGREDIENTS (Serves 4)
450g/1lb apricots
170g/6oz sugar
570ml/1pt water
Juice of half a lemon

1 Wash the apricots and cut them in half. Put them in a large shallow sauté pan with the stones.

2 In a saucepan dissolve the sugar in the water over gentle heat.

3 Pour over the apricots and add the lemon juice.

4 Bring to the boil and allow the syrup to bubble up over the fruit. (This is to prevent discolouring.)

5 Reduce the heat and poach gently until the apricots are soft but not mushy. This will take anything from 10—25 minutes depending on the ripeness of the fruit. Lift out the apricots with a perforated spoon and carefully remove their skins.

6 Put the apricots into a glass dish and strain over the sugar syrup. Leave to cool.

7 Crack the stones and take out the kernels. Remove the brown skins and chop the kernels. Roughly scatter over the apricots. Serve well chilled.

MACAROONS

INGREDIENTS (Makes 25)
110g/4oz ground almonds
170g/6oz caster sugar
1tsp plain flour
2 egg whites
2 drops vanilla flavouring
Rice paper for baking

FOR DECORATION
Split almonds

☐ *Take care that the macaroons are stone cold before storing in an airtight container — they will soften if stored while warm.*

1 Set the oven to 180°C/350°F/Gas 4.

2 Mix the ground almonds, sugar and flour together.

3 Add the egg whites and vanilla. Beat very well.

4 Lay a sheet of rice paper or vegetable parchment on a baking sheet and with a teaspoon put on small heaps of the mixture, well apart.

5 Place a split almond on each macaroon and bake for 20 minutes. Allow to cool.

NOTE 1 To use this recipe for petits fours, the mixture must be put out in very tiny blobs on the rice paper. Two macaroons can then be sandwiched together with a little stiff apricot jam and served in petits fours paper cases.

NOTE 2 Whole blanched almonds ground in a pestle and mortar make very much better flavoured and textured macaroons but they are time-consuming. Grind the nuts and then gradually beat in the sugar, flour and egg whites. Do not try to grind the nuts in a liquidizer — they will become too oily.

<u>MENU LESSON 29</u> *(see p.176)*
Doubling or tripling the quantities would give you a perfect cold summer buffet. *Clockwise from top left:* Damson ice cream, apple, avocado and bacon salad, Cumberland sauce, veal and ham pie and seafood and pasta salad.

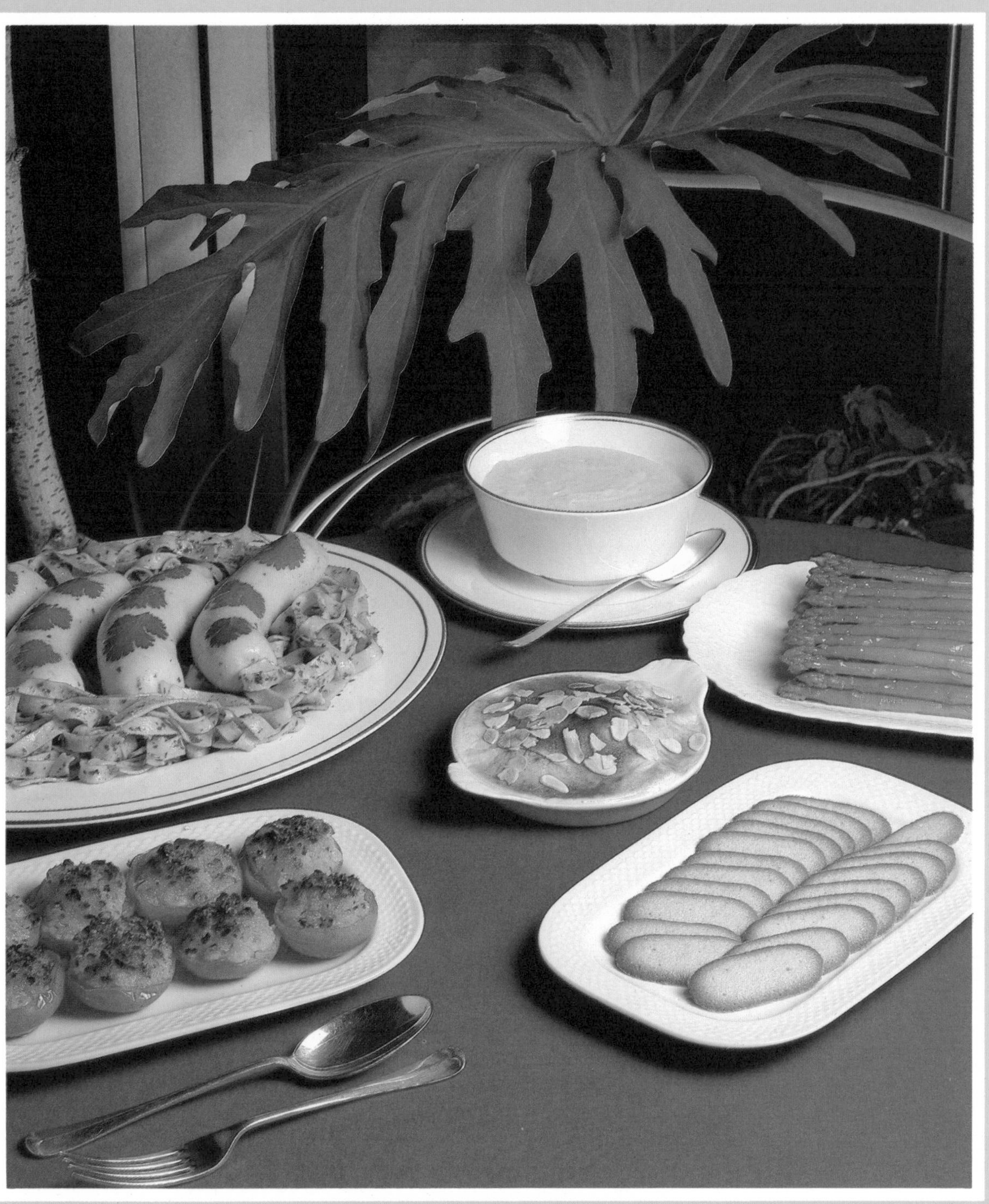

MENU LESSON 30 *(see p.182)*
Classic recipes from France and Italy combine to make this menu. *Clockwise from top left:* Boudin blanc on a bed of pasta with pesto, hollandaise sauce, asparagus, langues de chat, tomatoes Provençale, (*centre*) gratin aux fruits.

PHOTOGRAPH ON P.154

This menu emphasizes the techniques of soufflé making, stewing (the Navarin), and baking (the tart) but all are particularly simple versions of these skills. A true beginner could manage this menu with very little trouble.

MENU LESSON 27

Twice-baked soufflé

Navarin of lamb

Mashed potatoes (see p.101)

Green salad (see p.139)

Treacle tart

Yoghurt-and-custard

WORK PLAN

• Make the treacle tart, basic baked soufflés (without the sauce), lamb navarin and mashed potato in advance. Even the lettuce can be pre-prepared. This leaves only the re-baking of the soufflés, dressing the salad and the reheating for the last minute.
• Do not worry if the guests keep the soufflé waiting in the oven for a few minutes. It will not dry out as it is literally soaking in cream and if the top is browner than intended it will taste no worse for that.
• Do not overheat the treacle tart. Boiling treacle is dangerously hot. The tart is best served lukewarm.

TWICE-BAKED SOUFFLE

INGREDIENTS (Serves 4)
290ml/½pt milk
Slice of onion
Pinch of nutmeg
Knob of butter
55g/2oz butter
55g/2oz flour
Pinch of dry English mustard
170g/6oz strong Cheddar cheese, grated
4 eggs plus 1 entire egg white
Salt and freshly ground black pepper
350ml/12fl oz single cream

1 Heat the milk slowly with the onion and nutmeg.

2 Set the oven to 180°C/350°F/Gas 4. Butter 6 small teacups.

3 Melt the butter, add the flour and mustard. Cook for 30 seconds. Remove from the heat and leave to cool for one minute. Strain in the milk. Stir well and return to the heat. Bring gradually up to the boil and simmer, stirring continuously for 30 seconds.

4 Add three quarters of the cheese.

5 Separate each of the eggs: have two cups to hand. Crack the egg gently in the middle and break it in half. Allow the white to slip into a cup whilst catching the yolk in one of the half egg shells. Slip the yolk into the other half shell, allowing any white to slip into the cup. Continue to transfer the yolk from shell to shell, letting the white drop into the cup until there is none left in either shell. Put the egg yolk into the other cup (see illustration on p.280).

6 Add the egg yolks to the cheese sauce. Taste and season as necessary.

7 Whisk the egg whites until stiff: put the egg whites into a clean, dry bowl and with a large dry balloon whisk, whisk the whites until stiff but not dry (see p.285). Whisk slowly to begin with and gradually build up speed. Do not stop whisking or leave the whites sitting around — they will liquefy and not re-whisk.

8 Fold the egg whites into the soufflé base mixture: mix a spoonful of the egg whites into the base. Mix it in thoroughly, to 'loosen' the mixture. With a large metal spoon held near the bowl, not at the end, fold the remaining egg whites in. Be gentle but firm to ensure that they are completely incorporated without knocking out all the air. Think of it as drawing a three dimensional figure of 8 as you cut and fold. Do not forget to take your spoon right down to the bottom of the bowl.

9 Spoon into the cups, which the mixture should fill to two thirds at the most. Stand the cups in a roasting tin of boiling water and bake for 15 minutes or until the mixture is risen and set. Allow to sink and cool.

☐ *If egg and cheese soufflés soaked in double cream seems excessively rich, a simple béchamel sauce (p.279) can be used instead of the cream, or cream and béchamel could be mixed together.*

10 Butter a shallow ovenproof serving dish. Run a knife round the soufflés to loosen them. Turn them out onto your hand, giving the cups a sharp jerk. Put them, upside down, on the dish.

11 Twenty minutes before supper, set the oven to 220°C/425°F/Gas 7. Sprinkle the remaining cheese on top of the soufflés.

12 Season the cream with the salt and pepper and pour all over the soufflés, coating them completely. Bake for 10 minutes until a pale gold. Serve at once.

NAVARIN OF LAMB

INGREDIENTS (Serves 4)
1kg/2lb middle neck of lamb
Salt and freshly ground black pepper
2tbsp dripping
1tbsp flour
860ml/1½pt stock
1 garlic clove, crushed
2tbsp tomato purée
Bouquet garni (parsley, bay leaf and celery tied together with string)
12 button onions, peeled
Pinch of sugar
3 carrots, cut into sticks
1 turnip, cut into sticks
3 potatoes, cut into chunks

1 Cut the lamb into neat pieces and season with salt and pepper.

2 Heat 2tbsp dripping in a heavy saucepan and brown the meat on all sides. Pour off most of the fat into a frying pan, leaving only 1tbsp. Sprinkle the meat in the saucepan with the flour. Cook for one minute, then stir in the stock, garlic and tomato purée. Add the bouquet garni. Stir until boiling, then simmer for one hour. Skim off any surface fat.

3 Heat the fat in the frying pan and brown the onions with the sugar, then the carrots, turnip and potatoes, adding dripping as needed.

4 Add the browned vegetables to the meat stew, cover tightly and continue cooking over gentle heat, or in a moderate oven, for a further 30 – 40 minutes or until the meat is tender. Taste for seasoning.

5 Remove the bouquet garni. Allow the navarin to stand for 5 minutes, then skim off the surface fat and spoon the stew into a warmed dish.

NOTE Fresh peas or beans are sometimes added to the navarin.

TREACLE TART

INGREDIENTS (Serves 4)
170g/6oz flour-quantity shortcrust pastry (see next recipe)
3-4 slices white bread
Grated rind of ½ lemon and 2tsp juice
Pinch of ground ginger (optional)
About 4 large tbsp golden syrup

1 Set the oven to 190°C/375°F/Gas 5.

2 Roll the pastry out to 0.5cm/¼ inch thick, and line a pie plate or flan ring with it. Prick the bottom with a fork. Leave to relax in the refrigerator for 30 minutes.

Continued on p.168

MENU LESSON 31 *(see p.187)*
Expensive, rich and wonderful for a special occasion, this menu is still slightly old fashioned. But none the worse for that. *Clockwise from top left:* Artichoke and bacon soup, strawberry tartlets, fillet steak with Chinese mushroom sauce and Connaught vegetable 'frou-frou', and pommes dauphinoise.

MENU LESSON 32 *(see p.190)*
Paella is a classic Spanish dish, but it does well to be surrounded by other international dishes in a menu. *Clockwise from top left:* Gem lettuce and mint salad, sauce grelette, leek and bacon flan with mustard, paella and melon with ginger wine.

☐ *The trick with filling a treacle tart is not to attempt to spread the treacle with a spoon or to touch it at all. Just pour it over the crumbs as instructed. It works infallibly. Serve with yoghurt-and-custard if at the end of a rich meal, or with whipped cream or real custard (crème anglaise), p.232, if not.*

3 Trim the crusts from the bread and turn the rest into breadcrumbs.

4 Fill the flan, evenly and to the top, with crumbs, but do not push down. Sprinkle the grated lemon rind and juice over the crumbs, and also the ginger if used.

5 Pour golden syrup (straight from the tin if warm enough to flow easily, otherwise warm a little in a saucepan or by putting the whole tin in a gentle oven) over the crumbs so that all of the top layer is covered. Do not worry that the crumbs underneath might not be syrup-soaked. The syrup will seep down during cooking. (Do not be tempted to fork or spoon on the syrup — that will just pick up crumbs and make a mess. Just pour carefully until all the crumbs are under syrup.)

6 Bake for about 30 minutes or until the filling is almost set and the edge of the pastry is brown. The filling should be a little wet if the tart is to be eaten cold, because it hardens as it cools. Serve lukewarm.

SHORTCRUST PASTRY

INGREDIENTS
165g/6oz plain flour
Pinch of salt
30g/1oz lard
55g/2oz butter
Very cold water

1 Sift the flour with the salt. Rub in the fats as shown.

2 Add 2tbsp water to the mixture. Mix to a firm dough — first with a knife, and finally with one hand. It may be necessary to add more water, but the pastry should not be too damp. (Though crumbly pastry is more difficult to handle, it produces a shorter, less tough result.)

3 Chill, wrapped, for 30 minutes before using. Or allow to relax after rolling out but before baking.

RUBBING FAT INTO FLOUR

1 With well-floured fingertips, gently squash (or 'rub') dice-sized lumps of fat, dropping them back into the bowl as soon as they stick to the fingers.

2 Stop when the mixture resembles coarse breadcrumbs. The best action involves tentative rather than firm squashing, and dropping from a good height, which cools and aerates the mixture.

1

2

YOGHURT-AND-CUSTARD

INGREDIENTS (Serves 4)
1 heaped tsp custard powder
1 heaped tsp sugar
290ml/½pt milk
150g/5fl oz carton plain yoghurt

1 Blend the custard powder, sugar and 1tbsp milk together.

2 Boil the rest of the milk. Pour some of it on to the custard mixture, and tip back into the milk pan. Stir until boiling and thickened.

3 Pour into a bowl and cover the custard with polythene to prevent a skin forming.

4 When cold, whisk the custard until smooth and stir in the yoghurt.

NOTE This is an excellent sweet sauce when cream or proper egg custard (crème anglaise) would be too rich. Both are delicious with treacle tart but after such a rich first course they would not be a good idea. Also the tartness of the yoghurt counters the sweetness of the syrup very well.

PHOTOGRAPH ON P.159

This menu teaches the importance of good-looking presentation. The salad first course is very simple but prettily arranged on individual plates. It amounts to something quite special.

The Salmon in pastry is a classic. It can of course be more simply presented — the pastry could be a plain roll or decorated less elaborately with a fine lattice of pastry strips. But done as directed it makes a spectacular party dish.

The Noix au café requires the cook to master the making of Italian meringue — a useful technique which occurs frequently in cake and confectionery making.

MENU LESSON 28

Smoked chicken salad

Salmon in pastry with tarragon sauce

OR

Salmon en papillote

Cucumber and dill salad (see p.64)

Mangetout peas

Noix au cafe

WORK PLAN

- The chicken salad, except the dressing, can be prepared in advance and snap-wrapped to preserve freshness. Keep cool but take out of the refrigerator half an hour before adding the dressing.
- The salmon should be bought on the day of making, though the pastry (if it is home-made) can be well wrapped and stored overnight in the refrigerator. Assemble the fish en croûte several hours before baking if liked, but brush with egg and bake at the last minute. The dish does reheat well but both fish and pastry are better if freshly cooked.
- Mangetout peas may be blanched and refrigerated ahead of time and reheated rapidly in a microwave or by tossing in butter over moderate heat. Do not attempt to keep mangetout warm (they go an unattractive khaki), or to cook or reheat too large a quantity together. Rapid cooking or heating is essential.
- The Noix may be made several days in advance. So may the butter cream. But do not put the two together more than 2 hours before dinner.

SMOKED CHICKEN SALAD

INGREDIENTS (Serves 4)
1 small smoked chicken
85g/3oz butter
1tsp chopped parsley
Salt and pepper
Radicchio and lamb's lettuce leaves
French dressing (see p.193)
1tsp dry English mustard

☐ *When choosing smoked chicken, look for moist and not dry flesh.*

1 Separate the legs from the body of the chicken.

2 Mince or pound the leg flesh (without the skin) in a food processor with the butter and parsley. Season with salt and pepper.

3 Shape this pâté into a cylinder and roll up in a piece of foil. Chill, then unwrap and cut into slices.

4 Carve the chicken breast in thin slices and divide them between 4 dessert or side plates, overlapping the slices attractively.

5 Add a slice or two of the pâté to each plate and a few crisp salad leaves.

6 Add the mustard to the French dressing and whisk until smooth. Spoon a little dressing over each salad before serving.

FILLETING THE FISH
1 Cut off the head just below the gills. Use a sharp, flexible knife to ease the top fillet away from the backbone.

2 Use the blade to loosen lateral bones from the top fillet. Pull it away and cut the skin along the belly to free it completely.

3 To loosen the bottom fillet, cut through the backbone at the tail end.

4 With the help of a filleting knife, pull the back bone up and away gently.

5 Take as many small bones as possible with the backbone. Any remaining small bones can be removed with pliers or large tweezers (see p.17).

6 To skin, lay the fillet skin side down, loosen the skin at the tail, grip it firmly (salt helps) and 'push' the flesh away. Keep the cutting edge close to skin and use flat of knife to push.

SALMON IN PASTRY WITH TARRAGON SAUCE

INGREDIENTS (Serves 8-10)
One 2.3kg/5lb salmon
450g/1lb flour-quantity puff pastry (p.85)
a few tbsp fine semolina
Butter
Lemon juice
About 20 tarragon leaves
Salt and white pepper
Beaten egg
Tarragon sauce

FOR THE STOCK
2 slices onion
1 bay leaf
Small bunch of parsley
6 peppercorns
Salt
Bones, skin and head from the salmon
570ml/1pt water

1 Fillet the fish, keeping the four fillets intact. Skin the fillets.

2 Use the bones and other trimmings for the stock; put all the ingredients into a saucepan and simmer for 30 minutes. Strain into a measuring jug. Make up to 290ml/½pt with water if necessary, or boil down to reduce if there is too much fluid.

3 Heat the oven to 230°C/450°F/Gas 8.

4 Roll out a third of the pastry into a long thin piece, about the thickness of a coin. Cut out a fish shape.

5 Place on a wet baking sheet, and prick all over. Leave in a cool place for 15 minutes. Bake it in the hot oven until brown and crisp. Cool. Follow the illustrations for the rest of the sequence.

6 Bake for 15 minutes in the hot oven to brown and puff up the pastry, then turn down the oven to 150°C/300°F/Gas 2 for a further 30 minutes to cook the fish. Cover the crust with wet greaseproof paper if the pastry looks in danger of over-browning. To test if the fish is cooked, push a skewer through the pastry and fish from the side; it should glide in easily.

SALMON IN PASTRY WITH TARRAGON SAUCE

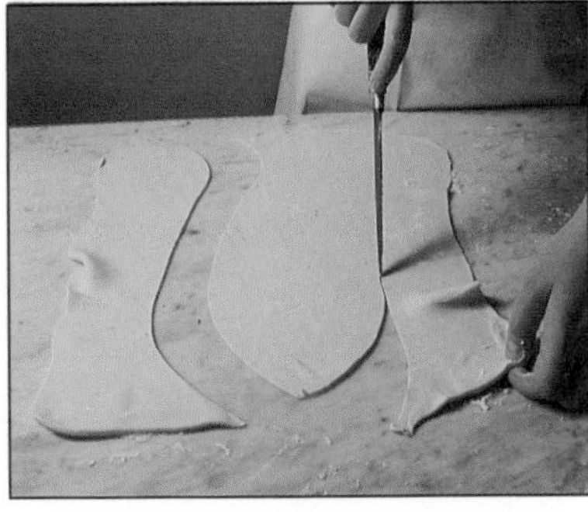

MAKING THE PASTRY CASE

1 Cut a fish shape (with a fairly wide tail) out of one third of the puff pastry, roughly the size of the original fish.

2 Prick it all over to restrict rising and to make it rise evenly. Bake until crisp. If when turning it over it is soggy underneath, return it to the oven, upside down, for a few minutes.

3 Once baked, sprinkle it heavily with semolina which will prevent the fish juices making the pastry soggy.

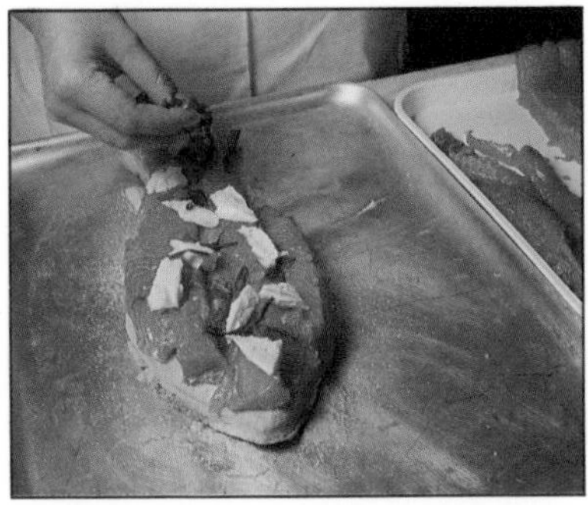

4 Cover the pastry base with the salmon and add lemon juice, tarragon leaves, salt and pepper, and plenty of butter. Take care not to leave the tail section empty.

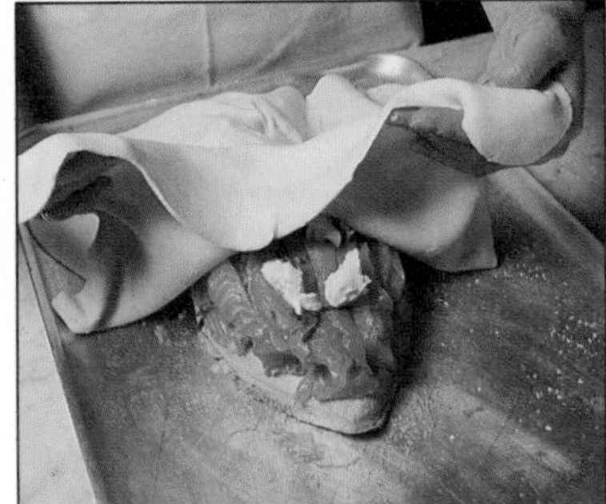

5 Cover the fish with the remaining paste, rolled to a large sheet. Cut round it, leaving a good 2.5cm/1 inch margin.

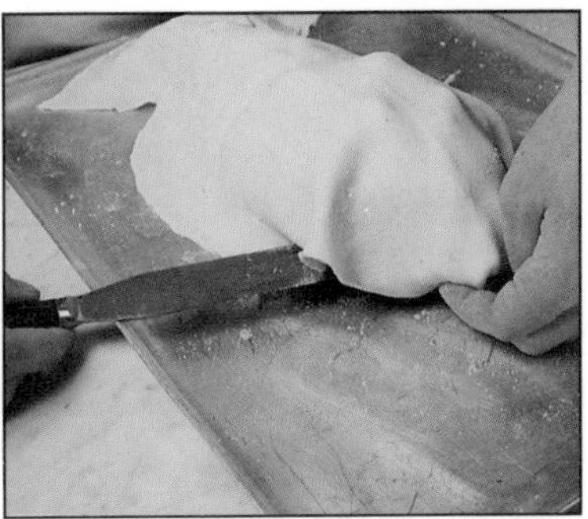

6 Using your fingers and a palette knife, gently lift the base and tuck the margin under it. Brush all over with egg.

7 To decorate, use a teaspoon to deeply mark fish-scales on the body. Use bits of the leftover pastry to make a line for the 'gills' and give the fish an eye.

8 Finally, decorate the tail with strips of pastry and brush again with egg.

7

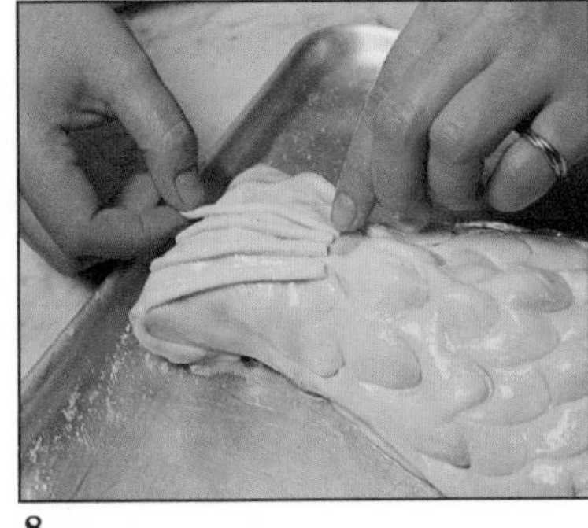

8

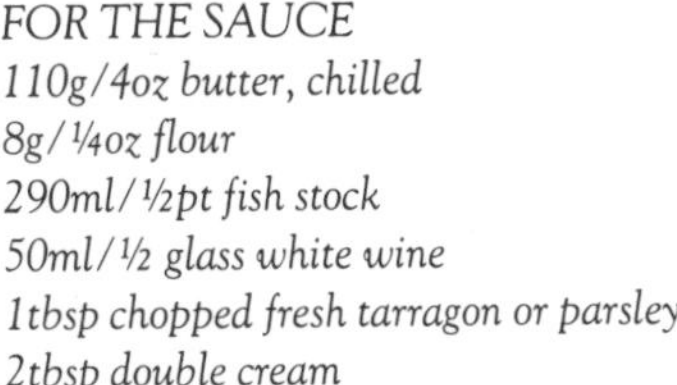

FOR THE SAUCE
110g/4oz butter, chilled
8g/¼oz flour
290ml/½pt fish stock
50ml/½ glass white wine
1tbsp chopped fresh tarragon or parsley
2tbsp double cream

7 TO MAKE THE SAUCE, melt 30g/1oz of the butter in a saucepan, add the flour and cook, stirring, for one minute or until the butter and flour are pale biscuit coloured and foaming. Draw off the heat then add the 290ml/½pt stock and the wine. Return to the heat and stir until boiling and smooth. Boil rapidly until you have a sauce of coating consistency.

8 Cut the rest of the chilled butter into 1cm/½ inch dice. Whisk them into the boiling sauce one by one, waiting for one to be incorporated before adding the next. The sauce will thicken perceptibly.

☐ *Salmon is expensive. For a cheaper variation use farmed pink trout or any firm-fleshed white fish, such as haddock or turbot.*

9 Add the chopped tarragon and the cream. Season with salt and pepper as necessary. Pour into a warmed sauceboat.

10 TO SERVE, slide the salmon en croûte onto a board or salmon dish.

11 Hand the sauce separately, or slit the salmon down the middle, lift one side of the pastry case, and pour the sauce inside.

SALMON EN PAPILLOTE

INGREDIENTS (Serves 2)
280g/10oz fillet of salmon, skinned
55g/2oz butter
1tbsp very finely shredded white of leek
1tbsp very finely shredded carrot
55g/2oz very white button mushrooms
1tsp freshly chopped tarragon or fennel leaves
Salt and freshly ground black pepper
2tbsp white wine
Lemon juice
Oil for brushing baking sheet and paper

1 Heat the oven to 250°C/500°F/Gas 9.

2 Cut out two 'papillotes' as shown.

3 Melt half the butter and add the leek and carrot to it. Cook slowly without browning for 2 minutes, then add the mushrooms. Cook one more minute, then add the tarragon or fennel, and season with salt and pepper.

4 Cut the salmon fillet into two pieces of even thickness.

5 Brush the inside of the paper rounds with oil. Lay one fish slice on each papillote and cover with the vegetables. Sprinkle each with 1tbsp of wine and a few drops of lemon juice. Dot with the remaining butter and add salt and pepper.

6 Fold the free half of the papillote paper over to make a parcel rather like an apple turnover, and twist to make an airtight seal.

7 Lightly brush a baking sheet with oil and put it into the oven for 5 minutes to heat. Then carefully put the papillotes on the baking sheet, taking care that they do not touch each other. Bake for 5 minutes.

8 Serve immediately on hot flat plates. Each diner unwraps his own puffed-up parcel, or the cook may serve it for him.

NOTE 1 Halibut, haddock, trout, and indeed almost any fish can be cooked in this way. Whole trout weighing 340g/12oz will take 15 minutes to cook. Breast of chicken, boned and skinned, is good too (20 minutes for a piece, 15 if in slices).

NOTE 2 For a richer dish serve with beurre blanc (see p.202).

NOTE 3 Papillotes are generally made from circular papers, as in the above recipe, but are better made from heart-shaped pieces if whole small fish or long fillets of fish are to be enwrapped.

MANGETOUT PEAS

INGREDIENTS
675g/1½lb mangetout peas
Salt and pepper
Melted butter

1 Wash, top and tail the mangetout peas but do not attempt to pod them. They are eaten whole.

2 Cook in a pan of boiling salted water until just tender — about 5 minutes.

3 Drain and serve with pepper and melted butter.

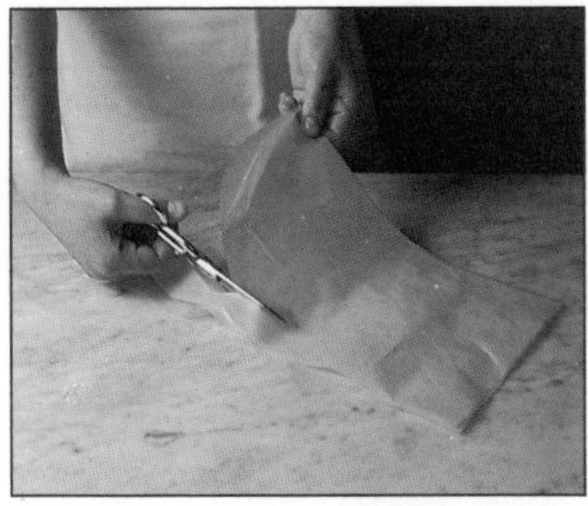

SALMON EN PAPILLOTE

1 Fold a large sheet of greaseproof paper in half and cut a semi-circle from it to make a 40cm/16 inch circle when the sheet is opened out.

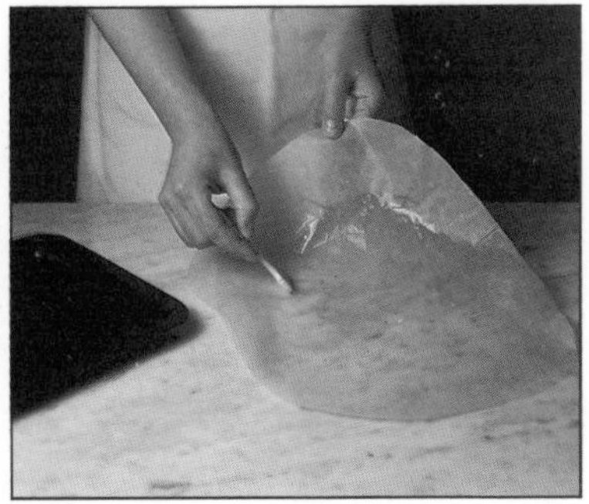

2 Brush with oil or melted butter, taking care to leave a margin without fat.

3 Put the fish and flavouring ingredients onto one side of the papillote and dot with butter.

4 Fold over the parcel to a half-moon shape enclosing the fish. Starting at one corner and working round the edge to the other, fold the two sheets of paper over together twice to seal.

5 Make neat, tiny folds — like rolling the edge of a silk scarf. Press each fold down hard to prevent unravelling. Make sure you fold the ends in, too.

6 The parcel will puff up swiftly as it bakes and, if the top is brushed with oil before baking, will brown attractively.

NOIX AU CAFE

INGREDIENTS (Makes 12-16)
225g/8oz sugar
6-7tbsp water
4 egg whites
1tsp coffee essence

1 Put the sugar and water into a heavy saucepan. Dissolve over a gentle heat and then cook quickly, without stirring, to 125°C/250°F. Use a sugar thermometer for this, or wait until it gets to the hardball stage.

2 Whisk the egg whites until stiff. Pour on the sugar syrup. Pour it steadily onto the egg whites, whisking all the time, but taking care that the syrup does not strike the whisk wires (where it would cool and set solidly). Continue whisking until all the sugar has been absorbed, and the meringue is completely cool. Beat in the coffee essence.

3 Set the oven to 140°C/275°F/Gas 1. Line 2 baking sheets with bakewell paper (vegetable parchment). It can be held in place with a few dots of the uncooked meringue.

4 Reserve a quarter of the mixture for the filling. Place the remaining mixture in a forcing bag fitted with a medium sized plain nozzle. Pipe walnut sized mounds on the prepared baking sheets. Bake for 1 – 1½ hours or until dry and crisp, when they will lift easily off the paper.

5 When completely cool, sandwich them together with the reserved coffee meringue mixture.

MENU LESSON 33 *(see p.194)*
The shaping of tortellini and the making of a fairly difficult soufflé are two of the tricky techniques to be learnt here *(below)*. *Clockwise from top left:* New potatoes, hot chocolate soufflé, hot spinach tortellini, braised shin of veal with oranges and turned carrots and potatoes and tomato salad.

MENU LESSON 34 *(see p.197)*
Spectacular to look at, this menu (*left*) is very delicious and almost indecently rich. *Clockwise from top left:* Boned chicken stuffed with leeks and potatoes sautéed with rosemary, creamy hot vegetable sauce, creamed peas and carrots and tarte Normande.

PHOTOGRAPH ON P.162

MENU LESSON 29

Seafood and pasta salad

Veal and ham raised pie

Cumberland sauce

Apple, avocado pear and bacon salad

Damson ice cream

This menu would be suitable for a cold summer buffet. The guests could have either the seafood salad or the pie, or, which is most likely, a little of each, one after the other. If doubling or tripling the quantities for such a party take care not to over-mix the seafood salad, which can easily become mushy, and do not make a raised pie more than twice the recipe size — it will take too long to get the middle cooked. Use a loose bottomed cake tin or a spring-form pie mould rather than the jar method — or use an ordinary deep cake tin as a mould. A large raised pie is better wide and shallow than tall and narrow.

The hot water crust for the pie is not the classic eggless and butterless one. We have, we believe, improved the flavour of the pastry while keeping the characteristic method of making and moulding. Any pie filling can be used instead of the traditional one we have included.

The art of raising a pie crust takes a little patience to master but is satisfying to do.

The seafood is simple to prepare, but the steps in the preparation of mussels must be carefully followed. Dead mussels are often poisonous, so take the time to check they are all alive before you cook them.

Draining and drying the pasta well is important if it is to be served cold — it can so easily become soggy in the dressing if overcooked or mixed while wet.

The technique of ice cream making using the Italian meringue method is learned in the Damson ice cream recipe.

WORK PLAN

- The salad ingredients can be cooked the day before but should be kept separate (covered and refrigerated) until just before the party. Oil the pasta to prevent it sticking.
- The pie must be made a day at least in advance. Fill it with savoury jelly while it is just tepid. If it is too cold the jelly sets as it runs into the pie and blocks the channels and spaces, so preventing more jelly flowing in. If it is put in while hot, or while the pie is hot, it is so liquid it makes the pastry soggy.
- The Cumberland sauce will keep a week if refrigerated.
- The ice cream is best made not more than 2 days in advance, and allowed to soften in the refrigerator for half an hour before serving.

SEAFOOD AND PASTA SALAD

INGREDIENTS (Serves 4)
450g/1lb green and white fettucine
85g/3oz smoked salmon
110g/4oz cooked peeled prawns
Lemon juice
Salt and freshly ground black pepper
110g/4oz squid
290ml/½pt mussels, live
1 small onion, chopped
50ml/½ glass white wine
French dressing (see p.139)
1tbsp chopped fresh dill
½ carton soured cream

1 Cook the pasta in plenty of boiling salted water, to which 2tbsp oil have been added, until just tender. Drain well, rinse off any excess starch with plenty of boiling water and leave to drain and cool. (Do not rinse in cold water as this prevents the pasta 'steaming off' and drying.)

2 Chop the smoked salmon. Sprinkle the prawns with lemon juice and pepper. Set aside.

3 Clean and slice the squid as illustrated.

4 Wash the mussels, scrub well and remove the threadlike 'beards' hanging from them (see p.37 for illustration). Throw away any mussels which remain open when tapped.

PREPARING SQUID

1 Cover a chopping board with greaseproof paper to prevent it becoming 'fishy'. Pull the head of the squid away from the body. It will bring the entrails with it.

2 Sever the head from the tentacles. Discard the head and entrails but keep the tentacles if the squid is a large one.

3 Remove the transparent cuttle-bone from the body and discard.

4 Cut off, but do not discard, the fins.

5 Scraping with a knife, carefully remove the skin from the body. Skin the fins as well.

6 If dealing with large squid, scrape the tentacles too. Do not bother with very tiny ones.

7 Wash the prepared squid thoroughly and put clean greaseproof paper on the cutting board. Cut the body into thin rings.

8 Cut the fins into strips. If using the tentacles, cut them into short lengths.

1 2 3 4 5 6 7 8

5 Place the squid in a saucepan with the onion and wine. Cover with a lid and poach very gently for one minute (more will toughen the flesh). Remove with a perforated spoon.

6 Put the mussels into the wine in the pan. Cover and cook gently for about 5 minutes or until all the shells have opened. Throw away any mussels that have not opened. Drain the mussels but cover them with a damp tea towel to prevent drying out as they steam dry.

7 Mix together the French dressing, dill and soured cream. Add it to the pasta, squid, smoked salmon and prawns. Mix well and check the seasoning. Transfer to a clean dish and put the mussels on top. (Remove the mussels from their shells if they are to be eaten at a stand-up party with a fork. Otherwise leave them in their shells and arrange them on top of the salad where they will look most attractive unshelled.)

☐ *Rinse pasta in boiling or very hot water, especially if it is to be served cold. Also spread it out in a layer to dry off. Hot pasta dries more thoroughly than cold pasta, which holds the water.*

VEAL AND HAM RAISED PIE

INGREDIENTS (Serves 4)
675g/1½lb boned shoulder of veal
110g/4oz ham
Salt and pepper
1 onion, finely chopped
2tbsp chopped parsley
1 hard boiled egg (see p.257)
450g/1lb flour quantity hot water crust pastry (see next recipe)
1 egg, beaten
570ml/1pt savoury jelly (see p.180)

1 Set the oven to 170°C/325°F/Gas 3.

2 Cut the veal and ham into very small cubes. Season with a little salt, plenty of pepper, onion and parsley. Leave on one side while you make the pastry and mould the base as shown.

3 Fill the pie, pushing the filling well into the corners, with half the seasoned meat. Press in the hard-boiled egg and cover with the remaining meat. Shape the filling so that there is a central dome.

4 COVER THE PIE with the pastry reserved for the lid. Using a little water secure the lid to the sides of the pie. Press firmly together. Cut off any excess pastry and 'crimp' the top edge as shown.

5 Secure a double piece of greaseproof paper around the whole pie with paper clips at top and bottom to prevent the sides from bulging.

6 Make a few pastry leaves from any pastry trimmings. Brush the top of the pie with egg white. Make a neat hole (for the steam to escape) in the middle of the lid and decorate the top with the pastry leaves.

7 Bake for 2 hours. After 1½ hours remove the greaseproof paper and brush the sides evenly with the egg glaze. Remove from the oven and allow to get completely cold on a wire rack, but do not refrigerate yet.

8 Warm the savoury jelly until just runny. Using a funnel, fill the pie with jelly. The jelly will take some time to filter through the meat so keep repeating the topping up process until you are sure that it is absolutely full. Leave to cool and set before serving.

☐ *Veal stock as used in our pie makes the most delicious jelly. But clear chicken broth set with gelatine would do too, though it does not keep as well. Pork jelly is unsatisfactory — murky in flavour and difficult to clear. If, when adding the jelly, an unsuspected crack or hole in the pastry allows the liquid to escape, just plug it firmly with butter, suitably coloured with gravy browning to the correct brown colour.*

MAKING PASTRY LEAVES

1 For curly leaves cut diamonds from a wide pastry strip. Use a knife blade held at a non-cutting angle to mark the leaf 'veins', while pulling the leaf into a curved shape.

2 Thicker, more robust leaves can be curved in situ. The leaves can be glazed with egg to stick them in place and to give them a shine when baked.

1

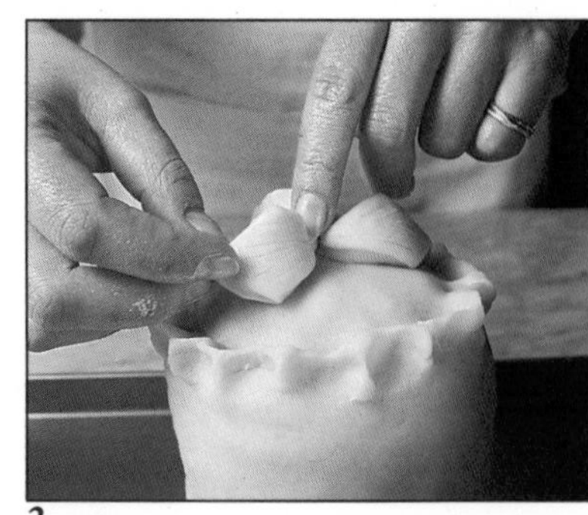
2

HOT WATER CRUST PASTRY

INGREDIENTS
450g/1lb plain flour
1tsp salt
2 beaten eggs
200ml/7fl oz water
70g/2½oz butter
70g/2½oz lard

1 Wrap a large piece of greaseproof paper around the outside of a tall, wide jar. Smooth it down as well as possible and try to cover the jar tightly. Leave upside down while you make the pastry.

2 Sift the flour and salt into a bowl. Make a dip in the middle of it, break the eggs into it and toss a liberal covering of flour over the egg.

3 Put the water, butter and lard into a saucepan and bring to the boil.

4 Once the liquid is boiling, pour it onto the flour, mixing with a knife as you do. Knead until the pastry is smooth.

5 Wrap in a piece of polythene and refrigerate for 15 minutes.

6 Reserve about a quarter of the paste for the lid, keeping it covered. Roll out the remaining paste to a round and shape to cover the upturned jar. Leave to chill until really firm, about 20 minutes.

7 When hard turn the jar over and remove it carefully, leaving the greaseproof paper inside the pastry case. Trim and carefully remove the greaseproof paper from the pastry.

8 Stand the pastry case on a baking sheet and fill as required.

HOT WATER CRUST PIE CASE

1 Wrap a sheet of greaseproof paper smoothly and tightly around an upturned jar. Tuck into the mouth of the jar to hold in place.

2 Sift the flour and salt into a bowl. Make a deep well in the middle. Break the egg into it and toss a liberal coating of flour over it.

1

2

3 Bring the water, butter and lard slowly to the boil.

4 Once the fat has melted and the liquid is boiling, pour it on to the flour—mixing with a knife as you do so.

3

4

5 Knead until all the egg streaks have gone and the pastry is smooth. Wrap in polythene and refrigerate for 15 minutes.

6 Reserve a quarter of the pastry for the lid. Roll out the rest into a circle and drape it over the upturned jar. Mould it to shape. Do not allow the pastry to get too thin at the corners.

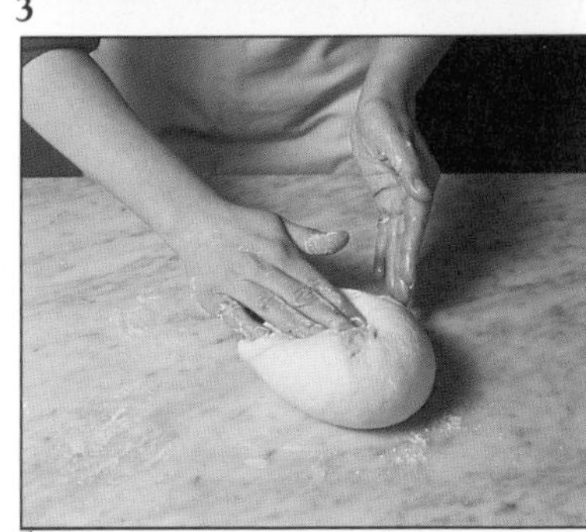
5

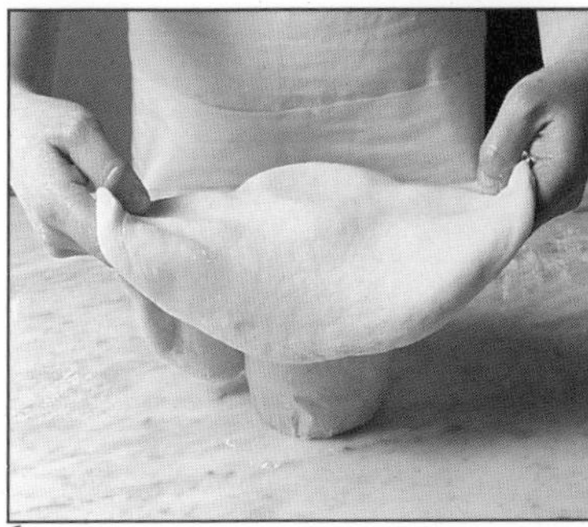
6

7 Chill until the pastry is really firm (20 minutes or so). Then carefully remove the jar, leaving the paper in place. Trim off most of the paper with scissors.

8 Very carefully draw the paper away from the pastry. When it is all loosened take it out.

7

8

9 Stand the pie case on a baking sheet and spoon in the filling. Use the reserved pastry to make a lid. Trim off excess pastry, wetting the edges where the pastry joins.

10 Use the finger and thumb of one hand and the forefinger only of the other to pinch and crimp the edge.

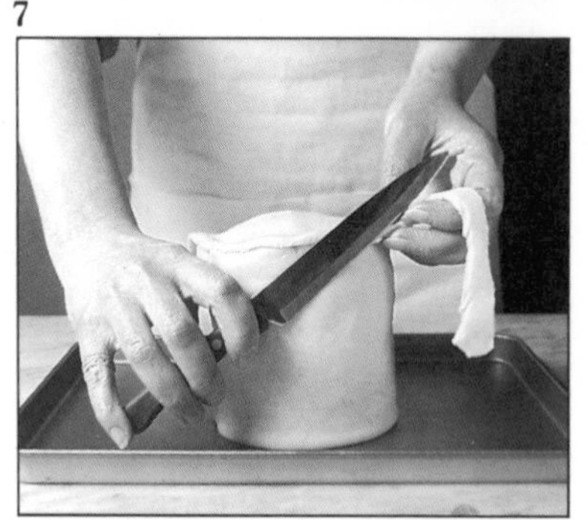
9

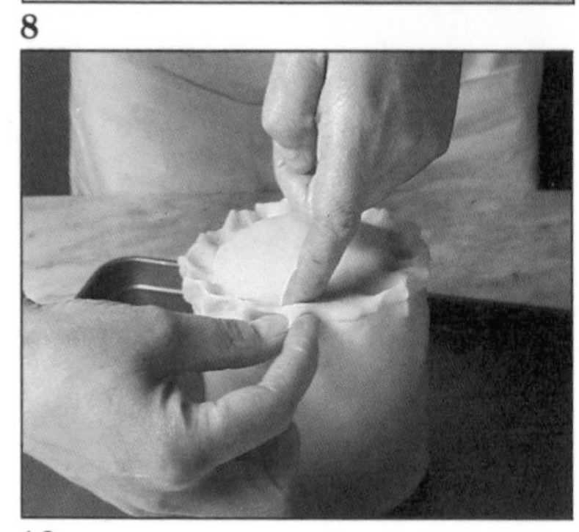
10

SAVOURY JELLY

INGREDIENTS (Makes about 600ml/1pt)
500g/1lb broken veal or beef
1 calves foot
1.5litres/3pt water
1 onion, sliced
Stick of celery
Pinch of thyme
Bunch of parsley
1 bay leaf

1 Wash the veal and bones well and put them in a saucepan with the water. Bring gradually to the boil and skim off any scum.

2 Add the other ingredients and simmer very slowly for 3 hours, skimming frequently.

3 When the liquid is reduced to about 600ml/1pt, strain it.

NOTE If when refrigerated the jelly does not set firmly, sprinkle on 1 level tsp gelatine for every 290ml/½pt stock, leave to soak for 10 minutes, then reheat until dissolved.

CUMBERLAND SAUCE

INGREDIENTS
1 shallot, finely chopped
4tbsp wine vinegar
6 black peppercorns
1 orange
1 lemon
150ml/¼pt white stock
55ml/2fl oz port
2tbsp redcurrant jelly
1tsp Worcestershire sauce

1 Put the shallot into a saucepan with the vinegar and peppercorns. Boil rapidly until reduced by two thirds.

2 Peel the orange and lemon finely, removing only the outer skin but no pith. Cut the rind into very fine needleshreds.

3 Squeeze all the fruit juice and add it to the shallot mixture with the white stock, port, redcurrant jelly and Worcestershire sauce. Bring to the boil and simmer for 10 minutes.

4 Strain, add the needleshreds and simmer for a further 10 minutes until syrupy and shiny. Leave to cool.

APPLE, AVOCADO PEAR AND BACON SALAD

INGREDIENTS (Serves 4)
110g/4oz rindless back bacon rashers
2 green apples
2 ripe avocado pears

FOR THE DRESSING
½ carton soured cream
1tbsp lemon juice
Bunch of chives, finely chopped
Salt and freshly ground black pepper
2tbsp olive oil

1 Heat the grill and cook the bacon until crisp. Drain and cut into strips.

2 Combine all the dressing ingredients, but for a few chopped chives, and mix well with a small whisk.

3 Cut the apple into thin slices, unpeeled. Put straight into the dressing.

4 Peel and cut the avocado pear into cubes and turn carefully, with the apple, in the dressing until completely coated.

5 Just before serving add most of the bacon. Mix well and tip into a clean bowl. Garnish with the remaining chives and bacon and serve immediately.

DAMSON ICE CREAM

INGREDIENTS (Serves 6-8)
450g/1lb damsons
340g/12oz caster sugar
150ml/¼pt water
2 large egg whites
Juice and finely grated rind of 1 small orange
290ml/½pt double cream

☐ Damson stones are more easily removed from cooked damsons if the flesh is cut open down the length of the fruit before poaching.

1 Wash the damsons and put them, still wet, with 110g/4oz sugar in a thick-bottomed saucepan. Stew gently, covered, over very gentle heat or bake in the oven until soft and pulpy.

2 Push through a sieve and remove the stones.

3 Dissolve the remaining 225g/8oz sugar in the water and bring to the boil.

4 Boil steadily for 5 minutes.

5 While the syrup is boiling beat the egg whites in an electric mixer or by hand until stiff. Pour the boiling syrup onto the egg whites, whisking as you do so, but taking care not to pour the syrup directly onto the whisk where it will cool and set stickily. The mixture will go rather liquid at this stage, but keep whisking until you have a thick meringue.

6 Stir in the orange rind and juice, and the purée.

7 Whip the cream until thick but not solid and fold it into the mixture.

8 Freeze. It is not necessary to re-whisk the ice cream during freezing.

NOTE The damson purée can be replaced by a purée of cooked plums, greengages, rhubarb, dried apricots or prunes, or a raw purée of soft fruit, apricots or peaches.

PHOTOGRAPH ON P.163

This menu leaps about among the classic recipes of France and Italy, but is none the worse for that. The cook making hollandaise learns the technique of adding cold butter to a hot sauce without the mixture separating. The principles of sausage making are tackled and the result is that most elegant and sophisticated of sausages, boudin blanc. A good pesto sauce is easy to achieve, especially with a modern processor or liquidizer. The gratin aux fruits is luxuriously rich, but easy to make. Langues de chat provide the cook with a lesson in French biscuit making. It's all simpler than it looks.

MENU LESSON 30

Asparagus with hollandaise sauce

Boudin blanc

Pasta with pesto

Tomates Provençale

Gratin aux fruits

Langues de chat

WORK PLAN

- The biscuits and the pesto can be made days in advance if preferred.
- The hollandaise sauce will stand quite stable for 20 minutes in a bowl or pan of hot water.
- The asparagus should be cooked at the last minute unless there is a microwave oven available (in which case 30 seconds will reheat them without damage).
- Pasta is best freshly made but will stay warm quite happily for half an hour if oiled or buttered.
- The gratin aux fruits, sadly, requires a cook in the kitchen while the diners are at table. It takes about 15 minutes of last-minute work.

ASPARAGUS WITH HOLLANDAISE SAUCE

INGREDIENTS (Serves 4-6)
48 thin or 24 fat asparagus stems
Hollandaise sauce (see next recipe)

1 Wash the asparagus, remove the hard ends as shown and peel a little of the tough outer skin from the base.

2 Tie in bundles and place upright in a tall pan of boiling salted water. The heads should be above the water level, where they will cook slowly in the steam while the stems cook fast in the boiling water. Cook for 10 to 15 minutes.

3 Drain well and serve with the hollandaise sauce handed separately.

NOTE An average bundle of bought fresh asparagus is enough for 3 or 4 people.

☐ *If an asparagus pan is not available, make sure the stems of the asparagus are properly peeled (see p.99) (this speeds up cooking) then lay the asparagus — not in bundles — in a frying pan or wide sauté pan of boiling water to cook. Lift out carefully with a fish slice.*

PREPARING ASPARAGUS
1 Hold asparagus spears points-down and tap lightly on the chopping board to get the tips level.

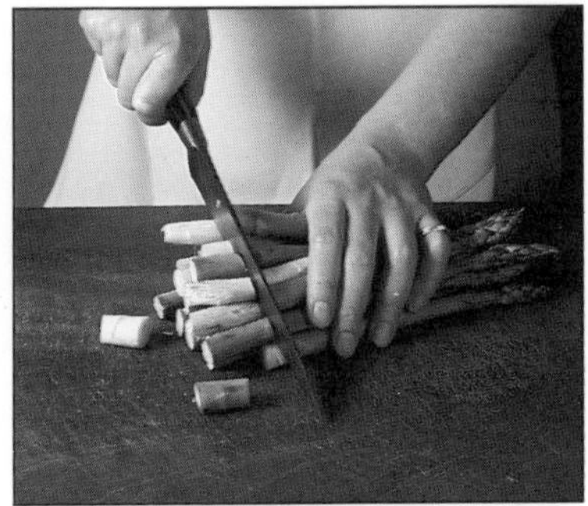

2 Chop off the tough, woody ends at the level of the shortest one. If the stalks are very tough, they can be peeled (see p.99).

HOLLANDAISE SAUCE

INGREDIENTS
3tbsp wine vinegar
6 peppercorns
1 bay leaf
Blade of mace
2 egg yolks
Salt
110g/4oz softened butter
Lemon juice

1 Place the vinegar, peppercorns, bay leaf and mace in a small heavy saucepan and reduce to 1tbsp by boiling.

2 Beat the egg yolks with a pinch of salt and a nut of butter in a small bowl. Set this is a roasting tin full of hot water on a gentle heat. With a wooden spoon, beat the mixture until slightly thickened, taking care that the water immediately around the bowl does not boil. Mix well.

3 Strain on the reduced vinegar. Mix well. Beat in the softened butter bit by bit, increasing the temperature to keep the sauce warm as you add more butter and the mixture thickens, but take care that the water does not boil against the bowl.

4 When the sauce has thickened take if off the heat and beat or whisk for 1 minute. Taste for seasoning and add lemon juice, and salt if necessary. Keep warm by standing the bowl in hot water. Serve warm.

NOTE *Instant hollandaise* If a liquidizer or food processor is available, a speedy hollandaise can be made. Reduce the flavoured vinegar and strain it, hot, onto the egg yolks while the machine is running. Then add the butter (just warm and melted, not in cold pieces) in a thin steady stream.

☐ *Hollandaise sauce will set too firmly if allowed to get cold and it will curdle if overheated. If it does begin to curdle, quickly drop in a spoonful of crushed ice to cool it. If the sauce is badly 'split', tip it into a jug and beat a further egg yolk in another clean bowl. Stand in the bain marie and add the curdled mixture to it, drop by drop, whisking steadily with a small wire whisk.*

HOLLANDAISE SAUCE
1 Put a knob of butter into the reduced vinegar at the 'quiet' end of a bain marie set over heat, and beat or whisk as it melts.

2 Continue adding knobs of butter, one at a time, beating continuously. Do not add the next knob until the previous one is incorporated.

3 The sauce will gradually thicken and become paler. Move it nearer the hot end of the bain marie as more cold butter is added. The sauce should be warm, but not hot.

4 When all the butter has been incorporated the sauce should be light-coloured, thick and shiny.

BOUDIN BLANC

INGREDIENTS (Makes about 900g/2lb sausages)
1.25m/1¼yd pork intestine or sausage casing
150ml/¼pt double cream
100g/3½oz fresh fine white breadcrumbs
225g/8oz boneless pork belly
225g/8oz lean veal
225g/8oz chicken breast meat
1 onion, minced or very finely chopped
3 eggs
1 level tsp ground allspice
Salt and pepper

FOR COOKING
1¼litres/2pt water
570ml/1pt milk

1 Soak the pork intestine in cold water.

2 Heat the cream to boiling and pour over the breadcrumbs. Leave to cool.

3 Mince the meats through the fine mincer plate or chop in a processor until smooth.

4 Put the mixture into a bowl and gradually beat in the onion, breadcrumb mixture and eggs. Season with allspice, salt and pepper. Taste — it should be fairly spicy. (If you do not like the idea of tasting raw meat, shape a little into a ball, fry it and then taste for seasoning.) The mixture should be very smooth.

5 Drain the pork intestine — it should be pliable. Tie one end, insert the sausage filler or funnel in the other and introduce the filling, easing it down the skins. Do not overfill or they will burst during cooking. Tie into 15cm/6 inch sausages.

6 Bring the water and milk to the boil in a large saucepan. Lower in the sausages, cover and poach very gently for 20 minutes. Do not cook them too fast or they will burst. Allow to cool to tepid in the liquid, then drain and leave to cool completely. They can be cooked up to 24 hours in advance and kept covered in the refrigerator.

☐ *Sometimes sausage casing comes in unmanageable lengths. Cut it into pieces which are no longer than 1.25m/1¼yd. Failing proper sausage skins, the boudin mixture can be cooked in buttered foil rolled up to a sausage shape. They will need to be steamed, rather than poached, however. They are done when they feel firm, not squashy, to the touch.*

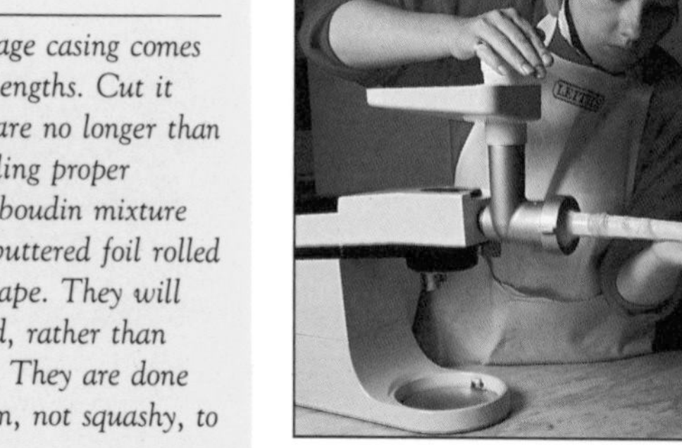

FILLING SAUSAGES
Support the sausage skin as the machine fills it and twist it into links. Do not overfill or the skin will burst. When using a machine with a sausage-filler attachment, wet the whole length of the tube before slipping the sausage casing on. This will prevent snagging.

PASTA WITH PESTO

INGREDIENTS (Serves 4)
225g/8oz pasta
Oil
Salt

FOR THE PESTO SAUCE
2 cloves garlic, peeled
2 large cups fresh basil leaves (about 30g/1oz)
55g/2oz fresh Parmesan or Pecorino cheese, finely grated
150ml/¼pt olive oil
Coarse salt
55g/2oz pinenuts

1 First PREPARE THE PESTO SAUCE If you have a liquidizer simply whizz together the garlic and basil and then gradually add the cheese, oil and plenty of salt. If not, pound a little of the garlic and some of the basil leaves together in a mortar, with a little salt. Gradually add more garlic, basil and salt but only when you have obtained a good pulp. Gradually work in the cheese and then as much oil as it will take whilst retaining a good thick texture.

2 COOK THE PASTA in plenty of rapidly boiling salted water to which 3tbsp oil have been added. Drain when just tender and pour over boiling water and a little oil.

3 Toss in the pesto sauce and serve sprinkled with pinenuts.

NOTE 1 Pesto can be kept for several weeks in a covered jar in the refrigerator. If some of it is used, pour in enough olive oil to completely cover and seal the sauce.

NOTE 2 Ground pinenuts may be added to the paste instead of sprinkled on top as here.

NOTE 3 Almonds make a good, if different-tasting, alternative to pinenuts, especially ground and added to the paste.

TOMATES PROVENCALE

INGREDIENTS (Serves 4)
4 medium tomatoes
55g/2oz butter
1 onion, finely chopped
½ garlic clove, crushed
4tbsp stale white breadcrumbs
Salt and freshly ground black pepper
Pinch of nutmeg
2tsp chopped fresh parsley
1tsp chopped tarragon

TO GARNISH
Chopped parsley

1 Heat the oven to 200°C/400°F/Gas 6.

2 Cut the tomatoes in half horizontally and remove the insides with a teaspoon. Reserve.

3 Melt half the butter and gently cook the onion until soft. Add the garlic and cook for one more minute.

4 Mix the breadcrumbs, seasoning, nutmeg, herbs and onion mixture together with a fork. Strain in enough of the tomato flesh to just bind together.

5 Pile the breadcrumb mixture into the tomato shells and place a knob of the remaining butter on each.

6 Put the tomatoes in an ovenproof dish and bake in the oven for about 20 minutes or until the breadcrumbs are golden.

7 Sprinkle with chopped parsley.

GRATIN AUX FRUITS

INGREDIENTS (Serves 4)
2 ripe peaches
4 ripe plums
4 ripe apricots
2 eggs
2 egg yolks
85g/3oz caster sugar
Dash of Kirsch
55g/2oz toasted flaked almonds

1 Peel and slice the peaches. Stone and slice the plums and apricots. Arrange on 4 small gratin dishes.

2 Heat the grill.

3 Put the eggs, egg yolks and sugar into a bowl. Set over a pan of simmering water. Whisk for 10-15 minutes until thick and creamy. Stir in the Kirsch.

4 Spoon the sauce over the fruits. Grill until evenly browned, then sprinkle with flaked almonds. Serve immediately.

LANGUES DE CHAT

INGREDIENTS (Makes 30)
100g/3½oz butter
100g/3½oz caster sugar
3 egg whites
100g/3½oz plain flour

1 Set the oven to 200°C/400°F/Gas 6. Grease and flour a baking sheet.

2 Soften the butter by beating with a wooden spoon and add the sugar gradually. Beat until pale and fluffy.

3 Whisk the egg whites slightly and add gradually to the mixture, beating thoroughly between each addition.

4 Sift the flour and fold into the mixture with a metal spoon. Put into a forcing bag fitted with a medium sized plain nozzle. Pipe into fingers on a greased and floured baking sheet.

5 Tap the baking sheet sharply on the table to release any large air bubbles. Bake for 5-7 minutes or until biscuit coloured in the middle and brown at the edges.

LANGUES DE CHAT
1 Pipe 5cm/2 inch lengths of mixture, well apart. If the piping bag is large, wind the unfilled end round the hand to prevent it flapping and spoiling your sight-line. To break off each langue de chat (the mixture is sticky), reverse direction at the end and then jerk up.

2 During baking these blobs will flatten to give the langues de chat their characteristic shape. Lift the biscuits off the baking sheet and cool on a wire rack.

PHOTOGRAPH ON P.166

MENU LESSON 31

Artichoke and bacon soup

Fillet steaks with Chinese mushroom sauce

Pommes dauphinoise

Connaught vegetable 'frou-frou'

Strawberry tartlets

This is something of an oldfashioned meal and none the worse for that. It is expensive, rich and wonderful for a special occasion. The cook learns the simple and endlessly repeatable principles of the vegetable cream soup, how to fry the perfect steak, and how to achieve a truly great Dauphinoise — rich, soft and velvety underneath, brown and crisp on top.

The tartlets are a fiddle, requiring time and care to get right. But they look and taste like the most exquisite luxury (which they are). So why not try?

WORK PLAN

- The soup, dauphinoise and tartlets can all be made several hours in advance.
- The vegetables can be cooked and refreshed for later reheating in a microwave oven or tossing in butter.
- The mushroom sauce can be cooked, reduced and strained, and left ready for last-minute adding to the steak pan and enriching with butter.
- The steaks, of course, must be cooked at the last minute.

ARTICHOKE AND BACON SOUP

INGREDIENTS (Serves 4)
675g/1½lb Jerusalem artichokes
2tbsp lemon juice
110g/4oz streaky, rindless bacon
30g/1oz butter or bacon fat
1 onion, sliced
570ml/1pt milk
570ml/1pt water
Salt and ground white pepper
2tbsp cream (optional)

TO GARNISH
Finely chopped young chives

1 Peel the artichokes as shown overleaf and leave in a bowl of cold water acidulated with the lemon juice to prevent discolouration.

2 Cut the bacon into strips. Fry it gently in the fat for 3 minutes. Add the onion and cook until soft but not coloured.

3 Dry the artichokes, slice and add to the pan. Continue cooking, covered, for about 10 minutes, giving an occasional stir.

4 Add the milk and water, season well and simmer for a further 20 minutes.

5 Liquidize, then push through a sieve. Check for seasoning — remember that bacon is often salty.

6 Reheat, add the cream, pour into a warmed soup tureen and garnish with chopped chives.

JERUSALEM ARTICHOKES
Choose the smoothest, largest most even-shaped artichokes you can find (the small knobbly ones are tiresome and time consuming to peel). Peel them with a potato peeler, and drop immediately into a bowl of cold, acidulated water. This will prevent the artichokes becoming discoloured.

FILLET STEAKS WITH CHINESE MUSHROOM SAUCE

INGREDIENTS (Serves 4)
1litre/1¾pt very good brown stock (see p.268)
1 large clove garlic, peeled and chopped
1 shallot, peeled and chopped
55g/2oz Chinese mushrooms, soaked in boiling water for 20 minutes
Oil for frying
Four 2½cm/1 inch fillet steaks
110g/4oz unsalted butter, chilled and cut into small pieces

TO GARNISH
Bunch of watercress

1 Put the stock, garlic and shallot together in a large saucepan. Simmer for 20 minutes. Add the mushrooms, roughly chopped, and simmer for a further 30 minutes.

2 Strain into a clean saucepan, pushing hard at the mushrooms to extract their juices but not too much of the pulp.

3 Reduce, by boiling rapidly, to 6tbsp. Set aside.

4 Brush a frying pan with a little oil. Heat until smoking. Fry the steaks as fast as you dare on both sides. Cook them to the degree you like. Generally they need about 1 – 1½ minutes a side for blue, 1½ – 2 minutes for rare, 2–2½ minutes for medium rare and 2½–3 minutes for medium. Remove them to a dish and keep warm while finishing the sauce.

5 Pour off the fat from the frying pan and pour in the reduced stock. Bring to the boil, reduce the heat and quickly whisk in the unsalted butter bit by bit. The sauce should remain just below simmering point and should thicken considerably within a minute or two.

6 Garnish the steaks with watercress and hand the sauce separately.

POMMES DAUPHINOISE

INGREDIENTS (Serves 4)
675g/1½lb potatoes
Butter
1 clove garlic, crushed
Nutmeg, grated
Salt and freshly ground black pepper
200ml/⅓pt single cream

☐ Grated Gruyère cheese and fresh breadcrumbs can be mixed and sprinkled on the top before baking to give a crunchy crust.

1 Set the oven to 170°C/325°F/Gas 3.

2 Butter a gratin dish and sprinkle with the crushed garlic.

3 Peel and slice the potatoes. Do not soak them in cold water.

4 Arrange a layer of overlapping slices of potato in the bottom of the dish. Season with salt, pepper and nutmeg. Add enough cream to just cover the potatoes. Continue to layer the potatoes with the seasoning and cream finishing with the cream. Bake for 2 hours, or until tender right through, and brown on the top.

NOTE 1 For a less cream-laden and cheaper version, half-cook the potato slices covered in milk in a saucepan. They will absorb most of the milk. Then put them in the buttered dish with the seasonings and garlic and pour over a little cream. Bake as above until tender and golden.

NOTE 2 For less solid dauphinoise, rinse the potato slices in water before cooking.

CONNAUGHT VEGETABLE FROU-FROU

INGREDIENTS (Serves 4)
1 medium courgette
55g/2oz French beans
55g/2oz mangetout peas
1 head broccoli
1 small cauliflower
2 small carrots
Melted butter
Salt and pepper

This is the popular 'mixed vegetables' offered to restaurant customers by chef Michel Bourdin.

1 PREPARE THE VEGETABLES Slice the courgette, top and tail the beans and mangetouts, break the broccoli and cauliflower into the smallest possible florets, peel and slice the carrots into fine rounds.

2 Cook all the vegetables in separate pans of boiling salted water until just tender. Drain and refresh. Drain again well.

3 When ready to serve, mix the vegetables together and toss in melted butter over moderate heat until just hot, then serve at once.

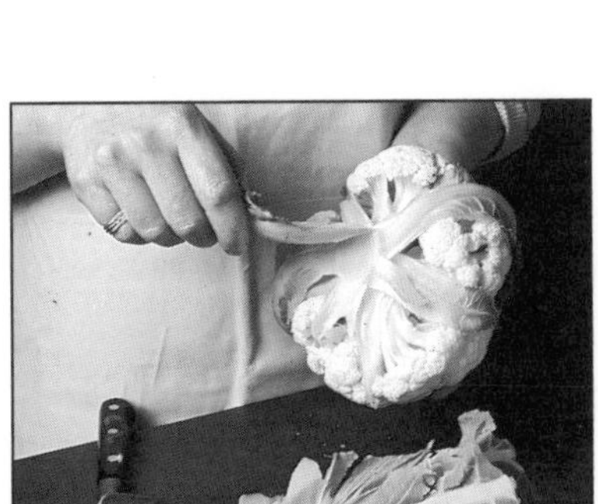

PREPARING CAULIFLOWER
1 Pull off the outer leaves.

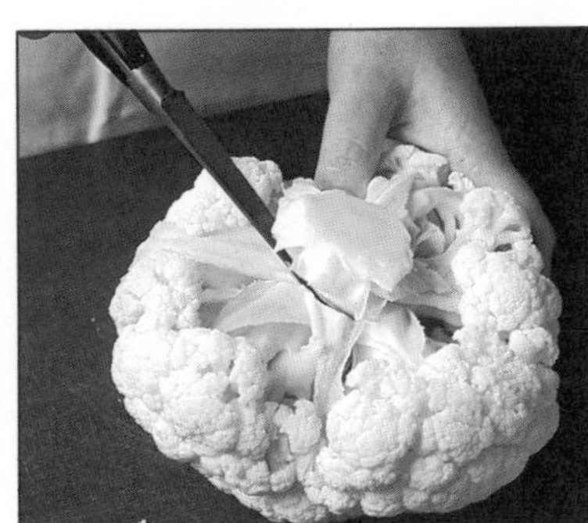

2 Cut around the tough core to extract a cone-shaped middle section.

3 Break off the florets. Do not cut through the flower 'curls' — it spoils their shape and makes them crumble and break during cooking.

STRAWBERRY TARTLETS

INGREDIENTS (Serves 4)
170g/6oz flour-quantity pâte sucrée (p.156)

FOR THE FILLING
225g/8oz petit Suisse cheese
55g/2oz caster sugar
450g/1lb strawberries, hulled
4tbsp redcurrant jelly

1 Set the oven to 190°C/375°F/Gas 5.

2 Roll out the pastry thinly and use it to line the tartlet tins. Bake blind for about 15 minutes or until a pale biscuit colour. Remove the papers and the 'blind' beans. If the pastry is not quite cooked, return to the oven for 5 minutes. Carefully take out the pastry cases and leave to cool on a wire rack.

3 Cream the cheese with the caster sugar and place 1tsp of this mixture at the bottom of each case. Arrange the strawberries, cut in half if necessary, on top of the cheese and brush lightly with melted redcurrant jelly, just cool enough to coat the fruit fairly thickly.

USING A PASTRY CUTTER
Press the cutter down firmly into the paste and twist it sharply (or push it a little to and fro) to loosen the circle before lifting.

PHOTOGRAPH ON P.167

This Menu Lesson teaches the cook the decorative and delicious Paella by the traditional method. Many 'Paellas' consist of cooked rice mixed with other cooked ingredients. But a true Paella is cooked as this one, the rice absorbing the stock and the steam from it cooking the fish and chicken. The sauce, however, is far from classic. But refreshing cold tomato is surprisingly good with the hot paella.

MENU LESSON 32

Leek and bacon flan with mustard

Paella

Sauce grelette

Gem lettuce and mint salad

Melon with ginger wine

WORK PLAN

The grelette sauce, salad and melon can all be prepared in advance, but both the flan and the paella are best if freshly made.

LEEK AND BACON FLAN WITH MUSTARD

INGREDIENTS (Serves 4)
170g/6oz flour-quantity rich shortcrust pastry (see next recipe)

Continued on p.191

1 Line a 20cm/8 inch flan ring with the pastry and leave it in the refrigerator to relax for 30 minutes.

2 Set the oven to 190°C/375°F/Gas 5.

3 Bake the pastry case blind. Remove from the oven and turn it down to 170°C/325°F/Gas 3.

MAKING A FLAN CASE

1 Roll out the pastry on a floured surface to a round 5cm/2 inches larger than the flan ring. Lay the rolling pin gently on the pastry and fold one side over it.

2 Lift up the pastry on the rolling pin. Brush off excess flour.

3 Drape the pastry carefully over the flan ring by turning the pin slowly to allow it to fall gently over the ring. Do not let the pin touch the ring or it may cut through the pastry. Do not stretch the pastry or it will shrink back once in the oven.

4 Ease the pastry into the corners with the back of a finger.

1

2

3

4

5 Alternatively, ,you can use a small ball of paste to push it well into the corners.

6 Roll the pin over the top of the flan ring to cut off the excess pastry.

7 Gently dislodge the pastry edge with a fingernail if it sticks to the flan ring — this will prevent it sticking in the oven.

8 To bake blind, prick the bottom of the flan case to prevent bubbling up while baking.

9 Line with greaseproof paper (crumpling the paper first will ensure that you do not damage the pastry) and fill with 'blind beans' (here we have used a mixture of dry rice and pasta). 'Blind beans' may be re-used indefinitely. Remove the paper and beans when the case is half-baked.

10 Remove the flan ring once the case is almost cooked and return to the oven to allow the sides to brown.

5 6 7 8 9 10

FOR THE FILLING
The white of 5 small or 3 large leeks
55g/2oz bacon
15g/½oz butter
2 egg yolks
150ml/¼pt double cream
Salt and pepper
Dijon mustard
1tbsp freshly grated Parmesan cheese

4 TO MAKE THE FILLING, wash and chop the leeks (see p.192). Remove the rind from the bacon and chop.

5 Fry the bacon in its own fat and when beginning to brown add the leeks with the butter and cook until soft.

6 Mix together the egg yolks, cream, leek and bacon. Season to taste with salt and pepper.

7 Spread a layer of mustard on the base of the flan and then pour in the filling. Sprinkle evenly with freshly grated Parmesan cheese. Bake for 30 minutes or until the filling is set and golden brown.

PREPARING LEEKS

1 Cut off tough green ends and roots, but not the root base which will help to prevent unravelling during cooking if the leeks are to be served whole.

2 Split the leeks lengthways from about 5cm/2 inches above the root end.

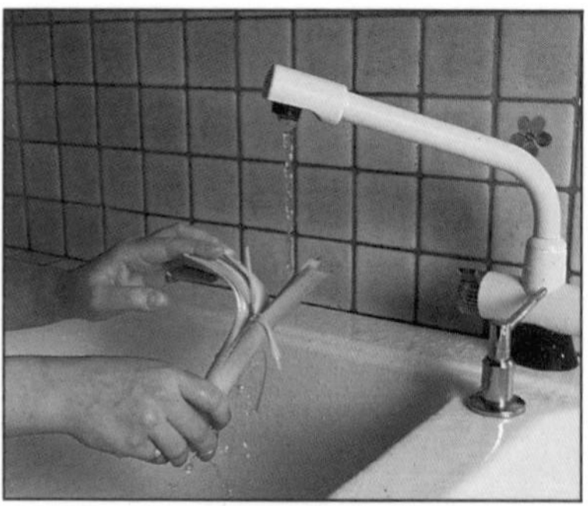

3 Riffle the split leaves under running cold water to wash out any grit or mud.

RICH SHORTCRUST PASTRY

INGREDIENTS
170g/6oz plain flour
Pinch of salt
100g/3½oz butter
1 egg yolk
Very cold water

1 Sift the flour with the salt and rub in the butter as shown on p.168.

2 Mix the yolk with 1tbsp water and add to the mixture.

3 Mix to a firm dough — first with a knife, and finally with one hand. It may be necessary to add more water, but the pastry should not be too damp. (Though crumbly pastry is more difficult to handle, it produces a shorter, less tough result.)

4 Chill, wrapped, for 30 minutes before using or allow to relax after rolling out but before baking.

PAELLA

INGREDIENTS (Serves 4)
3tbsp olive oil
170g/6oz long grain rice
1 onion, sliced
8 shreds of saffron, soaked in hot water
4 joints chicken, skinned, boned and cut up
170g/6oz squid, cleaned and cut in rings
4 crayfish tails, uncooked
1 pimento, sliced
2tbsp peas, cooked
570ml/1pt white stock (see p.268)
290ml/½pt unshelled cooked prawns
Chopped parsley

1 Heat the oil in a deep sided frying pan or paella dish. Add the rice and onion. Stir until the rice begins to whiten.

2 Add the soaked saffron. Mix well. Arrange the chicken, squid, crayfish, pimento and peas on top of the rice. Season well. Pour over the stock.

3 Bring to the boil. Cover with greaseproof paper and simmer or bake at 180°C/350°F/Gas 4 for 35 minutes.

4 De-vein the cooked prawns if they are large (see illustrations) and add them to the paella. Cook for a further 5 minutes. Serve dusted with plenty of chopped parsley.

SOAKING SAFFRON

1 Pour a few tablespoons of hot water onto the saffron shreds.

2 After a few minutes the liquid will be bright yellow and ready for use. Strain and use the liquid, or add saffron shreds and liquid together.

1

2

☐ *Mussels, oysters, Spanish sausage, langoustine or almost any fish may be added to the Paella to ring the changes.*

DE-VEINING PRAWNS
1 If serving prawns in shells, slit down the back with a sharp knife.

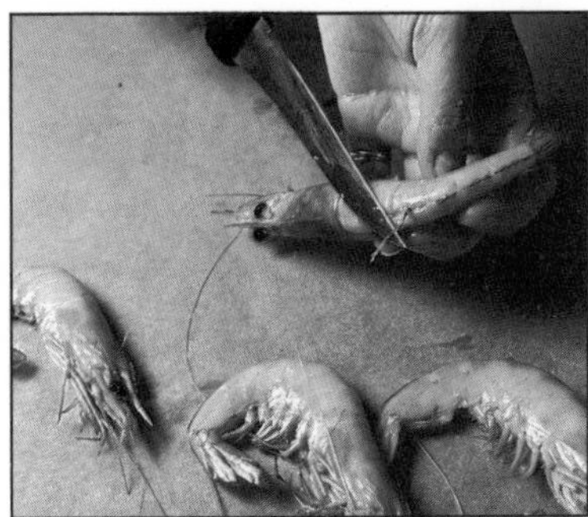

2 Remove the black thread that runs the length of the prawn. Remove the legs and any roe (coral) if preferred.

SAUCE GRELETTE

INGREDIENTS
3 tomatoes
3tbsp double cream
1tsp lemon juice
1tsp Dijon mustard
1tbsp finely chopped tarragon
1tbsp finely chopped parsley
1tsp finely chopped chervil
1tsp brandy
Salt, pepper and tabasco

1 Peel the tomatoes (see p.134). Cut into quarters. Remove the seeds and chop finely. Place in a sieve and salt lightly. Leave to drain.

2 Put the cream into a bowl with the lemon juice and mustard. Whisk lightly. Add the herbs, brandy, tabasco and tomatoes. Taste and season, if necessary, with salt and pepper.

GEM LETTUCE AND MINT SALAD

INGREDIENTS (Serves 4)
3 gem lettuces
A few sprigs mint, roughly chopped
French dressing (see p.139)

☐ *Gem lettuce are small, crisp, very well flavoured lettuces, like tiny Cos or Romaine. Use any crisp lettuce if they cannot be found.*

1 Wash and spin-dry the lettuces. Break the large leaves into smaller pieces and leave the small ones whole.

2 Toss in French dressing with the herbs and serve immediately.

MELON WITH GINGER WINE

INGREDIENTS (Serves 4)
Two 2-portion sized Ogen or Charentais melons
4tbsp ginger wine

1 Cut the melons in half and scoop out the seeds.

2 Pour 1tbsp ginger wine into each. Chill well before serving.

NOTE 1 This is much nicer than melon with port.

NOTE 2 If you don't have any ginger wine, make a strong syrup with 4tbsp sugar, 2tbsp sherry, 1tsp lemon juice, and 2tbsp water. Boil until tacky, then add 1tsp dry ginger.

PHOTOGRAPH ON P.175

MENU LESSON 33

Hot spinach tortellini with tomato salad and thyme

Braised shin of veal with oranges

New potatoes (see p.221)

Hot chocolate soufflé

Two tricky techniques are covered in this Menu Lesson — the folding and shaping of tortellini, and the making of a fairly difficult soufflé. Folding the convoluted tortellini (legend has it that their shape was inspired by that of Venus' navel) is a slow business at first, but the cook quickly speeds up with practice.

Chocolate soufflés are more difficult. The secret of success is to have absolutely everything ready (tools, ingredients, buttered dish, oven hot and cleared except for the shelf you will use — a rising soufflé can easily hit the shelf above it with disastrous results) before melting the chocolate and starting on the eggs.

If the mixture has to sit about after making, or is undercooked, it will tend to separate. Unlike savoury soufflés, sweet ones need to be fairly dry or they taste sickly.

The combination of hot pasta and cold tomato salad is surprisingly good, but of course either of these recipes would be a very adequate first course on its own.

WORK PLAN

- The tortellini can be stuffed and shaped the day before eating and refrigerated overnight.
- The tomato salad benefits from an hour or so in the dressing.
- The veal stew is excellent made in advance and reheated. It also keeps warm well.
- New potatoes are best freshly cooked but they keep warm for half an hour or so without deteriorating.
- The soufflé, of course, is a last-minute affair.

SPINACH TORTELLINI WITH TOMATO SALAD AND THYME

INGREDIENTS (Serves 4)
5 egg-quantity egg pasta (p.124)
450g/1lb fresh spinach
170g/6oz ricotta cheese
2 eggs, lightly beaten
55g/2oz fresh Parmesan cheese, grated
Salt and pepper
Unsalted butter

1 Prepare the pasta and set aside.

2 Wash the spinach and remove the stalks. Put into a saucepan without any water. Add salt and cook, gently shaking the pan occasionally for 5 – 7 minutes. The spinach should reduce in quantity by about two thirds. Drain thoroughly by squeezing between two plates.

3 Chop the spinach very finely and mix it with the ricotta, eggs and half the Parmesan cheese. Chopping and mixing may be done in a food processor. Season to taste.

4 Roll out the pasta dough and make tortellini, as illustrated. Lay the completed tortellini on a floured tea towel; be sure that they are not touching as they may stick together. Leave them to dry out for a few minutes before cooking.

5 Drop the tortellini into rapidly boiling salted water to which 1tbsp oil has been added. Cook for 5 – 6 minutes or until the pasta has lost its floury taste.

6 Drain well and rinse with plenty of boiling water to remove excess starch and prevent sticking.

7 Toss quickly in melted unsalted butter, fresh grated Parmesan cheese and ground black pepper.

☐ Ready-made tortellini are available in various flavours. They are a reasonable substitute for the real thing if you are short of time.

MAKING TORTELLINI

1 Cut the rolled-out pasta dough into 7.5cm/3 inch rounds. Put a teaspoon of stuffing into the middle of each one. Moisten the edges with water.

2 Fold them over to form stuffed semi-circles. Press the edges together.

3 Take each half-circle in both hands and curve it gently round the middle of the index finger. The ends should almost, but not quite, touch. Roll the sealed curved edge of the tortellini over to make a groove around the edge.

4 Slip the tortellini off the finger and press the ends of the curled half-moon firmly together so that the tortellini cannot unroll.

1

2

3

4

TOMATO SALAD WITH THYME

INGREDIENTS (Serves 4)
6 tomatoes
Fresh thyme
Sea salt
Coarsely ground black pepper

FOR THE DRESSING
Hazelnut oil
Lemon juice

Many tomato salad recipes call for virgin olive oil and fresh basil. A classic and delicious combination. This one of tomatoes, hazelnut oil and very fresh thyme is good too, especially with hot pasta.

1 Peel 1½ tomatoes per head (see p.134) and slice.

2 Dress well in advance with a dressing made with hazelnut oil and a drop or two of lemon juice.

3 Just before serving, sprinkle with fresh thyme leaves removed from the stalk, coarsely ground black pepper, and sea salt.

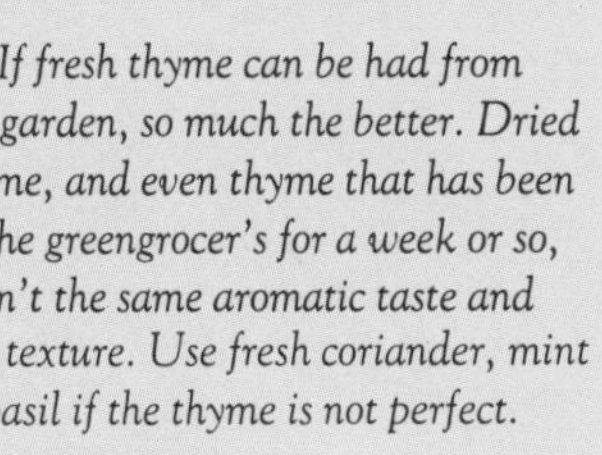

☐ *If fresh thyme can be had from the garden, so much the better. Dried thyme, and even thyme that has been in the greengrocer's for a week or so, hasn't the same aromatic taste and soft texture. Use fresh coriander, mint or basil if the thyme is not perfect.*

SLICING TOMATOES
When slicing peeled tomatoes, cut across rather than from top to tail. Discard the stalk end.

BRAISED SHIN OF VEAL WITH ORANGES

INGREDIENTS (Serves 4)
900g/2lb shin of veal, on the bone

Continued on p.196

1 Trim the veal (see p.196). Place in a large dish.

2 Add the marinade ingredients, cover and leave, turning occasionally, for 12 hours.

3 Drain the veal (but reserve the marinade) and pat dry.

FOR THE MARINADE
1 small onion, chopped
3 cloves, bruised
1 bay leaf, crumbled
1 parsley stalk, bruised
1 blade mace
Juice of 2 oranges
Juice of 1 lemon
6 peppercorns

FOR COOKING
Oil for frying
Knob of butter
290ml/½pt white stock (see p.268)
Salt and freshly ground black pepper
8 baby turnips, peeled
8 button onions, peeled
8 turned carrots (see p.150)
1tbsp sugar

TO GARNISH
1 orange

4 Heat the oil in a large flameproof casserole, add a knob of butter and in it brown the shin of veal evenly all over.

5 Remove the pan from the heat, strain in the marinade and add the chicken stock. Season with salt and pepper. Return to the heat, bring to the boil, cover tightly and cook in the oven for 1½ hours, at 170°C/325°F/Gas 3.

6 Add the turnips, onions and carrots and return to the oven until the meat is very tender and the vegetables still firm (about 30 minutes).

7 Meanwhile prepare the garnish: peel the orange (see p.38) and cut into segments. Reserve the juice.

8 Take the veal out of the oven. Carve into neat slices and arrange on a warm serving dish. Surround with the vegetables. Strain the liquid.

9 Dissolve the sugar in a small, heavy saucepan with 1tbsp water. Then boil rapidly until lightly caramelized. Add the strained liquid and reserved orange juice and boil again until all the lumps have disappeared. Reduce by boiling rapidly, until slightly syrupy, add the orange segments and pour over the sliced veal.

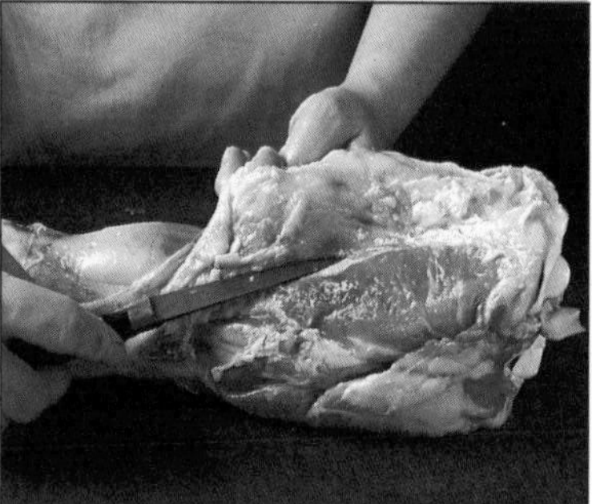

TRIMMING VEAL
With a sharp knife and your fingers carefully lift and cut away as much fat, membrane and gristle as possible.

HOT CHOCOLATE SOUFFLE

INGREDIENTS (Serves 4)
Unsalted butter
A little caster sugar
110g/4oz dark chocolate
1tbsp brandy
55g/2oz caster sugar
4 eggs, separated
Icing sugar

1 Set the oven to 200°C/400°F/Gas 6. Place a baking sheet on the middle shelf and remove any shelves above it. Prepare a soufflé dish by greasing the inside with butter and dusting it with caster sugar.

2 Chop the chocolate into small even-sized pieces and place in a bowl over a pan of simmering water, without allowing the bottom of the bowl to touch the water. Stir as the chocolate melts.

3 Whisk the sugar and egg yolks together and when pale in colour and mousse-like add the warm chocolate and brandy.

4 Whisk the egg whites until they will stand in soft peaks (see p.285). Gently but thoroughly fold them into the mixture.

5 Turn into the soufflé dish. With a large palette knife cut through the mixture to make sure that there are no over-large pockets of air. Run your finger round the edge of the dish (this is to help get the 'top hat' finish) and bake, on the pre-heated baking sheet, for 18– 20 minutes.

6 Test by giving the dish a slight shake or push. If it wobbles alarmingly it needs further cooking; if it is fairly steady, it is ready. Sift over a dusting of icing sugar and serve at once.

PHOTOGRAPH ON P.174

MENU LESSON 34

Boned chicken stuffed with leeks

Potatoes sautéed with rosemary (p.138)

Creamed carrots and peas

Tarte Normande

This menu is spectacular to look at, and very delicious. It takes a good two hours of work however, and, because the dessert is almost indecently rich and is bound to promote second helpings, there is no first course. For a lighter menu, you might substitute a plain green vegetable or a salad for the buttery purées.

Two techniques learned here are the boning of a chicken, and the making of a ballotine (a ballotine is a stuffed boned rolled-up bird or joint that is baked or roasted with very little, if any, stock. A galantine is similar but poached in plenty of liquid). If serving the chicken cold, the cook also learns the useful art of fine aspic glazing. Properly applied aspic can be elegant and pretty. Clumsily executed aspic is unattractive — like a PVC overcoat encasing the food.

WORK PLAN

- If the chicken is to be eaten cold it can with advantage be cooked and decorated the day before eating.
- Both chicken (covered in foil) and sauce will keep warm happily for an hour. Slice the chicken at the last minute.
- Sautéed potatoes keep warm in a cool oven in an open dish for an hour or so, and creamed vegetables re-heat well in a microwave oven or stirred over direct heat.
- Make the tarte on the morning of the dinner and re-heat to lukewarm.

BONED CHICKEN STUFFED WITH LEEKS

INGREDIENTS (Serves 8)
1 × 1.35kg/3lb chicken
Salt and white pepper
1tbsp mixed chopped fresh thyme and marjoram
5 small leeks
Lemon juice
2 courgettes, peeled
4 sticks celery
6 juniper berries
225g/8oz quark or fromage blanc

TO SERVE COLD
7g/¼oz gelatine
Cucumber peel
150ml/¼pt aspic made from aspic powder

TO GARNISH
Bunch of watercress

1 TO BONE THE CHICKEN, see the illustrations on p.198.

2 Open out the chicken, skin side down. Season with salt, pepper and some of the thyme and marjoram.

3 Clean the leeks thoroughly (see p.192), removing coarse leaves and most of the green part, and place 4 down the centre of the chicken. Season well with salt, pepper, lemon juice and herbs. Roll up the chicken and wrap in muslin (see p.199).

4 Coarsely chop the remaining leek, courgette and celery. Put them in a large saucepan and barely cover with water. Add the juniper berries, remaining herbs, salt and pepper.

5 Place the chicken on top of the vegetables. Cover tightly and braise gently for 1 hour. The chicken is cooked when it feels firm and solid.

TO SERVE HOT
6 Remove the chicken to a warm serving dish. Discard the juniper berries from the stock and liquidize the vegetables with enough of the liquid to give a creamy sauce. Strain into a clean saucepan, whisk in the fromage blanc or quark, and season to taste. Do not boil lest it curdle.

7 Unwrap the chicken and cut across into slices. Garnish with watercress. Hand the sauce separately.

TO SERVE COLD
6 Tighten the muslin wrapping round the chicken and leave to get quite cold, then refrigerate. Remove the muslin.

7 Remove the juniper berries from the stock and liquidize together the vegetables, juices (including any from the chicken) and the cheese.

8 In a small, heavy saucepan put 3tbsp water and sprinkle over the gelatine. Allow to soak for 10 minutes, and then warm gently until runny and clear.

9 Stir into the vegetable sauce. Cool, stirring occasionally until on the point of setting and use to coat the chicken, spooning it over the bird.

10 Cut the cucumber peel into fine strips or diamond shapes. Plunge

BONING A CHICKEN

1 Put the chicken breast-side down on a board. Cut through to the backbone.

2 Feel for the fleshy 'oyster' at the top of each thigh and cut round it. Cut and scrape the flesh from the carcass with a sharp knife held as close as possible to the bone.

3 Continue along both sides of the backbone until the rib-cage is exposed. At the joint of the thigh and pelvis, cut between the bones at the socket so that the legs stay attached to the flesh and skin, and not to the body carcass.

4 Keep working right round the bird then use scissors to cut away most of the rib cage, leaving only the cartilaginous breast-bone in the centre.

5 Using a heavy knife cut through the foot joints to remove the knuckle end of the drumsticks.

6 Working from the inside thigh end scrape one leg bone clean, pushing the flesh down towards the drumstick until you can free the thigh bone. Repeat on the other leg.

7 Working from the drumstick ends, scrape the lower leg bones clean in the same way and remove them. Remove as many tendons as possible from the legs as you work.

8 Now for the wings. Cut off the pinions with a heavy knife.

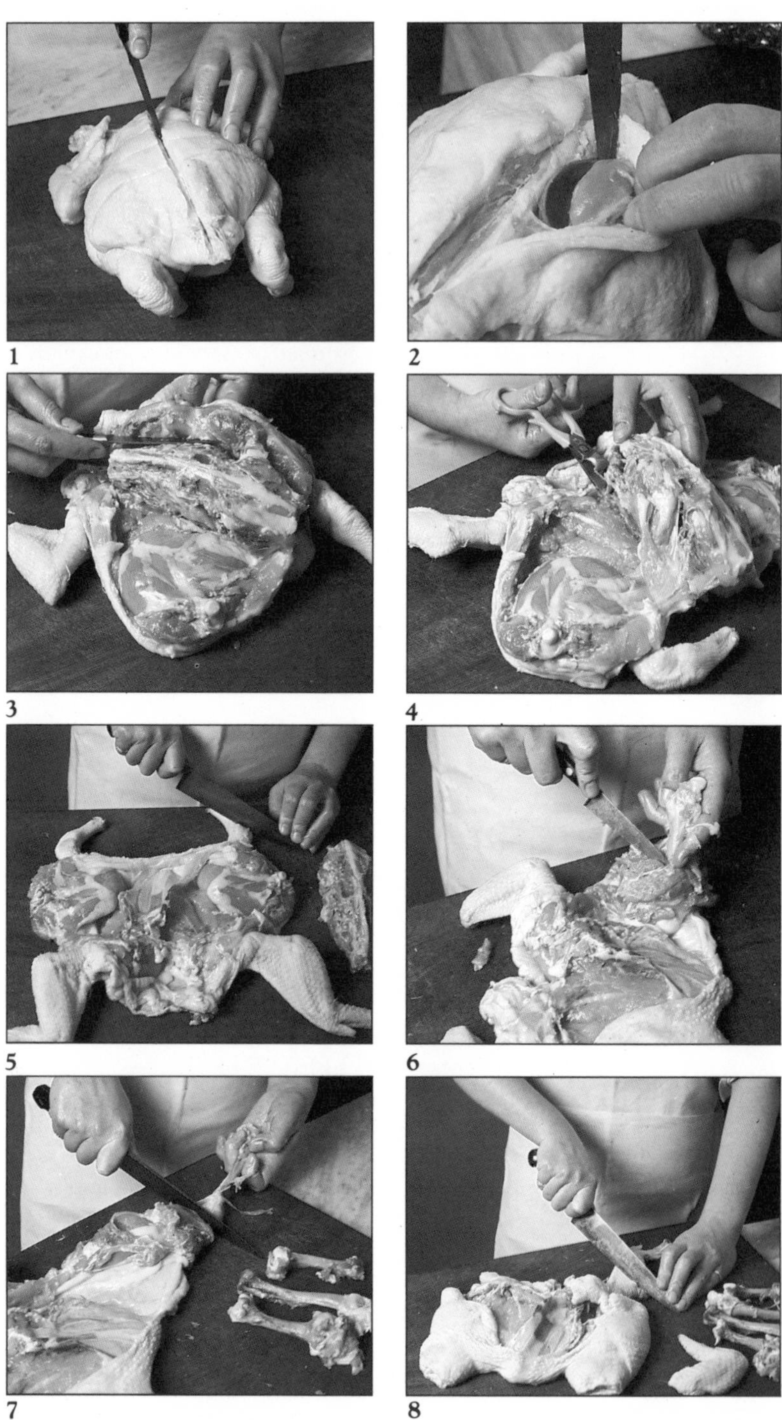

1 2 3 4 5 6 7 8

them into boiling water for 1 minute to soften them. Rinse under cold water, drain and dry. Use to decorate the ballotine.

11 Melt the aspic and cool until on the point of setting. Using a large metal spoon held close to the spoon-bowl, glaze the chicken with the aspic, taking care not to dislodge the decoration. If the aspic sets too fast, stand the aspic container in a bowl of warm water to re-melt it. You will then need a bowl of iced water handy to get it setting again. The perfect moment when the aspic is thick and syrupy but not yet set does not last long, so use it the second it reaches the right consistency.

9 Scrape the wing bones clean as you did the leg bones.

10 Carefully free the breastbone with the knife, working from the middle of the bird towards the tail.

11 Take great care not to puncture the skin, which has no flesh under it at this point so is easily torn.

12 You should now have a beautifully boned bird. Keep the neck flap of skin intact to fold over once the chicken is stuffed.

STUFFING AND ROLLING

1 Lay the leeks down the centre of the chicken and season with salt, pepper, lemon juice and herbs.

2 Fold over the ends, then the sides, to make a neat parcel. Roll in a piece of muslin or a pressed paper kitchen cloth. (Do not use a red one as the dye will run.) Twist the ends. The cloth should be wrapped tightly round the chicken twice.

3 Tuck the ends under. Place the parcel on top of the vegetables and cover the saucepan tightly.

4 The chicken is cooked when it feels firm and solid — not squashy — when pressed. A skewer will glide through it easily. Test before unwrapping and check again after. If piercing with a skewer allows the escape of pink rather than clear juices, rewrap and cook further.

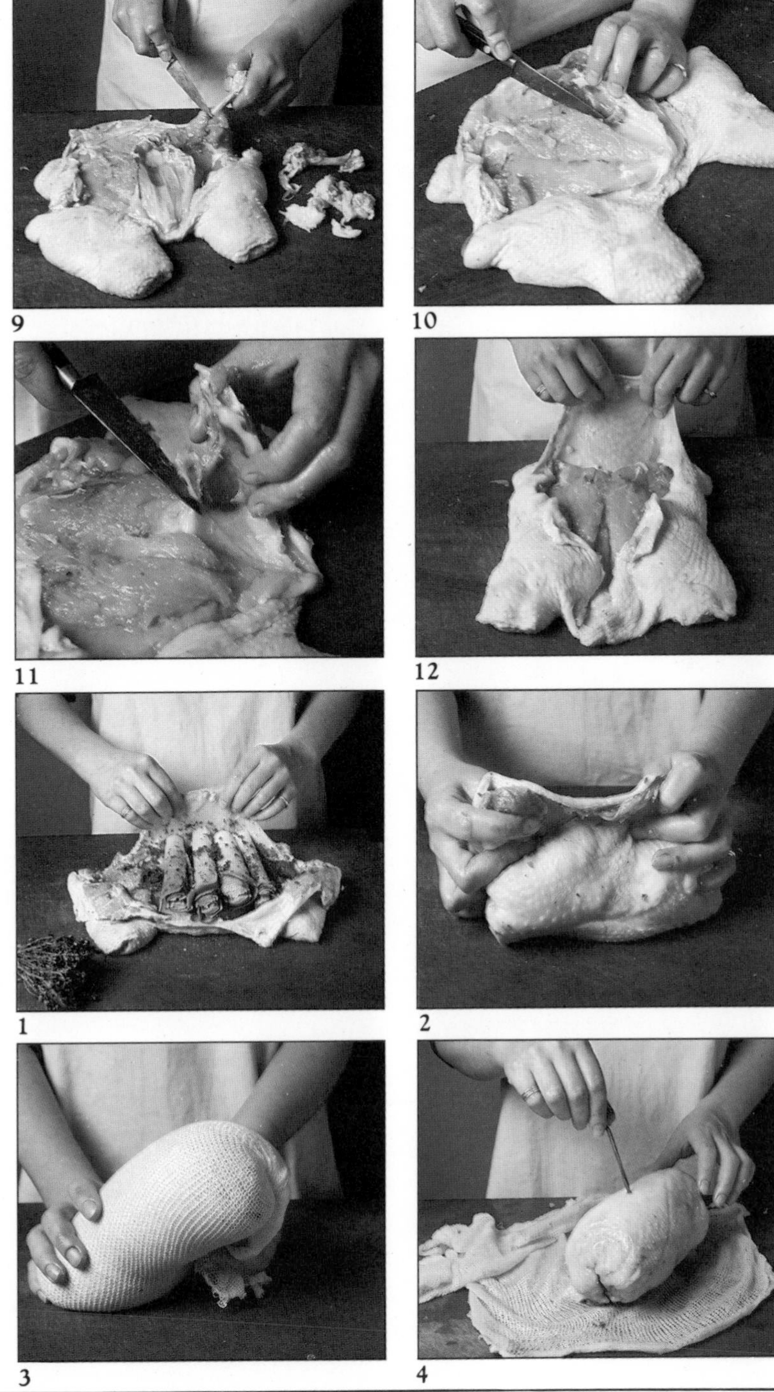

9 10 11 12 1 2 3 4

CREAMED CARROTS AND PEAS

INGREDIENTS (Serves 4-6)
450g/1lb peas
450g/1lb carrots
110g/4oz butter
1tsp sugar
Salt and pepper
Pinch dried ginger
2tsp chopped mint

1 Boil the peas and carrots in separate pans of salted water until tender right through — not crisp at all. Drain well.

2 Push the vegetables through sieves into two bowls, and add half the butter to each. Flavour the peas with a pinch of sugar, salt, pepper and mint, the carrots with sugar, salt, pepper and a pinch of ginger. (Alternatively they can be 'whizzed' in a processor.)

3 Put the carrot purée into one end of an ovenproof dish with the pea purée at the other.

4 Mark a criss-cross pattern on the top with a fork, and keep warm and covered until serving.

TARTE NORMANDE

INGREDIENTS (Serves 8)
225g/8oz flour-quantity rich shortcrust pastry (see p.192)

FOR THE ALMOND CREAM
110g/4oz unsalted butter
110g/4oz caster sugar
1 egg
1 egg yolk
55g/2oz plain flour
110g/4oz ground almonds
1tbsp cream

FOR THE FILLING
5 small ripe eating apples
4tbsp smooth apricot jam
1tbsp lemon juice

1 Make up the pastry and use it to line a 25cm/10 inch flan ring (see p.190). Prick lightly with a fork and chill in the refrigerator for 20 minutes.

2 Set the oven to 220°C/425°F/Gas 7.

3 PREPARE THE ALMOND CREAM Beat the butter and when soft add the sugar. Beat until pale and creamy. Add the egg, egg yolk, flour, almonds and cream. Spread mixture into the pastry case.

4 Peel the apples. Halve from the stalk down through the core and remove the core, keeping the apple halves intact.

5 Slice the half-apples, keeping all the slices together in their original order. Arrange as many half-apples in the almond cream round the edge of the dish, rounded side up, as will fit. Press each apple half so that the slices overlap slightly. Put a last half apple in the middle and press firmly into the cream.

6 Melt the jam slowly with the lemon juice. Spoon about half of it over the apples.

7 Bake for 15 minutes. Turn the oven down to 180°C/350°F/Gas 4 and bake for a further 20 minutes.

8 Remove from the oven when the pastry is crisp, the apples cooked and the almond cream risen and brown.

9 Brush the flan top with more melted jam and return to the oven for a further 10 minutes. Serve lukewarm.

☐ *The pastry for the tarte is so rich it can easily be pressed into the fluted flan ring rather than rolled out. Do not worry if it is a little uneven — the filling will disguise all.*

☐ *Both the pastry and the almond cream can be made quickly in a food processor. Make the pastry first, then, without washing the bowl or knife, proceed with the almond cream.*

PHOTOGRAPH ON P.210

MENU LESSON 35

Quails eggs en croustade

Braised pheasant with calvados

Mashed potatoes (see p.101)

Braised fennel

Cold lime soufflé

Quails eggs, though tasting very little different from hens eggs, are small enough to look very pretty in a tiny tartlet 'nest'. The sophisticated beurre blanc sauce gives the dish richness and sophistication and is a sauce well worth mastering.

Two different techniques of braising are used to produce the main pheasant dish and the Florence fennel.

The lime soufflé emphasizes the importance of getting the correct texture of the basic mousse mixture, the whisked egg whites and the cream — the closer they are to each other in consistency the easier they will be to lightly fold together. Equally, if the mousse is barely warm when the warm gelatine goes in they will combine without trouble.

WORK PLAN

- The croustade and duxelle for the first course may be prepared a few hours in advance but they should not be put together until the last minute, when the eggs are just poached.
- The beurre blanc, if properly made, will stand for 20 minutes or so without separating.
- The main course is best cooked just before serving but pheasant, fennel and potatoes will keep warm satisfactorily. The potatoes will reheat well, especially in a microwave oven.
- The cold soufflé is best made on the morning of serving. Overnight refrigeration tends to make the texture slightly rubbery, though the taste will of course remain delicious. On no account decorate the soufflé the day before however. Whipped cream easily picks up a stale 'fridge' taste if kept.

QUAILS EGGS EN CROUSTADE

INGREDIENTS (Serves 4)
4 thin slices bread
Unsalted butter, melted
1 shallot, finely chopped
1 rasher streaky rindless bacon, finely chopped
85g/3oz flat mushrooms, finely chopped
Chopped parsley
Salt and freshly ground black pepper
8 quails eggs
Half quantity beurre blanc (see next recipe)

TO GARNISH
Fresh chives (optional)

1 TO MAKE THE CROUSTADE, cut each bread slice into one long, or two small, rounds with a pastry cutter.

2 Dip the bread rounds into melted butter and press into patty tins.

3 Bake at 190°C/375°F/Gas 5 for 15 minutes. Remove from the tins and bake for a further 10 minutes.

4 Meanwhile, PREPARE THE DUXELLE. Cook the shallot and bacon in a little butter. Squeeze the mushrooms in a cloth and add to the pan. Cook for a further 2 minutes. Add the parsley and season to taste with salt and pepper.

5 POACH THE QUAILS EGGS Break the eggs onto a flat plate, keeping them separate. Heat a wide sauté or frying pan filled with water. When boiling, push the eggs, one by one, into the water so they are not all clustered together. Poach for 1 minute. Lift out with a perforated spoon and drain.

TO MAKE CROUSTADES
1 Cut out rounds of bread with a fluted cutter and dip them in the melted butter.

2 Press the rounds into patty tins. If possible place another patty tray on top to hold the bread rounds in shape.

3 Bake with the top tray in place (several trays can be stacked in one pile if making many croustades), then remove while hot. Cool on a wire tray.

6 TO SERVE, Lift the duxelle from the saucepan with a draining spoon. Divide the mixture between the croustades. Place 2 eggs on top of each and coat with the beurre blanc.

NOTE If serving the croustades on individual plates, you could garnish them with fresh chives as shown in the photograph, on p.210.

BEURRE BLANC

INGREDIENTS
110g/4oz butter, unsalted
½tsp very finely chopped shallot
1 bay leaf
1½tbsp wine vinegar
1½tbsp water
Salt and white pepper
Squeeze of lemon
1tbsp double cream (optional)

1 Chill the butter, then cut it in three lengthways, then across in thin slices. Keep cold.

2 Put the shallot, bay leaf, vinegar and water into a thick bottomed sauté pan or small shallow saucepan. Boil slowly until about 2tbsp liquid remain.

3 Using a small wire sauce whisk gradually add the butter piece by piece. When the last of the butter is beaten in, the sauce should be warm rather than hot. (As the proportion of fat to vinegar increases, the danger of separating increases if the sauce is too hot.) The process should take about 4 minutes. Add salt, pepper and lemon juice. Stir in the cream if used.

☐ *Stand the beurre blanc saucepan in warm water and give it an occasional whisk if it must be kept warm before serving.*

BEURRE BLANC
1 Boil the vinegar very gently with the shallot, peppercorns and bay leaf until two tablespoons of liquid remain. (The reduction must be cooked slowly to allow time for the shallot to soften and flavour the vinegar.)

2 Strain and return to the heat (or leave unstrained if preferred, but remove the peppercorns and bayleaf). Use plenty of vigorous action while beating in the chilled butter a few pieces at a time. Do not stop whisking throughout the process.

3 The liquid should be allowed to boil at first.

4 Lower the temperature as more butter is added. When the last lump of butter is added, the sauce should be very warm rather than hot, and pale, thick and creamy.

BRAISED PHEASANT WITH CALVADOS

INGREDIENTS (Serves 4)
2 pheasants
45g/1½oz unsalted or clarified butter (see p.75)
2tbsp calvados
1 large onion, finely sliced
2 sticks celery, chopped
1 carrot, peeled and chopped
2tsp flour
290ml/½pt dry cider
150ml/¼pt white stock (see p.268)
Salt and pepper
Bouquet garni (see p.344)

TO GARNISH
Chopped parsley

☐ *When flaming alcohol, stand well back in case the flames leap high. If they do, don't try to move the pan. Wait for the flames to die down or extinguish them with a pan lid.*

1 Set the oven to 180°C/350°F/Gas 4.

2 Wipe the pheasants and trim away any feathers. Heat the butter in a large flameproof casserole, and fry the pheasants gently until well browned all over.

3 Heat the calvados in a ladle, light it with a match and pour it, flaming, over the pheasants. Shake the pan until the flames have died down. If by any chance the flames become too high, turn off the source of heat (do not move the pan) and cover with a lid.

4 Add the onion, celery and carrot to the pan and cook until beginning to soften, but not brown.

5 Add the flour, stir well and cook for 30 seconds. Add the cider and chicken stock. Bring gradually up to the boil. Simmer for 2 minutes. Season with salt and pepper, add the bouquet garni, cover and bake for 1 hour. Remove the bouquet garni.

6 TO SERVE Lift out the pheasants and joint them as you would a chicken (see p.96). Keep warm on a serving dish.

7 Boil the sauce rapidly to reduce to a syrupy consistency. Pour over the pheasants, and sprinkle with chopped parsley.

BRAISED FENNEL

INGREDIENTS (Serves 4)
675g/1½lb Florence fennel (vegetable, not herb)
30g/1oz butter
1tbsp chopped fresh mint
1tbsp chopped fresh parsley
Juice of ½ lemon

1 Discard any discoloured outside leaves and quarter the heads of fennel neatly.

2 Lay the pieces in a roasting pan or ovenproof dish. Melt the butter and add the chopped herbs and lemon juice. Brush this over the fennel.

3 Cover tightly with a lid or foil and bake in the oven for about 1½ hours at 180°C/350°F/Gas 4 until the fennel is quite tender.

NOTE The fennel may be served on the same dish as the pheasant or by itself.

COLD LIME SOUFFLE

INGREDIENTS (Serves 4)
7g/¼oz gelatine
3tbsp water
3 eggs
140g/5oz caster sugar
Juice and rind of 4 limes
150ml/¼pt double cream, lightly whipped

FOR THE DECORATION
Icing sugar
Coarsely chopped pistacchio nuts

1 Tie a double-band of oiled paper round the top of a 12.5cm/5 inch soufflé dish so that it projects about 3cm/1½ inch above the rim.

2 Put the 3tbsp water into a very small saucepan. Sprinkle the gelatine over evenly and set aside until spongy in texture (about 10 minutes).

3 Separate the eggs. Place the yolks and sugar in a large mixing bowl and whisk together with an electric mixer (or with a balloon whisk or rotary beater with the bowl set over a saucepan of simmering water). Whisk until very thick. Gradually add the lime juice and rind. If whisking by hand over hot water, remove from the heat and whisk for a few minutes longer (until the mixture is lukewarm).

4 Dissolve the gelatine over a gentle heat and when clear and warm add it to the mousse mixture. Stir gently, occasionally, until the mixture is on the point of setting, then fold in the cream.

5 Whisk the egg whites until stiff but not dry and fold them into the soufflé with a large metal spoon.

6 Pour the mixture into a soufflé dish. It should come about 2.5cm/1-inch up the paper, above the top of the dish. Leave to set in the refrigerator for 2–3 hours.

7 Not more than half an hour before serving decorate the top.

NOTE A drop of green colouring can be added to the soufflé to give it a lime-coloured appearance. Take great care not to add too much lest it look garish.

TO DECORATE A COLD SOUFFLE

1 Carefully peel off the paper using a palette knife to ease the soufflé off the paper and prevent it sticking.

2 Dredge the top heavily with icing sugar sifted through a wire sieve.

1

2

3 Heat several skewers over a gas flame until red hot. Drag the skewers through the icing sugar to produce the first parallel lines.

4 Repeat to create a diagonal lattice pattern. Press the chopped nuts into the exposed sides with a palette knife.

3

4

PHOTOGRAPH ON P.211

The cook learns, in this menu, to make a simple combination of vegetables into a spectacular looking baked mould, to poach trout to perfection and to produce one of the prettiest of flans, the classic Tarte Française.

MENU LESSON 36

Aubergine pie

Poached trout with watercress sauce

New potatoes (see p.221)

Cucumber and mint salad

Tarte Française

WORK PLAN

- The aubergine pie is best made on the day of serving, but it needs to cool to room temperature. It could be made 5 – 8 hours in advance.
- The sauce for the fish can be made and reheated, but the trout must be poached immediately before serving.
- The Tarte pastry case can be made the day before but should not be filled or glazed until an hour or so before serving.

AUBERGINE PIE

INGREDIENTS (Serves 6-8)
2 large aubergines
Salt and freshly ground black pepper
1tbsp oil
1 onion, finely chopped
1 clove garlic, crushed
20 tomatoes, peeled, quartered, seeded and diced
1 small bunch fresh basil, finely chopped
225g/8oz plain low fat yoghurt

1 Wash and slice the aubergines. Sprinkle with salt and leave to stand in a colander for 30 minutes. Rinse well and pat dry.

2 Meanwhile cook the onions and garlic in the oil for 3 minutes. Add the tomatoes, salt and pepper and cook for a further 25 minutes or until a thickish pulp. Add the basil.

3 Heat the oven to 180°C/350°F/Gas 4.

4 STEAM THE AUBERGINES Place the slices in a large steamer and put this over a saucepan of boiling water. The water must not touch the aubergines. Cook until tender. This may take up to 20 minutes. Drain well on absorbent paper.

5 Oil a charlotte or cake tin and arrange a close fitting layer of aubergines along the bottom and sides. Layer the remaining aubergines with the tomatoes and yoghurt, finishing with a layer of aubergines.

6 Cover with wet greaseproof paper, place on a baking sheet and bake in the centre of the oven for 20 – 25 minutes. Remove the greaseproof paper. Leave to cool in the tin.

7 To turn out, put a plate over the mould, turn both over together, give a good firm shake, down and away from yourself, and remove the mould.

8 Soak up the liquid, which runs out, with successive layers of absorbent paper. Any extra tomato sauce or yoghurt can be mixed together and handed separately.

☐ *Aubergine pie makes an excellent vegetarian main course.*

POACHED TROUT WITH WATERCRESS SAUCE

INGREDIENTS (Serves 4)
4 one-portion cleaned trout (see p.264)
Court bouillon (see p.270)
Watercress sauce (see next recipe)

TO GARNISH
Watercress
A few of the court bouillon vegetables

☐ *The freshest trout have shiny skins, bulging eyes, bright gills and are as slippery as eels. They should have hardly any 'fishy' smell.*

1 Place the trout in a large saucepan or fish kettle. Pour over the cool court bouillon. Bring very slowly up to simmering point and poach (this means that no bubbles at all rise to the surface, but the water trembles very slightly — it is cooler than simmering) for 4 minutes.

2 The fish should now be done. The dorsal fin will pull out easily and the eyes will look very white and prominent.

3 Lift the fish from the liquid, drain them and arrange on a large, warm serving dish. Decorate with a few of the court bouillon vegetables and the watercress and hand the sauce separately.

WATERCRESS SAUCE

INGREDIENTS (Serves 4)
2 shallots
30g/1oz butter
2 bunches of watercress
1 glass white wine
1tbsp wine vinegar
570ml/1pt white stock (see p.268)
75ml/2½fl oz double cream
Salt and pepper

1 Chop the shallots and cook slowly in half of the butter.

2 Meanwhile pick over the watercress and finely chop the leaves and very tender stalks. Add two thirds of it to the saucepan with the wine and vinegar. Boil until reduced to about a third of its original quantity.

3 Add the chicken stock and boil until reduced to a third of a pint.

4 Add the cream. Reheat without boiling. Season and stir in the remaining butter and chopped watercress.

CUCUMBER AND MINT SALAD

INGREDIENTS (Serves 4)
1 extra large cucumber
Salt and freshly ground black pepper
3tbsp plain yoghurt
1tbsp fresh mint, finely chopped

TO GARNISH
Whole small mint leaves (optional)

1 Wash the cucumber, and grate coarsely, skin and all. Place in a colander , sprinkle with salt and leave to dégorge for 30 minutes. Rinse very well and pat dry.

2 Mix together the cucumber, yoghurt, mint, salt and pepper and serve within one hour.

TARTE FRANCAISE

INGREDIENTS (Serves 4)
170g/6oz flour-quantity rough puff (see next recipe) or puff pastry (p.85)

FOR THE FILLING
1 egg, lightly beaten
4tbsp apricot jam
Squeeze of lemon juice
2 oranges
85g/3oz black grapes
2 bananas
1 green apple
1 red plum

1 Roll out the pastry into a rectangle about 25×20cm/10×8 inches. It should be the thickness of a coin. Prick lightly all over. Cut out a border 2cm/¾ inch wide from the remaining pastry, to exactly fit the rectangle. Brush the outside edge of the rectangle with a little beaten egg and place the border on top.

2 Flour the blade of a knife and use this to 'knock up' the sides of the pastry: try to slightly separate the leaves of the pastry horizontally; this means that the edge will flake readily when cooking (see p.70).

3 With the back of the knife blade mark a pattern on the border of the pastry case. Try not to cut through the pastry.

☐ *The secret of a good looking Tarte Française is tightly packed neatly overlapping rows of fruit — be generous with both fruit and jam glaze. Remember the jam is the only sweetening the dish is to get so the cook can afford a deep shiny layer. In the autumn a tart can be made with a combination of dark fruits, which look spectacular — blueberries, raspberries, figs, damsons, dark plums, redcurrants, blackcurrants and blackberries.*

4 Brush the pastry border carefully with the beaten egg. Avoid the knocked up sides — if they are covered with egg the pastry will be prevented from rising.

5 Bake at 220°C/425°F/Gas 7 for 20 minutes or until golden brown and cooked. Leave to cool on a wire rack.

6 TO MAKE THE GLAZE, heat the apricot jam with 2tbsp water and the lemon juice in a small saucepan and push through a sieve. Brush a small quantity of this glaze over the base of the pastry. Keep the rest warm.

7 PREPARE THE FRUIT Peel the oranges with a knife as you would an apple, making sure that all the pith is removed. Divide into segments (see illustration p.38) and drain well. Cut the grapes in half and remove the pips. Peel and slice the bananas. Core the apple but do not peel it. Cut into slivers. Cut the plum into small neat segments.

8 Lay the fruit in rows on the pastry as neatly and closely together as possible. Be careful to get contrasting colours (do not put the apple next to the banana). As each row is laid down, spoon over warm apricot glaze. This is most important, especially with fruit that discolours such as apples and bananas. The glaze should be fairly deep.

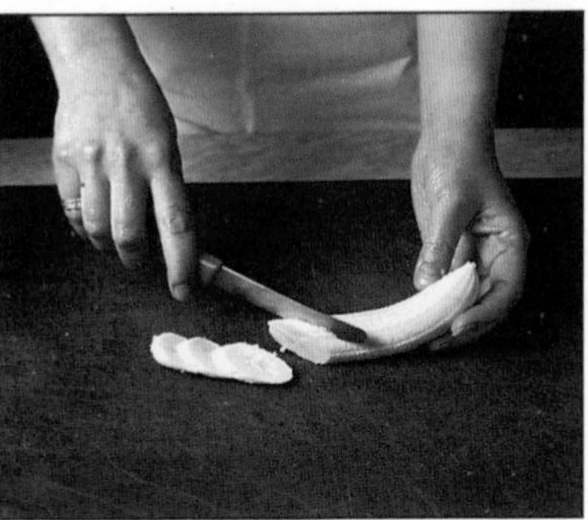

SLICING BANANAS
To get near-identical slices of banana that will lie evenly when overlapping, hold the banana like a boat, with ends up (rather than lying flat), then slice with neat parallel cuts.

GLAZING A TART
Bring melted jam glaze to the right temperature to give a just-liquid syrupy consistency. (Redcurrant jelly needs to be almost cold to be at the right consistency, but apricot jam needs to be warmer.) Spoon slowly over the fruit, allowing the glaze to cover the fruit and fill the hollows. To ensure a steady hand, hold the spoon near the bowl. If the fruit is of the kind that discolours easily, spoon the glaze on as soon as the row is in place.

ROUGH PUFF PASTRY

INGREDIENTS
170g/6oz plain flour
Pinch of salt
105g/3¾oz butter
Very cold water

1 Sift the flour and salt into a cold bowl. Cut the butter into knobs about the size of a sugar lump and add to the flour. Do not rub in but add enough water to just bind the paste together. Mix first with a knife, then with one hand.

2 Wrap the pastry up and leave to relax for 10 minutes in the refrigerator.

ROUGH PUFF PASTRY

3 On a floured board, roll the pastry into a strip about 15×10cm/6×4 inches. This must be done carefully: with a heavy rolling pin, press firmly on the pastry and give short sharp rolls until the pastry has reached the required size. The surface of the pastry should not be over-stretched and broken.

4 Fold the strip into three and turn so that the folded edge is to your left, like a closed book.

5 Again roll out into a strip 1cm/½-inch thick. Fold in three again and leave, wrapped, in the refrigerator for 15 minutes.

6 Roll and fold the pastry as before then chill again for 15 minutes.

7 Roll and fold again, by which time the pastry should be ready for use, with no signs of streakiness.

8 Roll into the required shape.

9 Chill again before baking.

ROUGH PUFF PASTRY

1 Cut butter into small pieces about the size of sugar-lumps and add them to the flour. Do not rub in.

2 Add enough water to bind together, mixing with a knife as you do so.

1

2

3 Gather the paste into a ball with one hand, wrap up and refrigerate for about 10 minutes.

4 Roll out on a floured board into a rectangle 15×10cm (6×4 inches). Be very careful not to overstretch the pastry.

3

4

5 Fold the strip of pastry into three lengthways.

6 Give it a half turn so the fold is on your left. Roll and fold as above three times, chilling the paste if the fat shows signs of melting or breaking through the flour.

5

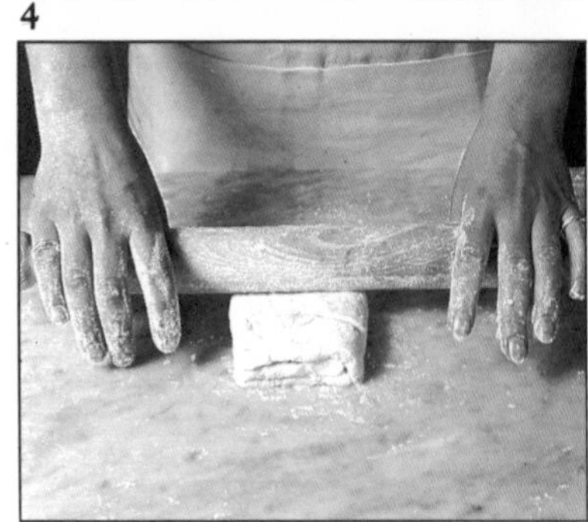

6

PHOTOGRAPH ON P.211

To make a good meatball the cook needs to be prepared to taste the raw mixture (in fact raw mixtures are surprisingly good) in order to adjust the seasoning. If this is impossible, fry a teaspoon and taste it cooked, before rolling the meatballs.

The technique of 'turning' mangoes is a neat and useful trick, making a simple dessert festive and easy for the diner to eat.

MENU LESSON 37

Spinach and ricotta cheese strudels with carrot and tomato purée

Meatballs with coriander and tomato sauce

Stir-fried vegetables

Spicy basmati rice (see p.97)

Fresh turned mangoes

WORK PLAN

- The strudels can be prepared well in advance but are best freshly baked.
- Meatballs positively improve on reheating, and freeze excellently.
- Stir-fried vegetables are a last-minute, but very quick dish. The rice can easily be timed to be ready when needed, and the mangoes can be cut a few hours in advance. Do not refrigerate once cut however — they will make any milk, butter or cream in the refrigerator taste of mango.

SPINACH AND RICOTTA CHEESE STRUDELS

INGREDIENTS (Serves 4)
450g/1lb fresh spinach
225g/8oz ricotta cheese
1 egg, lightly beaten
Salt and black pepper
Grated nutmeg
280g/10oz flour-quantity strudel pastry
30g/1oz melted butter

TO SERVE
Carrot and tomato purée (see next recipe)

☐ *Perfectly good strudel pastry (filo or phylo pastry) can be bought from specialist Greek food shops. It freezes well, so although the pack will contain more pastry than this recipe requires, it will not be wasted. It comes ready rolled in thin sheets.*

1 MAKE THE FILLING Wash the spinach and remove the stalks. Put still wet into a pan, but without added water. Cover and cook gently, shaking the pan occasionally for 5-7 minutes. The spinach will reduce in quantity by about two thirds. Drain well by squeezing between two plates, and chop finely.

2 Put the cheese into a bowl, add the spinach and beat together, adding the egg. Season to taste with salt, pepper and nutmeg.

3 Set the oven to 200°C/400°F/Gas 6.

4 TO MAKE THE STRUDELS, divide the dough into 4 pieces. Keep 3 of them covered. Dredge a teatowel with flour, put the pastry on top and roll it out as thinly as possible. Now put your hand, lightly floured, under the pastry and, keeping your hand firmly flat, gently stretch and pull until the pastry is paper thin (see p.77). Cut off the thick edges.

5 Brush immediately with butter. Spread a quarter of the mixture over the pastry and roll up rather like a Swiss roll, using the teatowel to help. Roll onto a greased baking sheet. Curve into a horseshoe shape.

6 Roll out, fill and shape the remaining strudels.

7 Brush with butter and bake for 15 minutes.

8 Hand the purée separately.

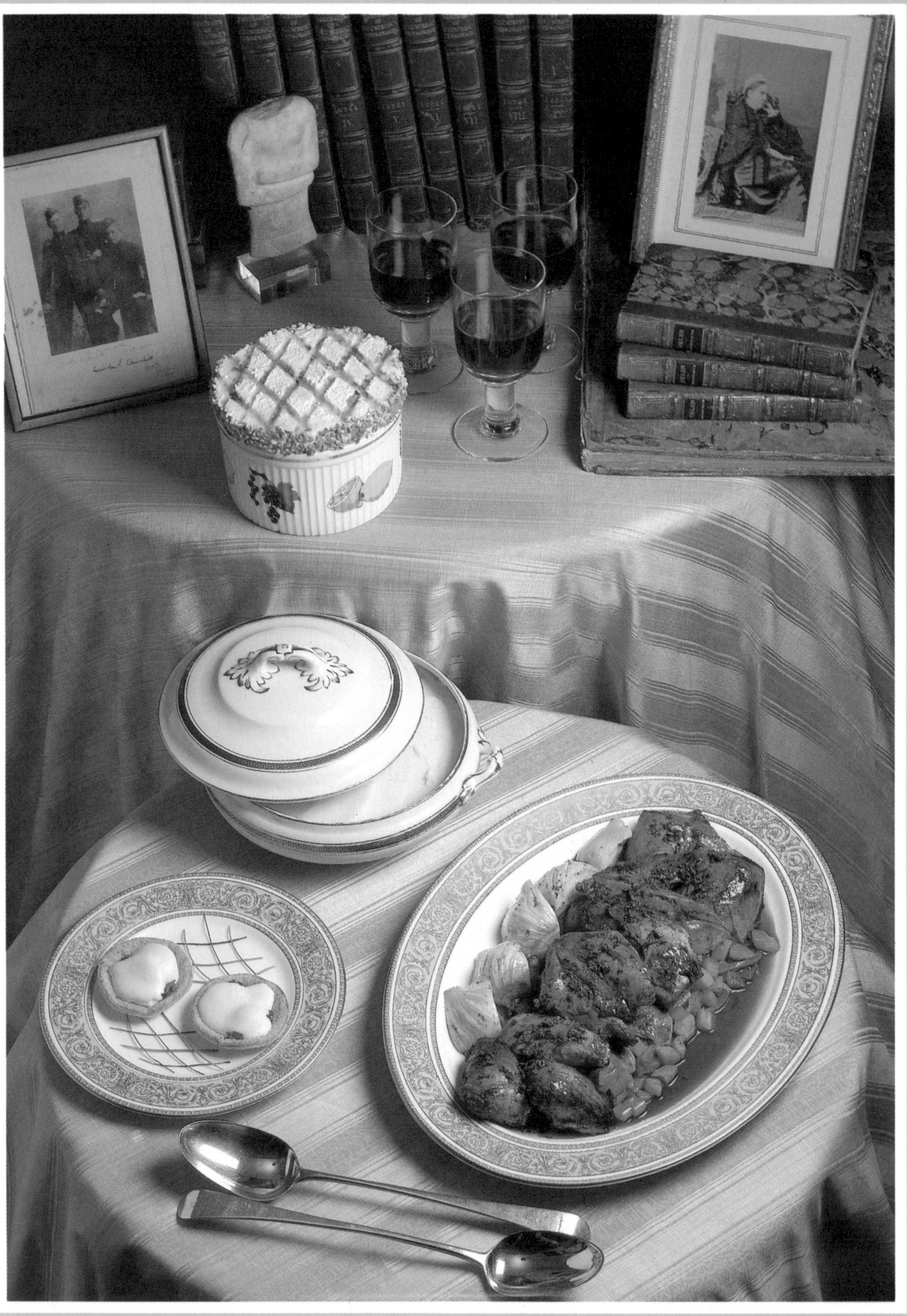

MENU LESSON 35 *(see p.201)*
A rich and expensive menu (*left*), but the lime soufflé should cleanse the palate. *Clockwise from top left:* Cold lime soufflé, braised pheasant and braised fennel, quails eggs en croustade and mashed potatoes.

MENU LESSON 36 *(see p.205)*
This menu (*right*) builds up, by degrees, to the classic dessert tarte Française. *Clockwise from top left:* Cucumber and mint salad, tarte Française, aubergine pie, poached trout, watercress sauce and new potatoes.

MENU LESSON 37 *(see p.209)*
Meatballs are hard to master — and so is turning mangoes (*above*). *Clockwise from top left:* Spicy Basmati rice, meatballs with fresh coriander, tomato sauce, stir-fried vegetables, turned mangoes with lime garnish, spinach and ricotta cheese strudels, and (*centre*) carrot and tomato purée.

CARROT AND TOMATO PUREE

INGREDIENTS (Serves 4)
6 large carrots
3 cardamom pods, crushed
1 tomato, peeled, seeded and quartered
4tbsp Greek yoghurt

1 Peel and slice the carrots. Cook them in boiling salted water, with the cardamom pods, until tender.

2 Drain and discard all but a few seeds from the cardamoms.

3 Put the carrots and tomato into a processor with the seeds and purée briefly. Add the yoghurt and mix until smooth.

NOTE This is a delicious accompaniment to the strudels and also makes an excellent dip for raw vegetable crudités.

MEATBALLS WITH CORIANDER AND TOMATO SAUCE

INGREDIENTS (Serves 4)
560g/1 ¼lb lean beef, eg shin
1tbsp chopped coriander leaves
5 spring onions, finely chopped
1 clove garlic, crushed
1tsp soy sauce
Salt and freshly ground black pepper

TO SERVE
Fresh tomato sauce (see next recipe)
Roughly chopped fresh coriander leaves

☐ *Take care when pounding meat in a processor. Overworking produces a meat paste which cooks to rubbery toughness — a common fault with hamburgers.*

1 Mince the beef, or chop briefly in a food processor. Add the coriander, spring onions, garlic and soy sauce. Knead by hand, or pound briefly in the processor. Season to taste with salt and pepper.

2 Shape into balls about the size of a pingpong ball. Fry slowly in a little oil for 10 minutes. Lift out with a draining spoon and tip into the tomato sauce. Reheat together.

3 Pile into a serving dish and garnish with the chopped coriander.

FRESH TOMATO SAUCE

INGREDIENTS
1 large onion, finely chopped
1tbsp oil
10 tomatoes, cut into quarters
Pinch of sugar
150ml/¼pt white stock (see p.268)
1tsp chopped fresh thyme leaves
Salt and pepper

1 Cook the onion in the oil for 3 minutes. Add the sugar and tomatoes and cook for a further 25 minutes.

2 Liquidize and push through a sieve.

3 Add enough of the stock to achieve the required consistency.

4 Add the thyme and season to taste with salt and pepper, and more sugar if necessary.

CHOPPING ONIONS

1 Slice the unpeeled onion lengthwise through the core, then peel both halves. Do not remove the root-end, which will serve to hold the 'leaves' together when chopping.

2 Put one half of the onion flat on the board. Using a thin, sharp knife make horizontal parallel cuts towards the root, without cutting through to the root end.

3 Make a series of parallel vertical cuts down to the board, again avoiding the root end.

4 Finally, slice the onion, making the cuts at right angles to the previous two sets of cuts. Put the root-end into the stock pot or chop it separately like parsley (see p.160).

1

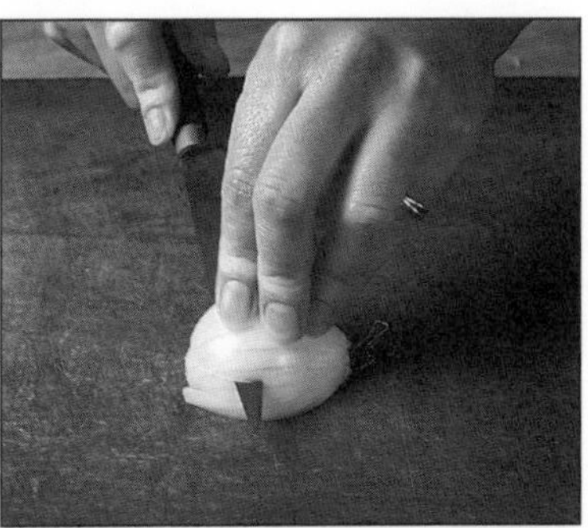
2

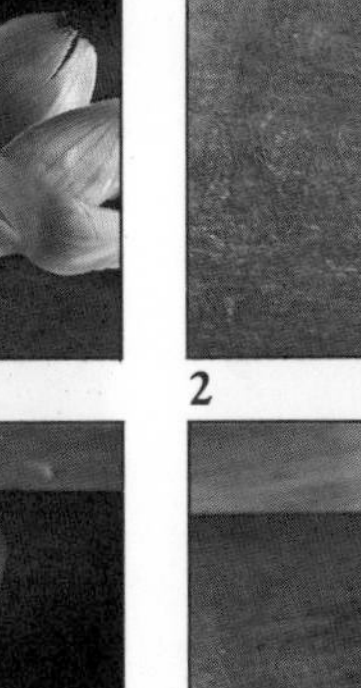
3

4

STIR-FRIED VEGETABLES

INGREDIENTS (Serves 4)
2tbsp sunflower oil
1 clove garlic, peeled and sliced
2.5cm/1 inch piece fresh root ginger, finely shredded
110g/4oz Chinese mushrooms, soaked in warm water for 20 minutes
225g/8oz spring greens, shredded
225g/8oz bean sprouts
1 small can water chestnuts, drained and cut in half
2tbsp soy sauce
Pinch of sugar
Sesame oil

☐ *Almost any vegetables are suitable for stir-frying. Add the firmest vegetables first, with the tenderer ones a few minutes later. To stir-fry large quantities of vegetables, blanching the tougher ones beforehand in water until just tender helps speed up the process. Sesame oil is one of the secrets of good stir-frying.*

In the absence of a wok use a large sauté pan or saucepan.

1 Heat the oil, add the garlic and ginger and fry until lightly browned.

2 Slice the mushrooms and add to the wok. Stir-fry for 1 minute. Add the spring greens and bean sprouts, stir-fry for 2 minutes. Add the water chestnuts, soy sauce, and sugar. Sprinkle with sesame oil and serve immediately.

STIR FRYING

The trick with stir frying is to stir with a Chinese ladle, strainer or wooden spoon with one hand while shaking and jerking the wok with the other to keep the ingredients dancing about in the hot pan.

MENU LESSON 38 *(see p.217)*
Unusual, delicious and adventurous, this menu would make a spectacular dinner party. *Clockwise from top left:* Blinis, floating islands, new potatoes, boned stuffed shoulder of veal with Mosimann's courgettes, caviar, and soured cream and butter.

FRESH TURNED MANGOES

INGREDIENTS (Serves 4)
2 ripe mangoes
2 limes, cut in quarters

Delicious as mangoes are, they are usually difficult to eat. This method makes tackling them with a spoon and fork possible. Allow half a ripe mango and 2 lime wedges a head.

1 Slice the two 'cheeks' from the mango as close to the flat stone as possible.

2 With a small sharp knife make diagonal parallel cuts through the flesh. Repeat to produce a lattice pattern.

3 Push the middle of each cheek up from underneath.

4 Serve each 'domed' mango cheek with 2 lime wedges.

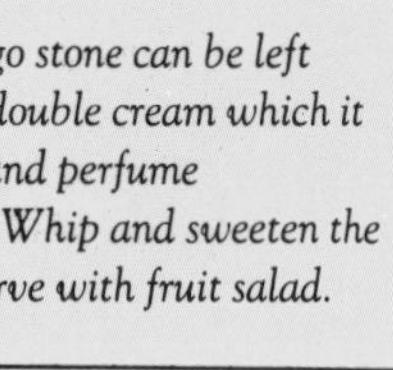

☐ *The mango stone can be left overnight in double cream which it will flavour and perfume wonderfully. Whip and sweeten the cream and serve with fruit salad.*

TURNED MANGOES
1 Slice close to either side of the mango stone to produce two full 'cheeks'. Using a sharp knife, cut into the flesh, but not through the skin in a lattice pattern. The cuts can be fairly large, as here, or very fine, as on p.211.

2 Hold the cut cheek in both hands and use the fingertips to press the skin up from underneath.

PHOTOGRAPH ON P.215

This menu would make a spectacular dinner party — unusual, delicious and adventurous. It is extremely expensive however, so take great care to get it right. The techniques taught are those of batter making with yeast (an interesting and satisfying process), the stuffing, tying and pot-roasting of veal, and the tricky business of poaching meringues for the Floating islands — the trick here is not to overcook them — once they are inflated and just firm to the touch of a finger they are done. Too much cooking produces rubber-like egg white. English custard gives problems to the most experienced cooks, but once a true custard made with creamy milk and eggs is mastered, packet custard will never seem the same again.

MENU LESSON 38

Blinis with caviar and soured cream

Boned stuffed shoulder of veal with green peppercorns

New potatoes

Mosimann's courgettes

Floating islands

WORK PLAN

• The veal may be prepared and stuffed in advance but should not be reheated.
• The Floating islands keep well for as much as a day, but should not be put on their lake of custard until the last minute.
• As the custard must be cold it has to be made in advance. Re-whisk it gently before straining into the dish in case it has formed a skin or lumps.
• Blinis are best made freshly — not more than an hour or so before eating. If they must be made several hours in advance, do not refrigerate them, which gives them a doughy texture. They are best just warm — but not so hot that the butter (which is spread on them in unhealthy amounts) melts too fast.

BLINIS WITH CAVIAR AND SOURED CREAM

INGREDIENTS (Serves 4)
225g/8oz buckwheat flour
45g/1½oz fresh yeast
2tsp sugar
720ml/1¼pt warm milk
225g/8oz plain flour
Salt
3 eggs
Lard

TO SERVE
Butter
Soured cream
Caviar

1 Put the buckwheat flour into a warm dry mixing bowl.

2 Cream the yeast with the sugar and add half the milk. Mix well.

3 Pour the yeasty milk into the buckwheat flour and mix to a paste.

4 Cover the bowl with a sheet of greased polythene or a damp cloth and leave in a warm place to rise for 45 minutes.

5 Sift the plain flour with a good pinch of salt into another basin. Make a hollow in the centre and drop in the 2 whole eggs and 1 egg yolk, reserving 1 egg white.

6 Gradually mix to a batter, bringing in the surrounding flour, and adding the melted butter and the rest of the milk. Beat well.

7 Beat this batter into the yeasty one, cover again with the greased polythene or cloth and leave in a warm place for 2 hours.

8 Just before cooking whip the remaining egg white and fold it in to the mixture.

Continued on p.220

FREDA
19
79
CLINCH

MENU LESSON 39 *(see p.225)*
An all-American chowder is combined with an old fashioned roast (*below*). *Clockwise from top left:* Sweetcorn chowder, Brussels sprouts purée, sweet port gravy, lamb en ballon with potatoes, creamed cheese with fruit.

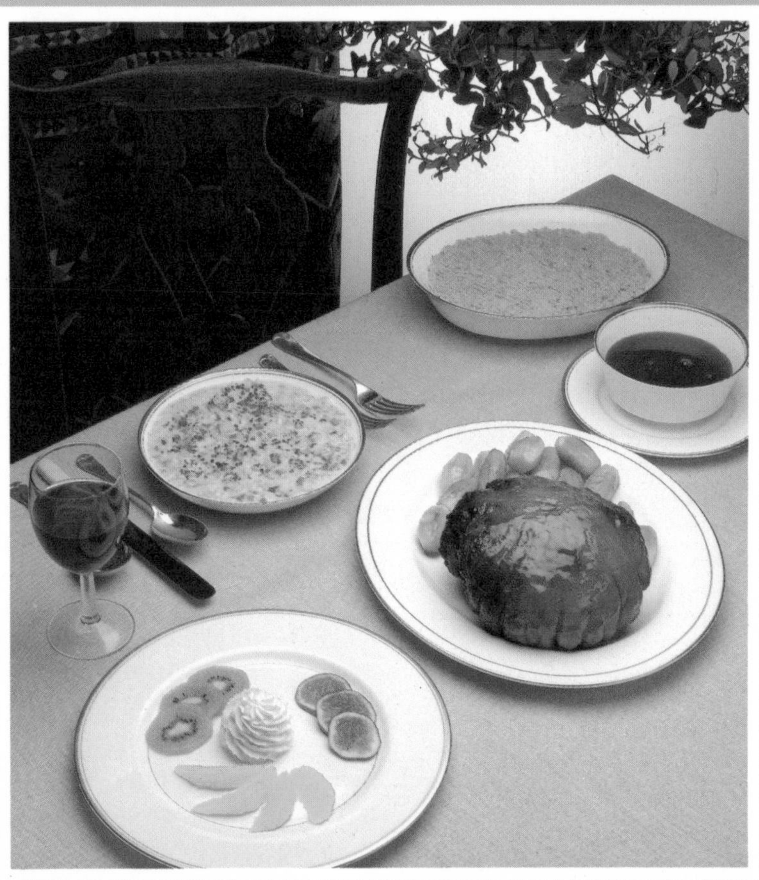

MENU LESSON 40 *(see p.228)*
A simple Sunday dinner (*left*)? It's more difficult than organizing army manoeuvres. *Clockwise from top left:* Apple and sultana crumble, roast potatoes and parsnips, carrots and peas, Yorkshire pudding, horseradish, beef, egg custard and (*centre*) gravy.

☐ *For the blinis — smoked salmon would be cheaper and just as delicious as caviar, and smoked eel or pickled herring are cheaper still. Blinis do not have to be topped with caviar, splendid though it is.*

9 Grease a heavy frying pan lightly with lard. Heat it gently over steady heat.

10 When the pan is hot pour enough of the batter on to the surface to make a blini the size of a saucer. When bubbles rise, turn over and cook the other side to a good brown.

11 TO SERVE Butter the warm blinis, place a spoonful of caviar on each and top with soured cream. Serve at once.

BONED STUFFED SHOULDER OF VEAL WITH GREEN PEPPERCORNS

INGREDIENTS (Serves 10)
1 × 2 kg/4½lb piece of shoulder of veal, boned and opened out flat

FOR THE STUFFING
1 onion, finely chopped
30g/1½oz butter
110g/4oz button mushrooms, sliced
1 small green pepper, chopped
1 clove garlic, crushed
70g/2½oz fresh white breadcrumbs
Salt and freshly ground black pepper
450g/1lb belly of pork, minced
1 heaped tsp green peppercorns, well rinsed
1tbsp chopped fresh mixed sage, mint and parsley
1 egg, lightly beaten
30g/1oz unsalted or clarified (see p.75) butter
1 glass dry white wine
150ml/¼pt double cream

TO GARNISH
Bunch of watercress

1 Trim off most of the fat from the shoulder of veal.

2 MAKE THE STUFFING Cook the onion in the butter until soft but not brown. Add the mushrooms, green pepper and garlic and cook for a further 2 minutes.

3 Mix with the breadcrumbs, salt, pepper, pork, peppercorns and herbs. Add the egg and beat very well (this helps to make a light stuffing).

4 Lay the veal out flat, season with pepper and spread with the stuffing. Roll and tie up as shown.

5 Set the oven to 180°C/350°F/Gas 4.

6 Melt the butter in a large flameproof casserole. When hot add the meat and brown evenly all over. Add the wine, cover and bake for 1¾ hours.

7 Remove the meat from the casserole, turn off the oven and return the meat to the cooling oven while you make the sauce.

8 Skim off *all* the fat from the casserole. This will take some time as there will be a great deal, but it is essential not to have a greasy sauce. Remove the last vestiges of the fat by laying successive sheets of absorbent paper on the surface of the liquid.

ROLLING AND TYING VEAL
1 Lay the boned veal skinned-side down on a board and spread with the stuffing. Do not lay stuffing too close to the edges.

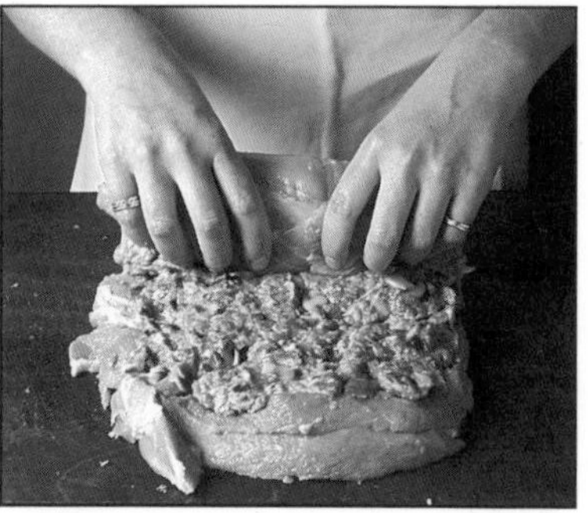

2 Roll up from one side into a neat cylindrical roll.

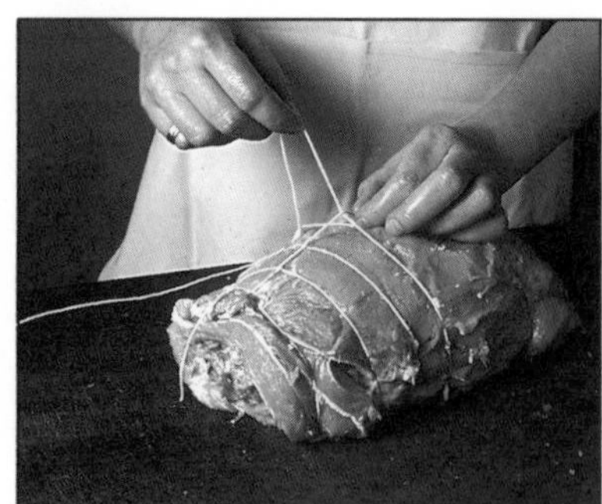

3 Tie with one continuous piece of string, as shown, or at 2½cm/1 inch intervals with short lengths.

- ☐ *The best veal is milk-fed and very expensive. Grass-fed veal is cheaper but lacks the delicacy of taste and texture.*
- ☐ *Rinse tinned peppercorns under a cold tap to remove the brine.*

9 Add the cream. Taste, season lightly if necessary and then boil rapidly, stirring occasionally to prevent the sauce from 'catching', until the right creamy consistency is achieved.

10 Remove the meat from the oven. Untie the string and carve. Serve in overlapping slices. Garnish with the watercress. Hand the sauce separately.

NEW POTATOES

INGREDIENTS (Serves 4)
675g/1½lb new potatoes
Salt
Fresh mint
Butter

1 Prepare the potatoes and cook in boiling salted water with a sprig of mint until tender. This will take anything between 8 and 15 minutes.

2 Drain well and serve with extra chopped mint and melted butter.

NOTE There is always controversy about peeling new potatoes. The best, very new pale ones need little more than washing. Most need scraping and some — usually large, dark and patently not very new — need peeling after cooking.

MOSIMANN'S COURGETTES

INGREDIENTS (Serves 4)
450g/1lb medium sized courgettes
340g/12oz cylindrical carrots (not cone-shaped, if possible) slightly smaller than the courgettes
Salt

1 Peel the carrots and boil them whole in salted water until fairly tender: about 8 minutes. They should be cooked but not soft.

2 Using an apple corer, remove the middle of the whole courgettes. If they are too long, cut them in half across.

3 Push the cooked carrots into the holes in the courgettes. They must be a tight fit or they will come to pieces when sliced.

4 Steam the stuffed courgettes for 8—10 minutes, or boil them in salted water for 5 minutes or until the courgettes are just tender.

5 Drain the courgettes and slice them across into rings.

FLOATING ISLANDS WITH CARAMEL

INGREDIENTS (Makes 6-8)

FOR THE CUSTARD
425ml/¾pt milk
290ml/½pt cream
2tsp caster sugar
Vanilla pod or 3 drops vanilla flavouring
2 level tsp cornflour
4 egg yolks

Continued on p.224

1 TO MAKE THE CUSTARD, place half the milk, the cream and the sugar in a saucepan with the vanilla. Bring gently to the boil, remove from the heat and leave to infuse for 30 minutes. Remove the vanilla pod.

2 Mix the cornflour with a little water. Stir a few tbsp of the hot milk mixture into it and then pour it back into the milk. Place over a gentle heat and bring slowly to the boil, stirring continuously. Simmer for 4 minutes to cook the cornflour and thicken the custard.

3 Beat the egg yolks then pour the cream mixture onto the yolks in a thin stream, beating well all the time. The custard will probably thicken at once to the consistency which will coat the back of a wooden spoon. If it does not, return to the saucepan and stir steadily over very gentle heat until it does. Take care not to boil, or it will curdle. Pour into a shallow wide serving dish, and cover with plastic film to prevent a skin forming.

Continued on p.224

MENU LESSON 41 *(see p.233)*
Serve your guests small portions of each course. This is not one of the lightest of meals. *Clockwise from top left:* Noodles and red peppers, French beans, veal escalopes with cream and marsala, saucisse en brioche and pears in honey.

MENU LESSON 42 *(see p.237)*
Cooking Christmas dinner can appear a daunting task. *Clockwise from top left:* Roast potatoes, boned turkey stuffed with ham, Brussels sprouts purée, port and prune ice cream, Christmas pudding, brandy butter, cranberry sauce, bread sauce and gravy.

FOR THE MERINGUE
3 egg whites
Salt
170g/6oz caster sugar

FOR THE CARAMEL
85g/3oz sugar

4 Meanwhile, MAKE THE ISLANDS Put the remaining milk plus 570ml/1pt of water into a deep frying pan and set over the heat.

5 Whisk the whites with a pinch of salt until stiff. Fold in the caster sugar (see p.285).

6 The milk and water mixture should now be simmering. Put 1tbsp meringue mixture into the frying pan and cook gently for only 30 seconds on each side. (Do not add more than 3 or 4 islands at a time.) Drain completely on a wire rack or teatowel. Lay the islands carefully on the 'lake' of custard.

7 MAKE THE CARAMEL Place the sugar in a heavy pan and set over a gentle heat until the sugar has dissolved and cooked to a golden brown. Remove from the heat and immediately trickle over the islands already in the custard.

NOTE Alternatively you can flavour the custard with coffee or orange:

FOR COFFEE CUSTARD, proceed as for Floating islands but dissolve 1tsp coffee in 2tsp boiling water and add it to the custard sauce just before removing it from the heat.

FOR ORANGE CUSTARD, proceed as for Floating islands but omit the vanilla and pare the rind from an orange, being careful to discard all the pith. Infuse the rind in the cream and milk mixture in place of the vanilla pod. Add 1tbsp Grand Marnier to the custard before pouring into the serving dish.

FLOATING ISLANDS
1 Shape the meringue with two large spoons. Follow the instructions for shaping sorbets on p.130.

2 Lower the shaped tablespoons of mixture into the simmering liquid and poach for 30 seconds. Turn over and cook the other side, also for 30 seconds.

3 When cooked they will have nearly doubled in size and feel just firm when pressed with a finger. Do not overcook or they will be rubbery. Lift out with a perforated spoon and leave on a wire rack or tea towel to drain.

PHOTOGRAPH ON P.219

This Menu Lesson combines the making of an all-American traditional chowder with oldfashioned roast lamb given a new look by clever butcher's stringing. The result looks professional and sophisticated, but is not hard to achieve. Carving is easy too — you just cut it like a cake.

Vegetable purées are delicious, pretty and allow the cook to get ahead before serving — the sprout one here is a good example. 'Turning' potatoes to obtain elegant shapes is a chef's skill that is worth acquiring for the look of the dish. The creamed cheese is a cheat's version of the French Coeurs à la crème — but is just as delicious, just as pretty to look at and rather quicker to do.

MENU LESSON 39

Sweetcorn chowder

OR

Corn on the cob

Shoulder of lamb 'en ballon' with sweet port gravy

Château potatoes

Brussels sprouts purée (see p.241)

Creamed cheese with fresh fruit

WORK PLAN

- The chowder may be made the day before and reheated successfully.
- The potatoes can be shaped (but not cooked) ahead of time and kept in a bowl of cold water to prevent them discolouring.
- The purée reheats well, and the cheese and fruit can be prepared a few hours in advance.
- That leaves only the roasting of the lamb, gravy making, cooking of the potatoes and reheating of the purée for the cook's pre-dinner attention.

SWEETCORN CHOWDER

INGREDIENTS (Serves 4)
1 potato
3 sticks celery
1 onion
110g/4oz streaky bacon
1 green pepper
30g/1oz butter
1 bay leaf
20g/¾oz flour
570ml/1pt milk
4 ears corn on the cob
Salt and pepper
Chopped fresh parsley

☐ *If the chowder seems too time-consuming the corn could be served on the cob. See next recipe.*

1 Wash and peel the potato.

2 Cut it, and the celery, onion and streaky bacon, into dice.

3 Remove the seeds from the pepper and dice the flesh.

4 Fry the bacon in the butter. When brown but not brittle add the diced vegetables and the bay leaf. Turn down the heat and cook slowly until the onion looks soft and transparent.

5 Draw the pan from the heat; mix in the flour and then the milk.

6 Return the pan to the heat and stir steadily until boiling.

7 Scrape the kernels from the cobs and add them to the soup. Press the cobs to extract all the juice and add this too. Season with salt and pepper to taste. Simmer for 5 minutes or until the vegetables are soft but not broken.

8 Serve sprinkled with chopped parsley.

SWEETCORN CHOWDER
1 Scrape the kernels from the raw cob with a sharp knife.

2 Press the cob firmly with a sharp knife and push hard to extract the juices.

CORN ON THE COB

INGREDIENTS (Serves 4)
4 young sweetcorn
Pinch of salt and pepper
Pinch of sugar
Butter

1 Remove the outside leaves and silk from the sweetcorn.

2 Bring a large pan of water with salt and sugar added to the boil and add the corn. Boil rapidly for 4-8 minutes. The corn is cooked when the kernels are easily pierced with a needle or knife-tip.

3 Drain them and serve hot with butter and freshly ground black pepper.

NOTE Serve the butter cold, not melted. It will melt as the guest spreads it on the corn. To avoid greasy fingers spread a little butter on each mouthful of corn as it is about to be eaten. But fingerbowls are a wise precaution anyway.

SHOULDER OF LAMB 'EN BALLON' WITH SWEET PORT GRAVY

INGREDIENTS (Serves 6-8)
1 boned shoulder of lamb
Butter
Sprig of rosemary
290ml/½pt stock or water
Salt and pepper
2 glasses port

FOR THE STUFFING
2tbsp parsley, chopped
85g/3oz green bacon, chopped
chopped Salt and pepper

FOR THE GLAZE
2tbsp redcurrant jelly

TO GARNISH
Watercress (optional)

1 Set the oven at 190°C/375°F/Gas 5.

2 Mix the stuffing ingredients together and push into the lamb, or (if the lamb has been opened out) spread it on one half and fold the other half over to cover it.

3 Using a long piece of string, tie the shoulder so that the indentations made by the string resemble the grooves in a melon or the lines between segments of a beachball.

4 Weigh the lamb.

5 Smear all over with butter and sprinkle with salt and pepper. You could scatter a few rosemary leaves on top. Pour the stock into the pan.

6 Roast for 25 minutes to the pound. Half an hour before the cooking time is up smear the lamb with 2 level (or 1 heaped) tbsp redcurrant jelly and return to the oven.

7 Remove the strings carefully and lift the lamb onto a warm serving dish. Leave to rest for 15 minutes before serving. (It will retain heat even if not put into a warming cupboard.)

LAMB 'EN BALLON'

1 Spread the stuffing on one half of the boned lamb shoulder and fold the other half close up over to cover it. If the shoulder has been boned but not opened out, push the stuffing into it.

2 Turn the shoulder over, skinned side up. Tie the end of a 3m/9ft piece of string firmly round the shoulder, making a knot in the middle at the top.

3 Take the string round again, but this time at right angles to the first line, again tying at the first knot.

4 Continue this process until the 'ball' is trussed about 8 times. Tuck in any loose flaps of meat or skin.

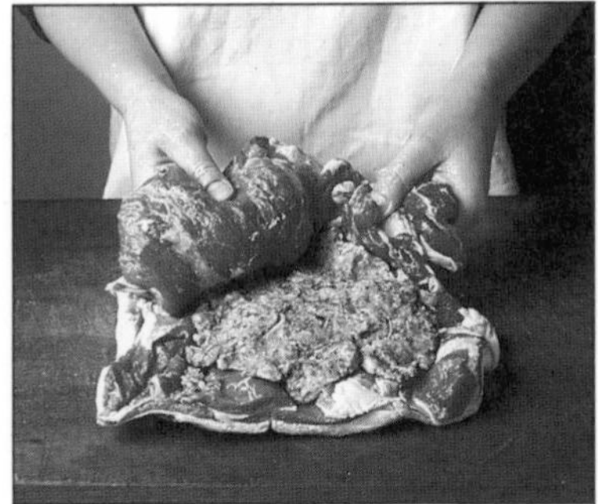
1

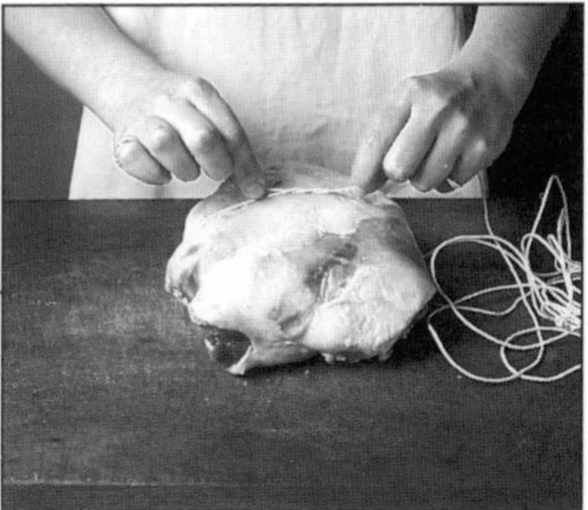
2

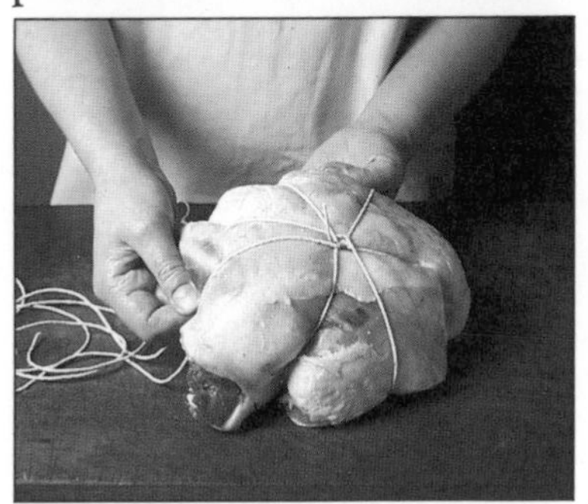
3

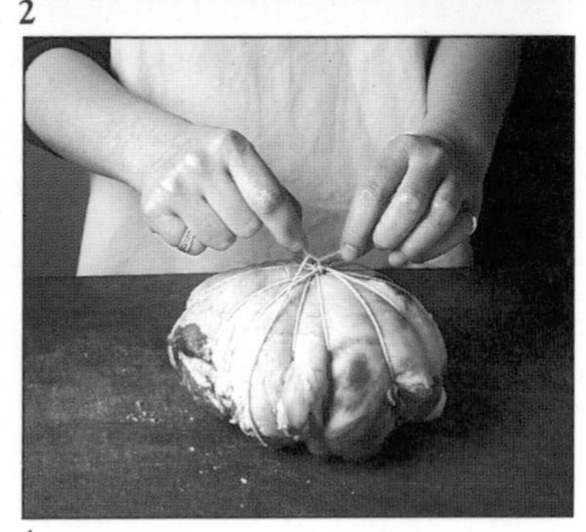
4

☐ *Make sure you have plenty of string — the 'ballon' takes at least 3m/9ft to achieve. Use soft string if possible.*

8 Meanwhile, MAKE THE GRAVY Skim the fat from the juices in the pan (see p.229).

9 Add the port and bring to the boil. Boil vigorously until the sauce is syrupy and reduced to about a third of a pint. Taste and add salt and pepper if necessary. Strain into a gravy boat.

CHATEAU POTATOES

INGREDIENTS (Serves 4)
675g/1½lb small, even sized potatoes
Oil or beef dripping
Salt and freshly ground black pepper

☐ *The secrets of neatly barrel-shaped château potatoes are patience, practice and starting with an even-sided regular rectangular block (see p.150).*

1 Wash and peel the potatoes. Trim each one into a barrel shape about 3.5cm/1½ inches long and 2cm/¾ inch wide (see p.150).

2 Set the oven to 190°C/375°F/Gas 5.

3 Heat a few spoons of oil or dripping in a sauté pan. Add the potatoes and fry gently on all sides (shaking the pan constantly) until they are just brown. Season with salt and pepper.

4 Cover the pan and place in the oven for about 45 minutes or until the potatoes are tender. Alternatively, they can be cooked on the hob, but care must be taken to prevent burning: shake the pan frequently. Do not remove the lid as this allows the steam to escape, and the potatoes will fry rather than cook gently.

CREAMED CHEESE WITH FRESH FRUIT

INGREDIENTS (Serves 8-10)
225g/8oz cottage cheese
55g/2oz icing sugar
290ml/½pt double cream, lightly whipped
Vanilla flavouring
4 figs, sliced
4 kiwi fruit, peeled and sliced
4 oranges, peeled and segmented (see p.38)

1 Push the cheese through a sieve. Sift in the icing sugar. Fold in the lightly whipped cream and a few drops of vanilla flavouring.

2 TO SERVE Pile into a large oval dish and shape into a shallow mound. Arrange the prepared fruit on top of the cheese. Alternatively, put the cheese into a piping bag with a large fluted nozzle, and pipe a conical whirl onto each plate. Arrange the fruits beside or around the cheese.

PHOTOGRAPH ON P.218

This may sound like a simple Sunday dinner, but cooking the traditional roast is like organizing army manoeuvres — efficiency is essential. The recipes assume that there is only one oven available, and no help for the cook. The principal techniques covered in this Menu Lesson are roasting meat, mixing a batter, making a simple crumble and thickening a custard with eggs. Read pp.244 and 280 on roasting and custards.

MENU LESSON 40

Roast beef

Yorkshire pudding

Roast potatoes

Roast parsnips

Carrots and peas

Horseradish sauce

Apple and sultana crumble

English egg custard

WORK PLAN

As this is a difficult menu, more preparation than usual should be done the day before, especially if the cook is inexperienced. We have suggested here the sort of work programme you should make for any menu if there is a chance of muddle or panic. We have, for example, suggested preparing vegetables well in advance, which is not ideal, but is sensible if a delicious meal is to be on the table by 1.15pm.

THE DAY BEFORE
- Peel and cut up the potatoes, carrots and parsnips. Leave in bowls of cold water, refrigerated.
- Make the horseradish cream.
- Make the English egg custard.
- Make the crumble.

ON THE DAY
10.30am • Heat the oven.
• Place the beef on the wire rack and spread with mustard.
10.45 • Put the beef into the oven.
• Parboil and drain the potatoes and parsnips.
11.05 • Reduce the oven temperature. Baste.
11.30 • Make the Yorkshire pudding batter. Leave to rest.
11.45 • Tip off all the fat from the roast.
• Brown the potatoes and parsnips in beef dripping.
• Lay the table and do all the incidental lunch preparations — putting a jug of water into the refrigerator, opening the wine, etc.
12.20 • Heat up the dripping for the Yorkshire pudding by putting the pan in the oven under the beef.

12.30 • Remove the beef from the oven and leave to stand somewhere warm. Turn the oven up high (220°C/425°F/Gas 7).
• Put Yorkshire pudding and potatoes and parsnips in the oven, the vegetables below the pudding.
12.35 • Make the gravy.
• Warm the plates.
• Put on the water for the carrots.
12.45 • Cook the carrots.
12.55 • Drain the carrots and peas and keep warm.
1-1.15 • When the Yorkshire pudding is ready, serve up the main course and put the crumble into the oven to warm while eating the roast beef.

ROAST BEEF

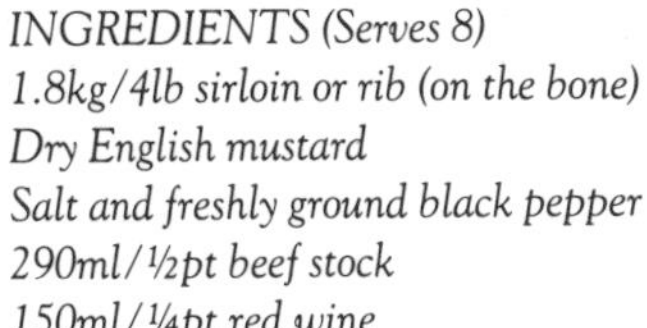

INGREDIENTS (Serves 8)
1.8kg/4lb sirloin or rib (on the bone)
Dry English mustard
Salt and freshly ground black pepper
290ml/½pt beef stock
150ml/¼pt red wine

1 Set the oven to 220°C/425°F/Gas 7.

2 Weigh the beef and establish the cooking time. Allow 45 minutes per kilo (20 minutes to the lb) for medium rare meat and 35 minutes per kilo (15 minutes to the lb) for rare meat.

3 Place the beef, fatty side uppermost, on a wire rack over a roasting tin and sprinkle with dry English mustard and plenty of pepper but no salt.

4 Roast for 20 minutes. Turn the oven down to 160°C/325°F/Gas 3 and time the joint from now.

5 Baste occasionally as it roasts.

6 Halfway through cooking tip off the dripping, which will be used for cooking the Yorkshire pudding, potatoes and parsnips.

7 When the beef is cooked, sprinkle it with salt and leave it standing in a warm place for 20-30 minutes to allow the meat juices to flow outwards evenly through the meat and to begin to set. (During roasting the intense heat drives the juices to the centre.) If allowed to rest like this the joint will be evenly coloured and much easier to carve. It will taste more succulent and will only be fractionally cooler. It also means that the oven can be turned up and the vegetables and Yorkshire pudding cooked whilst the meat stands.

SKIMMING GRAVY
To remove the last vestige of fat from the top of gravy liquid, tip the pan slightly, allowing the liquid to settle. Lay successive sheets of absorbent paper on the surface to soak up the layer of fat.

8 TO MAKE THE GRAVY With a large basting spoon, carefully skim off all the fat from the roasting pan without losing any of the brown juices. Lift the last vestige of fat from the liquid using a sheet of absorbent paper. Add the red wine and rapidly boil to reduce the quantity of liquid by half. This lessens the alcoholic taste of the wine while giving a stronger flavoured and richer liquid. Add the stock and bring to the boil, scraping the bottom of the pan to loosen any sediment. Boil briefly, taste and add salt and pepper. Strain into a warmed sauceboat. If a slightly thicker gravy is required, add a little mustard and whisk well.

NOTE Traditional British gravy is thickened with flour: skim off all but 1tbsp of the fat from the pan. Whisk in 1tbsp flour. Stir over heat for a minute, then proceed as for unthickened gravy. Boil the sauce hard (to give it a shine and to eliminate any floury taste) before straining.

YORKSHIRE PUDDING

INGREDIENTS (Makes enough pudding for 8 small or 4 large slices or 8 small individual puddings)
110g/4oz plain flour
Good pinch of salt
2 eggs
150ml/¼pt water] *mixed together*
150ml/¼pt milk]
4tbsp beef dripping

1 Sift the flour and salt into a large wide bowl. Make a well or hollow in the centre of the flour and break the eggs into it.

2 With a whisk or wooden spoon, mix the eggs to a paste and very gradually draw in the surrounding flour, adding just enough milk and water to the eggs to keep the central mixture a fairly stiff paste. When all the flour is incorporated, stir in the rest of the liquid. The batter can more speedily be made by putting all the ingredients together in a liquidizer or food processor for a few seconds, but take care not to over-whisk or the mixture will be bubbly. Leave to 'rest' at room temperature for 30 minutes before use. This allows the starch cells to swell, giving a lighter, less doughy final product.

3 Turn the oven to 220°C/425°F/Gas 7.

4 Heat the dripping until smoking hot in a roasting tin, ovenproof dish or Yorkshire pudding tin. This will take 10 minutes in the oven or a few seconds over direct heat, and is vital for a well-risen pudding.

5 Pour in the batter. Bake for 30 minutes or until the pudding is risen and golden.

NOTE If using individual patty moulds, the Yorkshire puddings will be cooked in 15 minutes.

MAKING A BATTER
Use a large bowl. Make a good-sized 'well' in the flour before dropping in the eggs.

ROAST POTATOES

INGREDIENTS (Serves 8 if other vegetables are offered, 4 if not)
900g/2lb potatoes
Beef dripping
Salt and freshly ground black pepper

☐ *Round off sharp edges of cut potatoes with a peeler for a more professional looking result.*

This recipe produces brown, but not leathery potatoes. They are achieved, not by true roasting, but by a combination of boiling, frying and baking. It sounds troublesome but the results are excellent, will keep warm without becoming hard and unattractive, and take much less cooking time than if simply roasted with the meat. However, if there is room in the oven, they can be par-boiled as here, then roasted slowly next to the meat or in a tray beneath it. If they are not a good colour by the time the meat comes out they can be browned over direct heat at this stage.

1 Wash the potatoes and peel them. Cut them into three if large.

2 Set the oven to 200°C/400°F/Gas 6.

3 Bring them to the boil in salted water and boil hard for 5 minutes.

4 Drain them in a sieve and toss and shake them gently so that they begin to look crumbly.

5 Heat the dripping in a heavy frying pan, add the potatoes and brown lightly, frying gently over direct heat, shaking the pan and turning the potatoes frequently as they fry. After 15 minutes they should be nearly, but not quite, cooked through. Season with salt and pepper.

6 Transfer them, with their fat, to the roasting tin (with the parsnips if following our menu) and bake in the oven for 30-45 minutes, or until tender and well browned. For an even colour roll them over at half time.

ROAST PARSNIPS

INGREDIENTS (Serves 8 if other vegetables are offered, 4 if not)
675g/1½lb parsnips
Beef dripping
Salt and pepper

1 Heat the oven to 220°C/425°F/Gas 7.

2 Wash and peel the parsnips — cut in half lengthwise, into quarters, and across into short lengths if large.

3 Boil in salted water for 5 minutes. Drain well.

4 Heat the dripping in a heavy frying pan. Add the parsnips and brown over direct heat, turning frequently to get an even colour.

5 Transfer to a roasting tin and bake for 30 minutes.

NOTE Once browned the parsnips can be cooked in the same pan as the potatoes.

CARROTS AND PEAS

INGREDIENTS (Serves 8 if other vegetables are offered, 4 if not)
225g/8oz frozen peas
450g/1lb carrots
Salt and freshly ground black pepper
1tbsp butter
2tsp fresh chopped mint (optional)

1 Peel and slice the carrots.

2 Place in a saucepan of boiling salted water and cook for 5-10 minutes (depending on size and youth) or until just tender.

3 Add the peas. Bring to the boil again. Drain well.

4 Melt the butter in the empty, still-hot pan. Add the vegetables and mint. Put on the lid and shake vigorously to mix well. Tip into a warm serving dish.

HORSERADISH SAUCE

INGREDIENTS (Serves 8)
150ml/¼pt double cream
1-1½ heaped tbsp grated fresh horseradish
2tsp wine vinegar
½tsp English mustard
Salt and freshly ground black pepper

1 Lightly whip the double cream and fold in the remaining ingredients.

NOTE If fresh horseradish is not available use ½ tsp grated horseradish from a jar, or mix bottled horseradish sauce with whipped cream, omitting the other flavourings.

APPLE AND SULTANA CRUMBLE

INGREDIENTS (Serves 4-6)

FOR THE CRUMBLE
170g/6oz plain flour
Pinch of salt
110g/4oz butter
55g/2oz caster sugar

FOR THE FILLING
900g/2lb cooking apples
Butter
3tbsp demerara sugar
2tbsp sultanas
Squeeze of lemon juice
Pinch of cinnamon

☐ *For the crumble, use a deep dish that takes apple and topping easily. The apple swells slightly as it cooks and can push bits of crumble off the top if the dish is overfilled, or the juices may overflow.*

1 Set the oven to 200°C/400°F/Gas 6.

2 MAKE THE CRUMBLE Sift the flour into a bowl with the salt. Rub in the butter until the mixture resembles coarse breadcrumbs. Stir in the sugar.

3 PREPARE THE FILLING Peel, quarter, core and slice the apples thinly into a deep buttered pie dish. Mix in the sultanas, sugar, lemon juice and cinnamon. Press down firmly to flatten.

4 Sprinkle the crumble mixture evenly over the apple so that it is well sealed. Bake for 30 minutes until golden brown.

ENGLISH EGG CUSTARD

INGREDIENTS (Serves 4-6)
290ml/½pt milk
1tbsp caster sugar
1 small vanilla pod
2 egg yolks

☐ *If custard curdles strain it immediately into a cold saucepan and whisk vigorously.*

1 Heat the milk with the sugar and vanilla pod. Bring slowly to the boil.

2 Beat the egg yolks in a bowl, using a wooden spoon — if a whisk is used the custard will be too frothy. Remove the vanilla pod and pour the milk onto the egg yolks, stirring steadily. Mix well and return to the pan.

3 Stir over a gentle heat until the mixture thickens so that it will coat the back of a spoon: do not boil or the custard will curdle. Pour into a cold bowl.

NOTE 1 A skin can be prevented from forming on the custard by sprinkling a fine layer of caster sugar on the hot surface of the custard which can be whisked in later. Or the custard can be closely covered with clingwrap.

NOTE 2 The keen cook *should* master the difficulties of custard making without resorting to packet custard or cornflour. But a teaspoon of cornflour or of custard powder added to the egg yolks will greatly lessen the chances of curdling without drastically affecting the flavour.

PHOTOGRAPH ON P.222

MENU LESSON 41

Saucisse en brioche

Veal escalopes with cream and Marsala

Noodles and red pepper

French beans

Pears in honey

This is not the lightest of meals, so serve smallish slices of the first course, and not too large veal escalopes. The principles of working with yeast are emphasized here, and the less confident cook should read the chapter on bread-making on p.311 before launching into brioche — which is one of the richest and most satisfying of breads to make.

The veal escalopes require the last-minute cooking of the true sauté. The dish is a typical sauté in that the sauce is made quickly in the pan in which the meat is cooked, and is served at once. A salad could very easily replace the noodles and French beans, although the combination of noodles and creamy veal is excellent.

The pears are rich and sticky. They are perhaps even better served with cream, but in this menu that would be more than gilding the lily. For a lighter last course just serve perfect fresh pears with top-grade parmesan cheese, bought in the piece.

WORK PLAN

- The pears can be cooked the day before, but may need reboiling if the juice becomes murky and dull. It is essential that it has a deep syrupy shine.
- The Saucisse en brioche should be made a few hours before eating so that it has cooled to lukewarm when served. It is better fresh than reheated.
- The noodles and peppers are quick to do, especially if the pepper and garlic oil is ready in advance. But the whole dish can be made, cooled and reheated in the oven or microwave.
- The beans can be blanched, refreshed and reheated if necessary, but they do not take long to cook.
- The veal, of course, *must* be served as soon as it is made.

SAUCISSE EN BRIOCHE

INGREDIENTS (Serves 4)
7g/¼oz fresh yeast
1 level tsp sugar
2tbsp warm water
225g/8oz plain flour
Pinch of salt
2 eggs, beaten
55g/2oz butter, melted
225g/8oz garlic sausage
Beaten egg to glaze

1 Mix together the yeast, sugar and water. Leave to dissolve.

2 Sift the flour into a large bowl. Add the salt, eggs, melted butter and yeast. Mix to a soft but not sloppy dough. Knead on an unfloured board for 5 minutes or until smooth, elastic and shiny.

3 Put into a clean bowl, cover and leave to rise in a warm place for 1 hour or until doubled in bulk.

4 Return to the board (still unfloured) and knead again for 2 minutes. Roll into a piece large enough to encase the sausage. Brush with beaten egg.

5 Skin the garlic sausage but leave in the piece. Put it on the dough.

6 Brush the sausage with beaten egg and then dust with flour. Roll up the brioche rather like a Swiss roll. Seal the edges firmly. Place in a greased and floured (or non-stick) 900g/2lb loaf tin with the seams underneath. Leave in a warm place to prove (rise again) for 30 minutes.

☐ *The Saucisse en brioche makes an excellent informal lunch dish with salad.*

7 Set the oven to 220°C/425°F/Gas 7.

8 Brush the egg glaze over the brioche and bake for 25 – 30 minutes. Leave to cool on a wire rack.

9 Slice thickly and serve warm.

NOTE The fattier the sausage, the more likely there is to be a gap between sausage and bread when the slices are cut. Raw sausage which must cook in the dough loses most fat, leaving the greatest gap, but the taste and smell of sausage cooked within the dough is very good. Cooked or smoked sausages or not-too-fatty pâtés shrink less, although there is almost always a slight unavoidable gap.

VEAL ESCALOPES WITH CREAM AND MARSALA

INGREDIENTS (Serves 4)
4×170g/6oz veal escalopes
30g/1oz unsalted butter
4tbsp Marsala
150ml/¼pt single cream
Lemon juice
Salt and freshly ground black pepper

1 Trim away any fat from the veal escalopes. Lay them between two sheets of greaseproof paper or polythene and beat gently until evenly thin.

2 Melt the butter. When hot and foaming add 1 or 2 escalopes and brown lightly on both sides, resisting the temptation to move them around too much (which inhibits browning) or to pierce with a fork (which allows the juices to escape). Leave them as still as you dare, turning them only after 2 or 3 minutes. They should be just pink inside — they will feel firm (neither squashy nor tough) when pressed with a finger. Keep warm while the remaining escalopes are fried.

3 TO MAKE THE SAUCE, take the pan off the heat. Add the Marsala. Return to the heat and bring to the boil, scraping the bottom of the pan with a wooden spoon. This is called deglazing and is done to draw the sediment into the sauce to add colour and flavour to the final dish. Boil to reduce to 2tbsp. Add the cream and bring to the boil. Add a few drops of lemon juice and season with salt and black pepper.

4 Arrange the veal escalopes in overlapping slices on a warm flat plate. Pour over the cream and Marsala sauce.

☐ *The best veal is milk-fed and very expensive. It has a tenderness and creaminess not found in grass-fed veal. If the best veal is out of the question, use good quality very pale pork, or turkey breast or chicken breast. All can be beaten out as described for veal escalopes.*

NOTE Do not try to halve this sauce recipe — the frying pan would be too large and all the Marsala would evaporate — rather halve the meat quantity and serve plenty of sauce. If frying more than four escalopes, double the sauce ingredients and use two frying pans.

BEATING OUT ESCALOPES
Put the veal slices between sheets of plastic. Beat each slice gently and evenly with a rolling pin or meat mallet. Do not hurry the process, and do not beat the escalopes too hard or the flesh will tear.

NOODLES AND RED PEPPER

INGREDIENTS (Serves 4)
1 medium sweet red pepper
225g/8oz tagliatelli noodles
2tbsp olive oil
1 clove garlic

☐ *Canned pimento (red capsicums) are cooked red peppers and are as good, if not better, in flavour than the fresh ones, but they lack the crisp texture. Either is good with the noodles.*

1 Wash the red pepper. Cut off the stalk end and remove all the seeds, which are sometimes too peppery. Cut the flesh into fine slices. Boil the pepper strips in salted water for 2 minutes. Cool (ie refresh) under running water to retain the colour and prevent the pepper from cooking further. Drain well.

2 Boil the pasta in plenty of rapidly boiling salted water, with 1tbsp oil, until tender but not too soft — about 5 minutes if the noodles are dried, 2 minutes if fresh. Drain well and rinse with boiling water to prevent the pasta sticking together. Tip into a warmed serving dish.

3 While the pasta is boiling, crush the garlic.

4 Heat the oil, add the garlic and pepper, shake over the heat until sizzling. Mix with the pasta. Season with plenty of freshly ground black pepper.

RINSING PASTA
Rinse excess starch from just-cooked pasta with *boiling* water. The pasta then remains hot and dries off quickly. All types of pasta benefit from this treatment.

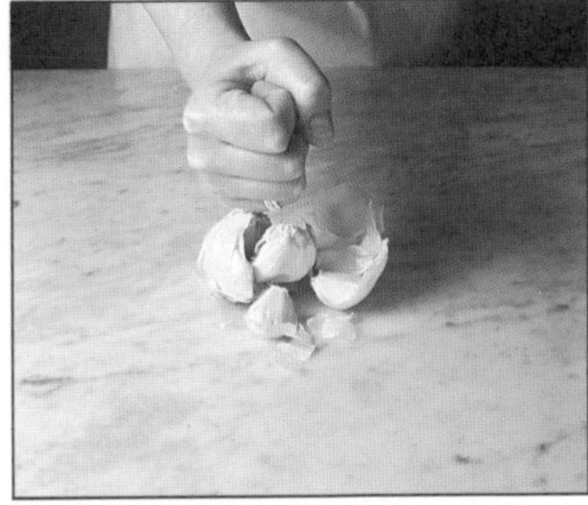

CRUSHING GARLIC
1 If using many cloves, split a head of garlic with a solid punch of the fist. (Put greaseproof paper on the board if you want to avoid having to scrub the board later.)

2 To skin a single clove, place it near the edge of a chopping board and lay the flat of a heavy knife over the clove with the handle overlapping the edge of the board. Use a fist to punch down hard on the knife to slightly crush the clove and loosen the skin.

3 The papery skin of the half-crushed garlic clove can now be easily peeled off.

4 To make garlic paste, use the tip of a round-bladed firm knife and a good quantity of salt to crush the clove, working from tip to 'root' end.

5 Continue the process of crushing and mixing until the paste is smooth.

FRENCH BEANS

INGREDIENTS (Serves 4)
450g/1lb French beans
20g/¾oz butter
Salt and freshly ground black pepper

1 Wash and top-and-tail the beans.

2 Place the beans in a pan of boiling salted water and cook, uncovered, until just tender. They should take between 3 and 6 minutes, depending on how young they are. Beans should be served with a little 'bite' to them, but they should be cooked reasonably well for the full flavour of the bean to develop — raw beans do not taste of much. Drain and serve with a little melted butter, salt and pepper.

TOPPING AND TAILING BEANS
1 Take a handful of beans, ensuring that the ends are level by tapping them all on the chopping board. Cut off the ends at a stroke.

2 Tap the other end of the bunch of beans on the board to level them up.

3 When the ends are aligned, slice them off at a stroke.

PEARS IN HONEY

INGREDIENTS (Serves 4)
570ml/1pt water
225g/8oz granulated sugar
Juice of ½ lemon
4 firm pears
1tbsp runny Greek honey
30g/1oz browned almond flakes

1 Place the water, sugar and lemon juice together in a thick-bottomed saucepan. Heat gently until the sugar has dissolved. (Boiling hard before dissolving encourages crystallization. Do not stir, as sugar will get deposited on the sides of the pan and this also tends to start a chain reaction of crystallization, giving a cloudy syrup. The acid in the lemon juice helps to prevent crystallization, and also inhibits the discolouration of the fruits to be poached in the syrup.)

2 Peel the pears very neatly without removing the stalks. Immediately place in the pan of syrup. They should then be kept completely covered in syrup to prevent discolouration. If this is not possible, wet the pears in the mixture thoroughly and turn them during cooking. Use wooden spoons and fingers rather than metal tools to avoid damaging the fruit.

3 Remove the pears from the pan and place in a glass bowl. Reduce the sugar syrup by rapid boiling to a light syrupy consistency. Add the honey. Pour over the pears. Allow to cool. Chill in the refrigerator.

4 Sprinkle over the browned nuts just before serving.

NOTE When making this dish for 8 people, the sugar syrup quantity is 860ml/1½pt water, 340g/12oz granulated sugar, 1½tbsp honey.

PHOTOGRAPH ON P.223

There is nothing particularly difficult to cook in the traditional Christmas lunch. But somehow, especially for the cook who is also the mother or father of the family, the host and the organizer of festivities, it can be a daunting task. As always the secret of success is in the planning and preparation. This menu is traditional in content — turkey, ham, sprouts and Christmas pudding, but the presentation is a little more stylish than usual. The turkey is boned and stuffed with boned ham, the sprouts are puréed to a luxurious cream and the Christmas pudding is a round one and served with Port and prune ice cream.

The techniques the cook will practise are those of boning a bird (easier with a turkey than with smaller birds), making gravy and boiling the pudding. But the real skill is in the careful following of a pre-determined time plan, and in keeping calm in the face of the excitement and importance of the occasion, and the sheer quantity of the food. Our menu assumes 12 diners at the feast.

MENU LESSON 42

Boned turkey stuffed with ham

Cranberry sauce

Bread sauce (see p.272)

Roast potatoes (see p.230)

Brussels sprouts purée

Cannon ball Christmas pudding

Brandy or rum butter

Port and prune ice cream

WORK PLAN

Because Christmas generally involves the cook in more than culinary matters, we have tried to include other jobs that will need doing. But no two families are quite alike so make your own work plan, working backwards from dishing-up time, and writing everything down. Stick the paper at eye level on door or wall and follow it step by step, religiously.

AS EARLY AS YOU LIKE

1 Make the Christmas pudding, ice cream and brandy butter. Suspend the pudding in a cool place or freeze it, supported by a bowl (see illustration). Once frozen it will not lose its round shape. If unfrozen do not put on a flat surface — it will develop a flat bottom.
2 Make a detailed shopping list.
3 Order turkey and anything likely to be difficult to get just before Christmas (extra milk, eggs, cream etc).
4 Buy charms or get new coins from the bank for the pudding.
5 Make the stuffing. Freeze in a shallow tray to facilitate quick thawing.

THREE DAYS AHEAD

If the turkey is frozen put in a cold place (eg refrigerator, larder, garage) to thaw.

TWO DAYS AHEAD

1 Do the shopping.
2 Remove the plastic wrap from the thawing turkey. Cover it with a damp, clean cloth instead.
3 Cook the bacon joint or ham. Refrigerate.
4 Put the frozen stuffing into the refrigerator to thaw.
5 Put the brandy butter (if frozen) into the refrigerator to thaw.

6 Make extra ice cubes for drinks. Store in polythene bag.
7 Turn the fridge to a colder than normal setting — it is going to work overtime for the next few days.

CHRISTMAS EVE MORNING

1 Remove the packet of giblets from inside the turkey.
2 Bone and stuff the turkey, working in a cool place so that the bird does not get too warm. Weigh it, and calculate cooking time. Soak clean muslin in melted butter and use to double-wrap the turkey (see recipe). Put in roasting pan. Return to the refrigerator.
3 Make turkey stock with the bones and giblets (except the liver). See p.267. Strain if necessary.
4 Make the bread sauce, doubling the quantities on p.272.
5 Thaw the pudding if frozen.

CHRISTMAS EVE AFTERNOON OR EVENING

1 Lay the table and decorate it. Put red wine and children's drinks etc, on it. Add corkscrew and bottle opener. Put chocolates, liqueurs, cigars on sideboard. Cover with sheet to preserve the surprise and keep off the dust. (The family must now picnic off their knees for supper and breakfast, but laying the table on Christmas morning is best avoided.)
2 Put the cranberry sauce, mustard, bread sauce and cream into jugs or pots and cover with plastic wrap. Keep cool.
3 Put sprigs of holly, matches, brandy bottle and ladle for flaming pudding near the cooker.
4 Sharpen the carving knife.
5 Wash charms or coins for the pudding. Do not cook them in the pudding (coins discolour and charms get lost) but insert them surreptitiously when dishing up.
6 Make the sprout purée. Cover and refrigerate.
7 Peel 2kg/5lb potatoes. Boil 10 minutes. While hot shake them roughly in a wire sieve (this will give a crisp, crumbly edge when roasted and they will stay warm for hours without getting leathery). Brush all over with melted butter to prevent discolouring. Put in greased roasting tin. Keep cool.
8 Suspend the pudding in a pan ready for tomorrow. (See recipe.)
9 Check through menu and get out relevant plates, vegetable dishes, gravy jugs etc. Think:
- what will it be taken to the table in?
- what serving implements are necessary?
- what is it to be eaten on?

Put plates, serving dishes etc. in the warmer if you have one. Otherwise into a plastic bowl or sink to be warmed under hot water.
10 Set the pre-lunch drinks things in the living room; check glasses, drinks, minerals, openers, sliced lemon, etc.
11 Put the white wine or champagne in the refrigerator.
12 Lay the after-lunch coffee tray.

CHRISTMAS MORNING

9.00am • Set oven to 180°C/350°F/Gas 4.
• Set the cranberry sauce and mustard on the table. Finish laying the table if necessary. Put brandy butter, cream, pudding plates, and servers on the sideboard.
9.30am • Add a cup of water to the turkey pan. Put it into the centre of the oven.

• Put the pudding on to boil. Refill kettle (for topping up).
10.00am Top up the pudding water and refill the kettle.
10.45am Top up pudding water. Refill kettle.
11.30am Move turkey to the bottom of the oven. Put potatoes in on top shelf. Top up the pudding water. Refill kettle.
12.30pm • Reheat the bread sauce, adding more milk or butter if too solid. Leave saucepan covered, but off the heat.
• Check the turkey. If cooked, dish up and return to the switched off oven.
• Dish up the potatoes. Do not cover them. Keep warm.
• Make the gravy. Leave in saucepan for last-minute heating.
• Remove plastic wrap from sauces on sideboard, and dust covers from table.
• Top up pudding water.
• Put plates in to warm.
• Put ice cream into the refrigerator to soften.
1.00pm Have a pre-lunch drink with the other revellers.
1.15pm • Reheat the sprouts in microwave oven or over gentle heat in frying pan or saucepan. Dish up.
• Dish up the warm bread sauce.
• Reheat and dish up the gravy.
• Light candles on the table. Open wine.
• Top up the pudding water.
1.30pm Serve the meal, mentally checking: turkey, gravy, bread sauce, potatoes, sprouts, warm plates.
2.30pm Dish up the pudding. Warm the brandy in the kitchen. Carry pudding and warm brandy into the dining room. Put the holly into the pudding, light the brandy and pour flaming over the top. Put on the table with the ice cream. (Carrying the pudding ready flaming from the kitchen is a mistake: the draught might blow it out before any satisfactory clapping is heard.)

THAWING AND COOKING TIMES FOR TURKEYS

WEIGHT OF BIRD (whether boned, stuffed or empty)	**THAWING TIME** at room temperature 17.5°C/65°F	in refrigerator 5°C/40°F	**COOKING TIME** at 180°C/350°F/ Gas 4	at 170°C/325°F/ Gas 3
4-5kg/8-10lb	20 hours	65 hours	2-2½ hours	3-4 hours
5.5-6.5kg/11-13lb	24 hours	70 hours	2½-3 hours	4-5 hours
7-8kg/14-16lb	30 hours	75 hours	3-4 hours	5¼-6 hours
8.5-10kg/17-20lb	40 hours	80 hours	4-5 hours	6¼-7 hours
11-12kg/21-24lb	48 hours	96 hours	5-6 hours	7½-8½ hours

NOTE Thawing in a warm room (over 17.5°C/65°F) or under warm water is not recommended, as this will encourage the growth of micro-organisms, which might result in food poisoning (see p.331).

BONED TURKEY STUFFED WITH HAM

INGREDIENTS (Serves 12)
2kg/4lb piece boneless gammon or ham
One 5.5kg/12lb turkey
225g/8oz butter
Muslin or thin cotton cloth

FOR THE STUFFING
30g/1oz butter
1 large onion, finely chopped
450g/1lb sausagemeat
225g/8oz unsweetened chestnut purée
110g/4oz fresh white breadcrumbs
½tsp dried sage
2tbsp chopped parsley
Salt and freshly ground black pepper
1 egg, lightly beaten

FOR ROASTING
225g/8oz butter

FOR THE GRAVY
2tbsp fat from roasting pan
2tbsp flour
425ml/¾pt turkey stock

FOR THE GARNISH
Holly sprigs

☐ *Do not use pressed paper kitchen cloths to wrap the turkey — they burn if cooked for very long. Use muslin or a thin cotton cloth, like an old tea towel.*

1 TO COOK THE HAM, put it into a saucepan that easily takes it. Cover with water.

2 Bring very slowly to the boil. Throw away the water and replace it with fresh. (Most ham today is only mildly cured and will not be too salty without long soaking.)

3 Simmer the ham gently for 1¾ hours. Allow to cool in the liquid. (To speed up the process, see illustration on p.331.)

4 When the ham is lukewarm, lift it out of the liquid and remove the skin and most of the fat. Refrigerate, covered, until ready to stuff the turkey.

5 BONE THE TURKEY Keep the knife as close to the bone as possible, scraping and easing the flesh away carefully. (See p.198.)

6 Turn the bird breast side down and cut through the skin, along the backbone, from the parson's nose to the neck. Work the skin and flesh away from the bones, peeling back the flesh as you go, gradually exposing the rib cage. When you get to the legs and wings, cut through the tendons close against the carcase at the joints. This will mean the wings and legs stay attached to the skin — not to the carcass. Continue working round the bird, taking special care when boning the breast where the skin and bone are very close.

7 Now bone the wings and legs. Chop off the wing pinions and the knuckle-end of the drumsticks. Working from the thicker end of the joints, ease the bones out, scraping the flesh from them carefully. You may need to work from the drumstick or wing tip ends as well, but most of the work should be done from the body side.

8 Cut off any excess fat, especially from near the parson's nose. When all the bones are out, scrape off any flesh still adhering to them and add it to the stuffing. Put the turkey in the fridge, loosely covered with foil, until ready to stuff.

9 TO MAKE THE STUFFING melt the butter, add the onion and cook until soft, but not coloured.

10 When cold, mix with the sausagemeat, chestnut purée, breadcrumbs, sage, parsley, salt and pepper. Add enough egg to bind the mixture together, but do not allow it to become sloppy.

11 TO STUFF THE TURKEY open up the bird, skin side down. Put the ham on it, cut into two thick chunks if necessary. Spread the stuffing all over the ham to fill in the gaps to make an even mound.

12 Bring up the sides of the bird to enclose the ham and stuffing and sew from neck to tail with string.

13 You should have an even-shaped object, like an overstuffed pillow. Weigh it and calculate the cooking time (see chart). Put in a greased roasting tin.

14 Melt 225g/8oz butter. Calculate how much muslin or cloth you will need to completely cover the bird with a double layer (probably 1m/3ft muslin). Dip the cloth into the butter so that it is completely soaked. Use this to cover the turkey. Refrigerate until ready to roast.

15 Roast as in the work plan or until the juices will run clear when the flesh is deeply punctured with a skewer.

16 Remove the wrappings and dish up the turkey.

17 TO MAKE THE GRAVY, pour off all but 1tbsp fat from the roasting pan and lift onto the top of the cooker. Stir in a tablespoon or so of flour to absorb the remaining fat. Add 425ml/¾pt turkey stock and whisk until the sauce boils. Boil 2 minutes, then drain into a warmed gravy boat.

18 Decorate the turkey with the holly.

CRANBERRY SAUCE

INGREDIENTS
450g/1lb frozen cranberries
170g/6oz sugar
150ml/¼pt water

1 Put the cranberries and sugar in a heavy saucepan and add the water.

2 Simmer gently, stirring occasionally, for 30 minutes, until it looks like fairly liquid jam. Serve cold or warm.

BRUSSELS SPROUTS PUREE

INGREDIENTS (Serves 12)
900g/2lb Brussels sprouts, cooked
290ml/½pt very fresh double cream
Salt and freshly ground black pepper
Grated nutmeg

☐ *Any green vegetables can be treated as the sprouts — spinach is particularly delicious.*

1 Liquidize or blend sprouts to a purée while still hot, to allow steam to escape. If they are very wet, stir the purée over direct heat to dry off.

2 Boil the cream in a small heavy saucepan until reduced in quantity by about a third. It will thicken. Stir frequently to prevent burning.

3 Mix the cream with the sprouts, adding salt, pepper and nutmeg to taste. Serve in a warmed serving dish.

NOTE This dish may be prepared the day before serving. Allow sprouts and cream to cool before mixing. Reheat by tossing in a heavy frying pan over gentle heat, or in a shallow buttered dish in a hot oven, or best of all, rapidly in a microwave oven.

CANNON BALL CHRISTMAS PUDDING

INGREDIENTS (Serves 12)
225g/8oz sultanas
225g/8oz stoned raisins
225g/8oz currants
1tsp mixed spice
170g/6oz shredded suet
225g/8oz soft brown sugar
280g/10oz fresh brown breadcrumbs
170g/6oz carrot, grated
1 small cooking apple, peeled and chopped
2tbsp black treacle
4 large eggs, beaten

For a perfectly round Christmas pudding, pack the mixture into both sides of a Chinese hinged round rice steamer, and enclose the steamer in a stout polythene bag, tied so as to eliminate as much air as possible. In the absence of a rice steamer the pudding can be boiled in polythene bags as described in the recipe, suspended by string so that it does not touch the bottom of the pan. A preserving pan with a handle that can be fixed in the upright position is good, or a wooden spoon or cooling rack laid across the top of a deep saucepan and the pudding suspended from that.

1 Mix everything together and pack into a greased rice boiler or a heavy-duty greased polythene bag, and tie securely. Put into another similar bag (a precaution in case the first one bursts) and tie securely with a long piece of strong string. If the shape is not round make a bag for it out of a piece of cloth and tie tightly to get a good shape. If not attempting the round-shaped pudding, pack the mixture into a 2litre/4pt greased pudding basin, tie down (see p.57) and boil (see p.79).

2 Choose a pan that will easily take the pudding with a good 2.5cm/1 inch of space around, below and above it when it is suspended.

3 Suspend the pudding in the correct position (it should not touch the bottom, and the top should be well below the level of the pan rim).

4 Bring a kettle of water to the boil and pour into the pudding pan. Repeat if necessary until the pudding is submerged.

5 Keep the pudding simmering steadily for 8 hours, topping up the water every 45 minutes or so as necessary to keep it under water.

6 Pour away the water and leave the pudding suspended to cool.

7 Once cold, the pudding will be solid and will retain its shape fairly well, but it is best stored suspended in a larder or lying in a bowl that will support its round shape (if left on a flat surface it may end up with a flat bottom). Store in a cool dry place, or freeze.

8 If frozen, remove from the freezer the day before serving.

9 Suspend the pudding in the saucepan as before.

10 Four hours before serving, fill the pan with boiling water, and simmer steadily, topping the water up at 45 minute intervals.

11 Lift out the pudding. Carefully unwrap it and ease it onto a serving dish. Stick a piece of real holly into the top.

12 TO FLAME THE PUDDING Heat a glass of brandy in a metal ladle or small saucepan over direct heat. Carry warm brandy and matches into the dining room. Light the brandy, and pour, flaming, over the pudding.

☐ *To flame a pudding successfully, warm the brandy in a small saucepan and carry it into the dining room before lighting it. If the brandy is hot it will light easily and if the pudding does not have to be carried through draughty doors the flames will not blow out.*
A little leftover Christmas pudding or Christmas mincemeat beaten into softened vanilla ice cream and refrozen, makes an excellent cassata.

CANNONBALL PUDDING

1 Pack the greased bags and seal them so they are watertight. Wrap in cloth and tie securely with a long piece of string.

2 Tie the pudding to a wooden spoon and suspend it in a large pan so that it does not touch the bottom. Cover with boiling water and simmer for 8 hours. Keep the pudding submerged.

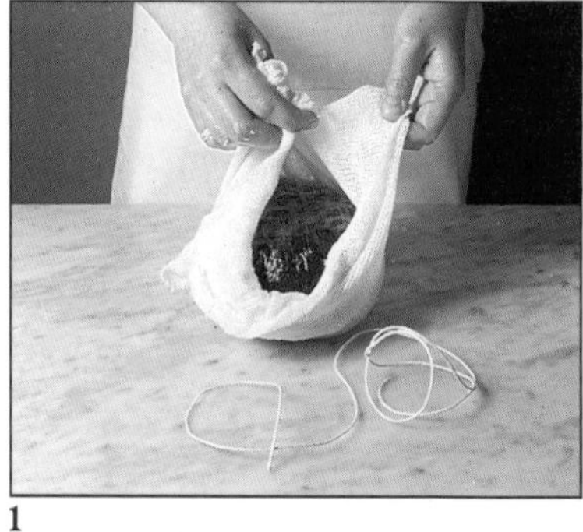

1

2

BRANDY OR RUM BUTTER

INGREDIENTS
225g/8oz unsalted butter
110g/4oz caster sugar
2tbsp brandy or rum

1 Beat the butter and sugar together until creamy and pale.

2 Beat in the brandy or rum gradually.

PORT AND PRUNE ICE CREAM

INGREDIENTS (Serves 12)
Rich vanilla ice cream (see p.144), softened
225g/8oz prunes
2tbsp port

1 Put the prunes in a saucepan and just cover with water. Leave to soak until soft (anything from 30 minutes to 8 hours depending on the dryness of the fruit).

2 Simmer gently until pulpy. Drain and remove the stones. Chop to a rough paste.

3 Mix with the port. Stir into the ice cream and refreeze.

TECHNIQUES AND METHODS

BASIC TECHNIQUES

This chapter is about the *processes* of cooking, the methods and techniques that produce the best results. Grilling is a better method of cooking a lamb cutlet than steaming it. Steaming is a better cooking method for carrots than grilling them, which wouldn't work at all. Why? How is the cook to choose? To understand what happens to food when it is cooked is important, because that knowledge allows the cook to be inventive and creative, to make adaptations and changes to a recipe, to right something patently going wrong and to judge what will work and what will not.

ROASTING

A large whole roasted bird or joint makes an impressive main course. The same meat cut into individual portions and grilled or pan fried, however delicious, never has quite the same impact.

Roasting means cooking in an oven with no other liquid than fat. Once, however, roasting and grilling were almost the same process carried out in front of an open fire where both large and small cuts of meat were spit-roasted. Provided that the meat was of a uniform shape and thickness, spit cooking made sure no part of the meat dried out, because the fat and meat juices ran over the surface as the meat turned. Today's ovens dispense with the long and arduous job of turning a spit, though some ovens or grills have electrically operated spits, known as rôtisseries, built into them.

ROASTING TABLE

If using a fan (convection) oven, reduce the cooking times by 15 percent or lower the oven temperature by 20°C/40°F.
Meat If sealing by browning in a frying pan first, omit the sealing in the oven and simply follow roasting times.
Poultry and game birds It is important that turkey and chicken are cooked through, or the flesh is unattractively slimy when eaten cold. When the bird is done, the thigh bone will feel loose and will wobble independently of the body when moved.
Pre-braising or oven sealing is not necessary with birds.

MEAT		TEMPERATURE °C	°F	Gas	COOKING TIME per kg	per lb
Beef	seal	220	425	7	20 mins +	
	rare roast	160	325	3	35 mins	15 mins
	medium roast				45 mins	20 mins
Pork	seal	—	—	—	65 mins	25 mins
	roast	200	400	6	65 mins	25 mins
Veal	seal	220	425	7	20 mins +	
	roast	180	350	4	55 mins	25 mins
Lamb	seal	220	425	7	20 mins +	
	roast	190	375	5	55 mins	20 mins
Chicken		200	400	6	35-45 mins	15-20 mins
NOTE Few chickens however small will be cooked in much under an hour.						
Turkey	small (Under 5kg/12lb)	200	400	6	25 mins	12 mins
	large	180	350	4	35 mins	15 mins
NOTE For more detailed timings see chart on p.239.						

MEAT		TEMPERATURE °C	°F	Gas	COOKING TIME per kg	per lb
Duck, goose	small (Under 2.5kg/5lb)	190	375	5	45 mins	20 mins
	large	180	350	4	55 mins	25 mins
Pigeon		200	400	6	25-35 minutes	
Grouse		190	375	5	25-35 minutes	
Guinea fowl		190	375	5	70 minutes	
Partridge		190	375	5	20-25 minutes	
Pheasant		190	375	5	45-60 minutes	
Wild duck		200	400	6	30-35 minutes	
Woodcock		190	375	5	20-25 minutes	
Quail		180	350	4	20 minutes	

In modern well insulated and thermostatically controlled ovens, even without rôtisseries, roasts need little attention other than occasional basting (unless the meat has a top layer of fat which eliminates even the need for this) to prevent the upper part of the meat drying out and to enhance the flavour. Potatoes and other root vegetables may also be roasted in the fat which melts and runs from the meat while it cooks. Another bonus is that a simple pan gravy, perfect to serve with the meat, can be made from the meat juices which collect in the pan during roasting. By skimming off the fat and boiling up with a little stock and/or wine the gravy can be made while the meat 'rests' before carving.

While the meat roasts, economize on heat and time by using any available oven space to cook other dishes. Yorkshire pudding and apple or berry pie are good choices for this traditional economy.

The following are general rules in checklist form for roasting meat:

1 Weigh the meat to calculate the time and temperature needed to roast it (see chart).

2 Preheat the oven to the required temperature.

3 As with grilling, it is essential to seal the surface of the raw meat quickly to keep in the juices while the meat roasts. The crisp surface will also add colour and flavour. You can seal or 'seize' meat such as beef, veal or lamb by putting it into a very hot oven for the first 20·minutes or so before reducing to the normal roasting temperature, or by browning quickly in a frying pan. For the latter method, put the meat into really hot fat and leave it there until one surface is completely browned, then repeat on each side until the whole roast has been seared. This will seal the meat effectively.

4 Place the browned meat on the roasting rack or trivet in a roasting pan and put it in the pre-heated oven. The rack or trivet keeps the meat off the bottom of the pan, preventing the bottom of the roast frying in its own fat and allows the heat to penetrate the meat more evenly.

5 Halfway through the cooking time, check the meat. Turn it over if it is well browned on top and baste with the melted fat and juices that have collected in the bottom of the pan.

6 When the cooking time is up, stand the roast on a warm serving platter in a warm place or leave it in the switched-off oven with the door wide open. This 'resting' period makes carving easier as the meat fibres relax from the taut state induced by the intense heat. In large roasts the heat drives the juices into the centre, and resting it is necessary to allow these juices some time to seep back into the outer layers giving an even colour and juiciness throughout. With small domestic roasts long resting is not really necessary; the time taken to make the gravy is enough.

7 Make the gravy in the roasting pan.

TO BARD
Tie a piece of fat on to a lean cut of meat. It will baste the meat as it cooks.

BASTING, BARDING AND LARDING Very lean meats such as veal and game birds should not be roasted without extra fat or they will become unpalatably dry. Continual basting is time-consuming and the repeated opening of the oven door lowers the temperature. The answer is to make a roast 'self-basting' and there are several ways to do this.

1 Bard the roast by wrapping it in pork fat. As the fat melts it bastes the meat and protects it from the drying effects of the oven.

SELF-BASTING ROASTS
Soak a piece of muslin thoroughly in melted butter. Fold it in half and lay it, like a blanket, over the fish or fowl.

2 Lard the roast by threading thin strips (lardons) of back fat through it. (See p.248.) This is not suitable for meat to be served rare.

3 Cover turkeys and whole very large round fish with a double layer of muslin which has been thoroughly soaked in melted butter or oil before roasting. This allows the skin to become crisp and brown.

Very lean meats benefit from slow roasting as well as from barding and/or larding. Less lean meats and poultry, such as beef and chicken benefit from a coating of butter and/or oil before going into the oven.

If the joint does have a fat layer, always start the roasting with the fat uppermost so that it will baste the meat as it melts. Although lamb shoulders and legs and well marbled joints of beef do not have an obvious layer of fat, they contain plenty of invisible fat and so need only a light coating of butter and/or oil before roasting.

Sometimes a cupful of liquid is added to the roasting pan to prevent the desirable pan juices from scorching to bitterness.

FLAVOURED ROASTS There are interesting variations on the plain roast such as stuffing with a meat or cereal mixture, or boning and rolling the joint to ensure a neat shape and easy carving. Other variations include spreading the meat with savoury mixtures such as mustard and/or spices, tucking fresh herbs or garlic between the outer skin and the flesh of the roast or flavouring the meat by steeping it in a marinade, then using it to baste the meat and to make the sauce.

COOKING TIMES are meant only as a general guide. Obviously, a long thin piece of meat will take less time to cook than a thick round one of the same weight. The essential thing is that the meat must reach an internal temperature of 60°C/140°F to be rare, 70°C/150°F to be medium pink and 80°C/175°F to be well done. The meat thermometer stuck into the centre of the meat eliminates guesswork. The thermometer should be positioned when the roasting is almost complete. Make sure that it does not touch a bone or the roasting pan.

If using a fan (convection) oven, reduce the cooking times by 15 per cent or lower the oven temperatures by 20°C/40°F.

If sealing meat by browning in a frying pan as described above, omit the sealing in the oven and simply follow roasting times.

POULTRY AND GAME BIRDS It is important that turkey and chicken are cooked through, or the flesh is unattractively slimy when eaten hot and can carry food poisoning bacteria if eaten cold. When the bird is done, the thigh bone will feel loose and will wobble independently of the body when moved.

Pre-browning or oven sealing is not necessary with birds.

MAKE GRAVY from the pan juices as follows:

1 Pour or skim off the fat from the top of the other liquids in the pan.

2 Off the heat, add just enough flour to absorb any remaining fat and thicken the gravy slightly. Stir with a wooden spoon to incorporate the flour.

3 Put the pan over gentle heat and scrape the bottom of the pan well to release any stuck sediment and cooked meat juices or glaze.

4 Add a cupful or two of stock or water. Stir all the time until the sauce thickens. Boil hard for a minute or two. Season to taste.

NOTES ON GRAVY

1 The pan juices will probably have enough flavour for water to be used, but stock will give the gravy more flavour and body.

2 When the meat has been roasted to a good brown colour there will probably be enough colour in the juices and the small pieces of meat stuck to the bottom of the pan to give the gravy a good final colour. If not, use commercial gravy browning, or cook about ½tsp sugar to a dark caramel in the dry roasting tin before adding the liquid.

3 If adding wine, port, cider or any alcoholic beverage to the gravy, reduce it first by rapid boiling to eliminate any harsh flavour. Red wine can be poured over a joint half way through the cooking — the alcohol will evaporate and the flavour of the meat will improve.

4 Gravy should run easily off the back of a spoon. One teaspoonful of flour is enough to slightly thicken 300ml/½pt gravy.

5 If there is enough natural liquid in the pan after roasting the meat, gravy may not be necessary at all, but the juices should be skimmed to remove the fat. (See p.229.)

6 Though many people like *slightly* fatty gravy, all traces of fat can be removed from the top of the gravy by laying sheets of absorbent paper on the surface to soak up the fat.

7 If serving gravy with game or goose — rich meat which benefits from a little sweetness — add 1tsp redcurrant, plum or similar sharp-flavoured jam to the reduced gravy. The preserve also helps to thicken the gravy.

8 Perfect gravy always looks shiny and never floury. Try to use a minimum of flour and get the gravy to the right consistency by reducing it. Boiling down also helps ensure the gravy has a clearer, shinier look.

POT-ROASTING

Pot-roasting is not really roasting at all, but baking food enclosed in a pot, either in the oven or over a low heat. It is an old, economical method of cooking that was much used in the days before there were many domestic ovens. Roasting proper is a much faster, 'dry' method, used for cooking choicer, more tender cuts of meat and poultry by exposing them to direct heat. Pot-roasting involves cooking meat and poultry in its own juices and might be better called a simpler, quicker version of braising.

Traditionally there is very little liquid in a pot-roast, other than the fat needed for browning, as moisture from the meat provides most of the liquid during cooking. With poultry, a few spoons of liquid are usually added after browning.

A casserole with a tightly fitting lid creates a small oven. Steam is formed inside the pot from the moisture given off by the added liquid or by the food itself, and this steam slowly tenderizes and cooks the meat. If the lid does not fit tightly, the steam can escape. Similarly, if the casserole or pan is too large, the liquid spreads over too large an area and is more likely to boil away. To make sure a lid fits tightly, cover the top of the pan with a piece of greaseproof paper and place the lid on top, jamming it down firmly.

If the casserole is flameproof, or if an ordinary saucepan is used, browning on the hob and pot-roasting on the hob or in the oven can be done in one vessel. Otherwise, brown the meat in a frying pan and transfer it (with all the pan juices) to a casserole for pot-roasting.

One traditional 'trick' in pot-roasting is to cook the browned meat on a piece of pork rind. This adds flavour, and prevents any scorching of the meat on the bottom of the pan or casserole. Coarsely cut root vegetables are sometimes placed under the meat for the same purpose. They can either be raw or browned in the same fat as the meat, though the meat should be removed from the pan while browning the vegetables. Once cooked, they can be served with the meat.

One way to ensure tender meat is to marinade it before cooking. A mixture of oil, wine and other flavourings penetrates the outer layer of the meat when it is left to marinade overnight in the refrigerator. The acid in the marinade also helps to break down tough fibres, and the oil prevents moisture evaporation and adds richness. Save some of the marinade to use as the cooking liquid.

LARDING LEAN MEAT
Use a larding needle with a clamp at the end. Pull strips of fat through the flesh with the grain at 2cm/1 inch intervals. Trim off protruding strips.

Another way to make sure that a large piece of pot-roasted meat is succulent is to lard it. This is especially important with some lean joints such as the beef 'leg of mutton' cut. Do this by cutting thin strips of pork back fat longer than the joint and threading them all the way through the meat about 1cm/½ inch apart. This is easily done with a larding needle which, when removed, leaves the strips of fat in place. As the meat cooks the fat partially melts, making the meat juicy and adding flavour and richness to the sauce. As long as the meat cooks very slowly, the liquid in the pan is not likely to boil or, more importantly, evaporate. This liquid becomes a richly flavoured sauce for the meat after cooking. Any vegetables cooked with the meat will help to thicken it.

Transfer the pot-roasted joint or bird to a warmed serving dish or board to carve and remove any strings or skewers. If there is too much liquid left in the pan, simply reduce it by boiling or thicken it with beurre manié (p.344). Hand it separately.

GRILLING

PREPARING CHOPS
To prevent steaks, chops or bacon rashers curling up during grilling, snip through the fat at regular intervals.

Intense heat is the secret of successful grilling. Although this method requires active attention from the cook, its advantages are that the food cooks quickly and the charred surface gives great flavour.

To produce succulent, perfectly grilled meat with a crisp brown outside and pink juicy inside, it is absolutely essential to preheat the grill to its highest setting. This may take 10 or even 20 minutes for a grill on a good domestic cooker. Under a cooler grill, the meat's surface will not brown quickly and flavourful juices will leak out, leaving the meat dry, tasteless and unattractive by the time it is cooked through. If the grill cannot be adequately preheated to quickly seal meat and fish, save it for toast and fry the steaks instead.

Over an open charcoal fire, it may take two hours before the embers are flameless yet burn with the necessary intensity. But their fierce heat will cook a small lamb cutlet perfectly in two minutes and the charcoal will give it a wonderfully smoky flavour. Charcoal, when ready, glows bright red in the dark and has an ashy grey look in daylight.

Unlike braising, grilling will not tenderize meat, so only tender, choice cuts should be grilled. They should not be much thicker than 5cm/2 inches because of the high temperatures involved. Any thicker and the

COOKING TIMES FOR STEAKS

	Minutes on each side	
	Fillet	**Sirloin**
Blue	2	2½
Rare	2½	3
Medium rare	3	3½
Medium	3½	4
Well done	5	5½

Rump As sirloin, but allow up to 30 per cent longer in each case

meat would remain cold and raw when the outside was black. Even so, unless the cut of meat is fairly thin, once it browns it must be moved further away from the heat source so the interior can cook before the surface burns. Basting with the delicious pan juices or with olive oil or butter adds flavour and shine. Turning is necessary for even cooking, and should be done half-way through the estimated cooking time, when the first surface is attractively brown.

The following points should be remembered when grilling:

1 Take food out of the refrigerator or freezer in plenty of time to have it at room temperature before grilling. An almost frozen steak will still be cold inside when the outside is brown and sizzling. This is particularly important if the steak is to be served very rare (blue).

2 Do not salt food much in advance. The salt draws moisture from the food. Salt after, during, or immediately before grilling.

3 Brush the food with butter, oil or a mixture of the two to keep it moist and to speed the browning and sealing process. This is also essential to keep delicate foods such as fish from sticking.

4 The more well done meat or fish is, the tougher it will be to the touch and the palate.

5 To avoid piercing the meat and allowing the juices to escape, turn the grilling food with tongs or spoons, not a sharp instrument.

6 Serve immediately. Grilled food, even if well sealed, inevitably loses moisture, dries up and toughens if kept hot for any length of time.

GRILLING STEAKS All grilled meats should be well-browned on the surface but the varying degrees of 'doneness' are defined as follows:

BLUE The inside almost raw (but hot)

RARE Red inside with plenty of red juices running freely

MEDIUM RARE As rare, but with fewer free-flowing juices and a paler centre

MEDIUM Pink in the centre with juices set

WELL DONE The centre beige but the flesh still juicy.

The best way to tell if meat is done is by its texture. Feel the meat by pressing firmly with a finger. Rare steak feels soft, almost raw; medium steak is firmer with some resilience to it; well done steak feels very firm. With practice there will soon be no need to cut-and-peep.

COOKING TIME FOR STEAKS varies with the heat of the grill, the distance of the food from the heat, the thickness of the cut and its fat content. The density of the meat also affects the cooking time. Open textured steak such as sirloin will cook faster than the same thickness and weight of the closer textured rump. The following table assumes a grill capable of being heated to 260°C/500°F with a 2.5cm/1 inch steak held 7.5cm/3 inches from the heat source and then, if necessary, at 15cm/6 inches until cooked to the required degree.

GRILLING FISH Lay the fish steaks and fillets on greased foil on the grill rack, and set close under the preheated grill. This prevents the delicate flesh from sticking to the rack and breaking up when turned.

When grilling over, rather than under heat, use a fine grill rack, or wire mesh grill to support delicate cuts of fish and grease the grill rack or mesh well. (Fish cuts *can* be wrapped in greased foil and cooked over heat, but they then cook in their own steam rather than grill in the true sense.)

GRILLING FISH
Slash large fish to speed cooking. Hold the knife-blade parallel to the worktop and cut down to the backbone on both sides. Brush with butter, then grill.

FRYING AND SAUTEING

Frying, sometimes referred to as 'shallow frying', and sautéing are both quick cooking methods, which are suitable for small, not-too-thick, tender pieces of meat and other foods. The difference in the two methods is the amount of fat used in cooking. For sautéing, an almost dry pan with no more than a tablespoon of fat is used; for frying, food is cooked in up to 0.5cm/¼ inch of fat.

The processes are similar in effect to that of grilling but when grilling small pieces of meat, some fat is lost into the pan juices which may or may not then be eaten with the meat. In frying, the meat cooks in fat and at least some of it is eaten with the meat. For this reason the fat used for frying is an important consideration as its distinctive flavour — or lack of it — will affect the taste of the dish. Olive oil, butter, bacon dripping, lard and beef dripping will each flavour fried foods, while corn, safflower, peanut and most other vegetable oils have little or no flavour.

Care should therefore be taken in choosing frying fat; for instance, potatoes fried in goose fat may taste delicious, but not when they are served with fish. When choosing a fat, remember that some of them can be heated to much higher temperatures than others before they break down and start to burn. For example, clarified butter — butter with all its milk solids removed (see p.75) can be heated to a higher temperature than untreated butter; pure bacon dripping, lard, beef dripping and solid frying fat can generally withstand more heat than margarine, butter or vegetable oil. Fats tend to lose their molecular structure ('break down') if heated for too long and this causes them to smoke (and smell) unpleasantly at a lower temperature than when fresh. Eventually they will give an unpleasant flavour to any food fried in them. However, even solid fresh fats (if they contain an emulsifier) will smoke and burn at cooler temperatures than pure fats without additives.

FRYING Techniques vary depending on the texture and size of the food and the effect the cook wishes to achieve. For instance, when frying steaks or chops remember to:

1 Fry in an uncovered wide pan. (A lid traps the steam and the food stews or steams rather than frying crisply.)

2 Preheat the fat. If the fat is cool when the food is put into it, the food will not brown and form the necessary skin to trap the interior juices. They will escape and the meat will become dry and tasteless. Even if the fat is subsequently heated to the right temperature, the juices will already have run from it, preventing it from browning well and frying properly. And the food might absorb some of the cool fat and become too greasy.

3 Fry a little at a time. Adding too much food at one time to hot fat lowers the temperature and, again, hinders the browning.

4 Fry fast until the meat is completely sealed on all sides. Then turn down to moderate heat to cook the inside through.

Fried food should be served as soon as possible after cooking. Juices gradually seep from even well browned meat and fish, making them dry up and toughen on standing; potatoes lose their crispness, becoming leathery and tough skinned; fritters deflate, and everything loses its newly-fried shine.

Fish is cooked à la meunière by dusting it with flour and shallow frying in butter until it is brown on both sides. (See Lemon sole with cucumber,

STIFFENING
Very tender cuts of meat, such as calves liver, should be fried in hot melted butter until stiff but tender and lightly browned. The liver will be cooked but still rare when semi-firm to the touch.

FRYING SAUSAGES
Loosen sausages stuck in the frying pan with the back of a fish slice — used the right way up it tends to break the sausage skins.

p.116.) The fish is then put on a warm platter. Chopped parsley, lemon juice, salt and pepper are added to the butter in the pan and, once sizzling, this is poured over the fish. Dusting like this with flour (à la meunière), is a common practice with fish or slices of veal, chicken, or liver. The slight coating of flour helps to prevent sticking and adds crispness to the skin.

STIFFENING Some recipes require gentle frying without a coating of flour. When this method is used the fat, though hot, is not fearsomely so and the food can be gently fried to a very pale brown, or cooked without browning. This is particularly useful with kidneys and liver which tend to burst and become grainy if fried too fast, with shellfish, which toughens if subjected to fierce heat and with thin slices of fish (say salmon to be served in a sorrel sauce), where the cook requires the taste of butter-frying, but does not want a browned surface.

ENGLISH BREAKFAST FRYING Eggs should be fried in clean fat. Frying them in a pan in which bacon or sausages have been cooking leads to sticking and possible breaking of the yolks. If eggs are to be fried in the same pan as other items, fry the bacon, ham, sausages, potatoes, mushrooms and bread first as these will all keep in a warm oven for a few minutes. Tip the fat into a cup. Rinse the pan, removing any stuck sediment, dry it, then pour the fat back into the pan. Using enough sizzling fat to spoon over the eggs speeds up the process and prevents the edges of the whites overcooking before the thicker parts are set.

Sausages generally have skins which, as the stuffing expands in the hot pan, can burst or split open. Avoid this by pricking them carefully all over with a thin needle (large holes like those made by the prongs of a fork provide weak points where the skin will split) and/or by cooking slowly. Shake the pan with rapid but careful side-to-side or forward-and-back movements; this will dislodge any pieces that are stuck with less damage than a prodding utensil. Fry the sausages slowly until evenly browned all over and firm to the touch.

Bacon rashers can be fried in an almost dry pan as they readily produce their own fat. However, they cook faster and more evenly in shallow fat.

GLAZING VEGETABLES Vegetables are sometimes given a final shiny, slightly sweet glaze by frying them in a mixture of butter and sugar. The sugar melts and caramelizes to a pale toffee and the vegetables brown in the butter and caramel mixture. Constant shaking of the pan is necessary to prevent burning and sticking. This method is particularly successful with shallots, baby onions, mushrooms and root vegetables.

SAUTEING is used on its own to cook foods such as chicken pieces, mushrooms or apple rings, but is most frequently used in conjunction with other forms of cooking. For example, whole small onions may be sautéed to brown them before they are added to liquid in a stew or a sauce. Sautéing is also employed after boiling to give cooked or partially cooked foods, such as potatoes, a lightly browned and buttered exterior.

Browning gives a sautéed dish its essential character. After browning, some meats, such as liver or veal slices, are often removed and then served with a relatively small amount of well flavoured sauce, which has been made in the same pan. Meats such as pork chops or chicken pieces may be given an initial browning and then be cooked with added ingredients which will eventually form the sauce. The range of such sauces is almost endless — as various as the liquids and other flavourings that can be used in making them. Good examples in this book are Pork fillets with red and green peppers on p.74, and Veal escalopes with cream and marsala on p.234. Stages in sautéing are as follows:

1 Fry the main ingredient together with any others, browning them in minimal fat. Remove them from the pan and keep them hot.

2 Deglaze (see p.255) the pan with a liquid such as stock, cream or wine.

3 Add the flavourings for the sauce.

4 If the initial browning has cooked the main ingredients sufficiently, reduce the sauce by rapid boiling and pour it over the dish. Garnish and serve immediately.

5 If the main ingredients need further cooking, simmer them in the sauce until they are tender, then proceed as above.

EGG-AND-BREADCRUMBING is a technique used both to protect moist food from the sizzling heat of deep fat (see p.253) and because it produces the most delicious crisp crusty coating — the perfect contrast to the succulent interior. The following recipe is a classic, but the technique can be used for veal escalopes, chicken breasts, brains, sweetbreads, seafood or fish — anything that is commonly grilled or fried.

BREADED LAMB CUTLETS

INGREDIENTS (Serves 4)
8 well trimmed lamb cutlets
Flour
Salt and pepper
Beaten egg
Dry white breadcrumbs
Oil and butter for frying

TO SERVE
Cumberland sauce (see p.180)

TO GARNISH
Bunch of watercress

1 Trim off any excess fat from the cutlets. Season about 55g/2oz flour with ½tsp each salt and pepper.

2 Dust the cutlets lightly with the seasoned flour. Season the beaten egg with salt and pepper. Dip the floured cutlets in the egg, then in the dry breadcrumbs, coating both sides well. Keep them well separated or they may 'weep' where they touch.

3 Heat 3tbsp oil in a large frying pan and when hot add 4 large tbsp butter — enough fat to come at least half way up the cutlets. Fry for about 3 minutes a side. Drain well on absorbent paper. Dish on a warm serving plate, garnish with watercress and hand the sauce separately.

NOTE The cutlets may also be deep fried for 3 to 4 minutes.

1

2

BREADED LAMB CUTLETS
1 Remove all traces of meat and membrane from the rack so that only the 'eye' of the meat is left on the bone. Slice into neat cutlets.

2 Dip first in seasoned flour and shake off excess. Then dip in seasoned beaten egg. Finally, dip into dry crumbs. Press lightly to adhere. Make sure to coat both sides well. Sieve crumbs to remove lumps if necessary.

DEEP FRYING Deep frying is one of the fastest possible methods of cooking small tender cuts of meat and fish. It is also suitable for many vegetables, and for dough mixtures such as fritters and doughnuts.

Because of the very high temperatures the fat reaches, most foods are given a protective coating before frying. This seals in their juices and prevents overcooking as well as too much spluttering of the hot fat, which would be caused by moisture rapidly vaporizing on the surface of uncoated wet food.

Some foods, such as potato crisps, are in and out of the hot fat so quickly that they do not need any coating. Other uncoated foods, such as chips, are given a first frying at a low temperature to cook them through, then a second frying at a higher temperature to brown them.

Most other foods need a coating, either of flour or crumbs or a flour-and-liquid batter. While the coating fries to a crisp brown, the food inside stays moist and tender. One of the pleasures of deep fried food is the contrast between interior and exterior. For the driest and crispest coating, drain off all excess fat on absorbent paper after cooking and serve as soon as possible.

If the coating covers the food completely, as it should, the flavour of the fried food will not contaminate the fat, which may then be used again. Filter the fat clean of any food particles after frying. As soon as it shows signs of breaking down, by becoming dark, odorous or cloudy, it should be replaced. Such fat smokes and burns at a lower temperature than fresh fat, smells stale and gives an unpleasant flavour to anything cooked in it. For an egg-and-crumb crust see Breaded lamb cutlets, p.252.

BATTER Batter is a farinaceous mixture of a thick liquid consistency. It is used to give a crisp protective coating to food that might otherwise burn or splatter when deep or shallow fried. The classic method of mixing a batter by hand is on p.319.

USING A DEEP FRYER

1 If the deep fryer is not thermostatically controlled, use a thermometer or test the temperature of the fat by dropping a cube of bread into it. If the bread browns in 60 seconds, the fat is about 182°C/360°F and suitable for gentle frying; if it browns in 40 seconds, the oil is moderately hot, about 190°C/375°F; if it browns in 20 seconds, the fat is very hot, about 195°C/385°F. If the bread cube browns in 10 seconds, the fat is dangerously hot and should be cooled down. Turn off the heat and fry several slices of bread in it to speed up the cooling.

2 Cook food in small amounts. Adding too many pieces at one time lowers the temperature of the fat so that the coating will not form a crisp crust. The food then absorbs fat and loses its juices into the cooking fat. This is particularly important if you are frying frozen food (such as fish fingers, commercially prepared chips or Chinese spring rolls) while still frozen — which will of course greatly cool the fat. However, do not attempt to remedy this problem by frying in very hot fat. Comparatively cool fat is needed (about 180°C/350°F) to allow the inside to thaw and cook before the coating browns.

3 Drain the cooked food well on absorbent paper.

4 If the food is not served right away, spread it out in a single layer on a hot baking sheet or tray and keep it uncovered in a warm oven with the door ajar to allow the free circulation of air. Covering or enclosing the food will make the crust soggy. Try not to fry far ahead of serving.

5 Add salt (or a sprinkling of caster sugar if the food is sweet) after frying. This accentuates the flavour and the dry, crisp texture.

6 After use, cool the fat and strain it through muslin or a coffee filter paper. This removes food particles which, if left in the fat, will become black and burned with repeated fryings. As soon as the fat becomes at all dark, it should be changed, as it is beginning to break down, will smoke readily and give a rancid flavour to fried food.

BRAISING

MIREPOIX FOR BRAISING
Fry the diced vegetables in a tablespoon of fat until evenly coated and pale brown. If braising in a metal casserole, the preliminary cooking can be done in the pot. If not, do it in a frying pan.

Braising, in the true sense of the word, is a method of slowly cooking meat on a mirepoix (a thick bed of finely diced mixed vegetables with the addition of strong stock). In practice, the term braising is often confused with pot-roasting, as in both methods food is cooked slowly in a pan with a tightly-fitting lid to give deliciously tender results. The main difference is that pot-roasted food is cooked with little if any liquid other than the fat used for browning the ingredients, and braising involves some liquid and at least some cut-up vegetables to add moisture to the pan, even if a true mirepoix is not used. A pot-roast should taste 'roasted' and be decidedly fattier than a braise, which is closer to a stew and depends more on juices and stocks than on fat for flavour.

Braising is also often confused with sweating as some 'braised' food is cooked only by sweating. This is a method of gently cooking vegetables, frequently onions and shallots, in butter or oil in a covered pan, which is shaken frequently to prevent burning and sticking. Once cooked through, softened and exuding their juices but not coloured, the vegetables are usually added to stews, sauces or soups, to which they give a subtle flavouring but no colouring. For example, to 'braise' red cabbage, a finely chopped onion is sweated in butter until tender, then shredded cabbage, a little vinegar, sugar, apple and seasonings are added. These are left over a low heat, covered tightly, to sweat for 2 to 3 hours. The red cabbage is then 'braised', even though neither meat nor mirepoix have been included.

Occasionally the term braising is used to mean baking in a covered pan with only a little liquid. 'Braised' celery heart, for example, consists of quarters of celery head cooked in a little stock in a covered pan in the oven. 'Braised' fennel is cooked with lemon juice, butter and stock.

Beef fillet and sirloin or lamb best-end should be roasted or grilled, but otherwise whole joints or smaller pieces of meat can with advantage be braised. The meat should be fairly lean and any fat that melts into the stock should be skimmed off before serving. Poultry may be braised unless it is old and tough, when stewing or poaching are more suitable cooking methods allowing all the flesh, which will tend to be stringy and dry, to be submerged in liquid.

The vegetables for the mirepoix should be browned quickly in hot fat, and stirred constantly to ensure even colouring, then transferred to a heavy-based casserole or pan. The meat can be browned in the same fat before it is placed on top of the vegetables and stock is added. As the vegetables cook they will disintegrate, helping to thicken the stock.

Making a strong, reduced, well flavoured stock is time-consuming, but it is one of the key factors in good braising. The best stock is one made from chopped up beef shin bones which have been browned all over and then simmered and skimmed frequently for hours. See p.267.

As with pot-roasting, meat may be marinaded overnight in the refrigerator and large pieces of exceptionally lean meat may also be larded to ensure that they remain moist. Dry the meat well before browning it.

The exacting and by no means easy steps for braising red meat so it has the ideal tenderness and almost sticky juiciness are as follows:

1 Fry the mirepoix of vegetables (and a few tbsp diced salt pork or bacon) slowly in oil and butter, shaking the pan and stirring until they are evenly browned all over.

2 Brown the meat on all sides and place it on top of the vegetable bed in a heavy casserole.

3 Add stock, made from gelatinous meats such as knuckle of veal or beef shin bones, to cover the meat. If the stock is not rich and solidly set when cold the braise will not have the correct 'melting' stickiness. Then stew, without basting, until half cooked.

4 Lift out the meat, strain the stock, and discard the mirepoix (which has by now imparted all of its flavour).

5 Return the meat to the casserole and reduce the stock by rapid boiling until it is thick and syrupy, then pour it over the meat.

6 There will no longer be enough stock to cover the meat and there is a danger, even in a covered pan, of the exposed top drying out, so turn the meat every 15 minutes and baste it with the stock.

By the end of the cooking time, when the meat is tender, the stock should be so reduced as to provide a shiny coating that will not run off the meat. It will penetrate the flesh, moistening it and giving it the slightly glutinous texture of perfectly braised meat.

STEWING

The term 'stew' is so widely used it can mean almost anything. A 'stew' is essentially food that has been slowly and gently cooked in plenty of liquid. Most cooks envisage meat cut into smallish pieces before cooking, as in our Beef stew with suet crust (p.56), but the term is sometimes used for sliced, sautéed meat or poultry served in a sauce, or for a whole joint or bird poached in liquid. Many stews require preliminary frying of the meat (and sometimes of onions, shallots, carrots or mushrooms too) to give a richer flavour to the ingredients themselves and to add colour and flavour to the sauce, which will be made on top of the browned sediment and dried-on juices sticking to the pan after frying. These are called 'brown' stews. 'White' stews are made without preliminary browning and are less rich, less fatty, altogether gentler (and more easily digestible) than brown ones.

Both brown and white stews are served in their cooking liquid, usually thickened to a syrupy sauce.

The principles of shallow frying (see p.250) apply to the preliminary frying for a brown stew. If the sauce is not to taste insipid, and be pale in colour, you must start with a good even colour on both sides of each slice or all sides of each cube of meat. Good stews are made or lost in the early stages — so take care to fry only a few pieces at a time, to keep the temperature hot enough to sizzle and to prevent the escape of juices (which will happen if the fat is too cold) and to take the time to get an even colour — over-brown on one side and anaemic on the other won't do. Deglaze the pan (see left) as often as necessary. Deglazing serves three essential purposes: it prevents the stuck sediment in the pan

DEGLAZING
After frying or sautéeing, deglaze the pan by pouring a few spoonfuls of stock or wine into the hot pan. Stir vigorously to loosen stuck sediment.

burning, it allows the capture of the flavour of that sediment and its incorporation into the sauce, and it cleans the pan ready for the next batch of meat.

The Beef stew with suet crust is a traditional stew, classically made. But the same principles can be used to make a Lamb navarin for example. Follow the same procedure, using lean cubes of lamb instead of the beef and omitting the suet crust. Young spring vegetables such as broad beans, French beans, tiny whole carrots, peas or sprigs of cauliflower, can be added to the stew for the last 10 minutes of stewing time to give a Navarin d'agneau Printanier. See p.165.

BOILING AND POACHING

BOILING is a blanket term for cooking food submerged in liquid by one of several techniques: from fast, agitated bubbling — a rolling boil — to a gentle simmer, when bubbles will appear in one part of the pan only, or to the barest tremble of the liquid, which is poaching. The techniques suit different foods and achieve different effects.

Cooking green vegetables quickly in rapidly boiling water in an open pan tenderizes them, yet makes sure they retain their crispness and bright colours. The water should be well salted (1 level tbsp for every 1.75litres/3pt) as it then boils at a higher temperature, cooking the vegetable even more quickly.

Rapid boiling in an open pan protects the vivid colours of some vegetables, such as artichokes, while enhancing the colours of others, such as peas and spinach. When covered, discolouration can be caused by enzymes from the vegetables, which collect in the condensation on the lid and fall back into the water. The best method is to bring the water to the boil without the vegetables, add the vegetables and cover with a lid to bring them back to the boil as fast as possible, then remove the lid to allow the escape of steam.

Vegetables that would be damaged by vigorous boiling are cooked by the more gentle simmering methods. Vegetables unlikely to discolour, like potatoes, carrots, parsnips, beetroot and other root vegetables are traditionally cooked in a covered pan to preserve heat and contain fuel costs. Hence the adage — if it grows in the light, cook it in the open; if it grows in the dark, keep it covered.

REFRESHING Once cooked, 'refresh' the vegetables by rinsing them briefly under cold water, then put them in a warm serving dish. 'Refreshing' prevents further cooking by the heat retained in the vegetables, and thus sets the colour. Vegetables which hold their colour well, such as carrots, or small quantities of vegetables, such as French beans for four people, do not need refreshing, but for large quantities it is vital, especially if there is to be any delay before serving. They can be reheated briefly before serving by any of the following methods: by being dipped in boiling water; by rapid steaming; by being given 30 to 60 seconds in a microwave oven; by being tossed quickly in butter over high heat. Slow reheating in the oven will discolour most green vegetables, frozen peas being the exception — although even these will eventually lose their brilliant hue.

BLANCHING Some foods, especially vegetables and fruit, are immersed in boiling water without being fully cooked. This is called 'blanching' and has various uses:

• To remove strong flavours, eg from liver or kidney before frying
• To facilitate the removal of skin, eg from tomatoes or peaches
• To lessen the salt content, eg from ham before cooking
• To destroy enzymes in vegetables destined for the freezer (which would otherwise discolour them)
• To shorten the roasting time of vegetables such as potatoes, onions and parsnips by parboiling first
• Simply to semi-cook or soften food, eg fennel in salad.

FAST BOILING Rice and pasta cook well at a good rolling boil. The boiling water expands the starch granules and makes them tender, while the rapid agitation keeps the pieces of pasta, or rice grains, from sticking together or to the pan. Adding a tablespoon of oil to the water also helps to prevent sticking. Long-grain rice boiled in a large pan of heavily salted water takes 10 or 11 minutes to cook. The grains should then mash to a paste when pressed between the thumb and index finger, though a little 'bite' is preferable to all-over soft texture.

Similarly, pasta should always be cooked al dente, ie firm to the bite. Do remember that fresh or homemade pasta (which already contains moisture) cooks four times faster than the dried commercial equivalents. The cooking time also depends on the thickness. Dried vermicelli cooks in two or three minutes, while dried lasagne takes 15 to 16.

Sometimes rapid boiling is used to drive off moisture and reduce liquids to a thicker consistency. With sugar mixtures, the essential high temperatures are most rapidly achieved by a galloping boil.

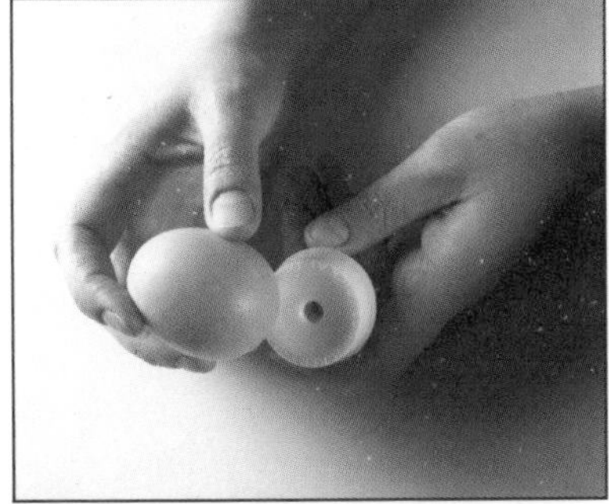

PRICKING EGGS
Prick the rounded end of the raw egg with an egg pricker to allow the air under the shell to escape. This will prevent cracking when boiling.

EGGS are often boiled, yet there is considerable confusion about the correct method of doing this. The easiest and most foolproof is as follows:

1 Holding the egg so that the rounded end is pricked, press onto egg-pricker or pierce carefully with a needle to allow air to escape.

2 Bring a pan of water to the boil. Have the eggs at room temperature. (If chilled add 30 seconds to cooking time.)

3 Carefully lower the eggs into the water using a perforated spoon.

4 Time the cooking from that moment, keeping the water simmering or gently boiling, not boiling too vigorously, which tends to crack the shells and toughen the whites.

THREE MINUTES will cook a medium sized egg until the white is barely set — indeed, the white closest to the yolk will still be slightly jelly-like. *FOUR MINUTES* gives a runny yolk and a just-set white. *SIX MINUTES* gives a well set white and moist but runny yolk (set on the rim and thick but wet inside).*EIGHT MINUTES* gives a nicely hard-boiled egg. *TEN MINUTES* will give a yolk sufficiently cooked to be dry and crumbly when mashed. *FIFTEEN MINUTES* will give a yellow-green rim to the dry yolk and make the white tough and unpalatable.

BOILING EGGS
Fresh eggs take longer to cook than stale eggs. Add 30 seconds if the eggs are new and 30 seconds if they are straight from the refrigerator. These eggs were 10 days old and at room temperature.

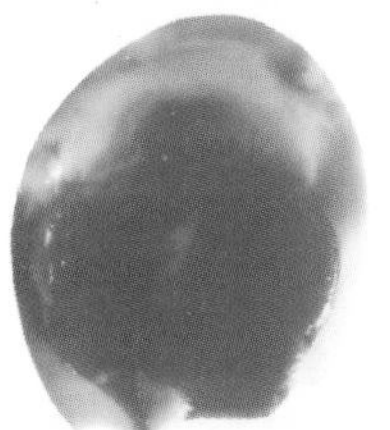

3 MINUTES

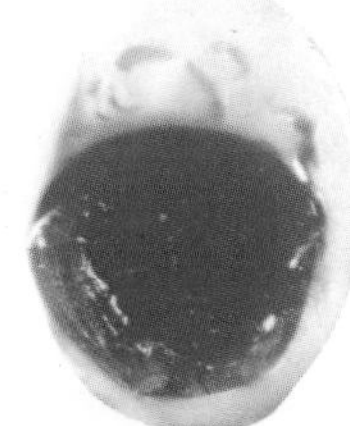

4 MINUTES

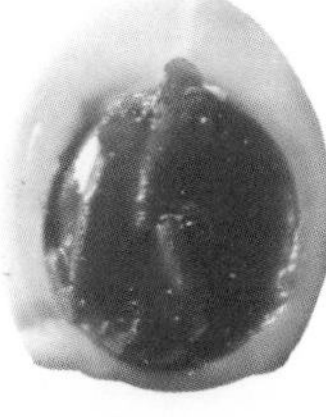

6 MINUTES

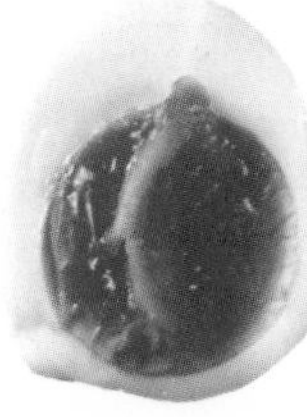

8 MINUTES

10 MINUTES

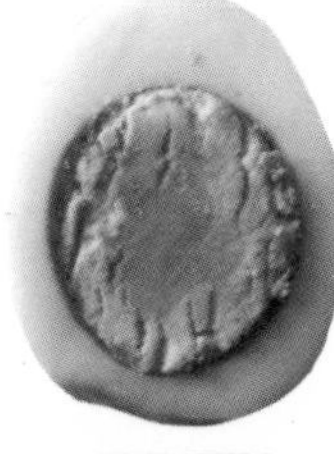

15 MINUTES

SIMMERING Dried pulses are also cooked by boiling. As there is no colour loss to worry about, and the process is a long one, they may be simmered rather than fast-boiled. (Rapidly boiling water evaporates very fast, risking boiling dry and burning.) They may even, with advantage, be slowly stewed — cooked in a covered pan in liquid that only partially covers them — either on top of the stove or in the oven. If the proportion of liquid to pulses is right, they absorb all the liquid during cooking and there is nothing to throw away and thus little loss of taste and nutrients. The amount of water needed obviously depends on the age (and therefore dryness) of the pulses and the speed of boiling, but twice the volume of water to pulses is a good guide.

It is often recommended that pulses be soaked in water before cooking, but this is not always necessary, especially if the pulses are last season's crop. Dried beans that are known to be two or three years old *can* be cooked without any prior soaking, but they will absorb more water, take longer to become tender, and will not taste as good as fresher pulses. As a general rule soaking is a good idea, especially for the larger beans.

Pressure cooking works well for pulses and eliminates the need for soaking. Pressure cookers vary and it is obviously sensible to consult the manufacturer's instructions. As a general rule, 450g/1lb of dried peas or beans, unsoaked, will need 1litre/1¾pt water and will cook in 30 minutes at 7kg/15lb pressure.

WARNING

Red kidney beans can be toxic if eaten raw or cooked at very low temperatures such as in a 'slow-cooker' or bottom oven of an Aga. If cooking by these methods, give them 10 minutes boiling first.

Like pulses, some vegetables can be slowly stewed until all the liquid is either absorbed or has evaporated. For example, even sized pieces of carrot can be put in very lightly salted water with a lump of butter. The carrots are cooked slowly so that when all the water has evaporated they are just tender, and coated in the butter. They are called Vichy carrots.

VICHY CARROTS

1 'Turn' the carrots (see p.150). Or slice them or cut lengthwise into even sticks.

2 Put everything except the pepper and herbs into a saucepan and boil rapidly until the water has almost evaporated. Then turn down the heat and allow the carrots to brown slightly in the remaining butter and sugar, shaking the pan to ensure even glazing.

3 Season with pepper and mix in the herbs.

NOTE It is important not to oversalt the water. When the water has evaporated the entire quantity of salt will remain with the carrots.

POACHING is also long, slow, gentle cooking, but the food is generally completely submerged in liquid that is barely trembling, either on top of the stove or in the oven. It is an excellent method for delicate items, such as fish or soft fruit, which would break up if subjected to vigorous agitation. See p.60 for poached salmon, p.206 for poached trout and p.113 for poached pears.

POACHED EGGS Use very fresh eggs straight from the refrigerator: fill a wide pan with water and add 1tbsp vinegar. Bring to simmering point. Break an egg into a cup. Slip the egg into the water and immediately increase the temperature of the water so that the bubbles help to draw the white around the yolk. Lower the temperature and poach for 2 to 3 minutes. Lift out with a perforated spoon and trim any ragged edges.

TO POACH EGGS

1 Break a very fresh egg into a cup. Simmer water in a wide, shallow saucepan or deep frying-pan. Slip egg in.

2 Immediately turn the heat up so the bubbling water draws the white round the yolk and prevents it sticking to the bottom. Once it turns opaque, reduce the heat.

3 Poach gently for 2-3 minutes. When cooked, lift the egg out of the water with a perforated spoon. Trim off ragged edges with scissors.

NOTE Poached eggs for last-minute dishes can be kept under cold water and reheated in simmering water for 30 seconds. Soft poached eggs destined for cold dishes would be poached for 3½ minutes (long enough to allow the yolk to thicken slightly), then cooled in a bowl of cold water to prevent further cooking.

Tough meat becomes more tender and succulent the more slowly it is cooked. A cut such as oxtail takes at least three hours of simmering on top of the stove until it is acceptably tender. Poached in the oven at 150°C/300°F/Gas 2 for five hours, it would be even more tender, falling from the bone and gelatinous.

A ham or large piece of bacon is cooked when the meat has shrunk back from the bone or, if boneless, when the whole thing has visibly shrunk in size by about one fifth. The rind or skin will then peel off easily and a skewer will penetrate the meat unimpeded. But until experienced and confident, it is wise to stick to the cooking times given in recipes.

STEAMING

Steaming is the cooking of food in hot vapour over boiling liquid (usually water) rather than *in* liquid. It occurs to some extent in braising and pot-roasting's closed pans with the relatively small amounts of liquid used. In true steaming, however, the food never touches the liquid, so the loss of many vitamins is significantly reduced. Furthermore, steamed food is not browned first, so it can be cooked without fat. This makes the food more easily digestible and particularly suitable for invalids and those on low-fat diets. The method has regained great favour with the new-wave Nouvelle Cuisine chefs because of its simplicity and purity. But excellent ingredients are essential for steaming — there is no help to be had from browning, so the food must taste good without such assistance.

A variety of equipment for steaming food is available. Most common are oval or round steamers, which are like double saucepans, except that the top has holes in its base. Steam from boiling water in the lower pan rises through the holes to cook the food, while the lid on the upper pan keeps in the steam.

Another popular steaming device is a stainless steel or aluminium basket that opens and folds shut and is used with an ordinary lidded saucepan. The basket stands on its own short legs to keep it clear of the boiling water. It fits inside most saucepans and is particularly suitable for foods that do not need much cooking time as the water underneath the short legs would otherwise have to be replaced too frequently. The saucepan must have a tightly fitting lid.

VEGETABLES are the food most commonly steamed, as they cook quickly and retain more of their colour and texture this way. Careful timing is essential as steamed food can be tasteless if even slightly overcooked. Today steaming times for vegetables are short, giving bright coloured, al dente, palpably fresh results. Some vegetables can be steamed in their own juices. Spinach, for example, may be trimmed and put wet from washing into a covered saucepan over medium heat, and shaken occasionally until limp and cooked cut still very green — about five minutes.

Potatoes that tend to break up when boiled before they are done are best steamed; choose potatoes that are about the same size as they cook at the same time. If they are very large or of different sizes, cut them into bite-sized pieces before steaming. For most other root vegetables such as turnips, parsnips and swedes, cut them into 1cm/½ inch dice and steam them until tender before seasoning and adding butter to serve.

FISH AND POULTRY Steaming fish is simple and quick and always produces a delicate result if the fish is not allowed to overcook. Put the food on a piece of muslin or cheesecloth to prevent it sticking to the steamer bottom. Oval steamers and folding baskets are suitable for small quantities of fish, but for larger fish or cooking many small fish, shellfish, fish steaks or fillets, a fish kettle (usually used for poaching fish) may be used. Made of metal, these come in sizes to take whole fish on a perforated rack inside the kettle. Ramekins can be placed under the rack to keep it well above the boiling liquid underneath. With fish kettles, whole fish can be stuffed and cooked over liquid in the covered kettle on top of the stove. Allow about 8 minutes per 450g/1lb weight of fish.

Delicate poultry such as chicken breasts or whole small quail may be steamed similarly.

Plate steaming is an excellent method of cooking small quantities of fish in their own juices. Put the fish, fillets or steaks on a lightly buttered plate, season well and cover with another upturned buttered plate or buttered aluminium foil. Set the covered plate on top of a pan of gently boiling water or on a trivet inside a large frying pan of bubbling water and cook for 8-10 minutes depending on the thickness of the fish.

STEAMED PUDDINGS Traditional English sweet and savoury puddings (particularly suet crust puddings) are also cooked by steaming, but here the food is cooked in a container heated by steam. This gives the suet mixture its distinctive soft, open texture. The easiest way to cook the pudding is to put its container in a saucepan with hot water that comes half way up the sides of the container. The pan is covered and cooked over low heat to steam gently for a long time, and water is added to the pan as necessary. Take care to put a band of folded foil under the basin with ends projecting up the sides to act as handles.

CHINESE COOKING traditionally involves a good deal of steaming. Fish, shellfish and tender cuts of meat, often wrapped in pastry or vegetable leaves, are quickly steamed. Food in one or more stacked rattan or modern metal baskets with a lid is placed over steaming liquid in a pan or wok for quick steaming. The Pigeon balls on p.124 could be cooked using this method.

HANDLE FOR STEAMING
To lift a steamed pudding from the steamer or saucepan easily, put a wide strip of cloth or folded foil under it like a sling. Use the two ends as handles.

MEAT

Modern nutritionists are rather against meat, especially in large quantities and when well-larded with fat. But there's no doubt that a diet with neither 'fish nor fowl nor good red meat' would deny the cook some of the great traditional skills of the kitchen, and the diner some of the great pleasures of the table. Meat in moderation is in fact good for you, providing protein and vitamins. There is no reason why meat should always play the dominant role in a dish; a few teaspoons of chopped ham, a few slices of duckbreast or a single lamb's kidney cut paper-thin can transform an otherwise meatless main-course dish into something interesting and delicious without over-burdening it with animal fat.

But, of course the roasts and sautés of the classic kitchen should stay in the cook's repertoire — at least for high days and holidays.

TEXTURE AND FLAVOUR

The tenderness of meat, rather than its flavour, is the foremost consideration among customers today. The tenderest — and most expensive — cuts come from the less active parts of the animal's body. The tender loin and rump cuts, for instance, cost more than the neck and leg cuts. Younger (and therefore less muscular) animals have more tender flesh generally, while older muscular animals have richly flavoured, tougher meat. This is because muscular tissues contain substances that, when cooked, become particularly succulent and tasty. To get the best of both, meat producers try to limit the exercise the animals take while allowing them to grow toward, if not into, maturity.

The diet as well as the maturity of any animal affects the flavour of its meat. A wild animal's diet will make its flesh taste stronger than that of its domesticated cousin feeding on specially formulated pellets. A third factor affecting its flavour is the length of time meat is hung before butchering, because the longer the meat is hung, the stronger and more gamey its taste will be.

In the case of game birds, meat is hung both to tenderize it and to increase its flavour. Domestic animals need less hanging than in the past, because they are bred, reared and fed for maximum tenderness.

Meat hung at 2°C/35°F will become increasingly tender with hanging. If the meat is hung at higher temperatures, it tenderizes faster, but the higher temperatures encourage bacterial growth and might cause the meat to go bad before it becomes tender. Young game birds do not need to hang any longer than for them to relax out of rigor mortis, though they are sometimes well hung, perhaps for a week, to develop that gamey flavour. Older game birds should be hung for at least five days.

The taste and tenderness of all meat depends somewhat on the method used to cook it. And to some extent this is determined by how tough or tender the meat is to begin with. Tough meat from, say, the neck or leg of an ox is tenderized by long slow cooking, while the *less* a prime cut such as sirloin steak is cooked, the more tender it is. This is because the tougher (and more muscular) a cut of meat is, the more connective tissue it contains and it is this that becomes meltingly soft during slow stewing, braising or other moist cooking. So that, ironically, it is the toughest cuts of meat (such as oxtail) which can be cooked to the most tender of all. Such cuts are tough precisely because of the amount of muscle and connective tissue they contain. This tissue is transformed in long moist cooking into gelatine, giving the meat a soft, almost sticky succulence.

Tender cuts such as sirloin steak have relatively few connective tissues.

As they cook they become tougher, because the meat fibres shrink and lose moisture. When overcooked, the juices finally dry up and a once-tender piece of meat becomes well done, tough and dry. The 'tenderness' of such cuts is simply the softness of raw meat — quite unlike the tenderness derived from the protracted cooking of connective tissue.

STORING MEAT

Once meat is bought, especially if it has been minced or sliced, it should be cooked within 24 hours or it will lose flavourful juices and become slimy, thus creating conditions where bacteria will easily grow. If mincing or grinding meat at home, make sure utensils are spotlessly clean, and refrigerate the mince as soon as possible. When storing cuts of meat, do not put them directly on top of each other, but lay them side by side and cover them loosely with foil so some air can circulate. Take care not to trap stale air in tightly stretched polythene to create a 'greenhouse' effect. If cuts of meat must be kept for several days, either freeze them, or rub the surface with dry mustard to retard deterioration, or cover them with a film of fat (oil or butter) to exclude air and micro-organisms. If the meat begins to smell high, wash it in cold running water, then smell it again. If the smell has not gone, cut away a thin layer of the outer flesh. The inside will almost certainly still be fresh. If not, discard the meat. (See p.331.)

PREPARING AND COOKING MEAT

STRETCHING BACON
Cut off rind then use the flat of a knife to 'stretch' the rasher.

CUTTING MEAT Before cooking meat, pull or cut off any thin membrane that may surround or be attached to it, because the membrane shrinks and becomes tough on cooking. When cutting meat for cooking, use a sharp knife so that the cells will be cleanly cut, not mashed — the meat will bleed less. Cut across the grain (the direction of the meat fibres) so that the meat will look better, keep its shape better and feel more tender. Cutting with the grain produces long stringy fibres which tend to curl during cooking, are difficult to chew and get stuck in the teeth. Trim steaks and chops neatly so there is not too much fat. When preparing meat for stewing, trim off all sinews, any membrane and fat and cut it into 2.5cm/1 inch cubes — no smaller, or the meat will break up.

POUNDING MEAT Prime cuts of lean meat are suitable for beating out thinly for quick cooking, as with veal or pork escalopes or minute steak Diane. To prevent the thin meat from tearing, put it between two sheets of plastic wrap moistened with water before pounding. Tough steaks can also be tenderized by beating them all over with a blunt instrument just before cooking. This bruises the cells and breaks the fibres.

SCORING FOR CRACKLING
Use a very sharp knife to score through pork rind and fat. Score evenly and thoroughly for crisp crackling.

ROASTING Roast meat joints with the fatty part uppermost. If the cut is lean, or if roasting poultry other than duck or goose (which are fatty), cover ('bard') with pork back fat or fatty bacon and secure with string.

For crispy pork crackling that is easy to carve, either make sure that the butcher has scored the skin all round so that the cuts go through the fat (but not into the flesh) or do this yourself. Rub a little salt and oil into the crackling and do not baste during cooking. A high temperature will produce bubbly crisp and crumbly crackling. For perfect results every time, lift off the crackling half way through and finish it separately.

Tie meat or truss poultry with strong, non-synthetic string. Use metal skewers for grilling or roasting. Wooden skewers can be used in the oven.

FISH AND SHELLFISH

Fish and shellfish, being low in animal fats and comparatively easy to digest, have become very popular with the new breed of health-conscious cooks. In addition, the tenderness and adaptability of fish makes it the perfect ingredient for nouvelle-cuisine cooks, who value its short cooking times, fresh delicate flavours, and the way it blends easily to make tender mousses and terrines.

A good fishmonger is increasingly rare — many so-called wet fish shops sell fish which was bought frozen and thawed to be sold as fresh. If truly fresh fish cannot be had, it is better to buy it frozen and thaw it at home.

BUYING AND STORING FISH

Buy fresh whole fish that have been kept iced or chilled and that smell and look fresh. The fish should have tight scales, be shiny, slippery and difficult to grip. The eyes should be shiny-bright; sunken, dull or opaque eyes indicate that the fish has been stored too long. The gills should be reddish or pink — definitely not brownish or dry. The flesh should be tight and feel firm when pressed. If an impression of your finger remains after a few seconds, the fish is not in prime condition.

Fish should be eaten as fresh as possible, at least within 24 hours of purchase. Otherwise it should be cleaned, gutted and frozen. Fish fillets and steaks can be prepared up to 12 hours in advance, loosely covered in foil and refrigerated. Longer than this is not advisable as the flesh loses moisture and generally deteriorates. Fishmongers hold fish for longer periods under crushed ice in special refrigerated drawers kept just above freezing point. But this is hardly practicable at home.

PREPARING FISH

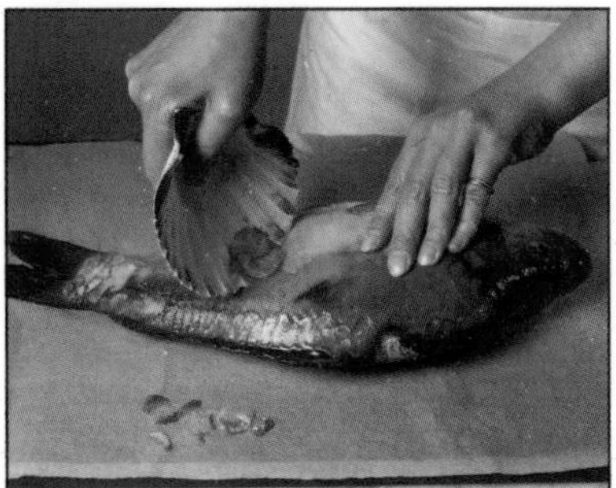

SCALING FISH
Use the back of a large knife or a scallop shell to scrape the scales from a whole fish.

For preparing fish, a knife that is not too large but is very sharp and flexible for filleting (see illustration p.339) and for cutting flesh and skin is essential. Other useful tools are a heavy, non-flexible knife, a scallop shell or pastry scraper to remove scales, a pair of tweezers or pliers to remove small bones and a clean cloth to get a good grip on the fresh slippery fish when doing fine boning, skinning and cutting jobs.

Prepare the fish on a large board, preferably positioned near running water as it, and all the tools, and the fish, will need frequent rinsing, especially if the fish has not been descaled by the fishmonger. Alternatively, put a piece of greaseproof paper over the board to protect it from fish smells, tucking the ends under the board. You will have to change the paper frequently, but the board will stay clean.

TO REMOVE FISH SCALES, use the heavy non-flexible knife or scallop shell or pastry scraper to scrape the fish from the tail to the head, against the line of the scales. Then trim or cut the fins off with scissors or a knife. (If cooking large round fish such as salmon, whole, leave the dorsal (back) fin in place. When it will pull out easily, the fish is cooked.)

TO SKIN DOVER SOLE, follow the illustrations on p.264. Finish by trimming off the fins with scissors. Other flat fish must be skinned after filleting (see p.116 for illustrations).

FILLET FLAT FISH by carefully cutting with a sharp flexible knife blade held (or slightly bent) firmly down against the rib bones and with the tip of the blade against the backbone, lifting the fillet up as you cut. Remove the second fillet. Turn over and repeat. Skin the fillets, if necessary.

SKINNING DOVER SOLE

1 Place the fish dark side up and cut through the skin at the tail.

2 Ease up the skin. Grip the tail with one hand and the skin with the other.

1

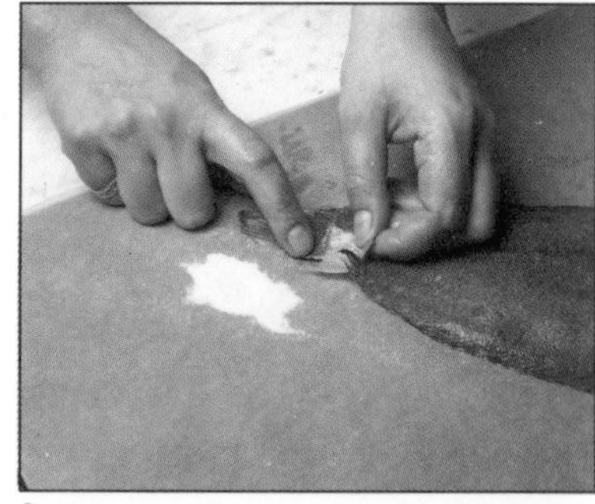

2

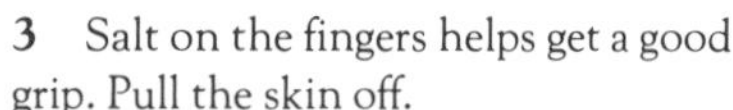

3 Salt on the fingers helps get a good grip. Pull the skin off.

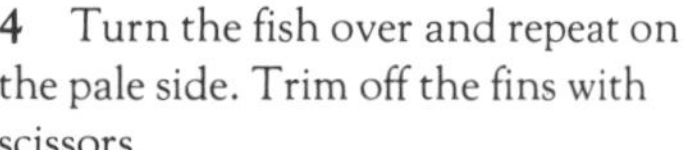

4 Turn the fish over and repeat on the pale side. Trim off the fins with scissors.

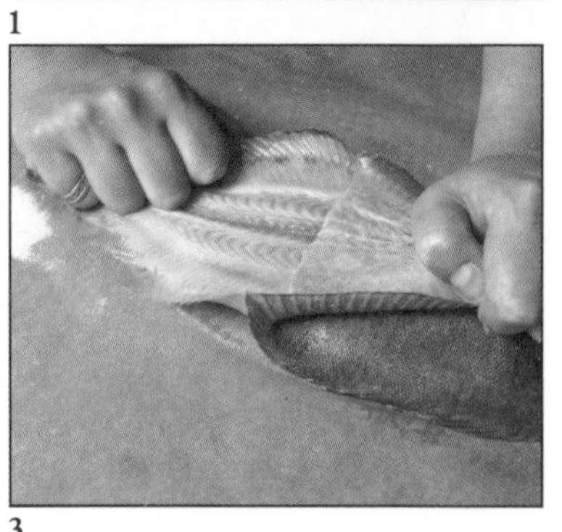

3

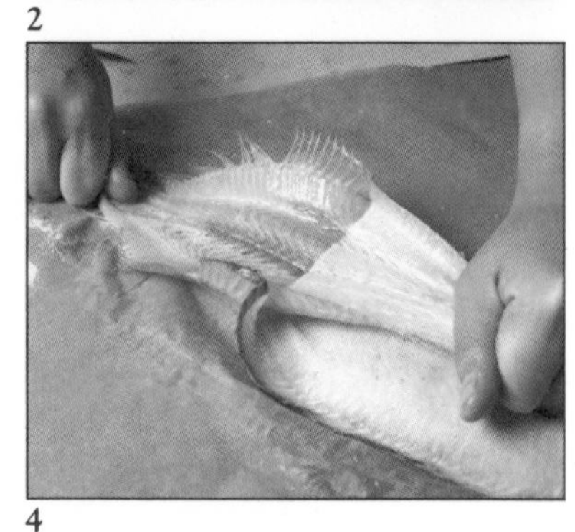

4

FILLET A ROUND FISH by cutting the head off below the gills. Cut down the length of the back, keeping the knife just above the central (back) bones and the flexible knife blade flat against them. With your fingertips, lift the top fillet and work it away from the ribs and backbone, using a stroking action repeatedly down the backbone with the blade of the knife. Then cut along the back again, this time just below the central bones, so you can then lift away the backbone and ribs. Run your fingertips along the filleted flesh to locate any remaining bones and remove them with tweezers or pliers.

If necessary, carefully remove the skin of the fillets by laying them flat, skin side down and, holding a knife with a large blade at right angles to the fish, slice between the skin and flesh, starting at the tail. Once started, keep the skin held down on the work surface and hold the knife blade angled so that it half cuts, half pushes the flesh away from the skin.

CLEANING FISH

1 Slit the belly from the head towards the vent. The belly of a round fish is near its tail; that of a flat fish is near its head.

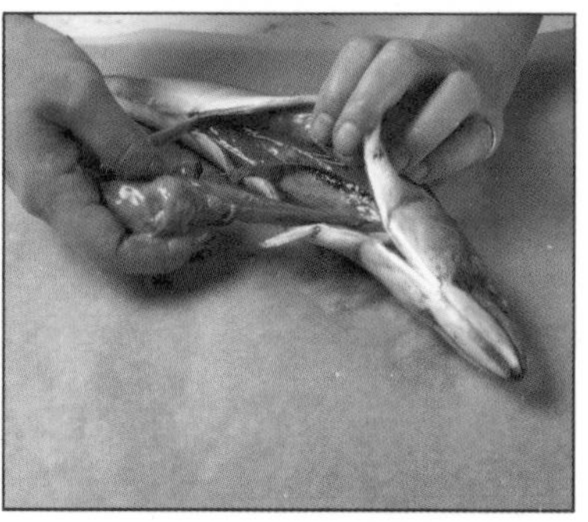

2 Open up and remove entrails. Rinse under cold running water.

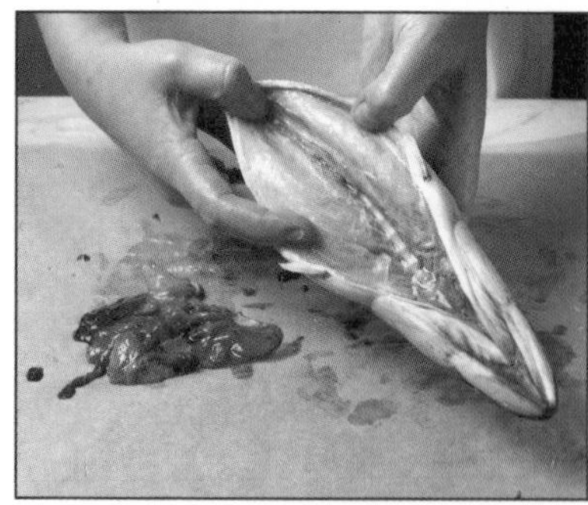

3 Use thumbnail or knife tip to scrape out the black blood channel down the backbone which would give the fish a bitter taste. Rinse again. Cut off head below the gills, or cut away the gills leaving the head intact.

PREPARING SHELLFISH

Shellfish, unless they are eaten very fresh, are dangerous as they deteriorate quickly. For this reason do not eat shellfish if at all 'high'.

OYSTERS should be chilled, while still live, in a bucket or tray of crushed ice, and opened just before serving. Keep them rounded side down so that the salty juices (much prized by oyster lovers) do not escape. To open an oyster, grip it firmly using a coarse cloth. Push an oyster knife into the hinge and twist to lever open the oyster.

CLEANING CLAMS AND MUSSELS Clams and mussels, if very fresh, are likely to have sand in their digestive tracts. To get rid of it, place them in cold water for several hours with some barley or fish food.

TO PREPARE CLAMS Discard any open ones which do not immediately close on tapping. Open as shown. For soups and stews,clams can be opened and killed in a hot oven or boiling water. They are only opened by hand for eating live, like oysters. Long (razor or steamer) clams are usually cooked briefly in a covered pan with a little liquid. The cooked clams are then served with a little of the liquid.

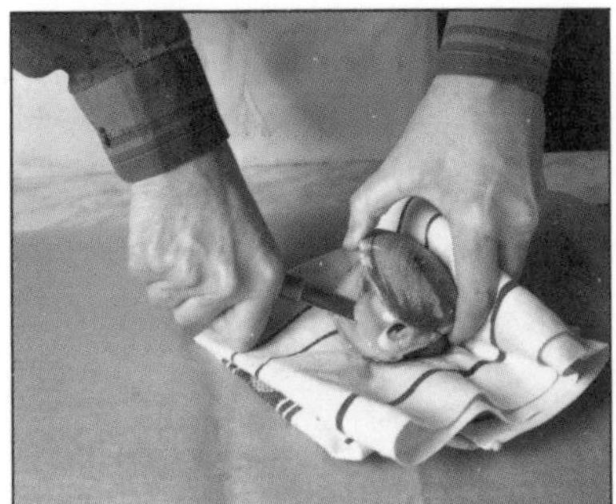

OPENING CLAMS
Large clams are difficult to open. Put them in a cool oven very briefly. When they begin to open, insert a clam knife between the shells and twist. Use cloth to protect your hands.

MUSSELS should be discarded if the shells do not close when tapped sharply on sink or table edge. The chances are they are dead and likely to be toxic. Scrub the shells with a hard brush or scrape with a knife or a metal pot scraper to remove loose shell encrustations. Tug sharply at any seaweed-like 'beard' to pull it away from the shell (see p.37), then rinse the shells before cooking them.

LOBSTERS, if live, should be killed immediately before cooking, or by the cooking process itself, when boiling them. If opting to kill the lobster before cooking it, grip its back firmly. To kill the creature painlessly pierce through firmly with a sharp heavy knife at the central cross clearly visible on the head. Halve the head, then split the lobster in half along the body which may continue to move although the lobster is dead. Then pull out the stomach (the transparent bag near the head) and the intestinal tract (the thin grey thread) running down the tail. Do not confuse a thick line of black roe with the thin grey intestine. The roe becomes red when cooked, excellent for flavouring and colouring sauces.

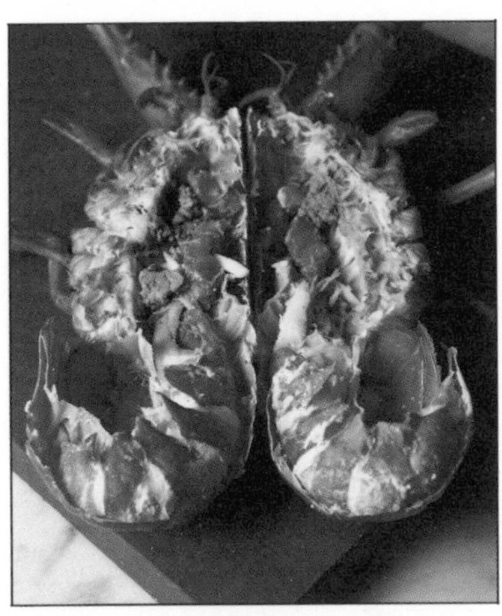

SERVING LOBSTER
Remove the tail meat from each shell. Turn it over and replace, round side up, on the opposite shell.

TO PREPARE A COOKED LOBSTER, lay it on its back and split the shell along the belly with a heavy knife. Cut the lobster in half through the head and body and pull the sides apart. Pull out the stomach sac and the intestinal tract. Remove the tail meat from each half of the body, then turn each piece over and put it in the opposite side of the body, with the pink side, which was next to the shell, uppermost and showing.

TO KILL AND PREPARE DUBLIN BAY PRAWNS (SCAMPI OR LANGOUSTINES) OR SMALL CRAYFISH (ECREVISSES) to be cooked and served whole, hold each one down with one hand and grip the middle tail fin with the other. Twist and quickly pull the tail fin to remove the digestive tract which will come out with the fin. The method kills and cleans the animal in one movement. More squeamish cooks should dunk the animals live in boiling water for a few seconds, then split them and remove the tract as for lobster (above).

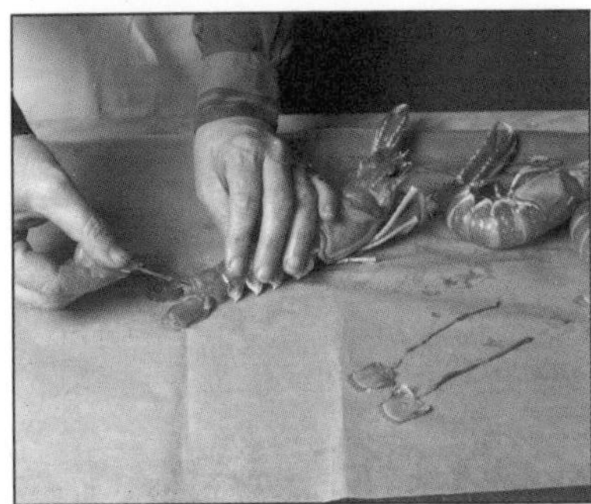

LANGOUSTINES
To extract the gut from live langoustines without splitting them, grasp the middle tail fin firmly, twist and pull.

TO SHELL COOKED PRAWNS OR SHRIMP, pinch off the legs and remove any roe from the underside of the body (see illustration on p.143). Remove the shell by peeling it back from the underside and discard it. Pull the meat away from the head and discard the head. Remove any visible intestinal tracts from large prawns. If the tracts are pale and barely noticeable do not bother.

TO COOK LARGE LIVE CRABS drop them into boiling water, and simmer for 6 minutes to the 450g/1lb. Small crabs take about 8 minutes. TO SHELL AND DRESS LARGE HARD SHELLED CRABS see illustration. Soft shelled crabs (crabs that have just shed one shell and not had time for the next to form) should be killed and cleaned by the fishmonger. They are then dipped in seasoned flour, fried briefly in butter and served with the pan juices (to which a little lemon juice and chopped parsley has been added) boiled up and poured over them.

DRESSING CRAB

1 Lay the crab on its back and twist off the claws. Then twist off the legs — do not pull them.

2 Prise the apron up by pulling at the pointed end near the mouth to remove the body from the shell.

3 Remove the dead men's fingers. These are soft and spongy and are found at the sides of the body and stomach sac which lies behind the head.

4 Strip out any cartilaginous membrane from the shell and discard it.

5 Remove the brown meat from the shell and put it aside. Do not mix it with the white meat from the body, legs and claws.

6 With the thumbs, break the shell along the visible lines to enlarge the opening. Use a hammer if it is tough. Wash out the shell and scrub it if necessary.

7 Remove the white meat from the body, claws and legs. Crack the claws and legs with a hammer or lobster cracker. Use a lobster pick or skewer to help you extract all the flesh.

8 Mix brown meat with a little mayonnaise (and brown breadcrumbs if you like). Spoon it down centre of shell. Put white meat at each end. Cover dark meat with lines of parsley, chopped egg white and yolk.

1 2 3 4 5 6 7 8

STOCKS AND SAUCES

STOCKS Behind every great soup and behind many a sauce, stands a good strong stock. Stock is flavoured liquid, and the basic flavour can be fish, poultry, meat or vegetable. There is not much wrong with stock cubes and bouillon mixes, except that they are over salty and they lack the intensely 'real' flavour of properly made stock. Also, they generally come in two universal flavours, chicken and beef, making much of the cook's food taste the same. As an emergency measure, or to strengthen a rather weak stock, they are most useful. But a good cook should be able to make a perfect stock.

BROWNING FOR STOCK
Vegetables and bones should be evenly well browned — but not burned — to make good brown stock.

MAKING A STOCK

The secret of stocks is slow gentle simmering. If the liquid is the slightest bit greasy, vigorous boiling will produce a murky fatty-tasting stock. Skimming, especially for meat stocks, is vital too — as fat and scum rise to the surface they should be lifted off with a perforated spoon, perhaps every 10 or 15 minutes.

Brown, rich-tasting stocks are made by first frying or baking the ingredients (bones, vegetables, scraps of meat) until a good, dark, even brown. Only then does the cook proceed with the gentle simmering. Care must be taken not to burn the bones or vegetables however — one burned carrot can ruin a gallon of stock. Brown stocks are usually made from red meats or veal, and sometimes exclusively from vegetables for vegetarian dishes.

White stocks are more delicate and are made by simmering only. They are usually based on white poultry or fish, or vegetables only. The longer meat stocks are simmered the better flavoured they will be. A stockpot will simmer all day in a restaurant, being skimmed or topped up with water as the chef passes it, and only strained before closing time. However, it is important not to just keep adding bits and pieces to the stock pot and keep the thing going on the back burner for days because the pot will become cluttered with cooked-out bones and vegetables that have long since given up any flavour. Eight hours over the gentlest flame, or in the bottom oven of an Aga is plenty.

The latter method is so gentle that skimming is unnecessary — as the liquid hardly moves there is no danger of fat being bubbled into the stock, and it sits docilely on the top from where it can be lifted when cold. But the ideal of eight hours is seldom possible and most stocks develop a good flavour in three hours.

Fish stocks should never be simmered for more than 30 minutes. After this the bones impart a bitter flavour to the liquid. For a stronger flavour the stock can be strained, skimmed of any scum or fat, and then boiled down to reduce and concentrate it.

Similarly, vegetable stocks do not need long cooking. As they will contain very little fat, even if the vegetables have been browned in butter before simmering, they're easily skimmed, and can then be boiled rapidly to extract maximum flavour. An hour's simmering or half an hour's rapid boiling is generally enough.

COOKED BONES OR RAW? Most households rarely have anything other than the cooked bones from a roast available for stocks. These will make good stock, but it will be weaker than that made with raw bones. Raw bones are very often free from the butcher, or can be had very cheaply. Get them chopped into manageable small pieces in the shop. A little raw meat, the bloodier the better, gives a rich, very clear liquid.

JELLIED STOCK Veal bones produce a particularly good stock that will set to a jelly. A pig's trotter added to any stock will have the same jellying effect. Jellied stock will keep longer than liquid stock, but in any event stocks should be re-boiled every two or three days if kept refrigerated, or every day if kept in a larder, to prevent them going bad.
SALT Do not add salt to stock. It may be used later for something that is already salty, or boiled down to a concentrated glaze, in which case the glaze would be over-salted if the stock contained salt. (Salt does not boil off with the water, but remains in the pan.)
STORAGE Stocks are time consuming to make so it is a sensible idea to make a good quantity, but large jugs are cumbersome to store. The answer might be to boil down the stocks to double strength, and to add water to them only when using. Or the process can be taken further and the stock boiled down to a thick syrupy glaze, which can be used to flavour dishes rather like modern stock cubes are — a few tablespoons to a pint or so of water. Many cooks freeze the glaze in ice cube trays, then turn the frozen cubes into a plastic box in the freezer. They will keep for at least a year if fat-free.

WHITE STOCK

INGREDIENTS (Makes 1 litre/2pt)
2 medium onions, peeled and sliced
1 medium carrot, sliced
2 sticks celery, sliced
1 leek, sliced
Handful of parsley stalks
1 bay leaf
½tsp peppercorns
2 chicken carcases, broken up, with any skin, but no fat
1 veal bone
1 sprig of fresh thyme OR ¼tsp dried thyme
About 2 litres/4pt water

1 Put all the solid ingredients into a large saucepan. Cover with the water and bring slowly to the boil. Skim off any scum or fat.

2 Simmer for 3 hours, skimming occasionally.

3 Strain, cool, and lift off any remaining fat.

BROWN STOCK

INGREDIENTS (makes 1 litre/2pt)
2 medium onions
2tbsp beef dripping
2 medium carrots, chopped
2 sticks celery, chopped
1 medium turnip, chopped
2kg/4½lb marrow bones (or beef, veal or bacon bones or duck carcases (but not pork, mutton or lamb))
225g/8oz raw meat, preferably beef and rather bloody (eg heart, ox cheek)
Handful of parsley stalks
1 bay leaf
½tsp peppercorns
1 sprig of fresh thyme OR ¼tsp dried thyme
About 2 litres/4pt water

This is a generally useful stock, which is why mutton or lamb bones — which have too distinctive a flavour — are not used. But the same stock can be made with lamb bones if to be used in a specifically lamb dish — such as Scotch broth or a lamb casserole. Similarly, pork bone stock is only suitable for pork pies or pork dishes.

1 Peel the onion, but keep the skin (it will help to give a good brown colour to the stock.) Chop the onion.

2 In a large, heavy based saucepan melt the dripping. Add the chopped vegetables and fry them very slowly until soft and evenly brown all over. They will need very frequent shaking and stirring, and careful watching. They must get to a good dark even colour.

3 Meanwhile, put the bones in a hot oven in a roasting pan. Turn them occasionally to ensure that they roast to an all-over brown.

4 Cut the meat up into large cubes and add them to the roasting pan,

spread out, so they will brown all over. (Alternatively, if the vegetables are brown, lift them out and use the saucepan to fry the meat over a fierce heat, turning them all the time.) Keep any beef blood. It will help to clarify the stock later.

5 When vegetables, bones and meat are all brown, put them in the saucepan and add the other ingredients, including the onion skin but not the beef blood.

6 Bring very slowly to the boil, and skim off any scum as it rises to the surface.

7 Simmer for at least 3 hours, preferably longer, skimming occasionally and keeping the water level topped up to cover the bones.

8 Strain the stock, skim off any remaining fat (or lift off with absorbent paper see p.229) then return to the pan with the beef blood.

9 Stir while bringing slowly to the boil. As the blood heats it will coagulate into scummy threads, and collect solid particles in the stock, helping to clear any murkiness.

10 Once boiling, lift off all the scum and fat and boil the stock hard to reduce it to about 1 litre/2pt. Cool.

FISH STOCK

INGREDIENTS (makes 1 litre/2pt)
1 onion, peeled and sliced
1 small carrot, sliced
1 stick celery, sliced
1 leek, sliced
1 slice lemon
Handful of parsley stalks
1 bay leaf
Sprig of fresh thyme OR ½tsp dried thyme
1½ litres/3pt water
6 white peppercorns
1-1½kg/2-3lb fish bones, skin, heads or tails, crustacean shells (prawn, lobster or crab shells, mussel shells, etc)

1 Put everything in a large saucepan and bring slowly to the boil.

2 Turn down to a gentle simmer, and skim off any scum.

3 Simmer for 20 minutes if the bones are small, 30 minutes if large, then strain immediately.

4 For stronger flavoured stock boil the strained stock down to reduce its water content and concentrate the flavour.

VEGETARIAN WHITE STOCK

INGREDIENTS (makes 1 litre/2pt)
1kg/2lb any suitable vegetables, or vegetable trimmings eg:
1 onion
2 carrots
1 leek
Few leaves cabbage
450g/1lb pea pods, broad bean pods
12 asparagus stalks (the inedible ends)
Leaves or stalks from 1 cauliflower
1½ litres/3pt water
Handful of parsley stalks
Sprig of fresh thyme OR ½tsp dried thyme
1 bay leaf

1 Chop, slice or shred everything up small.

2 Put in a saucepan with the water, and simmer gently for an hour. Strain.

VEGETARIAN BROWN STOCK

INGREDIENTS (makes 1 litre/2pt)
2 onions
2tbsp oil
1 aubergine, sliced
2 carrots, chopped
1 turnip, chopped
2 sticks celery, chopped
1 small parsnip, chopped
55g/2oz mushrooms OR stalks OR peelings
1 clove garlic
1tbsp tomato purée
Handful of parsley stalks
1 bay leaf
Sprig of thyme OR ¼tsp dried thyme
12 peppercorns
1½ litres/3pt water

1 Peel the onion, but keep the skin. Chop the flesh.

2 Heat the oil in a large, heavy based saucepan and fry the aubergine slices on both sides until evenly and well browned. Lift them out and set aside.

3 Put the onions, carrots, turnip, celery and parsnip in the pan (with a little more oil if necessary) and fry them slowly, shaking the pan and stirring frequently, until they are all evenly dark brown. Take care not to burn them.

4 Add the mushroom, garlic, tomato purée, herbs, peppercorns and onion skin and return the aubergine slices.

5 Cover with the water, and stir. Bring to the boil, and simmer for 1 hour, skimming occasionally.

6 Strain. For a richer-tasting, thicker and more soupy (but not clear) stock, press the vegetables in the sieve hard with a wooden spoon to extract the maximum juice from them.

MEAT AND FISH GLAZES

Professional chefs, who are able to make gallons of stock at a time, will reduce brown stock by steady boiling to obtain a concentrated essence or glaze. This is usually impractical in domestic kitchens unless the cook is able to start with at least 4 litres/7pt stock, which will reduce to about 300ml/½pt glace de viande. The glaze is then stored in small pots and covered tightly. It will keep for weeks in the refrigerator (or almost indefinitely frozen) and is used to strengthen weak soups or sauces.
FISH GLAZE (GLACE DE POISSON) is easier for the home cook as it thickens to syrupy consistency more readily. A litre/2pt fish stock will boil down to 4 or 5tbsp fish glaze and will make an excellent base for the fashionable butter-mounted sauces (see p.277).

COURT BOUILLON

INGREDIENTS (makes about 1 litre/2pt)
1 litre/2pt water
150ml/¼pt wine vinegar
1 carrot, sliced
1 onion, peeled and sliced
1 stick celery, sliced
12 peppercorns
2 bay leaves
½ lemon, sliced
1tbsp oil
1tsp salt

A court bouillon is not really a stock, being much weaker — it is a slightly acidic water in which fish is cooked.
THE CLASSIC METHOD Bring everything to the boil, simmer for 20 minutes then allow to cool. Fish is usually put into a cold court bouillon and brought to simmering point slowly, but the court bouillon may be used hot to poach small fish or fish steaks.
THE QUICK METHOD Omit the par-boiling of the court bouillon ingredients. Simply combine them and poach the fish in the resulting liquid. This method is only suitable for large fish. Small cuts cook so quickly that the liquid will not have time to develop and impart flavour.

SAUCES A sauce, defined by Larousse as 'liquid seasoning for food' can be anything from the juices in the frying pan to complicated and sophisticated emulsions taking real skill to prepare.

COMBINATION SAUCES

These are simple mixtures of ingredients, sometimes heated together, sometimes just combined. Included here too are 'hard sauces' — butter-based mixtures which set firmly when chilled and melt on the hot food. The following are further sauces of this kind.

APPLE SAUCE

INGREDIENTS
450g/1lb cooking apples
Finely grated rind of ¼ lemon
3tbsp water
1tsp sugar
15g/½oz butter
Pinch of cinnamon

1 Peel, quarter, core and slice the apples.

2 Place in a heavy saucepan with the lemon rind, water and sugar. Cover with a lid and cook very slowly until the apples are soft.

3 Beat in the butter and cinnamon. Serve hot or cold.

MINT SAUCE

INGREDIENTS
Large handful of fresh mint
2tbsp caster sugar
2tbsp hot water
2tbsp vinegar

1 Wash the mint and shake it dry.

2 Remove the stalks, and chop the leaves finely. Place in a bowl with the sugar.

3 Pour in the hot water and leave for 5 minutes to dissolve the sugar.

4 Add the vinegar and leave to soak for 1—2 hours.

NOTE When mint is plentiful it is a good idea to chop a quantity of it and mix it with golden syrup. This base can then be used for instant mint sauce (vinegar and boiling water being added when the sauce is required).

SOURED CREAM AND SPRING ONION SAUCE

INGREDIENTS
2 cartons soured cream
1 bunch well washed spring onions
Salt and freshly ground black pepper

1 Put the soured cream into a bowl.

2 Discard the roots and tough green leaves of the spring onions and chop the rest finely.

3 Mix the onions with the soured cream and season to taste with salt and pepper.

YOGHURT AND MUSTARD SAUCE

INGREDIENTS
290ml/½pt plain yoghurt
1tbsp good quality made mustard, preferably Dijon

Simply mix the yoghurt and mustard together. You may find that you need more or less mustard depending upon its strength.

BREAD SAUCE

INGREDIENTS
1 peeled onion
290ml/½pt milk
6 cloves
1 bay leaf
10 peppercorns OR a pinch of white pepper
Pinch of nutmeg
Salt
55g/2oz fresh white breadcrumbs
55g/2oz butter
2tbsp cream (optional)

1 Cut the onion in half. Put the onion pieces, the milk, cloves and bay leaf into a saucepan. Add the peppercorns, a pinch of nutmeg, and a good pinch of salt.

2 Leave to stand for 30 minutes or more if you can. If not, bring very slowly to the boil, and then simmer for 10 minutes. If you have had time to let the milk infuse (stand with its flavourings) you will not need to simmer it. But bring it to the boil very slowly just the same.

3 Strain the hot milk onto the breadcrumbs. Add the butter and cream. Mix and return to the saucepan.

4 Reheat the sauce carefully without reboiling.

5 If it has become too thick by the time it is needed, beat in more hot milk. It should be creamy.

SAVOURY BUTTERS

Flavoured butters are good served with grilled or fried fish or shellfish, or with plainly grilled chicken or meat dishes, and also excellent with hot toast or bread.

After preparation, the butter should be shaped into a cylinder, rolled up in foil or damp greaseproof paper and chilled in the refrigerator. It can then be sliced and used as required. If it is to be kept for more than two days it should be frozen.

ALMOND BUTTER

INGREDIENTS
110g/4oz butter
55g/2oz ground almonds
Squeeze of lemon
Salt and white pepper

1 Beat the butter to a light cream. Mix the almonds with the lemon juice and beat this paste into the softened butter. Season to taste.

2 Roll up as described above, and chill.

GREEN BUTTER

INGREDIENTS
4 sprigs of watercress
4 sprigs of fresh tarragon
1 sprig of parsley
4 small spinach leaves
110g/4oz butter
1 shallot, minced
Salt and pepper

1 Blanch the watercress, tarragon, parsley and spinach for 30 seconds in boiling salted water. Refresh under running cold water. Drain well and pat dry. Chop very finely.

2 Cream the butter and beat in the shallot, chopped green herbs and spinach. Add salt and pepper.

3 Roll up as described above and chill.

MAITRE D'HOTEL BUTTER

INGREDIENTS
110g/4oz butter
1tbsp lemon juice
2tsp finely chopped parsley
Salt and pepper

1 Cream the butter, stir in the lemon juice and parsley and season to taste.

2 Roll up as described above and chill.

GARLIC AND CHIVE BUTTER

INGREDIENTS
110g/4oz butter
1 clove garlic, crushed
1tbsp chopped chives
Salt and black pepper
Squeeze of lemon juice

1 Cream the butter to soften it. Mix the garlic and chives with the butter and season with salt, black pepper and lemon juice.

2 Roll up as described above and chill.

See also the recipe for Anchovy butter on p.160.

VINEGARS

Vinegars can sometimes be a disappointment. Avoid buying beautifully shaped bottles of wine vinegar filled with herbs, chillies etc. They cost the earth, and you can easily put those good-looking ingredients into any vinegar bottle yourself at a fraction of the price, or even make your own vinegar (see recipe below.) Buy flavoured vinegars (raspberry, tarragon, sherry, etc.) in plain small bottles and experiment with these. (See recipe for raspberry vinegar overleaf.)

HOME-MADE VINEGAR

The best vinegar is made by the slow and, to the commercial producer, expensive process of leaving nature to turn wine into vinegar. It can be done at home, though results tend to be better in summer when the vinegar mould grows more easily. The surest method is by adding an already established piece of mould (the vinegar 'mother') to the wine. However, given the right acid, warm conditions, the mould can appear spontaneously.

1 Leftover wine (including home-made wine), cider, sherry or port can be used to start and to top up the vinegar but it must be 'sound'. 'Off' or bad wine, or wine that has oxidized to the point of not being drinkable, or thick wine lees (sediment or dregs), should not be used. Put the wine into a large non-metal container, preferably with a tap at the bottom for drawing off the vinegar when it is made.

2 Add a good dash of vinegar to increase the acidity of the wine and also to preserve it. (Acid helps the vinegar mould grow and prevents the air oxidizing and spoiling the wine before it has had time to develop its own acid.) It does not matter how much vinegar you add, but it should be at least the equivalent of 10 per cent of the wine volume.

3 Keep the container in a warm room, covered loosely (you want a little air to enter, but a very wide mouth will cause too much evaporation). A skin of mould will appear on the surface of the liquid and may grow, like a plant, down into the wine. After a few weeks (usually four to five) the liquid will smell strongly and when run off will taste more vinegary than vinous. If during the process a very thick skin of white mould forms, carefully remove it, leaving only the pinkish skin beneath. Too heavy a crust of mould will prevent the air getting to the moulds beneath and they will die.

4 Drain off the vinegar (or syphon off if the container has no tap), taking care to leave only sediment and mould behind. Filter the vinegar through coffee filter papers (or, for crystal clear vinegar, clear it with egg-white as described for Aspic on p.100).

5 Once clear (it need not be crystal clear — the taste is what matters) bottle the vinegar in small screw top bottles. Protect metal screw tops from acid corrosion by using a layer of plastic film. Vinegar left in the open loses its acetic acid, so ensure the bottles are full, and tightly shut.

6 Keeping the original jar and mould, start the next batch. Do not top up half-made vinegar with large quantities of new wine just before bottling. It will give an over-strong taste of wine and is likely to go murky if not fully converted to vinegar. Draw off and bottle before starting the new batch. (To store leftover wine before adding it, pour it into small screw-top bottles, add a dash of vinegar and keep refrigerated.)

RASPBERRY VINEGAR

INGREDIENTS
450g/1lb raspberries
290ml/½pt white wine vinegar
Granulated sugar to taste

This is a strongly flavoured sweetened fruit vinegar, which should be used sparingly — perhaps mixed with five parts salad oil and a little salt and pepper and served as a dressing for cold meats or meat pies. For a less sweet, or unsweetened fruit vinegar, reduce or eliminate the sugar, but bring the strained juice and vinegar to the boil before bottling it.

1 Wash the fruit only if dusty. Put it into a glass or plastic bowl and mash well with a fork. Pour on the vinegar and leave for five days in a cool place (larder or refrigerator), and stir occasionally.

2 Set a fine nylon sieve over a measuring jug and tip the fruit into it. Allow to drain without forcing or stirring — about 4 hours.

3 Note the quantity of fruit juice, then pour it into a saucepan with 225g/8oz sugar for every 290ml/½pt juice.

4 Bring slowly to the boil, and simmer for a minute or two. Skim off any scum, and pour into clean warm screw-top bottles. Tighten the lids while the vinegar is still piping hot.

NOTE Any soft fruit may be substituted for the raspberries.

EMULSIONS are liquids which contain tiny droplets of oil or fat evenly distributed in a stable suspension.

STABLE EMULSIONS

MAYONNAISE is the best known of the cold emulsion sauces and is dealt with in detail in Menu Lesson 6. It may be altered dramatically by changing oils or combining them. A few spoons of hazelnut or walnut oil added to a tasteless peanut (arachide) oil makes a most interesting change. Olive oil gives a rich, heavy and voluptuous mayonnaise.

If mayonnaise is made in a processor or blender, the tireless speed of the blades means that it is possible to include the egg white as well as the yolk in the base of the mayonnaise, giving a much lighter, less rich but thinner mayonnaise. Many sauces can be made with a base of mayonnaise, by combining two sauces (such as the soured cream and spring onion sauce, or the yoghurt and mustard sauce) 50-50 with mayonnaise.

GREEN MAYONNAISE (makes 300ml/½pt)
Boil 75g/3oz spinach leaves (without stalks) in salted water for a minute or until limp. Drain and dry well and liquidize them with 300ml/½pt mayonnaise.

HERB MAYONNAISE (makes 300ml/½pt)
Combine 2tbsp any chopped herbs (basil, mint, tarragon, chervil, parsley, coriander are the best) with 300ml/½pt mayonnaise. Herbs are best used singly rather than all together. The sauce can be coloured green with spinach or by the addition of finely chopped watercress leaves.

CUCUMBER MAYONNAISE (makes just over 300ml/½pt)
Chop half a cucumber up roughly. Sprinkle it with 1tsp salt and leave in a nylon or stainless steel sieve to drain for an hour. Rinse under the tap, then pat dry. Liquidize or push through a sieve. Add to 300ml/½pt thick unsalted mayonnaise. Taste and add more salt (the cucumber, remember, was salty) if necessary. For a chunkier sauce, cut the cucumber carefully into tiny dice. Proceed as above but do not liquidize or sieve the cucumber. Cucumber mayonnaise can be coloured green with spinach as described above if liked.

AVOCADO MAYONNAISE
Add a ripe mashed or liquidized avocado pear, or one cut into neat tiny dice, to 300ml/½pt mayonnaise.

ELIZABETH MAYONNAISE
Combine 300ml/½pt mayonnaise with 3tbsp cream and 2tbsp Elizabeth sauce (p.278).

REMOULADE
This is a mustard-flavoured mayonnaise, and because mustard is a good vehicle for an emulsion, it is possible to use less egg yolk. Follow the mayonnaise recipe on p.61, substituting 1 heaped tbsp Dijon mustard for one of the egg yolks.

AVOCADO CREAM DRESSING

INGREDIENTS (makes about 450ml/¾pt)
1 ripe avocado
1 clove garlic, crushed
150ml/¼pt salad oil
Juice of ½ lemon
1tbsp onion juice
150ml/¼pt double cream
Salt and freshly ground black pepper

In this recipe the avocado forms the base, and the cream and oil are added to form the emulsion. It is good served as a salad dressing on raw skinned tomatoes, boiled potatoes, cooked broad beans, rice salads or as a dip for crudités or biscuits.

1 Mash the avocado flesh and push it through a sieve into a liquidizer or processor bowl, or, if making by hand, a pudding basin.

2 Beat in the garlic, and then add the oil drip by drip and beating all the time. As the oil is incorporated, it can be added less cautiously, and if using a machine, a steady thin stream while the machine is running will not end in disaster.

3 Gradually beat in the lemon and onion juices, and then the double cream. Season well with salt and pepper.

WARM EMULSIONS

The most stable warm emulsions, like the cold ones, are based on egg yolks. The best known is hollandaise, which is taught in detail on p.183. Variants of it, in classic cuisine, are:

BEARNAISE SAUCE

INGREDIENTS
3tbsp wine vinegar
6 peppercorns
1 bay leaf
1 small shallot, chopped
Sprig of fresh tarragon
Sprig of fresh chervil
2 egg yolks
Salt and pepper
110g/4oz softened butter
1tsp chopped fresh tarragon
1tsp chopped fresh chervil

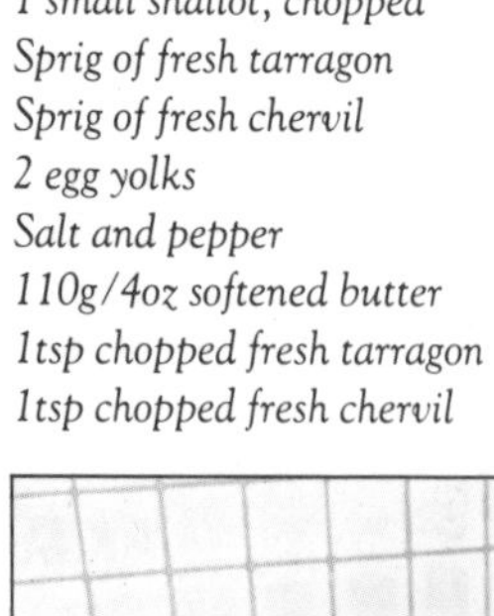

1 Place the vinegar, peppercorns, bay leaf, shallot, tarragon and chervil in a heavy saucepan and reduce over medium heat to 1tbsp.

2 In a small bowl, beat the egg yolks with a pinch of salt and a nut of butter. Set the bowl in a bain marie over a gentle heat. With a wooden spoon, beat the mixture until slightly thickened.

3 Strain on the reduced vinegar. Mix well. Beat in the softened butter bit by bit, increasing the temperature as the sauce thickens and you add more butter, but take care that the water does not boil immediately round the bowl.

4 When all the butter is added, stir in the chopped tarragon and chervil. Taste for seasoning.

MAKING WARM EMULSIONS
For sauces such as Hollandaise, start beating in the cool end of a bain marie. As more butter is added, move the bowl closer to the heat.

CHORON
As Béarnaise, but with 1 heaped tbsp tomato purée added to the finished sauce to colour and flavour it.

MOUSSELINE
As hollandaise, but with one whisked egg white and 2tbsps whipped double cream folded together and whisked in at the last minute to give lightness to the sauce.

MOUTARDE
Hollandaise lightly flavoured with Dijon mustard.

UNSTABLE EMULSIONS

Some sauces, such as French dressing (vinaigrette), will form a temporary emulsion if vigorously whisked or blended in a liquidizer, but will soon separate again into oil above and liquid (in the case of vinaigrette, vinegar or lemon juice) below. Vinaigrette dressing is taught on p.139. There are many variations of it: flavourings, such as chopped herbs, spring onions, crushed garlic, mustard and sugar may be added at the cook's whim. Green herbs should be added at the last minute, as they lose their colour in the vinegar. Onion benefits from an hour's maceration to allow it to soften in the sauce. Do not add garlic or onion to vinaigrette more than a day in advance, as the flavour can spoil. The best plan for the busy cook is to have a quantity of basic vinaigrette made up (oil, vinegar, salt and pepper) and kept in a screw topped bottle. The bottle can then be shaken hard to form a temporary emulsion, a few tablespoons poured out as needed, and flavoured as required.

EGGLESS EMULSIONS

WHEN TO USE A FLAT WHISK
For whisking small amounts in a shallow saucepan, a flat whisk is ideal.

Eggless emulsions are today's most fashionable butter sauces. They are less stable and lighter tasting than the egg-based thick hollandaise family, but still consist mostly of butter, and sometimes cream, and should, for the sake of good nutrition, be served in moderation.

To make them, butter is beaten into a base, exactly as for making hollandaise and béarnaise, but the base consists of reduced vinegar, reduced fish stock, or the reduced juices from frying pan or roasting tin. To obtain a good thick emulsion, without risk of separating, the butter should be very cold when beaten in. This means that each lump will take a while to melt and the cook will have time to whisk it into an emulsified state. If a large lump of softened butter hits the hot sauce, it will be melted before it can be incorporated smoothly, and will start a chain reaction with all the previously incorporated fat separating out and floating on the top of the sauce. Butter-mounted sauces are taught throughout the book. The darling of nouvelle cuisine, the classic Beurre blanc is on p.202.

The beginner who has not made butter-mounted sauces before, might be wise to cheat for the first time: If the base (reduced fish stock or, say, chicken gravy in a sauté pan) is very slightly thickened with a teaspoon of cornflour or plain flour, the starch will help to hold the emulsion as the butter is beaten in, and the sauce will stay stable until served without risk of separating. For example:

TARRAGON BUTTER SAUCE FOR ROAST CHICKEN

INGREDIENTS
Juices from the pan in which the chicken was roasted
Juice of ½ lemon
1tsp cornflour
110g/4oz unsalted butter, chilled and cut into small dice
2 sprigs of tarragon
Salt and pepper

1 Pour off as much fat from the roasting pan as possible.

2 Mix the lemon juice with the cornflour and 3tbsp water. Stir into the juices in the pan and stir until boiling. There should be about 150ml/¼pt barely thickened sauce. If there is less, and the sauce is at all like thick gravy, add a spoon or two more water.

3 Now set the roasting pan over a moderate heat so that the sauce is gently bubbling and briskly whisk in the first cube of butter. Once in, add another, and keep going until the sauce is a creamy emulsion. The secret is rapid whisking. As more butter is added, lower the temperature to below boiling.

4 Add the tarragon leaves and salt and pepper to taste.

HOLDING A SAUCE If warm emulsions are made in advance they are best kept warm in a bain marie as direct heat or reheating once cold can curdle them.

SAUCES THICKENED BY REDUCTION

Many sauces are thickened by the simple process of boiling down until so much water evaporates that the sauce is thick and syrupy, but to do this the cook needs very large quantities of good strong stock to start with. Brown demi-glaze is a classic of the professional kitchen, but is simply not feasible at home. Reduced sauces *can* be made if, for example, the vegetables of a brown stock are pushed through the sieve when the stock is strained. They will, of course, prevent the stock from being crystal clear, but they add body and flavour to the liquid, which, if simply boiled down vigorously, will be a good sauce without the addition of flour. It may then be mounted with spoon or two of butter, to give it richness and a sheen. (See previous recipe for how to 'mount' with butter). Other examples of thick sauces made by reduction are as follows:

TOMATO SAUCE

INGREDIENTS
400g/14oz can of peeled plum tomatoes
1 small onion, chopped
1 carrot, chopped
1 stick celery, chopped
½ garlic clove, crushed
1 bay leaf
Fresh parsley stalks
Salt and pepper
Juice of ½ lemon
Dash of Worcestershire sauce
1tsp sugar
1tsp chopped fresh OR 1 pinch dried basil or thyme

1 Put all the ingredients together in a thick bottomed pan and simmer over medium heat for 30 minutes.

2 Sieve the sauce and return it to the pan.

3 If it is too thin, reduce by boiling rapidly. Check the seasoning, adding more salt or sugar if necessary.

ELIZABETH SAUCE

INGREDIENTS
1 small onion, chopped
2tsp oil
2tsp curry powder
½tsp tomato purée
3tbsp water
1 small bay leaf
½ wineglass red wine
Salt and pepper
2tsp apricot jam
1 slice lemon
1tsp lemon juice

This sauce was invented by the staff at the Cordon Bleu School for the Coronation in 1953 and has become a classic. Use it as a base to flavour mayonnaise or other sauces.

1 Cook the onion gently for 4 minutes in the oil.

2 Add the curry powder and fry gently for 1 minute.

3 Add the tomato purée, water, bay leaf, wine, salt, pepper, jam, lemon slice and juice, and simmer for 8 minutes.

4 Strain the mixture, pushing as much as possible through the sieve.

PAN SAUCES

Many sauces are made in the frying or sauté pan in which meat, fish or poultry has been cooked. They can be thickened with flour as an English gravy, or mounted with butter as above. (See Tarragon butter sauce p.277.) But they can also be deglazed with wine, madeira, stock or cream and boiled rapidly, while the cook scrapes the bottom of the pan to detach and incorporate any sediment or fried-on juices to make a delicious impromptu sauce. The following are examples:

RED WINE REDUCTION (for liver, steak or lamb cutlets)
When the liver has been cooked, lift it out and set aside. Pour a glass of red wine into the bottom of the pan and stir over the heat while scraping the base to loosen any stuck-on matter. Add 1tsp redcurrant jelly and enough stock to give a thin dark gravy. Mount with butter if liked.

BERCY REDUCTION (for chicken or veal kidneys)
Deglaze the pan as described above with white wine. Add a finely chopped shallot and sweat until soft. Beat in 1tsp lemon juice, 1tbsp

diced bone marrow and 2tbsp parsley and mount with 2tbsp butter.

MUSTARD AND CREAM REDUCTION (for kidneys, pork/veal chops) Deglaze the pan with double cream, boil up and scrape the pan base. Add Dijon mustard, salt and pepper.

FLOUR-THICKENED SAUCES

The commonest English sauces are thickened with flour, and they are undoubtedly the most practical for the home cook.

The secret is not to make them too thick and to give them a good hard boil after they have thickened to give them a shine. They will also look professionally shiny if whizzed in a liquidizer after making, or if a tablespoon of butter is beaten in at the end.

WHITE SAUCE

INGREDIENTS
20g/¾oz butter
20g/¾oz flour
Pinch of dry mustard
290ml/½pt creamy milk
Salt and white pepper

1 Melt the butter in a heavy saucepan.

2 Add the flour and the mustard and stir over gentle heat for 1 minute. Draw the pan off the heat, pour in the milk gradually and mix well or whisk until smooth.

3 Return the sauce to the heat and stir or whisk continually until boiling.

4 Simmer for 2 – 3 minutes and season with salt and pepper.

BECHAMEL SAUCE

Proceed as for white sauce but omit the mustard and heat the milk first with bayleaf, sprig of thyme and slice of onion. Cool it and strain into the roux.

MORNAY SAUCE

INGREDIENTS
20g/¾oz butter
Large pinch of dry English mustard
20g/¾oz flour
290ml/½pt milk
25g/½oz grated Parmesan cheese
Cayenne pepper
Salt and pepper

1 Melt the butter in a heavy saucepan. Add the mustard and flour. Stir over a gentle heat for 1 minute.

2 Remove from the heat. Add the milk gradually and mix well or whisk until smooth.

3 Return the sauce to the heat and stir or whisk continuously until boiling. Simmer for 2 minutes.

4 Add all the cheese and mix well, but do not reboil.

5 Season with cayenne, salt and pepper.

VELOUTE SAUCE

INGREDIENTS
20g/¾oz butter
20g/¾oz flour
290ml/½pt white stock
2tbsp double cream
Salt and pepper
A few drops of lemon juice

1 Melt the butter, add the flour and cook, stirring, over a gentle heat until pale brown. Remove from the heat.

2 Add the stock. Bring to the boil, stirring, and simmer until slightly syrupy and semi-clear. Taste and add cream, seasoning and lemon juice.

ALL ABOUT EGGS

It is hard to imagine what European cooking would be without eggs. We use them as a main food in egg dishes, as a thickening or setting agent in sauces, custards and moulds. The yolks are used for their smooth richness, and the whites, with their magical property of holding air when whisked, give lightness to cakes, meringues, soufflés and mousses.

Their various uses are covered in the Menu Lessons, but understanding the different properties of yolks and whites will allow the cook to use them with intelligence and excellent results when cooking without a recipe or when altering recipes.

YOLKS

Yolks, as they are heated, change from the liquid to the solid state. The half thickened and the solid state interest the cook most.

SEPARATING EGGS Hold the egg in one hand and crack it sharply across its equator against a sharp edge. Hold the cracked egg vertically over a bowl and prise the top half off. The white will flow into the bowl and the yolk will stay in the lower egg shell half. By tipping the yolk from one shell to the other it is possible to get 90 per cent of the white into the bowl. If the white is very fresh, it might hang like a curtain over the side of the egg shell. Use the broken edge of the empty shell to cut it off. If specks of yolk get into the white, use the egg shell to scoop it out.

SEPARATING EGGS
1 Hold the egg in one hand and crack it sharply across its equator against a glass bowl. Separate the shells and let the egg white fall into the bowl.

2 Tip the yolk from one shell-half to the other, allowing all the white to drop into the bowl.

3 Use the broken edge of the empty egg shell to cut off any reluctant white.

SPECIALIST LESSON 1 THICKENING LIQUIDS

THE EGG AND CREAM LIAISON
To thicken and enrich 300ml/½ pint of sauce (say thinnish chicken sauce): stir 2 yolks into 2tbsp cream in a teacup. Add a ladleful of the hot sauce, stir well, and return to the pan. Stir over very gentle heat, but on no account boil — the idea is to thicken up those yolks without cooking them into hard curdled (or scrambled) lumps.

POURING CUSTARD (see p.232)
The same principle is used here but as the yolks are the only thickening used (unlike the chicken sauce above, which is already slightly thickened and therefore more stable and less liable to curdle), the process should be very gradual and careful — the liquid must be uniformly heated to allow thickening without scrambling. The more yolks, the richer and thicker the custard will be.

BACK OF THE SPOON TEST
To test for coating consistency, dip a wooden spoon into the custard and turn it over. The sauce should be thick enough to stay on the back of the spoon and for a line drawn with the finger to stay clear.

CHEAT'S EGG CUSTARD
If the milk used to make the custard is pre-thickened with a little cornflour or custard powder, or if 1tsp cornflour or custard powder is added to the yolks before pouring on the hot milk, the mixture will be slightly more stable and less liable to curdle. The yolks and vanilla will still give the true flavour of a proper egg custard and the cornflour or custard powder is undetectable.

CREME BRULEE
Although this most luxurious and wicked of puddings looks like a baked custard, the yolks are only cooked to thicken the cream, not to completely set it. Mix 8 yolks with 570ml/1pt of cream, sweeten with 2tbsp sugar, and add a vanilla pod. Stir continuously over very gentle heat until the mixture will coat the back of the spoon. Pour into a shallow dish and bake in a bain marie for 12 minutes — long enough to give it a skin but not to set the custard too solidly. Leave, without touching the skin, until the next day. Get the grill blazing hot. Stand the dish on a large try and, using a cook's sieve, sprinkle an even thick (0.5cm/¼ inch) layer of caster sugar on top using broad even passes and letting the tray catch the sugar falling wide. (Many people use brown sugar, which is cheating, but easier. The brown sugars taste more caramel-like, but look duller. A perfect glassy shine is only possible with caster sugar.) Then immediately put the custard under the grill, as close as possible, and watch it carefully while the sugar melts and browns. If the custard bubbles up the sides and burns there are five possible causes: the custard was not sufficiently thick with a good firm skin: the sugar layer wasn't even and thick enough; the grilling was not done as soon as the sugar was in place; the grill was not hot enough or evenly heated; the dish was not quite horizontal under the grill. For Almost crème brûlée, see Menu Lesson 1 on p.36.

CHEAT'S CREME BRULEE
This is a simple baked custard, solidly set with egg whites. Use half cream and half milk, and add 3 eggs and 2 extra yolks per 570ml/1pt. Sweeten with 3tbsp sugar and add 3 drops vanilla flavouring. Cook as for baked custard, then cool, without breaking the skin.

Make caramel by dissolving 4tbsp sugar and 1tsp lemon juice in 4tbsp water in a heavy pan, then boil without stirring until evenly brown. Cool slightly by carefully dipping the base only of the pan into cold water for a second or two, then pour over the custard in an even layer.

SAVOURY SET CUSTARDS
Modern fashionable nouvelle cuisine has revived many of the delicate savoury custards. Our Spinach timbales on p.128 and our Three-flavour omelette on p.53 are examples of a mixture set with eggs. The same is true for nearly all quiche fillings, which are savoury ingredients mixed with egg custards, and baked in a gentle oven to ensure a smooth filling.

CONFECTIONER'S CUSTARD OR CREME PATISSIERE
In this custard there is so much flour (both cornflour and plain wheatflour) that the yolks, even when boiling, are prevented from scrambling in a most magical way. The mixture does go into alarming lumps, but the end result is smooth as silk.

LEMON CURD

INGREDIENTS
2 large lemons
85g/3oz butter
225g/8oz granulated sugar
3 eggs

Lemon curd is thickened with eggs, and, like the yolks in the confectioner's custard above, they can be simmered without scrambling. This time it is the high degree of acid in the lemon juice which, like the flour in the custard, interferes with their tendency to scramble. But, as with confectioner's custard, the cook must stir vigorously and unremittingly as the mixture is heated.

1 Grate the rind of the lemons on the finest gauge on the grater, taking care to grate rind only, not pith.

2 Squeeze the juice from the lemons.

3 Put the rind, juice, butter, sugar and lightly beaten eggs into a heavy saucepan or double boiler and heat gently, stirring all the time, until the mixture is thick.

4 Strain into a bowl and allow to cool.

NOTE This curd will keep in the refrigerator for about 3 weeks.

SPECIALIST LESSON 2 USING EGGS TO SET FOODS SOLIDLY

Because egg whites set solidly even faster than yolks, unseparated eggs are generally used if the object is to get a solid set. Yolks on their own can be used if there are enough of them (as many as 8 yolks to 600ml/1 pt) and they will give a particularly attractive not-quite-solid silky set. The following recipe uses 5 yolks and 1 white, and the mixture just sets.

CHOCOLATE POTS

INGREDIENTS (serves 6)
85g/3oz dark bitter chocolate
150ml/¼pt milk
290g/½pt single cream
70g/2½oz caster sugar
4 yolks
1 egg

1 Set the oven to 150°C/300°F/Gas 2.

2 Melt the chocolate without allowing it to get more than warm. Do this on a plate over a pan of simmering water, or in the top of a double boiler, or by heating briefly in a microwave oven.

3 Bring the milk and cream to the boil with the sugar. Cool for 1 minute and add the chocolate. Whisk until smooth.

4 Beat the egg yolks and the egg together. Pour on the chocolate milk.

5 Strain to remove any threads from the eggs.

6 Pour into small china pots, coffee cups or ramekin dishes and cover with lids, or a single piece of foil laid on top of the pots.

7 Stand the chocolate pots in a roasting tin of near-boiling water and put in the oven.

8 Bake for 45 minutes or until there is a definite skin on the top, and the middle of each custard is just set, although it will still wobble if the ramekins are jiggled. The custards will firm up as they cool. Refrigerate once they are cold.

NOTE The top skin of chocolate custards often has a speckled or dark appearance when cooked, but this will not affect taste or texture. Coffee or vanilla custards can be made similarly. Replace the chocolate with 3tsp instant coffee, or 1tsp vanilla flavouring. They will cook in about 35 to 40 minutes — slightly less time than the chocolate pots.

BAKED CUSTARD
Generally made with 4 eggs to 570ml/1pt milk, sweetened with sugar and flavoured with vanilla, the resulting set custard is solid but smooth. The trick is to bake the custard standing in a pan of water (au bain marie), because this will prevent the outer edges overcooking and degenerating into holes before the middle is set.

BREAD-AND-BUTTER PUDDING
This is made in the same way, the custard being poured over slightly overlapping slices of bread and butter (with a handful of sultanas under them in the bottom of the buttered shallow dish). The pudding is baked au bain marie until the custard sets. For a crisp crust it is best to then sprinkle sugar all over the top, and grill it, rather than bake in a hot oven in the first place. Baking in fierce heat, while giving a good brown top, will overcook the custard.

CREME CARAMEL
This is simply an egg custard poured into the pan in the bottom of which is a layer of caramel (see p.106). It is cooked exactly as a baked custard, and when cold turned out into a deep flat dish.

BAKED CHARLOTTE
A deep mould or pudding basin is buttered and lined with strips of cake or sponge fingers, or slices of Swiss roll (which look very pretty) before the custard is poured in. Then it is baked au bain marie, turned out and eaten warm.

SPECIALIST LESSON 3 USING EGG TO FIRM UP SOLID MIXTURES

Whole eggs are often used to 'bind' stuffings and minced or puréed mixtures. If a mixture is very buttery, say mashed potatoes, the addition of egg will make it, when cooked, more solid. For this reason Duchess potatoes (mashed potatoes piped onto a buttered baking sheet and baked until brown) contain egg. If they were just potato and butter or cream they would soften as the butter melted in the oven rather than stiffen, and the result would be flat and unappetizing.

For the same reason stuffings for roasts and poultry often contain a beaten egg, which will harden during cooking and stiffen up the stuffing. This can be confusing for cooks because it is natural to think that breadcrumbs make stuffings stodgy and that the liquid egg will make it creamy — because it visibly loosens the mixture when added to it. But, in fact, a high proportion of breadcrumbs in stuffing will give a soft and tender stuffing, and too much egg will cook to a stodgy one.

☐ *Paint beaten egg onto cracks or small holes in a cooked flan or quiche case and return it to the oven. The egg will cook solidly and seal the gap. Then the liquid filling can be poured in and baked without danger of leaking.*

EGG WHITES

The chief joy of the egg white is that it will hold amazing quantities of air (8 times its own volume) when whisked. As it is practically tasteless, it is the ideal air-incorporating vehicle for savoury or sweet dishes.

SPECIALIST LESSON 4 WHISKING AND FOLDING

The best method of getting the maximum volume of air into egg whites is to use a steel balloon whisk in a copper bowl. The copper reacts with the egg white (especially if a little vinegar or lemon juice is added — which is why copper bowls are often wiped out with a cut lemon before whisking) and a mass of chains or tunnels of small stable air bubbles are produced. An electric whisk works faster, but produces bigger bubbles that burst and disintegrate faster. But the difference is not vital — perfectly good whisked egg white can be produced by machine, and in commercial kitchens today copper bowls are not used as much as chefs and catering colleges would have us believe. Apart from being very hard work, copper bowls have another disadvantage — the egg white frequently discolours as a result of the contact with the copper, and even when the bowl is assiduously cleaned beforehand the egg whites will often look greenish grey. But this colour disappears on cooking, and is nothing to worry about.

If using an electric machine, hand whisk or mixer, a metal bowl with the machine running at half pace produces the best results. Rapidly whisked whites produced in a glass or ceramic bowl will be the least voluminous, and the least likely to hold their air for any length of time. But even whites whisked like this, if they are immediately incorporated into soufflés, cakes, or mousses, are perfectly adequate.

Raw egg whites are used in cooking at all stages from un-whisked to whisked until stiff and dry.

UN-WHISKED As they come from the shell. Used to paint rose or geranium petals if making crystallized petals. The egg white must not be at all frothy or the coating will be bubbly. Perfect dry fresh petals are painted on both sides with the egg white. The petal is then dusted lightly on both sides with caster sugar and left on a sheet of greaseproof paper in a warm room (or above the boiler or radiator) for about 24 hours until dry and brittle, when they can be stored in an airtight tin or used at once for cake or pudding decoration. They must be fully dried out before storing or they will soften and go mouldy.

FROTHY Whisked, usually with a fork, just enough to mix them and prevent them plopping out of the jug separately. This makes them easier to add gradually to mixtures.

SOFT PEAK Whisked until the egg white will just hold its shape when the whisk is lifted, the points that are dragged up by the rising whisk flopping over softly. Used to add to fairly liquid mixtures such as cake batters or whipped cream.

MEDIUM PEAK Whisked until the egg white will stand in peaks when the whisk is lifted, but with the tips of the peaks just flopping over like wilted leaves. For incorporating in soft mixtures such as soufflés, ice creams, sorbets. The idea is to have the two mixtures the cook is combining as close to each other in consistency as possible. It is very difficult to add over-whisked (too stiff and too dry) egg whites to, say, a soft chocolate mousse mixture — the egg whites break up into islands and by the time the cook has stirred and struggled to get the mixture smooth, most of that carefully incorporated air has been knocked out.

STIFF PEAK Whisked until the egg white will stand up in rigid pointed (not floppy) peaks when the whisk is lifted. Used mainly for meringue, at which point the sugar is added.

HOLDING EGG WHITES If stiffly-whisked egg whites must stand before being folded into the mixture, liquefication can be delayed by excluding the air which causes the disintegration, either by stretching polythene across the bowl or turning the bowl right over on the work

HOLDING EGG WHITES
Eggs are 'held' by excluding the air which causes liquefication. One method is to turn the bowl upside down on the work surface.

surface (the whisked whites will stick to the bowl). Alternatively, if sugar is to form part of the mixture, as in meringue or sweet puddings, some, or all of it folded into the whites will keep them stable for 15 minutes or so.

FROTHY

SOFT PEAK

MEDIUM PEAK

STIFF PEAK

THE TECHNIQUE OF FOLDING Egg whites, and other mixtures into which air has been carefully incorporated (such as sifted flour, creamed sugar-and-butter mixtures, whipped cream) are often 'folded' into something else. The difference between folding and simple mixing is that, with folding, great care is taken to preserve the trapped air in the mixture. Simple stirring or vigorous beating could easily break the bubbles and let out the air. The technique of folding is easier to learn than to describe, but here are the essential points:

1 Use a bowl rather than a flat-bottomed container. Make sure the bowl is large enough to hold the completed mixture comfortably. (Working in a small bowl is awkward and leads to lumps of egg white spilling out.) Add first a spoon of egg white to the base mixture, beating it in to soften the mixture. Then tip in the rest of the egg whites and fold.

2 Use a large metal cook's spoon, not a wooden spoon and not an ordinary tablespoon. It should be metal because that will cut neatly and cleanly through the mixture with as little disturbance of the air bubbles as possible. A wooden spoon is too clumsy, does not cut through cleanly, and has not a big enough head to lift sufficient mixture.

3 Hold the spoon near the head, not halfway up the handle.

4 Do not stir round and round but using the spoon edge like a knife cut down to the bottom of the bowl, then turn the spoon to lift up the maximum amount of mixture from the bottom and bring it to the top. Turn the spoon over to drop the mixture when it comes to the top, and repeat the action in various parts of the bowl, always lifting the mass, bottom to top. Many cooks develop a 'figure of eight' motion, and it is

HOLDING SPOON FOR FOLDING
Hold the spoon (use a metal spoon, not a wooden one) near the head, not halfway up the handle. This will give you better control when folding.

helpful to use the non-folding hand to turn the bowl.

5 Do not overdo it. It is far better to have a few pockets of badly folded mixture, or lumps of unmixed egg white, than to risk stirring out the air. As the mixture is tipped into a soufflé dish or cake tin, any very large patches can be broken up with spatula or spoon.

SPECIALIST LESSON 5 MERINGUE

Meringue is whisked egg white with sugar added to it (usually in the proportion of 50g/2oz sugar to each egg white). Sometimes a few drops of vinegar are added to encourage volume on whisking. It is used in countless ways, and there are three main types of meringue, all used folded into various mousses, ice creams and desserts, or baked in the oven as pie-toppings or crisp meringue.

SWISS MERINGUE

Swiss Meringue is probably the nicest to eat if made into classic meringues — light, airy, crumbly and crisp. It also makes the best and lightest meringue topping for pies etc. The disadvantage is that, because the sugar is added at the last minute, and is dry, it is not as stable as the other varieties, and the cook must get it into the oven fairly fast. The Lemon meringue pie on p.120 is made with Swiss meringue.

TO MAKE SWISS MERINGUE

1 Whisk the egg whites to stiff peaks but take care not to over-whisk — the whites can break down and lose their volume.

2 Fold in 1tsp sugar per egg white and whisk again until stiff once more, and this time rather shiny. Half the sugar can be beaten with the whites if a strong electric machine is used, but beating whites and a lot of sugar to the correct solid consistency by hand is almost impossible. It is essential that the mixture at this point should not be at all runny. It should form a solid bridge between whisk and bowl if the whisk is brought up 2.5-5cm/1-2 inches above the mixture.

3 Then fold the rest of the sugar into the mixture, and use at once. Do not let it stand about because, after about 15 minutes, it will begin to 'weep'.

4 Swiss meringue can take 3 hours in a cool oven to dry out and often ends up pale biscuit-coloured with a slightly toffee-like centre — delicious.

5 A good variation of Swiss meringue is made by substituting soft brown sugar for half of the caster sugar. The resulting meringue is slightly caramel flavoured and, if eaten with whipped cream and lemon curd (see p.282) or filled with ginger-flavoured cream, is unusual and excellent.

ITALIAN MERINGUE

This meringue is much more laborious to make than Swiss meringue but it has the advantage that once mixed it is extremely stable. Provided it is covered with polythene or a damp cloth to prevent drying out, the cook can leave it for hours before using it without risk of disintegration and, as it hardly swells at all in the oven, it is ideal for piped meringue baskets, vacherins etc. It cooks rather faster than Swiss meringue, is chalkier and more powdery, and stays a brilliant white. Not as nice to eat as Swiss meringue, but useful if catering for large numbers, and delicious if filled with strawberries and cream.

TO MAKE ITALIAN MERINGUE

1 Put the sugar in a heavy saucepan, add enough water to just wet it and a squeeze of lemon juice to prevent it crystallizing.

2 Without stirring, bring it slowly to the boil. If sugar crystals get stuck to the side of the pan, brush them down into the syrup with a clean wet brush. Use a sugar thermometer if available.

TESTING SUGAR SYRUP
1 To avoid crystallization when syrups are boiling, brush the sides of the pan with a brush dipped in clean water to wash down any sugar crystals.

2 To test syrup, drop a teaspoonful into a cup of cold water. If the syrup has reached the right temperature it will set into a soft ball which can be squashed between the fingers.

3 If the syrup forms a hard ball — like a hard-boiled sweet — it has reached too high a temperature to make Italian meringue.

3 The syrup is ready when it reaches 116°C/240°F. Alternatively, test for the 'soft ball' stage.

4 While the syrup is gently boiling to the correct stage, whisk the egg whites to stiff peaks.

5 If the whites are in a machine, pour the bubbling hot syrup onto them in a steady stream while whisking, taking care not to pour the syrup onto the wires of the whisk — it cools fast against the cold metal and can harden and stick to the whisk. If whisking the whites by hand, and in the absence of anyone to pour as you whisk, pour the syrup onto the whites in stages, about one third at a time, whisking hard between each addition and working as fast as possible. The syrup must be bubbling hot as it hits the egg white to partially cook it.

6 Once the syrup is all in, whisk hard until the mixture is stiff and shiny and absolutely stable. If the whisk is lifted, the meringue should not flow at all.

7 Keep covered with polythene or a damp cloth if not using at once.
NOTE The Noix au café on p.173 are made with Italian meringue.

MERINGUE CUITE

'Cooked' meringue is a professional chef's meringue used largely for frosting petits fours, for fruit pie tops and for unbaked frosting for cakes. It is only worth making if an electric whisk is handy, when it is easy. It produces an even chalkier and finer-textured meringue than Italian meringue and, if used on baked confections, comes out of the oven shiny, smooth and pale biscuit coloured. Like Italian meringue, meringue cuite is very stable in the oven, hardly swelling at all and unlikely to cook out of shape. For this reason it is often used for intricate work such as the meringue basket on p.69. When baked at very low temperatures it emerges smooth and shiny-white. The proportions of egg white to sugar are the same as for most meringue, but the sugar used is confectioner's (icing) sugar, rather than caster. Sometimes a 50-50 mixture of caster and icing sugar is used and occasionally, when the meringue is for a fine cake frosting that will not be baked, the sugar content can be increased above the normal 50g/2oz per small egg white to 75g/3oz.

TO MAKE MERINGUE CUITE

1 Use a whisking bowl that will fit snugly on a saucepan of water, without the bottom of the bowl being in direct contact with the water.

2 Whisk the whites until stiff, set them over a pan of simmering water.

3 Add the sifted icing sugar (it flies about in sugar-dust clouds so take care). Whisk until thick and absolutely stable — there should be no movement at all when the whisk is lifted.

4 Keep covered with polythene or a damp cloth if not using at once.

NOTE If the mixture is whisked in a strong machine a good result can be had without beating over heat. But it takes a good 15 minutes to get a perfect 'cuite' consistency.

SPECIALIST LESSON 6 THE SOUFFLE

There is a certain amount of myth and mystique about soufflés but, in truth, they are easy things to make. They are satisfyingly untemperamental. They rise because the air inside them expands but sink fast if the mixture cools while still uncooked. To stay up permanently they must be rigid and overcooked. Chefs have solved this problem. They overcook the soufflé, then serve a sauce with it.

TO MAKE A PERFECT SOUFFLE (See also pp.157 and 164).

1 Make the base: this can be done in advance, but should be warmed before folding in the egg whites or it will be too stiff. It should be of a soft, not-quite-pouring consistency. If it is too solid it will take too much vigorous stirring, as opposed to light folding, to incorporate the whites, and much air will be lost resulting in a too-heavy soufflé. If it is too liquid, the mixture will rise unevenly, not dry out satisfactorily and sink fast. Soufflé bases almost always include egg yolks, so stir the base over gentle heat when re-heating to prevent scrambling. Stop when the mixture is warm and soft. Season and flavour the base very well.

2 Get the oven hot. Most soufflés are cooked at 190°C/375°F/Gas 5. Put a flat baking sheet on the middle shelf to heat too. When the soufflé is put on this it will give the bottom a good burst of heat and help it rise evenly. Make sure there is no shelf above the one to be used.

3 Brush out the soufflé dish with butter and dust with dried breadcrumbs. This helps the mixture glide easily up the sides and gives a crisp crust at the finish. For an impressively straight-sided soufflé tie a collar of greaseproof paper round the dish and grease that too. It is not strictly necessary — a well made soufflé will rise above the rim anyway, but it helps even rising if the oven is at all uneven or draughty. Whisk the whites to medium peak (see p.285).

4 If necessary, briskly stir a single spoonful of the whites into the base to further loosen and soften it. Using a spatula scrape all the egg white into the base mixture and fold in with a metal spoon (see p.285).

5 Pour the mixture into the soufflé dish. It should not be more than three-quarters full. Smooth the top. Give the whole dish a sharp crack on the table top. This will burst any over-large air bubbles.

6 Bake, without opening the door until 5 minutes before the estimated end of the cooking time.

7 Test for 'doneness' by giving the dish a sharp shove. If the soufflé wobbles easily it is still liquid in the middle and should be left in the oven. If it is rock solid, it is dry and cooked right through. A slight tremble is best — it means a just moist centre. Remove the paper collar. Serve as fast as feasible.

TO MAKE A SOUFFLE

1 Fold not-too-stiffly whisked whites into the base. Continue until there are no large patches of egg white, then stop. Do not overmix.

2 Brush out the soufflé dish with melted butter, then — for a crusty edge — dust with breadcrumbs. Fill dish only two-thirds full.

3 A paper collar — also buttered and breadcrumbed — pinned in place will allow the soufflé to rise to the top of the dish.

4 Draw a knife through the mixture, first one way then at angles to break up any air pockets.

5 Running a finger around the edge of the soufflé mixture ensures a top-hat shape when baked.

6 Peel away the collar, if used, carefully before serving.

CAKES

Successful cake making is a most satisfying activity for the cook. It is also most demanding on account of the accuracy needed in measuring the ingredients and the skill necessary in preparing certain cakes. Confidence is best built by beginning with the easier types, such as gingerbread or fruit cakes. The first attempt at making more difficult cakes such as a genoise sponge are often disappointing. Happily, practice — with good ingredients, proper utensils, careful weighing and measuring, precise oven temperatures and exact timing (in short careful attention to detail) — makes perfect.

Most cakes are made by mixing fat, sugar, flour, eggs and liquid. Air or another gas is incorporated to make the mixture rise while baking. As it bakes, strands of gluten in the flour are stretched by the gas until the heat finally hardens the cake. It is even rising that gives a cake a light sponge-like texture.

INGREDIENTS

FATS Butter makes the best flavoured cakes. Margarine, particularly the soft or 'tub' variety, has its place in baking both for speed and (if the margarine is high in polyunsaturated fats) for health reasons, though it has less flavour than butter. Vegetable shortenings are flavourless but give light cakes. Lard cakes are often delicious but heavy and for this reason lard is little used in cake making. Oils are not used much as they do not easily hold air when they are creamed or beaten, and the resulting cakes can therefore be heavy.

SUGARS The finer creaming possible with caster (fine granulated) sugar makes it most suitable for cake making. Very coarse granulated sugar can give a speckled appearance to a finished cake unless the sugar is ground down first in a blender or food processor. Soft brown sugars give colour and flavour to dark cakes like gingerbread, but they give sponge cakes a drab look and a too-caramel flavour.

Golden syrup, honey, treacle or molasses are used in cakes made by the melting method. Such cakes are cooked relatively slowly as these thick liquid sugars tend to caramelize and burn at higher temperatures.

EGGS Unless specified, most recipes assume a medium sized egg weighing about 55-60g/2oz (size 3 in UK). The eggs should be used at room temperature — cold eggs tend to curdle the mixture and this results in the cake having a tough, coarse, too open texture. When using whisked egg whites in a cake, be sure that not even a speck of yolk gets into the whites. Any yolk, or fat on the whisk, will prevent proper whisking (and therefore the air-holding ability) of the whites and thus reduce the lightness of the finished cake.

FLOURS Plain white flour is used in cake making unless otherwise specified. The high proportion of 'soft' or low-gluten wheat used in European plain flour makes it particularly suitable for cake making. In North America, plain or 'all-purpose' flour is made with more 'hard' than soft wheat, so corn flour which is also weak (low in gluten) is sometimes substituted for some of the all-purpose flour, or special soft 'cake flour' is used. Although a little gluten is needed to allow the mixture to stretch and expand as it rises, too much would give a tough chewy cake. For more information on gluten see p.312.

SELF-RAISING FLOUR has a raising agent (baking powder) added to it and should only be used if specified in the recipe. All flours, even if labelled 'ready-sifted' should be sifted before use to eliminate any lumps and to incorporate air.

RAISING AGENTS

AIR is incorporated into cake mixtures by agitating the ingredients. Methods include sifting the flour, beating the butter and beating or creaming it again with the sugar to a fluffy, mousse-like consistency, and whisking the eggs. The heat of the oven causes the air trapped in the mixture to rise and leaven or lighten the cake, either by itself or in conjunction with other raising agents.

STEAM raises some mixtures even when air has not been beaten into them. Flour mixtures with a high proportion of liquid in them, like Yorkshire pudding, will rise in a hot oven since, as the water vaporizes and the steam rises, the uncooked flour mixture rises with it. While in this puffed-up state, the mixture hardens in the oven heat with the steam trapped inside. The pockets of air created by steam are uneven and very open as in choux pastry (see p.306), so steam is not used on its own for making cakes. But steam is a contributing factor in raising wet cake mixtures such as gingerbread.

BICARBONATE OF SODA, or baking soda, is a powder which, when mixed into cake mixtures, quickly gives off half its substance as carbon dioxide gas. In a cake the trapped gas causes the mixture to puff up. Heat sets the mixture once it has risen. By the time the cake cools, the gas will have escaped and will have been replaced by air. Unfortunately, the unused portion of bicarbonate of soda remaining can give a cake a slightly unpleasant smell and taste, and a yellowish colour. For this reason, bicarbonate of soda is most often used in strongly tasting cakes such as gingerbread and those flavoured with chocolate, treacle or molasses. The carbon dioxide reaction is speeded up by acidic substances, so bicarbonate of soda is usually used in cake mixtures with ingredients such as sour milk, vinegar, buttermilk, soured cream, cream of tartar and yoghurt. This makes it especially suitable for quickly mixed items like fruit cakes, scones, soda bread and gingerbread. It also gives them a soft texture and spongy crust with a deep colour. Unfortunately the process destroys some of the vitamins present in the flour.

BAKING POWDER in commercial forms consists of bicarbonate of soda and an acid powder which varies according to the brand, plus a starch filler, usually cornflour, arrowroot or ground rice. The starch keeps the mixture dry by absorbing any dampness in the air which might cause the soda and acid in the powder to react. The presence of the filler explains why more commercial baking powder than mixed 'bi-carb' and cream of tartar would be needed to raise the same cake. A 'delayed action' or 'double action' baking powder is sold in the USA which needs heat as well as moisture to produce carbon dioxide gas. It is not widely known in Europe. The advantage of it is that it can be added to mixtures in advance of baking — it only starts to work once in the oven.

YEAST Cakes caused to rise by the growth of yeast cells are really sweetened enriched breads. They are traditional in East European cookery. Gugelhopf, which appears on p.316 in the chapter on yeast, is a classic example.

PREPARING A CAKE TIN

All tins should be greased before use to prevent the cake mixture from sticking or burning at the edges or bottom. Melted lard or oil are the most suitable fats. Always turn the tin upside down after greasing to allow any excess fat to drain away. Use a paint brush to get a thin layer.

Bread tins and non-stick sandwich tins need no preparation other than greasing. Tins for cakes made by the melting or creaming methods should be greased, then the base lined with greaseproof paper, cut exactly to size and the paper brushed out with more melted lard or oil. (To cut the paper accurately draw round the tin, then cut just inside the line.) For cakes made by the whisking method, a dusting of caster sugar and flour should be given after lining and greasing.

For fruit cakes, grease the tin, then line the sides and base with greaseproof paper as follows:

1 Cut two pieces of greaseproof paper to fit the base of the cake tin.

2 Cut another piece long enough to go right round the sides of the tin and to overlap slightly. It should be 2cm/1 inch deeper than the height of the cake tin.

3 Fold one long edge of this strip over 2cm/1 inch all along its length.

4 Cut snips at right angles to the edge and about 1cm/½inch apart, all along the folded side. The snips should just reach the fold.

5 Grease the tin, place one paper base in the bottom and grease again.

6 Fit the long strip inside the cake tin with the folded cut edge on the

PREPARING A FRUIT CAKE TIN
1 Cut a length of greaseproof paper long enough to encircle the cake tin and overlap slightly.

2 Fold the paper along one side to give a 2cm/1 inch margin. Make small cuts along its length up to the margin line, as shown. Cut 2 circles of greaseproof paper to fit bottom of tin.

3 Brush the tin with melted butter or oil and fit one of the paper circles in the bottom. Brush with butter or oil.

4 Fit the strip of paper around the edge of the tin, allowing the cut flanges to lie flat on the bottom.

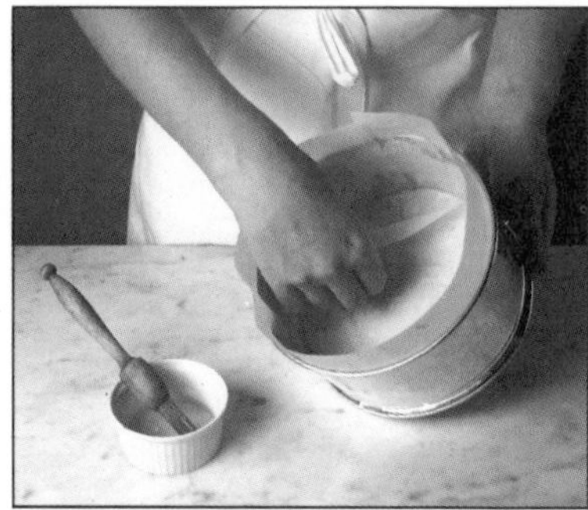

5 Fit the second paper circle in the bottom to keep the cut flanges flat. Brush the side and base of the lined tin with butter or oil.

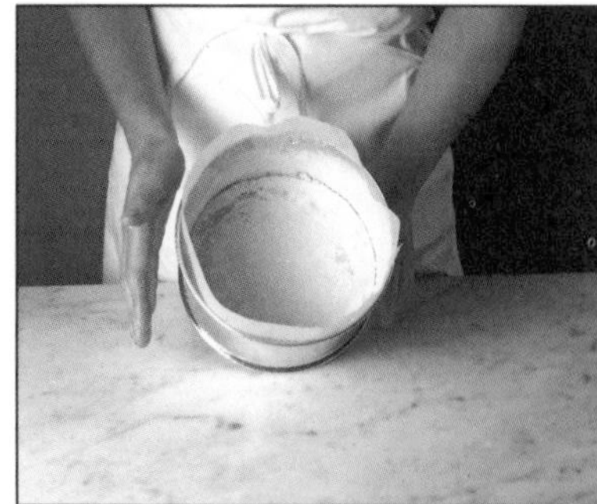

6 Finally, dust the inside of the tin lightly with flour, shaking out any excess.

bottom (the flanges will overlap slightly) and the main uncut part lining the sides of the tin. Press them well into the corners.

7 Grease the paper and lay the second base on top of the first.

8 Brush the base again with more melted lard or oil and dust the lined pan with flour.

There are five methods of cake making, each featured below.

SPECIALIST LESSON 1 A RUBBING-IN METHOD CAKE

The rubbing-in method gives a fairly substantial cake with a crumbly moist texture. The raising agent is always bicarbonate of soda. In this example the agent is in the self-raising flour. The cake is delicious served sliced and spread with butter, or eaten as a warm pudding with custard.

MARMALADE LOAF

INGREDIENTS
225g/8oz self-raising flour
½tsp salt
110g/4oz butter
55g/2oz caster sugar
2 eggs, lightly beaten
3tbsp orange marmalade
3tbsp milk

TO SERVE
Butter

1 Heat the oven to 180°C/350°F/Gas 4.

2 Grease a medium size (675g/1½lb) loaf tin or 15cm/6 inch cake tin or charlotte mould.

3 Sieve the flour and salt into a bowl and rub in the butter: to do this first cut the butter with a knife into tiny dice, and stir them into the flour with a knife, so that each piece is floured and separate. Then using the tips only of well floured fingers, gently rub a few dice at a time to break them up, dropping them back into the flour as soon as they are squashed or crumbled. Keep dipping your fingers into the flour and dropping the butter pieces from a height into the bowl — this both cools them and aerates the mixture. See p.305 for the correct position for the hands.

4 When the mixture resembles coarse breadcrumbs stir in the sugar, eggs, marmalade and milk. Mix well.

5 Turn into the prepared tin and bake for about 55 minutes, or until a skewer inserted into the middle of the cake will emerge clean.

6 Allow to cool in the tin for 10 minutes, then turn out and cool, right side up, on a wire rack.

7 Serve sliced and spread with butter.

SPECIALIST LESSON 2 A MELTING METHOD CAKE

The melting method is used for very moist cakes like gingerbread. The fat, sugar, syrup and any other liquid ingredients are heated together to melt, then they are cooled slightly. The flour and other dry ingredients are sifted together and the warm sugar mixture is stirred, not beaten, into the dry mixture along with the eggs. The raising agent is always bicarbonate of soda. These cakes are the perfect cake for the beginner — easy, reliable and delicious.

GINGERBREAD

INGREDIENTS
110g/4oz preserved ginger
85g/3oz butter
170g/6oz golden syrup
110g/4oz brown sugar
225g/8oz plain flour
1 level tsp ground ginger
½ level tsp salt
150ml/¼pt milk
1 egg, beaten
½ level tsp bicarbonate of soda
½ level tsp cream of tartar

1 Prepare a shallow rectangular cake tin: grease the bottom and sides and then line the bottom with greaseproof paper and grease again. Set the oven to 170°C/325°F/Gas 3.

2 Chop the preserved ginger finely.

3 Melt the butter, syrup and sugar together without boiling.

4 When the sugar has dissolved add the ginger and allow to cool.

5 Sift the flour into a bowl with the ground ginger and salt. Make a well in the centre.

6 Warm the milk and pour it into the egg. Add it to the treacle mixture.

7 Slowly beat the treacle mixture into the flour, pouring a little at a time into the well, and drawing the flour in from the sides as you mix.

8 When all the flour is incorporated in the treacle mixture, stir in the bicarbonate of soda and cream of tartar.

9 Turn the mixture into the prepared tin and bake for about 1 hour. The gingerbread should feel moist and slightly tacky but firm.

10 Let it cool before turning it out. It will keep for about 2 weeks in an airtight container, and freezes perfectly.

SPECIALIST LESSON 3 CREAMING METHOD CAKES

CLASSIC CREAMING METHOD The creaming method, ie the creaming of fat and sugar to a mousse-like consistency (and thereby incorporating air) is the secret of lightness in this type of cake, although a little chemical raising agent is usually added to ensure rising. First the butter or margarine is creamed (beaten) until it is smooth and very light in colour, but the fat is never allowed to melt (if it did the carefully incorporated air beaten into it would escape). The sugar is then beaten in by degrees until the mixture is pale and fluffy.

The eggs are lightly beaten and added, also by degrees, to the creamed mixture. The mix is beaten after each addition to thoroughly incorporate them. At this point the batter can curdle — usually caused by too-cold eggs — but beating in a tablespoon of sifted flour taken from the recipe after each addition of eggs should prevent this. Cakes made from curdled mixtures are acceptable, but they have a less delicate, more open and coarse texture than those made from uncurdled mixture.

Plain flour, if used, should be sifted with the baking powder and salt. Self-raising flour should be sifted with salt. The flour mixture is then folded carefully into the creamed mixture with a metal spoon and with as little mixing as possible to ensure a minimum loss of air in the batter.

VICTORIA SANDWICH CAKE

INGREDIENTS
110g/4oz butter
110g/4oz caster sugar
2 eggs, at room temperature
110g/4oz self-raising flour
Milk, if necessary

1 Set the oven to 190°C/375°F/Gas 5. Lightly oil 2 sandwich tins and line the bottom with greaseproof paper. Brush again with oil.

2 Beat the butter until soft. Add the sugar and beat again until light and creamy. It should look fluffy and pale.

3 Beat the eggs in a separate bowl until smooth. Gradually add the

FOR THE FILLING
Raspberry jam
Icing sugar

beaten egg to the butter mixture, beating well all the time. If the mixture begins to curdle add a little of the flour.

4 Sift the remaining flour and fold it into the cake mixture using a large metal spoon. The mixture should be of dropping consistency. That is, it should drop reluctantly off a spoon. If it sticks obstinately it is too thick. Add enough milk to achieve the correct consistency.

5 Divide the mixture between the tins and bake for 20 minutes or until the cakes are well risen, golden and feel spongy to the fingertips.

6 Allow the cakes to cool for a few minutes in the tins, then turn out onto a wire rack. Remove the baking papers and allow to cool.

7 Sandwich the cakes with the jam. Sift a little icing sugar over the top of the cake.

ALL-IN-ONE CREAMING METHOD The all-in-one method is any easy version of the creaming method, because all the ingredients are beaten together at the same time, but a strong electric mixer is necessary to make these cakes really successfully, and soft 'tub' margarine gives a lighter result than butter.

CHOCOLATE ALL-IN-ONE CAKE

INGREDIENTS
110g/4oz soft butter
110g/4oz caster sugar
2 eggs
30g/1oz cocoa powder, sifted
85g/3oz self-raising flour
Milk, if necessary

FOR THE FILLING
Chocolate butter icing
A little icing sugar

This cake is made with an electric beater.

1 Set the oven to 190°C/375°F/Gas 5. Lightly oil 2 sandwich tins and line the bottom with greaseproof paper. Brush out with oil.

2 Put all the ingredients except the milk into the bowl of a strong electric mixer or processor and beat until smooth. Start beating slowly — otherwise the flour will shoot out of the bowl. Gradually build up speed.

3 The mixture should be of dropping consistency. That is, it should drop reluctantly off a spoon. If it sticks obstinately it is too thick. Add enough milk to achieve the correct consistency.

4 Divide the mixture between the tins and bake for 20 minutes or until the cakes are well risen and feel spongy to the fingertips.

5 Allow to cool for a few minutes in the tins, then turn out onto a wire rack, remove the baking papers and allow to cool completely.

6 Sandwich the cakes with the chocolate butter icing. Dust the top of the cake with a little icing sugar.

CHOCOLATE BUTTER ICING

INGREDIENTS
110g/4oz plain chocolate
55g/2oz unsalted butter
110g/4oz icing sugar, sifted
1 egg yolk

1 Break the chocolate into small, equal sized pieces. Place on a plate and set over a saucepan of simmering water until completely melted.

2 Beat the butter. When soft add sugar. Beat until light and fluffy.

3 Beat in the egg yolk followed by the melted and cooled chocolate.

NOTE If the chocolate is hot when added it will melt the butter, which will then lose the beaten-in air that makes the icing fluffy. This also happens if the butter or icing is beaten too long (and consequently over-heated) in processor. In this case leave till cool and solid, then beat again.

CREAMING METHOD FRUIT CAKE Fruit cakes use another version of the creaming method. Softened butter and sugar are creamed in a mixing bowl to incorporate air. The eggs and any other liquid are gradually beaten into the creamed mixture, with the flour added with the last few additions of egg to reduce the risk of curdling. After the mixture is well combined, the dry fruit is folded in well to distribute it throughout the cake. The mixture should have a soft dropping consistency (it should fall reluctantly off a spoon given a slight shake — neither sticking obstinately nor running off) and be spread out evenly in the prepared tin, with a slight dip in the centre of the mixture to counteract the cake 'peaking'. Because these cakes are generally large and dense and contain a high proportion of fruit (which burns easily), they are cooked extremely slowly. To prevent burning they can be placed on a folded newspaper in the oven and can be covered in several layers of greaseproof or brown paper — but not foil, which traps the steam and produces too doughy a result.

RICH FRUIT CAKE

INGREDIENTS
225g/8oz butter
225g/8oz soft brown sugar
280g/10oz self-raising flour
1tsp salt
4 large eggs, lightly beaten
80g/3oz ground almonds
30g/1oz mixed candied peel
30g/1oz chopped glacé cherries
280g/10oz stoned raisins
280g/10oz sultanas
280g/10oz currants
1tsp mixed spice
290ml/½pt dark beer or stout (For an even richer flavour replace half the beer with rum or brandy)

1 Set the oven to 180°C/350°F/Gas 4. Line a cake tin as described on p.292.

2 Beat the butter and sugar together until light, fluffy and pale in colour. This is easily achieved in a machine. If doing it by hand start with the butter, soft but not melted, and beat hard for a few minutes, then add the sugar and continue for a good 10 minutes more.

3 Sift the flour with the salt and stir it into the butter mixture with the eggs, adding first a spoon of flour, then a spoon of egg, and so on.

4 Now add all the rest of the ingredients, alternating spoons of fruit or dry ingredients with the beer. Once all is in, beat the mixture briefly to ensure even mixing.

5 Turn into the prepared cake tin and bake for 1 hour.

6 Turn the oven down to 150°C/300°F/Gas 2. Cover the cake with a sheet or two of greaseproof paper and bake for a further 3 hours or until a skewer will emerge clean when pushed into the cake.

7 Allow the cake to cool in the tin.

8 Once cold store in an airtight container.

SPECIALIST LESSON 5 WHISKED METHOD CAKES

In the whisking method, the only raising agent is air that has been trapped in the cake batter during mixing. As the air expands in the heat of the oven, the cake rises.

The simplest whisked sponge contains no fat. Sugar and eggs are whisked together until they are thick and light, then flour is folded in gently to keep in as much air as possible. In a lighter but more complicated whisked sponge, the eggs are separated and the yolks are whisked with the sugar and the flour added. The whites are whisked in another bowl, then folded into the batter. Sometimes half the sugar is whisked with the yolks, and half with the whites to give a meringue.

To make these sponges, the sugar and eggs (or egg yolks only) are

WHISKED 'TO THE RIBBON'
A mixture is whisked 'to the ribbon' when a lifted whisk will leave a thick ribbon-like trail on the surface of the mixture.

whisked in a bowl set over a pan of barely simmering water. Make sure that the bowl does not touch the water or the heat will scramble the eggs.

The gentle heat from the steam speeds up the dissolving of the sugar and slightly cooks and thickens the eggs, so encouraging the mixture to hold the maximum number of air bubbles. The mixture should change from yellow to almost white in colour and increase to four times its original volume. The mixture is ready when a lifted whisk will leave a ribbon-like trail. Whisking is traditionally done with a balloon whisk but a hand-held electric one works excellently. If a powerful food mixer is used, the heat can be dispensed with, though this process is speeded up if the mixture is put into a warmed bowl.

When the flour is folded in, great care should be taken to fold rather than stir or beat, as the aim is to incorporate the flour without losing any of the beaten-in air which alone will raise the cake. The correct movement is more of lifting the mixture and cutting into it, rather than stirring it. See p.285.

Although they are light and springy, a drawback to these cakes is that they stale quickly. Always plan to make fatless sponge on the day of serving, or freeze the cake once it is cool.

THE GENOISE is a whisked sponge that has just-runny butter folded into it with the flour. Butter gives it flavour and richness and makes it keep a day or two longer than fatless sponges. A richer genoise cake (Genoise fine) has a greater proportion of butter to flour, and the egg whites are whisked separately and folded in after the butter. The butter for both types of genoise sponges should be poured in a stream around the edge of the bowl and then folded in. If the butter is poured heavily on top of the whisked mixture, it forces out some of the air, and needs excessive mixing, with the danger of loss of more air.

Whisked cakes are cooked when the surface will spring back when pressed with a finger. The cakes should be cooled a few minutes in the tin and then turned out onto a cake rack. The baking paper should be carefully peeled off to allow the escape of steam.

WHISKED SPONGE

This sponge mixture is made without fat.

INGREDIENTS
3 eggs
85g/3oz caster sugar
85g/3oz plain flour
Pinch of salt

FOR THE FILLING
Strawberry jam
Double cream, lightly whipped
Icing sugar

1 Set the oven to 180°C/350°F/Gas 4. Prepare a deep sandwich tin or moule-à-manquer: grease the tin with oil, then line the base with greaseproof paper, cut exactly to size. Brush again with oil. Dust with caster sugar and then flour. Shake out any excess sugar or flour.

2 Place the eggs and sugar in a bowl and fit it over (not in) a saucepan of simmering water. With a balloon whisk (or hand-held electric one) whisk the mixture until it has doubled in bulk and will leave a thick 'ribbon' trail on the surface when the whisk is lifted. Start whisking slowly and gradually build up speed. It is essential that the eggs and sugar are not allowed to get too hot — do not let the water get above simmering point and take care that it does not touch the bowl.

3 Remove the bowl from the heat and whisk occasionally until cool.

4 Sift the flour and salt. With a large metal spoon sprinkle it evenly over the surface of the mixture, then fold it in gently but thoroughly. See p.285 for folding movements.

5 Turn into the prepared tin and bake in the middle of the oven for about 25 to 30 minutes. When the cake is cooked it will be risen and brown with the edges slightly shrunk from the edge of the tin and crinkled. When pressed gently with a finger, it will spring back, and will feel spongy. The cake will sound 'creaky', if held close to the ear.

6 Leave to cool for a few minutes in the tin and then turn out onto a wire rack. Remove the greaseproof paper and leave to cool.

7 Split in half with a large sharp bread knife. Spread the bottom half with jam and spoon on the cream. Sandwich together again. Dust the top of the cake with a little icing sugar.

GENOISE COMMUNE

INGREDIENTS
4 eggs
125g/4½oz caster sugar
125g/4½oz plain flour
Pinch of salt
55g/2oz very soft but not melted butter

1 Set the oven to 190°C/375°F/Gas 5. Prepare a moule-à-manquer or deep sandwich tin as shown.

2 Place the eggs and sugar in a bowl and fit it over (not in) a saucepan of simmering water. With a balloon whisk (or hand-held electric one) whisk until the mixture has doubled in bulk, and will leave a thick 'ribbon' trail. Start whisking slowly, and gradually build up speed.

3 Remove the bowl from the heat and whisk occasionally until cool.

4 Sift the flour with the salt and dust it evenly and lightly over the egg mixture. Fold it in gently with a large metal spoon. (See p.285.)

5 Beat the butter until it is soft enough to be just liquid without being clear or melted. It should still be opaque and have the consistency of half-whipped cream. Pour it as thinly as possible round the edge of the bowl. (Dumping it in a lump on the surface requires too much mixing and consequent loss of air.) Fold in gently.

6 Pour the mixture into the prepared tin. Bake for 30 - 35 minutes. The cake is cooked when risen and golden brown, with the edges slightly shrunk from the tin edge and crinkled. The surface will feel spongy and will spring back when pressed with a finger and the cake will sound 'creaky' if held close to the ear.

7 Cool for a few minutes in the tin and then turn out onto a wire rack. Remove the greaseproof paper and leave to cool.

GENOISE COMMUNE
1 Cut a circle of greaseproof paper to fit the base of the tin. Brush the tin with oil or melted lard.

2 Put the greaseproof paper in the tin and brush with oil or lard.

3 Dust evenly all over with caster sugar. Shake off the excess. Then dust with plain flour and again shake out the excess.

4 Place eggs and sugar in a bowl over simmering water. Whisk the eggs and sugar together, slowly at first, then gradually build up speed.

5 Whisk until the mixture has doubled in bulk and will leave a thick ribbon behind when the whisk is lifted. Remove from the heat and whisk occasionally until cool.

6 Dust the flour and salt over, keeping the sieve as close to the egg and sugar mixture as possible.

7 Fold in the flour with a large metal spoon. Turn the bowl with your left hand and use a three-dimensional figure-of-eight movement to ensure an even fold.

8 Pour in the softened butter around the edge of the bowl. Fold in gently. Pour into the prepared tin and bake for 30 to 35 minutes.

9 Leave to cool on a wire rack. Remove the greaseproof paper and cut the cake in half with a bread knife.

NOTE The cake may be split and filled as Whisked sponge (p.297), filled and iced with either of the following butter creams or eaten plain.

CREME AU BEURRE MOUSSELINE

A rich, creamy cake filling.

INGREDIENTS
55g/2oz granulated sugar
4tbsp water
2 egg yolks
Grated rind of ½ lemon
110g/4oz unsalted butter

1 Dissolve the sugar in the water and when completely clear, boil rapidly to about 105°C/215°F. At this point the syrup, if tested between finger and thumb, will form short threads. Take off the heat immediately.

2 Whisk the yolks and lemon rind and pour on the syrup. Keep whisking until thick and cool.

3 Soften (but do not melt) the butter and whisk into the mixture slowly. Allow to cool.

CREME AU BEURRE MERINGUE

A light soft frosting for cakes.

INGREDIENTS
2 egg whites
110g/4oz icing sugar
170g/6oz unsalted butter

1 Put the egg whites with the sugar into a mixing bowl and set it over a pan of simmering water. Whisk until the meringue is thick and will hold its shape. Remove from the heat and whisk until slightly cooled.

SUGGESTED FLAVOURINGS
Grated lemon or orange rind
Melted chocolate
Coffee essence

2 In a large bowl beat the butter until soft and gradually beat in the meringue mixture.

3 Flavour to taste as required.

CHOCOLATE FEATHER SPONGE CAKE WITH CHESTNUTS

INGREDIENTS
3 eggs, separated
Pinch of cream of tartar
200g/7oz caster sugar
50ml/2fl oz vegetable oil
1tsp vanilla flavouring
75ml/3fl oz water
110g/4oz plain flour
30g/1oz cocoa powder
¼tsp baking powder
½tsp salt

FOR THE FILLING
290g/½pt double cream
8 marrons glacés or chestnuts in syrup
1tbsp icing sugar

TO SERVE
Hot chocolate sauce

This cake is a non-classic whisked one and can be made by hand, but is time- and labour-intensive. With the help of an electric whisk and a food processor or liquidizer, it is simplicity itself. It can be served plainly dusted with icing sugar for tea, or as a pudding with a chestnut cream filling and hot chocolate sauce. It is interesting because a variety of raising methods are used: a meringue is made with the egg whites (the acid cream of tartar being added to improve volume); a mousse-like emulsion is made with the oil and yolks; the powder ingredients are sifted to aerate them; and a tiny quantity of baking powder is added to guarantee lightness.

1 Set the oven to 190°C/375°F/Gas 5.

2 Separate the eggs.

3 Put the egg whites and pinch of cream of tartar into a bowl and whisk until they will hold their shape, then add about half the sugar and whisk until stiff and glossy. (This is only possible with an electric whisk. In the absence of one, whisk the whites to stiff peak (see p.285) and fold in the sugar carefully without further beating.)

4 Put the egg yolks with the oil, vanilla flavouring and water into the processor or liquidizer and beat until creamy, pale and smooth. If doing this by hand, use a balloon whisk and beat well.

5 Sift the flour, cocoa, baking powder and salt together and stir in the rest of the sugar. Add to the liquid mixture and whisk until smooth.

PIPING

Piping mixtures into patterns is easily mastered with a little practice. Problems arise when the bag is held at too much of an angle, or too far away from the dish or cake top, or if there are air bubbles in the bag. Wearing rubber gloves while piping provides excellent insulation which prevents ice cream mixtures or cream melting, or very hot mixtures burning the hands.

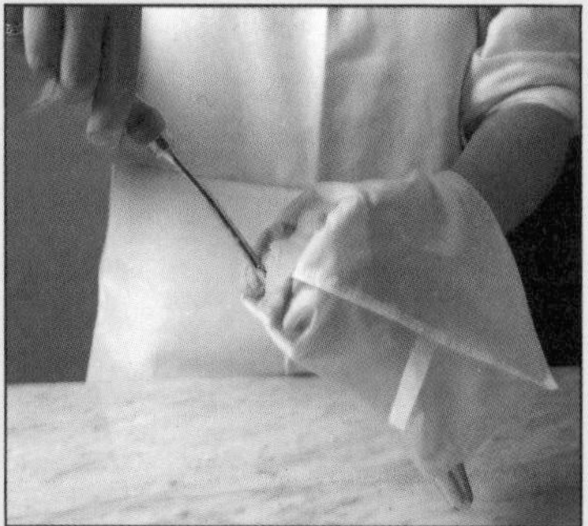

FOR PERFECT PIPING
1 Turn the piping bag over the whisk like a cuff so that you can easily spoon the piping mixture into the bottom of the bag. Do not overfill.

2 Press the mixture down into the bag slowly to eliminate any airpockets.

6 Fold into the meringue mixture.

7 Turn carefully into an ungreased 20cm/8 inch angel cake or tube tin, or ring tin, or into a loose bottomed 22cm/9 inch cake tin, prepared as for whisked cakes (p.298).

8 Bake for 50 minutes or until the cake has slightly shrunk from the sides of the tin and feels springy to the touch.

9 Allow to cool and shrink in the tin, then turn out and transfer to a cooling rack. Do not attempt to turn it out before it is cool — it will stick and break.

10 Whip the cream stiffly. Chop three of the chestnuts roughly. Mix into the cream.

11 Split the cake horizontally with a bread knife and carefully remove the top layer. Use half the whipped cream to sandwich the two layers together, and fill the central hole with the rest. (If the cake has been made in an ordinary, rather than ring shaped, tin use all the cream to sandwich it.)

12 Sift the icing sugar over the top of the cake, and decorate with the remaining five whole candied chestnuts.

13 Serve the sauce separately if the cake is to be eaten as a pudding.

HOT CHOCOLATE SAUCE

INGREDIENTS
3tbsp cocoa powder
290ml/½pt water
2tsp cornflour
3tbsp golden syrup

1 Mix the cocoa powder with 2tbsp water in a saucepan until smooth.

2 In a cup mix the cornflour with 1tbsp water until smooth.

3 Add the syrup and water and slaked cornflour to the pan and stir until boiling.

3 Twist the bag to prevent the mixture squeezing up; this also makes holding the bag easy.

4 Support the nozzle end with the fingertips of one hand and, holding the nozzle close to the surface to decorated, gently press the full bag with the fingers of the other.

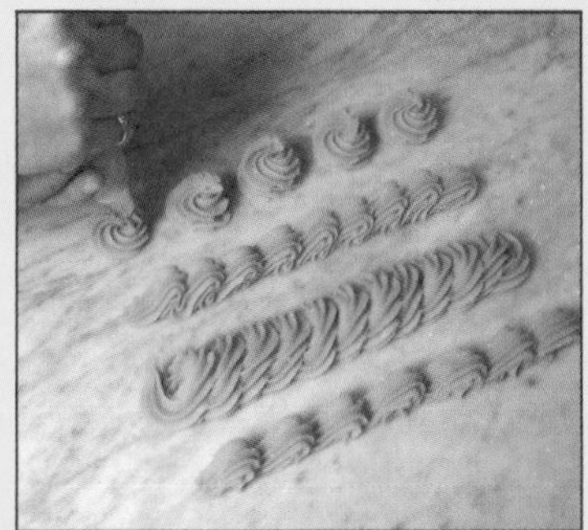

5 Keep the nozzle fairly low and the bag almost upright as you guide it. Very little practise makes perfect.

BISCUITS

Biscuits, called cookies in the United States from a Dutch word meaning 'little cakes', are rich baked pastry-like mixtures, usually small enough to be eaten in a mouthful or two. Cold fat, usually butter but sometimes butter and margarine, is rubbed into plain flour and any other dry ingredients. Because of their richness, biscuit doughs need little liquid other than, possibly, an egg or a drop or two of flavouring or, for certain biscuits, syrup or honey. Always follow the recipe carefully as it is the proportion of ingredients that gives a finished biscuit its texture.

MAKING BISCUITS

As with pastry, cool hands and a firm but quick touch produce the lightest biscuits. Overworking causes the fat to melt, producing a greasy uneven-textured biscuit.

When rolling out the biscuit dough do not work in too much flour as this will alter the proportions of flour to fat. But to facilitate the stamping out of shapes do dip the biscuit cutter in flour first. It is best to bake the biscuits on a baking sheet or on a shallow-sided baking tray to allow the heat to reach the biscuits evenly. Because of the richness of the dough, the sheet does not usually need greasing, but the sheet itself should be cool so the biscuits do not melt and immediately lose their shape when they are put on the baking sheet. Biscuits containing cheese, which burns easily (eg cheese straws see p.310), should be baked on a piece of greaseproof paper. The paper will protect the bottom and edges of the dough from the fierce heat of the metal and prevent them burning.

Time the baking carefully and check that the biscuits are cooking evenly, for they burn quickly. As soon as the biscuits are cooked, transfer them with a palette knife to a cooling rack so that they cool apart and keep their shape. Many biscuits emerge from the oven still doughy and soft in the centre, and become crisp on cooling. Do not store until stone cold. Most biscuits keep well for several days — sometimes for weeks — in an airtight container.

SPECIALIST LESSON 1 *FLAPJACKS*

INGREDIENTS
110g/4oz butter
110g/4oz demerara sugar
110g/4oz golden syrup
225g/8oz rolled porridge oats
Oil for greasing

This recipe is simplicity itself. The mixture is simply baked in a shallow Swiss roll tin, then cut into bars while still warm and soft from the oven. It hardens as it cools.

1 Set the oven to 180°C/350°F/Gas 4. Grease a Swiss roll tin lightly.

2 Melt the butter, sugar and syrup together. Pour onto the oats and mix well.

3 Press into the greased tin with the flat of your hand making sure that the middle is no higher than the edges and that there are no air spaces.

4 Bake for 20 minutes or until golden brown.

5 Cool for 5 minutes, then cut into fingers and loosen the edges. Leave to cool in the tin.

6 Store for up to a week in an airtight container.

SPECIALIST LESSON 2 PEANUT BUTTER COOKIES

INGREDIENTS (makes about 60 biscuits)
140g/5oz butter
110g/4oz caster sugar
110g/4oz soft brown sugar
1 large egg, beaten
110g/4oz crunchy peanut butter
½tsp vanilla flavouring
200g/7oz plain flour
½tsp salt
1tsp baking powder

This recipe is slightly more time consuming than the first, but not at all difficult. The technique of rolling the mixture into small balls and flattening with a fork is common to many biscuit recipes.

1 Heat the oven to 180°C/350°F/Gas 4.

2 Cream the butter and both sugars together until smooth and soft. Beat in the egg, then the peanut butter, and add the vanilla.

3 Sift the flour with the salt and the baking powder into the mixture and stir until smooth. Do not over-beat or the dough will be oily.

4 Roll the mixture into small balls with the fingers and place well apart on three ungreased baking sheets. Flatten with the prongs of a fork.

5 Bake for 10 - 15 minutes, to an even, not too dark, brown.

6 While hot, ease off the baking sheets with a palette knife or fish slice and cool on a wire rack. Once stone cold and crisp, store in an airtight container.

PEANUT BUTTER COOKIES
1 Roll the dough into small balls and place well apart on the baking sheet.

2 Flatten the balls by pressing firmly with the prongs of a fork.

1

2

SPECIALIST LESSON 3 ICED BISCUITS

INGREDIENTS (makes about 40 biscuits)
110g/4oz unsalted butter
110g/4oz caster sugar
1 egg, beaten
A few drops vanilla flavouring
280g/10oz plain flour
Pinch of salt

FOR THE GLACE ICING
225g/8oz icing sugar
Boiling water
Colouring (optional)

This is a classic rich iced biscuit, the dough rolled out and stamped into shapes with a biscuit cutter.

1 Set the oven to 190°C/375°F/Gas 5.

2 Beat the butter and when soft, add the sugar and beat again until light and fluffy. Gradually beat in the egg. Add the vanilla flavouring.

3 Sift the flour with the salt and mix it into the butter, sugar and egg.

4 Roll the paste out thinly (about the thickness of a heavy coin) and stamp into rounds with a cutter. Place on an ungreased baking sheet.

5 Bake for 8 - 10 minutes until just beginning to brown at the edges. Leave to cool on a wire rack.

6 Make the glacé icing: Sift the icing sugar into a bowl. Add enough boiling water to mix to a fairly stiff consistency.

7 Colour the icing as required.

8 Spoon the icing smoothly and evenly over the top of the biscuit. Leave to dry and harden.

PASTRY

Pastry comes in many forms. All of them are made from a mixture of flour and liquid, and usually contain fat. Variations in quantities and the ingredients themselves give each type its distinctive texture and taste.

The three commonest types of pastry are short (or crumbly), flaky, and choux pastry, all of which have variations. The degree of shortness (or crisp crumbliness) depends on the amount and type of fat (the shortening factor) incorporated into the flour and the way in which the uncooked pastry, or 'paste', is handled.

THE INGREDIENTS

FATS: BUTTER gives a crisp, rich shortcrust pastry with excellent flavour. SOLID MARGARINE gives a similar result which is slightly less rich and flavourful. LARD gives very short but rather tasteless pastry. It gives excellent results when used with butter. Solid cooking fat and vegetable shortening give a crust similar to lard. SUET is only used in suet crust, which is a soft and rather heavy pastry. A raising agent is usually added to the flour to combat the pastry's doughiness, and to make it more cake-like in texture.

FLOUR in shortcrust pastry is usually plain, all-purpose flour. Weak or cake flour is also suitable for pastry making. Wholemeal flour produces a delicious, nutty flavoured crust, but is more absorbent than white flour and will need more liquid, which makes it harder and heavier. For this reason, a mixture of wholewheat and white flour, usually half and half, is generally used to make 'wholemeal' pastry. Self-raising flour is occasionally used in pastry making. It produces a soft, thicker, more cakey crust. It is also sometimes used to lighten cheese dough and other heavy pastes like suet crust. Whatever the flour, it should be sifted, even if it has no lumps in it, to incorporate air and give the pastry lightness.

LIQUID The less used in pastry making the better. Some very rich doughs, such as almond pastry, which contains a high proportion of butter and eggs, can be kneaded without any water or milk at all. Others need a little liquid to bind them. Water gives the pastry crispness and firmness. Too much makes pastry easy to handle but gives a concrete hard crust that shrinks in the oven. The addition of egg or egg white instead of water will give a firm but not hard crust. Egg yolk on its own produces a rich, soft and crumbly crust.

MAKING PASTRY

RUBBING IN Shortcrust pastry is made by rubbing fat into sifted flour and other dry ingredients with the fingertips — then adding other ingredients such as egg yolks and any liquid. Everything should be kept as cool as possible. If the fat melts, the finished pastry may be tough. Cut the fat, which should be firm and cold straight from the refrigerator, into tiny pieces using a small knife and floured fingers. The flour prevents the fat from sticking to the fingers and beginning to melt, and the smaller the pieces of fat, the better the chances of even distribution.

Mix the pieces of fat into the flour, then rub in, handling the fat as quickly and lightly as possible so the fat does not stick to the fingertips. Keep them well floured to facilitate this. Pick up a few pieces of floury fat and plenty of flour with the fingertips and thumbs of both hands. Hold your hands about 25cm/10 inches above the bowl, thumbs up and little

RUBBING FAT INTO FLOUR
Using the fingertips and thumbs of both hands, rub the fat into the flour as lightly and quickly as possible. The fingertips should be kept well floured to ensure that the fat does not stick to them. Continue rubbing in until the mixture looks like coarse breadcrumbs.

fingers down, and gently and quickly rub the little pieces of fat into the flour, squashing the fat lightly as you go. See illustration. Do not try to mash each piece of fat; a breadcrumb texture, not doughy lumps, is what is wanted. Drop the floury flakes of fat from a height; this cools the fat and aerates it, making the finished pastry lighter. Shake the bowl regularly so that the big unrubbed pieces of fat come to the surface. When the mixture looks like very coarse — not fine — breadcrumbs, stop.

ADDING LIQUID Rich shortcrust pastry (with a higher proportion of fat) needs little if any water added. Although over-moist pastry is easy to handle and roll out, the baked crust will be tough and may well shrink in the oven as the water evaporates in the heat. The drier and more difficult to handle the pastry is, the crisper the shortcrust will be.

Add only as much water as is needed to get the pastry to hold together, and sprinkle it, a teaspoonful at a time, over as large a surface as possible.

MIXING Mixing should be kept to a minimum. Mix the pastry with a fork or knife so you handle it as little as possible. As soon as it holds together in lumps, stop mixing. Lightly flour your hands and quickly and gently gather into a ball, rolling it around the bowl to pick up crumbs.

RELAXING It is important to chill pastry for at least half an hour before rolling it out, or at least before baking. This allows cells to swell and absorb the liquid evenly. 'Relaxed' pastry will not shrink drastically or unevenly as just-made pastry will. Most pastries benefit from chilling, especially in hot weather, or if they are used to line tart tins, when shrinkage can spell disaster. Relaxing is less important, though still a good idea, for pastes used to cover pies. To prevent the surface of the pastry from drying out and cracking in the dry atmosphere of the refrigerator, cover it lightly with clingfilm or a damp cloth.

ROLLING OUT *Lightly* dust the work surface with flour. Do not use much as this can alter the proportion of flour to the other ingredients. Once rolled, allow the pastry to relax in a cool place before baking, especially if it was not relaxed before rolling out.

TYPES OF PASTRY

For *CLASSIC SHORTCRUST* see p.168, for *RICH SHORTCRUST* see p.192, for *SWEET PASTRY* see p.310.

SUET CRUST PASTRY

This is made like shortcrust pastry except that the fat (suet) is generally chopped or shredded before use. Because self-raising flour (or plain flour and baking powder) is used in order to produce a less heavy, doughy pastry, it is important to cook the pastry soon after making while the raising agent is at its most active. During cooking the raising agent causes the dough to puff up and rise slightly and as the paste hardens during cooking, air will be trapped. This makes the suet crust lighter and more bread-like. See p.79 for suet crust.

PATE SUCREE (p.156), *ALMOND PASTRY AND PATE A PATE*

These and other very rich pastries are extreme forms of rich shortcrust — with all the liquid replaced by fat or eggs. Traditionally they are made by working the egg yolks and fat, and sometimes sugar, together, using the fingertips, until soft and creamy. See p.156. The flour is then gradually incorporated until a soft, very rich paste is achieved.

To mix the paste, use only the fingertips of one hand. (Using both hands, or the whole hand, leads to sticky pastry and the cook getting, literally, into a mess.) The warmth of the fingertips is important for softening the fat, but once that is done the mixing and kneading should be as light and quick as possible. Because of the high proportion of fat, no water is added. A buttery, friable and delicate textured rich pastry results.

Modern processors have enabled the most unskilled cook to make these pastries in seconds. Simply put all the ingredients (the fat in smallish pieces) into the machine and process until the paste forms a ball. This may take a minute or so — the mixture first becomes crumbly, then as it warms up the butter softens and largish lumps appear. When these are gathered into one or two cohesive lumps the paste is made. Do not over-process as the paste will become sticky and taste greasy.

These pastries become crisp as they cool. When biscuit coloured and cooked they will feel soft in the centre. When completely cool, slide off the baking sheet using a palette knife.

PROCESSOR PASTRY

1 Put the fat (cut into lumps) into the bowl with the flour and any liquid if used. When processed the mixture will first go crumbly. At this stage, it is suitable for use as a crumble topping.

2 Continue processing until the crumbs are gathered into one lump in the bowl. The mixture is now suitable for pastry. Take care not to overprocess the paste.

1

2

HOT WATER CRUST

This is made by heating water and fat together and mixing them into the flour. Because of the high proportion of water, this pastry is inclined to be hard. Its strength and firmness allows it to encase heavy mixtures, such as English pork pie, without collapsing. Also, as the fat used is generally lard, the pastry can lack flavour, so add a good spoon of salt. Many old recipes recommend throwing the pastry away uneaten once it has done its duty as container. Our recipe for Veal and ham pie (p.178) is a better-tasting modification of hot water crust, containing butter and egg.

Do not allow the water to boil before the fat has melted. If the water reduces by boiling, the proportion of water to flour will not be correct.

Quickly mix the water and melted fat into the flour in a warm bowl, then keep it covered with a hot damp cloth. This prevents the fat from becoming set and the pastry flaking and drying out.

CHOUX PASTRY

Like Yorkshire pudding batter, this pastry contains water and eggs and depends on the rising of the steam within it to produce a puffy hollow pastry case. It is easy to make if the recipe is followed closely. The following points are particularly important:

1 Measure ingredients exactly. Proportions are important with choux.

2 Do not allow the water to boil until the butter has melted, but when it has, bring it immediately to a full rolling boil. Boiling the water too soon will cause too much evaporation.

3 Have the sifted flour ready in a bowl so that the minute the rolling

boil is achieved, you can tip in the flour, all in one go.

4 Beat fast and vigorously to get rid of lumps before they cook hard.

5 Do not over-beat. Stop once the mixture is leaving the sides of the pan.

6 Cool slightly before adding egg — otherwise you'll scramble them.

7 Do not beat in more egg than is necessary to achieve a dropping consistency. If the mixture is too stiff, the pastry will be stodgy. If it is too thin, it will rise unevenly into shapeless lumps.

8 Bake until it is a good even brown, otherwise the inside of the pastry will be uncooked.

9 If the pastry is to be served cold, split the buns/rings, or poke a hole in each of them with a skewer to allow the steam inside to escape. If steam remains trapped inside, the pastry will be soggy and a little heavy. Opened-up pastry or small buns with holes in them can be returned to the oven, hole uppermost, to dry out further.

10 Serve the pastry on the day it is made (or store frozen), as it stales rapidly. See p.109 for Chocolate profiteroles recipe; see also the illustrations on that page.

FLAKY PASTRY AND PUFF PASTRY

These are made rather like the first stage for preparing shortcrust pastry, though the consistency of these pastries is initially softer and less 'short', containing a high proportion of water. Then more fat, either in a solid block or small pieces, is incorporated into the paste, which is rolled, folded and re-rolled several times. This process creates layers of pastry which, in the heat of the oven, will rise into light thin leaves. For instance, puff pastry, which is folded in three and rolled out six times, will have 729 layers.

As the whole aim is to create the layers without allowing the incorporated fat to melt, start with everything cool, including the bowl, the ingredients and even the worktop if possible. Short, quick strokes (rather than long steady ones) allow the bubbles of air so carefully incorporated in the pastry to move about while the fat is gradually and evenly distributed in the paste. Work lightly and do not stretch the paste — or the layers you have built up will tear and allow the air and fat to escape. Chill the pastry between rollings or at any point if there is a danger of the fat breaking through the pastry, or if the pastry becomes sticky and warm. It sounds like a complicated business, but it is a lot easier done than said — follow the instructions on p.85 (puff pastry), p.207 (rough puff pastry) and p.308 (flaky pastry).

Pastry rises evenly to a crisp crust in a steamy atmosphere. For this reason flaky and puff pastries (which are expected to rise in the oven) are generally baked with a roasting tin full of water at the bottom of the oven, or on a wet baking sheet. The oven temperature is set high to cause rapid expansion of the trapped layers of air and quick cooking of the dough before the fat has time to melt and run out.

STRUDEL PASTRY

This differs from most other pastries in that it actually benefits from heavy handling. It is beaten and stretched, thumped and kneaded. This treatment allows the gluten to expand and promotes elasticity in the dough. The paste is rolled and stretched on a cloth (the bigger the better) until it is so thin that you should be able to read fine print through it. Keep the paste covered and moist when not in use. When the pastry is pulled out, brush it with butter or oil to prevent it cracking and drying, or keep it covered with a damp cloth. Strudel pastry can be bought in ready rolled leaves from specialist food shops, especially Greek-owned ones. Called 'phyllo' or 'filo' pastry, it is used to make the Middle Eastern baklava. Detailed instructions for strudel paste appear on p.76.

Almost all the classic pastries are taught in the Menu Lessons. Below are a few that are not. Read the relevant notes on the type of pastry you are tackling before starting, then follow the instructions religiously. Good pastry is almost sure to result.

SPECIALIST LESSON 1 *ALMOND PASTRY*

INGREDIENTS
110g/4oz plain flour
Pinch of salt
45g/1½oz ground almonds
45g/1½oz caster sugar
1 egg yolk OR ½ egg, beaten
2 drops vanilla flavouring
85g/3oz unsalted butter, softened

Care must be taken when making this pastry because if it is over-kneaded the oil will run from the almonds and make it greasy.

1 Sift the flour with the salt onto a board or tabletop. Scatter over the ground almonds. Make a large well in the centre and put in the sugar, beaten egg or yolk and vanilla flavouring.

2 Using one hand only 'peck' the egg and sugar with your fingertips. (See p.156.) When creamy, add the softened butter and continue to mix, gradually drawing in the flour and almonds.

3 Knead gently to a paste and chill. Allow to relax for 30 minutes before baking.

SPECIALIST LESSON 2 *PATE A PATE*

INGREDIENTS
225g/8oz plain flour
Pinch of salt
140g/5oz butter
2 small egg yolks
Up to 3tbsp water

1 Sift the flour and salt onto a board or tabletop. Make a large well in the centre and put the butter and yolks in it. 'Peck' the yolks and butter together with the fingers of one hand and gradually draw in the surrounding flour (see p.156), adding the water only if required to give a soft but not sticky paste.

2 Wrap and leave to rest in the refrigerator for 30 minutes. Use as required.

SPECIALIST LESSON 3 *FLAKY PASTRY*

INGREDIENTS
225g/8oz plain flour
Pinch of salt
85g/3oz butter
150ml/¼pt cold water
85g/3oz lard

1 Sift the flour with a pinch of salt. Rub in half the butter. Add enough cold water to mix with a knife to a doughy consistency. Turn out onto a floured board and knead until smooth.

2 Roll into an oblong about 12×25cm/5×10 inches. Cut half the lard into tiny pieces and dot them evenly all over the top two thirds of the pastry, leaving a good margin.

3 Fold the pastry in three as illustrated.

4 Repeat the rolling and folding process (without adding any fat) once more so that the folded, closed edge is on your left.

5 Roll out again, dot with butter as before, fold and seal as before.

MAKING FLAKY PASTRY
1 Sift the flour and the salt. Rub in half the butter with your hands. Add enough water to bind the mixture. Knead until smooth.

2 Roll the pastry into a rectangle and dot the top two-thirds with small pieces of lard. Fold the pastry in three. Fold the unlarded third up, then the top larded third down.

3 Press the edges well to seal them. This prevents the fat escaping during rolling.

4 Turn the pastry through ninety degrees and roll it flat again.

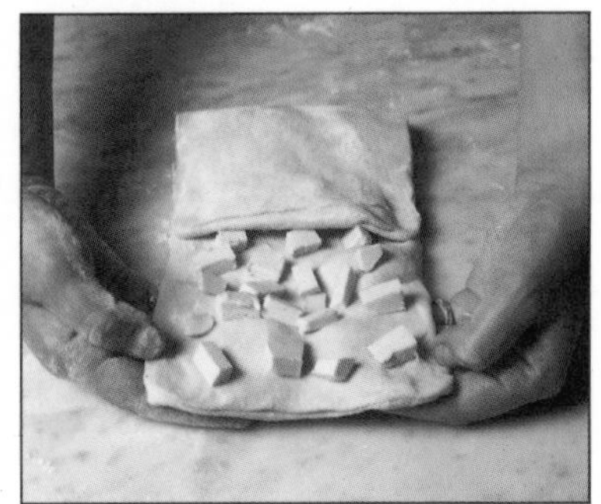

5 Once you've rolled the pastry out into a rectangle again, dot with butter and fold as before. Turn and dot with the remaining lard. Fold, seal and roll once more.

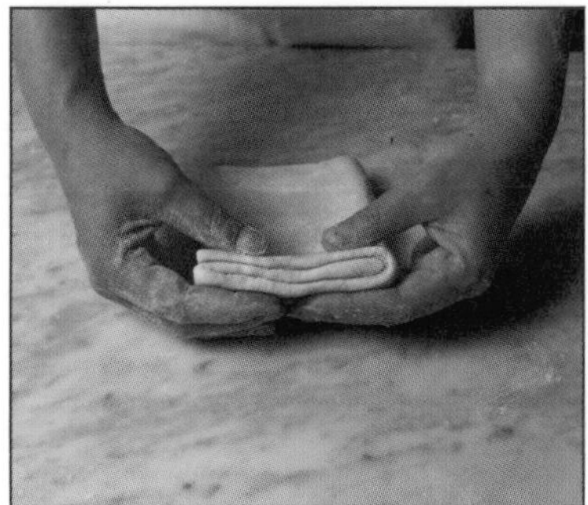

6 Leave to chill for 15 minutes. Roll and fold once more.

6 Roll out again, dot with the rest of the lard, fold, seal and roll once more.

7 Fold, wrap the pastry and 'relax' (or chill) for 10-15 minutes.

8 Roll and fold once again (without adding any fat) and then use as required.

NOTE 1 As a general rule flaky pastry is rolled out thinly, and baked at about 220°C/425°F/Gas 7.

NOTE 2 If the pastry becomes too warm or sticky and difficult to handle, wrap it up and chill it for 15 minutes before proceeding.

SPECIALIST LESSON 4 *WHOLEMEAL PASTRY*

INGREDIENTS
140g/5oz butter
110g/4oz wholemeal flour
110g/4oz plain flour
Pinch of salt
1 egg yolk
Water

1 Rub the butter into the flours and salt until the mixture looks like coarse breadcrumbs. (See p.305.)

2 Mix the yolk with 2tbsp water and add to the mixture.

3 Mix to a firm dough — first with a knife and then with one hand. It may be necessary to add more water, but the pastry should not be too damp. (Although crumbly pastry is more difficult to handle, it produces a shorter, less tough result.)

4 Chill in the refrigerator for at least 30 minutes before using, or allow the rolled-out pastry to relax before baking.

NOTE To make sweet wholemeal pastry, mix in 2 level tbsp sugar once the fat has been rubbed into the flour.

SPECIALIST LESSON 5 *SWEET PASTRY*

INGREDIENTS
170g/6oz plain flour
Large pinch of salt
½tsp baking powder
100g/3½oz unsalted butter
55g/2oz caster sugar
1 egg yolk
55ml/2fl oz double cream

This pastry is suitable for fruit flans etc.

1 Sift the flour, salt and baking powder into a large bowl.

2 Rub in the butter until the mixture looks like coarse breadcrumbs. Stir in the sugar.

3 Mix the egg yolk with the cream and add to the mixture.

4 Mix to a firm dough—first with a knife and finally with one hand. Chill, wrapped, for 30 minutes before using; or allow to relax after rolling out but before baking.

SPECIALIST LESSON 6 *CHEESE STRAWS*

INGREDIENTS (Makes 30)
170g/6oz self-raising flour
Pinch of salt
85g/3oz butter
55g/2oz grated Parmesan and Gruyère cheese
1 egg yolk
Salt and pepper
Pinch of cayenne pepper
Pinch of dry English mustard
Beaten egg

This pastry uses self-raising flour. The raising agent lightens pastry that might otherwise be slightly heavy, on account of the cheese.

1 Set the oven to 190°C/375°F/Gas 5.

2 Sift the flour into a basin with a pinch of salt. Rub the butter into the flour until the mixture looks like coarse breadcrumbs. Add the grated cheese, egg yolk, salt, pepper, cayenne and mustard. Mix to a stiff dough with the beaten egg. Chill for 15 minutes.

3 Line a baking sheet with greaseproof paper. Roll the paste into a large rectangle and cut into strips about 1cm/½ inch wide. Twist each strip two or three times like a barley sugar stick and press the ends down on the paper firmly to prevent unravelling.

4 Bake for 10-15 minutes. They should be biscuit brown. Leave to cool on a wire rack.

CHEESE STRAWS
Bake any mixture with a high cheese content — and therefore likely to burn — on greaseproof paper. If twisting the cheese straws, press the ends down firmly to prevent unravelling.

BREAD, BUNS AND SCONES

Almost all cooks would agree that yeast-cookery is a particularly satisfying craft. Whether it is the homely folk-memory of floury-handed Grandma kneading and slapping, or the noble notion that one is producing the staff of life, of the fascination or the magically rising dough, or just the unequalled smell of baking bread, yeast-cookery once embarked on is seldom abandoned. Breadmakers tend to make bread for the rest of their days, even if only very occasionally, just to recapture the reliable pleasure of it.

But for all its inherent romance, baking is a very practical, chemical, logical business, and the better the cook understands the process, the better the bread will be.

YEAST

Bakers' yeast, the most usual leavening agent for bread, is a one-celled organism that thrives in warm, moist conditions in sweet and starchy food. There, it reproduces spectacularly fast, giving off carbon dioxide gas. In baking mixtures, this is trapped.

Brewers' yeast, used in wine and beermaking, is not suitable for baking. Bakers' yeast is available 'compressed' and as 'active dried yeast'.

FRESH YEAST should be beige, crumbly-soft and sweet-smelling. It is usually thought of as the most satisfactory form of bakers' yeast as it is less likely to produce 'beery' bread. Fresh yeast keeps for 5 days or so, wrapped loosely in the refrigerator and can be frozen for short periods though results after freezing are unpredictable. If it is difficult to obtain, use dried yeast, or buy fresh yeast in a suitable quantity, divide it into 30g/1oz pieces, wrap them individually, then overwrap and freeze. Use as soon as the yeast thaws, and do not keep frozen more than a month.

DRIED YEAST is bought in granular form in airtight sachets. It will remain active for about six months in a cool dry place. If substituting dried for fresh yeast when following a recipe, halve the weight of yeast called for. Dried yeast takes slightly longer to work than fresh yeast, and must be first 'sponged' in liquid, partly to reconstitute it, partly to check that it is still active. To avoid any beery taste, use rather less than the estimated amount of dried yeast and allow a long rising and proving time. Using too much yeast generally means too fast a rise, resulting in bread with a coarse texture that makes the loaf stale quickly.

'EASY BLEND' DRIED YEAST is mixed directly with the flour, not reconstituted in liquid first. Sold in small airtight packages, it is also usually included in bought bread mixtures. One 7.5g/¼oz package usually equals 15g/½oz conventional dried yeast or 30g/1oz fresh yeast.

Yeast grows best in gentle warmth. Cold or draughts slow its growth, while strong heat kills it. The amount of yeast used in a recipe depends on the richness of the dough, the rising time allowed and the method of mixing. In ordinary bread dough, less yeast is needed when the dough is given a long slow rise — by far the best method for good bread. Conversely bread doughs given little time to rise, such as pizza base, contain more yeast. In enriched dough, eg for Danish pastries, which contain more sugar and a high proportion of fat, more yeast is needed, and the yeasted dough is kept cool and rises slowly.

FLOUR

Flour is the main ingredient in bread. It is differences in the flours used that largely account for the variety of breads. Wheat flour is the most common because it contains a large amount of gluten, a form of protein which absorbs liquid to produce elastic strands in the dough. As the yeast works, it gives off carbon dioxide which is trapped in the expanding dough, making it rise and puff up. When the loaf is cooked and set rigidly, the gas leaks out and is replaced by air.

Rye, maize, millet and other flours contain less (and different kinds of) gluten to that in wheat flour. Because these flours lack the essential elasticity of wheat gluten, some wheat flour is usually added to the dough to produce a light textured, well risen loaf.

Even wheat flours have differences that make some of them more suitable for bread making than others.

WHITE FLOUR is ground from wheat with the outer bran and inner germ removed, leaving 70-75 per cent of the original wheat. Removing the wheatgerm means the flour keeps longer, while removing the bran makes the flour lighter and finer. On the other hand, it will have fewer vitamins. For this reason white flours, whether bleached or unbleached, have B vitamins and other nutrients added to them in most countries. With or without such additions, bread made from white flour will have less flavour and less fibre than that made from whole grain flour.

STRONG FLOUR is white flour made from varieties of wheat (known as 'hard' wheat) which contain a particularly high proportion of gluten. Also called bread flour, the best comes from North America and is usually known as durum wheat. This makes it highly suitable for bread making, giving the dough a remarkable capacity to expand and rise and produce a light, well risen, springy loaf.

WEAK, SOFT OR HOUSEHOLD FLOUR is made from wheat mainly grown in Europe. It has less expansive gluten, produces a less elastic dough and bakes to a heavier, more crumbly bread. It makes excellent cakes and biscuits, where crumbliness and non-elasticity are advantages.

PLAIN FLOUR is a general, all-purpose flour claimed to be suitable for sauces, cakes and breads even though it does not have the high gluten content of strong flour. In Europe where plain flour contains more soft wheat, it is less suitable for making breads than the plain or all-purpose flour used in North America, which contains more hard wheat.

SELF-RAISING FLOUR is usually made from soft wheat. A raising agent — usually a mixture of bicarbonate of soda and cream of tartar — is mixed with the flour. It is not used in yeast cookery, though some 'breads' such as wholemeal soda bread are made with it. (See p.318.)

WHOLEMEAL, OR WHOLEWHEAT, FLOUR is milled from the whole grain so that it contains the germ and the bran. Most of the B vitamins are in the wheatgerm, while bran provides roughage necessary for the digestive system. Bread made from wholemeal flour is undoubtedly healthier, but regardless of its natural gluten, it produces a heavier loaf. Also, the oil in the wheatgerm means that the bread will not keep as well as a white loaf. A mixture of wholemeal and white flour is a good compromise.

STONEGROUND FLOUR is usually wholemeal flour that has been milled between stone rollers rather than by modern milling methods. It is definitely a coarser and heavier flour, even in its white version, than factory-milled flour, so more yeast (or a longer rising time) is needed to make it rise. It is claimed that more of the wheat's nutrients are retained as the grain is kept cooler during stone-grinding.

WHEATMEAL FLOUR, as the name implies, should refer to any wheat flour. But the term is used by commercial bakers to describe brown bread flour that is not wholemeal. The colour may simply come from dye. Containing little or no bran or wheatgerm, it makes a lighter loaf. It is usually no more nutritious or 'healthy' than refined white flour.

OTHER BREAD INGREDIENTS are the liquid, salt and sometimes sugar and fat. Water is usually called for; it gives bread crispness. Beer gives bread a malty taste, while milk gives it a richer crumb and a golden coloured crust. A little sugar or molasses is often included in bread recipes to encourage rapid yeast growth, and to add a touch of sweetness. A surprising amount of salt is needed for bread to taste right, but too much slows down yeast growth. Two level teaspoons (15g/½oz) per 450g/1lb is about right, though of course tastes vary. Fat, usually butter, is used in some breads to add richness and flavour.

MAKING BREAD

To create the right conditions for the yeast to grow and for the maximum elasticity in the dough to accommodate the carbon dioxide it gives off, it is important to prepare the dough properly. If the yeast is fresh, first cream it in a warm, not hot, cup with about a teaspoonful of sugar until smooth, then with a spoonful of lukewarm water. Dried yeast should be mixed with a little sweetened lukewarm water and left in a warm place for about 15 minutes. When the yeast looks frothy, you know it is working. If not, the yeast is dead and will have to be replaced before going to the trouble and expense of making the dough. Once the yeast liquid is frothy, or 'sponges', add it to the flour, and any remaining ingredients specified.

Some recipes, usually those enriched with fat and sugar, require the yeast mixture and all the liquid to be beaten with a small proportion of the flour to a yeasty batter (called the starter) and left in a warm place until it 'sponges'. Then the rest of the flour is added and the mixing completed. This method used to be common to all breads. The process takes longer but is said by old fashioned bakers to produce the best, lightest, most even textured bread.

KNEADING, or manipulating the dough, is the next stage. It is necessary in order to distribute the yeast cells evenly and promote the dough's elasticity. The length of time for kneading varies according to the type of flour and the skill of the kneader, but the dough must lose its stickiness and become smooth, elastic and shiny — this usually takes about 15 minutes. Techniques vary, but the most common one is to push the lump of dough down and away with the heel of the hand, then to pull it back with the fingers, slap it on the worktop and repeat the process, turning the dough slightly with each movement. (See p.67.)

Table-top electric mixers with dough hooks or robust food processors can also be used for kneading. They take less time than kneading by hand, but follow the manufacturer's instructions closely.

Once kneaded, the dough is formed into a ball and put into a lightly oiled, warm — not hot — bowl, turning the dough to coat it evenly with grease to prevent hardening and cracking. The bowl is covered with a piece of cling film, oiled polythene or a damp cloth and put in a warm (32°C/90°F) draught-free place and left until doubled in bulk. The dough should spring back when pressed lightly with a floured finger. (See illustration p.67.) The longer the rising takes the better. Too rapidly risen, or over-risen bread has a coarse texture and a beery smell.

KNOCKING BACK is the next process. The risen dough is knocked down, or punched with the knuckles to push out air that may have formed large, unevenly shaped holes. Punched to its original size, it is then kneaded briefly to make it pliable. Any more sugar or dried fruit are usually added at this point, before the dough is shaped and put into a loaf tin or onto a baking sheet.

PROVING is the second rising of the dough. When completed, the loaf will have doubled in bulk and should look the size and shape you hope the finished bread will be. Proving can be done in a slightly warmer place, about 40°C/100°F, for a shorter time (about 20 minutes), because the previous rising and further kneading will have made the dough even more elastic and it will rise more easily. With a second rising, the bread will be lighter when baked.

BAKING The bread will continue to rise in the oven for a short time partly because of rising steam in the loaf and partly because the yeast keeps working until the dough reaches 60°C/140°F. Then the heat of the oven will cook the dough into a rigid shape. Called 'oven spring', this final rising is likely to push the top crust away from the body of the loaf. To avoid much oven spring, bread is baked at a fairly high temperature to kill the yeast as quickly as possible.

TESTING FOR 'DONENESS' The baked bread should be golden brown and have shrunk slightly from the sides of the tin. To make sure that the bread is done, it should be turned out onto a cloth and tapped on the underside. If it sounds hollow, it is done. If not, it should be returned to the oven, on its side, without the tin. When done the bread is cooled on a wire rack. After two hours, the bread will slice easily. Once stone-cold it may be stored in a bread tin or a plastic bag. A lukewarm loaf stored in an airtight container will become soggy, if not mouldy.

SPECIALIST LESSON 1 BAKING WITH YEAST

The Saucisse en brioche (see p.233) and the Buckwheat blinis (see p.217) both teach the cook the principles of cooking with yeast. But they are rather unusual examples of the craft. Below are four classic bread recipes which, once mastered, will provide the technique and background principles for adventures in baking.

WHITE BREAD

INGREDIENTS (For a 450g/1lb loaf)
15g/½oz fresh yeast
290ml/½pt lukewarm milk
1tsp caster sugar
30g/1oz butter
450g/1lb plain flour
2tsp salt
1 egg, lightly beaten

1 Dissolve the yeast with a little of the milk and the sugar in a teacup.

2 Rub the butter into the sifted flour and salt as you would for pastry.

3 Pour in the yeast mixture, the milk and the beaten egg and mix to a stiffish dough.

4 Add a small amount of flour if the dough is too sticky. When the dough will leave the sides of the bowl, press it into a ball and tip it out on to a floured board.

5 Knead until it is elastic, smooth and shiny (about 15 minutes).

6 Put the dough back in the bowl and cover it with a piece of lightly greased polythene.

7 Put it somewhere warm and draught-free and leave it to rise until it

☐ *If using dried yeast,use half the amount called for, mix it with 3tbsp of the liquid (warmed to blood temperature) and 1tsp sugar. Leave until frothy, about 15 minutes, then proceed. If yeast does not go frothy it is dead and unusable.*

has doubled in size. This should take at least 1 hour. Bread that rises too quickly has a yeasty, unpleasant taste; the slower the rising the better — overnight in a cool larder is better than half an hour over the boiler.

8 Knead for a further 10 minutes or so.

9 Shape the dough into an oblong and put it into loaf tin.

10 Cover with the polythene again and allow to rise again until it is the size and shape of a loaf.

11 Set the oven to 220°C/425°F/Gas 7. Bake the loaf for 10 minutes, then turn the oven down to 190°C/375°F/Gas 5 and bake for a further 25 minutes or until it is golden and firm.

12 Turn the loaf out on to a wire rack to cool. It should sound hollow when tapped on the underside. If it does not, or feels squashy and heavy, return it to the oven, without the tin, for a further 10 minutes.

WHOLEMEAL ROLLS

INGREDIENTS (For 8-12 rolls)
20g/¾oz fresh yeast (for dried yeast see p.311)
290ml/½pt lukewarm milk
1tsp caster sugar
225g/8oz wholemeal flour
225g/8oz plain white flour
1tsp salt
55g/2oz butter
1 egg, lightly beaten

1 Dissolve the yeast with a little of the milk and the sugar in a teacup.

2 Warm a large mixing bowl and sift the flours and salt into it. Rub in the butter as you would for pastry.

3 Pour in the yeast mixture, the milk and the beaten egg and mix to a fairly slack dough.

4 When the dough will leave the sides of the bowl press it into a ball and tip it out onto a floured board. Knead it until it is elastic, smooth and shiny (about 15 minutes).

5 Put the dough back in the bowl and cover it with a piece of lightly greased polythene. Put it somewhere warm until it has doubled in size. This should take at least 1 hour, the longer the better.

6 Take the dough out of the bowl, punch it down and knead it again for 10 minutes.

7 Set the oven to 220°C/425°F/Gas 7.

8 Divide the dough into eight pieces and shape them into flattish ovals (using a rolling pin if you like). Put on a floured baking sheet and prove (allow to rise again) for 15 minutes.

9 Bake for 20 minutes or until firm.

CHELSEA BUNS

INGREDIENTS (For 8 buns)
15g/½oz fresh yeast
85g/3oz caster sugar
450g/1lb plain flour
1tsp salt
85g/3oz butter
1 egg
225ml/7½fl oz tepid milk
½tsp mixed spice
55g/2oz sultanas
55g/2oz currants

1 Cream the yeast with a teaspoon of the sugar.

2 Sift the flour into a warm dry bowl with the salt. Rub in half the butter and stir in half the sugar.

3 Beat the egg and add to the yeast mixture with the tepid milk. Follow the illustrations on pp.316-17 for the rest of the sequence.

CHELSEA BUNS
1 Make a well in the centre of the flour and pour in the yeasty liquid.

2 First draw in the flour gradually with a knife.

3 Then use your hand to draw the flour into the mixture.

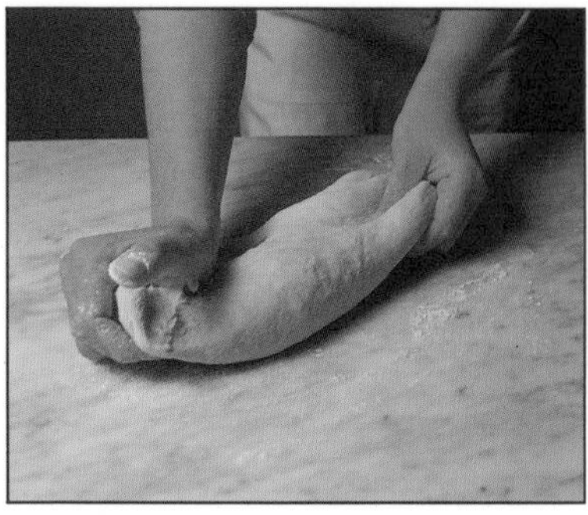

4 Knead until smooth. The dough should become smooth, elastic and shiny.

5 Return the dough to the bowl, cover and leave in a warm place for an hour.

6 The dough will double in bulk. Punch it down and knead again on a floured board for two minutes.

GUGELHOPF

INGREDIENTS
340g/12oz plain flour
1tsp salt
30g/1oz fresh yeast
225ml/7½fl oz lukewarm milk
30g/1oz caster sugar
2 small eggs, beaten
110g/4oz butter, softened
110g/4oz raisins and currants mixed
30g/1oz flaked almonds

1 Sift the flour and salt into a warmed bowl. Dissolve the yeast and sugar in the milk. Mix with the beaten eggs and the butter.

2 Mix the liquid into the flour. Now add the fruit and nuts.

3 Butter a gugelhopf tin (fluted round shape) and dust it out with sugar. Put in the mixture, which should three-quarters fill it. Put in a warm place to rise. Set the oven to 190°C/375°F/Gas 5.

4 When the mixture has risen to the top of the tin stand the tin on a baking sheet.

5 Bake for 45 minutes or until golden and firm. Remove from the tin and cool on a wire rack.

100% STONEGROUND WHOLEMEAL BREAD

This bread is exceptionally simple to make as it requires almost no kneading and only has one rising. As with all bread made purely from wholemeal flour it is heavier than that made from a mixture of white and wholemeal. But for a real 'health bread' 100 per cent wholemeal is preferable. For the same reason, buttermilk rather than milk is used,

7 Roll the dough out into a square, about 23cm/9inch across

8 Mix the remaining butter with half the remaining sugar and dot it over the dough. Fold the dough in half.

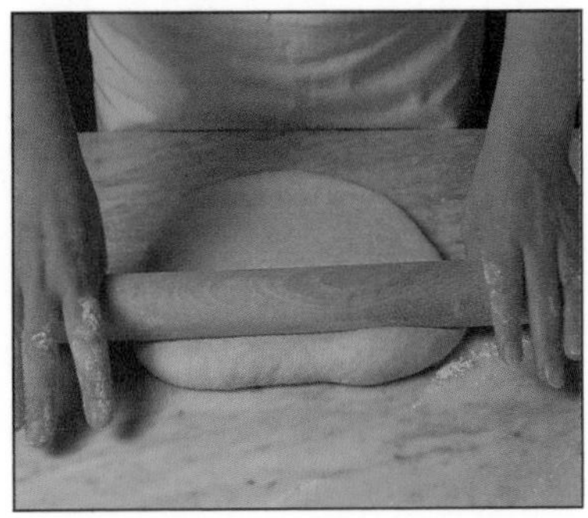
9 Roll the dough out into a square again. Set the oven to 220°C/425°F/Gas 7 and grease a baking sheet.

10 Sprinkle with the remaining sugar, spice and dried fruit. Roll up as you would a Swiss roll.

11 Cut into 3.5cm/1½ inch slices and arrange, cut side up, on the baking sheet. They should be nearly touching each other. Leave to prove for 15 minutes.

12 Sprinkle with sugar and bake for 20-25 minutes. Leave the buns to cool on a wire rack before separating.

INGREDIENTS (For 2x675g/1½lb loaves)
550-600g/1lb 4oz-1lb 6oz 100 per cent stoneground wholemeal flour
Large pinch of salt
15g/½oz fresh yeast
3tbsp buttermilk
290-340ml/10-12fl oz warm water

there is no fat, and only a minimum amount of salt is added. The flour and water quantities are approximations as the absorbency of flours varies.

1 Warm the flour and salt in a mixing bowl in the bottom of a low oven until it feels warm to the touch. Warm two 675g/1½lb loaf tins.

2 Mix together the yeast, buttermilk and three quarters of the water. Make a well in the centre of the flour, pour in the yeast mixture and mix to a moist soft dough (but not wet or sticky). Add extra liquid or flour as required. Knead lightly.

3 Fill the warmed tins three quarters full of dough. Smooth the tops and cover with greased polythene. Leave in a warm place for 45 minutes or until the dough has risen to the top of the tins. While the dough is rising heat the oven to 230°C/450°F/Gas 8.

4 Bake for 15 minutes. Reduce the heat to 190°C/375°F/Gas 5 and bake for a further 25 minutes. The bread is cooked when it sounds hollow when tapped on the underside. If it is not cooked, return to the oven without the tin, for a further 5 to 10 minutes. Leave to cool on a wire rack.

SPECIALIST LESSON 2 BREAD MAKING WITHOUT YEAST

Soda breads and scones are raised, like many cakes, by the action of bicarbonate of soda (see p.291). One of the best is the nutty flavoured wholemeal soda bread.

WHOLEMEAL SODA BREAD

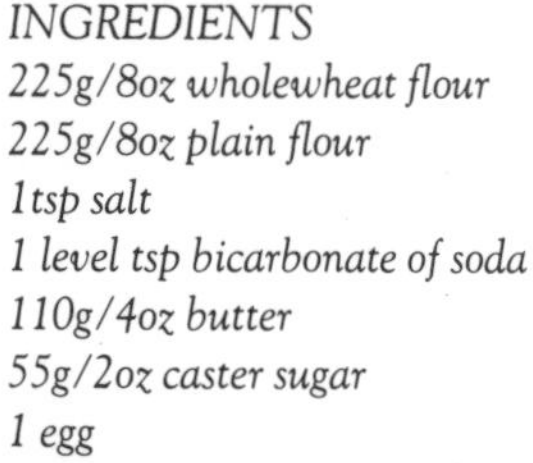

INGREDIENTS
225g/8oz wholewheat flour
225g/8oz plain flour
1tsp salt
1 level tsp bicarbonate of soda
110g/4oz butter
55g/2oz caster sugar
1 egg
290ml/½pt buttermilk

1 Set the oven to 200°C/400°F/Gas 6.

2 Sift the flours and salt into a warm dry bowl. Add the bicarbonate of soda.

3 Rub in the butter as you would for pastry (see p.305). Stir in the sugar.

4 Make a well in the centre and add the egg and enough of the buttermilk to make a stiff dough.

5 Shape into a large round about 5cm/2 inches thick. With the handle of a wooden spoon press a deep cross into the top of the loaf. The furrows should be about 2cm/¾ inch deep.

6 Bake on a lightly greased baking sheet for 45 minutes. Leave to cool on a wire rack.

NOTE Failing buttermilk, use half water and half milk and add 2tsp cream of tartar to the flour.

SODA BREAD FURROWS
With the handle of a wooden spoon press a deep cross in the top of the loaf. The furrows should be 2cm/¾ inch deep.

SULTANA SCONES

INGREDIENTS (For 8-10 scones)
225g/8oz plain flour
3 level tsp baking powder
½ level tsp salt
55g/2oz butter
55g/2oz sugar
30g/1oz sultanas
150ml/¼pt milk

FOR GLAZING
1 egg, beaten (optional)

1 Set the oven to 220°C/425°F/Gas 7. Lightly grease a baking sheet.

2 Sift the flour with the other powder ingredients.

3 Rub in the butter until the mixture resembles breadcrumbs. Stir in the sugar and sultanas.

4 Make a deep well in the flour, pour in all the liquid and mix to a soft, spongy dough with a palette knife.

5 On a floured surface, knead the dough very lightly until it is smooth. Roll or press out to about 1cm/½ inch thick and stamp into small rounds.

6 Heat the baking sheet in the oven.

7 Brush the scones with beaten egg for a glossy crust or sprinkle with flour for a soft one.

8 Bake the scones at the top of the hot oven until well risen and brown. Leave to cool on a wire rack, or serve hot from the oven.

BATTER

Batter is a versatile mixture of flour and liquid — usually milk and sometimes beaten egg — used to make pancakes, dropped scones and waffles, and also to give a protective coating to many foods which are deep fried (p.252). A crispy browned deep-fried batter coating is a delicious contrast to the soft hot food inside.

PANCAKES

THIN PANCAKES, or French crêpes, are made by pouring a thin layer of pancake batter into a hot greased pan about 20cm/8 inches in diameter, tipping to spread the batter evenly and pouring out the excess. The pancake is cooked fast to brown one side, turned to brown the other and when ready, wrapped around savoury or sweet fillings, or eaten simply with sugar and lemon juice.

BATTER FOR THICKER PANCAKES, sometimes called griddle (girdle) cakes or dropped scones, is mixed with baking powder or yeast. The raising agent causes the batter to rise in the pan to form thickish cakes which spread out only a little as they are fried on a greased hot griddle (girdle) or in a large frying pan. They are best eaten warm with plenty of butter. The blinis on p.217 are an example of a yeasted batter.

WAFFLES are also made from raised batter and cooked in a special iron device which holds the batter and gives the cooked waffles a thin, flat, indented shape on both sides. The waffle iron is heated over a gas flame if of the hand-held variety, or electrically if a table-top one, before the batter is poured in. This ensures that the waffles are crisp on the outside and soft on the inside, while the raised batter makes them light. As with the coating on deep fried foods, waffles must be eaten quickly or their crispness turns to limpness.

MAKING BATTER

The following recipes are examples of the main uses of batters. If the cook successfully manages these, no batter recipe should present any problems in the future.

1 Sift the flour into a large, wide bowl ensuring the absence of lumps.

2 Sprinkle the salt (or sugar or other dry ingredients) on top.

3 Using either a wooden spoon or your hand, make a well in the flour to expose the bottom of the bowl. The hole should be wide enough to mix in liquid ingredients (say, two eggs and a little milk) without bringing in too much of the surrounding flour.

4 Using a fork, whisk, wooden spoon or the fingertips of one hand, mix and stir the central liquid ingredients to a smooth paste.

5 Gradually incorporate the surrounding flour. With practice, the stirring action flips the liquid over the banks of flour and, as it runs back into the central well, it brings with it a thin film of flour. Pour more liquid into the centre as the batter gets thicker. The idea is to keep it at the consistency of thick cream — easier to keep lump-free than a runny mixture. Once all the flour is incorporated and the batter is absolutely smooth, beat in the remaining liquid.

6 Leave for 30 minutes, if possible, to allow time for the starch cells to

swell, giving a less doughy final product. If the mixture is left for more than an hour it might separate, but it is easily remixed. Do not make batter more than 12 hours in advance. It ferments easily.

WITH A FOOD PROCESSOR, batter making takes much less effort. Put any eggs and other liquid ingredients into a processor fitted with the metal blade, and spoon the flour and other dry ingredients on top. Turn on the machine for a second or two — just enough to blend them without creating too many bubbles.

SPECIALIST LESSON 1 *CREPES AU CITRON*

INGREDIENTS (Makes about 12)
110g/4oz plain flour
Pinch of salt
1 egg
1 egg yolk
290ml/½pt milk or milk and water mixed
1tbsp oil
Oil for frying

TO SERVE
Caster sugar
Lemon juice

This is the classic French pancake made with the thinnest of batters.

1 Sift the flour and salt into a bowl and make a well in the centre exposing the bottom of the bowl.

2 Into this well place the egg and egg yolk with a little of the milk.

3 Using a wooden spoon or whisk mix the egg and milk and then gradually draw in the flour from the sides as you mix.

4 When the mixture reaches the consistency of thick cream beat well and stir in the oil.

5 Add the rest of the milk — the consistency should now be that of thin cream. (Batter can also be made by placing all the ingredients together in a liquidizer for a few seconds, but take care not to over-whizz or the mixture will be bubbly.)

6 Cover the bowl and refrigerate for about 30 minutes. This is done so that the starch cells will swell, giving a lighter result.

7 Prepare a pancake pan or frying pan by heating well and wiping out

MAKING CREPES

1 Wipe the frying pan out with melted butter or oil. Heat the pan until smoking, then pour in enough batter to cover the surface, swirling the pan to spread the batter evenly.

2 Pour any excess batter back into the jug immediately and put the pan back on the heat. When the batter has set, cut off the lip created when pouring out the excess batter.

3 When cooked on one side, turn the pancake carefully with the fingers and cook the other side.

4 Lay the cooked pancake on sheets of greaseproof paper on a tea towel. The first side always looks better than the second, which is always spotty.

1

2

3

4

with oil. Pancakes are not fried in fat like most foods — the purpose of the oil is simply to prevent sticking.

8 When the pan is ready, pour in about 1tbsp batter and swirl about the pan until evenly spread across the bottom.

9 Place over heat and, after 1 minute, using a palette knife and your fingers, turn the pancake over and cook again until brown. (Pancakes should be extremely thin, so if the first one is too thick, add a little extra milk. The first pancake is unlikely to be perfect, and is often discarded.)

10 Make up all the pancakes, turning them out on to a plate.

11 Lay the pancakes spotty side (the second side to be fried) up, sprinkle them with a little sugar and lemon juice and roll up. Serve warm.

NOTE 1 Pancakes can be kept warm in a folded teatowel, on a plate over a saucepan of simmering water, in the oven, or in a warmer. If allowed to cool, they may be reheated by being briefly returned to the frying pan or by warming in an oven.

NOTE 2 Pancakes freeze well, but should be separated by pieces of greaseproof paper. They may also be refrigerated for a day or two.

SPECIALIST LESSON 2 *TOAD IN THE HOLE*

INGREDIENTS (Serves 8)
450g/1lb pork sausages
4tbsp beef dripping

FOR THE BATTER
110g/4oz plain flour
Good pinch of salt
2 eggs
150ml/¼pt water } *mixed together*
150ml/¼pt milk }

This unattractively named dish is one of the most delicious of inexpensive English family recipes. It is particularly good if served with meat gravy so is traditionally cooked the day after a roast dinner, when a little leftover gravy is available.

1 Sift the flour and salt into a large wide bowl. Make a well or hollow in the centre of the flour and break the eggs into it.

2 With a whisk or wooden spoon mix the eggs to a paste and very gradually draw in the surrounding flour, adding just enough milk and water to the eggs to keep the central mixture a fairly thin paste. When all the flour is incorporated, stir in the rest of the liquid. The batter can more speedily be made by putting all the ingredients together in a liquidizer or food processor for a few seconds, but take care not to over-whisk or the mixture will be bubbly. Leave to 'rest' at room temperature for 30 minutes before use. This allows the starch cells to swell, giving a lighter, less doughy final product.

3 Turn the oven to 220°C/425°F/Gas 7.

4 Heat 1tbsp dripping in a frying pan and in it fry the sausages until evenly browned all over, but do not cook them through.

5 Heat the rest of the dripping in an ovenproof shallow metal dish or roasting tin until smoking hot, either in the oven or over direct heat. Add the sausages to it and pour in the batter.

6 Bake for 40 minutes or until the Toad in the hole is risen and brown. Serve with hot gravy.

NOTE Toad in the hole can be made without preliminary frying of the sausages if skinless sausages are used, because the tops of the sausages will brown in the oven. But the submerged part of the sausages does not brown and unbrowned sausage skin is unpleasantly stringy.

SPECIALIST LESSON 3 *WAFFLES*

INGREDIENTS (Makes 10)
2 eggs
170g/6oz plain flour
Pinch of salt
3 level tsp baking powder
30g/1oz caster sugar
290ml/½pt milk
55g/2oz butter, melted
Vanilla flavouring
Extra melted butter

TO SERVE
Icing sugar

This is a thick batter with plenty of raising agent (bicarbonate of soda) so that it will puff up. The outside cooks to crispness, while the inside remains soft. Waffles can be served with maple syrup, jam or honey, with or without cream or topped with savoury foods like crispy grilled bacon or fried egg. Here they are served with a heavy dusting of icing sugar.

1 Separate the eggs. Sift the flour, salt, baking powder and sugar together. Make a well in the centre and drop in the egg yolks.

2 Stir the yolks, gradually drawing in the flour from the edges and adding the milk and melted butter until you have a thin batter. Add the vanilla flavouring.

3 Grease a waffle iron and heat it up.

4 Whisk the egg whites until stiff but not dry and fold into the batter.

5 Add a little melted butter to the hot waffle iron, pour in about 4tbsp of the mixture, close and cook for 1 minute per side. Do not worry if the first waffle sticks to the iron. It always does. Throw it away. The second one will come away cleanly.

6 Serve the waffles heavily dredged with icing sugar.

SPECIALIST LESSON 4 *BANANA FRITTERS*

INGREDIENTS (Serves 8)
8 small bananas
Oil for shallow frying
Icing sugar

FOR THE BATTER
125g/4½oz plain flour
Pinch of salt
2 eggs
150ml/¼pt milk
1tbsp oil
50g/1¾oz sugar

1 Sift the flour with the salt into a bowl. Make a well in the centre, exposing the bottom of the bowl.

2 Put one whole egg and one yolk into the well and mix with a wooden spoon or whisk until smooth, gradually incorporating the surrounding flour and the milk. A thick creamy consistency should be reached.

3 As the mixture thickens gradually add the milk to retain the creamy consistency.

4 Add the oil and sugar. Allow to rest for 30 minutes.

5 Whisk the egg white and fold into the batter with a metal spoon just before using.

6 Peel the bananas and cut in half lengthwise and dip immediately into the prepared batter.

7 Heat 6mm/¼ inch oil in a frying pan and when hot fry the fritters for about 2 minutes on each side until golden brown. Drain well and dust with icing sugar.

NOTE This batter can be speedily made in a blender. Simply put all the ingredients, except the egg white, into the machine and whizz briefly.

ICE CREAMS AND SORBETS

If ice creams contain a good proportion of fat, they freeze to smooth creaminess without much trouble. If they consist mostly of sugar and water or milk, they need frequent, if not constant, beating during the freezing process to prevent the formation of large icy crystals. In any event, the more a mixture is beaten or churned during freezing the more air will be incorporated, and the creamier in texture it will be.

MAKING AND STORING

AN ICE CREAM MAKER The best modern method of churning ice cream is with an ice cream maker with a built-in chiller and electric motor. These machines are expensive scaled-down versions of the commercial machines used by caterers. Their chief advantages are that they operate independently of the freezer, and are powerful and large enough to churn even a thick mixture to smoothness. The main disadvantages are the expense and the fact that they take up valuable work space when not in use (they are too heavy for cupboard storage).

AN ELECTRIC SORBETIERE is useful if making small quantities of ice cream from a fairly thin mixture — a custard or a syrup. But few are powerful enough to churn a mixture containing solid pieces (such as pieces of meringue or raisins for example) or thick mixtures made from, say, mashed bananas. Also, sorbetières must be put into a freezer as they have no built-in chilling equipment and care must be taken when setting up the machine that the lead that connects the churn placed in the freezer to the plug on the wall will not be damaged by the closing freezer door, nor prevent the door closing tight.

A FOOD PROCESSOR will not chill the mixture of course, but it is powerful enough to churn it to smoothness in a few minutes. Freeze the mixture in a shallow tray until solid, then break it up and process the frozen pieces, using the chopping blade, to pale creaminess. Return to the tray and refreeze.

BUCKET CHURNS can be bought with electric motors or with a handle for manual operation. Most have a good large capacity and are reliable and powerful, but they require a supply of ice and of salt. Coarsely crushed ice is packed in layers, sprinkled with coarse salt, between the metal ice cream container and the outer bucket. The ice cream in the container is churned steadily by a strong paddle for 25 minutes or so, until the ice cream is thick. It can be left, without fear of melting, in the churn for an hour or so after making.

MIXING ICE CREAMS BY HAND Finally, ice cream can be made without any special equipment. All that is needed is a shallow ice cube tray or roasting pan, a bowl, and a strong whisk. The ice cream is half frozen in the tray, then tipped into the bowl (which is chilled) and whisked until smooth. This is repeated until icy shards are eliminated.

SUGAR AND FLAVOURINGS Extreme cold inhibits our sense of taste, the tastebuds being too cold to operate effectively. For this reason ice creams must be sweetened or flavoured more than seems right when tasting the mixture at room temperature.

STORAGE Theoretically, ice cream can be stored for very long periods, but, certainly in a domestic freezer, there is some deterioration. Ice crystals may form on the surface of the ice cream after a week or so, meringue-based ices or ices containing gelatine may become rubbery, and if raw fruit (such as puréed peach) has been used, the colour will change for the worse. For total perfection, ice cream should be eaten the day it is made. But a few days' freezing is acceptable. If ices are frozen for longer periods, and obviously they often will be, poor texture can be rectified by allowing the ice cream to soften slightly, re-whisking it and re-freezing it. Or the frozen mixture can be re-beaten in a processor. If fruit ices are to be stored for longer than a few days, the fruit should be cooked to preserve the colour.

THAWING Unless the mixture is very soft, it is wise to put it into the refrigerator for half an hour before serving to allow the ice to soften slightly. Or it may be softened sufficiently to scoop into balls, then put into a chilled serving dish and returned to the freezer until needed.

PRESENTATION

Ice creams lend themselves to all sorts of exotic presentation. They can be served in filigree baskets (see p.150) served in a brandy snap cup (p.107) or in tuiles (p.145) or they can be spooned into a scooped-out melon shell, or into individual orange or lemon skins. Or they can be served in the now classic nouvelle cuisine manner, each person's three or five scoops of (probably various) ice creams arranged in star fashion on a frozen dessert plate, the gaps between the scoops of ice cream filled with tiny mounds of perfect fresh fruit at the last minute, or with a fruit or cream sauce elegantly 'feathered'. See illustrations.

TO MAKE A PAPER PIPING BAG
1 Cut a 15-inch square of greaseproof paper and fold it diagonally in half.

2 Hold the paper down with a finger in the middle of the long folded edge. Then bring one corner up to the apex opposite your steadying finger, and hold it, with the apex corner together.

3 Wrap the other side-corner right round the cone to join the other two. You should now have all three corners held together.

4 Fold the corners over together.

SPECIALIST LESSON 1 CUSTARD-BASE METHOD

The first lesson shows how to make an easy ice cream, containing plenty of butterfat.

CHOCOLATE ICE CREAM

INGREDIENTS (Serves 6)
110g/4oz sugar
150ml/¼pt milk
110g/4oz bitter, dark chocolate
4 egg yolks
290ml/½pt double cream

A simple handmade ice cream with a custard base.

1 Set freezer to coldest. Put in shallow tin tray, bowl and heavy whisk.

2 Put the sugar, milk and chocolate into a small saucepan and stir over gentle heat until the sugar and chocolate is dissolved. Bring to the boil.

3 Whisk the egg yolks until smooth, then pour the boiling chocolate mixture onto them, whisking all the time. Allow to cool. Strain into the shallow tray and freeze.

4 When the mixture is half frozen round the edges, but still soft in the

FEATHERING

5 Cut a tear in them so you have a lug or flange. Fold down this flange. This prevents the paper bag unravelling. Alternatively, use a paperclip.

1 Pipe parallel lines on base. Drag the point of a knife through crossways at 2cm/1 inch intervals. Then drag the knife through the lines in the opposite direction between the first lines.

2 This pattern is achieved by dragging the knife tip in only one direction through the piped lines. A slight angle gives a lattice effect.

6 Snip the tip of the cone to make a hole of the required size. If the mixture is fairly liquid (as it would be for feathering) do this only after the bag is filled.

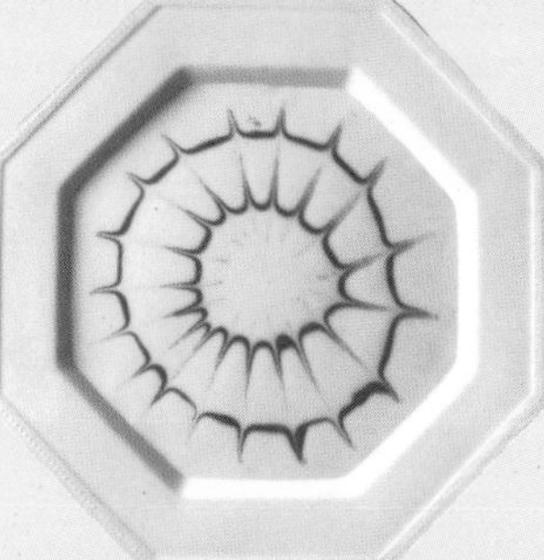

3 Pipe two concentric circles, then drag the knife tip from the centre outwards to give this star effect.

4 Again two concentric circles are piped, but the knife is dragged inwards and outwards. Drag the outward lines first, then the inward ones between them.

middle, whip the cream until it will hold its shape, but is soft rather than stiff.

5 Whisk the half frozen ice until smooth, and then quickly fold in the cream. Freeze again, whisking once more if texture is not smooth.

RICH COFFEE ICE CREAM

INGREDIENTS (Serves 6-8)
425ml/¾pt single cream
110g/4oz sugar
4 egg yolks
A few drops of vanilla flavouring
4tsp instant coffee powder

A custard-based ice, using the food processor for beating.

1 Set the freezer to coldest. Put the cream and sugar into a heavy saucepan and bring slowly to the boil.

2 Whisk the yolks and vanilla until smooth.

3 Remove the cream from the heat, stir in the coffee and immediately pour onto the yolks, whisking. Strain into a shallow roasting tin and leave to cool. Freeze until solid all through.

4 Turn the tin upside down on a board, and cover with a wettish cloth rung out in very hot water. This will melt the surface of the ice cream and dislodge it onto the board.

5 Using a meat cleaver, a very large knife, or a hammer and chisel, break the ice cream block into pieces.

6 Using the chopping blade of the processor, churn the ice cream, adding the frozen pieces a few at a time, until the mixture is smooth, pale and creamy. Working fast, spoon back into the ice tray and re-freeze.

NOTE The amount of coffee can be increased for a stronger flavour — for a less rich ice cream use 50 per cent milk and 50 per cent cream.

SPECIALIST LESSON 2 SIMPLE SORBET AND GRANITA

Sorbets (sherberts or water-ices) are made by freezing flavoured syrups or purées. The essential is to get the proportions right. Too much sugar and the sorbet will be oversweet, syrupy and too soft to hold its shape. Too little and it will be icy, crystalline and hard. Chefs use a saccharimeter to measure the amount of sugar in a syrup (a 'pèse-syrop' to get the desired 37 per cent sugar), but good results can be had if the mixture contains about one third sugar and two thirds other ingredients. Once this figure is in the cook's head, he or she can make almost any sorbet with two parts liquid (unsweetened) and one part sugar, bringing the syrup slowly to the boil, cooling it, and freezing it, whisking as necessary.

There is no question that a machine gives the best results. If no machine is available, the addition of a little gelatine (1tsp for every 300ml/½pt of liquid) or the addition of whisked egg whites does help prevent the formation of large ice crystals, and slows up melting.

If slightly less sugar is used, and the mixture is forked rather than beaten while freezing, a Granita results — a granular, fast-melting sorbet.

CLASSIC ORANGE SORBET

Made by hand, and using volume measures.

1 Set the freezer to coldest. Put a shallow tray, bowl and heavy whisk

INGREDIENTS (Serves 4)
Thinly pared rind of one orange
1 measuring cup water
1 measuring cup sugar
1 measuring cup orange juice
Juice of half a lemon

into the freezer to chill.

2 Put the rind, with no pith, into a saucepan with the water and sugar. Bring very slowly to the boil. Simmer for 5 minutes to extract the flavour of the rind.

3 Remove rind, and add the orange and lemon juice to syrup. Pour into chilled tray. Freeze until almost solid, but just soft in middle.

4 Scrape into the chilled bowl and whisk, working as fast as possible, until the large lumps have been beaten out. Return, either in the bowl or the tray, to the freezer.

5 Repeat beating once or twice to obtain a smooth creamy texture.

RED WINE GRANITA

INGREDIENTS (Serves 4)
110g/4oz sugar
100ml/3½fl oz water
425ml/¾pt red wine
2tbsp orange juice

☐ *Alcohol freezes at a lower temperature than water, so expect ices containing alcohol to stay softer and melt faster. This is especially true of alcoholic sorbets without cream or egg to keep them thick; too much sugar produces a syrupy over-soft sorbet, too little a rock-hard one.*

This mixture can be churned to smoothness in an electric ice cream machine and will have the texture of a soft sorbet. But for a true granita the ice should consist of tiny clear crystals of ice, and for this reason it is made as described. Because of the alcohol the granita melts very fast, so serve it in glasses that have been in the freezer for several hours, and serve as soon as it is dished up. It makes a refreshing course between savoury dishes in the middle of an elaborate meal.

1 Dissolve the sugar in the water over gentle heat. Once dissolved, bring to the boil and boil for a minute.

2 Cool the syrup and add it to the wine and orange juice.

3 Pour into a clean shallow roasting tin and freeze.

4 When the mixture is solid but not too hard mix it with a fork — the ice should be like gritty, rough snow.

5 Pile the granita into the frosted glasses and serve at once.

SPECIALIST LESSON 3 MOUSSE-BASED PARFAITS

In a mousse-based parfait the air that will give the creaminess to the frozen mixture is beaten into the egg base over heat before cooling and freezing. Which means that there is no need to churn or beat once the mixture is in the freezer, and it can be poured into a china soufflé dish with a paper collar tied round (see p.204) it so that it looks deceptively like a risen soufflé or an iced soufflé.

BLACKCURRANT PARFAIT

INGREDIENTS (Serves 4)
FOR THE PUREE
450g/1lb frozen, fresh or tinned blackcurrants
110g/4oz sugar

FOR THE ICE CREAM
150ml/¼pt water
125ml/4½oz sugar
3 eggs
150ml/¼pt double cream

1 Stew the blackcurrants gently with the sugar (no water) until the sugar has dissolved and the blackcurrants are soft. Liquidize and push through a sieve to extract the seeds.

2 Put the water and sugar together into a saucepan and bring to the boil slowly so that the sugar dissolves before it boils. Boil steadily until the temperature reaches 110°C/230°F, or until the syrup will form 2.5cm/1 inch threads. (To test, dip the tips of the pinching fingers of one hand in cold water, then immediately dip them into a spoon of the syrup — the cold water will prevent burning — and pinch syrup-coated thumb

and forefinger together. When drawn apart it should form long threads.)

3 Fit a basin over a pan of simmering water, making sure that it fits snugly and that the bottom of the bowl is not touching the water. In this whisk the eggs until frothy, then pour on the boiling syrup. Do not allow the hot syrup to touch the whisk. Whisk over the simmering water until the mixture is pale and mousse-like and the whisk will leave a ribbon trail in the mixture when lifted.

4 Remove from the heat and whisk until cool. To hurry things up stand the bowl first in a pan of cold water and then, when cool to the touch, in water with ice cubes in it.

5 Whip cream until thick, just holding its shape but not quite solid.

6 Fold the cream and fruit purée together, then fold into the mousse. Do not overstir or the air will be knocked out.

7 Pour into a mould and leave undisturbed until frozen — about 6 hours.

8 Remove from the refrigerator half an hour before serving to soften.

SPECIALIST LESSON 4 MERINGUE-BASED ICE CREAMS

These are similar to the mousse-based parfaits, but the air is incorporated into the egg whites, as for meringue, before the flavouring fruit purée is added. The method is suitable for fruit ice creams, where the acidity of the fruit nicely cuts the sweet meringue. Please read p. 287 on Italian meringue before you start this recipe.

RASPBERRY ICE CREAM

INGREDIENTS (Serves 6-8)
225g/8oz raspberries
225g/8oz caster sugar
150ml/¼pt water
4 egg whites
290ml/½pt double cream

1 Liquidize the raspberries, and sieve them, if liked, for a seedless purée.

2 Dissolve the sugar in the water slowly over a gentle heat, then boil fast to 'soft ball' or 116°C/240°F.

3 Whisk the egg whites to form stiff peaks and, while whisking, pour on the syrup. Continue to whisk until the meringue is absolutely stiff, shiny and will not flow at all.

4 Whip the cream until it will just hold its shape.

5 Fold meringue, cream and purée together carefully and freeze undisturbed for at least 4 hours.

6 If very hard to the touch remove from the refrigerator half an hour before serving.

SPECIALIST LESSON 5 FROZEN YOGHURTS

Yoghurt, because it is so low in fat, is not easy to freeze smoothly without the aid of a machine that beats or stirs constantly during freezing. It thaws and melts too fast for the processor method. The addition of large quantities of cream or sugar would make a smoother and more stable mixture but as frozen yoghurt is often served as a healthy alternative to a fattening dessert, such additions would defeat the cook's object. However, the addition of a little gelatine does help to prevent crystallization. The addition of milk powder gives a thicker mix which melts rather more slowly than it otherwise would.

FROZEN HONEY YOGHURT

INGREDIENTS (Serves 4)
2tbsp water
15g/½oz gelatine powder
570ml/1pt natural yoghurt
2tbsp runny honey
2tbsp skimmed or whole milk powder

1 Put the water into a small saucepan and sprinkle on the gelatine. Leave for 10 minutes to soak.

2 While the gelatine is soaking, tip the yoghurt into a saucepan, add the honey and milk powder and stir until just lukewarm and well mixed. Remove from the heat.

3 Put the gelatine over very gentle heat, without stirring, until smooth, runny and clear. Mix with the yoghurt.

4 Cool, then freeze in an ice cream maker, bucket churn or sorbetière.

FROZEN APRICOT YOGHURT

INGREDIENTS (Serves 4)
55g/2oz dried apricots
1tbsp apricot jam
570ml/1pt natural yoghurt
110g/4oz sugar
15g/½oz gelatine

1 Halve the apricots and put them with 150ml/¼pt water into a small saucepan.

2 Simmer them gently, covered, for 15 minutes or so until tender.

3 Lift the apricots out of the liquid with a perforated spoon, and chop them finely.

4 Stir them and the jam into the yoghurt, and, if the heat of the fruit has not warmed the yoghurt to at least room temperature, warm it slightly in a saucepan or microwave oven.

5 Add the sugar to the hot apricot liquid in the pan and stir until dissolved, heating gently if necessary.

6 Cool the apricot syrup and when lukewarm, sprinkle the gelatine on top of it. Leave to soak for 10 minutes.

7 Heat the apricot syrup and gelatine very gently, without stirring, until runny and clear, then stir briskly into the lukewarm yoghurt.

8 Freeze in an ice cream maker, bucket churn or sorbetière. A satisfactory texture cannot be achieved by hand.

SPECIALIST LESSON 6 THE ICE CREAM BOMBE

Proper bombe moulds, either round as a ball, or pudding shaped, can be bought, but a perfectly good bombe can be made in a pudding basin or in a round rice steamer available from some Chinese shops.

A bombe usually consists of two or more ice creams, set in layers in the mould, so that a cut slice has both or all the ice creams or sorbets in it.

If sorbet and ice cream are used together, the sorbet mixture should be the central one as it is softer and melts faster. If it is on the outside the central ice cream will still be rock hard when the sorbet has melted. Putting the sorbet in the middle allows the cook to take the bombe from the freezer to allow the ice cream to soften without risk of the sorbet melting.

Other fillings for bombes are crushed meringue, nuts (or chopped fruit) and whipped cream mixtures, or rich parfaits or mousses.

PRALINE AND CHOCOLATE BOMBE

INGREDIENTS (Serves 4-6)

FOR THE CHOCOLATE ICE CREAM
225g/8oz plain chocolate, cut up
290ml/½pt milk
1 egg
1 egg yolk
55g/2oz sugar
425ml/¾pt double cream
1tsp vanilla flavouring

FOR THE VANILLA ICE CREAM
80g/3oz sugar
100ml/3½fl oz water
3 egg yolks
425ml/¾pt double cream
1tsp vanilla flavouring

FOR THE PRALINE
A few drops of oil
55g/2oz unblanched (with the skins on) almonds
55g/2oz sugar

1 MAKE THE CHOCOLATE ICE CREAM Dissolve the chocolate in the milk over a gentle heat.

2 Beat egg and yolk together with sugar until light and fluffy.

3 When the chocolate has melted and the milk is almost boiling, pour onto the egg mixture while whisking steadily. Strain and allow to cool.

4 Whip the cream until it will just hold its shape and fold it into the chocolate mixture with vanilla flavouring. Pour into a flat tray and freeze.

5 When half frozen re-whisk and re-freeze.

6 TO MAKE THE VANILLA ICE CREAM Put the sugar and water into a saucepan and dissolve slowly over gentle heat.

7 Beat the egg yolks well.

8 Whip the cream until it will just hold its shape.

9 When the sugar has dissolved, bring the syrup to a good boil and boil for 5 minutes. Allow to cool for one minute.

10 Pour the sugar syrup onto the egg yolks while whisking them. (Do not let the sugar syrup hit the whisk or it will cool and set solidly.) Continue to whisk until the mixture is pale, thick and mousse-like.

11 Allow to cool, whisking occasionally.

12 When stone-cold, stir in vanilla flavouring. Fold in cream. Freeze. When ice cream is half frozen whisk again and return to freezer.

13 FOR THE PRALINE First oil a baking sheet, then put the almonds and sugar together in a heavy pan and set over gentle heat. Stir with a metal spoon as the sugar begins to melt and brown. When thoroughly caramelized, tip onto the oiled baking sheet and spread. Allow to cool completely, then pound to a coarse powder in a mortar or processor or blender.

14 TO ASSEMBLE THE BOMBE Pack the chocolate ice cream round the sides and bottom of a bombe mould or pudding basin. If the ice cream is too stiff to handle allow it to thaw until it is of the right consistency. Freeze until firm.

15 Mix the praline with the vanilla ice cream (slightly softened if necessary) and pack into the middle of the bombe. Cover with the bombe lid (or a piece of polythene if using a basin), and freeze.

16 TO UNMOULD THE BOMBE Remove the lid. Using a long trussing needle prick the mixture right through to the base to release any vacuum.

17 Invert plate over mould and turn mould and plate over together. Cover with a cloth wrung out in hot water. When it becomes cold wring it out again in hot water and replace over bombe.

18 Remove the cloth. The bombe case or pudding basin should now lift off easily. If it does not repeat the cloth process.

19 If the ice cream has melted slightly return the bombe to the freezer until firm. Cut as for a cake.

FOOD POISONING

Food poisoning is caused by the toxins present in large concentrations of micro-organisms. The commonest culprit is salmonella, and it has become more widespread with intensive farming where birds and animals easily re-infect each other. So it is almost inevitable that the germ will be brought into every kitchen, domestic or commercial. All the cook can do by prudent hygienic methods is to prevent the growth of the bacteria to poison-producing levels. The thing to remember is that bacteria need warmth, moisture and time to multiply, and if those three conditions are not present, they cannot get on with their evil work.

POINTS TO REMEMBER

1 Salmonella is generally on the surface of raw meat, chicken etc, so washing raw food will remove it. All meat that has been sitting about at room temperature for any length of time, or smells at all strongly, should be washed and dried on a clean cloth.

2 Heat kills bacteria, chilling slows up growth, and freezing halts reproduction without killing the organisms. So remember:
- Heat or cook food thoroughly. A lukewarm centre can harbour and encourage germs.
- As soon as food is cold, refrigerate or freeze it.
- Do not refreeze completely thawed food without cooking it first. Although the freezing does no harm it is easy to forget just how many periods at room temperature the food has had, and therefore how large the concentrations of bacteria now are.
- Do not cook large items (eg whole chickens) from frozen. When the bird looks cooked the inside (where salmonella is most likely to be present on the surface of the cavity) may be lukewarm and raw.
- Never leave cold cooked food at room temperature for more than two hours or so. Although the original cooking of the food will have destroyed any bacteria, the food can be re-infected and if left in a warm atmosphere can become very toxic in four hours.

3 Make sure knives, boards, tea towels, cloths, are clean. A damp cloth left over a warm cooker provides perfect incubation conditions for germs.

4 Cool large quantities of food fast. If a stew is left in a heavy pan the centre of it will provide perfect bacteria breeding conditions — warmth, moisture and time. Cool the pot as illustrated.

5 Do not leave food to cool covered with a heavy lid. Open food cools quicker. If you want to avoid drying out or a skin forming, place wet greaseproof paper (which is thin enough not to hinder cooling) flat on the surface of the food.

6 Take care wrapping hot food with polythene — if there are any air spaces between food and film, greenhouse-like perfect incubating conditions will be produced. Rather wrap the food loosely in foil and refrigerate as soon as cold.

7 Do not put hot food into the refrigerator. It will warm up the atmosphere and encourage any salmonella present on other food in the cabinet, to breed.

All this can be summed up simply: DON'T GIVE BUGS A CHANCE TO GROW.

RAPID COOLING
To cool large quantities of food rapidly, stand the container in a bowl of cold water. Arrange so that a thin, steady stream of cold tap water keeps the water in the bowl cool. Stir the hot food occasionally.

WEIGHTS AND MEASURES

WEIGHTS

Metric	Imperial
8 g	¼ oz
15 g	½ oz
20 g	¾ oz
25 g	1 oz
30 g	1 oz
45 g	1½ oz
50 g	1¾ oz
55 g	2 oz
75 g	2½ oz
85 g	3 oz
100 g	3½ oz
115 g	4 oz
125 g	4½ oz
140 g	5 oz
150 g	5½ oz
170 g	6 oz
175 g	6½ oz
200 g	7 oz
210 g	7½ oz
225 g	8 oz
250 g	8½ oz
255 g	9 oz
275 g	9½ oz
285 g	10 oz
300 g	10½ oz
325 g	11 oz
350 g	12 oz
375 g	13 oz
400 g	14 oz
425 g	15 oz
450 g	16 oz (1lb)
550 g	1¼ lb
675 g	1½ lb
700 g	1⅔ lb
800 g	1¾ lb
900 g	2 lb
1 kg	2¼ lb
1.35 kg	3 lb
1.5 kg	3½ lb
1.8 kg	4 lb
2 kg	4½ lb
2.3 kg	5 lb
2.5 kg	5½ lb
2.7 kg	6 lb
3 kg	6½ lb
3.2 kg	7 lb
3.5 kg	8 lb
4 kg	9 lb
4.5 kg	10 lb
5 kg	11 lb

VOLUME

Metric	Imperial		American
5 ml	—	1 tsp	1 tsp
10 ml	—	2 tsp	2 tsp
20 ml	—	1 tbsp	1½ tbsp
30 ml	1 fl oz	1½ tbsp	2 tbsp
50 ml	2 fl oz	3 tbsp	¼ cup
60 ml	2½ fl oz (½ gill)	3½ tbsp	¼C+2 tsp
75 ml	3 fl oz	4 tbsp	½C (6 tbsp)
100 ml	4 fl oz	¼ pint	½C (¼ pint)
150 ml	5 fl oz (1 gill)	¼ pint	¾C
175 ml	6 fl oz	—	¾C
200 ml	7 fl oz	—	—
250 ml	8 fl oz	⅓ pint	1C (½ pint)
300 ml	10 fl oz (2 gills)	½ pint	1¼ C
350 ml	12 fl oz	—	1½C
400 ml	14 fl oz	⅔ pint	1¾C
450 ml	15 fl oz	¾ pint	—
500 ml	16 fl oz	—	2C (1 pint)
550 ml	18 fl oz	—	2¼C
575 ml	20 fl oz	1 pint	2½C
600 ml	21 fl oz	—	2¾C
700 ml	25 fl oz	1¼ pint	3C
750 ml	27 fl oz	—	3½C
800 ml	28 fl oz	—	3⅔C
850 ml	30 fl oz	1½ pints	3¾C
900 ml	32 fl oz	1⅔ pints	4C
1 litre	35 fl oz	1¾ pints	4½C
1.1 litre	40 fl oz	2 pints	5C
1.3 litre	48 fl oz	2⅔ pints	6C
1.5 litre	50 fl oz	2½ pints	6¼C
1.66 litre	56 fl oz	2¾ pints	7C
1.75 litre	60 fl oz	3 pints	7½C
1.8 litre	64 fl oz	3¼ pints	8C
2 litre	72 fl oz	3½ pints	9C
2.1 litre	76 fl oz	3⅔ pints	9½C
2.2 litre	80 fl oz	3¾ pints	10C
2.25 litre	84 fl oz	2 quarts	10½C

TEMPERATURE

°C	°F	Gas mark
3	37	
10	50	
16	60	
21	70	
24	75	
27	80	
29	85	
38	100	
41	105	
43	110	
46	115	
49	120	
54	130	
57	135	
60	140	
66	150	
71	160	
77	170	
82	180	
88	190	
93	200	
96	205	
100	212	
107	225	¼ (vc)
110	228	
115	238	
120	250	½
130	275	1
140	285	
150	300	2 (c)
160	325	3 (w)
180	350	4
190	375	5 (m)
200	400	6 (lh)
220	425	7
230	450	8 (h)
250	475	9 (vh)
260	500	

LENGTH

Metric (cm)	Imperial (in)
0.3	⅛
0.6	¼
1	½
2	¾
2.5	1
5	2
15	6
30	12 (1ft)
46	18
92	36 (1yd)
100 (1m)	39

SPOON MEASURES

In American recipes, when quantities are stated as spoons, 'level' spoons are meant. European recipes and those in this book usually call for rounded (neither level, nor over-heaped) spoons, unless specifically stated otherwise. Also, American 'spoons' are standard cook's measuring spoons, whereas European 'spoons' tend to be any available kitchen or eating spoons. The best plan is to regard 2 American teaspoons or tablespoons as 1 English teaspoon or tablespoon. Dessertspoons are not often called for in recipes, but 1 dessertspoon is the equivalent of 2 teaspoons or half a tablespoon.

APPROXIMATE WEIGHT AND VOLUME EQUIVALENTS

Commodity	Metric	Imperial	American
Butter *(also margarine and lard)*	115 g	4 oz	½C
	225 g	8 oz	1C
	450 g	1 lb	2C
Breadcrumbs *(dry)*	90 g	3¼ oz	1 C
	175 g	6½ oz	2 C
Cheese *(hard fresh, like Cheddar, grated coarsely; Parmesan, grated)*	5 g	2 oz	1 C
	100 g	3½ oz	1 C
Dried fruit *(like raisins, sultanas and apricots)*	110 g	4 oz	½ C
	225 g	8 oz	1 C
	450 g	1 lb	2 C
Flours *(finely ground, including cornflour, wholewheat, and rice flour)*	115 g	4 oz	1 C
	170 g	6 oz	1½ C
	225 g	8 oz	2 C
Coarse meals *(including semolina, coarse oatmeal, coarse maize meal)*	115 g	4 oz	¾ C
	140 g	5 oz	1 C
	225 g	8 oz	1½ C
Nuts *(almonds, hazel-nuts, walnuts)*	75 g	2½ oz	½ C
	150 g	5½ oz	1 C
Ground nuts	50 g	2 oz	½ C
	115 g	4 oz	1 C
	225 g	8 oz	2 C
Rice *(uncooked)*	5 g	2 oz	¼ C
	115 g	4 oz	½ C
	225 g	8 oz	1 C
White sugar *(granulated and caster)*	115g	4 oz	½ C
	170g	6 oz	¾ C
	225g	8 oz	1 C
	350g	12 oz	1½ C
Brown sugar	115 g	4 oz	⅔ C
	170g	6 oz	1 C
	225 g	8 oz	1½ C
	350 g	12 oz	2 C
Icing sugar *(confectioners)*	140 g	5 oz	1 C
	170 g	6 oz	1¼ C
	225g	8 oz	1½ C
Treacle or golden syrup	85 g	3 oz	¼ C
	170 g	6 oz	1¼ C
	350 g	12 oz	1 C
Fish, meat, vegetables *(and other ingredients, when accuracy is not vital)*	250 g	½ lb	½ lb
	½ kilo	1 lb	1 lb
	1 kilo	2 lb	2 lb
	2 kilo	4 lb	4 lb
	3½ kilo	8 lb	8 lb
	4½ kilo	10 lb	10 lb
	5 kilo	11 lb	11 lb

EQUIPMENT AND UTENSILS

When buying kitchen equipment the basic rule for the big items is buy the best that you can possibly afford. They will probably last for 15 years. But when buying small or specialist equipment that might get lost or only be used once, be as economical or extravagant as your purse dictates.

The following is not intended to be a complete list of the kitchen equipment available, but includes all the utensils that the home cook could possibly want, while excluding certain specialist items like preserving equipment, cake decorating equipment, barbecues, smokers and storage equipment.

UTENSILS

The following items of equipment are essential:
1 cook's knife with 18cm/7 inch blade
1 cook's knife with 7.5cm/3 inch blade
1 filleting knife with 14cm/5½ inch blade
1 fruit knife
1 carbon-steel knife
1 palette knife
1 large saucepan 21cm/8½ inch diameter with lid
1 medium saucepan 19cm/7½ inch diameter with lid
1 small saucepan 12cm/5 inch diameter
1 frying pan with 20cm/8 inch diameter base
1 colander
2 wooden spoons
1 fish slice
1 rubber spatula
1 sieve (bowl strainer)
1 potato peeler
1 set of scales
1 measuring jug
1 pair poultry shears
3 gradated pudding basins
1 cheese grater
1 wooden board
1 roasting tin
1 salad bowl

KITCHEN EQUIPMENT

When setting up a kitchen, think about the following items. These cannot be rightly described as 'utensils' but they are very much a part of kitchen life.

Bottle stopper

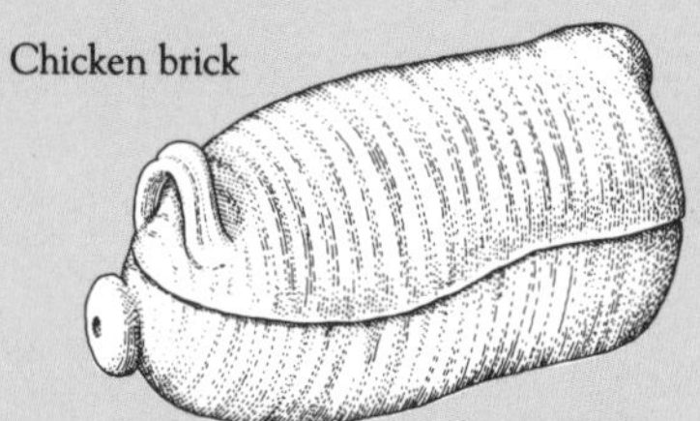
Chicken brick

Bottle opener
Bottle stopper
Bread board and knife
Can opener Wall-mounted ones are easiest to use and cannot be mislaid.
Casserole dishes Buy several sizes as food must be cooked in the right-sized pot or it will dry out during the long slow cooking. Make sure that the lids fit tightly. We recommend types made of enamelled cast iron (or other heavy duty metal) as they can be used on the hob and in the oven. Earthenware and heat resistant glass must not be put onto the hob.
Chicken brick Clay container for cooking chicken in its own juices. Makes for very succulent birds. Never

Cafetière

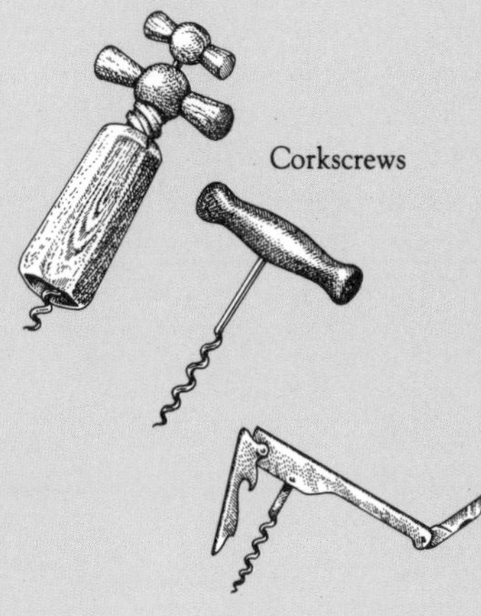
Corkscrews

wash with detergent which will be absorbed and taint food.

Clock

Coffee maker There are a huge variety of coffee machines available on the market, but almost the nicest and simplest way to make coffee is to pour boiling water into a large earthenware jug. Add 4 heaped tablespoons of medium ground coffee per 570ml/1pt water, stir once or twice with a large spoon and leave to stand and infuse in a warm place for 5 minutes. The coffee will sink to the bottom of the jug. Pour, through a small strainer, into pre-warmed cups.

Cafetière A cafetière is a glass jug with a central plunger. The coffee is made by infusion (as in jug method) but the plunger isolates the ground coffee and acts as a filter.

Filter Filter systems range from the simple drip filter with jug to electric machines. Use fine ground coffee. Experts say to choose a machine which doesn't use filter paper. The paper gives the coffee a poor flavour. The ultimate in coffee filter machines is the one that grinds and filters in one process — and no filter paper is used.

Percolator Does not make very good coffee — use medium ground beans.

Corkscrew Choose one with a very thin sharp coil that disturbs the wine as little as possible.

Electric kettle

Freezer Chest freezers are cheaper than upright freezers, but are less convenient to use and more energy is lost when a chest freezer is opened. Upright freezers take up less floor space than chest freezers.

Microwave oven Can be very useful for defrosting food (like loaves of bread and packets of butter), re-heating precooked vegetables and for melting butter, chocolate and jam. But they're not recommended for cooking unless you're in a rush.

Oven Choose the largest — think of the Christmas turkey! — and best oven that you can afford. You are not likely to be replacing it often. If you can, buy a double oven so that things can be

TYPES OF FUEL — ADVANTAGES AND DISADVANTAGES

	GAS	ELECTRICITY	SOLID FUEL
Expense	Cheaper than electricity	—	Cheaper than gas or electricity
Hobs	Quick to heat	Needs pre-heating	Provides a constant source of heat
	Any pans can be used	Some ceramic hobs need flat-based saucepans	Needs very flat, very heavy saucepans
Ovens	Drier heat than electricity therefore better for roasts, cakes and meringues	—	Excellent for long slow cooking
	Uneven heat — top of oven hotter than bottom, though this can be very useful	Even heat throughout oven	Temperature of oven can be guaranteed — but normally there are only three settings from which to choose
	The flame can go out at low temperature settings	Good for low simmering	Good for low simmering, but the hot plate is not always hot enough for fast frying
Additional points			Room heating effect — can make the kitchen too hot in the summer, but an excellent radiator in the winter

cooked at different temperatures. Gadgets can often be a snare — they go wrong. So choose an oven with only the gadgets that you are sure you will find useful. Make sure that it is easy to clean with no dirt traps. Ideally, buy one with a self-cleaning oven. Check that it has a good grill.

Fan-circulated ovens The less efficient fan-assisted ovens and convection ovens (rather than radiant ovens) heat up very quickly. Fan ovens can be run at up to 20 per cent lower temperatures.

Oven cloth/gloves

Refrigerator Choose the largest refrigerator that will fit into your kitchen; one can never have enough fridge space. Make sure that it is easy to clean and sturdy. The ice tray should be made of strong, flexible rubber.

Salad spinner Almost a 'spin-dryer' for salad leaves, operated by a handle; a cheap and very useful piece of kitchen equipment.

Salt and pepper mills Wooden with matt screw tops rather than with handles.

Tea towels

Timer Buy the type which you hang around your neck — that way it goes with you when you leave the kitchen.

Toaster Uses less energy than a grill.

Vegetable brush

MEASURING AND WEIGHING

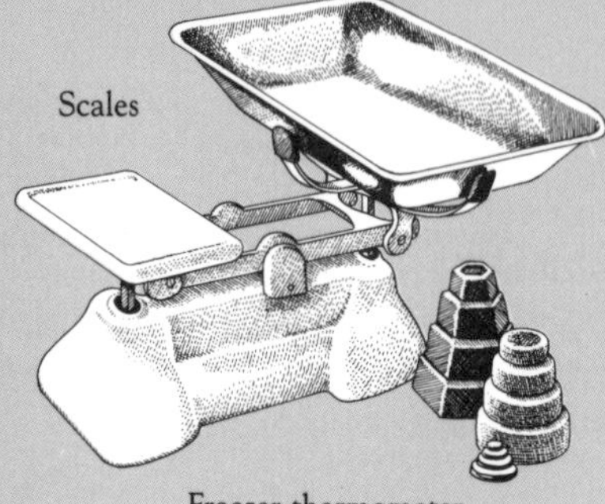

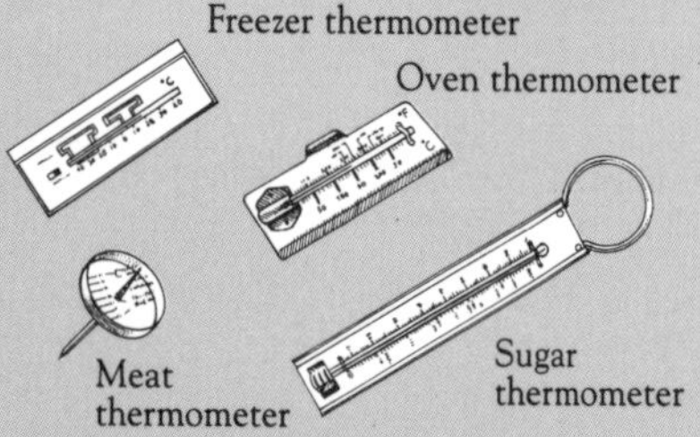

Having accurate weighing and measuring equipment is vital for successful cooking. Useful charts can be found on pp.332-333

American cup measures American recipes call for cups or part of a cup. A cup is 8fl oz. A set of cup measures are available in multiples of one cup.

Measuring jug Buy a large jug — so you can measure both large and small quantities with both imperial and metric gradations.

Scales Balance scales last a lifetime and are more accurate than any other type. They are used with expensive, but very accurate, metal weights — these can be imperial or metric.

Thermometers The thermometers on the market fall into the following broad categories:

Freezer thermometer To check that the freezer is running at the required temperature.

Meat thermometer Particularly useful when roasting a large joint — helps to indicate the degree of 'closeness'.

Oven thermometer For the accurate measurement of oven temperature.

Sugar or deep fat thermometer Gauges when fat is ready for deep-frying and indicates the degree of 'crack' of boiling sugar. Normally made of glass, so it should be warmed before use.

POTS, PANS AND OTHER VESSELS

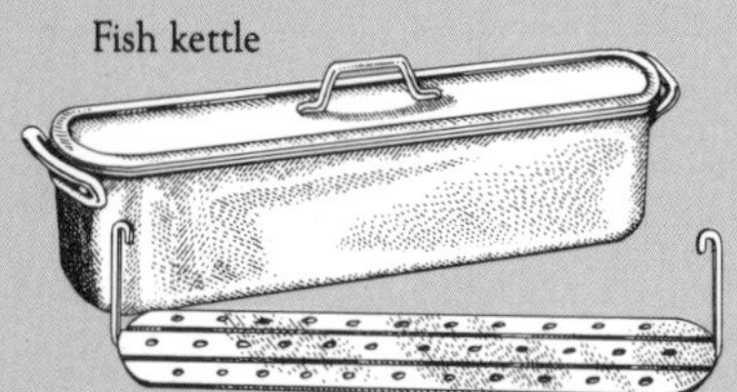

Always buy as heavy a pan as you can afford. The very best ones are made of copper with tin lining or heavy aluminium. Heavy pans conduct heat better and more evenly than light ones. A cheap pan might last two years, but it will dent and burn. A good, heavy pan could last fifty years and will not burn easily. Buy pans that are stable when empty, the right size for your burners and have lids which fit well.

Colander Choose a large standing colander; the legs keep the contents clear of draining liquid and it frees hands to empty heavy pans.

Double saucepan For making delicate sauces and melting chocolate. The bottom saucepan is very useful for boiling eggs if your other saucepans are made of heavy aluminium, which eggs tend to discolour. The handles of both pans are angled towards each other to facilitate picking up as one unit.

Fish kettle Buy a fish kettle with steaming platform. The kettle is made to match the shape of a large fish, and should be big enough to hold one at

least 50cm/20-inch long. The matching platform should fit well and have handles that stand proud of the liquid.

Frying pans For general use, choose a heavy duty pan with a 20cm/8 inch diameter base.

Crêpe pan Small, rounded edge frying pan only used for making French pancakes. The ideal size is 15cm/6-inch diameter base.

Deep fat frying pan Thicker than a roasting pan and deep. Make sure that your cooker is big enough for all your needs — including pieces of fish, etc — has good handles, and a fine mesh to keep the fat free of particles.

Omelette pan A small carbon steel frying pan with edges curving into the base, making the folding and serving of omelettes easier. Keep just for omelettes.

Girdle Heavy aluminium, iron, or steel plate for girdle (pronounced 'griddle') scones and crumpets. Make sure that the base is thick and quite flat. The handle should drop down for storage.

Heat diffuser Made of a circular piece of metal with wooden handle to reduce heat under glass and earthenware vessels on top of stove, and for controlled simmering.

Paella pan Broad, shallow, flat-bottomed, two-handled pan that gets its name from the traditional Spanish dish. (The paella is cooked and served in the pan.) Made of cast iron.

Pan rest Wooden triangle which prevents hot pans from marking work surfaces.

Pizza plate A round metal baking sheet with a slightly raised lip to support the edges of the pizza crust. Buy two. Normal size is 25cm/10 inch diameter.

Pressure cooker Extremely useful for speeding up cooking processes and wonderful for making preserves.

Roasting tin and racks Get several sizes, but make sure that the large one fits into your oven; a small roast in a large pan allows the juices to spread too thinly and burn. Choose ones made of heavy tin steel with rolled edges and high sides. Many ovens are supplied with roasting pans. Buy roasting racks to fit.

Saucepans Buy three or four saucepans ranging in capacity from 1l/2pt to 5½l/10-12pt. Saucepans should be deep and straight-sided to hold the heat well and minimize evaporation. A sloping-sided saucepan (without a lid) is invaluable for making sauces.

Sauté pan This is like a frying pan with deeper, straight sides which allow for vigorous shaking of food. Used for sauté dishes such as chicken casseroles. Buy one with a 30cm/12 inch diameter and one with a 20cm/8 inch diameter base.

Splash guard A fine wire mesh with long handle which covers pans but allows steam to escape. Very useful when frying.

Steamers You can buy steamers as a bottom saucepan with a second, perforated one on top. This is rather more expensive than the readily available perforated steamer top, with lid, with gradated bottom that fits onto any saucepan.

Chinese rice steamer Perforated aluminium, hinged, spherical container which is attached to the side of a saucepan for steaming rice.

Folding steaming platform This perforated platform that stands on legs with adjustable folding side panels is particularly useful for steaming small quantities of vegetables. It fits into any size of saucepan.

Steaming basket for wok Small bamboo cage that fits neatly into the wok, leaving about a 5cm/2inch gap between it and the base of the wok.

Stock pot Deep and straight sided for long slow cooking with minimum evaporation. It can be made of light aluminium as it will be used essentially for boiling. Choose one that holds at least 8.5l/15pt. Some pots have small taps near the bottom to draw off fat-free stock.

Wok Buy a wok set complete with a lid, stand and scoop. Made of carbon iron choose one with a round bottom, wooden handles and domed lid.
The best size is about 35cm/14 inch.

KNIVES AND CUTTING IMPLEMENTS

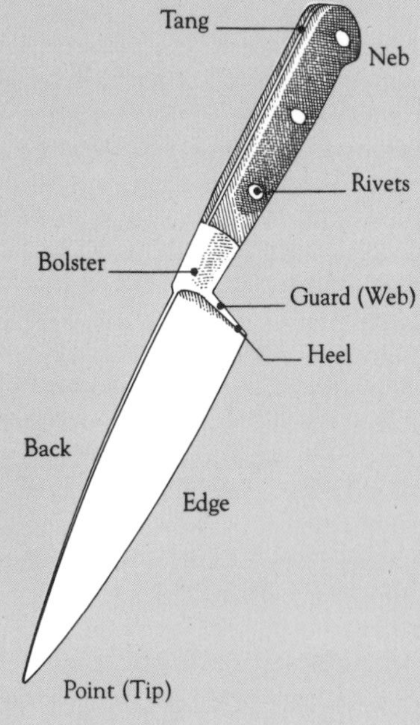

The basic principle when buying a knife is to choose one that feels comfortable in the hand, heavy and well balanced. Pivot the handle/blade junction on the edge of the open hand. The handle should fall gently back into the palm.

The part of the blade that extends into the handle of the knife is called the tang. The knives that have a full tang running the whole length of the handle give the best overall balance — blades that are not rivetted in place this way inevitably come loose. The heads of the rivets should be flush with the surface of the handle as this makes for easy cleaning.

Carbon-steel knives are easy to sharpen and stay sharp for a long time. However, they rust easily so must be wiped clean and dried immediately after use. They discolour, and are discoloured by, onions and highly acidic food. Stainless steel knives are strong, do not rust and can be used on onions and highly acidic food. Unfortunately, they are difficult to sharpen and blunt readily. High-carbon stainless steel knives have all the advantages of carbon-steel and stainless-steel knives and none of the disadvantages, but are very expensive.

Knives must be looked after carefully. Wipe clean and dry immediately after use. Sharpen them regularly with a steel suitable for the type of knife. Do not store them in a drawer. They will damage each other's blades and may cut your hands. Use a wooden knife block. When carbon steel knives get very stained clean them with half a lemon sprinkled with salt. If that does not work, use a scouring pad — but only occasionally. To remove rust, rub the blade with a burnt cork.

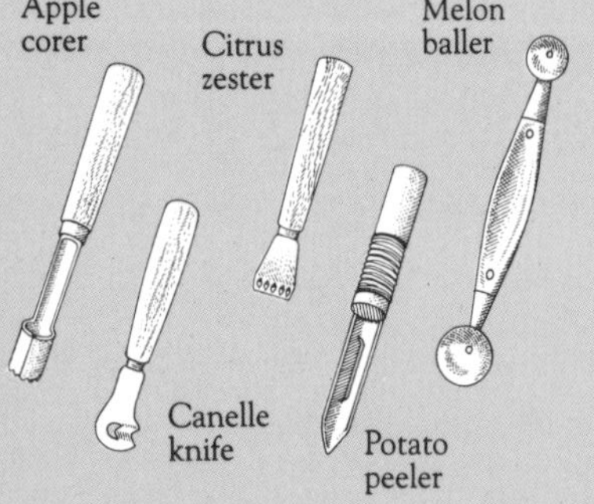

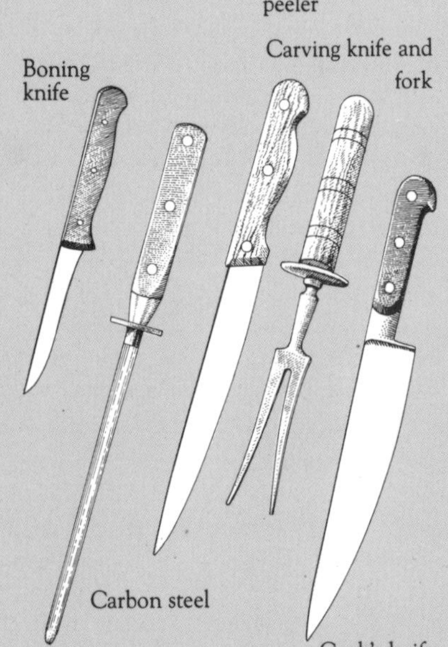

Apple corer Choose one with a sharp, strong and rigid stainless steel blade to withstand the force and torsion when coring.

Boning knife At least 10cm/4 inch long, the thin very rigid blade must be particularly sharp, especially at the tip which does most of the work.

Canelle knife Stainless steel blade with a sharpened notch for cutting decorative grooves.

Carbon steel The bigger the better. Choose one that has a good guard at the hilt and a handle with a good grip. Steels do eventually wear out, after several years.

Carving knife and fork The knife should have a broad and rigid blade at least 20cm/8 inch long. The fork should be about 25cm/10 inch long. If the prongs are curved, they can be useful for roasts — for larger roasts longer, straighter prongs are necessary. The guard, which is essential, protects against the knife slipping.

Cheese wire The simplest is a stainless steel wire with two wooden handles but they are only useful for slicing large pieces of cheese.

Cherry stoner Choose a sturdy stainless steel stoner, very useful for stoning both cherries and olives.

Chinese cleaver Similar to a meat cleaver but with a finer, sharper edge for precise slicing and chopping.

Chip cutter Only for people who eat a lot of chips. Potatoes are peeled and the chip cutter pushed down on top of each potato. Perfect chips emerge.

Citrus zester Wooden handled implement with stainless steel blade which has a row of holes with sharpened edges to remove the zest-filled top layer of citrus fruits, leaving the bitter pith behind. Various sizes are available.

Clam knife Similar to an oyster knife, but with longer, more blunted blade and rounded tip.

Cook's knife A cook's knife has a gentle curve from the blade to the tip, giving a neatly pointed end for fine work. Using the tip as a pivot, the blade gives an efficient chopping action. On a large cook's knife the broad, heavy flat of the blade makes a useful mallet. Cooks' knives come in a large variety of sizes from a 25cm/10 inch blade to 7.5cm/3 inch blade. The small one is particularly useful for

boning small birds and fine work like dicing shallots.

Double-handled herb chopper or 'mezzaluna' A double-handled knife with a wide curved stainless steel blade. Use for chopping herbs. It can come with up to four blades in parallel for chopping herbs in bulk.

Egg pricker These have a steel pin for pricking eggs to prevent cracking during boiling — invaluable.

Egg slicer A stainless steel wire cutter that will slice an egg without crumbling the yolk.

Filleting knife Choose a pointed straight-edged filleting knife with a fine, flexible blade that is about 14cm/5½ inch long.

Food mill A hand-operated mill for puréeing. Choose one with several discs of different gauges.

Freezer knife Rigid blade at least 30cm/12 inch long, serrated deeply on both sides and used like a saw. It has a hooked tip for prising and lifting.

Fruit knife Stainless steel blade with a serrated edge to cut through skins and 'saw' slices without squashing delicate insides and a sharp tip for piercing skins prior to peeling.

Grapefruit knife Stainless steel, slightly flexible blade, serrated and curved to fit the shape of the fruit.

Graters Hand-held graters come in a variety of shapes and sizes. We recommend a stainless box-shaped grater for general purposes, a tiny conical grater for nutmeg and a hand-operated rotary grater for cheese. Use a pastry brush rather than a knife to clean the faces of the graters.

Lobster crackers For cracking lobsters' legs. They look rather like pliers and can also be used to remove small bones from smoked salmon.

Lobster pick Steel prong for getting meat out of lobsters' legs and claws.

Mandoline A mandoline grater is useful both for slicing and grating. It has adjustable steel blades — one rippled, one straight, and is mounted on a wooden or plastic base. Food processers have, to a certain degree, replaced mandolines but they are still useful for small quantities.

Meat cleaver Buy one that is as heavy as you can handle with ease. For storage, hang by hole in the blade.

Melon baller, small Stainless steel metal scoop with a wooden handle used for making balls from potatoes and melons.

Mincers Choose one with a clamp rather than a suction base. Have blades sharpened or replaced regularly. Ensure that they come apart easily for cleaning.

Oyster knife For opening oysters. Short, rigid, pointed blade with a good grip and a guard to save hands if the knife slips.

Palette knife The blade should be sturdy and evenly flexible along its full length and have a blunt edge for easing under cakes and breads. They are also useful for smoothing iced surfaces. Buy a large one.

Paring knife Small stainless steel blade (7.5cm/3 inch) to peel soft fruit or vegetables.

Potato peeler There are two types of potato peeler: the swivel type has a blade which pivots freely to adapt to the shape of the item being peeled. One with a double cutting edge means that you can peel in both directions. The fixed blade type is used like a knife. Left-handed people must choose a left-handed peeler. This type can also be used for extracting bones from salmon. Both have pointed ends for clipping out eyes, but neither type can be sharpened well.

Poultry shears Can be used as both scissors and shears. They should be made of stainless steel because they are often in water and you don't want them to rust. They should be at least 25cm/10 inch long to cope with all varieties and sizes of birds. The notch cracks bones, the spring keeps the blade open between cuts and one blade is usually serrated for cutting cartilage.

Saw A lightweight saw can be very useful for sawing large thigh bones or frozen meat. Get the kind with a replaceable blade.

Scissors Choose kitchen scissors that can be unscrewed for easy cleaning and sharpening. Make sure that the blades meet smoothly along their full length.

Smoked salmon/ham knife Blade should be at least 25cm/10 inch long, and only slightly flexible. The blade often has indentations to cut down friction and keep thin slices intact.

BAKEWARE AND MOULDS

There is a large variety of moulds available on the market, many of which have been designed with a specific use in mind. Inevitably, they are not always used for that purpose. How many people own both a ring mould and a savarin mould? Moulds that are intended for baking, like terrines and cake tins, are made of a fairly heavy-duty material, while moulds that are intended for chilling are usually made of thinner more malleable metal.

The following list does not try and cover all moulds available, but only those that it would be fun to own. It also includes many of the large variety of cake tins, baking sheets and flan rings that are available.

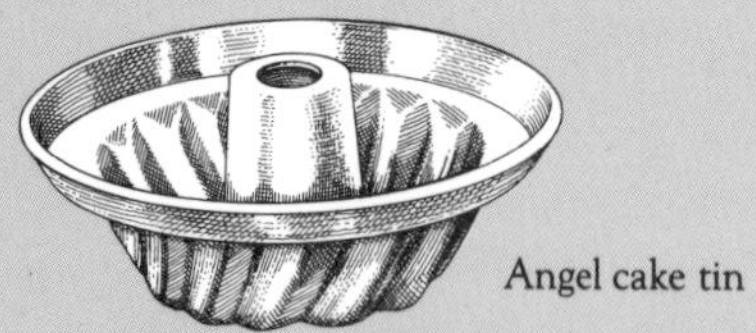
Angel cake tin

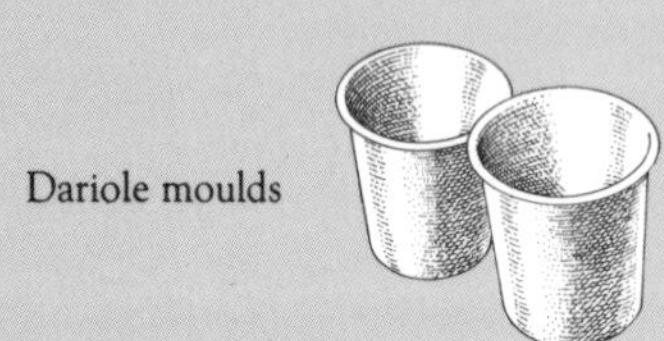
Dariole moulds

Flan rings

Flour sifters/ dredgers

Madeleine sheet

Angel cake tin The central funnel allows for better conduction of heat. Choose a non-stick tin as angel cakes tend to stick.

Baking sheets You will need several. Make sure that they fit into your oven. Heavy steel sheets with one lip are suitable for most uses — you can slide reluctant flans off them and the lip makes for easier handling. A lipped baking sheet is useful when there is the likelihood of an overflow.

Blind beans Ceramic baking beans are for baking blind and can be continually re-used. Uncooked rice is a perfectly good substitute.

Bombe mould For moulding ice cream and making ice cream bombes. The best ones have a vacuum release top — otherwise they are very difficult to dislodge.

Brioche tins Fluted, tinned metal moulds for making brioche. They come in a variety of sizes and some have funneled centres to aid the conduction of heat.

Cake moulds These are made of steel and come in a variety of shapes and sizes — chickens, rabbits, etc. They are held together by clips.

Cake racks They are either rectangular (for all types of baked food) or circular (specifically for cakes). Used for cooling cakes and biscuits without sweating. Buy one that is large and stands fairly high.

Charlotte mould Classic shaped mould for charlotte pudding. Can be used hot for apple charlotte, say, or cold for charlotte mousse.

Confectionery mould Rubber mould with 50 or more holes in several different shapes for sweet mixtures. Flexible for easy unmoulding.

Copper bowl An expensive and non-essential piece of kitchenware equipment. It is unlined and used solely for holding egg whites while they are being whisked. Some say that there is a chemical reaction between the egg whites and copper which aids beating.

Coeur à la crème mould Porcelain heart-shaped mould with a perforated base to drain the whey produced when making coeurs à la crème.

Dariole moulds Small, deep sloping-sided tins for individual hot mousses and timbales. Many people use ramekins instead, but these metal dariole moulds are better because the heat is conducted quickly throughout.

Deep cake tin Buy two — one square, one round — for fruit cakes. Make sure that they are heavy-duty for long, slow baking. Choose one with a loose bottom.

Easter egg moulds Stainless steel, glass or plastic moulds — either plain or patterned.

Fish mousse mould Metal or porcelain fish-shaped mould for fish mousses set with gelatine.

Flan rings Buy several flan rings, plain and fluted, of different sizes. They are preferable to porcelain flan dishes for pastry as they conduct heat well which prevents soggy pastry.

Flour dredger or sifter Buy one with a handle. Better still, buy two — one big one and one small holed one for heavy and light dredging.

Folding pâté tin Metal with folding sides for pies and pâté en croûte.

Jelly moulds There are a large variety of metal decorative jelly moulds, often made of copper with a tin lining. They are very rarely oven proof.

Loaf tin Can also be used for terrines.

Madeleine sheet Similar to a patty

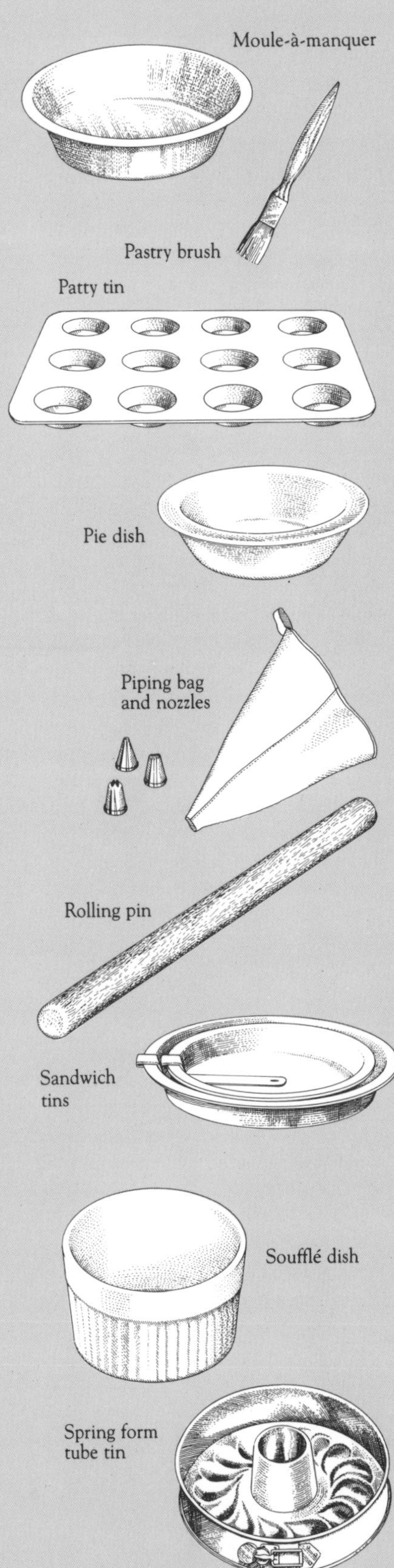

tin, but shaped for making madeleines.
Marble slab Ideal surface for making pastry on, as it keeps cool.
Mixing bowls Get about three or four different sizes of white china pudding basins and one larger ceramic mixing bowl.
Moule-à-manquer For French genoise cake. The sloping sides ease unmoulding and decoration.
Pastry brush Buy a good quality small paint brush with thick, tightly packed bristles which will not shed. A shaving brush also makes a good pastry brush as it is very soft and will stand upright when you are not using it.
Pastry cutters Buy an assortment of metal cutters, round, fluted, plain, animal shapes, ornamental shapes, etc. The top edge is rolled to safeguard fingers and to keep the shape rigid. The cutting edge must be sharp.
Pastry moulds Buy a variety of different shaped metal moulds for tarts, tartlets, boat-shaped moulds, petit fours moulds.
Patty tin The larger the better — all the moulds need not be filled.
Pie dishes Get a large and small pie dish — usually a deep, glazed ceramic dish. It must be deep so that the filling can cook before the crust burns.
Piping bag and nozzle Nylon bags with sewn seams last longer than plastic bags. Buy both a small and a large bag and a selection of metal nozzles.
Raised pie mould Wooden block to shape hot water crust pastry and make a traditional raised pie.
Raised pie tin Not for traditionally raised pies, but for pies that are to be decorated and made to look like a raised pie. The sides unclip and detach from the base. The advantage of these tins is that you can use a pâte à pâte pastry for making a raised pie; this rich pastry would not hold its shape if baked as a self-supporting raised pie.
Ramekin dishes Small soufflé dishes for individual servings.
Ring mould For jellies with a hole in the centre which can be filled with a suitable accompaniment.
Rolling pin Buy a wooden pin without handles which gives even pressure, covers the maximum surface area and is easy to wipe clean. Buy a fairly long one.
Sandwich tins Buy 2x20cm/8 inch diameter tins for Victoria sandwich cake. Ones with levers ease unmoulding.
Savarin mould or ring mould for jellies. The ring mould shape gives maximum surface for good heat conduction.
Soufflé dishes Get two or three souffle dishes ranging from ½l/¾pt to 1l/1¾pt. They must have straight sides, be good and deep for high rising and made of very fine porcelain to aid conduction of heat.
Sponge finger sheet Similar to a madeleine sheet, but shaped for making sponge fingers.
Spring form tin Use when unmoulding is difficult. The sides unclip.
Spring form tube tin For gugelhopf the funnel helps to get heat to the centre of the tin and the clips ease unmoulding.
Swiss roll tin Make sure that the sides are at least 2.5 cm/1 inch high. The tin should be 35×25cm/14×10 inch.
Terrine Make sure that the lid has a steam hole. A terrine can also be used as a pie dish.
Wooden board Choose a large, thick one made of maple or other hard wood. Make sure that it is reinforced. Ideally the grain on the main part should run in the opposite direction to that on the reinforced ends.

FOOD PROCESSING MACHINES

The following machines should be considered.

Deep fryer Buy an electric thermostatically controlled deep fryer with a charcoal filter lid, which prevents smells in the kitchen, and one that is easy to clean.

Food mixer Although food mixers have been superseded by food processors, they are remarkably versatile and have a huge variety of attachments, the most useful of which are: mincer, liquidizer, coffee grinder, electric sieve (which gives perfect mashed potatoes), can opener, sausage maker, dough hook and juice extractor. Buy a heavy duty model with rotating whisks that reach to the bottom of the bowl and are capable of whisking very small quantities.

Hand-held whisk An electric hand-held whisk is a very useful piece of kitchen equipment. Buy one with a heavy duty motor. Ideal for making whisked sponge cakes and mayonnaise.

Ice cream machines Electric ice cream machines make wonderful ice creams and sorbets and are very easy to use. They are expensive and take up a lot of space.

Liquidizer This often comes as an attachment to a food mixer but can be bought as a separate machine. Liquidizers are better for blending soups than food processors, but other than that they have become outdated. Choose a large liquidizer made of clear toughened glass or heavyweight plastic.

Pasta machine Buy a hand-operated machine for kneading, rolling and cutting pasta dough. It should be made of rust-resistant metal and be able to be clamped securely to a work surface. Choose one with rollers that adjust to several positions to alter the thickness of the dough and with rotary cutters that give a range of different widths of cut strips. Electric machines are available but are very expensive.

Processor and julienne attachment This is not an essential piece of equipment, but once you have used one you cannot live without it! It chops, slices, grates, minces, shreds, and beats. It does not whip egg whites successfully though. Choose the most compact model that you can find with as quiet a motor as possible. It should have a circuit breaker to prevent overheating or being burnt out. Choose one that will not operate unless the cover is in position.

HAND TOOLS AND SIEVES

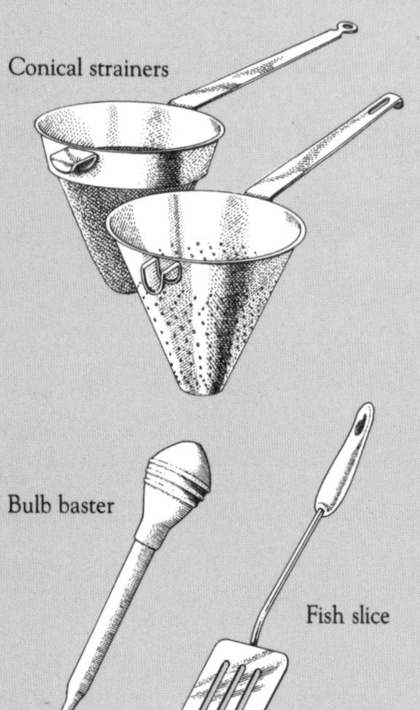

Basting spoon Choose a large one with a pierced or hooked handle if you want to hang it up. It should be heavy duty, deep and long-handled.

Bowl strainer (sieve) Choose a stainless steel sieve as carbon steel discolours some purées and nylon sieves break easily, sometimes melt and look old relatively quickly. Double mesh strainers are used for very fine puréeing. Make sure that the sieve will sit securely.

Bulb baster Syringe-type baster in plastic with rubber bulb. Also useful for skimming off fat or for extracting fat-free stock from under a layer of fat. Wash and dry carefully.

Conical strainer (Chinois or tammy strainer) There are two types of conical strainer, a firm metal one for heavy purées and a wire mesh one for straining large quantities of liquid into a single stream.

Drum sieve Good for sifting but not easy to clean so they are not suitable for making purées.

Fish slice Make sure that it has a pierced or hooked handle if you want to hang it up. Choose one that is broad enough to lift and turn large objects.

Fruit juice press Very useful for squeezing quantities of citrus fruits.

Funnel Get one that is heat resistant and with a wide flared top and a tube which fits narrow bottles.

Garlic press Best with thick handles and pivoted pressing foot. Some have cherry or olive stoners integrated in the handle. Garlic pressers are invaluable in the kitchen as the smell of garlic is difficult to remove from wooden boards or pestle and mortar.

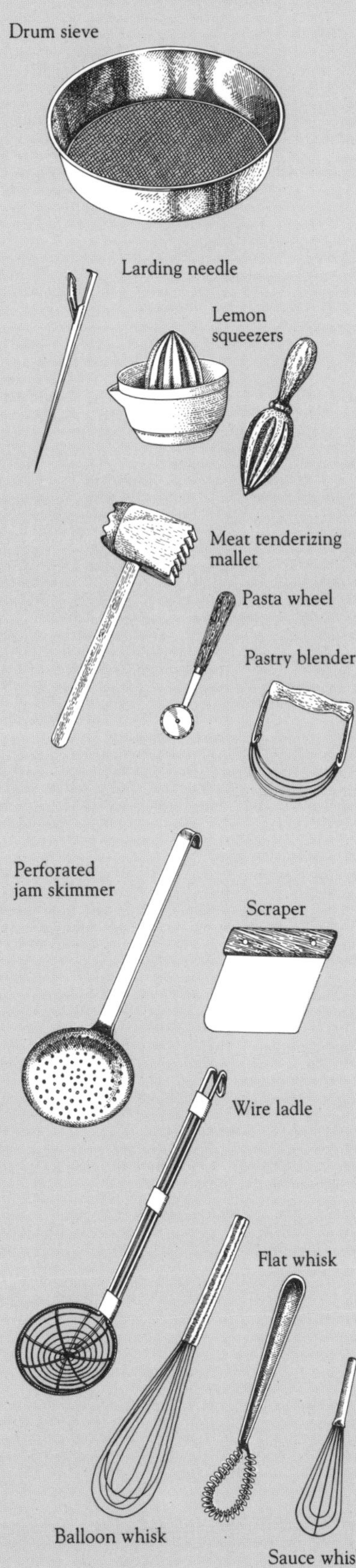

Ice cream scoop Spring action, moulds ice-cream or vegetable purées into ball shape.
Ladle Make sure that it has a pierced or hooked handle if you want to hang it up. Choose one with a large bowl and long handle.
Larding needle Lengths of lard are gripped by the teeth at the end of the needle. The lard is then threaded through the meat.
Lemon squeezer There are two types of lemon squeezer. One is made of glass or toughened plastic for squeezing citrus fruits. The plastic ones with a container underneath are the most useful. The other is a wooden gadget used to push into fruit halves for extracting a few drops.
Meat tenderizing mallet A spiked wooden mallet for flattening and tenderizing by breaking down the meat fibres.
Metal tongs For lifting and turning food, particularly useful when grilling. Make sure that the ends meet.
Pasta wheel Useful for cutting pasta.
Pastry blender Wooden handle with circular-shaped wires for easy blending.
Perforated jam skimmer A flat perforated spoon for removing fat from liquid and scum from jams and stock.
Perforated spoon Choose a large one with a pierced or hooked handle if you want to hang it up. Excellent for lifting poached food out of poaching liquid.
Pestle and mortar A pestle crushes herbs and spices in a mortar bowl. Stone is more effective than glass or wood — wooden mortars tend to absorb flavours. Stone is good and heavy and has an excellent rough texture for fine grinding. The pestle and mortar must be made of the same material as otherwise one will grind away the other.
Potato masher Although we recommend making potato purées by pushing the cooked potato through a bowl strainer, a potato masher can be very useful when you are in a hurry.
Scraper Steel with metal handle for scraping pastry boards clean. Also invaluable for scraping up vegetables after chopping.
Skewers Metal butchers' skewers are used to hold meat in place. Metal kebab skewers are used for grilling and should be about 40cm/16 inch long.
Spaghetti rake Looks like a giant wooden hairbrush. The spaghetti does not slip off the wooden prongs.
Spatulas These come in rubber or wood. The rubber variety is more effective than the wooden type. Choose one with a long wooden handle — ideal for getting last bits of food out of jars and for scraping bowls. A wooden spatula is particularly useful for use on non-stick saucepans.
Steak batt Flat and made of metal or wood.
Trussing needle Large metal needle with a large eye for sewing up stuffed meat and poultry.
Waffle iron Aluminium or cast-iron toaster or waffle iron for use on an open-flame burner. Check that the two halves fit smoothly and that the handles are long and insulated.
Whisk A device for beating air in and lumps out of a mixture. But you need the right type for the job.
Balloon whisk A simply designed whisk of several loops of wire. The large heavy duty ones with a wooden handle are the best for whisking in plenty of air.
Flat whisk A neat efficient whisk which is ideal for shallow whisking.
Sauce whisk A tiny flat whisk which is invaluable for whisking out lumps from sauces and mounting sauces with butter.
Wire 'spider' or ladle For lifting solids from liquids.
Wooden spoons Get a good assortment of sizes — the ones with long handles are sturdier and better beaters than short handled ones.
Wooden spoon with hole Allows liquid to pass through; prevents spillage during stirring.
Wooden spoon with square corner Particularly useful for getting into the corners of saucepans.

GLOSSARY

Bain marie A deep rectangular baking tin or 'water bath' in which delicate foods are stood in water while cooking. Direct fierce heat is thus prevented from curdling or otherwise spoiling the food, which cooks in a more gentle steamy atmosphere. Also, a similar container in which sauces, soups, etc, are kept hot.
Bake blind To bake a flan case while empty. In order to prevent the sides falling in or the base bubbling up the pastry is generally lined with paper and filled with 'blind' beans (see below).
Bard To wrap pork fat or fatty bacon over meat, game birds or poultry to prevent the flesh drying out while roasting, and reduce need for basting.
Baste To spoon fat or sometimes stock or wine over foods during cooking to prevent drying out and to promote flavour.
Bavarois Creamy dessert made with eggs and set with gelatine.
Beignets Fritters.
Beurre manié Equal quantities of flour and butter worked together to a paste and used as a thickening (or liaison) for liquids. Beurre manié is added to the boiling liquid in small pieces which are whisked in vigorously. As the butter melts it disperses the flour evenly so thickening it without causing lumps.
Beurre noir Black butter is a misnomer. The butter should be heated until dark brown, but by no means black. It is a slightly more nutty-flavoured version of beurre noisette (see below).
Beurre noisette Butter heated until it browns lightly. Care should be taken to pour it out of the pan immediately it reaches the right colour because the heat of the pan will continue to cook it until unpleasantly black.
Blanch Originally, to whiten by boiling; eg, briefly to boil sweetbreads or brains to remove traces of blood, or to boil almonds to make the brown skin easy to remove, leaving the nuts white. Now commonly used to mean parboiling (as in blanching vegetables when they are parboiled prior to freezing, or pre-cooked so that they need only be reheated before serving).
Blanquette Stew made without prior frying of the meat. Usually used for lamb, chicken or veal. The sauce is often thickened with yolk and cream.
Blind beans Dried beans, peas, rice or anything else (pebbles, pennies, marbles) used to temporarily fill pastry cases during baking. See 'Bake blind'.
Bouillon Uncleared stock. Broth.
Bouquet garni Small bunch of herbs usually consisting of a parsley stalk, small bay leaf, sprig of fresh thyme, celery stalk and sometimes leek leaf. Used to flavour stews, soups, etc. Removed before serving.
Braise To cook slowly in a covered pan on a bed of vegetables (see p.254).
Caramelize To cook sugar into toffee, either by boiling sugar to a liquid caramel or by heating sugar under a grill until brown and melted.
Chine To remove the backbone from a rack of ribs (veal, lamb, pork or beef) before cooking. Carving is almost impossible if the butcher has not chined the meat (see p.45).
Clarified butter Butter which has had the milk particles and other impurities removed from it. Clarified butter is clear and oily when heated, not cloudy, and can be heated to a greater temperature than unclarified butter without burning. See p.75.
Collops Small meat slices. Italian scaloppini.
Court bouillon Aromatic, slightly acidulated liquid used for poaching fish and seafood and occasionally vegetables or meat.
Crackling Scored, crisp section of roast pork. See p.262 for crackling.
Cream To beat ingredients such as fat and sugar together to a pale, creamy, mousse-like consistency.
Croustade Bread case dipped in butter or other fat and baked or fried until crisp. Used to contain hot savoury mixtures.
Dariole Castle-shaped, small mould used for shaping cake mixtures or mousses and sometimes for moulding rice salads.
Deglaze To add boiling liquid (usually water, stock or wine) to the sediment and browned juices stuck at the bottom of a pan to loosen and liquefy them. Essential technique for flavouring sauces made in the pan after frying meat.
Déglacer See 'Deglaze'.
Dégorger To extract the juices from meat, fish or vegetables, generally by salting then soaking or washing. Usually done to remove indigestible or strong-tasting juices.
Dépouille Anglicized version of dépouiller (see below).
Dépouiller To remove scum from a sauce or stock by adding a splash of cold stock to the pan which helps to bring the scum and fat to the surface, making it easier to remove.
Dropping consistency The consistency reached when a mixture will fall reluctantly from a spoon, neither running off nor adhering when the spoon is jerked (see p.110).
Duxelle Finely minced or chopped mushrooms sometimes mixed with chopped shallots or chopped ham and used raw or cooked to a dryish paste. Used for stuffing and flavouring.
Emulsion A stable suspension of fat and other liquid, eg, mayonnaise, hollandaise, beurre blanc (see p.202).
Escalope Very thin slice of meat, usually veal, sometimes beaten out flat to make it thinner and larger.
Farce Stuffing or forcemeat.
Fines herbes Chives, chervil, parsley and tarragon — the clasic combination of fresh herbs for an omelette.
Flamber To flame or to set alcohol alight, usually to burn it off but frequently done for dramatic effect. (Past tense 'flambé' or 'flambée'.)
Fold To mix with a gentle lifting motion rather than beating vigorously (see p.285).
Fromage blanc Low-fat, almost liquid, cheese.
Giblets Neck, gizzard, heart and liver of poultry. Generally used (except for liver) for flavouring stock.
Glace de viande (Meat glaze) Brown stock reduced by boiling to a syrupy consistency. Very strong in flavour, and used for adding colour and body to sauces (see p.270).
Glace de poisson (Fish glaze) As above, but of fish stock (see p.270).
Glaze To give a shine to a finished dish (eg, with jellied meat juices on a roast turkey, melted jam on a fruit flan or thick syrup on a cake or pudding).
Gluten Two proteins found in wheat and an important element in the making of risen breads. See p.312.

GLOSSARY

Gratiner To sprinkle breadcrumbs and melted butter on the surface of a dish and brown it under the grill. Sometimes used to denote browning without the breadcrumbs, or when cheese is thus browned.
Infuse To heat gently or to steep to extract flavour as when infusing milk with a vanilla pod or blade of mace.
Julienne Needle-fine shreds, generally of vegetables or citrus rind but can be of chicken, fish, etc. See p.46.
Knead To press, stretch and fold bread dough to evenly distribute the yeast. See p.67.
Knock down or knock back To knead or punch risen bread dough to expel the air. See p.314.
Knock up To slightly separate layers of raw puff pastry with the flat of a knife to encourage layered rising in the oven. See p.70.
Lard To thread strips of pork back fat or anchovy, or sometimes bacon fat, through meat with a special needle to give it flavour and juiciness.
Lard leaves Thin slices of pork back fat used for lining terrines and paté tins to prevent sticking to the pan and drying out.
Lardons Small cubes of pork back fat or bacon fat or salt pork (green bacon). Generally roasted or fried and used as a garnish.
Leavening or leavening agent Ingredient used to make mixtures rise during cooking, eg, yeast, baking powder, whisked egg whites.
Liaison Ingredient or combination of ingredients used to thicken liquids, eg roux (see beurre manié).
Macédoine Diced mixed vegetables or fruit.
Macerate To soak food in a liquid to allow flavours to mix, eg, to macerate strawberries in jams.
Marinade (noun) The liquid used for marinading (see below). Generally contains oil, onion and some acidic liquid like vinegar, lemon juice or wine.
Marinade (verb) To soak meat, fish or vegetables before cooking in acidulated liquid containing flavourings and herbs. This gives flavour and tenderizes the meat.
Médallions Small neat rounds of food, usually used of meat but sometimes of biscuits or vegetables, cut in flat discs.
Mirepoix The bed of vegetables used for braising.
Mousseline Little moulds made from poultry or fish, enriched with cream and served hot or cold. Also used to describe sauces with a mousse-like texture and added cream, or any light, whisked, frothy, creamed, mixture.
Needleshreds See 'Julienne'.
Noisette Hazlenut. Sometimes used to describe an amount, eg, a nut of butter, which means a nut-sized piece, or to describe the colour.
Noisette Neat rounds of boneless lamb taken from the best end.
Nouvelle cuisine Style of cooking that promotes light and delicate dishes using unusual combinations of very fresh ingredients, attractively arranged.
Oyster Small piece of meat found on either side of the backbone of the chicken or bird. Said to be the best flavoured flesh. Also, of course, a bi-valve mollusc.
Panade or Panada Thickened farinaceous mixture used as a base for souffles, fish cakes, etc.
Papillote Paper case in which fish or meat is cooked to contain the aroma or flavour (see p.173).
Parboil To half boil or partially soften by boiling. See also 'Blanch'.
Pass To push through a sieve.
Praline Almonds and sugar cooked together to a toffee. Sómetimes crushed to a powder and used for flavouring desserts.
Prove To allow yeasted dough to rise before baking.
Purée Sieved liquids or finely mashed food.
Quark Similar in texture to fromage blanc (see above) but made from skimmed milk.
Quenelles A fine minced mixture (usually fish) formed into small sausages or egg-shapes and poached. Generally served in a sauce or as a garnish to other dishes.
Reduce To boil rapidly so that moisture is driven off, flavour strengthened and quantity reduced.
Refresh To dunk green vegetables into cold water or to hold them under the tap to prevent further cooking in their own steam and loss of colour.
Relax or rest Of pastry: to set aside in a cool place to allow the gluten (which will have expanded during rolling) to contract. This lessens the danger of shrinking in the oven. Of batters: to set aside to allow the starch cells to swell, giving a lighter result when cooked.
Render To melt solid fat to produce dripping.
Ribbon, to the To whisk ingredients until the mixture is sufficiently thick to leave a ribbon-like trail on the surface when the whisk is lifted.
Rouille Emulsion of garlic and oil used to flavour Mediterranean soups.
Roux Thickening for a sauce or soup. Melted butter to which flour has been added and briefly cooked (the sauce liquid is then added and the whole stirred together over heat).
Sauter Frying in minimal fat. The food is continually shaken or tossed over high heat so that it browns quickly and evenly.
Scald Of milk: to heat until on the point of boiling. Of muslin, cloths, etc: to sterilize in boiling water.
Scalding point The moment immediately before boiling, when a liquid begins to tremble round the edges but is not yet bubbling.
Seal or seize To rapidly brown meat so as to form a cooked surface to trap interior juices.
Slake To mix farinaceous substances to a thin paste with water. Usually used of cornflour or custard powder.
Suprême Poultry breast.
Sweat To cook gently (usually in fat but sometimes in the food's own juices) without browning.
Terrine Pâté or minced mixture baked or steamed in a loaf tin-shaped terrine.
Timbale A dish which has been cooked in a castle-shaped mould, or a dish served piled up high.
Tomalley Greenish lobster liver. Creamy and delicious.
Tournedos Thick steak from the narrow end of beef fillet.
To turn vegetables To cut root vegetables to even olive shapes (see p.150).
Zest The coloured part of citrus skin. Generally pared thinly or grated and used for flavouring.

INDEX

Page numbers in *italic* refer to the illustrations

Q

R

S

T

BIBLIOGRAPHY

Beard, James, *Beard on Bread*, Michael Joseph, 1976
Bocuse, Paul, *The New Cuisine*, Granada, 1978
Boxer, Arabella, *Mediterranean Cookbook*, Dent, 1981
Campbell, Susan, *English Cookery New & Old*, Consumers Association, 1981
Carrier, Robert, *Cooking with Robert Carrier*, Hamlyn, 1978
Child, Julia, *From Julia Child's Kitchen*, Jonathan Cape, 1978
Christian, Glynn, *Glynn Christian's Delicatessen Food Handbook*, Macdonald, 1982
Conran, Terence & Caroline, *The Cookbook*, Mitchell Beazley, 1980
Costa, Margaret, *Four Seasons Cookery Book*, Nelson, 1970
David, Elizabeth, *French Provincial Cooking*, Michael Joseph, 1960
Davidson, Alan, *North Atlantic Seafood*, Macmillan, 1979
Dimbleby, Josceline, *Favourite Food*, Allen Lane, 1983
Dowell, Philip & Bailey, Adrian, *The Book of Ingredients*, Michael Joseph, 1980
Escoffier, Auguste, *The Complete Guide to the Art of Modern Cookery* (Translation of *La Guide Culinaire*), Heinemann, 1979
Freson, Robert, *The Taste of France*, Webb & Bower, 1983
Girardet, Fredy, *The Cuisine of Fredy Girardet*, William Morrow, 1985
Guerard, Michel, *Cuisine Gourmande*, Macmillan, 1978
Hanbury-Tenison, Marika, *Book of Afternoon Tea*, David & Charles, 1980
Haroutunian, Arto der, *Middle Eastern Cookery*, Century, 1982
Hume, Rosemary & Spry, Constance, *The Constance Spry Cookery Book*, Dent, 1956
Leith, Prue, *The Cook's Handbook*, Papermac, 1984
Lenotre, Gaston, *Lenotre's Desserts and Pastries*, Barron's, 1977
Montagne, Prosper, *Larousse Gastronomique* (English edition), Hamlyn, 1961
Mosimann, Anton, *Cuisine a la Carte*, Northwood, 1981
Pepin, Jacques, *La Methode*, Papermac, 1979
Pepin, Jacques, *La Technique*, Hamlyn, 1973
Rance, Patrick, *The Great British Cheese Book*, Macmillan, 1982
Readers Digest Cookery Year Book, Readers Digest Assoc'n Ltd, 1973
Roden, Claudia, *A Book of Middle Eastern Food*, Penguin, 1968
Root, Waverley, *The Food of France*, Papermac, 1983
Roux Brothers, *New Classic Cuisine*, Macdonald, 1983
Simon, Andre, *A Concise Encyclopædia of Gastronomy*, Allen Lane, 1983
Smith, Michael, *Cooking with Michael Smith*, Macmillan, 1981
So, Yan-Kit, *Classic Chinese Cookbook*, Dorling Kindersley, 1984
Stobart, Tom, *The Cook's Encyclopædia*, Batsford, 1980
The Sunday Times Complete Cookbook (presented by Arabella Boxer), Weidenfeld & Nicolson, 1983
Time Life, *The Good Cook Series*
Troisgros, Jean & Pierre, *The Nouvelle Cuisine*, Macmillan, 1980
Verge, Roger, *Cuisine of the Sun*, Macmillan, 1979